T0191572

Proceedings of COMPSTAT'2010

Yves Lechevallier · Gilbert Saporta
Editors

Proceedings of COMPSTAT'2010

19th International Conference on
Computational Statistics
Paris - France, August 22–27, 2010
Keynote, Invited and Contributed Papers

Physica-Verlag

Editors
Dr. Yves Lechevallier
INRIA Paris-Rocquencourt
Domaine de Voluceau
78153 Le Chesnay cedex
France
yves.lechevallier@inria.fr

Prof. Dr. Gilbert Saporta
CNAM
Chaire de Statistique Appliquée
292 rue Saint Martin
75141 Paris cedex 03
France
gilbert.saporta@cnam.fr

Additional material to this book can be downloaded from http://extras.springer.com

ISBN 978-3-7908-2603-6   e-ISBN 978-3-7908-2604-3
DOI 10.1007/978-3-7908-2604-3
Springer Heidelberg Dordrecht London New York

Library of Congress Control Number: 2010934004

Cover design: WMXDesign GmbH, Heidelberg

Printed on acid-free paper

Physica-Verlag is a brand of Springer-Verlag Berlin Heidelberg
Springer-Verlag is part of Springer Science+Business Media (www.springer.com)

Preface

The 19th Conference of IASC-ERS, COMPSTAT'2010, is held in Paris, France, from August 22nd to August 27th 2010, locally organised by the Conservatoire National des Arts et Métiers (CNAM) and the French National Institute for Research in Computer Science and Control (INRIA).
COMPSTAT is an initiative of the European Regional Section of the International Association for Statistical Computing (IASC-ERS), a section of the International Statistical Institute (ISI). COMPSTAT conferences started in 1974 in Wien; previous editions of COMPSTAT were held in Berlin (2002), Prague (2004), Rome (2006) and Porto (2008). It is one of the most prestigious world conferences in Computational Statistics, regularly attracting hundreds of researchers and practitioners, and has gained a reputation as an ideal forum for presenting top quality theoretical and applied work, promoting interdisciplinary research and establishing contacts amongst researchers with common interests.

Keynote lectures are addressed by Luc Devroye (School of Computer Science, McGill University, Montreal), Lutz Edler (Division of Biostatistics, German Cancer Research Center, Heidelberg) and David Hand (Statistics section, Imperial College, London). The conference program includes three tutorials: "Statistical Approach for Complex data" by Lynne Billard (University of Georgia, United States), "Bayesian discrimination between embedded models" by Jean-Michel Marin (Université Montpellier II, France) and "Machine Learning and Association Rules" by Petr Berka and Jan Rauch (University of Economics, Prague, Czech Republic). Each COMPSTAT meeting is organised with a number of topics highlighted, which lead to Invited Sessions. The Conference program includes also contributed sessions and short communications (both oral communications and posters).

The Conference Scientific Program Committee chaired by Gilbert Saporta, CNAM, includes:

Ana Maria Aguilera, Universidad Granada
Avner Bar-Hen, Université René Descartes, Paris
Maria Paula Brito, University of Porto
Christophe Croux, Katholieke Universiteit Leuven
Michel Denuit, Université Catholique de Louvain
Gejza Dohnal, Technical University, Prag
Patrick J. F. Groenen, Erasmus University, Rottterdam
Georges Hébrail, TELECOM ParisTech
Henk Kiers, University of Groningen

Erricos Kontoghiorghes, University of Cyprus
Martina Mittlböck, Medical University of Vienna
Christian P. Robert, Université Paris-Dauphine
Maurizio Vichi, Universita La Sapienza, Roma
Peter Winker, Universität Giessen
Moon Yul Huh, SungKyunKwan University, Seoul, Korea
Djamel Zighed, Université Lumière, Lyon

Due to space limitations, the Book of Proceedings includes keynote speakers'
papers, invited sessions speakers' papers and a selection of the best contributed papers, while the e-book includes all accepted papers.

The papers included in this volume present new developments in topics
of major interest for statistical computing, constituting a fine collection of
methodological and application-oriented papers that characterize the current
research in novel, developing areas. Combining new methodological advances
with a wide variety of real applications, this volume is certainly of great value
for researchers and practitioners of computational statistics alike.

First of all, the organisers of the Conference and the editors would like to
thank all authors, both of invited and contributed papers and tutorial texts,
for their cooperation and enthusiasm. We are specially grateful to all colleagues who served as reviewers, and whose work was crucial to the scientific
quality of these proceedings. A special thanks to Hervé Abdi who took in
charge the session on Brain Imaging. We also thank all those who have contributed to the design and production of this Book of Proceedings, Springer
Verlag, in particular Dr. Martina Bihn and Dr. Niels Peter Thomas, for their
help concerning all aspects of publication.

The organisers would like to express their gratitude to all people from CNAM
and INRIA who contributed to the success of COMPSTAT'2010, and worked
actively for its organisation. We are very grateful to all our sponsors, for
their generous support. Finally, we thank all authors and participants, without whom the conference would not have been possible.

The organisers of COMPSTAT'2010 wish the best success to Erricos Kontoghiorghes, Chairman of the 20th edition of COMPSTAT, which will be held
in Cyprus in Summer 2012. See you there!

Paris, August 2010

Yves Lechevallier
Gilbert Saporta

Stéphanie Aubin
Gérard Biau
Stéphanie Chaix
Marc Christine
Laurence de Crémiers
Séverine Demeyer
Thierry Despeyroux
Christian Derquenne
Vincenzo Esposito Vinzi
Ali Gannoun
Jean-Pierre Gauchi
Chantal Girodon
Pierre-Louis Gonzalez
Luan Jaupi
Ludovic Lebart
Ndeye Niang
Françoise Potier
Giorgio Russolillo
Julie Séguéla

Acknowledgements

The Editors are extremely grateful to the reviewers, whose work was determinant for the scientific quality of these proceeding. They were, in alphatbetical order:

Hervé Abdi
Ana Maria Aguilera
Massimo Aria
Josef Arlt
Avner Bar-Hen
Jean-Patrick Baudry
Younès Bennani
Petr Berka
Patrice Bertrand
Pierre Bertrand
Gerard Biau
Christophe Biernacki
Lynne Billard
Hans-Hermann Bock
Frank Bretz
Henri Briand
Maria Paula Brito
Edgar Brunner
Stephane Canu
Gilles Celeux
Andrea Cerioli
Roy Cerqueti
Ka Chun Cheung
Marc Christine
Guillaume Cleuziou
Claudio Conversano
Christophe Croux
Francisco de Assis De Carvalho
Michel Denuit
Christian Derquenne
Thierry Despeyroux
Gejza Dohnal
Antonio D'Ambrosio
Manuel Escabias
Vincenzo Esposito Vinzi
Christian Francq
Giuliano Galimberti

Ali Gannoun
Bernard Garel
Cristian Gatu
Jean-Pierre Gauchi
Pierre-Louis Gonzalez
Gérard Govaert
Patrick Groenen
Nistor Grozavu
Fabrice Guillet
Frederic Guilloux
Anne Gégout-Petit
Hakim Hacid
Peter Hall
André Hardy
Georges Hébrail
Harald Heinzl
Marc Hoffman
Moon Yul Huh
Alfonso Iodice d'Enza
Antonio Irpino
Junling Ji
François-Xavier Jollois
Henk A.L. Kiers
Dong Kim
Christine Kiss
Erricos Kontoghiorghes
Labiod Lazhar
Ludovic Lebart
Mustapha Lebbah
Yves Lechevallier
Seung Lee
Guodong Li
Olivier Lopez
Maria Laura Maag
Jean-Michel Marin
Claudia Marinica
Roland Marion-Gallois
Geoffrey McLachlan
Bertrand Michel

Martina Mittlboeck
Angela Montanari
Irini Moustaki
Shu Ng
Ndeye Niang
Monique Noirhomme
Francisco A. Ocaña
Matej Oresic
Chongsun Park
Franceso Palumbo
Fabien Picarougne
Jean-Michel Poggi
Tommaso Proietti
Pierre Pudlo
Jan Rauch
Marco Riani
Christian Robert
Nicoleta Rogovschi
Rosaria Romano
Fabrice Rossi
Anthony Rossini
Judith Rousseau
Laurent Rouviere
Giorgio Russolillo
Lorenza Saitta
Ryan Skraba

Gilbert Saporta
Seisho Sato
Roberta Siciliano
Francoise Soulie Fogelman
Matthias Studer
Laura Trinchera
Brigitte Trousse
Mariano J. Valderrama
Stefan Van Aelst
Gilles Venturini
Rosanna Verde
Maurizio Vichi
Emmanuel Viennet
Cinzia Viroli
Michal Vrabec
François Wahl
William Wieczorek
Peter Winker
Jingyun Yang
In-Kwon Yeo
Kam Yuen
Daniela Zaharie
Djamel A. Zighed
Lihong Zhang
Xinyuan Zhao

Sponsors

We are extremely grateful to the following institutions whose support contributes to the success of COMPSTAT'2010:

- Conseil Régional Ile de France

- Mairie de Paris

- Société Française de Statistique

- Association EGC (Extraction et Gestion des Connaissances)

- Société Francophone de Classification

- Electricité de France

- Institut National de la Recherche Agronomique

- Institut National de la Statistique et des Etudes Economiques

- IPSOS

- Orange Labs

- SAS-Institute

Sponsors

Contents

Part I. Keynote

Complexity Questions in Non-Uniform Random Variate Generation 3
  Luc Devroye

Computational Statistics Solutions for Molecular Biomedical
Research: A Challenge and Chance for Both 19
  Lutz Edler, Christina Wunder, Wiebke Werft, Axel Benner

The Laws of Coincidence 33
  David J. Hand

Part II. ABC Methods for Genetic Data

Choosing the Summary Statistics and the Acceptance Rate in
Approximate Bayesian Computation 47
  Michael G.B. Blum

Integrating Approximate Bayesian Computation with Complex Agent-Based Models for Cancer Research 57
  Andrea Sottoriva, Simon Tavaré

Part III. Algorithms for Robust Statistics

Robust Model Selection with LARS Based on S-estimators . . . 69
  Claudio Agostinelli, Matias Salibian-Barrera

Robust Methods for Compositional Data 79
  Peter Filzmoser, Karel Hron

Detecting Multivariate Outliers Using Projection Pursuit with
Particle Swarm Optimization 89
  Anne Ruiz-Gazen, Souad Larabi Marie-Sainte, Alain Berro

Part IV. Brain Imaging

Imaging Genetics: Bio-Informatics and Bio-Statistics
Challenges 101
  Jean-Baptiste Poline, Christophe Lalanne, Arthur Tenenhaus,
  Edouard Duchesnay, Bertrand Thirion, Vincent Frouin

The NPAIRS Computational Statistics Framework for Data
Analysis in Neuroimaging 111
Stephen Strother, Anita Oder, Robyn Spring, Cheryl Grady

Part V. Computational Econometrics

Bootstrap Prediction in Unobserved Component Models 123
Alejandro F. Rodríguez, Esther Ruiz

Part VI. Computer-Intensive Actuarial Methods

A Numerical Approach to Ruin Models with Excess of Loss
Reinsurance and Reinstatements 135
Hansjörg Albrecher, Sandra Haas

Computation of the Aggregate Claim Amount Distribution
Using R and Actuar 145
Vincent Goulet

Applications of Multilevel Structured Additive Regression Models to Insurance Data 155
Stefan Lang, Nikolaus Umlauf

Part VII. Data Stream Mining

Temporally-Adaptive Linear Classification for Handling Pop-
ulation Drift in Credit Scoring............................. 167
*Niall M. Adams, Dimitris K. Tasoulis, Christoforos
Anagnostopoulos, David J. Hand*

Large-Scale Machine Learning with Stochastic Gradient Descent 177
Léon Bottou

Part VIII. Functional Data Analysis

Anticipated and Adaptive Prediction in Functional Discriminant Analysis.. 189
Cristian Preda, Gilbert Saporta, Mohamed Hadj Mbarek

Bootstrap Calibration in Functional Linear Regression Models
with Applications.. 199
Wenceslao González-Manteiga, Adela Martínez-Calvo

Empirical Dynamics and Functional Data Analysis........... 209
  Hans-Georg Müller

Part IX. Kernel Methods

Indefinite Kernel Discriminant Analysis 221
  Bernard Haasdonk, Elżbieta Pękalska

Data Dependent Priors in PAC-Bayes Bounds 231
  John Shawe-Taylor, Emilio Parrado-Hernández, Amiran Ambroladze

Part X. Monte Carlo Methods in System Safety, Reliability and Risk Analysis

Some Algorithms to Fit some Reliability Mixture Models under Censoring 243
  Laurent Bordes, Didier Chauveau

Computational and Monte-Carlo Aspects of Systems for Monitoring Reliability Data 253
  Emmanuel Yashchin

Part XI. Optimization Heuristics in Statistical Modelling

Evolutionary Computation for Modelling and Optimization in Finance.. 265
  Sandra Paterlini

Part XII. Spatial Statistics / Spatial Epidemiology

Examining the Association between Deprivation Profiles and Air Pollution in Greater London using Bayesian Dirichlet Process Mixture Models...................................... 277
  John Molitor, Léa Fortunato, Nuoo-Ting Molitor, Sylvia Richardson

Assessing the Association between Environmental Exposures and Human Health 285
  Linda J. Young, Carol A. Gotway, Kenneth K. Lopiano, Greg Kearney, Chris DuClos

Part XIII. ARS Session (Financial) Time Series

Semiparametric Seasonal Cointegrating Rank Selection 297
Byeongchan Seong, Sung K. Ahn, Sinsup Cho

Estimating Factor Models for Multivariate Volatilities: An Innovation Expansion Method 305
Jiazhu Pan, Wolfgang Polonik, Qiwei Yao

Multivariate Stochastic Volatility Model with Cross Leverage. 315
Tsunehiro Ishihara, Yasuhiro Omori

Part XIV. KDD Session: Topological Learning

Bag of Pursuits and Neural Gas for Improved Sparse Coding 327
Kai Labusch, Erhardt Barth, Thomas Martinetz

On the Role and Impact of the Metaparameters in t-distributed Stochastic Neighbor Embedding 337
John A. Lee, Michel Verleysen

Part XV. IFCS Session: New Developments in Two or Highermode Clustering; Model Based Clustering and Reduction for High Dimensional Data

Multiple Nested Reductions of Single Data Modes as a Tool to Deal with Large Data Sets 349
Iven Van Mechelen, Katrijn Van Deun

The Generic Subspace Clustering Model 359
Marieke E. Timmerman, Eva Ceulemans

Clustering Discrete Choice Data 369
Donatella Vicari, Marco Alfò

Part XVI. Selected Contributed Papers

Application of Local Influence Diagnostics to the Buckley-James Model 381
Nazrina Aziz, Dong Qian Wang

Multiblock Method for Categorical Variables 389
Stéphanie Bougeard, El Mostafa Qannari, Claire Chauvin

A Flexible IRT Model for Health Questionnaire: an Application to HRQoL 397
Serena Broccoli, Giulia Cavrini

Multidimensional Exploratory Analysis of a Structural Model Using a Class of Generalized Covariance Criteria 405
Xavier Bry, Thomas Verron, Patrick Redont

Semiparametric Models with Functional Responses in a Model Assisted Survey Sampling Setting : Model Assisted Estimation of Electricity Consumption Curves 413
Hervé Cardot, Alain Dessertaine, Etienne Josserand

Stochastic Approximation for Multivariate and Functional Median 421
Hervé Cardot, Peggy Cénac, Mohamed Chaouch

A Markov Switching Re-evaluation of Event-Study Methodology 429
Rosella Castellano, Luisa Scaccia

Evaluation of DNA Mixtures Accounting for Sampling Variability 437
Yuk-Ka Chung, Yue-Qing Hu, De-Gang Zhu, Wing K. Fung

Monotone Graphical Multivariate Markov Chains 445
Roberto Colombi, Sabrina Giordano

Using Functional Data to Simulate a Stochastic Process via a Random Multiplicative Cascade Model 453
G. Damiana Costanzo, S. De Bartolo, F. Dell'Accio, G. Trombetta

A Clusterwise Center and Range Regression Model for Interval-Valued Data 461
Francisco de A. T. de Carvalho, Gilbert Saporta, Danilo N. Queiroz

Contributions to Bayesian Structural Equation Modeling 469
Séverine Demeyer, Nicolas Fischer, Gilbert Saporta

Some Examples of Statistical Computing in France During the 19th Century 477
Antoine de Falguerolles

Imputation by Gaussian Copula Model with an Application
to Incomplete Customer Satisfaction Data 485
   Meelis Käärik, Ene Käärik

On Multiple-Case Diagnostics in Linear Subspace Method 493
   Kuniyoshi Hayashi, Hiroyuki Minami and Masahiro Mizuta

Fourier Methods for Sequential Change Point Analysis in Autoregressive Models... 501
   Marie Hušková, Claudia Kirch, Simos G. Meintanis

Computational Treatment of the Error Distribution in Non-
parametric Regression with Right-Censored and Selection-
Biased Data 509
   Géraldine Laurent, Cédric Heuchenne

Mixtures of Weighted Distance-Based Models for Ranking
Data... 517
   Paul H. Lee, Philip L. H. Yu

Fourier Analysis and Swarm Intelligence for Stochastic Optimization of Discrete Functions.............................. 525
   Jin Rou New, Eldin Wee Chuan Lim

Global Hypothesis Test to Simultaneously Compare the Predictive Values of Two Binary Diagnostic Tests in Paired Designs: a Simulation Study 533
   *J. A. Roldán Nofuentes, J. D. Luna del Castillo, M. A. Montero
   Alonso*

Modeling Operational Risk: Estimation and Effects of Dependencies 541
   Stefan Mittnik, Sandra Paterlini, Tina Yener

Learning Hierarchical Bayesian Networks for Genome-Wide
Association Studies 549
   Raphaël Mourad, Christine Sinoquet, Philippe Leray

Posterior Distribution over the Segmentation Space 557
   G. Rigaill, E. Lebarbier, S. Robin

Parcellation Schemes and Statistical Tests to Detect Active
Regions on the Cortical Surface 565
   Bertrand Thirion, Alan Tucholka, Jean-Baptiste Poline

Robust Principal Component Analysis Based on Pairwise Correlation Estimators 573
   Stefan Van Aelst, Ellen Vandervieren, Gert Willems

Ordinary Least Squares for Histogram Data Based on Wasserstein Distance 581
Rosanna Verde, Antonio Irpino

DetMCD in a Calibration Framework 589
Tim Verdonck, Mia Hubert, Peter J. Rousseeuw

Separable Two-Dimensional Linear Discriminant Analysis 597
Jianhua Zhao, Philip L.H. Yu, Shulan Li

List of Supplementary Contributed and Invited Papers Only Available on springerlink.com 605

Index 617

Part XVII. Supplementary Contributed Papers

Clustering of Waveforms-Data Based on FPCA Direction 625
Giada Adelfio, Marcello Chiodi, Antonino D'Alessandro, Dario Luzio

Symbolic Data Analysis of Complex Data: Application to nuclear power plant 633
Filipe Afonso, Edwin Diday, Norbert Badez, Yves Genest

Different P-spline Approaches for Smoothed Functional Principal Component Analysis 641
Ana M. Aguilera, M. Carmen Aguilera-Morillo, Manuel Escabias, Mariano J. Valderrama

Peak Detection in Mass Spectrometry Data Using Sparse Coding 649
Theodore Alexandrov, Klaus Steinhorst, Oliver Keszöcze, Stefan Schiffler

A Comparison between Beale Test and Some Heuristic Criteria to Establish Clusters Number 657
Angela Alibrandi, Massimiliano Giacalone

Estimating Population Proportions in Presence of Missing Data 665
Encarnaciòn Álvarez-Verdejo, Antonio Arcos, Silvia González, Juan Francisco Muñoz, Maria Rueda

Sub-Quadratic Markov Tree Mixture Models for Probability Density Estimation 673
Sourour Ammar, Philippe Leray, Louis Wehenkel

Data Management in Symbolic Data Analysis 681
   Teh Amouh, Monique Noirhomme-Fraiture, Benoit Macq

Variable Selection for Semi-Functional Partial Linear Regression Models 689
   Germán Aneiros, Frédéric Ferraty, Philippe Vieu

Clustering Functional Data Using Wavelets 697
   Anestis Antoniadis, Xavier Brossat, Jairo Cugliari, Jean-Michel
   Poggi

Polynomial Methods in Time Series Analysis 705
   Félix Aparicio-Pérez

Cointegrated Lee-Carter Mortality Forecasting Method 713
   Josef Arlt, Markéta Arltová, Milan Bašta, Jitka Langhamrová

Empirical Analysis of the Climatic and Social-Economic Factors influence on the Suicide Development in the Czech Republic 721
   Markéta Arltová, Jitka Langhamrová, Jana Langhamrová

Yield Curve Predictability, Regimes, and Macroeconomic Information: A Data-Driven Approach 729
   Francesco Audrino, Kameliya Filipova

Socioeconomic Factors in Circulatory System Mortality in Europe: A Multilevel Analysis of Twenty Countries 737
   Sara Balduzzi, Lucio Balzani, Matteo Di Maso, Chiara
   Lambertini, Elena Toschi

 Comparing ORF Length in DNA Code Observed in Sixteen Yeast Chromosomes 745
   Anna Bartkowiak , Adam Szustalewicz

Influence of the Calibration Weights on Results Obtained from Czech SILC Data 753
   Jitka Bartošová, Vladislav Bína

Continuous Wavelet Transform and the Annual Cycle in Temperature and the Number of Deaths 761
   Milan Bašta, Josef Arlt, Markéta Arltová, Karel Helman

EM-Like Algorithms for Nonparametric Estimation in Multivariate Mixtures 769
   Tatiana Benaglia, Didier Chauveau, David R. Hunter

On the use of Weighted Regression in Conjoint Analysis 777
  Salwa Benammou, Besma Souissi, Gilbert Saporta

Wavelet-PLS Regression: Application to Oil Production Data. 785
  Salwa Benammou, Kacem Zied, Hedi Kortas, Dhifaoui Zouhaier

Variable Selection and Parameter Tuning in High-Dimensional
Prediction 793
  Christoph Bernau, Anne-Laure Boulesteix

A Generative Model for Rank Data Based on Sorting Algorithm 801
  Christophe Biernacki, Julien Jacques

"Made in Italy" Firms Competitiveness: A Multilevel Longitudinal Model on Export Performance 809
  Matilde Bini, Margherita Velucchi

Statistical Inference on Large Contingency Tables: Convergence, Testability, Stability 817
  Marianna Bolla

A Class of Multivariate Type I Generalized Logistic Distributions 825
  Salvatore Bologna

Adaptive Mixture Discriminant Analysis for Supervised Learning with Unobserved Classes 831
  Charles Bouveyron

Forecasting a Compound Cox Process by means of PCP 839
  Paula R. Bouzas, Nuria Ruiz-Fuentes, Juan Eloy Ruiz-Castro

Cutting the Dendrogram through Permutation Tests 847
  Dario Bruzzese, Domenico Vistocco

Design of Least-Squares Quadratic Estimators Based on Covariances from Interrupted Observations Transmitted by Different Sensors 855
  R. Caballero-Águila, A. Hermoso-Carazo, J. Linares-Pérez

Pseudo-Bayes Factors 863
  Stefano Cabras, Walter Racugno, Laura Ventura

Diagnostic Checking of Multivariate Normality Under Contamination 871
  Andrea Cerioli

On Computationally Complex Instances of the c-optimal Experimental Design Problem: Breaking RSA-based Cryptography via c-optimal Designs 879
Michal Černý, Milan Hladík, Veronika Skočdopolová

Estimation and Detection of Outliers and Patches in Nonlinear Time Series Models 887
Ping Chen

Two-way Classification of a Table with non-negative entries: Validation of an Approach based on Correspondence Analysis and Information Criteria 895
Antonio Ciampi, Alina Dyachenko, Yves Lechevallier

A Mann-Whitney Spatial Scan Statistic for Continuous Data . 903
Lionel Cucala

Quantile Regression for Group Effect Analysis 911
Cristina Davino, Domenico Vistocco

Regularized Directions of Maximal Outlyingness 919
Michiel Debruyne

A New Approach to Robust Clustering in $\mathbb{R}^p$ 927
Catherine Dehon, Kaveh Vakili

An Exploratory Segmentation Method for Time Series 935
Christian Derquenne

Using Auxiliary Information Under a Generic Sampling Design 943
Giancarlo Diana, Pier Francesco Perri

Improving Overlapping Clusters obtained by a Pyramidal Clustering 951
Edwin Diday, Francisco de A. T. de Carvalho, Luciano D.S. Pacifico

Visualizing and Forecasting Complex Time Series: Beanplot Time Series 959
Carlo Drago, Germana Scepi

M-estimation in INARCH Models with a Special Focus on Small Means 967
Hanan El-Saied, Roland Fried

Score Moment Estimators 975
Zdeněk Fabián

Testing the Number of Components in Poisson Mixture Regression Models 983
Susana Faria, Fátima Gonçalves

Support Vector Machines for Large Scale Text Mining in R .. 991
Ingo Feinerer, Alexandros Karatzoglou

Computation of the Projection of the Inhabitants of the Czech Republic by sex, age and the highest education level 999
Tomáš Fiala, Jitka Langhamrová

Two Kurtosis Measures in a Simulation Study 1007
Anna Maria Fiori

Clustering of Czech Household Incomes Over Very Short Time Period 1015
Marie Forbelská, Jitka Bartošová

Model-Based Nonparametric Variance Estimation for Systematic Sampling. An Application in a Forest Survey 1023
Mario Francisco-Fernández, Jean Opsomer, Xiaoxi Li

Thresholding-Wavelet-Based Functional Estimation of Spatiotemporal Strong-Dependence in the Spectral Domain 1031
María Pilar Frías, María Dolores Ruiz-Medina

Boolean Factor Analysis by the Expectation-Maximization Algorithm 1039
Alexander. A. Frolov, Pavel. Y. Polyakov, Dusan Húsek

Modeling and Forecasting Electricity Prices and their Volatilities by Conditionally Heteroskedastic Seasonal Dynamic Factor Analysis 1047
Carolina García-Martos, Julio Rodríguez, María Jesús Sánchez

Consensus Analysis Through Modal Symbolic Objects 1055
Jose M. Garcia-Santesmases, M. Carmen Bravo

Nonlinear Regression Model of Copper Bromide Laser Generation 1063
Snezhana Georgieva Gocheva-Ilieva, Iliycho Petkov Iliev

Random Forests Based Feature Selection for Decoding fMRI Data 1071
Robin Genuer, Vincent Michel, Evelyn Eger, Bertrand Thirion

Differentiation Tests for the Mean Shape and the Mean Variance of Renal Tumours appearing in early Childhood 1079
  Stefan Markus Giebel, Jens-Peter Schenk, Jang Schiltz

Local or Global Smoothing? A Bandwidth Selector for Dependent Data 1087
  Francesco Giordano, Maria Lucia Parrella

Panel Data Models for Productivity Analysis 1095
  Luigi Grossi, Giorgio Gozzi

A Stochastic Gamma Diffusion Model with Threshold Parameter. Computational Statistical Aspects and Application 1103
  Ramón Gutiérrez, Ramón Gutiérrez-Sánchez, Ahmed Nafidi, Eva Maria Ramos-Ábalos

On the Correlated Gamma Frailty Model for Bivariate Current Status Data 1111
  Niel Hens, Andreas Wienke

Evolutionary Stochastic Portfolio Optimization and Probabilistic Constraints 1119
  Ronald Hochreiter

Boosting a Generalised Poisson Hurdle Model 1127
  Vera Hofer

Fast and Robust Classifiers Adjusted for Skewness 1135
  Mia Hubert, Stephan Van der Veeken

Modelling the Andalusian Population by Means of a non-Homogeneous Stochastic Gompertz Process 1143
  Maria Dolores Huete Morales, Francisco Abad Montes

Neural Network Approach for Histopathological Diagnosis of Breast Diseases with Images 1151
  Yuichi Ishibashi, Atsuko Hara, Isao Okayasu, Koji Kurihara

Detection of Spatial Cluster for Suicide Data using Echelon Analysis 1159
  Fumio Ishioka, Makoto Tomita, Toshiharu Fujita

Time-Varying Coefficient Model with Linear Smoothing Function for Longitudinal Data in Clinical Trial 1167
  Masanori Ito , Toshihiro Misumi, Hideki Hirooka

Metropolis-Hastings Algorithm for Mixture Model and its
Weak Convergence 1175
  Kengo Kamatani

A Method for Time Series Analysis Using Probability Distribution of Local Standard Fractal Dimension 1183
  Kenichi Kamijo, Akiko Yamanouchi

Assessment of Scoring Models Using Information Value 1191
  Jan Koláček, Martin Řezáč

The Moving Average Control Chart Based on the Sequence
of Permutation Tests 1199
  Grzegorz Konczak

Depth Based Procedures for Estimation ARMA and GARCH
Models 1207
  Daniel Kosiorowski

Half-Taxi Metric in Compositional Data Geometry Rcomp ...1215
  Katarina Košmelj, Vesna Žabkar

LTPD Plans by Variables when the Remainder of Rejected
Lots is Inspected 1223
  J. Klufa, L. Marek

A Comparison between Two Computing Methods for an Empirical Variogram in Geostatistical Data 1231
  Takafumi Kubota, Tomoyuki Tarumi

Improvement of Acceleration of the ALS Algorithm Using the
Vector ε Algorithm 1239
  Masahiro Kuroda, Yuchi Mori, Masaya Iizuka, Michio Sakakihara

Unsupervised Recall and Precision Measures: a Step towards
New Efficient Clustering Quality Indexes 1247
  Jean-Charles Lamirel, Maha Ghribi, Pascal Cuxac

Performance Assessment of Optimal Allocation for Large Portfolios 1255
  Fabrizio Laurini, Luigi Grossi

Clustering of Multiple Dissimilarity Data Tables for Docu-
ments Categorization 1263
  Yves Lechevallier, Francisco de A. T. de Carvalho, Thierry
  Despeyroux, Filipe M. de Melo

Slimming Down a High-Dimensional Binary Datatable: relevant Eigen-Subspace and Substantial Content 1271
Alain Lelu

Comparing Two Approaches to Testing Linearity against Markov-switching Type Non-linearity 1279
Jana Lenčuchová, Anna Petričková, Magdaléna Komorníková

Numerical Error Analysis for Statistical Software on Multi-Core Systems...1287
Wenbin Li, Sven Simon

Sparse Bayesian Hierarchical Model for Clustering Problems .1295
Heng Lian

Data Mining and Multiple Correspondence Analysis via Polynomial Transformations 1303
Rosaria Lombardo

Structural Modelling of Nonlinear Exposure-Response Relationships for Longitudinal Data 1311
Xiaoshu Lu, Esa-Pekka Takala

Empirical Composite Likelihoods 1319
Nicola Lunardon, Francesco Pauli, Laura Ventura

A Fast Parsimonious Maximum Likelihood Approach for Predicting Outcome Variables from a Large Number of Predictors 1327
Jay Magidson

A Bootstrap Method to Improve Brain Subcortical Network Segregation in Resting-State FMRI Data 1335
Caroline Malherbe, Eric Bardinet, Arnaud Messé, Vincent Perlbarg, Guillaume Marrelec, Mélanie Pélégrini-Issac, Jérôme Yelnik, Stéphane Lehéricy, Habib Benali

The Problem of Determining the Calibration Equations to Construct Model-calibration Estimators of the Distribution Function..1343
Sergio Martínez, Maria Rueda, Antonio Arcos, Helena Martínez, Juan Francisco Muñoz

Dealing with Nonresponse in Survey Sampling: an Item Response Modeling Approach 1353
Alina Matei

Estimation of the Bivariate Distribution Function for Censored Gap Times 1359
Luís Meira-Machado, Ana Moreira

Two Measures of Dissimilarity for the Dendrogram Multi-Class SVM Model 1367
Rafael Pino Mejías, María Dolores Cubiles de la Vega

Visualizing the Sampling Variability of Plots 1375
Rajiv S. Menjoge, Roy E. Welsch

Empirical Mode Decomposition for Trend Extraction. Application to Electrical Data....................................1383
Farouk Mhamdi, Mériem Jaïdane-Saïdane, Jean-Michel Poggi

The Evaluation of Non-centred Orthant Probabilities for Singular Multivariate Normal Distributions.....................1391
Tetsuhisa Miwa

Variable Inclusion and Shrinkage Algorithm in High Dimension 1397
Abdallah Mkhadri, Mohamed Ouhourane

Application of a Bayesian Approach for Analysing Disease Mapping Data: Modelling Spatially Correlated Small Area Counts 1405
Mohammadreza Mohebbi, Rory Wolfe

Clusters of Gastrointestinal Tract Cancer in the Caspian Region of Iran: A Spatial Scan Analysis 1413
Mohammadreza Mohebbi, Rory Wolfe

The Financial Crisis of 2008: Modelling the Transmission Mechanism Between the Markets 1421
M. Pilar Muñoz Maria Dolores Márquez, Helena Chuliá

Determining the Direction of the Path Using a Bayesian Semiparametric Model 1429
Kei Miyazaki, Takahiro Hoshino,, Kazuo Shigemasu

Data Visualization and Aggregation 1437
Junji Nakano, Yoshikazu Yamamoto

Longitudinal Data Analysis Based on Ranks and its Performance 1445
Takashi Nagakubo, Masashi Goto

Multiple Change Point Detection by Sparse Parameter Estimation...1453
  Jiří Neubauer, Vítězslav Veselý

Quasi-Maximum Likelihood Estimators for Threshold ARMA
Models: Theoretical Results and Computational Issues 1461
  Marcella Niglio, Cosimo Damiano Vitale

A Case Study of Bank Branch Performance Using Linear
Mixed Models 1469
  Peggy Ng, Claudia Czado, Eike Christian Brechmann, Jon Kerr

Numerical Methods for some Classes of Matrices with Applications to Statistics and Optimization 1477
  Juan M. Peña

Maximum Margin Learning of Gaussian Mixture Models with
Application to Multipitch Tracking 1485
  Franz Pernkopf, Michael Wohlmayr

Low-Pass Filter Design using Locally Weighted Polynomial
Regression and Discrete Prolate Spheroidal Sequences.......1493
  Tommaso Proietti, Alessandra Luati

A Statistical Survival Model Based on Counting Processes....1501
  *Jose-Manuel Quesada-Rubio, Julia Garcia-Leal, Maria-Jose
  Del-Moral-Avila, Esteban Navarrete-Alvarez, Maria-Jesus
  Rosales-Moreno*

Bootstrapping Additive Models in Presence of Missing Data. .1509
  *Rocío Raya-Miranda, M. Dolores Martínez-Miranda, Andrés
  González-Carmona*

On Aspects of Quality Indexes for Scoring Models 1517
  Martin Řezáč, Jan Koláček

Data Clustering with Mixed Type Variables and Cluster Number Determination 1525
  Hana Řezanková, Dušan Húsek, Tomáš Löster

A General Strategy for Determining First-Passage-Time Densities Based on the First-Passage-Time Location Function 1533
  *Patricia Román-Román, Juan José Serrano-Pérez, Francisco
  Torres-Ruiz*

Rplugin.Econometrics: R-GUI for Teaching Time Series Analysis...1541
  Dedi Rosadi

Computational Statistics: the Symbolic Approach 1549
  Colin Rose

EOFs for Gap Filling in Multivariate Air Quality data: a FDA
Approach 1557
  Mariantonietta Ruggieri, Francesca Di Salvo, Antonella Plaia,
  Gianna Agró

A Transient Analysis of a Complex Discrete k-out-of-n:G System with Multi-State Components 1565
  Juan Eloy Ruiz-Castro, Paula R. Bouzas

Using Logitboost for Stationary Signals Classification 1573
  Pedro Saavedra, Angelo Santana, Carmen Nieves Hernández,
  Juan Artiles, Juan-José González

Test of Mean Difference for Longitudinal Data Using Circular
Block Bootstrap 1581
  Hirohito Sakurai, Masaaki Taguri

An Empirical Study of the Use of Nonparametric Regression
Methods for Imputation 1589
  Ismael R. Sánchez-Borrego, Maria Rueda, Encarnación
  Álvarez-Verdejo

A Simulation Study of the Bayes Estimator of Parameters in
an Extension of the Exponential Distribution 1597
  Samira Sadeghi

A Cluster-Target Similarity Based Principal Component Analysis for Interval-Valued Data 1605
  Mika Sato-Ilic

Bayesian Flexible Modelling of Mixed Logit Models 1613
  Luisa Scaccia, Edoardo Marcucci

A Decision Tree for Symbolic Data 1621
  Djamal Seck, Lynne Billard, Edwin Diday, Filipe Afonso

The Set of $3 \times 4 \times 4$ Contingency Tables has 3-Neighborhood
Property 1629
  Toshio Sumi, Toshio Sakata

Visualization Techniques for the Integration of Rank Data....1637
  Michael G. Schimek, Eva Budinská

Comprehensive Assessment on Hierarchical Structures of DNA
markers Using Echelon Analysis 1645
  Makoto Tomita, Koji Kurihara

Non-Hierarchical Clustering for Distribution-Valued Data 1653
  Yoshikazu Terada, Hiroshi Yadohisa

On Composite Pareto Models................................1661
  Sandra Teodorescu, Raluca Vernic

Visualisation of Large Sized Data Sets : Constraints and Improvements for Graph Design...............................1669
  Jean-Paul Valois

Selecting Variables in Two-Group Robust Linear Discriminant
Analysis 1677
  Stefan Van Aelst, Gert Willems

How to Take into Account the Discrete Parameters in the BIC
Criterion? 1685
  Vincent Vandewalle

Analysis of Breath Alcohol Measurements Using Compartmental and Generalized Linear Models 1693
  Chi Ting Yang, Wing Kam Fung, Thomas Wai Ming Tam

Fisher Scoring for Some Univariate Discrete Distributions 1701
  Thomas W. Yee

Constructing Summary Indexes via Principal Curves 1709
  Mohammad Zayed, Jochen Einbeck

Censored Survival Data: Simulation and Kernel Estimates 1717
  Jiří Zelinka

Part XVIII. Supplementary Invited Papers

Heuristic Optimization for Model Selection and Estimation ...1727
  Dietmar Maringer

General Index 1737

Part I

Keynote

Complexity Questions in Non-Uniform Random Variate Generation

Luc Devroye

School of Computer Science
McGill University
Montreal, Canada H3A 2K6
lucdevroye@gmail.com

Abstract. In this short note, we recall the main developments in non-uniform random variate generation, and list some of the challenges ahead.

Keywords: random variate generation, Monte Carlo methods, simulation

1 The pioneers

World War II was a terrible event. But it can not be denied that it pushed science forward with a force never seen before. It was responsible for the quick development of the atomic bomb and led to the cold war, during which the United States and Russia set up many research labs and attracted the best and the brightest to run them. It was at Los Alamos and RAND that physicists and other scientists were involved in large-scale simulations. John von Neumann, Stan Ulam and Nick Metropolis developed the Monte Carlo Method in 1946: they suggested that we could compute and predict in ways never before considered. For example, the Metropolis chain method developed a few years later (Metropolis, Rosenbluth, Rosenbluth, Teller and Teller, 1953) can be used to simulate almost any distribution by setting up a Markov chain that has that distribution as a limit. At least asymptotically, that is. But it was feasible, because the computers were getting to be useful, with the creation of software and the FORTRAN compiler.

To drive the Markov chains and other processes, one would need large collections of uniform random numbers. That was a bit of a sore point, because no one knew where to get them. Still today, the discussion rages as to how one should secure a good source of uniform random numbers. The scientists eventually settled on something that a computer could generate, a sequence that looked random.

The early winner was the linear congruential generator, driven by $x_{n+1} = (ax_n + b) \bmod m$, which had several well-understood properties. Unfortunately, it is just a deterministic sequence, and many of its flaws have been exposed in the last three decades. The built-in linear-congruential generator in the early FORTRAN package for IBM computers was RANDU. Consecutive pairs

Y. Lechevallier, G. Saporta (eds.), *Proceedings of COMPSTAT'2010*,
DOI 10.1007/978-3-7908-2604-3_1, © Springer-Verlag Berlin Heidelberg 2010

(x_n, x_{n+1}) produced by RANDU fall on just a few parallel lines, prompting Marsaglia (1968) to write a paper with the ominous title "Random numbers fall mainly in the plane". But bad linear congruential or related generators have persisted until today—the generator in Wolfram's Mathematica had a similar problem: their built-in generator Random uses the Marsaglia-Zaman subtract-with-borrow generator (1991), which has the amazing property that all consecutive triples (x_n, x_{n+1}, x_{n+2}) fall in only two hyperplanes of $[0, 1]^3$, a fact pointed out to me by Pierre Lecuyer. Many thousands of simulations with Mathematica are thus suspect—I was made aware of this due an inconsistency between simulation and theory brought to my attention by Jim Fill in 2010. The company has never apologized or offered a refund to its customers, but it has quietly started using other methods, including one based on a cellular automaton (the default). Hoewever, they are still offering linear congruential generators as an option. The story is far from over, and physical methods may well come back in force.

Information theorists and computer scientists have approached random-ness from another angle. For them, random variables uniformly distributed on $[0, 1]$ do not and can not exist, because the binary expansions of such variables consist of infinitely many independent Bernoulli $(1/2)$ random bits. Each random bit has binary entropy equal to one, which means that its value or cost is one. A bit can store one unit of information, and vice versa, a random bit costs one unit of resources to produce. Binary entropy for a more complex random object can be measured in terms of how many random bits one needs to describe it. The binary entropy of a random vector of n inde-pendent fair coin flips is n, because we can describe it by n individual fair coins.

For the generation of discrete or integer-valued random variables, which includes the vast area of the generation of random combinatorial structures, one can adhere to a clean model, the pure bit model, in which each bit operation takes one time unit, and storage can be reported in terms of bits. In this model, one assumes that an i.i.d. sequence of independent perfect bits is available. This permits the development of an elegant information-theoretic theory. For example, Knuth and Yao (1976) showed that to generate a random integer X described by the probability distribution

$$\mathbf{P}\{X = n\} = p_n, n \geq 1,$$

any method must use an expected number of bits greater than the binary entropy of the distribution,

$$\sum_n p_n \log_2(1/p_n).$$

They also showed how to construct tree-based generators that can be imple-mented as finite or infinite automata to come within three bits of this lower bound for any distribution. While this theory is elegant and theoretically important, it is somewhat impractical to have to worry about the individual bits in the binary expansions of the p_n's. Noteworthy is that attempts have been made (see, e.g., Flajolet and Saheb (1986)) to extend the pure bit model to obtain approximate algorithms for random variables with densities.

For integer-valued random variables with $\mathbf{P}\{X = n\} = p_n, n \geq 0$, the inversion method is always applicable:

```
X ← 0
Generate U uniform [0,1]
S ← p₀ (S holds the partial sums of the pₙ's)
while U > S do :     X ← X + 1, S ← S + pₓ
return X
```

The expected number of steps here is $\mathbf{E}\{X + 1\}$. Improvements are possible by using data structures that permit one to invert more quickly. When there are only a finite number of values, a binary search tree may help. Here the leaves correspond to various outcomes for X, and the internal nodes are there to guide the search by comparing U with appropriately picked thresholds. If the cost of setting up this tree is warranted, then one could always permute the leaves to make this into a Huffman tree for the weights p_n (Huffman (1952)), which insures that the expected time to find a leaf is not more than one plus the binary entropy. In any case, this value does not exceed $\log_2 N$, where N is the number of possible values X can take. The difference with the Knuth-Yao result is that one now needs to be able to store and add real numbers (the p_n's).

Even when taking bits at unit cost, one needs to be careful about the computational model. For example, is one allowed to store real numbers, or should we work with a model in which storage and computation time is also measured in terms of bits? We feel that the information-theoretic boundaries and lower bounds should be studied in more detail, and that results like those of Knuth and Yao should be extended to cover non-discrete random variables as well, if one can formulate the models correctly.

2   The assumptions and the limitations

Assume that we can indeed store and work with real numbers and that an infinite source of independent identically distributed uniform $[0,1]$ random variables, $U_1, U_2, \ldots$ is available at unit cost per random variable used. The random source excepted, the computer science community has embraced the so-called RAM (random access memory) model. While it unrealistic, designing random variate generators in this model has several advantages. First of all, it allows one to disconnect the theory of non-uniform random variate generation from that of uniform random variate generation, and secondly, it permits one to plan for the future, as more powerful computers will be developed that permit ever better approximations of the idealistic model. The subject of non-uniform random generation is to generate random variables with a given distribution—we call these random variates—, in (possibly random) finite time. We also assume that computations can be carried out with infinite precision, and we require that the results be theoretically exact.

For a given collection of operations (a computer language), one can define the collection of all distributions of random variables that can be generated in finite time using these operations. Classes of achievable distributions defined in this manner will be denoted by $\mathcal{D}$. For example, if we only allow addition and subtraction, besides the standard move, store and copy operations, then one can only generate the sums

$$c + \sum_{i=1}^{N} k_i U_i,$$

where $c \in \mathbf{R}$, and $N, k_1, \ldots, k_N$ are finite integers. This is hardly interesting. An explosion occurs when one allows multiplication and division, and introduces comparisons and loops as operators. The achievable class becomes quite large. We will call it the algebraic class.

The need for non-uniform random variates in Monte Carlo simulations prompted the post-World War II teams to seriously think about the problem. All probabilists understand the inversion method: a random variate with distribution function F can be obtained as

$$X = F^{\mathrm{inv}}(U),$$

where U is uniform $[0, 1]$. This inversion method is useful when the inverse is readily computable. For example, a standard exponential random variable (which has density $e^{-x}, x > 0$), can be generated as $\log(1/U)$. Table 1 gives some further examples.

Table 1. Table 1: Some densities with distribution functions that are explicitly invertible. Random variates can be generated simply by appropriate transormations of a uniform $[0, 1]$ random variable U.

Name	Density	Distribution function	Random variate
Exponential	$e^{-x}, x > 0$	$1 - e^{-x}$	$\log(1/U)$
Weibull (a), $a > 0$	$ax^{a-1}e^{-x^a}, x > 0$	$1 - e^{-x^a}$	$(\log(1/U))^{1/a}$
Gumbel	$e^{-x}e^{-e^{-x}}$	$e^{-e^{-x}}$	$-\log\log(1/U)$
Logistic	$\frac{1}{2+e^x+e^{-x}}$	$\frac{1}{1+e^{-x}}$	$-\log((1-U)/U)$
Cauchy	$\frac{1}{\pi(1+x^2)}$	$1/2 + (1/\pi)\arctan x$	$\tan(\pi U)$
Pareto (a), $a > 0$	$\frac{a}{x^{a+1}}, x > 1$	$1 - 1/x^a$	$1/U^{1/a}$

However, note that only the Pareto distribution for values of a that are inverses of an integer is in the algebraic class. One can attempt to create functions of a finite number of uniforms, and in this way, one notes that the Cauchy too is in the algebraic class. We leave it as a simple exercise to show that the following method works. Keep generating independent random pairs of independent uniforms, (U, U'), until for the first time $U^2 + U'^2 \leq 1$ (now (U, U') is uniformly distributed in the positive quarter of the unit circle). Then set $X = SU/U'$, where $S \in \{-1, +1\}$ is a random sign. One can ask if the normal distribution is in the algebraic class for example. In fact, a good description of the algebraic class is sorely needed.

Assume now a much more powerful class, one that is based upon all operations for the algebraic class, plus the standard mathematical functions, exp, log, sin (and thus cos and tan). Call it the standard class. All inversion method examples in Table 1 describe distributions in the standard class.

Since we did not add the inverse of the normal distribution function to the allowed operations, it would appear at first that the normal distribution is not in the standard class. For future reference, the standard normal density is given by $\exp(-x^2/2)/\sqrt{2\pi}$. This was of great concern to the early simulationists because they knew how to calculate certain standard functions very well, but had to make do with approximation formulas for functions like the inverse gaussian distribution function. Such formulas became very popular, with researchers outcompeting each other for the best and the latest approximation.

Amazingly, it was not until 1958 that Box and Müller showed the world that the gaussian distribution was in the standard class. Until that year, all normal simulations were done either by summing a number of uniforms and rescaling in the hope that the central limit theorem would yield something good enough, or by using algebraic approximations of the inverse of the gaussian distribution function, as given, e.g., in the book of Hastings (1955).

As in our Cauchy example, Box and Müller noted that one should only look at simple transformations of k uniform $[0, 1]$ random variates, where k is either a small fixed integer, or a random integer with a small mean. It is remarkable that one can obtain the normal and indeed all stable distributions using simple transformations with $k = 2$. In the Box-Müller method (1958), a pair of independent standard normal random variates is obtained by setting

$$(X, Y) = \left(\sqrt{\log(1/U_1)} \cos(2\pi U_2), \sqrt{\log(1/U_1)} \sin(2\pi U_2) \right).$$

For the computational perfectionists, we note that the random cosine can be avoided: just generate a random point in the unit circle by rejection from the enclosing square, and then normalize it so that it is of unit length. Its first component is distributed as a random cosine.

There are many other examples that involve the use of a random cosine, and for this reason, they are called polar methods. We recall that the beta

(a, b) density is

$$\frac{x^{a-1}(1-x)^{b-1}}{B(a,b)}, 0 \le x \le 1,$$

where $B(a, b) = \Gamma(a)\Gamma(b)/\Gamma(a + b)$. A symmetric beta (a, a) random variate may be generated as

$$\frac{1}{2}\left(1 + \sqrt{1 - U_1^{\frac{2}{2a-1}}}\cos(2\pi U_2)\right)$$

(Ulrich, 1984), where $a \ge 1/2$. Devroye (1996) provided a recipe valid for all $a > 0$:

$$\frac{1}{2}\left(1 + \frac{S}{\sqrt{1 + \frac{1}{\left(U_1^{-\frac{1}{a}} - 1\right)\cos^2(2\pi U_2)}}}\right),$$

where S is a random sign. Perhaps the most striking result of this kind is due to Bailey (1994), who showed that

$$\sqrt{a\left(U_1^{-\frac{2}{a}} - 1\right)}\cos(2\pi U_2)$$

has the Student t density (invented by William S. Gosset in 1908) with parameter $a > 0$:

$$\frac{1}{\sqrt{a}B(a/2, 1/2)\left(1 + \frac{x^2}{a}\right)^{\frac{a+1}{2}}}, x \in \mathbf{R}.$$

Until Bailey's paper, only rather inconvenient rejection methods were available for Student's t density.

There are many random variables that can be represented as $\psi(U)E^{\alpha}$, where ψ is a function, U is uniform $[0, 1]$, α is a real number, and E is an independent exponential random variable. These lead to simple algorithms for a host of useful yet tricky distributions. A random variable $S_{\alpha,\beta}$ with characteristic function

$$\varphi(t) = \exp\left(-|t|^\alpha \exp\left(-i(\pi/2)\beta(\alpha - 2\mathbf{1}_{\alpha>1})\operatorname{sign}(t)\right)\right)$$

is said to be stable with parameters $\alpha \in (0, 2]$ and $|\beta| \le 1$. Its parameter α determines the size of its tail. Using integral representations of distribution functions, Kanter (1975) showed that for $\alpha < 1$, $S_{\alpha,1}$ is distributed as

$$\psi(U)E^{1-\frac{1}{\alpha}},$$

where

$$\psi(u) = \left(\frac{\sin(\alpha\pi u)}{\sin(\pi u)}\right)^{\frac{1}{\alpha}} \times \left(\frac{\sin((1-\alpha)\pi u)}{\sin(\alpha\pi u)}\right)^{\frac{1-\alpha}{\alpha}}.$$

For general α, β, Chambers, Mallows and Stuck (1976) showed that it suffices to generate it as

$$\psi(U - 1/2)E^{1-\frac{1}{\alpha}},$$

where

$$\psi(u) = \left(\frac{\cos(\pi((\alpha - 1)u + \alpha\theta)/2)}{\cos(\pi u/2)}\right)^{\frac{1}{\alpha}} \times \left(\frac{\sin(\pi\alpha(u + \theta)/2)}{\cos(\pi((\alpha - 1)u + \alpha\theta)/2)}\right).$$

Zolotarev (1959, 1966, 1981, 1986) has additional representations and a thorough discussion on these families of distributions. The paper by Devroye (1990) contains other examples with $k = 3$, including

$$S_{\alpha,0}E^{\frac{1}{\alpha}},$$

which has the so-called Linnik distribution (Linnik (1962)) with characteristic function

$$\varphi(t) = \frac{1}{1 + |t|^\alpha}, 0 < \alpha \leq 2.$$

We end this section with a few questions about the size and nature of the standard class. Let us say that a distribution is k-standard (for fixed integer k) if it is in the standard class and there exists a generator algorithm that uses only a fixed number k of uniforms. The standard class is thus the union of all k-standard classes. Even more restrictive is the loopless k-standard class, one in which looping operations are not allowed. These include distributions for which we can write the generator in one line of code. The gaussian and indeed all stable laws are loopless 2-standard. We do not know if the gamma density

$$\frac{x^{a-1}e^{-x}}{\Gamma(a)}, x > 0,$$

is loopless k-standard for any finite k not depending upon the gamma parameter $a > 0$. Similarly, this is also unknown for the general beta family. Luckily, the gamma law is in the standard class, thanks to the rejection method, which was invented by von Neumann and is discussed in the next section.

It would be a fine research project to characterize the standard class and the (loopless) k-standard classes in several novel ways. Note in this respect that all discrete laws with the property that p_n can be computed in finite time using standard operations are 1-standard. Note that we can in fact use the individual bits (as many as necessary) to make all the necesary comparisons of U with a threshold. Only a random but finite number of these bits are needed for each variate generated. Let us define the class of distributions with the property that only a (random) finite number of bits of U suffice 0-standard. The full use of all bits in a uniform is only needed to create an absolutely continuous law.

Are absolutely continuous laws that are describable by standard operations k-standard for a given universal finite k?

Finally, it seems that even the simplest singular continuous laws on the real line are not in the standard class, but a proof of this fact would be nice to have. Take as an example a random variable $X \in [0,1]$ whose binary expansion has independent Bernoulli (p) bits. If $p = 1/2$, X is clearly uniform on $[0,1]$. But when $p \notin \{0, 1/2, 1\}$, then X is singular continuous. It is difficult to see how standard functions can be used to recreate such infinite expansions. If this is indeed the case, then the singular continuous laws, and indeed many fractal laws in higher dimensions, have the property that no finite amount of resources suffices to generate even one of them exactly. Approximations on the real line that are based on uniforms and standard functions are necessarily atomic or absolutely continuous in nature, and thus undesirable.

3   The rejection method

The Cauchy method described above uses a trick called rejection. The rejection method in its general form is due to von Neumann (1951). Let X have density f on $\mathbf{R}^d$. Let g be another density with the property that for some finite constant $c \geq 1$, called the rejection constant,

$$f(x) \leq cg(x), x \in \mathbf{R}^d.$$

For any nonnegative integrable function h on $\mathbf{R}^d$, define the body of h as $B_h = \{(x,y) : x \in \mathbf{R}^d, 0 \leq y \leq h(x)\}$. Note that if (X, Y) is uniformly distributed on B_h, then X has density proportional to h. Vice versa, if X has density proportional to h, then $(X, Uh(X))$, where U is uniform $[0,1]$ and independent of X, is uniformly distributed on B_h. These facts can be used to show the validity of the rejection method:

```
repeat
      Generate U uniformly on [0, 1]
      Generate X with density g
until Ucg(X) ≤ f(X)
return X
```

The expected number of iterations before halting is c, so the rejection constant must be kept small. This method requires some analytic work, notably to determine c, but one attractive feature is that we only need the ratio $f(x)/(cg(x))$, and thus, cumbersome normalization constants often cancel out.

The rejection principle also applies in the discrete setting, so a few examples follow to illustrate its use in all settings. We begin with the standard normal density. The start is an inequality such as

$$e^{-x^2/2} \leq e^{\alpha^2/2 - \alpha|x|}.$$

The area under the dominating curve is $e^{\alpha^2/2} \times 2/\alpha$, which is minimized for $\alpha = 1$. Generating a random variate with the Laplace density $e^{-|x|}$ can be done either as SE, where S is a random sign, and E is exponential, or as $E_1 - E_2$, a difference of two independent exponential random variables. The rejection algorithm thus reads:

```
repeat
      Generate U uniformly on [0, 1]
      Generate X with with the Laplace density
until Ue^{1/2-|X|} ≤ e^{-X^2/2}
return X
```

However, taking logarithms in the last condition, and noting that $\log(1/U)$ is exponential, we can tighten the code using a random sign S, and two independent exponentials, E_1, E_2:

```
Generate a random sign S
repeat Generate E₁, E₂
until 2E₂ > (E₁ − 1)²
return X ← SE₁
```

It is easy to verify that the rejection constant (the expected number of iterations) is $\sqrt{2e/\pi} \approx 1.35$.

The laws statisticians care about have one by one fallen to the rejection method. As early as 1974, Ahrens and Dieter showed how to generate beta, gamma, Poisson and binomial random variables efficiently. All these distributions are in the standard class. However, if the density f or the probability p_n is not computable in finite time using standard functions, then the distribution is not obviously in the standard class.

4   The alternating series method

To apply the rejection method, we do not really need to know the ratio $f(x)/(cg(x))$ exactly. Assume that we have computable bounds $\xi_n(x)$ and $\psi_n(x)$ with the property that $\xi_n(x) \uparrow f(x)/(cg(x))$ and $\psi_n(x) \downarrow f(x)/(cg(x))$ as $n \to \infty$. In that case, we let n increase until for the first time, either

$$U \le \xi(X)$$

(in which case we accept X), or

$$U \ge \psi_n(X)$$

(in which case we reject X). This approach is useful when the precise computation of f is impossible, e.g., when f is known as infinite series or when f can never be computed exactly using only finitely many resources. It was first developed for the Kolmogorov-Smirnov limit distribution in Devroye (1981a). For another use of this idea, see Keane and O'Brien's Bernoulli factory (1994).

```
repeat
      Generate U uniformly on [0,1]
      Generate X with density g
      Set n = 0
      repeat n ← n + 1 until U ≤ ξₙ(X) or U ≥ ψₙ(X)
until U ≤ ξₙ(X)
return X
```

The expected number of iterations in the outer loop is still c, as in the rejection method. However, to take the inner loop into account, let N be the largest index n attained in the inner loop. Note that N is finite almost surely. Also, $N > t$ implies that $U \in [\xi_t(X), \psi_t(X)]$, and thus,

$$\mathbf{E}\{N|X\} = \sum_{t=0}^{\infty} \mathbf{P}\{N > t|X\} \leq \sum_{t=0}^{\infty} (\psi_t(X) - \xi_t(X))$$

and

$$\mathbf{E}\{N\} \leq \sum_{t=0}^{\infty} \mathbf{E}\{\psi_t(X) - \xi_t(X)\}.$$

We cannot stress strongly enough how important the alternating series method is, as it frees us from having to compute f exactly. When ξ_n and ψ_n are computable in finite time with standard functions, and g is in the standard class, then f is in the standard class.

It is indeed the key to the solution of a host of difficult non-uniform random variate generation problems. For example, since the exponential, logarithmic and trigonometric functions have simple Taylor series expansions, one can approximate densities that use a finite number of these standard functions from above and below by using only addition, multiplication and division, and with some work, one can see that if a law is (k-)standard, then it is (k-)algebraic. Both gamma and gaussian are algebraic if one invokes the alternating series method using Taylor series expansions. To the programmer, this must seem like' a masochistic approach—if we have the exponential function, why should we not use it? But for the information theorist and computer scientist, the model of computation matters, and lower bound theory is perhaps easier to develop using more restricted classes.

But one can do better. Assume that a given density is Riemann integrable. Then it can be approximated from below by histograms. It takes only a moment to verify that such densities can be written as infinite mixtures of uniforms on given intervals. The mixture weights define a discrete law, which we know is 0-standard. A random variate can be written as

$$a_Z + b_Z U,$$

where Z is a discrete random variable, and $[a_i, b_i]$, $i \geq 1$, denote the intervals in the mixture decomposition. So, given one uniform random variable, first use a random number of bits from its expansion to generate Z, and then note that the unused bits, when shifted, are again uniformly distributed. This shows that Riemann integrable densities are 1-standard if we can compute the density at each point using only standard functions. In particular, the gamma and normal laws are 1-standard. This procedure can be automated, and indeed, several so-called table methods are based on such mixture decompositions. See, e.g., Devroye (1986a), or Hörmann, Leydold and Derflinger (2004).

5   Oracles

Oracles are a convenient way of approaching algorithms. Engineers call them "black boxes". One can imagine that one has an oracle for computing the value of the density f at x. Armed with one or more oracles, and our infinite source of uniforms, one can again ask for the existence of generators for certain dustributions.

For example, given a density oracle, is there an exact finite time method for generating a random variate with that density? Is there such a method that is universal, i.e., that works for all densities? The answer to this question is not known. In contrast, when given an oracle for the inverse of a distribution function, a universal method exists, the inversion method.

Given that we do not know the answer for the density oracle, it is perhaps futile at this point to ask for universal generators for characteristic function, Laplace transform or other oracles. It is perhaps possible to achieve success in the presence of two or more oracles. In the author's 1986 book, one can find partial success stories, such as a density oracle method for all log-concave densities on the line, or a combined density / distribution function (not the inverse though) moracle method for all monotone densities.

Complexity is now calculated in terms of the numbers of uniforms consumed and as a function of the number of consultations of the oracle. This should allow one to derive a number of negative results and lower bounds as well.

6   Open questions

We discussed the need for descriptions of operator-dependent classes, and the creation of models that can deal with singular continuity. The rejection and alternating series methods enable us to generate random variates with any distribution provided two conditions hold: we have an explicitly known finite dominating measure of finite, and we can approximate the value of the density or discrete probability locally by convergent and explicitly known upper and lower bounds. This has been used by the author, for example, to deal with distributions that are given by infinite series (Devroye, 1981a, 1997, 2009), distributions specified by a characteristic function (Devroye, 1981b, 1986b), Fourier coefficients (Devroye, 1989), a sequence of moments (Devroye, 1991), or their Laplace transforms. It should also be possible to extend this to laws whose Mellin transforms are known, or infinitely divisible laws that are specified in terms of Lévy or Khinchin measures (see Sato for definitions; Bondesson (1982) offers some approximative solutions). In all these examples, if a density exists, there are indeed inversion formulae that suggest convergent and explicitly known upper and lower bounds of the density.

It is hopeless to try to remove the requirement that a dominating measure be known—a characteristic function of a singular continuous distribution is a particularly unwieldy beast, for example. Some distributions have asymptotic distributional limits. As an example, consider

$$X = \sum_{i=0}^{\infty} \theta^i \xi_i,$$

where the ξ_i are independent Bernoulli (p), and $\theta \in (-1, 1)$. When $p = 1/2, \theta = 1/2$, X is uniform $[0, 1]$, while for $p \notin \{0, 1/2, 1\}$, $\theta = 1/2$, X is singular continuous. Using $\overset{\mathcal{L}}{=}$ for distributional identity, we see that

$$X \overset{\mathcal{L}}{=} \xi_0 + \theta X.$$

It seems unlikely that the distribution of X is in the standard class for all parameter values.

This leads to the question of determining which X, given by simple distributional identities of the form

$$X \overset{\mathcal{L}}{=} \phi(X, U)$$

are in the standard class. Note that the map $X \leftarrow \phi(X, U)$ defines in some cases a Markov chain with a limit. Using CFTP (coupling from the past; see Propp and Wilson (1996), Asmussen, Glynn and Thönnes (1992), Wilson (1998), Fill (2000), Murdoch and Green (1998)) or related methods, some progress has been made on such distributional identities if one assumes a particular form, such as

$$X \overset{\mathcal{L}}{=} U^{\alpha}(X + 1)$$

(its solutions are known as Vervaat perpetuities, Vervaat (1979). We refer to Kendall and Thönnes (2004), Fill and Huber (2009), Devroye (2001), and Devroye and Fawzi (2010) for worked out examples.

Identities like

$$X \overset{\mathcal{L}}{=} AX + B$$

occur in time series, random partitions, fragmentation processes, and as indirect descriptions of limit laws. Solutions are in the form of general perpetuities

$$X \stackrel{\mathcal{L}}{=} B_0 + \sum_{i=1}^{\infty} B_i \prod_{j=0}^{i-1} A_j,$$

where (A_i, B_i) are i.i.d. pairs distributed as (A, B). Necessary and sufficient conditions for the existence of solutions are known (Goldie and Maller, 2000; see also Alsmeyer and Iksanov, 2009, for further discussion). It suffices, for example, that

$$\mathbf{E}\{\log |A|\} \in (-\infty, 0), \mathbf{E}\{\log^+ |B|\} < \infty.$$

Yet one needs to describe those perpetuities that are in the standard class, and give algorithms for their generation.

Even more challenging are identities of the form

$$X \stackrel{\mathcal{L}}{=} \psi(X, X', U),$$

where X and X' on the right-hand-side are independent copies of X. Such identities do not lead to Markov chains. Instead, the repeated application of the map ψ produces an infinite binary tree. One should explore methods of random variate generation and constructively determine for which maps ψ, there is a solution that is in the standard class. A timid attempt for linear maps ψ was made by Devroye and Neininger (2002).

References

AHRENS, J.H. and DIETER, U. (1974): Computer methods for sampling from gamma, beta, Poisson and binomial distributions. *Computing, vol. 12, pp. 223–246.*

AKHIEZER, N.I. (1965): *The Classical Moment Problem*, Hafner, New York.

ALSMEYER, G. and IKSANOV, A. (2009): A log-type moment result for perpetuities and its application to martingales in supercritical branching random walks.' *Electronic Journal of Probability, vol. 14, pp. 289–313.*

ASMUSSEN, S., GLYNN, P. and THORISSON, H. (1992): Stationary detection in the initial transient problem. *ACM Transactions on Modeling and Computer Simulation, vol. 2, pp. 130–157.*

BAILEY, R.W. (1994): Polar generation of random variates with the t distribution (1994): *Mathematics of Computation, vol. 62, pp. 779–781.*

BONDESSON, L. (1982): On simulation from infinitely divisible distributions. *Advances in Applied Probability, vol. 14, pp. 855–869.*

BOX, G.E.P. and MÜLLER, M.E. (1958): A note on the generation of random normal deviates. *Annals of Mathematical Statistics, vol. 29, pp. 610–611.*

CHAMBERS J.M., MALLOWS, C.L. and STUCK, B.W. (1976): A method for simulating stable random variables. *Journal of the American Statistical Association, vol. 71, pp. 340–344.*

DEVROYE, L. (1981a): The series method in random variate generation and its application to the Kolmogorov-Smirnov distribution. *American Journal of Mathematical and Management Sciences, vol. 1, pp. 359–379.*

DEVROYE, L. (1981b): The computer generation of random variables with a given characteristic function. *Computers and Mathematics with Applications, vol. 7, pp. 547–552.*

DEVROYE, L. (1986a): *Non-Uniform Random Variate Generation*, Springer-Verlag, New York.

DEVROYE, L. (1986b): An automatic method for generating random variables with a given characteristic function. *SIAM Journal of Applied Mathematics, vol. 46, pp. 698–719.*

DEVROYE, L. (1989): On random variate generation when only moments or Fourier coefficients are known. *Mathematics and Computers in Simulation, vol. 31, pp. 71–89.*

DEVROYE, L. (1991): Algorithms for generating discrete random variables with a given generating function or a given moment sequence. *SIAM Journal on Scientific and Statistical Computing, vol. 12, pp. 107–126.*

DEVROYE, L. (1996): Random variate generation in one line of code. In: *1996 Winter Simulation Conference Proceedings*, Charnes, J.M., Morrice, D.J., Brunner D.T. and Swain J.J. (eds.), pp. 265–272, ACM, San Diego, CA.

DEVROYE, L. (1997): Simulating theta random variates. *Statistics and Probability Letters, vol. 31, pp. 2785–2791.*

DEVROYE, L., FILL, J., and NEININGER, R. (2000): Perfect simulation from the quicksort limit distribution. *Electronic Communications in Probability, vol. 5, pp. 95–99.*

DEVROYE, L. (2001): Simulating perpetuities. *Methodologies and Computing in Applied Probability, vol. 3, pp. 97–115.*

DEVROYE, L. and NEININGER, R. (2002): Density approximation and exact simulation of random variables that are solutions of fixed-point equations. *Advances of Applied Probability*, vol. 34, pp. 441–468.

DEVROYE, L. (2009): On exact simulation algorithms for some distributions related to Jacobi theta functions. *Statistics and Probability Letters*, vol. 21, pp. 2251–2259.

DEVROYE, L. and FAWZI, O. (2010): Simulating the Dickman distribution. *Statistics and Probability Letters, vol. 80, pp. 242–247.*

FILL, J. (1998): An interruptible algorithm for perfect sampling via Markov chains. *The Annals of Applied Probability*, vol. 8, pp. 131–162.

FILL, J.A. and HUBER, M (2009): *Perfect simulation of perpetuities*, To appear.

FLAJOLET, P. and SAHEB, N. (1986): The complexity of generating an exponentially distributed variate. *Journal of Algorithms, vol. 7, pp. 463–488.*

GOLDIE, C.M. and MALLER, R.A. (2000): Stability of perpetuities. *Annals of Probability, vol. 28, pp. 1195–1218.*

GREEN, P.J. and MURDOCH, D.J. (2000): Exact sampling for Bayesian inference: towards general purpose algorithms (with discussion). In: *Monte Carlo Methods*, Bernardo, J.M., Berger, J.O., Dawid, A.P. and Smith, A.F.M. (eds.), pp. 301–321, Bayesian Statistics, vol. 6, Oxford university Press, Oxford.

HASTINGS, C. (1955): *Approximations for Digital Computers*, Princeton University Press, Princeton, New Jersey.

HÖRMANN, W., LEYDOLD, J., and DERFLINGER, G. (2004): *Automatic Nonuniform Random Variate Generation*, Springer-Verlag, Berlin.

HUFFMAN, D. (1952): A method for the construction of minimum-redundancy codes. *Proceedings of the IRE, vol. 40, pp. 1098–1101.*

KANTER, M. (1975): Stable densities under change of scale and total variation inequalities. *Annals of Probability, vol. 3, pp. 697–707.*

KEANE, M.S., and O'BRIEN, G.L. (1994): A Bernoulli factory. *ACM Transactions on Modeling and Computer Simulation, vol. 4, pp. 213–219.*

KENDALL, W. (2004): Random walk CFTP. Thönnes ed., Department of Statistics, University of Warwick.

KNUTH, D.E. and YAO, A.C. (1976): The complexity of nonuniform random number generation. in: *Algorithms and Complexity,* Traub, J.E. (ed.), pp. 357–428, Academic Press, New York, N.Y..

MARSAGLIA, G. (1968): Random numbers fall mainly in the planes. *Proceedings of the National Academy of Sciences, vol. 60, pp. 25–28.*

MARSAGLIA, G. and ZAMAN, A. (1991): A new class of random number generators. *Annals of Applied Probability, vol. 1, pp. 462–480.*

METROPOLIS, N., ROSENBLUTH, A., ROSENBLUTH, M., TELLER, A., and TELLER, E. (1953): Equations of state calculations by fast computing machines. *Journal of Chemical Physics, vol. 21, p. 1087–1091.*

MURDOCH, D.J. and GREEN, P.J. (1998): Exact sampling from a continous space. *Scandinavian Journal of Statistics, vol. 25, pp. 483–502.*

PROPP, G.J. and WILSON, D.B. (1996): Exact sampling with coupled Markov chains and applications to statistical mechanics. *Random Structures and Algorithms, vol. 9, pp. 223–252.*

RÖSLER, U. and RÜSHENDORF, L. (2001): The contraction method for recursive algorithms. *Algorithmica, vol. 29, pp. 3–33.*

K. SATO (2000): *Lévy Processes and Infinitely Divisible Distributions,* Cambridge University Press, Cambridge.

ULRICH, U. (1984): Computer generation of distributions on the m-sphere. *Applied Statistics, vol. 33, pp. 158–163.*

VERVAAT, W. (1979): On a stochastic difference equation and a representation of non-negative infinitely divisible random variables. *Advances in Applied Probability, vol. 11, pp. 750–783.*

VON NEUMANN, J. (1963): Various techniques used in connection with random digits. *Collected Works,* vol. 5, pp. 768–770, Pergamon Press. Also in (1951): Monte Carlo Method. *National Bureau of Standards Series, Vol. 12, pp. 36-38.*

WILSON, D.B. (2000): Layered multishift coupling for use in perfect sampling algorithms (with a primer on CFTP). In: *Monte Carlo Methods,* Madras, N. (ed.), pp. 141–176, Fields Institute Communications, vol. 6, American Mathematical Society.

ZOLOTAREV, V. M. (1959): On analytic properties of stable distribution laws. *Selected Translations in Mathematical Statistics and Probability, vol. 1, pp. 207–211.*

ZOLOTAREV, V. M. (1966): On the representation of stable laws by integrals. *Selected Translations in Mathematical Statistics and Probability, vol. 6, pp. 84–88.*

ZOLOTAREV, V. M. (1981): Integral transformations of distributions and estimates of parameters of multidimensional spherically symmetric stable laws. In: *Contributions to Probability,* pp. 283–305, Academic Press.

ZOLOTAREV, V. M. (1986): *One-Dimensional Stable Distributions,* American Mathematical Society, Providence, R.I..

Computational Statistics Solutions for Molecular Biomedical Research: A Challenge and Chance for Both

Lutz Edler, Christina Wunder, Wiebke Werft, and Axel Benner

Department of Biostatistics-C060, German Cancer Research Center
Im Neuenheimer Feld 280, D-69120 Heidelberg, Germany,
edler@dkfz.de, c.wunder@dkfz.de, w.werft@dkfz.de, benner@dkfz.de

Abstract. Computational statistics, supported by computing power and availability of efficient methodology, techniques and algorithms on the statistical side and by the perception on the need of valid data analysis and data interpretation on the biomedical side, has invaded in a very short time many cutting edge research areas of molecular biomedicine. Two salient cutting edge biomedical research questions demonstrate the increasing role and decisive impact of computational statistics. The role of well designed and well communicated simulation studies is emphasized and computational statistics is put into the framework of the International Association of Statistical Computing (IASC) and special issues on Computational Statistics within Clinical Research launched by the journal Computational Statistics and Data Analysis (CSDA).

Keywords: computational statistics, molecular biomedical research, simulations, International Association of Statistical Computing, computational statistics and data analysis

1   Introduction

Statistical methods have been recognized and appreciated as unalterable tool for the progress of quantitative molecular biology and medicine (molecular biomedicine) as they were in physics, quantitative genetics and in clinical drug research. With the emergence of larger biomedical data sets, both in terms sample size (n) and number of individual characteristics (p), in particular when $p >> n$, novel and more efficient computational methods and data analysis approaches were needed, and valid conclusions and decision making required the company of statistical inference and statistical theory. Whereas from the beginning on, when molecular data appeared massively due to high-throughput techniques, extraordinary efforts and large investments were put into the quality of biomedical data and bioinformatics, much less was invested into the computational statistics methods for the information extraction. That neglect left gaps in biomedical research projects when the validity of both methods and results were questioned. Modern emerging biomedical approaches and complex models in biological, epidemiological

Y. Lechevallier, G. Saporta (eds.), *Proceedings of COMPSTAT'2010*,
DOI 10.1007/978-3-7908-2604-3_2, © Springer-Verlag Berlin Heidelberg 2010

and clinical studies require high quality computational and statistical support. We will address below how computational statistics, computing power, data analysis and data interpretation invaded in a very short time many cutting edge research areas of modern biomedicine and biomedical research. Therefore we will elaborate from two biomedical areas a salient cutting edge research question for which computational statistics plays now an increasing role with a decisive impact.

A statisticians work for biomedicine - name it biostatistics or biometrics - is defined by the biomedical problems and hypotheses as well as by the tools he/she has at hands to solve the corresponding mathematical and statistical problems. According to Finney (1974) it is the duty of a biostatistician *"to interpret quantitative biomedical information validly and usefully"*. He also noted that that the applied statistician should express him/herself in *"terms intelligible beyond the confines of statistics* in varying degrees of collaboration with persons being expert in the field, and stressing the fact that a *"substantial contribution from the statistician is essential"* when citing R.A. Fisher with *"when a biologist believes there is information in an observation, it is up to the statistician to get it out"*, one of the first statisticians who heavily calculated in Rothamsted for his collaborations with agriculture and genetics. This work has always been initiated and guided by data and required the use of computational methods for doing the calculations right and efficiently. Computational statistics has been an integral part of statistics from its beginning when statisticians had to do calculations and needed to simplify the computational work load, starting with numerical calculus using later statistical tables, mechanical calculators and electronic calculators, called computers, all overruled now by highly interactive computing systems which integrate statistics software with an almost uncountable number of applets acting during data input, data processing and data output. Victor (1984) discussed in a highly recognized essay the role of computational statistics for statistics and statisticians. Although he denied the attribute of a scientific discipline because of missing own methodology and own subject for investigation, he acknowledged the high relevance for applied statistics and its undisputable role for knowledge generation in all sciences. For a discussion of this concept, see e.g. Lauro (1996), also Nelder (1996), who distinguishes science from technology and locates computational statistics nearer to latter although it is performed by scientists. The most conciliatory definition of computational is found in Chambers (1999) citing John Tukeys defining of computational statistics as the *"peaceful collisions of computing with statistics"*.

In its growth period around 1970-1980 it became the irrevocable tool for statistics. Exact statistical inference methods and permutations, bootstrapping and interactive graphical methods were the dominant tools. The interaction of computational statistics with biostatistics from the view point how it developed in Germany was summarized in Edler (2005). The technological aspect has been emphasized in the German Region of the International Biometric Society when personal computers started to take over the main frame computers in 1990 by Bernd Streitberg. His vision at that time was that computational statistics has the chance to become the driving force for the progress of statistics and, in particular for biostatistics, if it will be possible to overcome fixation to program packages. At that time he already foresaw the innovative power of personal computers- now notebooks - for software development. It is fair to say that the R-project for statistical computing has made this vision coming true. Notably, he denounced software validation where he rather pessimistically stated that for many users and heads of institutes and companies that would not be an issue as long as all compute with the same software, notwithstanding whether that software calculated correct or incorrect. A second still relevant issue Streitberg indicated in 1989 was the wish that the computer has to become the standard test for the applicability and use of a statistical method: If a method cannot be programmed it is not relevant; if it is not programmed its is useless. This way of thought had been expressed already in 1981 by Jürgen Läuter who noted in the introduction to his software development that processes of thinking, decision making and production can be advanced by mathematics and computing techniques.

Concerning the high-dimensional molecular data all these thoughts seem to fit well for an intelligible interpretation of the data and the reduction of the data to their information content.

2   Screening Molecular Data for Predictors

A multitude of biomedical techniques provide high-throughput high-resolution data on the molecular basis of diseases. Most of these DNA microarray array data fall into one of the following categories:

- gene or expression
- allelic imbalance
- methylation imbalances.

These investigations aim at a better understanding of the underlying mechanisms of the genesis of the disease, e.g. of a specific cancer like the AML out of the class of leukaemia. Current biomedical knowledge postulates for most diseases, in particular for cancer, as of being heterogeneous and of different subtypes, on the clinical, histo-pathological and the molecular level. Heterogeneity at the molecular level lead to the development of prognostic and also to predictive gene signatures (also called gene expression profiles, biomarker sets etc) from which some have already been commercialized (for breast cancer see e.g., ONKOtypeDx, MammPrint, GGI) and used in attempts to personalize cancer treatment, although there exists still considerable uncertainty on the use of new molecular markers in routine clinical decision making. The need to examine their role in patient selection and for stratification for future clinical trials is obvious. For a review of the situation in breast cancer therapy see Kaufmann et al (2010). Urgent biomedical questions concern

- usefulness of currently available molecular biomarkers and biomarker based,
- the establishment of designs and design strategies which account for clinical, histo-pathological and molecular subtypes at the same time, and
- coherent collection, combination and processing of both biomedical information, being it collected prospectively or retrospectively.

The challenge for biostatistics arising from these questions is huge and starts conceptually at a clarification of the difference between prognostic and predictive markers (Sargent (2005)).

Biomedical research has always been targeted to develop e.g. prognostic models which may classifiy patients in different risk groups and so called prognostic marker guide therapy of groups of patients in a general way. Another clinical target is the development of predictive models which guide treatment and optimize therapy by guiding treatment decision in dependency of so-called predictive factors. Next to consider is the translation of the medical task into statistical approaches. For the prognostic models the biostatisticians task, almost exclusively performed in collaborative projects with biologists and clinicians is to build prediction models e.g. for classification in different risk groups based on such molecular data. Whereas formerly the statistical inferences were based on either statstical testing or on class discovery methods e.g. cluster analyses, regression techniques are now somehow rediscovered as the more appropriate approach to build those risk prediction models. Regularization methods are now widespread to solve the so called $p >> n$ problem (penalized regression approaches like the Lasso or the Elastic Net, the use of Support Vector Machines, Boosting etc.).

For the development of biomarkers as predictive factors guiding the choice of therapy, regression type analyses are applied on the outcome variable based on those high-dimensional predictors listed above. Efficient and non-overly conservative adjustment for multiple testing becomes crucial when focusing on a gene wise analysis. Multiple adjustments becomes crucial, see e.g. Dudoit and van der Laan (2007). Simulation studies analyze sample-size determination for the identification and validation of such predictive markers. The classical multivariable regression model works well for identifying prognostic factors and with regard to predictive factors one can go back to another classical tool, interactions between covariables.

2.1   Using the Analysis of Molecular Data for Identifying Predictive Biomarker

When screening for predictive factors in case of a dichotomous outcome the method of choice is conditional logistic regression. A gene wise interaction model has then the form

$$\text{Logit}(\mathbf{Y} = 1 | \mathbf{X_g}; \mathbf{Z}) = \beta_{0g} + \beta_{1g}\mathbf{X_g} + \beta_{2g}\mathbf{Z} + \beta_{3g}\mathbf{X_g}\mathbf{Z}$$

where $\mathbf{X_g}$ describes the continuous gene expression of gene g, $g = 1, \ldots, M$, and M is the number of gene expression varaiables, i.e. the number of hypotheses, analyzed in total $\mathbf{Z}$ is a binary treatment variable and $\mathbf{Y}$ is a binary response variable. An interaction effect is then tested with the null hypothesis H0: $\beta_{3g} = 0$ using e.g. likelihood ratio (LR) or the Wald test. When focusing on the multiple testing scenario for the M simultaneous hypotheses one would prefer to control the false discovery rate (FDR) introduced by Benjamini and Hochberg (1995) for such gene expression data as a certain proportion of false discoveries would be accepted. Control of the FDR could be for example obtained by linear step-up procedures such as the Benjamini-Hochberg or Benjamini-Yekutieli method. Lately, resampling-based multiple testing methods for FDR control have become an alternative approach see e.g. Dudoit and van der Laan (2007).

The next challenge arises when determining a sample size for such screening methods and when complexity has barricaded an analytical solution. Only simulations of several scenarios will help to get grip on the sample size estimation which is essential for all trial partners: those investing their time and career, those who invest resources and those who are responsible the sample size, namely the trial statistician. Since one is forced to analyze the system "statistical model" in detail valuable "fall outs" of the simulation approach can be obtained, e.g. a comparison of the performance of different statistical test procedures.

Actually there is now a problem of comparability of the results since the implementation of methods and simulation designs are almost always different. From a user-friendly point of view usage of available methods is impaired by different platforms, different implementations etc. Realized as a Harvest Programme of the PASCAL2 European Network of Excellence a group of researchers has recently come together for a unified, extensible interface covering a large spectrum of multiple hypothesis testing procedures in R: μTOSS (multiple hypotheses testing in an open software system), see Dickhaus et al. (2010). Intended as first step to overcome the problem of comparability of the results μTOSS aims at unifying implementation of methods and simulation platforms as an open source package addressing (i) multiple tests controlling the family wise error rate (single-step and stepwise rejection methods, resampling-based procedures), (ii) multiple adjustment procedures controlling the false discovery rate (classical and adaptive methods, Bayesian approaches as well as resampling-based techniques), (iii) multiplicity-adjusted simultaneous confidence intervals, and (iv) simulation platform to investigate and compare multiple adjustment methods. Features of μTOSS (http://mutoss.r-forge.r-project.org/) are

- Open Source code implementation (using R)

- Well-documented developer interfaces for new procedures to add-on
- Graphical user interface (GUI)
- Online user's guide on which procedure to use according to the user specification
- Inclusion of a large part of the known Multiple Comparison Procedure methods
- Inclusion of tested datasets for verification and exemplary purposes
- Simulation Platform
- Ongoing maintenance

There has been an ongoing discussion in the biomedical community on the best clinical trial design for the identification and validation of predictive biomarkers. At this time, there are three major classes of designs proposed for the evaluation of a biomarker-guided therapy and the assessment of biomarkers in clinical practice, see Sargent et al. (2005), Simon (2008), or Freidlin et al. (2010):

1. Targeted Trial Design (or Enrichment Design)
2. Biomarker Stratified Design
3. Biomarker Strategy Design

Sample size considerations for the biomarker stratified and biomarker strategy designs to assess the clinical utility of predictive biomarkers have been made by Richard Simon, see http://linus.nci.nih.gov/brb/samplesize/index1.html. Current recommendation and practice is to use the biomarker-stratified design since it validates predictivity of a marker best (Freidlin 2010). For the validation of predictive biomarkers one should

  i. provide reproducible biomarker information
 ii. test in a randomized setting before use in clinical practice
iii. apply a biomarker-stratified design.

However, it may take years until biomedicine will know whether the choice of the design today will have been the best one. Computational statistics should contribute to make this time span shorter.

2.2   Combining the Analysis of Molecular Data for Prognosis

The standard approach has been so far the application of a regression model based on a $n \times p$ data matrix $\mathbf{X}$ representing one single source of data, e.g. gene expression, where the sample size n range around 102 and the dimension of the individual observation between 104 and 106. Given the availability of multiple data sources it would be more awarding when searching for prognostic and predictive factors when all available data would be used in an integrative approach to generate one single risk prediction model based on a combination of different sources $\mathbf{X_a}$, $\mathbf{X_b}$, $\mathbf{X_c}$, etc. (e.g. methylation and gene expression data). Since a solution of this problem might be either not feasible at all or may lead to unstable results with unsatisfying prediction performance compared to single data source based prediction a strategy must be defined on how dealing with more than one data source. In biomedicine an integrative approach is not new at all. Since decades clinicians combined several types of data, e.g. data from physical examinations and hematological laboratory data. The role of the traditional hematological data can be thought of being taken over now by the array data, moving the hematological laboratory nearer to the traditional clinical data.

For future basic medical research it is relevant to know the added value provided by the molecular data. Since usage of p-values is no longer an option a measure characterizing prediction accuracy should inform in particular on the performance of future patients on the treatment selection. Binder and Schumacher (2008) used the bootstrap sampling without replacement for efficient evaluation of prediction performance without having to set aside data for validation. Conventional bootstrap samples, drawn with replacement could be severely biased and such translate to biased prediction error estimates, often underestimating the amount of information that can be extracted from high-dimensional data.

Combining clinical data with one high-dimensional data set (Boulesteix et al. 2008; Benner et al. 2010 or Bovelstad et al 2007) has been quite common since the availability of microarrays. Methods for pre-processing, dimension reduction and multivariable analysis are available as well. It has even become a business in advanced education when e.g. a Cold Spring Harbor Laboratory conference on "Integrative Statistical Analysis of Genome Scale Data", June 8 - 23, 2009 educates in a course for about 3500$ on how to combine different genomic data sources, e.g. to model transcriptional networks through integration of mRNA expression, ChIP, and sequence data.

More appropriate would be a comprehensive integrative approach of risk predictive modeling that would stepwise narrow down the list of candidate predictors. An open question is, however, in which order to proceed with the available data sources. Since the number of sources is small one could try all possible orderings, however the number of predictors could differ by orders of magnitude in this case. Another question would be whether it would be useful to link the data sources sequentially, e.g. by using information from the analysis of data from a first data source for modeling data from a second source, or how to analyze them in parallel. One should also not underestimate technical problems like model misspecification, limited number of replicates, limited computing time or the use of asymptotical test statistics. One has to outweigh the influence of the different factors when planning as well as when interpreting the results, elements of research which are often missing.

3   Outweighing Flexibility and Complexity Using Adaptive Designs

For handling an increasing number of new anticancer compounds, clinical drug testing is pressed by practical, economical and ethical demands for increasing degree of flexibility in the design and the conduct of a clinical study. Adaptive group sequential designs allowing e.g., sample size recalculation, have become critical for overcoming the bottleneck of treatment options and making drugs sooner available to patients. When using adaptive designs, the further course of the trial depends on the data observed so far, the decision about how to continue (effecting e.g. final sample size, selection of treatment arms, choice of data modelling).

Bretz et al. (2009) recommended adaptive designs in confirmatory clinical trials since *"It is a difficult, if not unsolvable problem to completely foresee at the design stage of a clinical trial the decision processes at an interim analysis since other consideration than the observed efficacy results may influence the decision"*. However, when evolving scientific expert knowledge and additional unknown background information not available at the planning phase becomes part of an adaptive design, it is essential to understand the operating characteristics before the start of an actual trial. Full scale clinical trial simulations are crucial to describe and analyse the features of such designs. Thus the behaviour of the decision rules can only be described by constructing "real" data for possible interesting scenarios and estimating design features, such as e.g. type I error rate, power, average sample number, from iterated computational simulations of the whole study course. This means there are three major challenges for computer simulations in evaluating the features of a specific adaptive design:

1. The potential decisions during the course of the study have to be specified in advance as detailed as possible to simulate scenarios which depict the closest the reality and hence will allow valid inferences.
2. Computer programs should be built in modules to allow easy implementation of different kind of adaptations. So the flexibility of the adaptive approach will be also maintained in the implementation. Figure 1 displays a study simulations scheme for two-stage adaptive design where design adaptations may be executed in one interim analysis.
3. There is an infinite number of scenarios or parameter settings under which the specific adaptive approach could be simulated. To get relevant results for the considered clinical study situation one has to identify parameter settings which will be probable to occur in reality (e.g. realistic accrual rate, probable true treatment effect, possible loss to follow-up, potential influence of nuisance covariates).

We report here experience with a simulation set up to enable an investigational randomized two arm phase II study for the rare subtype of non-clear cell renal cell carcinoma (ncc-RCC) when two novel molecularly targeted agents (Sunitinib and Temsirolinus) were examined for progression-free survival (PFS) as primary endpoint. At planning of that trial there little was known on the activity of each of the drugs in ncc-RCC patients as well as on the achievable difference of the activity between both. A restriction of the study were limitations in both funds and patient horizon which enforced a sample size not largely exceeding $n = 50$ per arm and $N = 100$ in total. Further, the study time was limited to three years accrual and one year follow-up. After about 30 patients, an interim look was foreseen with the possibility to stop for futility or unfeasibility (if the estimated necessary number of patients could not be recruited in the remaining accrual time) and with recalculation of the sample size for the second study stage if the trial continues. A two-stage group sequential design with type I and type II error spending was established where the second stage was adapted for sample size recalculation using the conditional rejection probability principle of Schäfer and Müller (2001). Since the endpoint of interest was a right-censored failure time, sample size recalculation for the second study stage has to account for patients where recruited in the first stage but will still be under observation the second. The sample size of such a failure time study is determined via the number of events needed to achieve the overall power $1 - \beta$ of the study and, when recalculated after the 1st stage as new number of events Δd needed to achieve the conditional power $1 - \beta_{\text{cond}}$ cond. For details see Wunder et al. (2010). The study course is depicted in Figure 2.

The restricted number of patients which could be recruited, enforces to execute simulations under conventional as well as "investigational" high type I and type II error probabilities $(\alpha, \beta) \in \{(0.5, 2), (0.1, 0.2), (0.05, 0.3), (0.1, 0.3), (0.2, 0.3), (0.2, 0.2), (0.3, 0.3)\}$. The "traditional" choices for the error probabilities lead to unachievable sample sizes and only when allowing for unconventionally high error rates the expected sample sizes are near 100 patients. Interim looks are implemented after 30%, 40% and 50% of the expected total event number to finally choose an interim analysis after approximately 30 patients. The uncertainty about the difference between treatment arms causes the need to simulate under a wide range of true treatment effects, i.e. log hazard ratios in $\{0, log(10/7), log(11/7), log(12/7), log(14/7)\}$ to assess the impact of true hazard ratios which differ from the clinically relevant effect of $log(11/7)$. This means, to cover all interesting and relevant design settings, 105 different simulation scenarios were executed.

A large scale simulation study was constructed for illustration of the design and for determining within a set of scenarios that design which meets the desired properties of the planning agreement between principle investigator, sponsor, funding partner and biostatistician. When interpreting simulation results, one has also to keep in mind that simulation results may deal with different sources of inaccuracy. For example, when analyzing type I error rates in adaptive survival trials there may be potential influence of misspecified

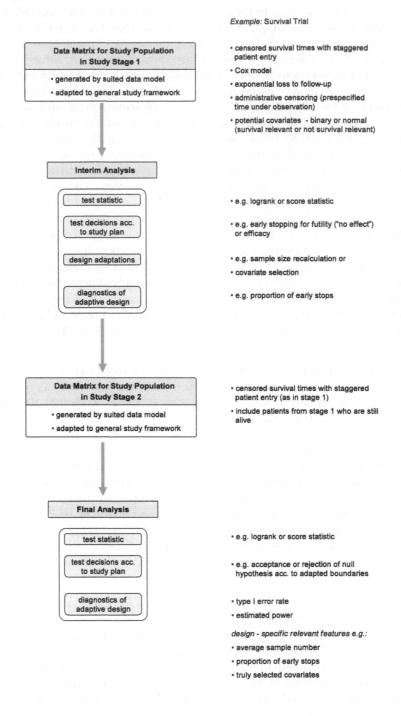

Fig. 1. Diagram of study simulations for two-stage adaptive designs where design adaptations may be executed in the interim analysis.

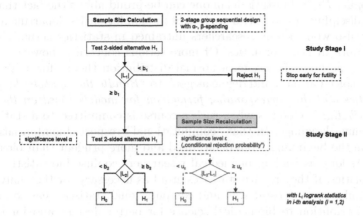

Fig. 2. Diagram of two-stage phase II study in ncc-RCC patients with possibility to stop for futility after the first stage and sample size recalculation for the second stage.

models (see e.g. Lagakos and Schoenfeld (1984)), simulation error (number of replicates may be limited by time) or asymptotical effects in the test statistics (e.g. when considering logrank or score tests, see e.g. Tsiatis et al. (1985). Thus, one has to outweigh the influence of different factors when interpreting simulation results.

4 Discussion

With the appearance of molecular sequence data and microarray data and with the intrinsic problems of screening and archiving these new and massive data sets grew in biomedicine the impression that bioinformatics tools would be the most appropriate methods to analyze these data. Data mining and clustering methods were overestimated in their potency and computer programs were just applied without a thorough statistical analysis of the research problems and the properties of ad hoc generated optimization algorithms. The two examples used above to illustrate the fruitful interaction between computational statistics and molecular biomedicine is the tip of the iceberg. There are many more examples and there are computational methods which are much more involved in those as well as in the examples above where one may look forward for further development.

The role of biostatistics and computational statistics has been recognized also in the bioinformatics community, see e.g. the announcement of courses in the internet with a list of contents like: *Descriptive statistics, Distributions, Study design, Hypothesis testing/interval estimation, Non-parametric methods, Analysis of variance, Linear regression, Multiple testing, The statis-*

tical program R. As biostatistician one can be proud about the fact that the classical disciplines of statistics are taught in bioinformatics departments but one may also wonder why researchers untrained in statistics actually could start to work in Bioinformatics. Of more serious concern is however, when instructors propose the usage of normal distribution theory for analysis of complex molecular data and define as goal: to *"Handle the symbolic language of statistics and the corresponding formalism for models based on the normal distribution"*. Good is when such a course is committed to a statistical programming language. In that "computational" respect, bioinformaticians were from the beginning more determined and more prudent than biostatisticians. As long as leading biomedical researchers confuse biostatistics with bioinformatics, if they realize statistics at all as necessary for the analysis of the molecular data, biostatistics and computational statistics has to articulate is contribution to biomedical science for better designs and for better analyses of high-dimensional genomic data. Computational statistics methods are strongly required for exploratory data analysis and novel means of visualizing high-dimensional genomic data as well as for quality assessment, data pre-processing, and data visualisation methods. The R packages and the Bioconductor project have taken a promising lead to improve the situation. Yet, one should recognize that computational statistics being it science, technology or something special in between is still young, below age 50 when one remembers the start in UK in December 1966 and in the USA on February 1967, and we should give it time.

Recently the journal "Computational Statistics & Data Analysis" (CSDA) launched a second special issues on "Computational Statistics within Clinical Research" where the call explicitly asks for submission of work for *"understanding the pathogenesis of diseases, their treatment, the determination of prognostic and predictive factors, and the impact of genetic information on the design and evaluation of clinical outcomes"*. Such activities at the interface between biomedicine and computational statistics may add further to bridge the gaps.

5   First Author's epilogue

When I started my career in biostatistics at the German Cancer Research Center three decades ago it took only a few months to realize the importance and relevance of computational statistics for both the research work in applied statistics and the biostatistical consulting of clients and partners coming from all relevant biomedical fields of experimental and clinical cancer research. At that time - just after the appearance of John Tukeys book on Explorative Data Analysis (Tukey (1977) resources on computational statistics methods and literature were rare.

The journal Computational Statistics & Data Analysis (CSDA) which later became the flagship publication of the International Association of Statistical Computing (IASC) as well as the journal "Computational Statistics Quarterly", now "Computational Statistics" were then just starting. However there were two easy accessible resources which imprinted my relationship with computational statistics for ever: the receipt of the "Statistical Software Newsletter"(SSN), founded already in 1975, with methods and algorithms at that time hardly needed for the rising computational needs for the analysis of clinical survival data (Edler et al. 1980), and the attendance of COMPSTAT conferences for the exchange with the colleagues interested at the interface between statistics and computing.

It was the 5th COMPSTAT in Toulouse in 1982 where I started to report methods developed for biostatistical applications and I enjoy now how COMPSTAT has grown and developed by 2010 and its 19th COMPSTAT in Paris, again in France. The passage of the years has not diminished my respect and my inclination to that forum of scientific exchange nor my pride of having had the honor to serve IASC as officer for some time, our society IASC which shields as member of the ISI family the COMPSTAT conference.

References

BENJAMINI, Y. and HOCHBERG, Y. (1995): Controlling the false discovery rate: a practical and powerful approach to multiple testing. *Journal of the Royal Statistical Society Series B 57, 289-300.*

BENNER, A., ZUCKNICK, M., HIELSCHER, T., ITTRICH, C. and MANSMANN, U.(2010): High-dimensional Cox models: the choice of penalty as part of the model building process. *Biometrical Journal 52, 50-69.*

BINDER, H. and SCHUMACHER, M. (2008): Adapting Prediction Error Estimates for Biased Complexity Selection in High-Dimensional Bootstrap Samples. *Statistical Applications in Genetics and Molecular Biology 7 (1) Article 12.* DOI: 10.2202/1544-6115.1346

BOULESTEIX, A.L., STROBL, C., AUGUSTIN, T., DAUMER, M. (2008): Evaluating microarray-based classifiers: An overview. *Cancer Informatics 6, 77-97.*

BOVEHSAD, H.M., NYGARD, M., STORVOLD, S., ALDRIN, H.L.L., BORGAN, O., FRIGESSI, A. and LINGGIAERDE, O.C.C. (2007): Predicting survival from microarray data - a comparative study. *Bioinformatics, 23(16), 2080-2087*

BRETZ, F., KOENIG, F., BRANNATH, W, GLIMM,E. and POSCH, M. (2009: Tutorial in biostatistics: Adaptive designs for confirmatory clinical trials, *Statistics in Medicine 28, 1181-1217.*

CHAMBERS, J. (1999): Computing with data: concepts and challenges. *The American Statistician 53, 73-84.*

DICKHAUS, T., BLANCHARD, G., HACK, N., KONIETSCHKE, F., ROHMEYER, K., ROSENBLATT, J., SCHEER, M. and WERFT, W. (2010): μTOSS - Multiple hypotheses testing in an open software system. 2nd Joint Statistical Meeting DAGSTAT Statistics under one Umbrella March 23-26, 2010, Technical University, Dortmund, p 77 (abstract).

DUDOIT, S, and Van DER LAAN, M. (2007) *Multiple Testing Procedures with Applications to Genomic.* Springer, New York

EDLER, L. (2005): Computational Statistics und Biometrie. Wer treibt wen? *GMDS Medizinische Informatik, Biometrie und Epidemiologie 1 (2)* doi10 - (20050620), 2005.

EDLER, L, WAHRENDORF, J. and BERGER, J. (1980): SURVIVAL. A program package for the statistical analysis of censored survival times. *Statistical Software Newsletter 6, 44-53*

FINNEY, D.J. (1974): Problems, data, and Inference (with discussion). *Journal of the Royal Statistical Society Series A 137, 1-22.*

FISHER R.A. (1925): *Statistical Methods for Research Workers.* Oliver & Boyd, Edinburgh.

FREIDLIN, B,, MCSHANE, L. and KORN, E.L.(2010): Randomized Clinical Trials With Biomarkers: Design Issues. *Journal National Cancer Institute 102, 152-160*

KAUFMANN, M., PUSZTAI, L., RODY, A., CARDOSO, F., DIETEL, M., EDLER, l., HAHN, M., JONAT, W., KARN T., KREIPE. H., LOI, S., VON MINCKWITZ, G., SINN, H.P. and VAN DE VIJVER (2010/11): Use of standard markers and incorporation of molecular markers into breast cancer therapy (to appear).

LAURO, N.C. (1996): Computational statistics or statistical computing, is that the question? *Computational Statistics and Data Analysis 23, 191-193.*

L€UTER, J. (1981): *Programmiersprache DIST. Dateneingabe und Datenstrukturierung.* Akademie Verlag, Berlin.

LAGAKOS, S. W. and SCHOENFELD, D. A. (1984): Properties of proportional-hazards score tests under misspecified regression models. *Biometrics 40,1037-1048.*

NELDER, J. (1996): Statistical computing. In P. Armitage and D. Hand (Eds.): *Advances in Biometry. 50 Years of the International Biometric Society.* Wiley, New York, 201-212.

POTTER, M. (2005): A permutation test for inference in logistic regression with small- and moderate-sized data sets. *Statistics in Medicine 24 (5), 693-708.*

TSIATIS, A., ROSNER, G. L. and TRITCHLER, D. L. (1985): Group sequential tests with censored survival data adjusting for covariates. *Biometrika 72(2), 365-373.*

SARGENT, D.J., CONLEY, B.A., ALLEGRA, C., et al. (2005): Clinical trial designs for predictive marker validation in cancer treatment trials. *Journal of Clinical Oncology 23(9), 2020-2027.*

SCHÄFER, H. and MÜLLER, H. (2001): Modification of the sample size and the schedule of interim analyses in survival trials based on data inspections. *Statistics in Medicine 20, 3741-3751.*

SIMON, R. (2008). Using genomics in clinical trial design. *Clinical Cancer Research 14, 5984-5993.*

VICTOR, N. (1984): Computational statistics - science or tool? (with discussion). *Statistical Software Newsletter 10, 105-125.*

WUNDER, C., KOPP-SCHNEIDER, A, and EDLER, L. (2010): *Adaptive group sequential trial to improve treatment in rare patient entities* (to appear).

TUKEY, J.W. (1977): *Exploratory Data Analysis.* Addison-Wesley, New York.

The Laws of Coincidence

David J. Hand

Imperial College London
and
Winton Capital Management
d.j.hand@imperial.ac.uk

Abstract. Anomalous events often lie at the roots of discoveries in science and of actions in other domains. Familiar examples are the discovery of pulsars, the identification of the initial signs of an epidemic, and the detection of faults and fraud. In general, they are events which are seen as so unexpected or improbable that one is led to suspect there must be some underlying cause. However, to determine whether such events are genuinely improbable, one needs to evaluate their probability under normal conditions. It is all too easy to underestimate such probabilities. Using the device of a number of 'laws', this paper describes how apparent coincidences should be expected to happen by chance alone.

Keywords: anomalies, coincidences, hidden forces

1 Introduction

Coincidence is God's way of remaining anonymous

Albert Einstein

Statistics is a dynamic discipline, evolving in response to various stimuli. One of these is the advent of new application domains, presenting novel statistical challenges. A glance back at the history of the development of statistical ideas and methods shows how areas such as psychology, engineering, medicine, and chemistry have impacted the discipline. However, once a tool or method has been developed to tackle a problem in one application area, its use typically spreads out to pervade other domains. We thus have a leapfrog effect, in which statistical methods enable understanding to grow in the areas to which they are applied, and then the challenges of these areas promote the development of new theory and methods in statistics.

More recently, however, a second stimulus has had a dramatic impact on statistics – an impact which can fairly be characterised as revolutionary. This is the development of the computer. The computer has completely changed the face of statistics, transforming it from a dry discipline, requiring substantial tedious effort to undertake even relatively simple analyses, to an exciting technology, in which the intellectual focus is on the use of high level tools for probing structure in data. Of course, the general public has not yet caught

Y. Lechevallier, G. Saporta (eds.), *Proceedings of COMPSTAT'2010*,
DOI 10.1007/978-3-7908-2604-3_3, © Springer-Verlag Berlin Heidelberg 2010

up with this revolution, though I believe we can see green shoots indicative of a beginning change in perceptions (Hand, 2009). The computer has enabled older statistical methods, which would have taken months of painstaking effort, to be applied essentially instantaneously (though this is not without its dangers - in the past one would have thought carefully about the appropriateness of an analysis before going to the effort of undertaking it). It has also enabled the development of entirely original methods, methods which would not have been conceived in earlier days because the computational effort would have rendered them totally impracticable. This has driven a huge blossoming of statistical methods.

The impact of the computer has manifested itself in several ways. One is the fact that huge numbers of (accurate) calculations can now be undertaken in a split second. Another is that electronic data capture technologies mean that streaming data are increasingly prevalent (data which are obtained in real-time, and which simply keep on coming, so that adaptive real-time analyses are needed). A third is the ability to store, manipulate, search, and analyse massive data sets. Here are some extreme examples which will convey this magnitude. The credit scoring company Fair Isaac has sold around 10^{11} credit scores. The Large Hadron Collider will generate about 15 petabytes of data per year (a petabyte is 10^{15} bytes). AT&T transfers around 16 petabytes and Google processes around 20 petabytes of data per day. To put this in context, the entire written works of humanity, in all languages, occupy about 50 petabytes. While most problems do not involve data sets quite as extreme as those, the analysis of gigabytes and terabytes is increasingly common. Such data sets arise in all applications, from the scientific to the commercial.

Vast data sets, in particular, present opportunities and challenges which cut across application domains (though always, of course, mediated by the particular problems and issues of the different domains) – see, for example Hand et al, 2001; Baldi et al, 2003; Ayres, 2007; Giudici and Figini, 2007. The opportunities include the potential for discovering structures and relationships which would not be apparent in small data sets. The challenges include housekeeping ones of efficiently manipulating and searching terabytes of data, and perhaps even also of accessing it (for example, if it is distributed over the web). But the challenges also include deep theoretical ones, such as the role of significance tests when the size of the data set mean that even very small underlying structures produce highly significant results. Just one example of the exciting developments which have arisen from such problems is the work on false discovery rate.

I find it useful to distinguish between two broad kinds of problems in the analysis of very large data sets. To use data mining analogy, we might regard these as analogous to coal mining and diamond mining. The first is the familiar one of modelling, though flavoured by the consequences of the data set size. The aim of modelling is to construct some kind of global summary of a set (or subset) of data, which captures its main structures or those structures which are relevant to some particular purpose. This is a familiar one for statisticians, since modern statistics is couched almost entirely in the language of "models" (just glance at any recent statistics text or journal). In many situations it is sufficient to work with a relatively small sample from the entire database – provided this can be drawn in an unbiased way (selectivity bias is often a danger when large data sets are involved). The required size of the sample will depend on the level of detail desired in the model. This relationship is something which merits further research.

The second broad kind of analytic problem is the detection of anomalies. While particular kinds anomaly detection problem have always been of interest (e.g., outlier detection - the first edition of Barnett and Lewis's classic book on outliers appeared in 1978), the advent of massive data sets has opened up new possibilities. As I have argued elsewhere (Hand and Bolton, 2004), many important discoveries are the consequence of detecting something unusual – that is, detecting a departure from what was expected or from the received wisdom – so that this represents a considerable opportunity. Examples of anomaly detection areas on which myself and my research team have worked include large astronomical data sets, earthquake clusters, adverse drug reactions, and fraud in credit card usage.

Unfortunately, however, anomalies in data can arise from multiple causes, not merely because there is some previously unsuspected genuine aspect of the phenomena under study. These include, but are not restricted to (see also Hand and Bolton, 2004), the following:

- Ramsey theory. This is a branch of mathematics which tells us that sometimes one is *certain* to find particular configurations in a data set. A familiar and trivial example is that, if there are six people in a room, it is *certain* that there are three who are either mutual acquaintances or who do not know each other.
- Data quality. The problems that poor data quality bring to the search for anomalies in large data sets are illustrated by Twyman's law, which states that *any figure that looks interesting or different is usually wrong*. Unfortunately, poor quality data are commonplace, to the extent that if the data appear perfect one might wonder what prior manipulation has occurred to remove the distortions, fill in the missing values, and so on.
- Chance. Curious configurations do arise by chance, and, as the size of the data set increases, so the opportunities for such chance occurrences likewise increase. It is this third of these causes which is the focus of this paper.

2 Chance and coincidence

To set the scene for how chance can provide anomalies and coincidences, here some examples.

Example 1: In the early 1980s, a New Jersey woman won a lottery twice in just 4 months. The odds of any particular person winning this lottery twice were reported as being just one in 17 trillion (that is, one in 10^{12}).

Example 2: More recently, on 6th and 10th September 2009, the same six numbers (4, 15, 23, 24, 35, and 42, though in different orders) were drawn in the Bulgarian lottery.

Example 3: UK plastic cards have four digit Personal Identification Numbers (PINs) associated with each card. Kevin Stokes, from Lancashire in the UK, had already changed the PIN on his Sainsbury's card to a number he could easily remember. By coincidence, when his new Barclaycard arrived, it had the same PIN as his Sainsbury's card. Then, when Kevin and his wife opened an Alliance and Leicester account, it also had the same PIN. As if this wasn't enough, in 2004 when Barclays sent Kevin a new card, it also had the same PIN.

Example 4: Golfers scoring holes in one are the stuff of folklore. But how about Joan Creswell and Margaret Williams both scoring holes in one, one immediately after the other, at the 13th hole at the Barrow Golf Club in 2005? And as if that wasn't enough, in 2007 Jacqueline Cagne hit her 14th hole in one. Local sportswriter Larry Bohannan had tracked down witnesses, and the last hole in one even occurred in front of television cameras, so there appears to be no doubt of the truth of the claim. (There is a downside to this: Ms Cagne says that she has spent several thousand dollars on celebratory champagne for her fellow golfers.)

Example 5: Lightning strikes, especially two strikes in the same place, are paradigms of coincidence. What then of the case of Major Walter Summerford, who was struck by lightning in 1918. Then again in 1924, And then again in 1930. He died in 1932 (not from a lightning strike). But then, as if to rectify the oversight, his gravestone was struck by lightning. And as if his case was not bad enough, Roy C. Sullivan, a park ranger from Virginia, was struck by lightning seven times.

The anecdotes above are all examples of coincidences. The *New Oxford Dictionary of English* defines a coincidence as '*a remarkable concurrence of events or circumstances without apparent causal connection*', and Diaconis and Mosteller (1989) define it as a '*surprising concurrence of events, perceived as meaningfully related, with no apparent causal connection*'. We see that these definitions contain two components: (i) that the event is highly improbable ('remarkable', 'surprising' in the above definitions); (ii) that there is no apparent causal connection.

The improbability of the concurrence, if one assumes no causal connection, prompts one to seek such a connection. This is simply a subconscious application of the *law of likelihood*, which says that evidence E supports explanation *H1* better than explanation *H2* whenever the likelihood ratio of *H1* to *H2* given E exceeds 1. So, if I obtain twenty heads in a row when tossing a coin, I might seek an explanation which leads to a greater probability of getting such an outcome (e.g. the coin is double-headed; the observed outcome would have probability equal to 1) than that the coin is fair (the observed outcome would have probability of around 10^{-6}). Thus one might extend the above definitions of coincidence to: *a concurrence of events which is apparently so improbable that one suspects there might be a hidden causal connection.*

The fact that the causal connection is *hidden* means that one may be unable to explain what it is – although the human brain seems to have a remarkable ability to conjure up sensible sounding explanations (even to the extent of managing to do so when it turns out that the observed data structure was a consequence of some error in the data).

The suspicion or belief that there may be a hidden causal connection leading to an anomaly or structure doubtless underlies many pre-scientific explanations for empirical phenomena – in superstitions, religions, miracles, Jung's synchronicity, and so on. And note that the term 'pre-scientific' does not mean that such explanations are no longer believed by many people. And, of course, it is true that sometimes there are unobserved forces or influences which manifest themselves without obvious mechanism – magnetism springs to mind.

In Hand (2009) I pointed out that the notion that statistics is solely concerned with mass phenomena – with aggregating, summarising, and describing data – is not really true. Many applications of statistics are aimed at the individual. In a clinical trial, for example, the ultimate aim is not really to make some general statement about the average effectiveness of a drug, but to decide which treatment is best for each individual. Nonetheless, and even in such applications, a first-stage modelling process is necessary, in which one tries to construct overall summaries, which can then be combined with data on the individual to draw some conclusion about the individual. Such statistical modelling relies on aggregate statistical laws, such as the law of large numbers and the central limit theorem. They are properties of multiple observations. Likewise, the laws of statistical physics (the gas laws, magnetism, heat, etc) are based on the aggregate behaviour of large numbers of objects. My aim in the next section is to make a first pass at compiling some 'laws' which apply at the other extreme, when we are concerned with individual unusual events – with anomalies.

3   The Laws of coincidence

The law of total probability: *One of an exhaustive set of possible events must happen.*
   This law is really a tautology: by the very meaning of the word 'exhaustive', one of the events must happen. Thus, in a 6/49 lottery, in which the winning number is a set of six different numbers random drawn from the integers 1 to 49, we know that one of the 13,983,816 possible sets of six

numbers must come up. This means that, if one buys a single ticket, the probability of winning is roughly 7×10^8 . It also means that if 13,983,816 individuals each buy tickets with different numbers, then one of them is *certain* to win the jackpot.

The law of truly large numbers: *With a large enough data set, any data configuration is likely to occur.*

Superficially, this law is straightforward: the more opportunities there are for an event to happen, the greater is the probability that it will happen, and this is true even if the probability that the event will happen at any individual opportunity is very small. While you might be surprised if an event with a one in a million probability happened to you, you would not be surprised if such an event happened to someone, somewhere on the planet. After all, there are around 7 billion people on the planet. With that sort of number of opportunities, one should expect around 7000 such 'one in a million' events to occur. Indeed, what would be really surprising is if no such events occurred. Such a lack of events would have a probability of around 10^{-3040} .

However, where this law really begins to bite as a law of coincidence is when one underestimates the number of opportunities. Example 2 above illustrates this. Lottery coincidences are typically calculated based on ignoring the fact that many lotteries are conducted around the world, that they take place week after week, and that a huge number of people buy lottery tickets, often more than one ticket. This means that we might expect to observe coincidences like the Bulgarian lottery of Example 2 at some time somewhere in the world. Indeed, again, it means it would be surprising if we did not. And, in fact, on July 9th and 11th 2007, the sets of five numbers picked in the North Carolina Cash 5 lottery were identical.

In some situations the underestimation is dramatic since the number of opportunities increases in an exponential way, and this may not always be obvious. It is this principle which underlies the counterintuitive nature of the classic 'birthday problem' or 'birthday paradox': in a group 23 people, the probability that some pair have a birthday on the same day is greater than $1/2$. The key point here is a confusion between the number of potential pairs each of which includes a specific individual (which is just 22 in the case of 23 people in a room), and the total number of potential pairs (which is 253, more than ten times as many).

The law of near enough: *Events which are sufficiently similar are regarded as identical.*

The birthday problem required an exact match, which was achievable because there is a finite number of discrete days in a year. Often, however, nature does not partition things up so conveniently, and it is left to us to decide on the divisions - or to decide if something is sufficiently like another thing to be regarded as of the same type. Since, in many cases, there is no hard and fast definition, there is plenty of scope for arbitrarily increasing the chance that two events will be concurrent. For example, we might regard it as a striking coincidence if I unexpectedly and accidentally meet my only brother in a town neither of us have visited before, but we would regard it as less of a coincidence if I unexpectedly bump into one of the set consisting of my several brothers, my cousins, my neighbours, my old school mates, my work colleagues, and my sports club friends.

Coincidences arising as a combined consequence of the law of truly large numbers and the law of near enough have been a source of entertaining numerology. Examples are Ramanujan's constant, $e^{\pi\sqrt{263}}$, which is equal to $(2 \times 10005^3) + 744$ to within 2.9×10^{-30}, $e^{\pi} - \pi$, which is very close to 20, and the trio of numbers 1782, 1841, and 1922 which, with exponent 12, come perilously close to disproving Fermat's last theorem. There is no limit to the number of combinations of mathematical operators and numbers which may be searched through, and sooner or later one will find some combination which lies within any specified accuracy limits: a rational number, a ratio of two integers, can be found which approximates any real number to any degree of accuracy that one wishes.

The law of search: *Keep seeking and you will find.*

The law of truly large numbers really comes into its own when the search space is unlimited. For example, the unlimited set of integers provide rich grounds in which to search for coincidences: one can fit the integers together in various ways and simply keep on increasing the size of the integers. In 2009, on the occasion of the 175th anniversary of the founding of the Royal Statistical Society, I noticed that $175 = 1^1 + 7^2 + 5^3$, but had it been some other anniversary I am sure we could have found another combination of the constituent integers which was striking.

The law of the lever: *A slight adjustment to a distribution can dramatically alter probabilities.*

Much of statistical modelling, whether Bayesian or frequentist, assumes an underlying distributional form. This might be fairly elaborate (e.g. a mixture distribution), but it will often belong to a family of distributions. Such distributional forms are fine for modelling, but, simply because the data are by definition sparser in the tails, accuracy may break down there. In particular, small changes to parameter values may have a negligible effect on the overall shape of a distribution, but a large effect in the tails.

A very simple, and familiar, illustration of this is the effect on the tail probability of a normal distribution when the mean is slightly shifted. For example, compare the probability of observing a value below -5 from a $N(0, 1)$ distribution with the probability of observing such a value from a $N(-0.135, 1)$ distribution. Although the standardised difference between the means is only 0.135, the first probability is only a half the size of the second. To take a more extreme case, the probability of observing a value below -10 from a $N(0, 1)$ distribution is only a quarter of the probability of observing so small a value if the mean is shifted by just 0.139.

This sort of phenomenon has been held to account for breakdowns in the financial markets, in which extreme events occur more often than expected. For mathematical convenience, normal distributions are often assumed to hold for various random variables, and yet empirical observation shows that the distribution tails are often fat: the probability of extreme values is much greater than would appear to be the case under the normal assumption. To illustrate the consequence of the difference, the ratio of the probability of taking a value greater than 10 for the lognormal and normal distribution is 1.40×10^{21}.

The law of the tortoise: *All journeys take place one step at at time.*

Imagine a square consisting of one million by one million smaller subsquares. The chance of alighting on a single specified subsquare at random in just one attempt is simply 10^{12}. However, if we randomly pick some subsquare at random and then walk towards the target, one step at a time, each step being a move to a neighbouring orthogonal subsquare, we are certain to arrive there within two million steps. A vanishingly small probability has become certainty. One can even relax the requirement that each step necessarily moves towards the target, and replace it by a probability greater than a half that each step so moves, and one is certain ultimately to end at the target.

Creationists often confuse the probability of producing a complex structure in one step with the probability of producing the structure by one incrementally step at a time. The 'miracle of the typing monkeys', in which a large enough number of monkeys, randomly hitting the keys of typewriters, eventually produce the works of Shakespeare, is of this kind.

The law of selection: *Paint the target round the arrow.*

The name of this law is derived from the story of the man who notices that the side of a barn has a number of targets painted on it, each of which has an arrow centred in the bull's eye. Such a configuration can be achieved in various ways. At one extreme, one can first paint the targets on the barn, and then shoot the arrows, hitting all the bull's eyes, so demonstrating either superb archery skills or that an event of extraordinarily low probability has occurred. At the other extreme, one can shoot the arrows into the barn and then paint the targets around them.

The latter situation is not all that uncommon and, indeed, to many, the phrase 'data mining' is synonymous with this sort of activity: if one's initial hypothesis is not supported by the data, then trawl through the data to find some unusual data configuration, and then devise a theory which 'explains' that configuration. The physicist Richard Feynman (Feynman, 1998) described such a situation in which a psychologist's rats did not behave as the theory predicted, but the psychologist noticed that they alternated in turning left and right unexpectedly often. For any experimental results, no doubt if he had searched for long enough, the psychologist could have found *some* configuration in the rats' behaviour which seemed non-random.

The law of selection has also been called the *Jeane Dixon Effect*, after the American psychic of that name. It refers to the practice of emphasising a few correct predictions after the fact, while ignoring the many incorrect predictions.

And finally, a law which does not exist: Borel's law: *Events with a sufficiently small probability never occur.*

This 'law' was proposed by the eminent mathematician Émile Borel in a popular book, originally published in 1943 (Borel, 1962). Borel is also said to be the originator of 'miracle of the typing monkeys'. This law is not to be confused with Borel's 'law of large numbers', which lies at the heart of probability, or the various other discoveries named after him. It was simply an attempt to communicate the notion of astronomically improbable events to his lay readers. Indeed, on page 3 of Borel (1962) he appends the above definition with the words: '*or at least, we must act, in all circumstances, as if they were impossible.*'

Borel says that if the works of Shakespeare and Goethe comprise about 10 million letters, the probability of producing them by random typing is 'equal to unity divided by a number of more than 10 million figures'. He then goes on to say:

'But in concluding from its extremely small probability that the typist's miraculous feat is impossible ... we leave the domain of mathematical science, and it must be recognised that the assertion, which seems to us quite evident and incontestable, is not, strictly speaking, a mathematical truth. A strictly abstract mathematician could even claim that the experiment *need only* be repeated a *sufficient* number of times, namely a number of times represented by a number of 20 million figures, to be sure, on the contrary, that the miracle will be produced several times in the course of these inumerable trials. But it is not humanly possible to imagine that the experiment can be so often repeated.'

To illustrate this, he produces some other small numbers with which the 20 million digits can be compared. Examples (not the ones he gave) are that the number of fundamental particles in the universe is estimated to be around 10^{80} and that the age of the universe, in seconds, is a number of around 10^{18}. These are a far cry from a number of the order of $10^{20,000,000}$.

With such numbers as context, he says:

'It is then clearly absurd to imagine experiments whose number would extend to more than a million figures; that is a purely abstract conception, a piece of mathematical juggling of no consequence, and we must trust our intuition and our common sense which permit us to assert the *absolute impossibility* of the typists miracle which we have described...

...the single law of chance carries with it a certainty of another nature than mathematical certainty, but that certainty is comparable to one which leads us to accept the existence of an historical character, or of a city situated at the antipodes ... it is comparable even to the certainty which we attribute to the existence of the external world.'

Another way of looking at this is to note that there are about 30 million seconds in a year. Suppose that our typist types at a rate of ten characters a second. Then, assuming constant typing (not stopping for sleep, etc), about 30 documents of the size of Shakespeare's complete works could be produced each year. To repeat the exercise $10^{20,000,000}$ times would require around $10^{19,999,980}$ times the length of the history of the universe (roughly speaking!). It seems perfectly reasonable, when one compares that length of time with the length of a human lifespan, to regard such events as impossible.

Borel's law then, while false within the abstract world of the pure mathematician, can only sensibly be regarded as true in anything remotely approaching a real world.

4   Conclusion

Borel's law, saying that events of absurdly small probability are impossible, implies that events which we actually observe – the coincidence examples in Section 2, for example – cannot be events of absurdly small probability. The laws of coincidence in Section 3 show how the probabilities associated with such events are in fact not absurdly small.

Familiar statistical theory is based on the aggregate behaviour of groups of objects, each behaving according to the laws of probability. These laws combine to produce overall laws for the aggregations, such as the laws of large numbers. However, anomalous behaviour, and in particular coincidences, can also often be explained in terms of certain laws based on basic probability. These laws may well remove the (natural, subconscious?) need to find a reason for apparent coincidences – no reason may be necessary, but just a proper calculation of the probabilities involved.

Principles similar to those outlined above also apply elsewhere to low probability events. A familiar one arises in screening for small subsets of a population (e.g. rare diseases, credit card fraud, terrorists, etc). A screening instrument which correctly identifies 99% of the rare class and also correctly identifies 99% of the majority class, when applied to a situation in which the rare class comprises just one in a million of the population, will be incorrect for about 99.99% of those it predicts belong to the rare class.

It follows that if unusual or unexpected events are to be used as indicators of possible unsuspected relationships, then the first step is to examine the events in the light of the 'laws' above. Having decided that the occurrence really is a very low probability event, under the standard assumptions, only then it is worthwhile seeking alternative explanations.

References

AYRES I. (2007): *Supercrunchers*. John Murray, London.

BALDI P., FASCONI P., and SMYTH P. (2003): *Modeling the Internet and the Web*. Wiley, Chichester.

BARNETT V. and LEWIS T. (1978): *Outliers in Statistical Data*. Wiley, Chichester.

BOREL É. (1962): *Probabilities and life*. Dover, New York.

DIACONIS, P. and MOSTELLER F. (1989): Methods for studying coincidences. *Journal of the American Statistical Association 84(408), 853-861*.

FEYNMAN R. (1998): *The Meaning of It All: Thoughts of a Citizen-Scientist*. McGraw-Hill, New York.

GIUDICI P. and FIGINI S. (2009): *Applied Data Mining*. Wiley, Chichester.

HAND D.J. (2009): Modern statistics: the myth and the magic. *Journal of the Royal Statistical Society, Series A, 172, 287-306*.

HAND D.J. and BOLTON R.J. (2004): Pattern discovery and detection: a unified statistical methodology. *Journal of Applied Statistics, 31, 885-924*.

HAND D.J., MANNILA H., and SMYTH P. (2001): *Principles of data mining*. MIT Press, Cambridge, Massachusetts.

Part II

ABC Methods for Genetic Data

Choosing the Summary Statistics and the Acceptance Rate in Approximate Bayesian Computation

Michael G.B. Blum[1]

Laboratoire TIMC-IMAG, CNRS, UJF Grenoble
Faculté de Médecine, 38706 La Tronche, France, *michael.blum@imag.fr*

Abstract. Approximate Bayesian Computation encompasses a family of likelihood-free algorithms for performing Bayesian inference in models defined in terms of a generating mechanism. The different algorithms rely on simulations of some summary statistics under the generative model and a rejection criterion that determines if a simulation is rejected or not. In this paper, I incorporate Approximate Bayesian Computation into a local Bayesian regression framework. Using an empirical Bayes approach, we provide a simple criterion for 1) choosing the threshold above which a simulation should be rejected, 2) choosing the subset of informative summary statistics, and 3) choosing if a summary statistic should be log-transformed or not.

Keywords: approximate Bayesian computation, evidence approximation, empirical Bayes, Bayesian local regression

1 Introduction

Approximate Bayesian Computation (ABC) encompasses a family of likelihood free algorithms for performing Bayesian inference (Beaumont et al. (2002), Marjoram et al. (2003)). It originated in population genetics for making inference in coalescent models (Pritchard et al. (1999)). Compared to MCMC algorithms that aim at providing a sample from the *full* posterior distribution $p(\phi|\mathcal{D})$, where ϕ denotes a possibly multi-dimensional parameter and $\mathcal{D}$ denotes the data, ABC targets a *partial* posterior distribution $p(\phi|S)$ where S denotes a p-dimensional summary statistic $S = (S^1, \ldots, S^p)$ typically of lower dimension than the data $\mathcal{D}$. Despite of this approximation inherent to ABC, its ease of implementation have fostered ABC applications in population genetics and evolutionary biology.

1.1 Rejection algorithm

To generate a sample from $p(\phi|S)$, the original ABC rejection algorithm is indeed remarkably simple (Pritchard et al. (1999)):

1. Generate a parameter ϕ according to the prior distribution π;

Y. Lechevallier, G. Saporta (eds.), *Proceedings of COMPSTAT'2010*,
DOI 10.1007/978-3-7908-2604-3_4, © Springer-Verlag Berlin Heidelberg 2010

2. Simulate data $\mathcal{D}'$ according to the model $p(\mathcal{D}'|\phi)$;
3. Compute the summary statistic S' from $\mathcal{D}'$ and accept the simulation if $d(S, S') < \delta$ where d is a distance between the two summary statistics and $\delta > 0$ is a threshold parameter.

It is the user's task to choose a threshold δ. Rather than choosing explicitly a threshold value δ, Beaumont et al. (2002) rather set the percentage of accepted simulations, the acceptance rate p_δ, to a given value. For a total of n simulations, it amounts to setting δ to the p_δ-percent quantile of the distances $d(S_i, S)$, $i = 1 \ldots n$. In the following, we choose $d(S, S') = ||S - S'||$ where $|| \cdot - \cdot ||$ denotes the Euclidean distance, and we consider that each summary statistic has been rescaled by a robust estimate of its dispersion (the median absolute deviation).

1.2   Regression adjustment

To weaken the effect of the discrepancy between the observed summary statistic and the accepted ones, Beaumont et al. (2002) proposed two innovations: weighting and regression adjustment. The weighting is a generalization of the acceptance-rejection algorithm in which each simulation is assigned a weight $W_i = K_\delta(||S - S_i||) \propto K(||S - S_i||/\delta)$ where K is a smoothing kernel. Beaumont et al. (2002) considered an Epanechnikov kernel so that simulations with $||S - S'|| > \delta$ are discarded as in the rejection algorithm.

The regression adjustment step involves a local-linear regression in which the least-squares criterion

$$\sum_{i=1}^{n}\{\phi_i - (\beta_0 + (S_i - S)^T \beta_1)\}W_i, \quad \beta_0 \in \mathbb{R}, \beta_1 \in \mathbb{R}^p, \tag{1}$$

is minimized. The least-squares estimate is given by

$$\hat{\beta}_{\text{LS}} = (\hat{\beta}_{\text{LS}}^0, \hat{\beta}_{\text{LS}}^1) = (X^T W_\delta X)^{-1} X^T W_\delta \phi, \tag{2}$$

where W_δ is a diagonal matrix in which the ith element is W_i, and

$$X = \begin{pmatrix} 1 & s_1^1 - s^1 & \cdots & s_1^p - s^p \\ \vdots & \cdots & \ddots & \vdots \\ 1 & s_n^1 - s^1 & \cdots & s_n^p - s^p \end{pmatrix}, \quad \phi = \begin{pmatrix} \phi_1 \\ \vdots \\ \phi_n \end{pmatrix}. \tag{3}$$

To form an approximate sample from $p(\phi|S)$, Beaumont et al. (2002) computed $\phi_i^* = \hat{\beta}_{\text{LS}}^0 + \epsilon_i$, where the ϵ_i's denote the empirical residuals of the regression. This translates into the following equation for the regression adjustment

$$\phi_i^* = \phi_i - (S_i - S)^T \hat{\beta}_{\text{LS}}^1. \tag{4}$$

To give an intuition about the benefit arising from the regression adjustment, look at the first and second weighted moments of the ϕ_i^*. The first moment of the ϕ_i^* is equal to the local linear estimate $\hat{\beta}_0$ and therefore provides an estimate of the posterior mean. Compared to the weighted mean of the ϕ_i's obtained with the rejection algorithm (the Nadaraya-Watson estimate in the statistics literature), $\hat{\beta}_0$ is *design adaptive*, i.e. its bias does not depend on the design $p(S)$ (Fan 1992). The second moment of the ϕ_i^* is equal to the second moment of the empirical residuals ϵ_i which is inferior to the total variance of the ϕ_i's. A shrinkage towards $\hat{\beta}_0$ is therefore involved by regression adjustment.

1.3   Potential pitfalls of ABC

Assume that we observe a sample of size $N = 50$ in which each individual is a Gaussian random variable of mean μ and variance σ^2. We are interested here in the estimation of the variance parameter σ^2. We assume the following hierarchical prior for μ and σ^2 (Gelman et al. (2004))

$$\sigma^2 \sim \mathrm{Inv}\chi^2(\mathrm{d.f.} = 1) \tag{5}$$
$$\mu \sim \mathcal{N}(0, \sigma^2), \tag{6}$$

where $\mathrm{Inv}\chi^2(\mathrm{d.f.} = \nu)$ denotes the inverse chi-square distribution with ν degrees of freedom, and $\mathcal{N}$ denotes the Gaussian distribution. We consider the the empirical mean and variance as the summary statistics. The data consists of the empirical mean and variance of the petal length for the viriginica species in the iris data.

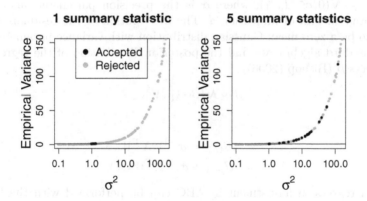

Fig. 1. Rejection algorithm for estimating σ^2 in a Gaussian model. In the left panel, the empirical variance is the single summary statistic in the rejection algorithm whereas in the right panel, we considered the five summary statistics. The horizontal line represents the observed empirical variance $s_N^2 = 1.144$.

1.4   Outline of the paper

In this paper, I will provide a criterion for 1) choosing a set of informative summary statistics among the p summary statistics $(S^1, \ldots, S^p)$, 2) choosing an acceptance rate p_δ, and 3) choosing if a summary statistic should be transformed or not. Here I will consider only log transformation but square root or inverse transformations could also be considered. The first section presents how to compute the $(p+1)$-dimensional parameter β of the local linear regression in a Bayesian fashion. In the context of Bayesian local regression, we define the evidence function that will provide us a rationale criterion for addressing questions 1-3. The second section presents two examples in which we show that the evidence function provides reasonable choices for p_δ, for the selection of the summary statistics, and for the choice of the scale (logarithmic or not) of the summary statistics.

2   Regression adjustment in a Bayesian fashion

2.1   Local Bayesian regression

Carrying out locally-linear regression in a Bayesian fashion has been studied by Hjort (2003). The linear regression model can be written as $\phi_i = \beta^0 + (S_i - S)^T \beta^1 + \epsilon$. The points (S_i, ϕ_i) are weighted by the $W_i = K_\delta(||S_i - S||)/K_\delta(0)$. By contrast to the least-squares estimate, Bayesian local regression is not invariant to rescaling of the W_i's. Here, a weight of 1 is given to a simulation for which S_i matches exactly S and the weights decrease from 1 to 0 as the $||S_i - S||$'s move from 0 to δ.

Here we assume a zero-mean isotropic Gaussian prior such that $\beta = (\beta^0, \beta^1) \sim \mathcal{N}(0, \alpha^{-1} I_{p+1})$, where α is the precision parameter, and I_d is the identity matrix of dimension d. The distribution of the residuals is assumed to be a zero mean Gaussian distribution with variance parameter σ^2. With standard algebra, we find the posterior distribution of the regression coefficients β (Bishop (2006))

$$\beta \sim \mathcal{N}(\beta_{\mathrm{MAP}}, V), \tag{7}$$

where

$$\beta_{\mathrm{MAP}} = \sigma^{-2} V X^T W_\delta \phi \tag{8}$$

$$V^{-1} = (\alpha I_{p+1} + \sigma^{-2} X^T W_\delta X). \tag{9}$$

Bayesian regression adjustment in ABC can be performed with the linear adjustment of equation (4) by replacing β_{LS}^1 with β_{MAP}^1. By definition of the posterior distribution, we find that β_{MAP} minimizes the regularized least-squares problem considered in ridge regression (Hoerl and Kennard (1970))

$$E(\beta) = \frac{1}{2\sigma^2} \sum_{i=1}^{n} (\phi_i - (S_i - S)^T \beta)^2 W_i + \frac{\alpha}{2} \beta^T \beta. \tag{10}$$

As seen from equation (10), Bayesian linear regression shrinks the regression coefficients towards 0 by imposing a penalty on their sizes. The appropriate value for σ^2, α, and p_δ, required for the computation of β_{MAP}, will be determined through the evidence approximation discussed below.

2.2   The evidence approximation

A complete Bayesian treatment of the regression would require to integrate the hyperparameters over some hyperpriors. Here we adopt a different approach in which we determine the value of the hyperparameters, by maximizing the *marginal likelihood*. The marginal likelihood $p(\phi|\sigma^2, \alpha, p_\delta)$, called the evidence function in the machine learning literature (MacKay (1992), Bishop (2006)), is obtained by integrating the likelihood over the the regression parameters β

$$p(\phi|\sigma^2, \alpha, p_\delta) = \int \left(\Pi_{i=1}^n p(\phi_i|\beta, \sigma^2)^{W_i} \right) p(\beta|\alpha) \, d\beta. \tag{11}$$

Finding the value of the hyperparameters by maximizing the evidence is known as *empirical Bayes* in the statistics literature (Gelman et al. (2004)). Here, we do not give the details of the computation of the evidence and refer the reader to Bishop (2006). The log of the evidence is given by

$$\log p(\phi|\sigma^2, \alpha, p_\delta) = \tfrac{p+1}{2} \log \alpha - \tfrac{N_W}{2} \log \sigma^2 - E(\beta_{\text{MAP}}) - \tfrac{1}{2} \log |V^{-1}| - \tfrac{N_W}{2} \log 2\pi, \tag{12}$$

where $N_W = \sum W_i$. By maximizing the log of the evidence with respect to α, we find that

$$\alpha = \frac{\gamma}{\beta_{\text{MAP}}^T \beta_{\text{MAP}}}, \tag{13}$$

where γ is the effective number of parameters (of summary statistics here)

$$\gamma = (p+1) - \alpha \text{Tr}(V). \tag{14}$$

Similarly, setting $\delta \log p(\phi|\sigma^2, \alpha, p_\delta)/\delta\sigma^2 = 0$ gives

$$\sigma^2 = \frac{\sum_{i=1}^n (\phi_i - (S_i - S)^T \beta)^2 W_i}{N_W - \gamma}. \tag{15}$$

Equations (13) and (15) are implicit solutions for the hyperparameters since β_{MAP}, V, and γ depend on α and σ^2. For maximizing the log-evidence, we first update β_{MAP} and V with equations (8) and (9), then we update γ using equation (14), and finally update α and σ^2 with equations (13) and (15). This updating scheme is applied in an iterative manner and stopped when the difference between two successive iterations is small enough. Plugging the values of these estimates for α and σ^2 into equation (12), we obtain the log-evidence for the acceptance rate $\log p(\phi|p_\delta)$.

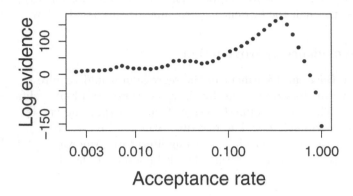

Fig. 2. Log of the evidence as a function of the acceptance rate for the generative model of equation (16). A total of $1,000$ simulation is performed and the optimal acceptance rate is found for $p_\delta = 37$.

3   The evidence function as an omnibus criterion

3.1   Choosing the acceptance rate

To show that the evidence function provide a good choice for the tolerance rate, we introduce the following toy example. We denote ϕ, the parameter of interest and S the data which is equal here to the summary statistic. The generative model can be described as

$$\phi \sim \mathcal{U}_{-c,c} \quad c \in \mathbb{R},$$

$$S \sim \mathcal{N}\left(\frac{e^\phi}{1 + e^\phi}, \sigma^2 = (.05)^2\right), \tag{16}$$

where $\mathcal{U}_{a,b}$ denotes the uniform distribution between a and b. We assume that the observed data is $S = 0.5$. For $c = 5$, Figure 2 displays that the evidence function has a maximum around $p_\delta = 37\%$. As seen in Figure 3, this value of p_δ corresponds to a large enough neighborhood around $S = 0.5$ in which the relationship between S and ϕ is linear. For increasing values of c in equation (16), the width of the neighborhood-around $S = 0.5$-in which the linear approximation holds, decreases. Figure 3 shows that the evidence function does a good job at selecting neighborhoods of decreasing widths in which the relationship between S and ϕ is linear.

3.2   Choosing the summary statistics

The evidence function can be used to choose a subset of predictor variables in a regression setting. For example, Bishop (2006) used the evidence to select

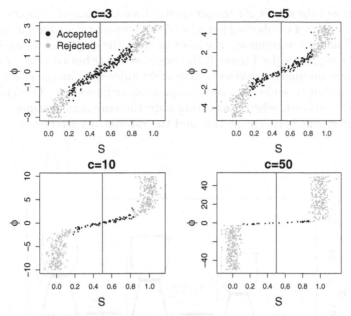

Fig. 3. Plot of the accepted points in the rejection algorithm for four different values of the parameter c. In the four plots, the acceptance rate is chosen by maximizing the evidence function $p(\phi|p_\delta)$.

the order of the polynomial in a polynomial regression. Here we show that the evidence function provides a criterion for choosing the set of informative summary statistics in ABC.

Plugging the optimal value for p_δ in equation (12), we obtain the evidence as a function of the set of summary statistics $p(\phi|(S^1,\ldots,S^p))$. To find an optimal subset of summary statistics, we use a standard stepwise approach. We first include the summary statistic S^{j_1} ($j_1 \in \{1,\ldots,p\}$) that gives the largest value of the evidence $p(\phi|S^{j_1})$. We then evaluate the evidence $p(\phi|(S^{j_1}, S^{j_2}))$ ($j_2 \in \{1,\ldots,p\}$) and include a second summary statistics if $\max_{j_2} p(\phi|(S^{j_1}, S^{j_2})) > p(\phi|S^{j_1})$. If a second summary statistics is not included in the optimal subset, the algorithm is stopped. Otherwise, the process is repeated until an optimal subset has been found.

To check the validity of the algorithm, we apply this stepwise procedure to the Gaussian model of Section 1.3 in which there are five different summary statistics. To estimate the posterior distribution of σ^2, we apply the linear correction adjustment of equation (4) to $\log \sigma^2$ and then use the exponential function to return to the original scale. This transformation guarantees that the corrected values will be positive. For each test replicate, we perform $n = 10,000$ simulations of the generative model of Section 1.3 and select an optimal subset of summary statistics with the stepwise procedure. Performing a total of one hundred test replicates, we find that the stepwise procedure always chooses the subset of summary statistics containing the empirical variance only. Figure 4 displays summaries of the posterior distribution obtained with ABC using five summary statistics or with the empirical variance only. As already suggested by Figure 1, the posterior distribution of σ^2 obtained with the five summary statistics is extremely different from the exact posterior distribution (a scaled inverse chi-square distribution, see Gelman et al. (2004)). By contrast, when considering only the empirical variance, we find a good agreement between the true and the estimated posterior.

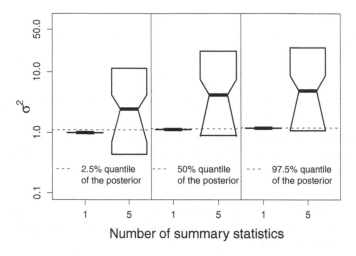

Fig. 4. Boxplots of the 2.5%, 50%, and 97.5% estimated quantiles of the posterior distribution for σ^2. ABC with one summary statistics has been performed with the empirical variance only. A total of 100 runs of ABC has been performed, each of which consisting of $n = 10,000$ simulations.

3.3   Choosing the scale of the summary statistics

Here we show that changing the scale of the summary statistics can have a dramatic effect in ABC. We perform a second experiment in which we replace the empirical variance by the log of the empirical variance in the set of five summary statistics. Performing a total of one hundred test replicates, we find that the stepwise procedure always chooses the subset containing the log of the empirical variance only. However, by contrast to the previous experiment, we find that the posterior distribution of σ^2 obtained with the five summary statistics is in good agreement with the exact posterior distribution (see Figure 5). As usual for regression model, this simple experiment shows that better regression models can be obtained with a good transformation of the predictor variables.

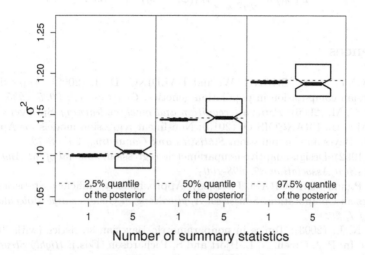

Fig. 5. Boxplots of the 2.5%, 50%, and 97.5% estimated quantiles of the posterior distribution for σ^2. In the ABC algorithms the empirical variance has been log-transformed.

We test here if the evidence function is able to find a good scale for the summary statistics. In one hundred test experiment, we compare $p(\log \sigma^2 | s_N^2)$ to $p(\log \sigma^2 | \log(s_N^2))$. We find that the evidence function always selects $\log(s_N^2)$ showing that a good scale for the summary statistics can be found with the evidence function.

3.4   Using the evidence without regression adjustment

If the standard rejection algorithm of Section 1.1 is considered without any regression adjustment, it is also possible to use the evidence function. The local Bayesian framework is now $\phi_i = \beta_0 + \epsilon$ in which each points (S_i, ϕ_i) is weighted by $W_i = K_\delta(||S_i - S||)/K_\delta(0)$. Assuming that the prior for β_0 is $\mathcal{N}(0, \alpha)$, we find for the evidence function

$$\log p(\phi | \sigma^2, \alpha, p_\delta) = \tfrac{1}{2} \log \alpha - \tfrac{N_W}{2} \log \sigma^2 - E(\beta_{0,\mathrm{MAP}}) - \tfrac{1}{2} \log |\alpha + \sigma^{-2} N_W| - \tfrac{N_W}{2} \log 2\pi,$$

(17)

where

$$\beta_{0,\mathrm{MAP}} = \frac{\sigma^{-2}}{\alpha + \sigma^{-2}N_W} \sum_{i=1}^{n} W_i \phi_i \qquad (18)$$

$$E(\beta_0) = \frac{1}{2\sigma^2} \sum_{i=1}^{n} W_i(\phi_i - \beta_0)^2 + \frac{\alpha}{2}\beta_0^{\,2}. \qquad (19)$$

References

BEAUMONT, M. A., ZHANG, W. and BALDING, D. J. (2002): Approximate Bayesian computation in population genetics. *Genetics 162: 2025-2035.*

BISHOP, C. M. (2006): *Pattern recognition and machine learning.* Springer

BLUM, M.G.B., FRANÇOIS O. (2010): Non-linear regression models for Approximate Bayesian Computation. *Statistics and Computing, 20: 63-73.*

FAN, J. (1992): Design-adaptive nonparametric regression. *Journal of the American Statistical Association 87, 998-1004.*

JOYCE, P. and MARJORAM, P. (2008): Approximately Sufficient Statistics and Bayesian Computation. *Statistical Applications in Genetics and Molecular Biology 7, 26.*

HJORT, N. L. (2003): Topics in nonparametric Bayesian statistics (with discussion). In: P. J. Green, N. L. Hjort and S. Richardson (Eds.): *Highly Structured Stochastic Systems.* Oxford University Press, 455-487.

GELMAN, A., CARLIN J. B., STERN H. S. and RUBIN D. B. (2004): *Bayesian Data Analysis.* Chapman & Hall/CRC.

HOERL, A. E. and KENNARD, R. (1970): Ridge regression: biased estimation for nonorthogonal problems. *Technometrics 12, 55-67.*

MACKAY, D. J. C. (1992): Bayesian interpolation. *Neural Computation 4, 415-447.*

MARJORAM, P., MOLITOR, J., PLAGNOL, V. and TAVARÉ, S. (2003): Markov chain Monte Carlo without likelihoods. *Proceedings of the National Academy of Sciences USA 100, 15324-15328.*

PRITCHARD, J. K., SEIELSTAD, M. T., PEREZ-LEZAUN, A. and FELDMAN, M. W. (1999): Population growth of human Y chromosomes: a study of Y chromosome microsatellites. *Molecular Biology and Evolution 16, 1791-1798.*

Integrating Approximate Bayesian Computation with Complex Agent-Based Models for Cancer Research

Andrea Sottoriva[1] and Simon Tavaré[2]

[1] Department of Oncology, University of Cambridge, CRUK Cambridge Research Institute, Li Ka Shing Centre, Robinson Way, Cambridge CB2 0RE, UK, *as949@cam.ac.uk*

[2] Department of Oncology and DAMTP, University of Cambridge, CRUK Cambridge Research Institute, Li Ka Shing Centre, Robinson Way, Cambridge CB2 0RE, UK, *st321@cam.ac.uk*

Abstract. Multi-scale agent-based models such as hybrid cellular automata and cellular Potts models are now being used to study mechanisms involved in cancer formation and progression, including cell proliferation, differentiation, migration, invasion and cell signaling. Due to their complexity, statistical inference for such models is a challenge. Here we show how approximate Bayesian computation can be exploited to provide a useful tool for inferring posterior distributions. We illustrate our approach in the context of a cellular Potts model for a human colon crypt, and show how molecular markers can be used to infer aspects of stem cell dynamics in the crypt.

Keywords: ABC, cellular Potts model, colon crypt dynamics, stem cell modeling

1 Introduction

1.1 Agent-based modeling in cancer research

In recent years, cancer research has become a multi-disciplinary field. As well as biological and medical advances, mathematical and computational modeling and advanced statistical techniques have been employed to deal with the ever-increasing amount of data generated by experimental labs.

Recently, the concept of mathematical oncology has taken shape as an emerging field that integrates cancer biology with computational modeling, statistics and data analysis (Anderson and Quaranta (2008)). However, the use of mathematical modeling in cancer research is not completely new; since the 1960s population growth models have been developed to explain the growth kinetics of tumors (cf. Laird (1964), Burton (1966)).

Despite the importance of these models in explaining the basic growth dynamics of solid malignancies, they often fail to represent the intricate underlying mechanisms involved in the disease. Cancer is in fact driven by

Y. Lechevallier, G. Saporta (eds.), *Proceedings of COMPSTAT'2010*,
DOI 10.1007/978-3-7908-2604-3_5, © Springer-Verlag Berlin Heidelberg 2010

a large number of complex interactions spanning multiple space and time scales. All these interactions among molecules, such as transcription promoters and repressors, and among cells, such as cell-to-cell signaling, give rise to several emergent behaviors of tumors, most importantly tissue invasion and metastasis (Hanahan and Weinberg (2000)).

In this scenario, multi-scale agent-based models become necessary to study many of the mechanisms involved in cancer formation and progression. In particular, hybrid cellular automata models (Anderson et al. (2006), Sottoriva et al. (2010a)) and cellular Potts models (Jiang et al. (2005), Sottoriva et al. (2010b)) have proved suitable to model cancer cell proliferation, differentiation, migration, invasion and cell signaling. These models aims to represent cancer as an evolutionary process (Merlo et al. (2006)) with emergent behaviour that results from the interplay of several underlying mechanisms at the cellular and extra-cellular level.

1.2   Coupling biological data and models with ABC

Approximate Bayesian Computation (ABC) provides a valuable tool to infer posterior distributions of parameters from biological data when using stochastic models for which likelihoods are infeasible to calculate. Agent-based models are able to incorporate many of the processes occurring in cancer, most of which show non-linear behavior and are therefore impossible to treat analytically. The integration of ABC and agent-based models therefore seems natural, yet there are some important issues to discuss.

In the past ABC has been extensively and successfully employed with population genetics models (Beaumont et al. (2002), Marjoram and Tavaré (2006)). In such applications the models are often relatively simple because they aim to simulate a few crucial underlying processes. In contrast, in some cancer modeling scenarios the models are complex and computationally expensive; even with large computational resources simulating the model millions of times is infeasible. In this paper we discuss how to make use of ABC with complex agent-based models by exploiting parallelization and by reducing the complexity of the ABC algorithms to the minimum. We illustrate our approach using the human colon crypt as an example.

2   Material and methods

2.1   Methylation data

To study the evolutionary dynamics of a human colon crypt we first need to collect data that contain information about the basic processes occurring in it, such as proliferation, differentiation and migration of cells. Neutral methylation patterns have proved to be suitable candidates to be used as molecular clocks of the cells in the crypt (Yatabe et al. (2001)). By using a population genetics model combined with Markov chain Monte Carlo, Nicolas et al. (2007) showed that it is possible to infer the parameters regulating some of the mechanisms occurring in the human colon crypt.

Nicolas et al. (2007) collected methylation patterns from a total of 57 colon crypts from 7 male patients aged between 40 and 87 years. The dataset is divided into two subgroups: the first contains 8 cells sampled from each of 37 crypts obtained from 5 distinct individuals, the second has 24 cells sampled from each of 20 crypts taken from 3 individuals; one individual is common to both subsets. Each sampled pattern is 9 CpGs long and has been sequenced from a 77 bp locus upstream of the BGN gene on the X chromosome. Because BGN is not expressed in neoplastic or normal colon tissue (Yatabe et al. (2001)) we consider it an epigenetically neutral locus.

2.2 Modeling the colon crypt

Colorectal cancer is one of the most common cancers in humans and it is known to originate from cells in a colon crypt, the units responsible for renewing the colon lining (Barker et al. (2009)). These tubular structures form the colon epithelium and continuously generate new cells that repopulate the fast-renewing colon tissue. At the base of the colon crypt there are stem cells that generate a compartment of transient amplifying cells that in turn give rise to the fully differentiated colon cells. These cells migrate to the top of the crypt and become part the colon epithelial tissue before being shed into the colon lumen (Figure 1). Colorectal cancer is triggered by the disruption of some of the most important pathways that regulate crypt homeostasis, such as *Wnt* and *APC* (Barker et al. (2009), Reya and Clevers (2005)).

Despite the crucial role played by colon crypts in colorectal carcinogenesis, several mechanisms and parameters of crypt dynamics are unknown, including the number of stem cells present in the crypt, the number of transient amplifying stages and the rate of symmetrical division of stem cells in the crypt (Potten et al. (2009)).

Here we present a newly developed model that simulates cell proliferation, differentiation, migration in the colon crypt. In addition to these processes our model, which we call the *VirtualCrypt*, simulates the occurrence of methylation mutations at each cell division. To model the colon crypt, we unfold the crypt and represent it as a two-dimensional sheet of cells with periodic boundary conditions on the sides and fixed at the bottom (Figure 2A). Cells that exit the top of the lattice are shed into the colon lumen and are therefore deleted from the simulation.

The VirtualCrypt is a Cellular Potts Model that models the colon crypt as a two-dimensional lattice Ω with $N \times M$ sites. Each biological cell in the crypt has a unique identifier or spin σ, and adjacent lattice sites with the same spin define a single cell volume V_σ and its shape (Glazier and Graner (1993)). Each cell has also a type $\tau(\sigma)$ that identifies a cell as a stem cell, a transient amplifying (TA) cell or a differentiated cell (DC).

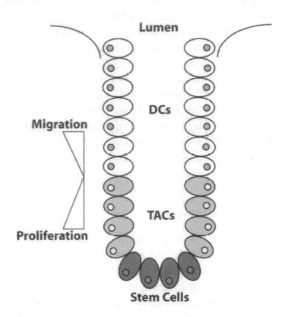

Fig. 1. Cartoon of a colon crypt. DC, differentiated cell; TAC, transient amplifying cell. Stem cells at the bottom of the crypt spawn all the other crypt cells that differentiate and migrate towards the top of the crypt to form the colon lining.

The evolution of the system is modeled using a thermodynamical approach borrowed from statistical mechanics in which all the components of the system seek the point of lowest energy. In other words, at each step we propose a large number of random variations to the system and we are more likely to accept those which are more advantageous, in terms of energy, for the cells. For example a cell will seek to expand to maintain its original volume when it is compressed, or it will tend to migrate along a chemotactic gradient if it is attracted by it.

In summary, we can describe the total energy of the system with a simple Hamiltonian:

$$H = E_v + E_a + E_c, \tag{1}$$

where E_v is the volume elastic energy, E_a is the cell membrane contact energy and E_c is the chemotactic energy. These values represent the energy cost of a certain cell state. The Volume Elastic Energy E_v is defined by

$$E_v = \sum_{\sigma} \lambda_{\tau(\sigma)} |V_\sigma - V_T|, \tag{2}$$

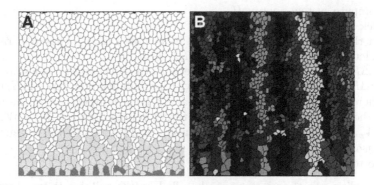

Fig. 2. The cellular Potts model. Panel A: stem cells are dark shade, transient amplifying cells intermediate shade, differentiated cells are white. Panel B: Methylation patterns in the cells in the crypt. Different shades correspond to different alleles in the BGN locus.

In the absence of external forces the cell volume V_σ is equal to its target volume V_T and therefore the cell elastic energy $E_v = 0$. When a cell is compressed or stretched its elastic energy increases proportionally to the change in volume and its elastic coefficient $\lambda_{\tau(\sigma)}$, which depends on the cell type. The Cell Adhesion Energy E_a is given by

$$E_a = \sum_{(i,j),(i',j') \text{ neighbours}} J(\tau(\sigma_{i,j}), \tau(\sigma_{i',j'}))(1 - \delta_{\sigma_{i,j}\sigma_{i',j'}}) \qquad (3)$$

A certain energy cost or credit $J(\tau_1, \tau_2)$ is associated with each contact point between cells, in a cell type dependent manner. The δ term in (3) ensures that only contact points between two different cells are considered and not points within the same cell. In this way we can simulate cell adhesion to neighboring cells or to other surfaces in an elegant and straightforward manner. The Chemotactic and Haptotactic Energy is given by

$$E_c = \sum_{(i,j)} \nu_{\tau(\sigma_{i,j})} C(i,j) \qquad (4)$$

The chemotactic or haptotactic response of cells to underlying concentration gradients is modeled by assuming that the energy cost of a certain cell state depends on the cell taxis coefficient ν and on the underlying chemical or extracellular matrix concentration $C(i,j)$. The higher the gradient and the migration coefficient, the less it would cost in terms of energy for the cell to migrate rather than stay still.

To evolve the system, at each time step τ we propose and eventually accept a certain number of random local changes in a Monte Carlo fashion, proceeding according to the following Metropolis algorithm (Beichl and Sullivan (2000)):

1. Compute system energy H
2. Pick a random lattice site (i, j)
3. Set the content σ of (i, j) to that of its neighbor (i', j'), chosen at random
4. Calculate the new energy $\Delta H = H_{\text{new}} - H$
5. If $\Delta H < 0$ accept the new state because the total energy is lower
6. If $\Delta H \geq 0$ accept the new state with probability $p = \exp(-\Delta H/(\kappa T))$, where κ is the Boltzmann constant and T is the temperature of the system
7. If the cell is growing, increase the target volume to $V_T = V_T + \delta V$
8. If $V_\sigma > 2V_T$ the cell divides (V_σ automatically tends to V_T, for energetic reasons)
9. Go to 1

In addition to the mechanisms handled by the cellular Potts algorithm, at each cell division we simulate the occurrence of methylation mutations with a rate μ (see Table 1). Each of the 9 CpG sites forming the methylation pattern we collected in the data has a probability μ of being methylated or demethylated at each cell division. If no methylation error occurs, the original methylation pattern is carried into the daughter cell from the mother.

2.3 Inferring colon crypt dynamics with ABC

With our cellular Potts model we are able to simulate the evolution of methylation patterns for long periods of time, up to the age of the patient from which the data have been collected. The two main parameters we are interested in inferring about the colon crypt are the number of stem cells N present in the bottom of it and their symmetrical division rate ρ. The rest of the parameters are assumed to be fixed and are reported in Table 1.

Parameter	Symbol	Value
TACs and DCs migration speed	ν	1000 (1 cell position per day)
Cell cycle time	t_c	24h (Potten and Loeffler (1990))
Methylation rate	μ	2×10^{-5} (Yatabe et al. (2001))
Methylation pattern length	γ	9 CpGs (Nicolas et al. (2007))

Table 1. Fixed parameters in the VirtualCrypt simulations.

To fit the two parameters to our methylation data we use Approximate Bayesian Computation. The prior distributions are taken to be uniform, with

$$N \sim U(2, 30), \quad \rho \sim U(0, 1).$$

Initially all cells in the crypts are assumed to be unmethylated (Yatabe et al. (2001)). To compare the multi-dimensional data from the simulations and the patients we define a summary measure $S(\cdot)$ by

$$S(d, p, w, u, g) = \sqrt{d^2 + p^2 + w^2 + u^2 + g^2}, \tag{5}$$

where d is the number of distinct patterns, p number of polymorphic sites, w the average pairwise distance between the patterns, u the number of completely unmethylated patterns and g the number of singletons (patterns that appear only once in a crypt). We note that these statistics are normalized to have common range before use. The ABC algorithm that we applied is as follows:

1. Sample a parameter set θ from the prior
2. Sample a random seed r for the simulation
3. Run the model until the correct patient age is reached
4. Repeat from step 2. until the number of simulated crypts is the same as in the data
5. Compute the average summary statistics $X = (d, p, w, u, g)$ of the observed data, averaged over all crypts
6. Compute the average summary statistics $X' = (d', p', w', u', g')$ from the simulated crypts
7. If $|S(X) - S(X')| < \epsilon$ accept θ as a sample from the posterior distribution
8. Go to 1

This simple ABC approach allows for heavy parallelization due to the independence of the simulations and the accept/reject step that can be performed a posteriori, together with other signal extraction techniques.

3 Results

We generated a total of 80,000 single colon crypt simulations, grouped in sets of 16 having the same parameter set but different random seeds (5000 different parameter sets in all). This allows us to compare the simulations with the data by reproducing the sampling performed on the patients, where up to 14 crypts were analyzed from a single patient. We are assuming crypts from a single patient have similar parameters. The posterior distributions obtained from each patient are plotted together in Figure 3.

Due to the heterogeneity of the methylation patterns present in the crypt, our study suggests a relatively high number of stem cells (Figure 3A). These findings confirm the results previously reported by our group using a population genetics model on the same dataset (Nicolas et al. (2007)).

Therefore, in contrast to the common assumption of a colon crypt driven by a small number of stem cells, our model indicates a crypt controlled by quite a large number of stem cells that are responsible for generating the heterogeneous methylation patterns that we observed. Our model indicates that the homeostasis in the crypt is rather more complex than expected, in the sense that it involves a significant number of stem cells, likely between 18 and 25.

Regarding the symmetrical division rate, our study is in agreement with the common assumption that symmetrical division is a relatively rare event,

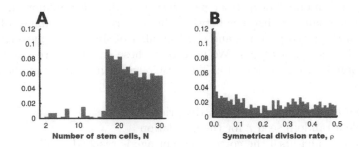

Fig. 3. Posterior histograms of the number of stem cells N and the symmetrical division rate ρ.

with a probability per cell division of $\rho \ll 1$. Our results suggest a value smaller than 0.02 (Figure 3B). Hence, crypt homeostasis appears to be driven by a population of stem cells at the bottom of the crypt that most of the time divide asymmetrically, but occasionally undergo symmetrical division, either for self-renewal or differentiation, about once in every 400 cell divisions.

4   Discussion

The role of the colon crypt as an initiator of colorectal carcinogenesis makes it a very important and interesting biological system to study. Nonetheless, characterizing the types of cells in the crypt using reliable biomarkers is often a challenging task. Using an in silico approach incorporating modeling and inference, here using methylation patterns as the marker, has proved a good complementary approach to wet lab techniques.

In this study we have shown that it is possible to infer biological features of a structure such as the colon crypt by using agent-based models that reduce the number of approximations and assumptions we need to make to simulate a biological system. We found that, in agreement with the classical stochastic model of proliferation in the crypt, the high level of methylation pattern heterogeneity observed in human colon crypts can be induced only by a relatively high number of stem cells, as also shown using a non-spatial model by Nicolas et al. (2007). Furthermore, we confirm the common assumption that stem cells undergo rare (< 0.025 times per cell division) events of symmetrical division that yields either stem cell self-renewal or the differentiation of both mother and daughter cells.

To our knowledge ABC methods have not previously been used for inference in agent-based models. This new framework needs a different approach to modeling and Bayesian inference itself. Agent-based models are often complex and include several processes to simulate; this makes them computationally slow even when extensive computational resources are available. In the past ABC has been employed with relatively simple population genetics models that do not contain complex inter-cellular or spatial communication but simply a population of individuals evolving in time. Such models are fast and easy to simulate, and have led to the development of adaptive ABC algorithms that allow posterior distributions to be obtained more rapidly (cf. Beaumont et al. (2009)).

In a scenario where a single simulation takes tens of minutes instead of mere seconds, the efficiency of the ABC technique is overwhelmed by the bottleneck induced by the model. In our study we found that adaptive ABC methods, developed to work with simple and fast population genetics models, are not suitable for computationally expensive models due to the slow convergence caused by the computation of the model.

Instead we found that a more convenient approach was to first run all the simulations in parallel with the parameters sampled from the priors. Then once a sufficient number of simulations have been computed, any rejection algorithm can be used to analyze the data, from a simple threshold method to more advanced signal extraction techniques.

Another advantage of the simple approach is that it is embarassingly parallel, and can be directly implemented in a high-performance computing environment by just scheduling the simulations independently. Using an adaptive scheme in a computer cluster may require complex job scheduling scripts that would be able to carry information throughout the process of adaptation.

References

ANDERSON, A. R. and QUARANTA, V. (2008): Integrative mathematical oncology. *Nature Reviews Cancer 8, 227–234.*

ANDERSON, A. R., WEAVER, A. M., CUMMINGS, P. T. and QUARANTA, V. (2006): Tumor morphology and phenotypic evolution driven by selective pressure from the microenvironment. *Cell 127, 905–915.*

BARKER, N., RIDGWAY, R. A., van ES, J. H., van de WETERING, M., BEGTHEL, H., van den BORN, M., DANENBERG, E., CLARKE, A. R., SANSOM, O. J. and CLEVERS, H. (2009): Crypt stem cells as the cells-of-origin of intestinal cancer. *Nature 457, 608–611.*

BEAUMONT, M., CORNUET, J.-M., MARIN, J.-M. and ROBERT, C. P. (2009): Adaptive approximate Bayesian computation. *Biometrika 96, 983–990.*

BEAUMONT, M. A., ZHANG, W. and BALDING, D. J. (2002): Approximate Bayesian computation in population genetics. *Genetics 162, 2025–2035.*

BEICHL, I. and SULLIVAN, F. (2000): The Metropolis algorithm. *Computing in Science and Engineering 2, 65–69.*

BURTON, A. C. (1966): Rate of growth of solid tumours as a problem of diffusion. *Growth 30, 157–176.*

GLAZIER, J. A. and GRANER, F. (1993): Simulation of the differential adhesion driven rearrangement of biological cells. *Physical Review E 47, 2128–2154.*

HANAHAN, D. and WEINBERG, R. A. (2000): The hallmarks of cancer. *Cell 100,* *57–70.*

JIANG, Y., PJESIVAC-GRBOVIC, J., CANTRELL, C. and FREYER, J. P. (2005): A multiscale model for avascular tumor growth. *Biophysics Journal 89, 3884–3894.*

LAIRD, A. K. Dynamics of tumor growth. (1964): *British Journal of Cancer 13, 490–502.*

MARJORAM, P. and TAVARÉ, S. (2006): Modern computational approaches for analysing molecular-genetic variation data. *Nature Reviews Genetics 7, 759–770.*

MERLO, L. M. F., PEPPER, J. W., REID, B. J. and MALEY, C. C. (2006): Cancer as an evolutionary and ecological process. *Nature Reviews Cancer 6, 924–935.*

NICOLAS, P., KIM, K. M., SHIBATA, D. and TAVARÉ, S. The stem cell population of the human colon crypt: analysis via methylation patterns. *PLoS Computational Biology 3, e28.*

POTTEN, C. S., GANDARA, R., MAHIDA, Y. R., LOEFFLER, M. and WRIGHT, N. A. (2009): The stem cells of small intestinal crypts: where are they? *Cell Proliferation 42, 731–750.*

POTTEN, C. S. and LOEFFLER, M. (1990): Stem cells: attributes, cycles, spirals, and uncertainties. Lessons for and from the crypt. *Development 110, 1001–1020.*

REYA, T. and CLEVERS, H. (2005): Wnt signalling in stem cells and cancer. *Nature 434, 843–850.*

SOTTORIVA, A., VERHOEFF, J. J. C., BOROVSKI, T., McWEENEY, NAUMOV, L., S. K., MEDEMA, J. P., SLOOT, P. M. A. and VERMEULEN, L. (2010a): Modeling cancer stem cell-driven tumor growth reveals invasive morphology and increased phenotypical heterogeneity. *Cancer Research 70, 46–56.*

SOTTORIVA, A., VERMEULEN, L. and TAVARÉ, S. (2010b): Modeling epigenetic mutations in hierarchically organized tumors. *In preparation.*

YATABE, Y., TAVARÉ, S. and SHIBATA, D. (2001): Investigating stem cells in human colon by using methylation patterns. Proceedings of the National Academy of Sciences of the United States of America 98, 10839–10844.

Part III

Algorithms for Robust Statistics

Part II

Algorithms for Robust Statistics

Robust Model Selection with LARS Based on S-estimators

Claudio Agostinelli[1] and Matias Salibian-Barrera[2]

[1] Dipartimento di Statistica
Ca' Foscari University
Venice, Italy *claudio@unive.it*
[2] Department of Statistics
The University of British Columbia
Vancouver, BC, Canada *matias@stat.ubc.ca*

Abstract. We consider the problem of selecting a parsimonious subset of explanatory variables from a potentially large collection of covariates. We are concerned with the case when data quality may be unreliable (e.g. there might be outliers among the observations). When the number of available covariates is moderately large, fitting all possible subsets is not a feasible option. Sequential methods like forward or backward selection are generally "greedy" and may fail to include important predictors when these are correlated. To avoid this problem Efron et al. (2004) proposed the Least Angle Regression algorithm to produce an ordered list of the available covariates (sequencing) according to their relevance. We introduce outlier robust versions of the LARS algorithm based on S-estimators for regression (Rousseeuw and Yohai (1984)). This algorithm is computationally efficient and suitable even when the number of variables exceeds the sample size. Simulation studies show that it is also robust to the presence of outliers in the data and compares favourably to previous proposals in the literature.

Keywords: robustness, model selection, LARS, S-estimators, robust regression

1 Introduction

As a result of the recent dramatic increase in the ability to collect data, researchers sometimes have a very large number of potentially relevant explanatory variables available to them. Typically, some of these covariates are correlated among themselves and hence not all of them need to be included in a statistical model with good prediction performance. In addition, models with few variables are generally easier to interpret than models with many ones. Model selection refers to the process of finding a parsimonious model with good prediction properties. Many model selection methods consist on sequentially fitting models from a pre-specified list and comparing their goodness-of-fit, prediction properties, or a combination of both. In this paper we consider the case where a proportion of the data may not satisfy the

Y. Lechevallier, G. Saporta (eds.), *Proceedings of COMPSTAT'2010*,
DOI 10.1007/978-3-7908-2604-3_6, © Springer-Verlag Berlin Heidelberg 2010

model assumptions and we are interested in predicting the non-outlying observations. Therefore, we consider model selection methods for linear models based on robust methods.

As it is the case with point estimation and other inference procedures, likelihood-type model selection methods (e.g. AIC (Akaike (1970)), Mallows' C_p (Mallows (1973)), and BIC (Schwarz (1978)) may be severely affected by a small proportion of atypical observations in the data. These "outliers" may not necessarily consist of "large" values, but might not follow the model that applies to the majority of the data. Model selection procedures that are resistant to the presence of outliers in the sample have only recently started to receive some attention in the literature. Seminal papers include Hampel (1983), Ronchetti (1985, 1997) and Ronchetti and Staudte (1994). Other proposals include Sommer and Staudte (1995), Ronchetti, Field and Blanchart (1997), Qian and Künsch (1998), Agostinelli (2002a, 2002b), Agostinelli and Markatou (2005), Morgenthaler, Welsch and Zenide (2003). See also the recent book by Maronna, Martin and Yohai (2006). These proposals are based on robustified versions of classical selection criteria (e.g. robust C_p, robust final prediction error, etc.). More recently Müller and Welsh (2005) proposed a model selection criterion that combines a measure of goodness-of-fit, a penalty term to avoid over-fitting and and the expected prediction error conditional on the data. Salibian-Barrera and Van Aelst (2008) use the fast and robust bootstrap of Salibian-Barrera and Zamar (2002) to obtain a faster boostrap-based model selection method that is feasible to calculate for larger number of covariates. Although less expensive from a computational point of view than the stratified bootstrap of Müller and Welsh (2005), this method, as the previous ones, needs to compute the estimator on the full model.

A different approach to variable selection that is attractive when the number of explanatory variables is large is based on ordering the covariates according to their estimated "importance" in the full model. Forward stepwise and backward elimination procedures are examples of this approach, whereby in each step of the procedure a variable may enter or leave the linear model (see, e.g. Weisberg (1985) or Miller (2002)). With backward elimination one starts with the full model and then finds the best possible submodel with one less covariate in it. This procedure is repeated until we fit a model with a single covariate or a criterion is reached. A similar procedure is forward stepwise, where we first select the covariate (say x_1) with the highest absolute correlation with the response variable y. We take the residuals of the regression of y on x_1 as our new response, project all covariates orthogonally to x_1 and add the variable with the highest absolute correlation to the model. At the same step, variables in the model may be deleted according to a criterion. These steps are repeated until no variables are added or deleted. Unfortunately, when p is large ($p = 100$, for example), these procedure becomes unfeasible for highly-robust estimators, furthermore these algorithms are known to be greedy and may relegate important covariates if they are correlated with those selected earlier in the sequence.

The Least Angle Regression (LARS) of Efron et al. (2004) is a generalization of stepwise methods, where the length of the "step" is selected so as to strike a balance between fast-but-"greedy" and slow-but-"conservative" alternatives, as those in stagewise selection (see, e.g. Hastie, Tibshirani and Friedman (2001)). It is easy to verify that this method is not robust to the presence of a small amount of atypical observations. McCann and Welsch (2007) proposed to add an indicator variable for each observation and then run the usual LARS on the extended set of covariates. When high-leverage outliers are possible, they suggest building models from randomly drawn subsamples of the data, and then selecting the best of them based on their (robustly estimated) prediction error. Khan, Van Aelst and Zamar (2007b) showed that the LARS algorithm can be expressed in terms of the pairwise sample correlations between covariates and the response variable, and proposed to apply this algorithm using robust correlation estimates. This is a "plug-in" proposal in the sense that it takes a method derived using least squares or L_2 estimators and replaces the required point estimates by robust counterparts.

In this paper we derive an algorithm based on LARS, but using a S-regression estimator (Rousseeuw and Yohai (1984)). Section 2 contains a brief description of the LARS algorithm, while Section 3 describes our proposal. Simulation results are discussed in Section 4 and concluding remarks can be found in Section 5.

2   Review of Least Angle Regression

Let (y_1, x_1), ..., (y_n, x_n) be n independent observations, where $y_i \in \mathbb{R}$ and $x_i \in \mathbb{R}^p$, $i = 1, \ldots, n$. We are interested in fitting a linear model of the form

$$y_j = \alpha + \beta' x_j + \epsilon_j \quad j = 1, \ldots, n,$$

where $\beta \in \mathbb{R}^p$ and the errors ϵ_j are assumed to be independent with zero mean and constant variance σ^2. In what follows, we will assume, without loss of generality that the variables have been centered and standardized to satisfy:

$$\sum_{i=1}^{n} y_i = 0 \qquad \sum_{i=1}^{n} x_{i,j} = 0 \qquad \sum_{i=1}^{n} x_{i,j}^2 = 1 \qquad \text{for } 1 \le j \le p .$$

so that the linear model above does not contain the intercept term.

The Least Angle Regression algorithm (LARS) is a generalization of the Forward Stagewise procedure. The latter is an iterative technique that starts with the predictor vector $\hat{\mu} = 0 \in \mathbb{R}^n$, and at each step sets

$$\hat{\mu} = \hat{\mu} + \delta \, \text{sign}(c_j) \, x_{(j)}$$

where $j = \arg\max_{1 \leq i \leq p} \text{cor}(y - \hat{\mu}, x_{(i)})$, $x_{(i)} \in \mathbb{R}^n$ denotes the i-th column of the design matrix, $c_j = \text{cor}(y - \hat{\mu}, x_{(j)})$, and $\delta > 0$ is a "small" constant. Typically the parameter δ controls the speed and "greediness" of the method: small values produce better results at a large computational cost, while large values result in a faster algorithm that may relegate an important covariate if it happens to be correlated with one that has entered the model earlier.

The LARS iterations can be described as follows. Start with the predictor $\hat{\mu} = 0$. Let $\hat{\mu}_{\mathcal{A}}$ be the current predictor and let

$$c = X' \left(y - \hat{\mu}_{\mathcal{A}}\right),$$

where $X \in \mathbb{R}^{n \times p}$ denotes the design matrix. In other words, c is the vector of current correlations c_j, $j = 1, \ldots, p$. Let $\mathcal{A}$ denote the active set, which corresponds to those covariates with largest absolute correlations: $C = \max_j\{|c_j|\}$ and $\mathcal{A} = \{j : |c_j| = C\}$. Assume, without loss of generality, that $\mathcal{A} = \{1, \ldots, m\}$. Let $s_j = \text{sign}(c_j)$ for $j \in \mathcal{A}$, and let $X_{\mathcal{A}} \in \mathbb{R}^{n \times m}$ be the matrix formed by the corresponding signed columns of the design matrix X, $s_j x_{(j)}$. Note that the vector $u_{\mathcal{A}} = v_{\mathcal{A}}/\|v_{\mathcal{A}}\|$, where

$$v_{\mathcal{A}} = X_{\mathcal{A}} \left(X'_{\mathcal{A}} X_{\mathcal{A}}\right)^{-1} \mathbf{1}_{\mathcal{A}},$$

satisfies

$$X'_{\mathcal{A}} u_{\mathcal{A}} = A_{\mathcal{A}} \mathbf{1}_{\mathcal{A}}, \tag{1}$$

where $A_{\mathcal{A}} = 1/\|v_{\mathcal{A}}\| \in \mathbb{R}$. In other words, the unit vector $u_{\mathcal{A}}$ makes equal angles with the columns of $X_{\mathcal{A}}$. LARS updates $\hat{\mu}_{\mathcal{A}}$ to

$$\hat{\mu}_{\mathcal{A}} \leftarrow \hat{\mu}_{\mathcal{A}} + \gamma u_{\mathcal{A}},$$

where γ is taken to be the smallest positive value such that a new covariate joins the active set $\mathcal{A}$ of explanatory variables with largest absolute correlation. More specifically, note that, if for each λ we let $\mu(\lambda) = \hat{\mu}_{\mathcal{A}} + \lambda u_{\mathcal{A}}$, then for each $j = 1, \ldots, p$ we have

$$c_j(\lambda) = \text{cor}\left(y - \mu(\lambda), x_{(j)}\right) = x'_{(j)}(y - \mu(\lambda)) = c_j - \gamma a_j,$$

where $a_j = x'_{(j)} u_{\mathcal{A}}$. For $j \in \mathcal{A}$, equation (1) implies that

$$|c_j(\lambda)| = C - \gamma A_{\mathcal{A}},$$

so all maximal current correlations decrease at a constant rate along this direction. We then determine the smallest positive value of γ that makes the correlations between the current active covariates and the residuals equal to that of another covariate $x_{(k)}$ not in the active set $\mathcal{A}$. This variable enters the model, the active set becomes

$$\mathcal{A} \leftarrow \mathcal{A} \cup \{k\},$$

and the correlations are updated to $C \leftarrow C - \gamma A_{\mathcal{A}}$. We refer the interested reader to Efron et al. (2004) for more details.

3   LARS based on S-estimators

S-regression estimators (Rousseeuw and Yohai (1984)) are defined as the vector of coefficients that produce the "smallest" residuals in the sense of minimizing a robust M-scale estimator. Formally we have:

$$\hat{\beta} = \arg \min_{\beta \in \mathbb{R}^p} \ \sigma(\beta) \, ,$$

where $\sigma(\beta)$ satisfies

$$\frac{1}{n} \sum_{i=1}^{n} \rho \left(\frac{r_i(\beta)}{\sigma(\beta)} \right) \ = \ b,$$

$\rho : \mathbb{R} \rightarrow \mathbb{R}_+$ is a symmetric, bounded, non-decreasing and continuous function, and $b \in (0,1)$ is a fixed constant. The choice $b = E_{F_0}(\rho)$ ensures that the resulting estimator is consistent when the errors have distribution function F_0.

For a given active set $\mathcal{A}$ of k covariates let $\hat{\beta}_\mathcal{A}, \hat{\beta}_{0\mathcal{A}}, \hat{\sigma}_\mathcal{A}$ be the S-estimators of regressing the current residuals on the k active variables with indices in $\mathcal{A}$. Consider the parameter vector $\theta = (\gamma, \beta_0, \sigma)$ that satisfies

$$\frac{1}{n-k-1} \sum_{i=1}^{n} \rho \left(\frac{r_i - x'_{i,k}(\hat{\beta}_\mathcal{A}\gamma) - \beta_0}{\sigma} \right) = b.$$

A robust measure of covariance between the residuals associated with θ and the j-th covariate is given by

$$\mathrm{cov}_j(\theta) = \sum_{i=1}^{n} \rho' \left(\frac{r_i - x'_{i,k}(\hat{\beta}_\mathcal{A}\gamma) - \beta_0}{\sigma} \right) x_{ij} \, ,$$

and the corresponding correlation is

$$\tilde{\rho}_j(\theta) = \mathrm{cov}_j(\theta) \ \bigg/ \ \sum_{i=1}^{n} \rho' \left(\frac{r_i - x'_{i,k}(\hat{\beta}_\mathcal{A}\gamma) - \beta_0}{\sigma} \right)^2 .$$

Our algorithm can be described as follows:

1. Set $k = 0$ and compute the S-estimators $\hat{\theta}_0 = (\mathbf{0}, \hat{\beta}_{00}, \hat{\sigma}_0)$ by regressing y against the intercept. The first variable to enter is that associated with the largest robust correlation:

$$\hat{\lambda}_1 = \max_{1 \leq j \leq p} \left| \tilde{\rho}_j(\hat{\theta}_0) \right| .$$

Without loss of generality, assume that it corresponds to the first covariate.

2. set $k = k + 1$ and compute the current residuals

$$r_{i,k} = r_{i,k-1} - x_{i,k-1}^t (\hat{\beta}_{k-1} \hat{\gamma}_{k-1}) - \hat{\beta}_{0,k-1}.$$

3. let $\hat{\beta}_k, \hat{\beta}_{0k}, \hat{\sigma}_k$ be the S–estimators of regressing r_k against x_k.
4. For each j in the inactive set find θ_j^* such that
   - $\lambda_j^* = |\tilde{\rho}_j| = |\tilde{\rho}_m|$ for all $1 \leq m \leq k$,
   - $\sum_{i=1}^n \rho' \left((r_{i,k} - x_{i,k}^t (\hat{\beta}_k \gamma_k^*) - \beta_{0k}^*)/\sigma_k^* \right) = 0$, and
   - $\sum_{i=1}^n \rho \left((r_{i,k} - x_{i,k}^t (\hat{\beta}_k \gamma_k^*) - \beta_{0k}^*)/\sigma_k^* \right) = b(n - k - 1)$.
5. Let $\hat{\lambda}_{k+1} = \max_{j>k} \lambda_j^*$, the associated index, say v corresponds to the next variable to enter the active set. Let $\hat{\theta}_k = \theta_v^*$.
6. Repeat until $k = d$.

Given an active set $\mathcal{A}$, the above algorithm finds the length γ_k^* such that the robust correlation between the current residuals and the active covariates matches that of an explanatory variable yet to enter the model. The variable that achieves this with the smallest step is included in the model, and the procedure is then iterated. It is in this sense that our proposal is based on LARS.

4   Simulation results

To study the performance of our proposal we conducted a simulation study using a similar design to that reported by Khan et al. (2007b). We generated the response variable y according to the following model:

$$y = L_1 + L_2 + \cdots + L_k + \sigma \epsilon,$$

where L_j, $j = 1, \ldots, k$ and ϵ are independent random variables with a standard normal distribution. The value of σ is chosen to obtain a "signal to noise" ratio of 3. We then generate d candidate covariates as follows

$$X_i = L_i + \tau \epsilon_i, \qquad i = 1, \ldots, k,$$
$$X_{k+1} = L_1 + \delta \epsilon_{k+1}$$
$$X_{k+2} = L_1 + \delta \epsilon_{k+2}$$
$$X_{k+3} = L_2 + \delta \epsilon_{k+3}$$
$$X_{k+4} = L_2 + \delta \epsilon_{k+4}$$

$$\vdots$$

$$X_{3k-1} = L_k + \delta \epsilon_{3k-1}$$
$$X_{3k} = L_k + \delta \epsilon_{3k},$$

and $X_j = \epsilon_j$ for $j = 3k, 3k+1, \ldots, d$. The choices $\delta = 5$ and $\tau = 0.3$ result in $\text{cor}(X_1, X_{k+1}) = \text{cor}(X_1, X_{k+2}) = \text{cor}(X_2, X_{k+2}) = \text{cor}(X_2, X_{k+3}) = \cdots = \text{cor}(X_k, X_{3k}) = 0.5$. We consider the following contamination cases:

a. $\epsilon \sim \mathcal{N}(0,1)$, no contamination;
b. $\epsilon \sim 0.90\,\mathcal{N}(0,1) + 0.10\,\mathcal{N}(0,1)/\mathcal{U}(0,1)$, 10 % of symmetric outliers with the Slash distribution;
c. $\epsilon \sim 0.90\,\mathcal{N}(0,1) + 0.10\,\mathcal{N}(20,1)$, 10 % of asymmetric Normal outliers;
d. 10% of high leverage asymmetric Normal outliers (the corresponding covariates were sampled from a $\mathcal{N}(50,1)$ distribution).

For each case we generated 500 independent samples with $n = 150$, $k = 6$ and $d = 50$. In each of these datasets we sorted the 50 covariates in the order in which they were listed to enter the model. We used the usual LARS algorithm as implemented in the R package lars, our proposal (LARSROB) and the robust plug-in algorithm of Khan et al. (2007b) (RLARS).

For case (a) where no outliers were present in the data, all methods performed very close to each other. The results of our simulation for cases (b), (c) and (d) above are summarized in Figures 1 to 3. For each sequence of covariates consider the number t_m of target explanatory variables included in the first m covariates entering the model, $m = 1, \ldots, d$. Ideally we would like a sequence that satisfies $t_m = k$ for $m \geq k$. In Figures 1 to 3 we plot the average t_m over the 500 samples, as a function of the model size m, for each of the three methods. We see that for symmetric low-leverage outliers LARSROB and RLARS are very close to each other, with both giving better results that the classical LARS. For asymmetric outliers LARSROB performed marginally better than RLARS, while for high-leverage outliers the performance of LARSROB deteriorates noticeably.

5   Conclusion

We have proposed a new robust algorithm to select covariates for a linear model. Our method is based on the LARS procedure of Efron et al. (2004). Rather than replacing classical correlation estimates by robust ones and applying the same LARS algorithm, we derived our method directly following the intuition behind LARS but starting from robust S-regression estimates. Simulation studies suggest that our method is robust to the presence of low-leverage outliers in the data, and that in this case it compares well with the "plug-in" approach of Khan et al. (2007b). A possible way to make our proposal more resistant to high-leverage outliers is to downweight extreme values of the covariates in the robust correlation measure we utilize. Further research along these lines is ongoing.

An important feature of our approach is that it naturally extends the relationship between the LARS algorithm and the sequence of LASSO solutions (Tibshirani (1996)). Hence, with our approach we can obtain a resistant algorithm to calculate the LASSO based on S-estimators. Details of the algorithm discussed here, and its connection with a robust LASSO method will be published separately.

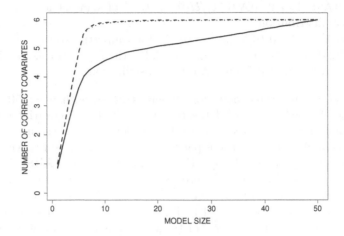

Fig. 1. Case (b) - Average number of correctly selected covariates as a function of the model size. The solid line corresponds to LARS, the dashed line to our proposal (LARSROB) and the dotted line to the RLARS algorithm of Khan et al. (2007b).

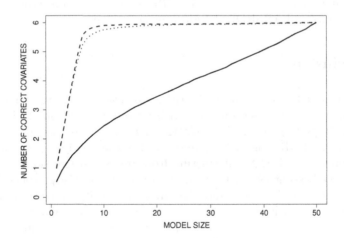

Fig. 2. Case (c) - Average number of correctly selected covariates as a function of the model size. The solid line corresponds to LARS, the dashed line to our proposal (LARSROB) and the dotted line to the RLARS algorithm of Khan et al. (2007b).

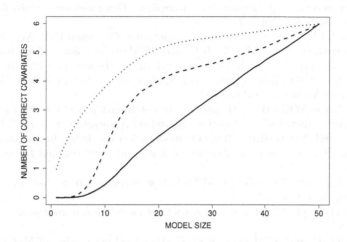

Fig. 3. Case (d) - Average number of correctly selected covariates as a function of the model size. The solid line corresponds to LARS, the dashed line to our proposal (LARSROB) and the dotted line to the RLARS algorithm of Khan et al. (2007b).

References

AGOSTINELLI, C. (2002a): Robust model selection in regression via weighted likelihood methodology. *Statistics and Probability Letters, 56 289-300.*

AGOSTINELLI, C. (2002b): Robust stepwise regression. *Journal of Applied Statistics, 29(6) 825-840.*

AGOSTINELLI, C. and MARKATOU, M. (2005): M. Robust model selection by cross-validation via weighted likelihood. *Unpublished manuscript.*

AKAIKE, H. (1970): Statistical predictor identification. *Annals of the Institute of Statistical Mathematics, 22 203-217.*

EFRON, B., HASTIE, T., JOHNSTONE, I. and TIBSHIRANI, R. (2004): Least angle regression. *The Annals of Statistics 32(2), 407-499.*

HAMPEL, F.R. (1983): Some aspects of model choice in robust statistics. In: *Proceedings of the 44th Session of the ISI, volume 2, 767-771.* Madrid.

HASTIE, T., TIBSHIRANI, R. and FRIEDMAN, J. (2001): *The Elements of Statistical Learning.* Springer-Verlag, New York.

KHAN, J.A., VAN AELST, S., and ZAMAR, R.H. (2007a): Building a robust linear model with forward selection and stepwise procedures. *Computational Statistics and Data Analysis 52, 239-248.*

KHAN, J.A., VAN AELST, S., and ZAMAR, R.H. (2007b): Robust Linear Model Selection Based on Least Angle Regression. *Journal of the American Statistical Association 102, 1289-1299.*

MALLOWS, C.L. (1973): Some comments on C_p. *Technometrics 15, 661-675.*

MARONNA, R.A., MARTIN, D.R. and YOHAI, V.J. (2006): *Robust Statistics: Theory and Methods.* Wiley, Ney York.

McCANN, L. and WELSCH, R.E. (2007): Robust variable selection using least angle regression and elemental set sampling. *Computational Statistical and Data Analysis 52, 249-257.*

MILLER, A.J. (2002): *Subset selection in regression.* Chapman-Hall, New York.

MORGENTHALER, S., WELSCH, R.E. and ZENIDE, A. (2003): Algorithms for robust model selection in linear regression. In: M. Hubert, G. Pison, A. Struyf and S. Van Aelst (Eds.): *Theory and Applications of Recent Robust Methods.* Brikhäuser-Verlag, Basel, 195-206.

MÜLLER, S. and WELSH, A. H. (2005): Outlier robust model selection in linear regression. *Journal of the American Statistical Association 100, 1297-1310.*

QIAN, G. and KÜNSCH, H.R. (1998): On model selection via stochastic complexity in robust linear regression. *Journal of Statistical Planning and Inference 75, 91-116.*

RONCHETTI, E. (1985): Robust model selection in regression. *Statistics and Probability Letters 3, 21-23.*

RONCHETTI, E. (1997): Robustness aspects of model choice. *Statistica Sinica 7, 327-338.*

RONCHETTI, E. and STAUDTE, R.G. (1994): A robust version of Mallows' C_p. *Journal of the American Statistical Association 89, 550-559.*

RONCHETTI, E., FIELD, C. and BLANCHARD, W. (1997): Robust linear model selection by cross-validation. *Journal of the American Statistical Association 92, 1017-1023.*

ROUSSEEUW, P.J. and YOHAI, V.J. (1984). Robust regression by means of S-estimators. In: J. Franke, W. Hardle and D. Martin (Eds.): *Robust and Nonlinear Time Series, Lecture Notes in Statistics 26.* Springer-Verlag, Berlin, 256-272.

SALIBIAN-BARRERA, M. and VAN AELST, S. (2008): Robust model selection using fast and robust bootstrap. *Computational Statistics and Data Analysis 52 5121-5135.*

SALIBIAN-BARRERA, M. and ZAMAR, R.H. (2002): Bootstrapping robust estimates of regression. *The Annals of Statistics 30, 556-582.*

SCHWARTZ, G. (1978): Estimating the dimensions of a model. *The Annals of Statistics 6, 461-464.*

SOMMER, S. and STAUDTE, R.G. (1995): Robust variable selection in regression in the presence of outliers and leverage points. *Australian Journal of Statistics 37, 323-336.*

TIBSHIRANI, R. (1996): Regression shrinkage and selection via the lasso. *Journal of the Royal Statistical Society, Series B: Methodological 58, 267-288.*

WEISBERG, S. (1985): *Applied linear regression.* Wiley, New York.

Robust Methods for Compositional Data

Peter Filzmoser[1] and Karel Hron[2]

[1] Vienna University of Technology
   Wiedner Hauptstraße 8-10, A-1040 Vienna, Austria, *P.Filzmoser@tuwien.ac.at*
[2] Palacký University, Faculty of Science
   tř. 17. listopadu 12, CZ-77146 Czech Republic, *hronk@seznam.cz*

Abstract. Many practical data sets in environmental sciences, official statistics and various other disciplines are in fact compositional data because only the ratios between the variables are informative. Compositional data are represented in the Aitchison geometry on the simplex, and for applying statistical methods designed for the Euclidean geometry they need to be transformed first. The isometric logratio (ilr) transformation has the best geometrical properties, and it avoids the singularity problem introduced by the centered logratio (clr) transformation. Robust multivariate methods which are based on a robust covariance estimation can thus only be used with ilr transformed data. However, usually the results are difficult to interpret because the ilr coordinates are formed by non-linear combinations of the original variables. We show for different multivariate methods how robustness can be managed for compositional data, and provide algorithms for the computation.

Keywords: Aitchison geometry, logratio transformations, robustness, affine equivariance, multivariate statistical methods

1 Compositional data and logratio transformations

Practical data sets are frequently characterized by multivariate observations containing relative contributions of parts on a whole. Examples are concentrations of chemical elements in a rock, household expenditures on various commodities from the monthly salary, or representations of various animal species in a study area in percentages. Often just percentages are used to express the mentioned relative magnitudes of the parts of the data and thus the simplex is usually referred to be the sample space. However, the situation is a more general one, because only the relevant information in the data is contained in the ratios between the parts. From this point of view, the percentages represent only a proper representation of the information, contained in the multivariate observations. These considerations led John Aitchison at the beginning of the eighties of the 20th century to introduce the term *compositional data* (or compositions for short) to characterize such kind of data and to propose possibilities for their statistical analysis using so-called logratio transformations.

The geometry of compositions, later denoted as the Aitchison geometry, follows their special properties and is based on special operations of perturbation, power transformation and the Aitchison inner product. In more detail,

Y. Lechevallier, G. Saporta (eds.), *Proceedings of COMPSTAT'2010*,
DOI 10.1007/978-3-7908-2604-3_7, © Springer-Verlag Berlin Heidelberg 2010

for D-part compositions $\mathbf{x} = (x_1, \ldots, x_D)'$ and $\mathbf{y} = (y_1, \ldots, y_D)'$ and a real number α, this results in compositions

$$\mathbf{x} \oplus \mathbf{y} = \mathcal{C}(x_1 y_1, \ldots, x_D y_D), \ \alpha \odot \mathbf{x} = \mathcal{C}(x_1^\alpha, \ldots, x_D^\alpha)$$

and a real number

$$\langle \mathbf{x}, \mathbf{y} \rangle_A = \frac{1}{D} \sum_{i=1}^{D-1} \sum_{j=i+1}^{D} \ln \frac{x_i}{x_j} \ln \frac{y_i}{y_j},$$

respectively. Using usual Hilbert space properties, the Aitchison inner product also leads to the definitions of the Aitchison norm and distance. Moreover, the symbol $\mathcal{C}$ denotes a closure operation that moves the sum of the compositional parts to any chosen constant κ without loss of information. As mentioned above, the constant κ is usually chosen as 1 or 100 in order to represent the compositions on the D-part simplex (of dimension $D - 1$),

$$\mathcal{S}^D = \{\mathbf{x} = (x_1, \ldots, x_D)', \ x_i > 0, \ \sum_{i=1}^{D} x_i = \kappa\}.$$

From the geometrical properties of compositional data it is easy to see that using standard statistical methods like principal component analysis, factor analysis or correlation analysis, designed for Euclidean space properties of standard multivariate data with absolute scale, can lead (and frequently does) to meaningless results. This has been demonstrated in various examples, e.g. the book Aitchison (1986), and further Aitchison et al. (2000), Filzmoser et al. (2009a), Filzmoser et al. (2009b), Pearson (1897).

Although the Aitchison geometry on the simplex has the usual properties that are known from the Euclidean geometry (Hilbert space), it is more natural to directly work in the Euclidean space. This means that a transformation of the compositional data from the simplex sample space to the Euclidean space is performed. In the transformed space the standard multivariate methods can be used. The main idea that leads to such transformations is to find a basis (or a generating system) and to express compositions in coefficients of such a basis (coordinate system). This class of mappings is widely known under the term logratio transformations. Nowadays three main approaches using the logratio family are used: additive, centered and isometric logratio transformations (coordinates). All of them move the operations of perturbation and power transformation to the usual vector addition and scalar multiplication. However, only the latter two transformations move the whole Aitchison geometry to the Euclidean one, i.e. including the Aitchison inner product. As the proposed transformations are one-to-one transformations, the obtained results are usually back-transformed to the simplex in order to simplify the interpretation.

The additive logratio transformation follows the idea to construct a (non-orthonormal) basis which is very easy to interpret. Thus, for a composition $\mathbf{x}$, a special case of the *additive logratio (alr) transformations* (Aitchison (1986)) to $\mathbf{R}^{D-1}$, is defined as

$$alr(\mathbf{x}) = \left(\ln \frac{x_1}{x_D}, \ldots, \ln \frac{x_{D-1}}{x_D} \right)'.$$

It is easy to see that also another part can be used as ratioing part in the denominator. It is usually chosen in such a way that the interpretation of the result is facilitated. Note that different alr transformations are related by linear transformations (see, e.g., Filzmoser and Hron (2008)).

Taking a generating system on the simplex leads to the *centered logratio (clr) transformation* (Aitchison (1986)) to $\mathbf{R}^D$,

$$clr(\mathbf{x}) = \left(\ln \frac{x_1}{\prod_{i=1}^{D} x_i}, \ldots, \ln \frac{x_D}{\prod_{i=1}^{D} x_i} \right)'.$$

This transformation has also a good interpretability, and the compositional biplot (Aitchison and Greenacre (2002)), nowadays a very popular exploratory tool, takes advantage of this property. However, as the dimension of the simplex is only $D-1$, the clr transformation is singular, namely, the sum of the obtained coordinates is equal to zero. As a consequence, this makes the use of the robust statistical methods mentioned in the following section impossible.

The last proposal refers to the *isometric logratio (ilr) transformations* (Egozcue et al. (2003); Egozcue and Pawlowsky-Glahn (2005)) from the simplex to $\mathbf{R}^{D-1}$, where the main idea is to express the coordinates in an orthonormal basis on the simplex. However, the corresponding coordinates are often not easy to interpret; one such choice of the orthonormal basis leads to

$$\mathbf{z} = (z_1, \ldots, z_{D-1})', \quad z_i = \sqrt{\frac{i}{i+1}} \ln \frac{\sqrt[i]{\prod_{j=1}^{i} x_j}}{x_{i+1}}, \quad i = 1, \ldots, D-1.$$

Thus, in spite of their advantageous geometrical properties, the ilr transformations are preferably used for methods where the interpretation is focused on the objects rather than on the single compositional parts, because in the latter case a consequent interpretation of the results in coordinates would be necessary. From the definition it is easy to see that all the ilr coordinates are mutually joined with orthogonal relations. An intuitive relation can be found also between clr and ilr transformations. Namely, the ilr coordinates are in fact coordinates of an orthonormal basis on the hyperplane $\mathcal{H}$, formed by the clr transformation. Thus also the relation $ilr(\mathbf{x}) = \mathbf{U}clr(\mathbf{x})$ holds, where the $(D-1) \times D$ matrix $\mathbf{U}$ contains in its rows the mentioned orthonormal basis on $\mathcal{H}$, and $\mathbf{U}\mathbf{U}' = \mathbf{I}_{D-1}$ (identity matrix of order $D-1$) is fulfilled.

Even more general, it has been shown that all three mentioned logratio transformations are mutually joined with linear relations (see, e.g., Filzmoser and Hron (2008)). This property is crucial for the robustification of statistical methods for compositional data.

2   Robustness for compositional data

Outliers and data inhomogeneities are typical problems of real data sets. This can severely affect classical multivariate statistical methods that ignore these problems, and the results might then even become meaningless. For this reason, robust statistical approaches were developed that reduce the influence of outliers and focus on the main data structure. An example is the estimation of multivariate location and covariance. The classical estimators, arithmetic mean and sample covariance matrix, are sensitive to outlying observations in the data set while robust estimators can resist a certain proportion of contamination. Among the various proposed robust estimators of multivariate location and covariance, the MCD (Minimum Covariance Determinant) estimator (see, e.g., Maronna et al. (2006)) became very popular because of its good robustness properties and a fast algorithm for its computation (Rousseeuw and Van Driessen (1999)).

Besides robustness properties the property of affine equivariance of the estimators of location and covariance plays an important role. The location estimator T and the covariance estimator C are called affine equivariant, if for a sample $\mathbf{x}_1, \ldots, \mathbf{x}_n$ of n observations in $\mathbf{R}^{D-1}$, any nonsingular $(D-1) \times (D-1)$ matrix $\mathbf{A}$ and for any vector $\mathbf{b} \in \mathbf{R}^{D-1}$ the conditions

$$T(\mathbf{A}\mathbf{x}_1 + \mathbf{b}, \ldots, \mathbf{A}\mathbf{x}_n + \mathbf{b}) = \mathbf{A}T(\mathbf{x}_1, \ldots, \mathbf{x}_n) + \mathbf{b},$$
$$C(\mathbf{A}\mathbf{x}_1 + \mathbf{b}, \ldots, \mathbf{A}\mathbf{x}_n + \mathbf{b}) = \mathbf{A}C(\mathbf{x}_1, \ldots, \mathbf{x}_n)\mathbf{A}'$$

are fulfilled. The MCD estimator shares the property of affine equivariance for both the resulting location and covariance estimator.

Since robust methods are usually designed for the Euclidean geometry and not for the simplex, a transformation of the raw compositional data is required. As mentioned earlier, the clr transformation is not useful for this purpose because robust estimators cannot deal with singular data. The alr and ilr transformations are thus possible transformations prior to robust estimation. However, it depends on the multivariate method and on the purpose of the analysis which of the alr and ilr transformations are useful. This issue will be discussed in more detail in the following sections for multivariate outlier detection, principal component analysis, and factor analysis.

2.1   Multivariate outlier detection

The Mahalanobis distance, defined for regular $(D-1)$-dimensional data as

$$\mathrm{MD}(\mathbf{x}_i) = \left[(\mathbf{x}_i - T)'C^{-1}(\mathbf{x}_i - T) \right]^{1/2},$$

is a popular tool for outlier detection (Maronna et al. (2006); Filzmoser et al. (2008)). Here, the estimated covariance structure is used to assign a distance to each observation indicating how far the observation is from the center of the data cloud with respect to the covariance structure. The choice of the location estimator T and the scatter estimator C is crucial. In case of multivariate normal distribution, the (squared) Mahalanobis distances based on the classical estimators arithmetic mean and sample covariance matrix follow approximately a χ^2 distribution with $D - 1$ degrees of freedom. In presence of outliers, however, only robust estimators of T and C lead to a Mahalanobis distance being reliable for outlier detection. Usually, also in this case a χ^2 distribution with $D-1$ degrees of freedom is used as an approximate distribution, and a certain quantile (e.g. the quantile 0.975) is used as a cut-off value for outlier identification: observations with larger (squared) robust Mahalanobis distance are considered as potential outliers.

Compositional data need to be transformed prior to computing Mahalanobis distances. The linear relations between the logratio transformations can be used to prove that the Mahalanobis distances are the same for all possible alr and ilr transformations. This, however, is only valid if the location estimator T and the covariance estimator C are affine equivariant (Filzmoser and Hron (2008)). If the arithmetic mean and the sample covariance matrix are used, this holds also for the alr, clr and ilr transformations, where the inverse of the covariance matrix in the clr case is replaced by its Moore-Penrose inverse.

2.2   Principal component analysis (PCA)

PCA is one of the most popular tools for multivariate data analysis. Its goal is to explain as much information contained in the data as possible using as few (principal) components as possible (see, e.g., Reimann et al. (2008)). In the case of compositional data, it is very popular to display both loadings and scores of the first two principal components by means of biplots. The compositional biplot is usually constructed for clr transformed data, where the resulting loadings and scores have an intuitive interpretation corresponding to the nature of compositions (Aitchison and Greenacre (2002)). However, it is not possible to robustify it because of the mentioned singularity of the clr transformation. As a way out, the ilr transformation can be used to compute the robust loadings and scores, which are then back-transformed to the clr space (Filzmoser et al. (2009a)). In more detail, the $n \times (D - 1)$ matrix $\mathbf{Z}_{ilr}$ of scores and $(D - 1) \times (D - 1)$ matrix $\mathbf{G}_{ilr}$ of loadings are transformed to $n \times D$ and $D \times D$ matrices

$$\mathbf{Z}_{clr} = \mathbf{Z}_{ilr}\mathbf{U} \text{ and } \mathbf{G}_{clr} = \mathbf{U}'\mathbf{G}_{ilr}\mathbf{U},$$

respectively. Thanks to the properties of the matrix $\mathbf{U}$ defined earlier in Section 1, and the affine equivariance of the MCD estimator, the resulting principal components correspond to the same nonzero eigenvalues for both ilr and clr. Thus, such a transformation of the loadings and scores can be used to obtain a robust compositional biplot of compositional data.

2.3   Factor analysis

Both PCA and factor analysis are based on the same objection, namely on reduction of the dimensionality, and the main principle is to decompose the multivariate data into loadings and scores. However, the more strict definition of factor analysis implies that the number of factors to be extracted is defined at the beginning of the procedure. In addition, an estimate of the proportion of variability has to be provided for each variable, which is not to be included in the factors but is considered unique to that variable (Reimann et al. (2008)). This often leads to a better interpretation of the (rotated) factors than (rotated) principal components. However, the definition of factor analysis and the uniquenesses induce problems in case of compositions, where the treatment of the single compositional parts seems to be questionable. Here the clr transformation offers again a reasonable solution, however, the procedure to estimate the 'clr-uniquenesses' and loadings must be performed in an iterative manner and also the estimation of scores has to overcome the singularity of the clr transformed data, see Filzmoser et al. (2009b), for details. The key to robustness is again contained in the estimation of the covariance matrix where the same approach as for PCA can be used.

3   Real data example

The methods are demonstrated in the following using a data example of mean consumption expenditures of households from 2008 in the countries of the European Union. The data set is available at http://epp.eurostat.ec.europa.eu at statistics_explained/index.php/Household_consumption_expenditure. The expenditures on food, alcohol and tobacco, clothing, housing, furnishings, health, transport, communications, recreation, education, restaurants and hotels, and on other goods and services are reported for the countries Austria (A), Belgium (B), Bulgaria (BG), Cyprus (CY), Czech Republic (CZ), Denmark (DK), Estonia (EST), Finland (FIN), France (F), Germany (D), Greece (GR), Hungary (H), Ireland (IRL), Italy (I), Latvia (LV), Lithuania (LT), Luxembourg (L), Malta (M), Netherlands (NL), Poland (PL), Portugal (P), Romania (R), Slovakia (SK), Slovenia (SLO), Spain (ES), Sweden (S), and United Kingdom (GB). These are compositional data because the expenditures are parts of the overall household incomes. For example, if more money is devoted to one part, typically less money will be left for the other parts, and thus not the absolute number but only their ratios are informative.

At first we apply multivariate outlier detection using Mahalanobis distances. Location and covariance are estimated in a classical way but also robustly using the MCD estimator. Both variants are applied to the original untransformed data, and to the ilr transformed data. The results are presented with distance-distance plots (Rousseeuw and Van Driessen (1999)) in Figure 1. The dashed lines correspond to the outlier cut-offs using the

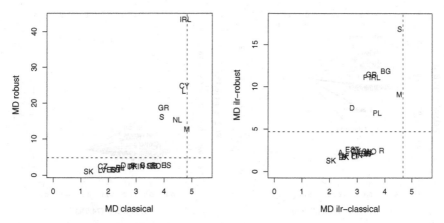

Fig. 1. Distance-distance plots for outlier detection using the untransformed (left) and the ilr transformed (right) data.

0.975 quantile of the corresponding χ^2 distributions. Both figures reveal several masked outliers, but they do not indicate the same outliers. Without any further inspection it would be difficult to interpret the results. Since the data are of compositional nature, only the distance-distance plot of the ilr transformed data is reliable.

A deeper insight into the multivariate data structure can be achieved by a PCA. We want to compare the classical and the robust (MCD) approach, as well as PCA for the untransformed and the ilr transformed data (back-transformed to the clr space). The resulting biplots are shown in Figure 2. We can see a typical phenomenon when analyzing compositional data with inappropriate methods: all variables are positively correlated for the untransformed data which is an artifact resulting from the underlying geometry. Note that a robust analysis cannot 'repair' this geometrical artifact. In contrast, the biplots based on the ilr ($\rightarrow$ clr) transformed data show quite different relations between the variables. Using the biplots, it is also possible to explain the multivariate outliers identified in Figure 1. The robust biplot for the ilr ($\rightarrow$ clr) transformed data shows striking differences for expenditures on health. It is also interesting to see that on the right-hand side of the plot we find potentially richer countries (with a higher GDP) whereas on the left-hand side the poorer countries are located. The latter devote a larger part of their expenditures to food, communication, and alcohol and tobacco.

Similar to PCA we apply factor analysis to the original and to the ilr ($\rightarrow$ clr) transformed data, and perform in both cases a classical and a robust analysis. The biplots for the untransformed data show again a degenerated behavior. The robust biplot for the ilr ($\rightarrow$ clr) transformed data shows almost contrasting priorities for the expenditures: Positive values on factor 1 are referring to education, while negative values refer to recreation, trans-

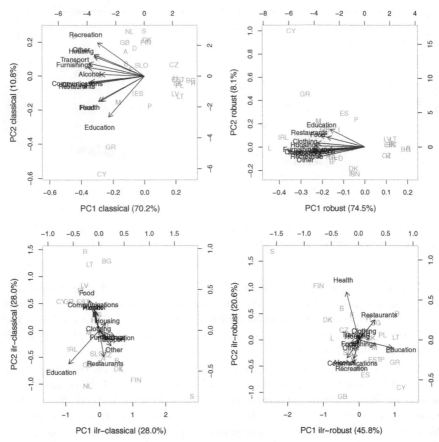

Fig. 2. Principal component analysis classical (left column) and robust (right column) using the original scaled (upper row) and the ilr ($\rightarrow$ clr) transformed data.

port, housing, furnishings, and other goods and services. Of course, expenses for education are usually set by the political system. Factor 2 reflects the differences in expenditures for restaurants and hotel, versus expenditures for more basic needs like food, alcohol and tobacco, communications, and health. The poorer countries devote a larger proportion of their expenses to these basic needs.

4   Conclusions

For compositional data an appropriate transformation is crucial prior to performing any multivariate data analysis. In environmental sciences, like typically in geochemistry, compositional data are frequently simply logarithmically transformed. This transformation, however, can only achieve symmetry

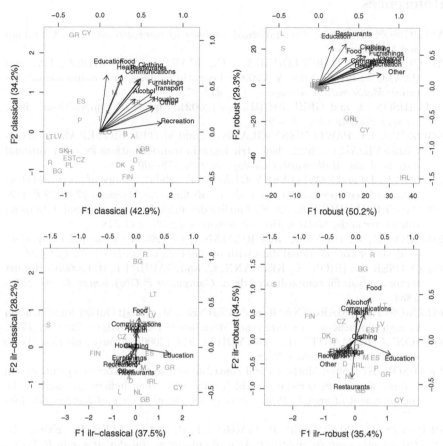

Fig. 3. Factor analysis classical (left column) and robust (right column) using the original scaled (upper row) and the ilr ($\to$ clr) transformed data.

of the single variables, but it does not transform the data from the simplex to the Euclidean space. Phenomena like positive variable relations as shown in the upper rows of Figure 2 and 3 are typical outcomes of such an approach.

Generally, the ilr transformation shows the best properties. For a robust analysis, one important property is that the ilr transformed data are in general non-singular, which allows for the application of robust covariance estimators. However, since the ilr variables are difficult to interpret, they usually need to be back-transformed to the clr space, like it has been demonstrated for the compositional biplot.

The transformations, the adapted multivariate methods, and various other representations and statistical methods for compositional data have been implemented in the R library `robCompositions` (Templ et al. (2009)).

References

AITCHISON, J. (1986): *The statistical analysis of compositional data.* Chapman and Hall, London.

AITCHISON, J., BARCELÓ-VIDAL, C., MARTÍN-FERNÁNDEZ, J.A. and PAWLOWSKY-GLAHN, V. (2000): Logratio analysis and compositional distance. *Mathematical Geology 32 (3), 271-275.*

AITCHISON, J. and GREENACRE, M. (2002): Biplots of compositional data. *Applied Statistics 51, 375-392.*

EGOZCUE, J.J., PAWLOWSKY-GLAHN, V. and MATEU-FIGUERAS, G., BARCELÓ-VIDAL, C. (2003): Isometric logratio transformations for compositional data analysis. *Mathematical Geology 35 (3), 279-300.*

EGOZCUE, J.J.and PAWLOWSKY-GLAHN, V. (2005): Groups of parts and their balances in compositional data analysis. *Mathematical Geology 37 (7), 795-828.*

FILZMOSER, P., HRON, K. (2008): Outlier detection for compositional data using robust methods. *Mathematical Geosciences 40 (3), 233-248.*

FILZMOSER, P., HRON, K. and REIMANN, C. (2009a): Principal component analysis for compositional data with outliers. *Environmetrics 20, 621-632.*

FILZMOSER, P., HRON, K., REIMANN, C. and GARRETT, R. (2009b): Robust factor analysis for compositional data. *Computers & Geosciences 35 (9), 1854-1861.*

FILZMOSER, P., MARONNA, R. and WERNER, M. (2008): Outlier identification in high dimensions. *Computational Statistics & Data Analysis 52, 1694-1711.*

MARONNA, R., MARTIN, R.D. and YOHAI, V.J. (2006): *Robust statistics: theory and methods.* Wiley, New York.

PEARSON, K. (1897): Mathematical contributions to the theory of evolution. On a form of spurious correlation which may arise when indices are used in the measurement of organs. *Proceedings of the Royal Society of London 60, 489-502.*

REIMANN, C., FILZMOSER, P., GARRETT, R. and DUTTER, R. (2008): *Statistical data analysis explained: Applied environmental statistics with R.* Wiley, Chichester.

ROUSSEEUW, P. and VAN DRIESSEN, K. (1999): A fast algorithm for the minimum covariance determinant estimator. *Technometrics 41, 212-223.*

TEMPL, M., HRON, K. and FILZMOSER, P. (2009): robCompositions: Robust estimation for compositional data, http://www.r-project.org, R package version 1.2, 2009.

Detecting Multivariate Outliers Using Projection Pursuit with Particle Swarm Optimization

Anne Ruiz-Gazen[1], Souad Larabi Marie-Sainte[2], and Alain Berro[2]

[1] Toulouse School of Economics (Gremaq et IMT),
21, allée de Brienne, 31000 Toulouse, France
ruiz@cict.fr
[2] IRIT, 21, allée de Brienne, 31000 Toulouse, France
larabi@irit.fr, berro@irit.fr

Abstract. Detecting outliers in the context of multivariate data is known as an important but difficult task and there already exist several detection methods. Most of the proposed methods are based either on the Mahalanobis distance of the observations to the center of the distribution or on a projection pursuit (PP) approach. In the present paper we focus on the one-dimensional PP approach which may be of particular interest when the data are not elliptically symmetric. We give a survey of the statistical literature on PP for multivariate outliers detection and investigate the pros and cons of the different methods. We also propose the use of a recent heuristic optimization algorithm called Tribes for multivariate outliers detection in the projection pursuit context.

Keywords: heuristic algorithms, multivariate outliers detection, particle swarm optimization, projection pursuit, Tribes algorithm

1 Introduction

The definition of outliers as a small number of observations that differ from the remainder of the data is commonly accepted in the statistical literature (Barnett and Lewis (1994), Hadi et al. (2009)). Most of the detection methods in continuous multivariate data are based either on the Mahalanobis distance or on Projection Pursuit. In the first approach, an observation is declared an outlier if its Mahalanobis distance is larger than a given cut-off value. Because the classical non-robust Mahalanobis distances suffer from masking, Rousseeuw and Van Zomeren (1990) propose to use robust location and scatter estimators. Moreover, reliable methods for defining cut-off points have been recently proposed (Cerioli et al. (2009)). The PP approach consists in looking for low dimensional linear projections that are susceptible to reveal outlying observations. In the following, we focus on this second approach which does not assume that the non-outlying part of the data set originates from a particular distribution (like elliptically symmetric distributions for the first approach). In general, exploratory PP gives insight about a multivariate

Y. Lechevallier, G. Saporta (eds.), *Proceedings of COMPSTAT'2010*,
DOI 10.1007/978-3-7908-2604-3_8, © Springer-Verlag Berlin Heidelberg 2010

continuous data set by finding and proposing to the analyst high revealing low-dimensional projections. A projection pursuit method is based on two ingredients: a projection index which measures the interestingness of a given projection and a strategy for searching the optima of this index. In the second section, we give a survey of the different projection indices that are aimed at detecting multivariate outliers. PP is computationally intensive and the choice of the strategy of "pursuit" together with the optimization algorithm are also important. In the third section, we present the existing "pursuit" strategies and propose a new strategy that relies on a optimization algorithm that can find several local minima in a reasonable time. We also investigate the pros and cons of the different strategies. In the fourth section, we present the Tribes algorithm which is a recent heuristic optimization algorithm (Clerc (2005), Cooren et al. (2009)). Heuristic optimization methods are attractive on the one hand, because they don't rely on strong regularity assumptions about the index and on the other hand, because they offer an efficient way to explore the whole space of solutions. But they usually imply the choice of some parameters. Tribes belongs to the family of Particle Swarm optimization (PSO) methods which are biologically-inspired optimization algorithms based on a cooperation strategy. Its main advantage relies on the fact that it is a parameter-free algorithm. We give some generalities concerning PSO and Tribes and propose to use it for the detection of outliers in an exploratory PP context. In the last section, we present the java interface we are currently developing for exploratory PP and give some perspectives.

2   Projection indices for detecting outliers

As said above a PP method assigns a numerical value (defined via an index) to low dimensional projections of the data. The index is then optimized to yield projections that reveal interesting structure. In the following, we review several one-dimensional indices that can be useful for the detection of outliers. We use the following notations: the data set is a n (observations) by p (variables) matrix X and X_i denotes the vector in R^P associated with the ith observation. For one-dimension exploratory PP, a real-valued index function $I(a)$ is defined for all projection vectors $a \in R^p$ such that $a'a = 1$ (where a' denotes the transpose of a). This function I is such that interesting views correspond to local optima of the function.

The most well-known projection index is the variance which leads to Principal Component Analysis (PCA). As detailed in Jolliffe (2002, section 10.1), observations that inflate variances will be detectable on the first principal components while outliers with respect to the correlation structure of the data may be detected on the last principal components. PCA is generally the first step in multivariate continuous data analysis but it is not specifically designed for the detection of outliers and further exploration with other PP indices are of interest. Moreover, in order to avoid masking as previously mentioned for Mahalanobis distances, it is advisable to consider as a projection index a robust variance estimator rather than the usual variance (Li and Chen (1985)). Such a method, called robust PP-based PCA, may detect outliers which inflate the variance (without the possible masking of the non-robust PCA) but is not aimed at detecting other types of outliers.

The definition of an "interesting" projection has been discussed in the founding papers on PP (Friedman and Tukey (1974), Huber (1985), Jones and Sibson (1987), and Friedman (1987)). Several arguments (see Friedman (1987) for details) have led to the conclusion that gaussianity is uninteresting. Consequently, as noted by Huber (1985), any measure of departure from normality can be viewed as a measure of interestingness and thus as a PP index. The objective of measuring departures from normality is more general than looking for projections that reveal outlying observations. However, several indices are very sensitive to departure from normality in the tails of the distribution which means that they will reveal outliers in priority. We will focus on such indices. In particular, the Friedman and Tukey (1974) and Friedman (1987) indices are known to be quite sensitive to the presence of outliers (see Friedman and Tukey (1974) and Hall (1989)). A detailed presentation of these indices can be found in Caussinus and Ruiz-Gazen (2009) and Berro et al. (2009).

As mentioned by Huber (1985, p. 446) and further studied by Peña and Prieto (2001), the kurtosis of the projected data is an index well adapted for detecting outliers. While heavy tailed distributions lead to high values of the kurtosis, bimodality leads to low values of the kurtosis. Thus, Peña and Prieto (2001) propose to detect outliers by looking at projections that minimize or maximize the kurtosis.

Recently, the Friedman index (Achard et al. (2004)) and the kurtosis index (Malpica et al. (2008)) have been used successfully for detecting anomalies in hyperspectral imagery. We also mention the index proposed in Juan and Prieto (2001) which is well suited for concentrated contamination patterns but which does not seem appropriate in other situations as detailed in Smetek and Bauer (2008) also in the field of hyperspectral imagery.

Another well-known projection index which is dedicated to the research of outliers is the measure of outlyingness defined independently by Stahel (1981) and Donoho (1982). For each observation $i = 1, \ldots, n$, we look for a projection that maximizes

$$I_i(a) = \frac{|a'X_i - \mathrm{med}_j(a'Xj)|}{\mathrm{mad}_j(a'X_j)}$$

where the "med" (resp. the "mad") corresponds to the median (resp. the median absolute deviation) of the projected data. The main difference between this index and the ones previously introduced is that the search of an optimal projection has to be done for each observation while the previous proposals consist in looking for the most interesting projections without refering to any particular observation. The Stahel-Donoho index is generally used as a first step in order to define weights of highly robust location and scatter estimators. But it may be used also in the exploratory PP context when the number of observations is small.

Finally, Caussinus and Ruiz-Gazen (1990, 2003), and Ruiz-Gazen (1993) proposed a generalization of PCA designed for the detection and the vizualization of outliers. The methodology is based on the spectral decomposition of a scatter estimator relative to another scatter estimator and has been recently revisited in a more general framework by Tyler et al. (2009). Contrary to usual and robust PP-based PCA, Generalized PCA (GPCA) cannot be defined as a problem of optimizing a function $I(a)$ of a projection vector a. Even if it is detailed as a projection pursuit method in Caussinus and Ruiz-Gazen (2009), there is no projection index associated with GPCA. Moreover, like PCA (and unlike robust PP-based PCA), the projections obtained by GPCA rely on spectral decomposition and do not need any pursuit. In the following we do not consider PCA and GPCA any further and focus on possible strategies for pursuit in the ususal exploratory PP context.

3   Different "pursuit" strategies

The structure of complex data sets in more than two dimensions is usually observable in many one-dimensional projections. So, as already stated in Friedman and Tukey (1974), PP should find as many potentially informative projections as possible. Consequently, the first strategy proposed by Friedman and Tukey (1974) and Jones and Sibson (1987) consists in using local optimization methods with several starting points. Useful suggested initial directions are the original coordinate axes, the principal axes but also some random starting points. This strategy is also the one followed by Cook et al. (1995) in their grand tour proposal but with the difference that the initial directions are chosen by the viewer in an interactive way. To our opinion, looking at rotating clouds as in Cook et al. (2007) may be tedious for the data-analyst.

A second strategy is proposed in Friedman (1987) and most of the literature on PP focus on this second strategy. The procedure repeatedly invokes a global optimization method, each time removing from the data the solutions previously found. Several global optimization methods have been considered in the literature (e.g. Friedman (1987), Sun (1993), Peña and Prieto (2001)). For continuously differentiable indices, such as the Friedman index with a smooth kernel or the kurtosis index, the global optimization procedure usually involves a local optimization step based on steepest ascent or quasi-Newton. Concerning the "structure removal", the simplest idea is to consider orthogonal projections as in PCA. This methods used in Peña and Prieto (2001) is easy to implement and greatly accelerates the procedure. However, as noticed in Huber (1985) and Friedman (1987), it may miss interesting oblique projections. Friedman (1987) proposed a more sophisticated "structure removal" procedure but it is not easy to implement and, as noticed in Nason (1992), the way it may affect the later application of PP is unclear.

We propose to go back to the first strategy and offer to the data-analyst several views of the data based on numerous starting directions and an efficient local optimization algorithm. The reasons we advocate for such a choice are the following:

(i) the aim of PP is to explore several local optima and global optimization methods that consider non-global local extrema as a nuisance are time consuming and not adapted,

(ii) the structure removal may miss some interesting projections or/and is also time consuming,

(iii) by using numerous starting directions and examining the plot of the index values, we can detect whether an extremum is found by accident (because of sampling fluctuations) or discovered several times.

The drawback of this strategy, as noticed in Friedman's discussion of Jones and Sibson (1987), is that it leads to numerous views of the data that are not imediately interpretable. One does not know the extent to which a new view reflects a similar or a different structure compared with the previous views. As detailed in the perspectives, in order to circumvent the problem, we propose several simple tools to analyse and compare the different views.

Concerning the Stahel-Donoho index, Stahel (1981) and Maronna and Yohai (1995) suggest to calculate the maximum over a finite set of vectors. The vectors are taken at random and there is no local optimization step. This idea of taking a finite set of projection directions is also used to derive algorithms for robust PP-based PCA. The Croux and Ruiz-Gazen (2005) algorithm uses the directions of the observations as projection vectors. Because the index is a (robust) measure of dispersion, directions that are pointing where the data are, lead to interesting results, at least when n is larger than p (see Croux et al. (2007) for further improvement). However, this algorithm is not relevant for other types of indices.

In order to be able to deal with unsmooth indices such as the Stahel-Donoho index and explore in the most efficient way the whole space of solutions, we propose to use a recent Particle Swarm optimization algorithm called Tribes.

4   Tribes: a parameter-free Particle Swarm optimization algorithm

Tribes is a recent heuristic optimization algorithm (Clerc (2005), Cooren et al. (2009)) which belongs to the family of Particular Swarm optimization (PSO). As explained in Gilli and Winker (2008) in a statistical context, heuristics optimization methods can tackle optimization problems that are not tractable with classical optimization tools. Moreover, such algorithms usually mimic some behavior found in nature. In the case of PSO, the algorithm mimics the behavior of a swarm of insects or a school of fish that is, the collective learning of individuals when they are in groups. There are two families of heuristic optimization methods: the trajectory methods (e.g. simulated annealing or Tabu search) which consider one single solution at a time and population based methods (e.g. genetic algorithms) which update a whole set of solutions simultaneously. For the second family of methods to which belongs PSO, the exploration of the whole search space is sometimes more efficient and this property is of importance given our objectives in the context of exploratory PP. Particle Swarm Optimization was introduced by Eberhart and Kennedy (1995) (see also Kennedy and Eberhart (2001)). The solution vectors of the population are called particles and the algorithm consists in updating the position of the particles of the swarm from one generation to another by adding an increment called velocity. More precisely, a particle is defined by a current position (which corresponds to a projection vector) and a velocity of moving in the search space. At each generation, the particle calculates the value of the function (index value). If this value is the best found so far, the particle memorizes the current position as the best position. The best value is called pbest. The particle looks also in its neighborhood the best value found. This value is called lbest. Then the particle changes its velocity toward its pbest and lbest positions in a stochastic way. Finally, she updates its position (which means that the projection vector is updated).

Recently, researchers have used PSO for solving various optimization problems (e.g. Gilli and Schumann (2009) for robust regression). But like other heuristics methods, PSO depends heavily on the selection of its parameter values which may be difficult to tune. In our case, the parameters depend notably on the number of observations and the number of variables. As described in Cooren et al. (2009), Tribes is a new adaptive PSO algorithm that avoids manual tuning by defining adaptation rules which aim at automatically changing the particles behaviors as well as the topology of the swarm. In particular, the strategies of moving are chosen according to the performances of the particles. A precise description of the Tribes algorithm is given in Larabi et al. (2009) for exploratory PP.

In Berro et al. (2009), we propose to use Genetic algorithm and standard PSO for exploratory PP but Tribes is clearly more adapted to the research of local optima. This feature is considered a drawback in a global optimization strategy ; but according to our strategy (see section 3), it is a clear advantage.

5 Perspectives

We are currently developing a java interface in order to propose to the data-analyst an efficient exploratory tool based on the PP strategy we have detailed in the third section and on the heuristics algorithms as detailed in the fourth section.

In Berro et al. (2009), we stress the importance of using numerous indices and looking at as many views as possible. Among the implemented indices, several ones are adapted to the detection of outliers such as the Friedman-Tukey, the Friedman and the kurtosis indices. The user can center and sphere the data, a preliminary process which may ease the discovery of interesting projections (see for instance Cook et al. (1995)). Following the strategy detailed in the third section, we divide the exploratory process in two stages: the first stage consists in running several times the Tribes algorithm and obtain several projections. This research of several local optima may be time consuming especially if the number of observations or the number of variables or the number of runs are large. But the statistician does not need to be in front of the computer during this first step! Moreover, because the different runs are independent, one could use parallel computing. During this research process, the potentially interesting projections obtained by optimization of a projection index are stored in an output file. At the second stage of the procedure, the statistician has many one-dimensional views of the data at his disposal and he can begin the analysis of the potential structure. Note that at this stage, there is no more need of computing power. The user can display either histograms or kernel density estimators of the univariate distributions of the projected data (see Figure 1 for an illustration of the interface on a simulated data set). These histograms or density estimators can be examined and outliers can be easily detected by vizualisation. Comparison of the different projections (similarities and differences) is more tricky and we propose several simple tools to help the user in this process. On Figure 1, some of the tools can be vizualised. First, the projections are ordered according to the decreasing values of the projection index and the values of the index are plotted so that the different local minima are easily detected (see the plot at the top right of Figure 1). Note that the data analysed on Figure 1 are simulated data with a majority of observations following a standardized gaussian distribution and a few points following a mean-shifted gaussian distribution in eight dimensions. For this artificial example, we know that there is only one interesting projection and if we exclude a small number of runs (see the right part of the index plot), all the runs have led to almost the same value of index (see Berro et al. (2009) for more details). By repeating the local search many times, we avoid considering spurious projections (due to sampling fluctuations) since interesting projections are usually recovered several times and associated with larger index values. But similar values of the index does not correspond necessarily to similar projection vectors. We add a plot of the cosines of the angles between any chosen projection vector and the other projection directions. This plot is very helpful in order to measure how far two projection directions are. Note that the different projections are simply obtained by mouse-clicking on the index or on the cosine plot and a selection

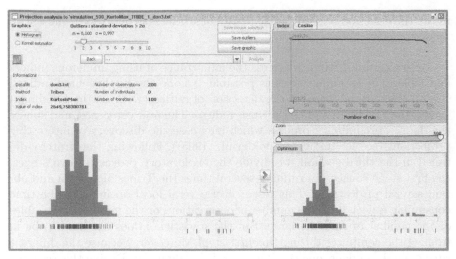

Fig. 1. A screenshot of the Java interface currently in development.

of the most interesting projections can be stored on the right bottom panel of the window (see Figure 1). In a general exploratory PP context, the analysis of many projections may be tricky and need some more dedicated tools that we are currently developing. But in the context of outliers detection, once defined an automatic rule to flag one-dimensional outlying observations, it is easy to save the outlying observations in a file together with the number of times they have been discovered on the different projections. As can be seen on Figure 1, the present version of the interface offers the possibility to declare as outliers, observations with an absolute distance to the mean larger than a certain number of times the standard deviation. The choice of the number of standard deviations is based on the vizualization of the histograms and can be changed interactively (on Figure 1, the choice is two standard deviations and the observations in yellow on the right of the histograms are identified as outliers). The interface will be soon available and will offer all the described possibilities.

Among the perspectives, we also plan to implement the Tribes algorithm for the Stahel-Donoho index in an exploratory PP context. Finally, in the context of outliers detection, we would like to compare our proposal with other existing detection methods on several data sets.

Acknowledgements

We thank Maurice Clerc, Salvador Flores, Marcel Mongeau and David Tyler for fruitful discussions.

References

ACHARD, V., LANDREVIE, A. and FORT, J.-C. (2004): Anomalies detection in hyperspectral imagery using projection pursuit algorithm In: L. Bruzzone (Ed): *Image and Signal Processing for Remote Sensing X*. Proceedings of the SPIE, Vol. 5573, 193–202.

BARNETT, V. and LEWIS, T. (1994): *Outliers in statistical data*, third edition. Wiley.

BERRO, A., LARABI MARIE-SAINTE, S. and RUIZ-GAZEN, A. (2009): Genetic and Particle Swarm Optimization for Exploratory Projection Pursuit. Submited.

CAUSSINUS, H., FEKRI, M., HAKAM, S. and RUIZ-GAZEN, A. (2003): A monitoring display of Multivariate Outliers. *Computational Statististics and Data Analysis 44, 237–252*

CAUSSINUS, H. and RUIZ-GAZEN, A. (1990): Interesting projections of multidimensional data by means of generalized principal component analysis, COMPSTAT 90, Physica-Verlag, 121–126.

CAUSSINUS, H. and RUIZ-GAZEN, A. (2009): Exploratory projection pursuit. In: G. Govaert: *Data Analysis (Digital Signal and Image Processing series)*. Wiley, 67–89.

CERIOLI, A., RIANI, M. and ATKINSON A. C. (2009): Controlling the size of multivariate outlier tests with the MCD estimator of scatter. *Statistics and Computing 19, 341–353*.

CLERC, M. (2005): *L'optimization par essaims particulaires*. Lavoisier.

COOK, D. , BUJA. A. and CABRERA, J. (1993): Projection Pursuit Indices Based on Orthogonal Function Expansions. *Journal of Computational and Graphical Statistics 2, 225–250*.

COOK, D. and SWAYNE, D. F. (2007): *Interactive and Dynamic Graphics for Data Analysis*. Springer Verlag, New York.

COOREN, Y., CLERC, M. SIARRY, P. (2009): Performance evaluation of TRIBES, an adaptive particle swarm optimization algorithm. *Swarm Intelligence 3, 149–178*.

CROUX C. and RUIZ-GAZEN, A. (2005): High Breakdown Estimators for Principal Components: the Projection-Pursuit Approach Revisited. *Journal of Multivariate Analysis, 95, 206-226*.

CROUX, C., FILZMOSER, P. and OLIVEIRA, M. R. (2007): Algorithms for projection-pursuit robust principal components analysis. *Chemometrics and Intelligent Laboratory Systems, 87, 218-225*.

DONOHO, D. L. (1982): Breakdown properties of multivariate location estimators. Ph.D. qualifying paper, Harvard University.

EBERHART, R. C. and KENNEDY, J. (1995): A new optimizer using particle swarm theory. In: Proceedings of the Sixth International Symposium on Micromachine and Human Science. Nagoya, Japan, 39–43.

FRIEDMAN, J. H. (1987): Exploratory projection pursuit. *Journal of the American Statistical Association, 82, 249–266*.

FRIEDMAN J. H. and TUKEY J. W. (1974): A projection pursuit algorithm for exploratory data analysis. *IEEE Transactions on Computers, Ser. C, 23, 881–889*.

GILLI, M. and SCHUMANN, E. (2009): Robust regression with optimization heuristics. Comisef Working paper series, WPS-011.

GILLI, M. and WINKER, P. (2008): Review of heuristic optimization methods in econometrics. Comisef working papers series WPS-OO1.

HADI, A. S., RAHMATULLAH IMON, A. H. M. and WERNER, M. (2009): Detection of outliers. *Wiley Interdisciplinary Reviews: computational statistics, 1, 57-70.*

HALL, P. (1989): On polynomial-based projection indexes for exploratory projection pursuit. *The Annals of Statistics, 17, 589-605.*

HUBER, P. J. (1985): Projection pursuit. *The Annals of Statistics, 13, 435-475.*

JOLLIFFE, I. T. (2002): *Principal Component Analysis*, second edition. Springer.

JONES, M. C. and SIBSON, R. (1987): What is projection pursuit? *Journal of the Royal Statistical Society, 150, 1-37.*

JUAN, J. and PRIETO, F. J. (2001): Using angles to identify concentrated multivariate outliers. *Technometrics 43, 311-322*

KENNEDY, J. and EBERHART, R. C. (with Yuhui Shi) (2001): *Swarm Intelligence.* Morgan Kaufmann.

LARABI MARIE-SAINTE, S., RUIZ-GAZEN, A. and BERRO, A. (2009): Tribes: une méthode d'optimisation efficace pour révéler des optima locaux d'un indice de projection. Preprint.

LI, G. and CHEN, Z. (1985): Projection-pursuit approach to robust dispersion matrices and principal components: primary theory and Monte Carlo. *Journal of the American Statistical Association, 80, 759-766.*

MALPIKA, J. A., REJAS, J. G. and ALONSO, M. C. (2008): A projection pursuit algorithm for anomaly detection in hyperspectral imagery. *Pattern recognition, 41, 3313-3327*

MARONNA, R. A. and YOHAI, V. J. (1995). The behavior of the Stahel-Donoho robust multivariate estimator. *Journal of the American Statistical Association, 90 (429), 330-341.*

NASON, G. P. (1992): *Design and choice of projections indices.* Ph.D. dissertation, University of Bath.

PEÑA, D. and PRIETO, F. (2001): Multivariate outlier detection and robust covariance matrix estimation. *Technometrics, 43, 286-310*

ROUSSEEUW, P. J. and VAN ZOMEREN, B. H. (1990): Unmasking multivariate outliers and leverage points. *Journal of the American Statistical Association, 85, 633-639.*

RUIZ-GAZEN, A. (1993): Estimation robuste d'une matrice de dispersion et projections révélatrices. Ph.D. Dissertation. Université Paul Sabatier. Toulouse.

SMETEK, T. E. and BAUER, K. W. (2008): A Comparison of Multivariate Outlier Detection Methods for Finding Hyperspectral Anomalies. *Military Operations Research, 13, 19-44.*

STAHEL, W. A. (1981): Breakdown of covariance estimators. Research report 31. Fachgruppe für Statistik, E.T.H. Zürich.

SUN, J. (1991): Significance levels in exploratory projection pursuit. *Biometrika, 78(4), 759-769.*

TYLER, D. E., CRITCHLEY F., DÜMBGEN L. and OJA, H. (2009): Invariant co-ordinate selection. *Journal of the Royal Statistical Society. Series B, 71(3), 549-592.*

Part IV

Brain Imaging

Imaging Genetics: Bio-Informatics and Bio-Statistics Challenges

Jean-Baptiste Poline[1], Christophe Lalanne[1], Arthur Tenenhaus[2], Edouard Duchesnay[1], Bertrand Thirion[3], and Vincent Frouin[1]

[1] Neurospin, Institut d'Imagerie Biomédicale, CEA, 91191 Gif sur Yvette Cedex, France. jbpoline@cea.fr, ch.lalanne@gmail.com, edouard.duchesnay@cea.fr, vincent.frouin@cea.fr

[2] SUPELEC Sciences des Systèmes (E3S)-Department of Signal processing and Electronics systems, 91192 Gif-sur-Yvette Cedex. arthur.tenenhaus@supelec.fr

[3] Neurospin, INRIA-Parietal, 91191 Gif sur Yvette Cedex, France. Bertrand.Thirion@inria.fr

Abstract. The IMAGEN study—a very large European Research Project—seeks to identify and characterize biological and environmental factors that influence teenagers mental health. To this aim, the consortium plans to collect data for more than 2000 subjects at 8 neuroimaging centres. These data comprise neuroimaging data, behavioral tests (for up to 5 hours of testing), and also white blood samples which are collected and processed to obtain 650k single nucleotide polymorphisms (SNP) per subject. Data for more than 1000 subjects have already been collected. We describe the statistical aspects of these data and the challenges, such as the multiple comparison problem, created by such a large imaging genetics study (i.e., 650k for the SNP, 50k data per neuroimage). We also suggest possible strategies, and present some first investigations using uni or multi-variate methods in association with re-sampling techniques. Specifically, because the number of variables is very high, we first reduce the data size and then use multivariate (CCA, PLS) techniques in association with re-sampling techniques.

Keywords: neuroimaging, genome wide analyses, partial least squares

1 Neuroimaging genetics and the IMAGEN project

Neuroimaging genetics studies search for links between biological parameters measured with brain imaging and genetic variability. These studies are based on the hypothesis that the brain endophenotype (e.g., size or activity of a brain region) is more linked to genetic variations than to behavioral or clinical phenotypes. There are several kind of neuroimaging genetics studies depending whether they address clinical or normal populations, which endophenotype is measured, or if family information is used. However, from both a statistical and a neuroscience point of view, an important classification is "how open are the genetic and imaging hypotheses?" Often the

Y. Lechevallier, G. Saporta (eds.), *Proceedings of COMPSTAT'2010*,
DOI 10.1007/978-3-7908-2604-3_9, © Springer-Verlag Berlin Heidelberg 2010

neuroimaging genetics study considers a specific hypothesis about one polymorphism (e.g. the serotonin transporter) and involves few brain images of a small group of subjects.

The current somewhat low cost of full genome data acquisition makes possible to perform brain and genome wide analyses (BGWA). Genome wide analyses (GWA) are already statistically challenging and often require a very large cohort, but the challenge is even bigger with the large number of potential endophenotypes (see the description below) associated with a relatively small number of subjects, as it is time consuming and costly to acquire neuroimaging data in a large cohort. In fact, it is practically impossible for a single neuroimaging center to acquire data on thousands of subjects.

Despite these challenges, several studies are on the way such as the IMA-GEN project which explores brain-genetic-behavior relations in a population of 2000 normal adolescents, with an emphasis on addiction disorders, including emotional, reward or impulsivity aspects. The consortium comprises eight Europeans neuroimaging centers, the data are centralized at Neurospin (CEA, I2BM) which deals with bioinformatics and biostatistics.

1.1   Genetic data: Single Nucleotide Polymorphisms (SNP)

GWAS focuses on the relationships between the genetic sequence information (i.e., the "genotype") and a trait or phenotype (e.g., cholesterol level) measured in vivo or in vitro in unrelated individuals. Single base pair changes occurring in at least 1% of the population are used as a proxy to reflect spatial loci of variability on the whole genome. In this data one must take into account the spatial correlation between markers on DNA strands; *linkage disequilibrium* (LD), which reflects the association between alleles present at each of two sites on a genome, because a set of SNPs may not directly explain the variations observed in the trait under consideration but may be correlated with a true disease creating variants of a known biomarker instead (for reviews see Cordell & Clayton (2005), and Ioannidis et al. (2009)).

However, GWAS are considered semi-exploratory and other techniques—relying on haplotypes, genes, and gene regulation pathways—are necessary to understand relations b etween genetic polymorphisms and a given phenotype.

To avoid spurious associations between the trait of interest and genetic data, population substructure are assessed and SNPs with low minor allele frequency, not in Hardy-Weinberg equilibrium, or with low genotyping rate are discarded.

1.2   Magnetic Resonance Imaging (MRI) data

We describe below some endophenotypes acquired with MRI.

T1 images: brain macroscopic structure and the issue of anatomical structures variability. Studies of sulco-gyral anatomical variability across subjects (Riviere et al. (2002)) established that variability is important even for normal subjects, and that the distance between two identical structures (e.g., sulci) can be as large as a centimeter after spatial normalization (i.e., "morphing") to a common template. These studies also showed that small structures may or may not be present in the brain of different subjects. However, characteristics of reproducible sulci can be heritable attributes and relevant endophenotypes in association studies (Rogers et al. (2010)).

A popular alternative to studying individually identified structures is to use Voxel-Based Morphometry (VBM). VBM uses a the spatial normalization of the subjects brains (e.g., the MNI brain template) and then estimates from the number of voxels quantities such as grey matter density or regional volume (Ashburner and Friston (2001)). This convenient method is, however, sensitive to the values of the parameters of spatial normalisation procedures.

Diffusion Weighted Images (DWI) measures, for a voxel, the amount of water molecule diffusion in several directions. The spatial resolution is often of the order of $8mm^3$ and the angular resolution (number of directions) varies from 6 to hundreds, but is often around 60 in standard settings. DWI is then used to reconstruct fiber tracks connecting brain regions (Assaf and Pasternak (2008)). As with T1 images, measurements can be made at the level of the voxel (mean diffusion, fractional anisotropy) or at the level of the fiber tracks reconstructed per subjects, or with hybrid strategies. The usefulness of the endophenotypes derived from DWI is still being assessed. Depending on the strategy, the number of features per subject ranges from a few (e.g., length of fiber tracks) to thousands (e.g., voxels).

fMRI processings. The Blood Oxygen Level Dependent (BOLD) signal measures the amount of brain regional blood flow and blood volume which correlates with neuronal activity at a spatial resolution of a few mms. In general, for a subject, an fMRI dataset is composed of several runs, each consisting of a few hundreds of three-dimensional scans acquired every few seconds. Prior to statistical analysis proper, a few essential pre-processing steps are necessary, such as intra-subject motion correction. Subject activation maps are then estimated (in general with the use of a linear model of the form $\mathbf{Y} = \mathbf{X}\beta + \epsilon$, with several variables included in $\mathbf{X}$ to model the expected time variation of $\mathbf{Y}$). This step is crucial because the results depend strongly on the model. The model usually includes time courses designed to account for variation due to experimental conditions and confounding factors (see Poline et al (2008)). To compares subjects, a spatial normalization procedure is applied on each subject data. The group inference results are then obtained at the voxel level after a spatial smoothing of the individual data using mixed effect (or simple random effects) models (see, e.g., Mériaux et al. (2006)).

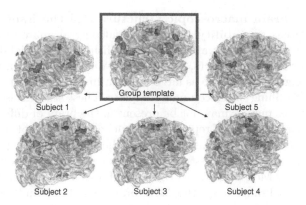

Fig. 1. How to build a model of the brain activity at the group level with a subject per subject representation (Thirion et al (2007)). This may provide more relevant endophenotypes than region of interest defined solely on the template space.

Parcellisation and functional landmarks techniques A parcellisation divides the brain into entities which are thought to correspond to well-defined anatomical or functional regions. In the context of group inference for neuroimaging, basing the analysis on parcels amounts to reducing spatial resolution to obtain a more reliable as well as interpretable matching of functional regions across subjects. Although atlas-based divisions are frequently used, their regions do not adapt to the individual functional anatomy.

An alternative to parcellisation is functional brain landmarks. Here, one searches individual topographical features and estimates their frequencies in a population of subjects. By contrast with traditional approaches, this kind of inference follows bottom-up strategy, where objects are extracted individually and then compared. Typically, structural features or patterns relevant for descriptions are local maxima of activity, regions segmented by watershed methods or blob models. Whatever the pattern used, the most difficult questions are to 1) decide if these patterns represent true activity or noise, and 2) infer a pattern common to the population of subjects.

Which endophenotype? From the description of fMRI above, it is clear that a large number of endophenotypes can be chosen from the imaging data. These endophenotypes can be differentiated into 1) voxel based approaches which use spatial normalization prior to measuring the activity of brain structures, and 2) individual landmark/structure approaches that provide individual measures. Voxel-based approaches have the advantage of being easy to automatize, but are less precise, and depend on the normalization procedures. Individual structure detection have the advantage that the endophenotype defined are more relevant and therefore more sensitive, but they are difficult to implement, rely on a model of the correspondence between subjects, and may not always define one endophenotype per subject.

The research to understand which endophenotypes are *heritable, sensitive, specific and reproducible* for association studies is only beginning and will certainly be a key aspect of imaging genetics in the near future.

Behavioral and clinical data. Clearly, imaging and genetic data have to be complemented by demographic, behavioral, and clinical data. Summarizing these data or constructing latent variables (e.g., with SEM or PLS) that can reveal association with genetic or imaging is also a challenge.

Indeed, using items as manifest variables to uncover the locations of a latent trait (e.g. extraversion, impulsivity) implies a measurement error whose magnitude depends on the reliability of the measurement scale. As a consequence, for example, correlations between latent constructs should be corrected for attenuation, group comparisons should account for possible differential item functioning (i.e., conditional on the true latent score, the probability of endorsing an item differs between the reference and a focal group, defined by external variables). As pointed by Ioannidis et al. (2009), these considerations apply when using latent variables in GWAS. However, higher-order latent variables should give a better account of the inter-subjects variance when integrated in a conceptual model, and so should constitute more sensitive indicators.

2   Biostatistics: challenges and methods

There are several challenges for the analyses[1] of these large datasets. The first challenge arises from the specificities of multiple complex types of data. To integrate these different types of data implies a good understanding of their acquisition, and pre-processing, as well as the neuroscience or clinical contexts. Second, the large number of variables requires appropriate statistical techniques (e.g., variable selections, use of sparse techniques). Third, there is an obvious multiple comparison issue. Fourth, it is not clear what should be the overall strategy of analysis. Figure 2 represents symbolically the data at hand and how they can be analysed.

2.1   Mappings one to many

Voxel based mappings: BWAS. The aim is to isolate brain regions or voxels associated with a genetic polymorphism or a trait/phenotype on the group of subjects. This corresponds to a simple standard statistical parametric mapping analysis in neuroimaging. The method consists in first computing

---

[1] The bioinformatics (database, computing) aspects of these large studies are not addressed here, but are vital.

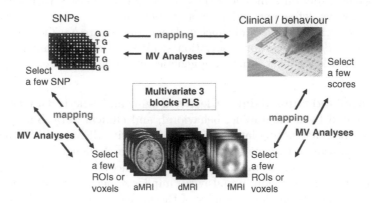

Fig. 2. The data available and how to combine them in mapping studies (one to many) or through multivariate PLS (many to many). Three PLS block can be used to integrate these data. Mappings and multivariate techniques often require variable selection or regularization because of the $N \ll P$ problem.

for each subject one brain volume summarizing the metabolic activity in one experimental condition (the so called contrast maps) and second to regressing for each voxel v the activity measured Y_v on one of the variables of interest that define the model X. The issue is then to select the brain regions with significant activity. This is done by first choosing a statistics (e.g., Fisher's F) and then estimating a threshold to correct for multiple comparisons involving 50k to 100k correlated voxels. The multiple comparison problem is often handled with random field techniques (Worsley (2003)) or permutation tests (Rorden et al. (2007)). This approach is reasonable only if a limited number of candidate SNPs or scores are tested against few contrast maps.

Genetic (SNP) based mappings. GWAS analysis seeks to isolate genetic markers that explain a significant part of the variance of a given trait for unrelated individuals. Usually, such associations are studied by analyzing SNPs with a GLM model in which the frequency of the minor allele predicts the trait under study. However, this amounts to run as many tests as there are SNPs and creates an obvious problem of multiple comparisons. To control for inflation of Type I error rate, FWER corrections (e.g., Bonferroni) will only retain SNP with a p-value as low as 5.10^{-8}. Such a drastically conservative approach is likely to mask functionally interesting variants with small effect size. Moreover, tests are not independent because adjacent loci are spatially correlated. Several authors (for a review, Dudoit and van der Laan (2008)) discussed alternative strategies to enhance signal to noise ratio and increase the likelihood of tagging reliable markers.

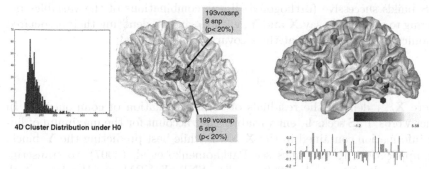

Fig. 3. Left: Constructing 4D clusters in a voxel × SNP space and permutation test. Right: Two blocks PLS. Loadings for the best 100 SNPs associated with 34 brain ROIs: positive (resp. negative) loadings in yellow (resp. red).

The voxels × SNPs challenge. Here we consider the endophenotype of an individual as the constructed 3D contrast map described above and study the association between all these voxels (approx. 50k voxel) and with each SNP within the set of more than 500k polymorphisms. For example the association of voxels with the allelic dosage (genetic additive model) for each SNP will generate around *25 billions* comparisons per contrast map.

In the QTL association study with SNP data, several techniques have been designed based on the idea that combining *p*-values of adjacent SNPs is more significant and more biologically relevant than considering SNPs independently. (e.g., Tippett's, Fisher's and Stoufers' methods). Recent contributions use a set of tests based on *p*-values aggregation (sliding window along the sequence or scan statistics). The multiple comparison issue is dealt with the usual techniques (e.g., Bonferroni, FDR, permutation tests). Theses ideas may be applied to imaging genetic data (voxel × SNPs) in order to detect contiguous brain regions linked to neighboring SNPs. The method detects clusters defined by a threshold in the product (4D) dataset, and calibrates the null hypothesis using permutations. While computationally intensive, this technique is conceptually simple, corrects for multiple comparisons in both imaging and genetic dimensions, and accounts for the spatial structure of the data. Preliminary results show that this method—illustrated in Figure 3— is efficient compared to other procedures.

2.2   Two-blocks methods

The main questions raised by two-blocks datasets with $N \ll P + Q$ are: 1) how to select the predictors of interest, 2) which multivariate model to choose, 3) how to evaluate its performance and 4) how to compare models.

Partial least squares (PLS) regression belongs to the type of methods used for modeling the association of original variables with latent variables. PLS builds successive (orthogonal) linear combinations of the variables belonging to each block, say $\mathbf{X}$ and $\mathbf{Y}$, with $\mathbf{u}_h$ and $\mathbf{v}_h$ denoting their associated canonical variates, such that their covariance is maximal:

$$\max_{|\mathbf{u}_h|=1,|\mathbf{v}_h|=1} \mathrm{cov}(\mathbf{X}_{h-1}\mathbf{u}_h, \mathbf{Y}\mathbf{v}_h)$$

where $\mathbf{X}_{h-1}$ denotes the residuals of $\mathbf{X}$ after deflation of component h. In other words, PLS seeks latent variables that account for the maximum of linear information contained in the $\mathbf{X}$ block while best predicting the $\mathbf{Y}$ block. For applications to genomics see Parkhomenko et al. (2007), to transcriptomics, see Lê Cao et al. (2009), and to SNPs X VBM, see Hardoon et al. (2009).

When predicting brain activation from SNPs, we face two issues created by the high-dimensionality of the problem. First we need to reduce the number of predictors and to design cross-validation procedures which avoid overfitting and facilitate interpretation of the resulting set of variables (Parkhomenko et al. (2007), Lê Cao et al. (2008)). Second, we need to evaluate the significance of the X–Y links (e.g., with appropriate permutation schemes).

Figure 3 (right) illustrates the results obtained when maximizing PLS criterion across training samples and estimating correlation between factor scores in test samples. The significance of this test statistic was assessed using a permutation procedure embracing the whole statistical framework (cross-validation including feature selection). These preliminary results indicate that it is possible to spot significant relationships between genetic and MRI data.

2.3   Multi block analyses: RGCCA

To estimate conjointly relationships between 3 or more blocks of variables, we use Regularized Generalized Canonical Correlation Analysis (RGCCA, see Tenenhaus & Tenenhaus, submitted). With the following notations:

- J blocks $\{\mathbf{X}_1, \ldots, \mathbf{X}_J\}$ of centered variables measured on N observations,
- a design matrix $\mathbf{C} = (c_{jk})$ describing a network of connections between blocks ($c_{jk} = 1$ for two connected blocks, and 0 otherwise),
- a function g equal to the identity, absolute value or square function,
- shrinkage constants $\tau_1, \ldots, \tau_J$,

RGCCA is the solution of the following optimization problem:

$$\begin{cases} \underset{\mathbf{w}_1,\mathbf{w}_2,\ldots,\mathbf{w}_J}{\mathrm{argmax}} \sum_{1 \leq j < k \leq J} c_{jk} g(\mathrm{cov}(\mathbf{X}_j\mathbf{w}_j, \mathbf{X}_k\mathbf{w}_k)) \\[2em] \text{with the constraints } (1 - \tau_j)\mathrm{var}(\mathbf{X}_j\mathbf{w}_j) + \tau_j\|\mathbf{w}_j\|^2 = 1, j = 1, \ldots, J \end{cases}$$

RGCCA builds block components (i.e., latent variables) $\mathbf{y}_j = \mathbf{X}_j\mathbf{w}_j$, $j = 1, ..., J$ which explain their own block and are well correlated to their connected components. The RGCCA algorithm requires to invert—for each block—the shrunk estimation of the covariance matrices. This is computationally intractable for large blocks. To overcome this problem, we split the SNP block in blocks corresponding to chromosomes and add one block for neuroimaging. The method gives, for each block, the value of the the highest correlations is then associated to SNPs of interest. Our preliminary results with RGCCA show good sensitivity and interpretable results.

2.4 Biostatistics challenges and strategies for data analysis

The analysis of a large database such as IMAGEN, is also challenging at the level of the overall strategy as well as the computational methods and tools. Specific difficulties methodological, or even sociological are:

- The data are acquired continuously (this is necessarily the case for large imaging data studies) or by batch (genotyping). What intermediary steps should be taken, what is the likelihood that those will be confirmed with the full dataset analyses, how those should influence or not the remaining cohort recruitment are generally open questions.
- There are several approaches to study a particular neuroscience question, and controlling for the overall risk of error is difficult.
- While multivariate links may be better investigated first, this approach is technically challenged by the large number of variables (SNP, voxels) available; as multivariate variable selection is NP-hard and entails a combinatorial explosion, univariate procedures are often used in practice as initial screening.

3 Conclusions

To conclude, we believe that neuroimaging genetics—a new field that emerges at the interaction of several domains such as neuroimaging, cognitive neuroscience, genetics, experimental psychology—is particularly challenging for computational statistics, because it requires to adapt, tailor, or even create statistical methods suitable for high dimensional and heterogeneous data but also to develop specific software and databasing tools.

Acknowledgements

We are very grateful to H. Abdi for his help in editing the manuscript. Support was provided by the IMAGEN project, which receives research funding from the European Community's Sixth Framework Programme (LSHM-CT-2007-037286). This manuscript reflects only the author's views and the Community is not liable for any use that may be made of the information contained therein.

References

ASHBURNER J., and FRISTON K.J. (2001): Why voxel-based morphometry should be used. *NeuroImage, 14, 1238-1243.*

ASSAF Y, and PASTERNAK O. (2008): Diffusion tensor imaging (DTI)-based white matter mapping in brain research: a review. *J Mol Neurosci, 34, 51-61.*

DUDOIT, S. and VAN DER LAAN, M. J. (2008): *Multiple Testing Procedures with Applications to Genomics,* Springer, New York.

CORDELL H.J., and CLAYTON D.G. (2005): Genetic association studies. *Lancet, 366, 1121-1131.*

HARDOON D.R., ETTINGER U., MOURÃO-MIRANDA J., ANTONOVA E., et al., (2009): Correlation-based multivariate analysis of genetic influence on brain volume. *Neuroscience letters, 450, 281-286.*

IOANNIDIS J.P., THOMAS G., and DALY MJ (2009): Validating, augmenting and refining genome-wide association signals. *Nature Reviews Genetics, 10, 318-329.*

LÊ CAO K.A., ROSSOUW D., ROBERT-GRANIÉ C., and BESSE P. (2008): A sparse PLS for variable selection when integrating omics data. *Statistical Applications in Genetics and Molecular Biology, 7, 35.*

MÉRIAUX S., ROCHE A., DEHAENE-LAMBERTZ G., THIRION B., and PO-LINE J.B. (2006): Combined permutation test and mixed-effect model for group average analysis in fMRI. *Hum Brain Mapp, 27, 402-410.*

PARKHOMENKO E., TRITCHLER D., and BEYENE J. (2007): Genome-wide sparse canonical correlation of gene expression with genotypes. *BMC Proceedings, 1, S119.*

POLINE J.B., ROCHE A., CIUCIU P., and THIRION B. (2008): Intra- and inter-subject aspects of fMRI data analysis. In Paragios N., Duncan J., Ayache N. (Eds.) *Handbook of Biomedical Imaging.*

ROGERS J., KOCHUNOV P., ZILLES K., SHELLEDY W., et al., (in press). On the genetic architecture of cortical folding and brain volume in primates. *Neuroimage.*

RORDEN C., BONILHA L., and NICHOLS T.E. (2007). Rank-order versus mean based statistics for neuroimaging. *NeuroImage, 35, 1531-1537.*

SMITH S.M., JENKINSON M., JOHANSEN-BERG H., RUECKERT D., et al., (2006): Tract-based spatial statistics: Voxelwise analysis of multi-subject diffusion data. *NeuroImage, 31, 1487-1505.*

TENENHAUS A., and TENENHAUS M. (in revision). Regularized generalized canonical correlation analysis, *Psychometrika.*

THIRION B., PINEL P., and POLINE, J.B. (2005): Finding landmarks in the functional brain: detection and use for group characterization. *Med Image Comput Comput Assist Interv Int Conf, 8, 476-483.*

THIRION B., PINEL P., TUCHOLKA A., ROCHE A., CIUCIU P., MANGIN J.-F., and POLINE J.-B. (2007): Structural analysis of fMRI data revisited: Improving the sensitivity and reliability of fMRI group studies. *IEEE Transactions on Medical Imaging, 26, 1256-1269.*

WORSLEY K.J. (2003): Detecting activation in fMRI data. *Stat Methods Med Res, 12, 401-418.*

The NPAIRS Computational Statistics Framework for Data Analysis in Neuroimaging

Stephen Strother[1][2], Anita Oder[1], Robyn Spring[1][2], and Cheryl Grady[1]

[1] Rotman Research Institute, Baycrest
   3560 Bathurst Street, Toronto, ON, Canada   *sstrother@rotman-baycrest.on.ca
[2] Department of Medical Biophysics, University of Toronto

Abstract. We introduce the role of resampling and prediction (p) metrics for flexible discriminant modeling in neuroimaging, and highlight the importance of combining these with measurements of the reproducibility (r) of extracted brain activation patterns. Using the NPAIRS resampling framework we illustrate the use of (p, r) plots as a function of the size of the principal component subspace (Q) for a penalized discriminant analysis (PDA) to: optimize processing pipelines in functional magnetic resonance imaging (fMRI), and measure the global SNR (gSNR) and dimensionality of fMRI data sets. We show that the gSNRs of typical fMRI data sets cause the optimal Q for a PDA to often lie in a phase transition region between gSNR $\simeq 1$ with large optimal Q versus SNR $\gg 1$ with small optimal Q.

Keywords: prediction, reproducibility, penalized discriminant analysis, fMRI

1 Introduction

Mapping of brain function is a major area of brain imaging. In the 1980s it was dominated by positron emission tomography (PET) and single photon emission tomography (SPECT) but since the discovery of the blood oxygenation level dependent (BOLD) signal in the 1990's, BOLD functional magnetic resonance imaging (fMRI) and related techniques now dominate the brain imaging literature. The early PET-based applications used some machine learning and neural networks techniques for the analysis of functional neuroimages, but most the current fMRI experimental and analysis paradigms are still based on simple univariate general linear models with inferential statistical tests, and in some instances their predictive, machine learning equivalent (e.g., Gaussian Naïve Bayes, Kjems et al. (2002); Pereira et al. (2009)). However, there has been a recent explosion of interest in using related multivariate classification approaches—dubbed "mind reading" by some.

2 Data-driven performance metrics

In brain mapping it is crucial to optimize and evaluate models and to select the most salient features. These tasks must be guided by a performance met-

Y. Lechevallier, G. Saporta (eds.), *Proceedings of COMPSTAT'2010*,
DOI 10.1007/978-3-7908-2604-3_10, © Springer-Verlag Berlin Heidelberg 2010

ric. A variety of possible performance metrics including crossvalidated prediction (p) are briefly reviewed in Afshinpour et al. (in press). Although prediction accuracy alone can be an effective metric for general machine-learning
problems, neuroimaging also demands that the spatial pattern (encoded by
the predictive model) be reproducible (r) or generalizable between different
groups of subjects or different scans of the same subject. The reproducibility of models' estimated parameters when optimizing prediction in such ill-
posed data sets (variables $\gg$ observations) is a neglected issue in the field
of predictive modeling. In some problems this is unimportant as prediction
performance may be the primary result that matters (Schmah et al. 2008).
However, in high-dimensional brain mapping problems the reliability of the
extracted brain maps and the voxels that influence prediction performance
are often the critical outputs of the modeling process that reflects underlying
brain processes. One approach is to include a greedy search procedure because this reduces the size of the voxel feature space to the subset relevant for
prediction. This may be iteratively driven by prediction metrics using classical machine learning approaches or simply based on a subset of voxels that
are detected with a separate voxel-based, general linear model (GLM). Some
tradeoffs of such purely prediction-driven analysis approaches are discussed
in Pereira et al. (2009). Together with prediction accuracy, reproducibility is
an important metric because it provides a data-driven substitute for receiver
operator characteristic (ROC) analysis. We also address model performance
in real data sets where the true SNR structure is unknown and ROC curves
cannot be measured. In particular, we illustrate the use of (p, r) metrics to
optimize the pipeline of image pre-processing steps for fMRI data sets before
data analysis, e.g., scan-to-scan registration, spatial and temporal filtering,
etc. (for a review see Strother (2006)). And we demonstrate the use of (p, r)
metrics to optimize subspace selection for a penalized discriminant analysis
(PDA) model built on a PCA basis.

3   Nonparametric, activation, influence and reproducibility resampling (NPAIRS)

NPAIRS provides a resampling framework for combining prediction metrics
with the reproducibility of the brain-activation patterns, or statistical parametric maps (SPM), as a data-driven substitute for ROCs. However, any
measure of similarity between patterns extracted from independent data sets
is subject to an unknown bias (Afshinpour et al., in press). To obtain combined prediction and reproducibility values Strother et al. (2002); Kjems et
al. (2002) proposed a novel split-half resampling framework dubbed NPAIRS
and applied it first to PET and later to fMRI (see Strother et al. (2004);
LaConte et al. (2003); Yourganov et al., in press). While NPAIRS may be
applied to any analysis model we have focused on LDA built on a regularized
PCA basis (i.e., PDA). This allows us to (1) regularize the model by choosing

soft (e.g., ridge) or hard thresholds on the PCA eigenspectrum or other basis set (e.g., tensor product splines) (2) maintain the link to covariance decomposition previously used with PET for elucidating network structures, and (3) easily produce robust whole-brain activation maps useful for discovering features of brain function and/or disease.

The basic outline of NPAIRS follows[1]. Consider an fMRI data set $\mathbf{S}$ of v voxels by NT scans for N subjects' data sets of T scans each. The independent observations of N subjects are split into two independent halves $\mathbf{S} = [\mathbf{S}_1, \mathbf{S}_2]$: training and test sets of size $\frac{N}{2}$. This split-half resampling represents a form of repeated, 2-fold cross-validation that has the benefits of smooth, robust metrics obtained with delete-d jackknife and the 0.632+ bootstrap (Efron and Tibshirani (1993, 1997)). Typically in neuroimaging we have $v \gg NT$, with $v = 10k - 100k$ voxels, and $N = 10s$ of subjects and $T = 50 - 100s$ of scans/subject. Consequently $\mathbf{S}$ is large and ill-posed and cannot be directly inverted. Therefore, we proceed with an initial dimensionality reduction step using PCA that also serves as a preliminary denoising process. Further the PCA ensures that we have captured at least the first order voxel interactions that represent the important functional connectivity of underlying brain networks. We can obtain estimates of the PCA basis components needed using a singular value decomposition (SVD) or equivalently from the eigenvalue decomposition (EVD) of the smaller outer-product covariance matrix (which is considerably faster than an SVD). We proceed as follows

1. Given the singular SVD, $\mathbf{S} = \mathbf{ULV}^T$, we compute the EVD, $\mathbf{S}^T\mathbf{S} = \mathbf{VL}^2\mathbf{V}^T$, and proceed with a reduced basis set, $\mathbf{X}^* = \mathbf{U}^{*T}\mathbf{S} = \mathbf{L}^*\mathbf{V}^{*T}$, where we typically retain 30% of the PCA components so that $\mathbf{X}^*$ has size $(0.3NT \times NT)$, assuming $v \gg NT$.

2. Randomly partition $\mathbf{X}^*$ into two independent split-half groups across the subjects to obtain $\mathbf{X}^* = [\mathbf{X}_1, \mathbf{X}_2] = \mathbf{U}^{*T}[\mathbf{S}_1, \mathbf{S}_2]$, where $\mathbf{X}_i$ has size $(0.3NT \times N_iT)$, $N_i = N/2$ for N even, or $N_i = N/2 \pm 0.5$ for N odd.

3. Given the SVD $\mathbf{X}_i = \mathbf{Y}_i\mathbf{L}_i\mathbf{R}_i^T$, we compute second-level EVDs $\mathbf{X}_i^* = \mathbf{Y}_i^{*T}\mathbf{X}_i = \mathbf{L}_i^*\mathbf{R}_i^T$, on $\mathbf{X}_1$ and $\mathbf{X}_2$, and retain Q components from each, so that $\mathbf{X}_i^*$ has size $(Q \times T_i)$ where $T_i = N_iT$. With Q typically $\leq \min(2 - 500, 0.3NT)$ we achieve a large dimensionality (and computational) reduction. For example from Strother et al. (2004) with $N = 16$, $T = 187$ scans and $v = 23{,}389$ brain voxels, $\mathbf{S}$ is $(23{,}389 \times 2992)$, but $\mathbf{X}_i^*$ is only $Q \times 1496$, and for PDA we only calculate $(Q \times Q)$ covariances with $Q \leq 500$.

4. Now apply the prediction model separately to $\mathbf{X}_1^*$ and $\mathbf{X}_2^*$ using a scan-label structure. This label structure may directly reflect the experimental design (i.e., number of experimentally defined conditions or brain states), or it may be chosen to reflect other possibilities, such as agnostic labels that will extract an unknown but common, data-driven temporal-covariance across subjects (e.g., Strother et al. (2004); Kustra and Strother (2001); Kjems et al. (2002); Evans et al. (2010)). For the rest of this paper we focus on Canonical

---

[1] Software available at http://code.google.com/p/plsnpairs/.

Variates Analysis (CVA, Mardia et al. (1979)), which reflects a Gaussian mixture model across classes with the strong regularization constraint that all class covariances are equal and may therefore be estimated using a pooled, within-class covariance estimate; this CVA is equivalent to LDA, although we further regularize by calculating CVA on a subspace of size Q, as in a PDA (Kustra and Strother (2001)). For $g = 1, \ldots, G$ classes, and $k = 1, \ldots, K_g$, with K_g the number of scans in class g, let $\mathbf{x}_{gk}$ represent a column of $\mathbf{X}_i^*$ with Q component features of the kth scan in class g. We calculate,

$$\mathbf{W}_i = \sum_{gk}^{GK_g} (\mathbf{x}_{gk} - \bar{\mathbf{x}}_g)(\mathbf{x}_{gk} - \bar{\mathbf{x}}_g)^T \tag{1}$$

$$\mathbf{B}_i = K_g \sum_g^G (\bar{\mathbf{x}}_g - \bar{\mathbf{x}})(\bar{\mathbf{x}}_g - \bar{\mathbf{x}})^T \tag{2}$$

where $\bar{\mathbf{x}}_g = \frac{1}{K_g} \sum_k^{K_g} \mathbf{x}_{gk}$ is the mean of scans in class g, and $\bar{\mathbf{x}} = \frac{1}{T_i} \sum_{kg}^{GK_g} \mathbf{x}_{gk}$ is the mean over all scans in split-half $\mathbf{X}_i^*$. The canonical variates that represent a penalized, generalized likelihood ratio solution of the G-class discriminant problem are obtained by the following EVD:

$$\mathbf{W}_i^{-1} \mathbf{B}_i \mathbf{C}_i = \mathbf{C}_i \mathbf{M}_i \tag{3}$$

where $\mathbf{C}_i$ has $G - 1$ columns of canonical variates, $\mathbf{c}_j$ with dimension Q, normalized such that $\mathbf{C}_i^T (\mathbf{W}_i / (T_i - G)) \mathbf{C}_i = \mathbf{I}$, and $\mathbf{M}_i$ is a $(G-1) \times (G-1)$ diagonal matrix containing eigenvalues, m_j. From $\mathbf{C}_i$ we obtain PCA-like, canonical-coordinate time series defined by

$$\mathbf{Z}_i = \mathbf{X}_i^{*T} \mathbf{C}_i \tag{4}$$

where $\mathbf{Z}_i$ has $G-1$ columns of $\mathbf{z}_j$, with time-series dimension T_i, and $\mathbf{z}_j^T \mathbf{z}_h = 0$ where $(j \neq h)$, and $\mathbf{z}_j^T \mathbf{z}_j = (T_i - G)(1 + m_j)$, since $\mathbf{X}_i^* \mathbf{X}_i^{*T} = \mathbf{B}_i + \mathbf{W}_i$. The associated canonical eigenimages are given by

$$\mathbf{E}_i = \mathbf{U}^* \mathbf{Y}_i^* \mathbf{C}_i \tag{5}$$

where $\mathbf{E}_i$ has $G - 1$ columns $\mathbf{e}_j$ with dimension v.

Prediction accuracy is defined as the posterior probability of a test-scan, $\mathbf{s}_{gk(\text{test})}$, being assigned to its true class label, g, given by $p\left(g | \mathbf{s}_{gk(\text{test})}; \theta_{\text{train}}\right)$, where θ_{train} are model parameters calculated in an independent training set. Assume the scans represented by the split-half set, $\mathbf{X}_1^*$, form a training set in which we calculate the PDA model parameters in Eqn. 5. The prediction accuracy for scans in the test set, $\mathbf{X}_2^*$, is given by

$$
\begin{aligned}
&p\left(g_{gk(2)} \middle| \mathbf{s}_{gk(2)}; \theta_{(1)}\right) \\
&= \tfrac{1}{a} \exp\left\{ -\tfrac{1}{2} \left(\mathbf{s}_{gk(2)} - \bar{\mathbf{s}}_{g(1)}\right)^T \mathbf{U}^* \mathbf{Y}_1^* \mathbf{W}_1^{-1} \mathbf{Y}_1^{*T} \mathbf{U}^{*T} \left(\mathbf{s}_{gk(2)} - \bar{\mathbf{s}}_{g(1)}\right) \right\} p(g_{gk(2)}) \\
&= \tfrac{1}{a'} \exp\left\{ -\tfrac{1}{2} \left(\mathbf{s}_{gk(2)} - \bar{\mathbf{s}}_{g(1)}\right)^T \mathbf{E}_1 \mathbf{E}_1^T \left(\mathbf{s}_{gk(2)} - \bar{\mathbf{s}}_{g(1)}\right) \right\} p(g_{gk(2)})
\end{aligned}
$$

from Eqn. 1 with $\mathbf{C}_1\mathbf{C}_1^T = (T_i{-}G)\mathbf{W}_1^{-1}$, ($a$ and a' are normalizing constants). In practice we swap training and test sets and average across all scans to obtain the average prediction value for a particular split-half.

Each independent split-half PDA produces a set of canonical eigenimages, $\mathbf{E}_i$, and canonical coordinate time series, $\mathbf{Z}_i$, which can have arbitrary signs and component ordering. To address this before comparing the split-half eigenimages we perform a PDA on the full data set $\mathbf{S}$ from step 1, without splitting, using $2Q$ components from the 2nd-level EVD in steps 3 and 4. This $\mathbf{Z_S}$ result provides a reference set against which we compare each $\mathbf{Z}_i$ set of canonical-coordinate time series using a Procrustes matching procedure restricted to sign changes and permutations of component order. The operations performed on the $\mathbf{Z}_i$ components are then also performed on the $\mathbf{E}_i$ components to match them across the spit-halfs. For a particular canonical component, the reproducibility of the two split-half eigenimages is defined as the correlation (r) between all pairs of the spatially aligned voxels. This correlation value r is directly related to the available SNR in each extracted pair of split-half SPMs. For transformed eigenimages of mean=0, and length=1, the two eigenvalues are equal to $1 + r$ (signal) and $1 - r$ (noise). Therefore, we define a global SNR metric for each split-half as

$$\text{gSNR} = \sqrt{((1 + \text{r}) - (1 - \text{r}))/(1 - \text{r})} = \sqrt{2\text{r}/(1 - \text{r})} \qquad (6)$$

Note that the Procrustes matching procedure is likely to make r positive but that low-reproducibility components will still reflect the distribution of r around 0. From Eqn. 6 we see that r maps the $[0, \infty]$ range of gSNR to $[0, 1]$. In general when the number of unique split-resamplings (i.e., $\frac{1}{2}{}^N C_{N/2}$) is large enough, we perform $\gg 10$ split-halfs and record the average, or median, of the p and r distributions across for a particular choice of Q. This procedure is then repeated as a function of Q to obtain the best (p, r) values possible as a function of Q. We recognize that the resulting p-values are biased upwards as a result of optimizing model parameters (i.e, Q) using only training and validation sets, and then biased downwards, relative to leave-one-out cross-validation, as a result of using split-half resampling. Finally, we obtain a single Z-scored SPM from each split-half pair of eigenimages (i.e., rSPM(z)). In the scatter plot used to calculate r we project all pairs of voxel values onto the principal axis to obtain a consensus rSPM. These projected rSPM values are then scaled by the pooled noise estimate, $(1 - r)$, from the minor axis. As this noise estimate is uncorrelated by construction the resulting rSPM(z) values will be approximately normally distributed; in practice this is a good approximation for brain imaging. Finally, this procedure is robust to heterogeneity across the split objects (e.g., subjects) as more heterogeneous split-half pairs produce smaller r's and larger $(1 - r)$ pooled noise estimates, and thus lower rSPM(z) values than more homogeneous splits. Then we average all rSPM(z)'s to obtain a robust, consensus technique for Z-scoring any prediction model that produces voxel-based parameter estimates.

4   Measuring pipeline performance

Figure 1 plots NPAIRS (p, r) curves for an 11-class CVA of 2992 fMRI scans from 16 subjects performing a static force task (Strother et al. (2004)). The two curves reflect a small change in a single preprocessing step: the number of half cosines used for removal of low-frequency trends in fMRI time series. The points on the curves are the number of PCA components from $1 - Q$ ($Q \in \{10, 25, 75, 100, 150, 200, 300, 500\}$). A full NPAIRS analysis with 50 split-halfs was run for each value of Q. In Figure 1 as the PDA parameterization initially increases with Q, both p and r (i.e., gSNR(r)) initially increase. Then at $Q = 50$, while p continues to slowly increase, r starts to decreases quite rapidly. This appears to be a fundamental feature of predictive modeling in ill-posed neuroimaging data sets. with p typically being optimized at larger values of Q than for optimal r, but both eventually decreasing. This (p, r) tradeoff has also been demonstrated in the context of parameterization of nonlinear hemodynamic models estimated using MCMC, with r replaced by a Kullback-Leibler measure on posterior distributions (Jacobsen et al. (2008)). The (p, r) plot provides a data-driven, ROC-like space where perfect performance is represented by the upper-right-hand corner with perfect prediction (p=1) and infinite gSNR ($r = 1$). For a given set of preprocessing steps and parameters our goal is to move the (p, r) curve closer to $(1, 1)$. As this is a relative change we assume that the p-value bias is approximately constant when measuring (p, r) curves that lie closer to $(1, 1)$. We have been experimenting with using the minimum Euclidian distance from $(1, 1)$ to define an optimal (p, r) tradeoff and a cost function for processing-pipeline optimization. In Fig. 1 if we generate (p, r) curves for each of the 16 subjects and record their mean distance from $(1, 1)$, $\bar{M}$, then the change, $\triangle \bar{M}$, across the 16 subjects and their standard deviation may be used to judge improved processing choices. In Fig. 1 we see that on average temporal detrending with a 1.5 cycle cosine will slightly improve (p, r) performance over using a 2.0 cycle cosine.

Zhang et al. (2009) has explored this approach in the context of the same fMRI data set with both a predictive GLM and two-class PDA analysis models (2c-CVA). Table 1 summarizes her greedy search results for the impact of several pipeline processing steps. Slice-timing correction (Step 1) has no significant impact regardless of analysis model. Within-subject motion correction (Step 2) significantly improves performance for 2c-CVA, but not for GLM because of the increased inter-subject heterogeneity. As expected spatial smoothing (Step 3), and high-pass temporal filtering (Step 4) of various sorts, all significantly improve performance, but with quite different subject heterogeneity depending on the analysis model and processing technique.

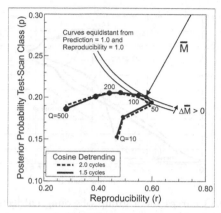

Fig. 1. NPAIRS split-half prediction (p) vs. rSPM(z) reproducibility (r) for an 11-class PDA model as a function of Q, and for a small change in low frequency temporal artefact removal: detrending with 1.5 vs. 2.0 cosine cycles per fMRI run. (Data from Strother et al. (2004)).

	Preprocessing steps	Data Analysis Model & Software	$\Delta\bar{M}$	Std. Dev.	$p = ^3$	$\Delta\bar{M}$ /(Std Dev)
1	Slice timing correction	GLM (NPAIRS)	-0.04	0.20	0.78	-0.21
		2c-CVA (NPAIRS)	0.07	0.20	0.14	0.36
2	Motion correction	GLM (NPAIRS)	-0.07	0.21	0.24	-0.34
		2c-CVA (NPAIRS)	0.08	0.094	0.00	0.85
3	Spatial smoothing	GLM (NPAIRS)	0.12	0.059	0.00	2.03
		2c-CVA (NPAIRS)	0.11	0.093	0.00	1.18
4	Temporal detrending	GLM (NPAIRS)	0.06	0.051	0.00	1.18
		2c-CVA (NPAIRS)	0.17	0.19	0.03	0.90
	High-pass filtering [1]	GLM (FSL)	0.04	0.049	0.00	0.82
	High-pass filtering [2]	2c-CVA (NPAIRS)	0.10	0.124	0.01	0.81

Table 1. Average change in optimal (p, r) curve distance from $(1, 1)$ (e.g., Fig. 1) for turning selected fMRI processing steps on and off across 16 subjects performing a parametric static force task (Zhang et al, (2008, 2009)). High-pass temporal filtering: detrending $\equiv$ removal of cosine cycles/run; [1]Sliding window running means. [2]Multi-Taper power spectrum. [3]Wilcoxon matched-pair per subject rank sum test

5 Measuring dimensionality

We generated 18 separate (p, r) curves from the multi-task, age-dependent data set acquired by Grady et al. (2006). The subjects belonged to three different age groups: young, middle-aged, and old. The experiment consisted of 6 separate task runs per subject of 4 memory encoding tasks (1-4), and 2 recognition tasks (5, 6). During the two recognition tasks, the subjects reported whether or not they recognized the presented stimulus. The BOLD fMRI was measured with a 1.5T MRI scanner. Standard image preprocessing was applied to the data. For each subject, one run was collected for every

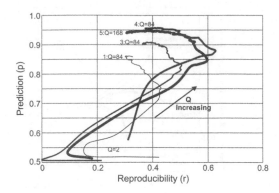

Fig. 2. NPAIRS (p, r) curves for a group of young subjects performing memory tasks: $1, 3, 4, 5. < Q$ is the regularizing PCA subspace of a PDA. (see text for details).

task (89 volumes for encoding tasks, and 166 volumes for recognition tasks). Each scan was described 50,308 voxels (for more details see Grady et al.).

Figure 2 shows example (p, r) curves for the 10 young subjects performing Tasks 1, 3, 4 and 5 and analyzed with a 2-class PDA to discriminate task from fixation scans. For each analysis the dimensionality of the 2nd-level PCA subspace on which the PDA was built ranged from $Q = 2$ to $Q = 84$ (Encoding tasks), and $Q = 168$ (Recognition tasks). At the largest values of Q, the PDA started to become unstable due to the large condition number (> 1000) of the within-class matrix $\mathbf{W}$.

The (p, r) curves in Fig. 2 display the same features as those in Fig. 1. For small values of increasing Q, both p and r increase until r is maximized at: Task 1, $Q = 24$; Task 3, $Q = 24$; Task 4, $Q = 12$; Task 5, $Q = 12$. In all cases p continues to rise with increasing Q, but r rapidly decreases as p is maximized at: Task 1, $Q = 76$; Task 3, $Q = 66$; Task 4, $Q = 64$; Task 5, $Q = 108$. We recorded the 18 values of Q that separately maximized r, p, and the Euclidean distance (M) from $(1, 1)$. These 54 values are plotted as a function of gSNR(r) in Figure 3. Here we see that dimensionality for optimum r (circle) and M (cross) values are often very similar, and fall on a curve with a vertical asymptote of gSNR $\simeq 1$ for $q >> 1$, and a horizontal asymptote with $Q \leq 20$ for gSNR ≥ 1.5. The horizontal asymptote with gSNR large enough (e.g., > 1.5) indicates that signal and noise eigenvalues are well separated in the eigenspectra of $\mathbf{X}_i^*$ (NPAIRS step 3), and occur in a relatively compact discrete subspace early in the PCA eigenspectrum. Conversely, the vertical asymptote indicates that as signal eigenvalues merge into the noise spectrum a phase transition occurs requiring large numbers of components from which to extract a discriminant signal, which is now relatively broadly distributed across many components of the PCA eigenspectrum.

This behavior matches recent analytic results from random matrix theory that indicate that such a phase transition occurs and is governed by the

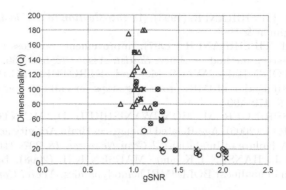

Fig. 3. For 18 NPAIRS (p, r) curves (Fig. 2) the PCA subspace size, Q, is plotted against gSNR(r) for optimal (1) prediction "$\triangle$", (2) reproducibility "O," and (3) Euclidean distance "X" (see Fig. 1). (see text for details)

ratio of variables (i.e., voxels) to observations (i.e., scans) for a particular signal strength. We have recently compared measurement of Q, across simulated and fMRI-data phase transitions with multiple dimensionality estimation approaches proposed in the literature (e.g., optimization of Bayesian evidence, Akaike information criterion, minimum description length, supervised and unsupervised prediction, and Stein's unbiased risk estimator: Yourganov et al., in press). None of the alternate approaches detect the phase transition indicating that they are suboptimal to obtain activation maps with $v \gg NT$.

Figure 3 shows that there is a shift of the distribution of Q values for maximum prediction towards higher dimensionality at a gSNR value of approximately 1. This suggests that irrespective of the underlying signal eigenstructure reflected in the possible gSNR (i.e., horizontal asymptote), optimal prediction tends to select a smaller gSNR with a solution typically built from a large number of PCA components. Examination of the associated rSPM(z) for maximum prediction shows that the reduced gSNR is partly a result of a reduced number of signal voxels (e.g., rSPM$(z) > 3$) compared to rSPM(z) for optimal reproducibility. We are exploring the possibly that this reflects the tendency for prediction to select low reliability voxel sets. It remains an unresolved and important issue whether or not optimal prediction based on preliminary voxel-based feature selection or recursive feature selection can detect highly reliable spatial patterns in neuroimaging. Our PDA results suggest that this may not be the case for linear multivariate models.

References

AFSHINPOUR B, HAMID S-Z, GHOLAM-ALI H-Z, GRADY C, and STROTHER SC. (In press). Mutual Information Based Metrics for Evaluation of fMRI Data Processing Approaches. *Hum Brain Mapp.*

EFRON B, and TIBSHIRANI R. (1993). *An Introduction to the Bootstrap*. London, U.K.: Chapman & Hall.

EFRON B, and TIBSHIRANI R. (1997). Improvements on cross-validation: The .632+ bootstrap method. *J. Amer. Statist. Assoc. 92*, 548–560.

EVANS JW, TODD RM, TAYLOR MJ, and STROTHER SC. (2010). Group specific optimisation of fMRI processing steps for child and adult data. *NeuroImage, 50*, 479–490.

GRADY C, SPRINGER M, HONGWANISHKUL D, MCINTOSH A, and WINOCUR G. (2006). Age-Related Changes in Brain Activity across the Adult Lifespan: A Failure of Inhibition? *J Cogn Neurosci, 18*, 227–241.

JACOBSEN D.J., HANSEN L.K. and MADSEN K.H. (2008): Bayesian model comparison in nonlinear BOLD fMRI hemodynamics. *Neural Comput, 20*, 738–55.

KJEMS U., HANSEN L.K., ANDERSON J., FRUTIGER S., MULEY S., SIDTIS J., ROTTENBERG D. and STROTHER S.C. (2002): The quantitative evaluation of functional neuroimaging experiments: mutual information learning curves. *NeuroImage, 15, 772–86*.

KUSTRA R. and STROTHER S.C. (2001). Penalized discriminant analysis of [15O]-water PET brain images with prediction error selection of smoothness and regularization hyperparameters. *IEEE Trans Med Imaging, 20, 376–87*.

LACONTE S., ANDERSON J., MULEY S., ASHE J., FRUTIGER S., REHM K., HANSEN L.K., YACOUB E., HU X., ROTTENBERG D. and STROTHER S. (2003): The evaluation of preprocessing choices in single-subject BOLD fMRI using NPAIRS performance metrics. *NeuroImage, 18, 10–27*.

MARDIA K.V., KENT J.T. and BIBBY J.M. (1979): *Multivariate Analysis*. San Diego: Academic Press.

PEREIRA F., MITCHELL T., and BOTVINICK M. (2009): Machine learning classifiers and fMRI: a tutorial overview. *NeuroImage, 45, 199–209*.

SCHMAH T., HINTON G., ZEMEL R.S., SMALL S.L., and STROTHER S.C. (2008): Generative versus discriminative training of RBMs for classification of fMRI images. *Neural Information Processing Systems*. Vancouver, Canada. p 1409–1416.

STROTHER S.C. (2006): Evaluating fMRI preprocessing pipelines. *IEEE Eng Med Biol Mag, 25, 27–41*.

STROTHER S.C., ANDERSON J., HANSEN L.K., KJEMS U., KUSTRA R., SIDTIS J., FRUTIGER S., MULEY S., LACONTE S. and ROTTENBERG D. (2002): The quantitative evaluation of functional neuroimaging experiments: the NPAIRS data analysis framework. *NeuroImage, 15, 747–71*.

STROTHER S.C., LA CONTE S., KAI HANSEN L., ANDERSON J., ZHANG J., PULAPURA S. and ROTTENBERG D. (2004): Optimizing the fMRI data-processing pipeline using prediction and reproducibility performance metrics: I. A preliminary group analysis. *NeuroImage, 23, 196–207*.

YOURGANOV G., XU C., LUKIC A., GRADY C., SMALL S., WERNICK M. and STROTHER S.C. (In press): Dimensionality estimation for optimal detection of functional networks in BOLD fMRI data. *NeuroImage*.

ZHANG J., ANDERSON J.R., LIANG L., PULAPURA S.K., GATEWOOD L., ROTTENBERG D.A. and STROTHER S.C. (2009): Evaluation and optimization of fMRI single-subject processing pipelines with NPAIRS and second-level CVA. *Magn Reson Imaging, 27, 264–78*.

Part V

Computational Econometrics

Bootstrap Prediction in Unobserved Component Models

Alejandro F. Rodríguez[1] and Esther Ruiz[1]

Departamento de Estaística, Universidad Carlos III de Madrid, 28903 Getafe (Madrid), Spain.

Abstract. One advantage of state space models is that they deliver estimates of the unobserved components and predictions of future values of the observed series and their corresponding Prediction Mean Squared Errors (PMSE). However, these PMSE are obtained by running the Kalman filter with the true parameters substituted by consistent estimates and, consequently, they do not incorporate the uncertainty due to parameter estimation. This paper reviews new bootstrap procedures to estimate the PMSEs of the unobserved states and to construct prediction intervals of future observations that incorporate parameter uncertainty and do not rely on particular assumptions of the error distribution. The new bootstrap PMSEs of the unobserved states have smaller biases than those obtained with alternative procedures. Furthermore, the prediction intervals have better coverage properties. The results are illustrate by obtaining prediction intervals of the quarterly mortgages changes and of the unobserved output gap in USA.

Keywords: NAIRU, output gap, parameter uncertainty, prediction intervals, state space models

1 Introduction

Unobserved component models have proven to be very useful for the description of the dynamic evolution of financial and economic time series; see, for example, the references in Durbin and Koopman (2001). One of the main advantages of these models is that they allow to obtain estimates of the underlying components which are often of interest in themselves. Furthermore, one may also obtain measures of the uncertainty associated with these estimates as their Prediction Mean Squared Errors (PMSE). The estimates of the underlying components and their PMSE can be obtained by using the Kalman filter with the true parameters substituted by consistent estimates and assuming Gaussian innovations. Furthermore, by running the Kalman filter, we can also obtain forecasts of future values of the observed series and their PMSE which can then be used to obtain prediction intervals. One limitation of this approach is that it does not incorporate the uncertainty due to parameter estimation and it relies on the Gaussianity assumption. This drawback can be overcome by using bootstrap procedures. In particular, Pfeffermann and Tiller (2005) proposed several bootstrap procedures to

Y. Lechevallier, G. Saporta (eds.), *Proceedings of COMPSTAT'2010*,
DOI 10.1007/978-3-7908-2604-3_11, © Springer-Verlag Berlin Heidelberg 2010

obtain the PMSE of the estimates of the unobserved states that incorporates the parameter uncertainty. However, their bootstrap procedures are based on obtaining unconditional PMSEs while the Kalman filter is designed to deliver conditional estimates of the components. In Rodríguez and Ruiz (2010), we propose new bootstrap procedures which simplifies those proposed by Pfeffermann and Tiller (2005) by taking into account that the filter is designed to deliver conditional estimates of the states and their PMSEs.

On the other hand, when dealing with prediction intervals for future values of the variables, Wall and Stoffer (2002) have also proposed using bootstrap procedures that incorporate the parameter uncertainty and are not based on any particular assumption on the error distribution. However, the procedure proposed by Wall and Stoffer (2002) relies on the backward representation which implies important limitations from the computational point of view. Furthermore, the procedure is restricted to models in which such representation exists. Consequently, Rodríguez and Ruiz (2009) propose a new bootstrap procedure to construct prediction intervals that does not require the backward representation.

In this paper, we revise the main bootstrap procedures proposed to obtain prediction intervals of the unobserved components and future observations in the context of the random walk plus noise model. We show that they deliver PMSEs of the unobserved components with smaller biases and prediction intervals with better coverage properties than those obtained with alternative procedures. Finally, the results are illustrated by obtaining prediction intervals of quarterly mortgages changes and of the unobserved output gap in USA.

The rest of the paper is organized a follows. Section 2 describes the random walk plus noise model and the Kalman filter. Sections 3 and 4 describe the bootstrap procedures proposed for PMSE of the unobserved components and prediction intervals of future observations respectively. The empirical applications appear in Section 5. Section 6 concludes the paper.

2   The random walk plus noise model and the Kalman filter

We consider the univariate local level or random walk plus noise model which has often be successfully considered to represent the dynamic evolution of many macroeconomic and financial time series; see. for example, Stock and Watson (2007) for an application to inflation. The local level model is given by

$$y_t = \mu_t + \varepsilon_t, \qquad (1)$$
$$\mu_t = \mu_{t-1} + \eta_t, \quad t = 1, \ldots, T$$

where ε_t and η_t are mutually independent white noises with variances σ_ε^2 and σ_η^2 respectively, and T is the sample size. The Kalman filter equations to estimate the underlying level, μ_t, and their corresponding PMSE are given by

$$m_{t+1|t} = m_{t|t-1} + \frac{P_{t/t-1} + \sigma_\eta^2}{P_{t/t-1} + \sigma_\eta^2 + \sigma_\varepsilon^2} \nu_t \tag{2}$$

$$P_{t+1|t} = (P_{t|t-1} + \sigma_\eta^2)\left(1 - \frac{P_{t/t-1} + \sigma_\eta^2}{P_{t/t-1} + \sigma_\eta^2 + \sigma_\varepsilon^2}\right),$$

where ν_t are the one-step ahead prediction errors or innovations, given by $\nu_t = y_t - m_{t/t-1}$; see Harvey (1989) for the starting values of the Kalman filter in (2).

Then, assuming conditional Gaussianity, the within-sample prediction intervals for the underlying levels are given by the following expression

$$\left[m_{t+1|t} \pm z_{1-\alpha/2}\sqrt{P_{t+1|t}}\right], \ t = 1, \ldots, T \tag{3}$$

where where $z_{1-\alpha/2}$ is the $\left(1 - \frac{\alpha}{2}\right)$-percentile of the Standard Normal distribution.

Assuming that future prediction errors are Gaussian, the k-step ahead prediction intervals for y_{T+k} are given by

$$\left[\tilde{y}_{T+k|T} - z_{1-\alpha/2}\sqrt{F_{T+k|T}}, \ \tilde{y}_{T+k|T} + z_{1-\alpha/2}\sqrt{F_{T+k|T}}\right], \tag{4}$$

where $\tilde{y}_{T+k|T}$ and $F_{T+k|T}$ are the k-steps ahead prediction of y_{T+k} and its PMSE given by

$$\tilde{y}_{T+k|T} = m_T, \tag{5}$$
$$F_{T+k|T} = P_{T/T-1} + (k+1)\sigma_\eta^2 + \sigma_\varepsilon^2, \ \ k = 1, 2, \ldots$$

Although, the random walk plus noise model in (1) has several disturbances, it is also possible to represent it in what is known as the Innovation Form (IF) which has a unique disturbance, ν_t. The IF, which will be very useful for the implementation of the bootstrap procedures described later in this paper, is given by the first equation in (2) together with

$$y_{t+1} = m_{t+1|t} + \nu_{t+1}. \tag{6}$$

The estimates of the underlying levels and their corresponding PMSE in (2) and the predictions in (5) are obtained assuming known parameters. However, in practice, the parameters are unknown and have to be substituted by consistent estimates, for example, Quasi Maximum Likelihood (QML) estimates. In this case, both the PMSE of the unobserved levels and future observations and, consequently, the corresponding prediction intervals in (3) and (4) do not take into in account the uncertainty caused by parameter estimation.

3   PMSE of unobserved components

Rodríguez and Ruiz (2010) propose to implement a very simple bootstrap procedure to obtain PMSE of the Kalman filter estimator of the underlying component. Denote by $\widehat{m}_{t/t-1}$ and $\widehat{P}_{t/t-1}$ the estimates of the state and their PMSE obtained as in (2) with the unknown parameters substituted by their QML estimates. First of all, it is important to realize that although $P_{t/t-1}$ is the PMSE of $m_{t/t-1}$, $\widehat{P}_{t/t-1}$ is not the PMSE of $\widehat{m}_{t/t-1}$ because it does not incorporate the parameter uncertainty of the latter. Note that the conditional PMSE of $\widehat{m}_{t/t-1}$ can be decomposed as follows

$$PMSE(\widehat{m}_{t/t-1}) = \underset{\theta}{E}\left\{\underset{t-1}{E}\left[(\widehat{m}_{t/t-1} - m_{t/t-1})^2|\theta\right]\right\} + \underset{\theta}{E}\left\{\underset{t-1}{E}\left[(m_{t/t-1} - \mu_t)^2|\theta\right]\right\} \tag{7}$$

where θ is the vector of unknown parameters. The PMSE in (7) can be approximated by generating bootstrap replicates of the parameters and taking the expectations along all these bootstrap replicates. In particular, the procedure proposed by Rodríguez and Ruiz (2010) consists on the following steps:

1) Estimate the parameters by QML, $\widehat{\theta}$, and compute the corresponding estimates of the innovations, $\widehat{\nu}_t$. Obtain a bootstrap replicate of the innovations $(\nu_1^*, ..., \nu_T^*)$ by resampling with replacement from the standardized innovations.

2) Construct a bootstrap replicate of the series as follows

$$y_t^* = m_{t|t-1}^* + \nu_t^* \tag{8}$$

$$m_{t|t-1}^* = m_{t-1|t-2}^* + \frac{P_{t-1/t-2}^* + \widehat{\sigma}_\eta^2}{P_{t-1/t-2}^* + \widehat{\sigma}_\eta^2 + \widehat{\sigma}_\varepsilon^2}\nu_t$$

and estimate the parameters by QML, $\widehat{\theta}^*$.

3) Using the bootstrap estimates of the parameters and the original observations, run again the Kalman filter to obtain a bootstrap replicate of the underlying level, $(\widehat{m}_{1/0}^*, ..., \widehat{m}_{T/T-1}^*)$ and the corresponding $(\widehat{P}_{1/0}^*, ..., \widehat{P}_{T/T-1}^*)$.

After repeating steps (1) to (3) a large number B of times, the bootstrap PMSE is given by

$$PMSE_{t/t-1}^* = \frac{1}{B}\sum_{j=1}^{B}\widehat{P}_{t/t-1}^{*(j)} + \frac{1}{B}\sum_{j=1}^{B}(\widehat{m}_{t/t-1}^{*(j)} - \widehat{m}_{t/t-1})^2. \tag{9}$$

To illustrate the performance of the bootstrap PMSE in (9), Figure 1 plots the Monte Carlo averages of the relative biases of the bootstrap procedure proposed by Rodríguez and Ruiz (2010) to estimate the PMSE of $\widehat{m}_{t/t-1}$ together with the biases obtained when the Kalman filter is run with estimated parameters or when the asymptotic approximation of the parameters as proposed by Hamilton (1986) is implemented or when implementing the bootstrap procedure proposed by Pfeffermann and Tiller (2005). Figure 1 illustrates that the biases in the estimation of the PMSE of the unobserved components is clearly reduced when implementing the procedure proposed by Rodríguez and Ruiz (2010).

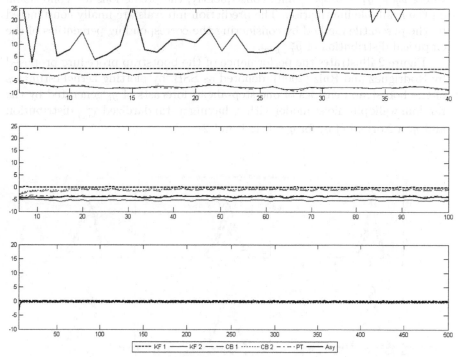

Fig. 1. Monte Carlo averages of the ratios $d_t = 100 \times \left(\frac{P_{t|t-1}}{PMSE_t} - 1 \right)$ for the RWN model with homoscedastic Gaussian error and $T = 40$ (first row), $T = 100$ (second row) and $T = 500$ (third row).

4   Prediction intervals of future observations

Rodríguez and Ruiz (2009) propose to construct prediction intervals for y_{T+k} by approximating directly its distribution using a bootstrap procedure. The procedure proposed is not based on the backward representation and, consequently, is much simpler than other alternative bootstrap procedures previously proposed in the literature as, for example, Wall and Stoffer (2002). The procedure proposed by Rodríguez and Ruiz (2009) consists on generating bootstrap replicates of the parameters as described in steps 1 and 2 of the previous section. Then, bootstrap replicates of future values of y_t are obtained as follows

$$\widehat{y}^*_{T+k/T} = \widehat{m}^*_{T|T-1} + \sum_{j=1}^{k-1} \widehat{K}^*_{T+j} F^{*-1}_{T+j} \nu^*_{T+j} + \nu^*_{T+k}$$

where $\nu^*_T = y_T - \widehat{m}^*_{T|T-1}$ and, consequently, the predictions are conditional on the available information. The prediction intervals are finally constructed by the percentile method by considering the corresponding percentiles of the empirical distribution of $\widehat{y}^*_{T+k/T}$.

Figure 2 illustrates the performance of the bootstrap procedure proposed by Rodríguez and Ruiz (2009), denoted as SSB, by plotting kernel estimates of the bootstrap densities of one-step-ahead forecasts of y_t generated by the random walk plus noise model with ε_t having a standardized $\chi^2_{(1)}$ distribution and η_t a Normal $(1,q)$ for $q = 0.1$, 1 and 2.

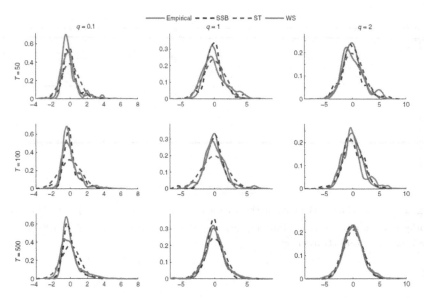

Fig. 2. Kernel estimates densities of y_{T+k} for $k = 1$. $\chi^2_{(1)}$ case.

Figure 2, which also plots the empirical conditional density of y_t and the densities obtained by using the standard Kalman filter based on assuming Gaussian errors, denoted as ST, and the bootstrap procedure proposed by Wall and Stoffer (2002), denoted as SW, shows that the density obtained with the SSB bootstrap procedure, is closer to the empirical mainly when the signal-to-noise ratio, q, is small and the sample size is large.

5   Empirical applications

5.1   Estimation of the NAIRU

In this subsection, we consider to implement the bootstrap procedure proposed by Rodríguez and Ruiz (2010) to estimate the PMSE associated with the NAIRU of US using quarterly data of the unemployment rate observed from 1948 Q1 until 2003 Q1; see Doménech and Gómez (2006) for details about the unobserved components model and the interest of analyzing the NAIRU. Figure 3 plots the observed rate of unemployment together the 90% confidence bounds of the unobserved NAIRU obtained using the PMSE given by the Kalman filter implemented with estimated parameters and the bootstrap PMSE. Figure 3 shows that the confidence intervals obtained using the bootstrap PMSE are clearly wider than the standard intervals. Furthermore, the unemployment rate is always within the bootstrap intervals but it is clearly out of the standard intervals in some periods of time. The fact that the unemployment rate is outsides the intervals of the NAIRU has been interpreted by some authors as the ability of the NAIRU to identify economic recessions; see Doménech and Gómez (2006). However, one the parameter uncertainty is taken into account, it seems that the NAIRU has not any ability as an indicator of economic recessions.

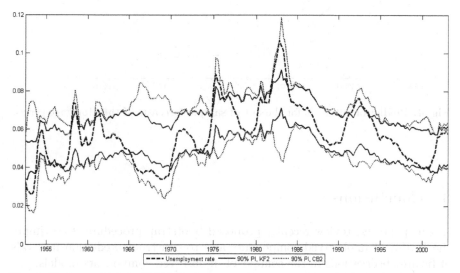

Fig. 3. Estimated of the NAIRU, the unemployment rate and prediction intervals.

5.2   Prediction of mortgage changes

In this subsection, we consider to illustrate the bootstrap procedure proposed by Rodríguez and Ruiz (2009) by constructing prediction intervals of future values of quarterly mortgages change in US's home equity debt outstanding, unscheduled payments. The data has been observed from Q1 1991 to Q1 2001 (estimation period) and from Q2 2001 to Q2 2007 (out-of-sample forecast period). Figure 4 plots the 95% prediction intervals obtained by using the standard Kalman filter and the bootstrap intervals obtained using the procedures proposed by Wall and Stoffer (2002) and by Rodríguez and Ruiz (2009). We can observe that both bootstrap intervals are very similar and clearly wider than the standard intervals that do not incorporate the parameter uncertainty. Furthermore, observe that 2 observations are not included in the standard intervals while they are contained in the bootstrap intervals.

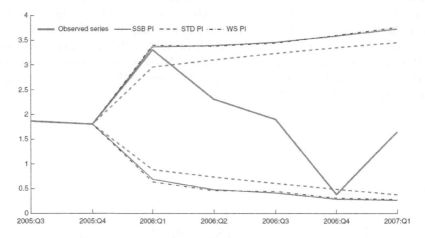

Fig. 4. Prediction intervals for the out of sample forecasts of the Mortgage series.

6   Conclusions

In this paper we review recently proposed bootstrap procedures to estimate the PMSE of unobserved components and to construct prediction intervals of future observations in the context of unobserved components models.

We show, by Monte Carlo experiments an empirical applications, that the bootstrap procedure proposed by Rodríguez and Ruiz (2010) to estimate the PMSE of the estimates of the underlying states obtained using the Kalman filter with estimated parameters has a clearly better behavior than alternative procedures previously available in the literature. Furthermore, in an empirical application, it is shown that incorporating the parameter uncertainty of the estimated unobserved components into their PMSEs may have important implications for the conclusions about the behavior of the underlying components.

We also show that the bootstrap procedure proposed by Rodríguez and Ruiz (2009) to construct prediction intervals of future observations improves over previous procedures in three ways:

1) It obtains in one-step the density of predictions, simplifying the computations

2) It does not rely on the backward representation so it can be extended to models without such representation

3) It allows the state to vary among bootstrap replicates incorporating a further source of uncertainty.

References

DOMÉNECH, R. and GÓMEZ, V. (2006): Estimating potential output, core inflation, and the NAIRU as latent variables. *Journal of Business and Economic Statistics 24, 354–365.*

DURBIN, J. and KOOPMAN, S.J. (2001): *Time Series Analysis by State Space Methods.* New York: Oxford University Press.

HAMILTON, J.D. (1986): A standard error for the estimated state vector of a state-space model. *Journal of Econometrics 33, 387–397.*

HARVEY, A. (1989): *Forecasting, Structural Time Series Models and the Kalman Filter.* Cambridge: Cambridge University Press.

PFEFFERMANN, D. and TILLER, R. (2005): Bootstrap approximation to prediction MSE for State-Space models with estimated parameters. *Journal of Time Series Analysis 26, 893–916.*

RODRÍGUEZ, A. and RUIZ, E. (2009): Bootstrap prediction intervals in State-Space models. *Journal of Time Series Analysis 30, 167–178.*

RODRÍGUEZ, A. and RUIZ, E. (2010): Bootstrap prediction mean squared errors of unobserved states based on the Kalman filter with estimated parameters. *WP 10-03(01), Universidad Carlos III de Madrid.*

STOCK, J.H. and WATSON, M.W. (2007): Why has U.S. inflation become harder to forecast? *Journal of Money Credit and Banking 39, 3–33.*

WALL, K.D. and STOFFER, D.S. (2002): A State Space approach to bootstrapping conditional forecasts in ARMA models, *Journal of Time Series Analysis, 23, 733–751.*

Part VI

Computer-Intensive Actuarial Methods

A Numerical Approach to Ruin Models with Excess of Loss Reinsurance and Reinstatements [*]

Hansjörg Albrecher[1] and Sandra Haas[2]

[1] Department of Actuarial Science, Faculty of Business and Economics,
University of Lausanne,
email: hansjoerg.albrecher@unil.ch
[2] Department of Actuarial Science, Faculty of Business and Economics,
University of Lausanne,
email: sandra.haas@unil.ch

Abstract. The present paper studies some computational challenges for the determination of the probability of ruin of an insurer, if excess of loss reinsurance with reinstatements is applied. In the setting of classical risk theory, a contractive integral operator is studied whose fixed point is the ruin probability of the cedent. We develop and implement a recursive algorithm involving high-dimensional integration to obtain a numerical approximation of this quantity. Furthermore we analyze the effect of different starting functions and recursion depths on the performance of the algorithm and compare the results with the alternative of stochastic simulation of the risk process.

Keywords: reinsurance, integral operator, ruin probability, high-dimensional integration

1 Introduction

Excess of loss (XL) reinsurance contracts are widely used in insurance practice and many results on optimal reinsurance schemes under different premium principles and objective functions can be found in the literature (for a survey, see for instance Albrecher & Teugels (2010)). In practice, the reinsurer rarely offers a pure excess of loss contract, but adds clauses, such as limiting his aggregate liability or adding reinstatements. Clauses limiting the aggregate claims of the reinsurer and its effects are well understood from a theoretical perspective. On the other hand, although reinstatements are quite common in practice (in particular for casualty insurance), literature dealing with a rigorous and quantitative approach to the subject is scarce. The main focus of the existing literature is on the calculation of premiums for these contracts under different premium principles, see e.g. Sundt (1991) for an early reference.

[*] Supported by the Swiss National Science Foundation Project 200021-124635/1.

Y. Lechevallier, G. Saporta (eds.), *Proceedings of COMPSTAT'2010*,
DOI 10.1007/978-3-7908-2604-3_12, © Springer-Verlag Berlin Heidelberg 2010

Mata (2000) studied the joint distribution for consecutive layers with rein-statements and applied the PH transform to calculate the premiums for free and paid reinstatements. For the discrete case, Walhin and Paris (2000) de-rived a multivariate Panjer's algorithm in order to approximate the resulting compound claim distribution for the cedent. A distribution-free approxima-tion in a market with incomplete information was given by Hürlimann (2005). Hess and Schmidt (2004) determine an optimal premium plan for reinsurance contracts with reinstatements by minimizing the expected squared difference between the loss and the premium income of the reinsurer.

In terms of effects of reinstatements on the solvency of the cedent, Wal-hin and Paris (2001) calculated the probability of ruin in a discrete-time risk model using recursive methods.

The goal in this paper is to determine the probability of ruin in a continuous-time risk model. Since one cannot expect analytical solutions for the resulting complicated dynamics, numerical techniques have to be applied. We will for-mulate a contractive integral operator whose fixed point is the required ruin probability in this model. Iterative application of this integral operator will lead to a high-dimensional integration problem to approximate the exact so-lutions. We investigate the feasibility of such an approach and illustrate the procedure with numerical results for exponentially distributed claim sizes based on an expected value principle for the calculation of the premiums. Fi-nally, we compare the results with approximations obtained from stochastic simulation of the underlying risk process.

2   XL reinsurance with reinstatements

Let the independent and identically distributed random variables X_i ($i = 1, \ldots, N_t$) denote individual claim sizes in an insurance portfolio, where the random variable N_t is the number of claims up to time t. N_t is assumed to be Poisson distributed with parameter λ, and X_i and N_t are independent. The surplus process of the insurance portfolio at time t in the classical risk model is defined by

$$R(t) = u + \beta t - \sum_{i=1}^{N_t} X_i,$$

where u is the initial capital of the cedent and β is the gross premium income per time unit.

Let $T_u = \inf\{t : R(t) < 0\}$ denote the time of ruin and $\psi(u) = \mathbb{P}(T_u < \infty)$ the infinite time ruin probability. The finite time ruin probability is defined by $\psi(u, T) = \mathbb{P}(T_u < T)$.

In a plain excess of loss contract with retention l, the reinsurer covers the part of each claim that exceeds l. In practice the reinsurer usually limits the covered part by an upper bound $l + m$, such that the reinsurer's part Z_i and the cedent's part C_i, respectively, are

$$Z_i = \begin{cases} 0, & X_i \le l \\ X_i - l, & l \le X_i \le l + m \\ m, & X_i \ge l + m \end{cases} \text{ and } C_i = \begin{cases} X_i, & X_i \le l \\ l, & l \le X_i \le l + m \\ X_i - m, & X_i \ge l + m \end{cases}.$$

The aggregate cover of the reinsurer up to time t is then $Z = Z(t) = \sum_{i=1}^{N_t} Z_i$. In addition, the reinsurer often limits this aggregate liability to an amount M, which usually is an integer multiple of the individual maximum cover, i.e. $M = (k+1)m$. In this case the reinsurer is said to offer k reinstatements. Under this setting, the reinsurer's part becomes $R_k = \min(Z, (k+1)m)$ and the cover of the j-th reinstatement is therefore $r_j = \min(\max(Z - jm, 0), m)$.

In this paper we assume a pro-rata-capita concept: At the beginning of the XL reinsurance contract the cedent pays an initial premium p_0 for the reinsurance cover $r_0 = \min(Z, m)$. If a claim X_i occurs which uses up part of the cover, the cover is reinstated and the cedent pays at this moment an additional premium P_j to reinstate the used up part of the layer. This premium is a multiple of the fraction of the cover used up of the last reinstatement r_{j-1}:

$$P_j = \frac{p_0 c}{m} \min(\max(Z - (j-1)m, 0), m),$$

where $c > 0$ is a percentage of the initial premium p_0.
Therefore it can happen that multiple claims use up one reinstated layer, but also that one claim uses two reinstatements ($r_{j'-1}$ and $r_{j'}$) partly. In this case the charged premium for the reinstatement of the cover is the sum of $P_{j'}$ and $P_{j'+1}$. For a numerical illustration of this procedure see e.g. Mata (2000).
The surplus process of the cedent is

$$R_{XL}(t) = u - p_0 + \beta t - \sum_{i=1}^{N_t} C_i - P_{XL}(t),$$

where $P_{XL}(t)$ is the amount of reinstatement premiums paid up to time t. The total amount of charged reinstatement premiums at the end of the period of cover is therefore $p_0 \left(1 + \frac{c}{m} \sum_{i=1}^{k} \min(\max(Z - (k-1)m, 0), m)\right)$. The resulting ruin probability is denoted by $\psi_{XL}(u, T)$.

In Albrecher et al. (2010) it is shown that the ruin probability is the fixed point of the following contractive integral operator.

$$\mathcal{A}h(u, y, T) = \int_0^T \lambda \exp(-\lambda t) \int_0^{x^*(u,y,t)} h\left(u + \beta t - x + l(x,y)_k - \frac{cp_0}{m} l(x,y)_{k-1}, \right.$$

$$\left. y + l(x,y)_k, T - t\right) dF_{X_i}(x) dt + \int_0^T \lambda \exp(-\lambda t) \int_{x^*(u,y,t)}^{\infty} 1 dF_{X_i}(x) dt,$$

where the following definitions are used:

- T is the observation period and t is the realization of the exponential inter-claim time.
- x denotes the occurred claim size and y is the reinsurance cover already used up,
- $x^*(u, y, t)$ is the solution (w.r.t. x) of

$$u + \beta t - x + l(x, y)_k - \frac{cp_0}{m} l(x, y)_{k-1} = 0, \tag{1}$$

with

$$\text{layer} = \min\left(\max\left(x - l, 0\right), m\right),$$
$$l(x, y)_k = \min\left(\text{layer}, (k+1)m - y\right).$$

Indeed, the operator $\mathcal{A}h$ is a contraction, because

$$\|\mathcal{A}h_1(u, y, t) - \mathcal{A}h_2(u, y, t)\|_\infty =$$
$$\left\| \int_0^T \lambda \exp(-\lambda t) \int_0^{x^*(u,y,t)} \left(h_1(k(u, y, t)) - h_2(k(u, y, t))\right) dF_{X_i}(x) dt \right\|_\infty$$
$$\leq \|h_1 - h_2\|_\infty \int_0^T \lambda \exp(-\lambda t) dt$$
$$= \|h_1 - h_2\|_\infty \cdot (1 - \exp(-\lambda T)),$$

where $k(u, y, t) = \left(u + \beta t - x + l(x, y)_k - \frac{cp_0}{m} l(x, y)_{k-1}, y + l(x, y)_k, T - t\right).$

To get an approximation for the ruin probability, the main idea is now to iterate the operator $\mathcal{A}$ d times on some starting function $h^{(0)}(u, y, t)$, i.e.

$$h^{(d)}(u, y, t) = \mathcal{A}^d h^{(0)}(u, y, t)$$

and evaluate the resulting $2d$-dimensional integral by Monte Carlo techniques. The appropriate choice of the starting function is discussed in Section 4.

3   A recursive algorithm for the numerical solution

In the following, we consider exponentially distributed claim sizes (parameter γ). Then the operator can be written as

$$\mathcal{A}h(u, y, T) = \int_0^T \lambda \exp(-\lambda t) \int_0^{x^*(u,y,t)} h\left(u + \beta t - x + l(x, y)_k - \frac{cp_0}{m} l(x, y)_{k-1},\right.$$
$$\left. y + l(x, y)_k, T - t\right) \gamma \exp(-\gamma x) dx dt$$
$$+ \int_0^T \lambda \exp(-\lambda t) \int_{x^*(u,y,t)}^\infty \gamma \exp(-\gamma x) dx dt,$$

To apply Monte Carlo methods in an effective way, we first transform the integration domain of the operator to the unit cube by applying the techniques of Albrecher et al. (2003) to the present set-up. This results in

$$\mathcal{A}h(u,y,T) = (1 - \exp(-\lambda T)) \int_0^1 \int_0^1 (1 - \exp(-\gamma x^*(u,y,t)))$$

$$h\left(u + \beta t - x + l(x,y)_k - \frac{cp_0}{m}l(x,y)_{k-1}, y + l(x,y)_k, T - t\right) dvdw$$

$$+ (1 - \exp(-\lambda T)) \int_0^1 \int_0^1 \exp(-\gamma x^*(u,y,t))dvdw.$$

Here t and x are defined by

$$\begin{aligned} t &= -\frac{\log(1-w(1-\exp(-\lambda T)))}{\lambda} \\ x &= -\frac{\log(1-v(1-\exp(-\gamma x^*(u,y,t))))}{\gamma} \end{aligned} \tag{2}$$

and $x^*(u,y,t)$ is the solution of equation (1) and can be calculated in every iteration step.

The integral operator is now applied d times onto $h^{(0)}(u,y,t)$ and the resulting multidimensional integral $h^{(d)}(u,y,t)$ is approximated by the Monte-Carlo estimate

$$h^{(d)}(u,y,t) \approx \frac{1}{N} \sum_{n=1}^{N} h_n^{(d)}(u,y,t), \tag{3}$$

where each $h_n^{(d)}(u,y,t)$ is based on a random point $\mathbf{x}_n \in [0,1]^{2d}$ (note that d will usually be quite large) and calculated by the recursion

$$\begin{aligned} h_n^{(0)}(u,y,t) &= h^{(0)}(u,y,t) \\ h_n^{(i)}(u,y,t) &= (1 - \exp(-\lambda t))(1 - \exp(-\gamma x^*(u,y,t_n^i))) \\ &\quad \cdot h_n^{(i-1)}\left(u + \beta t_n^i - x_n^i + l(x_n^i,y)_k - \frac{cp_0}{m}l(x_n^i,y)_{k-1}, y + l(x_n^i,y)_k, \right. \\ &\qquad\qquad \left. t - t_n^i\right) \\ &\quad + (1 - \exp(-\lambda t)) \exp(-\gamma x^*(u,y,t_n^i)). \end{aligned} \tag{4}$$

Here t_n^i and x_n^i are determined according to equation (2) for random deviates v and w of the uniform distribution in the unit interval.

4   Numerical illustrations

The recursive algorithm in formula (4) is implemented in Mathematica. It is essential that $\frac{cp_0}{m}l(x_n^i,y)_{k-1}$ is always larger or equal to 0, in order to avoid negative premiums. Therefore $\frac{cp_0}{m} \max\left(l(x_n^i,y)_{k-1},0\right)$ instead of purely $\frac{cp_0}{m}l(x_n^i,y)_{k-1}$ is used in the implementation.

We now illustrate the performance of the resulting algorithm for the parameters $\lambda = 10$, $\gamma = \frac{1}{5}$. Further, the security loading of the cedent is assumed to be $\alpha_{ced} = 0.2$ and of the reinsurer $\alpha_{re} = 0.3$. Both the cedent's premium and the reinsurance premium are determined by the expected value principle. Additionally, the initial capital of the cedent is assumed to be $u = 40$ and the covered layer within each reinstatement is $[l, l + m] = [6, 6 + 15]$. The reinsurance contract covers one year, i.e. $T = 1$.

The MC estimates are obtained using $N = 75000$, the confidence intervals are calculated to the level 95% and for the recursion depth we use three different choices ($d = 20$, $d = 35$ and $d = 70$) to assess the effect of the recursion depth on the performance. Consequently we generate up to 140-dimensional random numbers $\mathbf{x}_n$.

The random numbers are generated using the default algorithm `ExtendedCA` in `Mathematica 6.0`, which uses cellular automata to generate high-quality pseudo-random numbers. This generator uses a particular five-neighbor rule, so each new cell depends on five nonadjacent cells from the previous step.

We first choose the trivial starting function $h^{(0)} = h^{(0)}(u, y, t) = 0$, if $u \geq 0$. For $u < 0$ we set $h^{(0)} = h^{(0)}(u, y, t) = 1$. The following table shows the effect of excess of loss reinsurance (without reinstatements, but an upper coverage limit of 15) on the probability of ruin for $d = 70$. So in this case the

Ruin Probability without reinsurance	
$\psi(u, 1)$ using formula (5):	0.052907
Ruin Probability with reinsurance	
$\psi_{XL}(u, 1)$: 0.045820	Confidence interval: [0.044790, 0.046851]

Table 1. Effects of the excess of loss reinsurance on the probability of ruin

classical excess of loss reinsurance layer $[6, 21]$ (i.e. no additional reinstatements are available after the consumption of the reinsurance cover) improves the probability of ruin by 13%. If we now introduce reinstatement clauses in the reinsurance contract, this is also mostly an improvement over the case without reinsurance, but depending on the value of c (and hence the premiums for the additional reinstatement layers) the resulting situation can be more risky than without reinstatements. The following tables summarize the

$\psi_{XL}(u, 1)$ with $c = 0.$:	0.024310	Confidence interval: [0.023542, 0.025078]
$\psi_{XL}(u, 1)$ with $c = 0.5$:	0.029833	Confidence interval: [0.028979, 0.030686]
$\psi_{XL}(u, 1)$ with $c = 1.$:	0.033785	Confidence interval: [0.032877, 0.034694]
$\psi_{XL}(u, 1)$ with $c = 1.5$:	0.036809	Confidence interval: [0.035860, 0.037758]

Table 2. Effects of $k = 1$ reinstatements on the probability of ruin

probabilities of ruin of the cedent and the corresponding confidence intervals for different combinations of offered reinstatements k and charged premium percentages c. From Table 2 and 3 one sees that the ruin probability is not

$\psi_{XL}(u,1)$ with $c = 0.$: 0.014954	Confidence interval: [0.014319, 0.015589]
$\psi_{XL}(u,1)$ with $c = 0.5$: 0.032902	Confidence interval: [0.031982, 0.033821]
$\psi_{XL}(u,1)$ with $c = 1.$: 0.046573	Confidence interval: [0.045498, 0.047648]
$\psi_{XL}(u,1)$ with $c = 1.5$: 0.055864	Confidence interval: [0.054701, 0.057027]

Table 3. Effects of $k = 3$ reinstatements on the probability of ruin

monotone in k, i.e. an increase of the number of reinstatements does not automatically decrease $\psi(u)$. This comes from the balance between reduced risk due to higher reinsurance cover, but at the same time higher costs for the reinsurance premiums. In a straight-forward implementation of the recursion algorithm, each value given above needs approximately 1 hour computation time on a standard PC (this can certainly be improved by a more efficient vector implementation, but note also that the reinstatement clauses entail a lot of algebraic operations in each integration run). It is natural to ask whether a reduction of the recursion depth d (which obviously will decrease the computation time) can be afforded in this method in terms of accuracy. Table 4 shows indeed that for $d = 35$ the obtained results are very similar to those calculated with recursion depth $d = 70$ (and the computation time is approximately halved). One observes that for an increasing number of rein-

	$k = 1$	confidence interval	$k = 3$	confidence interval
$c = 0.$	0.023953	[0.023192, 0.024715]	0.014829	[0.014203, 0.015455]
$c = 0.5$	0.029335	[0.028491, 0.030179]	0.032423	[0.031506, 0.033340]
$c = 1$	0.033265	[0.032365, 0.034165]	0.045881	[0.044811, 0.046951]
$c = 1.5$	0.036260	[0.035320, 0.037200]	0.055094	[0.053936, 0.056252]

Table 4. The probability of ruin using a recursion depth of $d = 35$

statements k and fixed c, the difference between the results using $d = 70$ and $d = 35$ becomes smaller.

As Table 5 shows, a further decrease of recursion depth to $d = 20$ still leads to comparable results, but the third digit now is not accurate and it will depend on the concrete application whether this reduced accuracy is still acceptable. In absence of analytical solutions, we compare these results with simulated ruin probabilities using stochastic simulation of surplus paths of the underlying risk process according to the compound Poisson dynamics. Table 6 depicts the ruin probabilities for several combinations of k and c (in each case, the estimate is based on 500,000 simulation runs). The ruin probabilities (and corresponding confidence intervals) obtained by the recursive numerical method above are observed to nicely match the values obtained by simulation (as long as d is chosen sufficiently high) in the sense that the

	$k = 1$	confidence interval	$k = 3$	confidence interval
$c = 0.$	0.023648	[0.022898, 0.024397]	0.014474	[0.013848, 0.015099]
$c = 0.5$	0.029160	[0.028323, 0.029997]	0.032555	[0.031638, 0.033472]
$c = 1$	0.033178	[0.032283, 0.034073]	0.046310	[0.045235, 0.047384]
$c = 1.5$	0.036142	[0.035206, 0.037078]	0.055580	[0.054418, 0.056743]

Table 5. The probability of ruin using a recursion depth of $d = 20$

	$k = 1$	confidence interval	$k = 3$	confidence interval
$c = 0.$	0.024016	[0.023587, 0.024446]	0.015116	[0.014775, 0.015457]
$c = 0.5$	0.029784	[0.029306, 0.030262]	0.032588	[0.032088, 0.033088]
$c = 1$	0.033298	[0.032792, 0.033804]	0.045988	[0.045394, 0.046582]
$c = 1.5$	0.036634	[0.036104, 0.037165]	0.055636	[0.054982, 0.056290]

Table 6. The probability of ruin using the simulation of the risk process

obtained estimate is then usually in the simulation confidence interval.

In the following we investigate whether a more sophisticated starting function $h^{(0)}(u, y, t)$ leads to significantly improved results. A natural choice for a better starting function are the infinite and finite time ruin probability without reinsurance, $\psi(u)$ and $\psi(u, t)$. Since the claim size distribution is exponential (parameter γ), there exist closed-form expressions for the latter, namely $\psi(u) = \frac{\lambda}{\gamma\beta} \exp\left(-u\left(\gamma - \frac{\lambda}{\beta}\right)\right)$ and

$$\psi(u, t) = 1 - \exp(-\gamma u - (1 + \tau)\lambda t)g(\gamma u + \tau\lambda t, \lambda t), \tag{5}$$

where $\tau = \gamma\beta/\lambda$ and

$$g(z, \theta) = J(\theta z) + \theta J^{(1)}(\theta z) + \int_0^z \exp(z - v)J(\theta v)dv$$
$$- \frac{1}{\tau} \int_0^{\tau\theta} \exp(\tau\theta - v)J(z\tau^{-1}v)dv,$$

with $J(x) = I_0(2\sqrt{x})$ and $I_0(x)$ denotes the modified Bessel function (see e.g. Rolski et al. (1999)).

Table 7 gives the resulting ruin probabilities for $c = 100\%$ and recursion depths $d = 35$ and $d = 20$.

One can see from Table 7 that this new choice of $h^{(0)}(u, y, t)$ improves the performance of the algorithm in terms of d, i.e. a lower number of recursion steps (and hence a faster algorithm) already gives satisfying results.

One observes that for the starting function $h^{(0)}(u, y, t) = \psi(u)$ a recursion depth of $d = 20$ leads to slightly over-estimated values for the ruin probability. Increasing d and using the finite time ruin probability $\psi(u, t)$ as the starting function significantly improves these results. Note that the resulting ruin probabilities for this starting function and $d = 20$ are closer to the results

$d = 35$	$h^{(0)}(u,y,t) = \psi(u)$		$h^{(0)}(u,y,t) = \psi(u,t)$	
	probability	confidence interval	probability	confidence interval
$k = 1$	0.033501	[0.032595, 0.034407]	0.033382	[0.032487, 0.034277]
$k = 3$	0.046526	[0.045451, 0.047601]	0.046435	[0.045363, 0.047506]
$d = 20$	$h^{(0)}(u,y,t) = \psi(u)$		$h^{(0)}(u,y,t) = \psi(u,t)$	
	probability	confidence interval	probability	confidence interval
$k = 1$	0.034601	[0.033696, 0.035506]	0.033683	[0.032777, 0.034590]
$k = 3$	0.047735	[0.046652, 0.048818]	0.046518	[0.045445, 0.047592]

Table 7. The probability of ruin using different starting functions $h^{(0)}(u,y,t)$

of the simulation of the risk process, than the ruin probabilities calculated with the simple starting function and $d = 70$.

The numerical recursive method introduced above is a valuable alternative to stochastic simulation of the risk process which allows to obtain an independent estimate of the ruin probability in this risk model. In terms of comparing computation times of the recursive numerical method and simulation of the risk process, it seems that (unlike in the context of dividend models, cf. Albrecher et al. (2003)) the simulation method is in general more competitive. However, as shown above, an appropriate choice of the starting function can considerably decrease the dimension of the resulting integration and this may be an advantage in certain applications (for instance when using Quasi-Monte Carlo methods to speed up the simulation efficiency). In the above example, a 40-dimensional integral was sufficient for the recursive method, whereas simulation of the risk process usually needs dimensions beyond 100 (as each interclaim time and claim size variable needed for the simulation of one sample path represents one dimension). Further refinements in the choice of starting functions may improve this situation even further. This issue will be addressed in a future study.

References

ALBRECHER, H., FURIAN, N., HAAS, S. (2010): *Ruin Probabilities under Excess of Loss Reinsurance with Reinstatements: Piecewise Deterministic Markov Processes and a Numerical Approach*, Working paper, University of Lausanne.

ALBRECHER, H., KAINHOFER, R., TICHY, R. (2003): Simulation methods in ruin models with non-linear dividend barriers, *Math. Comput. Simulation 62(3-6), 277-287*.

ALBRECHER, H., TEUGELS, J. (2010): *Reinsurance: Actuarial and Financial Aspects*, Wiley, Chichester, to appear.

FURIAN, N. (2007): *Excess of Loss Reinsurance with Reinstatements*, Diploma Thesis, Graz University of Technology.

HESS, K.T., SCHMIDT, K.D. (2004): Optimal premium plans for reinsurance with reinstatements, *Astin Bulletin, 34(2), 299-313*.

HÜRLIMANN, W. (2005): Excess of loss reinsurance with reinstatements revisted, *Astin Bulletin, 35(2), 211-238.*

MATA, A.J. (2002): Pricing excess of loss reinsurance with reinstatements, *Astin Bulletin, 30(2), 349-368.*

ROLSKI, T., SCHMIDLI, H., SCHMIDT, V., TEUGELS, J. (1999): *Stochastic Processes for Insurance and Finance*, John Wiley and Sons.

SUNDT, B. (1991): On excess of loss reinsurance with reinstatements, *Bulletin of Swiss Actuaries, 1, 1-15.*

WALHIN, J.F., PARIS, J. (2002): The effect of excess of loss reinsurance with reinstatements on the cedent's portfolio, *Blätter der Deutschen Gesellschaft für Versicherungsmathematik, 24, 616-627.*

WALHIN, J.F., PARIS, J. (2001): Excess of loss reinsurance with reinstatements: Premium calculation and ruin probability for the cedent, *Blätter der Deutschen Gesellschaft für Versicherungsmathematik, 25, 257-270.*

Computation of the Aggregate Claim Amount Distribution Using R and Actuar

Vincent Goulet

École d'actuariat
Université Laval
Pavillon Alexandre-Vachon
1045, avenue de la Médecine
Québec, Québec G1V 0A6
Canada *vincent.goulet@act.ulaval.ca*

Abstract. **actuar** is a package providing additional Actuarial Science functionality to the R statistical system. This paper presents the features of the package targeted at risk theory calculations. Risk theory refers to a body of techniques to model and measure the risk associated with a portfolio of insurance contracts. The main quantity of interest for the actuary is the distribution of total claims over a fixed period of time, modeled using the classical collective model of risk theory.

actuar provides functions to discretize continuous distributions and to compute the aggregate claim amount distribution using many techniques, including the recursive method and simulation. The package also provides various plotting and summary methods to ease working with aggregate models.

Keywords: risk theory, aggregate models, compound distribution, R, actuar

1 Introduction

Risk theory refers to a body of techniques to model and measure the risk associated with a portfolio of insurance contracts. A first approach consists in modeling the distribution of total claims over a fixed period of time using the classical collective model of risk theory. A second input of interest to the actuary is the evolution of the surplus of the insurance company over many periods of time. In *ruin theory*, the main quantity of interest is the probability that the surplus becomes negative, in which case technical ruin of the insurance company occurs.

The interested reader can read more on these subjects in Klugman et al. (2008), Gerber (1979), Denuit and Charpentier (2004) and Kaas et al. (2001), among others.

This paper concentrates on the computation of the aggregate claim amount distribution using the functions found in the package **actuar** (Dutang et al. (2008)) for the R statistical system (R Development Core Team (2009)). The

Y. Lechevallier, G. Saporta (eds.), *Proceedings of COMPSTAT'2010*,
DOI 10.1007/978-3-7908-2604-3_13, © Springer-Verlag Berlin Heidelberg 2010

package also includes functions to compute ruin probabilities; see Goulet (2010).

The paper is based on version 1.0-1 of **actuar**, available from the Comprehensive R Archive Network[1]. The package contains two visible functions for the calculation of the aggregate claim amount distribution.

2   The collective risk model

Let random variable S represent the aggregate claim amount (or total amount of claims) of a portfolio of independent risks over a fixed period of time, random variable N represent the number of claims (or frequency) in the portfolio over that period, and random variable C_j represent the amount of claim j (or severity). Then, we have the random sum

$$S = C_1 + \cdots + C_N, \tag{1}$$

where we assume that $C_1, C_2, \ldots$ are mutually independent and identically distributed random variables each independent of N. The task at hand consists in evaluating numerically the cumulative distribution function (cdf) of S, given by

$$
\begin{aligned}
F_S(x) &= \Pr[S \leq x] \\
&= \sum_{n=0}^{\infty} \Pr[S \leq x | N = n] p_n \\
&= \sum_{n=0}^{\infty} F_C^{*n}(x) p_n,
\end{aligned}
\tag{2}
$$

where $F_C(x) = \Pr[C \leq x]$ is the common cdf of $C_1, \ldots, C_n$, $p_n = \Pr[N = n]$ and $F_C^{*n}(x) = \Pr[C_1 + \cdots + C_n \leq x]$ is the n-fold convolution of $F_C(\cdot)$. If C is discrete on $0, 1, 2, \ldots$, one has

$$
F_C^{*k}(x) =
\begin{cases}
I\{x \geq 0\}, & k = 0 \\
F_C(x), & k = 1 \\
\sum_{y=0}^{x} F_C^{*(k-1)}(x - y) f_C(y), & k = 2, 3, \ldots,
\end{cases}
\tag{3}
$$

where $I\{\mathcal{A}\} = 1$ if $\mathcal{A}$ is true and $I\{\mathcal{A}\} = 0$ otherwise.

3   Discretization of claim amount distributions

Some numerical techniques to compute the aggregate claim amount distribution (see Section 4) require a discrete arithmetic claim amount distribution;

---

[1] http://cran.r-project.org

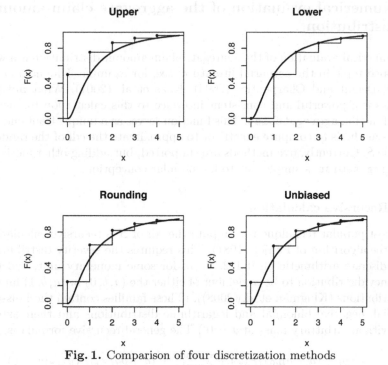

Fig. 1. Comparison of four discretization methods

that is, a distribution defined on $0, h, 2h, \ldots$ for some step (or span, or lag) h.
actuar provides function `discretize` to discretize a continuous distribution
with cdf $F(x)$. (The function can also be used to modify the support of an
already discrete distribution, but this requires additional care.)

Currently, `discretize` supports four discretization methods:

a. upper discretization, or forward difference of $F(x)$;
b. lower discretization, or backward difference of $F(x)$:
c. rounding of the random variable, or the midpoint method;
d. unbiased, or local matching of the first moment method.

See Dutang et al. (2008) and Klugman et al. (2008) for the details. Figure 1
compares the four methods graphically. It should be noted that although very
close in this example, the rounding and unbiased methods are not identical.

Usage of `discretize` is similar to R's plotting function `curve`. For example, upper discretization of a Gamma$(2, 1)$ distribution on $(0, 17)$ with a step
of 0.5 is achieved with

```
> fx <- discretize(pgamma(x, 2, 1), method = "upper",
+        from = 0, to = 17, step = 0.5)
```

4 Numerical evaluation of the aggregate claim amount distribution

The numerical evaluation of the aggregate claim amount distribution is a well developed topic in the actuarial literature; see, for example, Klugman et al. (2008), Denuit and Charpentier (2004), Kaas et al. (2001). What **actuar** provides is a powerful and consistent interface to this calculation by means of the function `aggregateDist`. This function serves as a unique front end for various methods to compute exactly or to approximate the cdf of the random variable S. Currently, five methods are supported, but adding other methods to `aggregateDist` is simple due to its modular conception.

4.1 Recursive calculation

The most popular technique to compute the cdf of S is recursive calculation using the algorithm of Panjer (1981). This requires the severity distribution to be discrete arithmetic on $0, 1, 2, \ldots, m$ for some monetary unit, and the frequency distribution to be a member of either the $(a, b, 0)$ or $(a, b, 1)$ family of distributions (Klugman et al. (2008)). (These families contain the Poisson, binomial, negative binomial and logarithmic distributions and their extensions with an arbitrary mass at $x = 0$.) The general recursive formula is:

$$f_S(x) = \frac{(p_1 - (a + b)p_0)f_C(x) + \sum_{y=1}^{\min(x,m)}(a + by/x)f_C(y)f_S(x - y)}{1 - af_C(0)},$$

with starting value $f_S(0) = P_N(f_C(0))$, where $P_N(\cdot)$ is the probability generating function of N. Probabilities $F_S(x)$ are computed until their sum is arbitrarily close to 1.

actuar implements the recursions in C to dramatically increase speed compared to a pure R solution. One difficulty the programmer is facing is the unknown length of the output. This was solved using a common, simple and fast technique: first allocate an arbitrary amount of memory and double this amount each time the allocated space gets full. The unused memory space is flushed at the end of the function call.

The recursive method fails when the expected number of claims is so large that $f_S(0)$ is numerically equal to zero. One solution proposed by Klugman et al. (2008) consists in dividing the appropriate parameter of the frequency distribution by 2^n, with n chosen such that $f_S(0) > 0$ numerically. One then computes the aggregate claim amount distribution using the recursive method as usual, and then convolves the resulting distribution n times with itself to obtain the final distribution. Function `aggregateDist` supports this procedure. The user has to choose n and adjust the frequency distribution parameter, but the function will carry out the convolutions and adjust the precision level automatically. Again, computations are done in C using a simple discrete convolution of two vectors.

Given a suitable discrete severity distribution, the recursive method is exact. In practice, severity distributions are rather continuous, but with lower and upper discretizations of the latter, the recursive method can provide lower and upper bounds for the true cdf of S.

4.2   Simulation

Another technique to compute the aggregate claim amount distribution that is gaining popularity with the general availability of fast computers is stochastic simulation. The idea is simple: simulate a sufficiently large random sample $x_1, \ldots, x_n$ from S and approximate $F_S(x)$ by the empirical cdf

$$F_n(x) = \frac{1}{n} \sum_{j=1}^{n} I\{x_j \leq x\}. \tag{4}$$

In **actuar**, the simulation itself is done with function `simul`. This function admits very general compound hierarchical models for both the frequency and the severity components; see Goulet and Pouliot (2008) for a detailed presentation.

4.3   Direct calculation

Exact calculation of the compound distribution function by numerical convolutions using (2) and (3) is conceptually feasible. This also requires a discrete severity distribution, but there is no restriction on the shape of the frequency distribution. In practice, this approach is limited to small problems only due to the large number of products and sums to carry out.

Function `aggregateDist` supports the direct calculation method, but merely implements the sum (2). The convolutions themselves are computed with R's function `convolve`, which in turn uses the Fast Fourier Transform.

4.4   Approximating distributions

Probably the simplest and easiest technique to compute $F_S(x)$ is by means of approximating distributions. The downside is the unknown level of accuracy and, usually, crudeness in the tails. Still, `aggregateDist()` supports two simple and popular approximating methods:

a. the normal approximation

$$F_S(x) \approx \Phi\left(\frac{x - \mu_S}{\sigma_S}\right), \tag{5}$$

where $\mu_S = E[S]$ and $\sigma_S^2 = \mathrm{Var}[S]$;

b. the Normal Power II approximation

$$F_S(x) \approx \Phi \left(-\frac{3}{\gamma_S} + \sqrt{\frac{9}{\gamma_S^2} + 1 + \frac{6}{\gamma_S} \frac{x - \mu_S}{\sigma_S}} \right), \qquad (6)$$

where $\gamma_S = E[(S - \mu_S)^3]/\sigma_S^{3/2}$. This approximation is valid for $x > \mu_S$ only and performs reasonably well when $\gamma_S < 1$. See Daykin et al. (1994) for details.

5 Interface

As mentioned earlier, function `aggregateDist` provides a unified interface to the calculation methods presented in the previous sections. Adding other methods is simple due to the modular conception of the function.

The arguments of `aggregateDist()` differs depending on the calculation method; see the help page for details. One interesting argument to note is `x.scale` to specify the monetary unit of the severity distribution. This way, one does not have to mentally do the conversion between the support of $0, 1, 2, \ldots$ assumed by the recursive and convolution methods and the true support of S. Also, the resulting distribution is convoluted n times with itself when argument `convolve` is equal to $n > 0$.

The result of `aggregateDist()` is slightly disconcerting at first. The function returns an object of class `"aggregateDist"` inheriting from the `"function"` class. In other words, the object is a *function* to compute the value of $F_S(x)$ in any x.

For illustration purposes, consider the following model: the distribution of S is a compound Poisson with parameter $\lambda = 10$ and severity distribution Gamma$(2, 1)$. To obtain an approximation of the cdf of S we first discretize the gamma distribution on $(0, 22)$ with the unbiased method and a step of 0.5, and then use the recursive method in `aggregateDist`:

```
> fx <- discretize(pgamma(x, 2, 1), from = 0, to = 22,
+     step = 0.5, method = "unbiased", lev = levgamma(x,
+        2, 1))
> Fs <- aggregateDist("recursive", model.freq = "poisson",
+     model.sev = fx, lambda = 10, x.scale = 0.5)
> summary(Fs)

Aggregate Claim Amount Empirical CDF:
   Min. 1st Qu.  Median   Mean 3rd Qu.    Max.
    0.0    14.5    19.5    20.0    25.0    71.0
```

Although useless here, the following is essentially equivalent, except in the far right tail for numerical reasons:

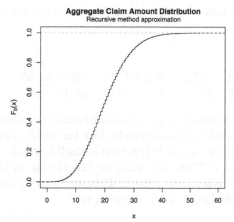

Fig. 2. Graphic of the empirical cdf of S obtained with the recursive method

```
> Fsc <- aggregateDist("recursive", model.freq = "poisson",
+      model.sev = fx, lambda = 5, convolve = 1, x.scale = 0.5)
> summary(Fsc)

Aggregate Claim Amount Empirical CDF:
   Min. 1st Qu.  Median    Mean 3rd Qu.     Max.
   0.0    14.5    19.5    20.0    25.0    103.0
```

We now return to object **Fs** for the rest of our presentation. The object contains an empirical cdf with support

```
> knots(Fs)

  [1]   0.0  0.5  1.0  1.5  2.0  2.5  3.0  3.5  4.0  4.5  5.0
 [12]   5.5  6.0  6.5  7.0  7.5  8.0  8.5  9.0  9.5 10.0 10.5
 ...
[122]  60.5 61.0 61.5 62.0 62.5 63.0 63.5 64.0 64.5 65.0 65.5
[133]  66.0 66.5 67.0 67.5 68.0 68.5 69.0 69.5 70.0 70.5 71.0
```

A nice graph of this function is obtained with a method of `plot` (see Fig. 2):

```
> plot(Fs, do.points = FALSE, verticals = TRUE, xlim = c(0, 70))
```

6   Summary methods

The package defines a few summary methods to extract information from `"aggregateDist"` objects. A first, simple one is a method of `mean` to easily compute the mean of the approximate distribution:

```
> mean(Fs)

[1] 20
```

A second is a method of `quantile` to obtain the quantiles of the aggregate distribution:

```
> quantile(Fs)
```

```
 25%   50%   75%   90%   95% 97.5%   99% 99.5%
14.5  19.5  25.0  30.5  34.0  37.0  41.0  43.5
```

For the normal and Normal Power approximations, the quantiles are obtained by inversion of (5) and (6), respectively. For the other methods, where the cdf is a step function, the quantile function is itself a step function by default. With option `smooth = TRUE`, the quantile function is rather the inverse of the ogive (Hogg and Klugman (1984)). This amounts to interpolate linearly between the knots of the cdf. Indeed, given that

```
> Fs(c(30, 30.5))
```

```
[1] 0.8985 0.9076
```

compare

```
> quantile(Fs, 0.9)
```

```
90%
 30.5
```

with

```
> quantile(Fs, 0.9, smooth = TRUE)
```

```
  90%
30.08
```

A method of `diff` gives easy access to the underlying probability mass function:

```
> diff(Fs)
```

```
 [1] 6.293e-05 8.934e-05 1.767e-04 2.954e-04 4.604e-04
 [6] 6.811e-04 9.662e-04 1.324e-03 1.760e-03 2.282e-03
 ...
[136] 5.432e-07 4.577e-07 3.854e-07 3.243e-07 2.726e-07
[141] 2.290e-07 1.923e-07 1.613e-07
```

Of course, this is defined (and makes sense) for the recursive, direct convolution and simulation methods only.

Finally, the package introduces the generic functions `VaR` and `CTE` (with alias `TVaR`) with methods for objects of class `"aggregateDist"`. The former computes the value-at-risk VaR_α such that

$$\Pr[S \leq \text{VaR}_\alpha] = \alpha, \tag{7}$$

where α is the confidence level. Thus, the value-at-risk is nothing else than a quantile. As for the method of CTE, it computes the conditional tail expectation (also called Tail Value-at-Risk)

$$\text{CTE}_\alpha = E[S|S > \text{VaR}_\alpha]$$
$$= \frac{1}{1-\alpha} \int_{\text{VaR}_\alpha}^{\infty} x f_S(x)\, dx. \tag{8}$$

Here are examples using object Fs obtained above:

```
> VaR(Fs)

 90%  95%  99%
30.5 34.0 41.0

> CTE(Fs)

  90%   95%   99%
35.42 38.55 45.01
```

We compute the conditional tail expectation by different means depending on the method used in `aggregateDist()`. For the normal approximation, we use the well known exact formula

$$\text{CTE}_\alpha = \mu + \sigma \frac{\phi(\Phi^{-1}(\alpha))}{1-\alpha}.$$

For the Normal Power approximation, we evaluate the integral in (8) numerically using R's function `integrate`. For the other methods, which yield step cdfs, we estimate (8) with

$$\widehat{\text{CTE}}_\alpha = \frac{\sum_{x > \text{VaR}_\alpha} x f_S(x)}{\sum_{x > \text{VaR}_\alpha} x}.$$

7 Conclusion

Computation of the cumulative distribution function of the total amount of claims in an insurance portfolio is central to the risk assessment process conducted by actuaries. Function `aggregateDist` of the R package **actuar** offers a convenient and unified interface to five different computation or approximating methods. Heavy calculations are implemented in C for speed. The function returns a function object to compute the cdf in any point and for which one can easily develop summary and plotting methods. The modular design of `aggregateDist()` makes extending the software simple.

The **actuar** package is Free software released under the GNU General Public License[2]. Contributions to the project are most welcome.

Finally, if you use R or **actuar** for actuarial analysis, please cite the software in publications. Use

---

[2] http://www.fsf.org/licensing/licenses/gpl.html

```
> citation()
```

and

```
> citation("actuar")
```

at the R command prompt for information on how to cite the software.

Acknowledgments

This research benefited from financial support from the Natural Sciences and Engineering Research Council of Canada and from the *Chaire d'actuariat* (Actuarial Science Chair) of Université Laval.

References

DAYKIN, C., PENTIKÄINEN, T. and PESONEN, M. (1994): *Practical Risk Theory for Actuaries*, Chapman and Hall, London.

DENUIT, M. and CHARPENTIER, A. (2004): *Mathématiques de l'assurance non-vie, Vol. 1: Principes fondamentaux de théorie du risque*, Economica, Paris.

DUTANG, C., GOULET, V. and PIGEON, M. (2008): **actuar**: An R package for actuarial science, *Journal of Statistical Software 25 (7)*. http://www.jstatsoft.org/v25/i07

GERBER, H. U. (1979): *An Introduction to Mathematical Risk Theory*, Huebner Foundation, Philadelphia.

GOULET, V. and POULIOT, L.-P. (2008): Simulation of compound hierarchical models in R, *North American Actuarial Journal 12, 401-412*.

GOULET, V. (2010): Evaluation of ruin probabilities using R and **actuar**. In preparation.

HOGG, R. V. and KLUGMAN, S. A. (1984): *Loss Distributions*, Wiley, New York.

KAAS, R., GOOVAERTS, M., DHAENE, J. and DENUIT, M. (2001): *Modern actuarial risk theory*, Kluwer Academic Publishers, Dordrecht.

KLUGMAN, S. A., PANJER, H. H. and WILLMOT, G. (2008): *Loss Models: From Data to Decisions*, Third Edition, Wiley, New York.

PANJER, H. H. (1981): Recursive evaluation of a family of compound distributions, *ASTIN Bulletin 12, 22-26*.

R DEVELOPMENT CORE TEAM (2009): *R: A Language and Environment for Statistical Computing*, R Foundation for Statistical Computing, Vienna. http://www.R-project.org

Applications of Multilevel Structured Additive Regression Models to Insurance Data

Stefan Lang[1] and Nikolaus Umlauf[1]

University of Innsbruck, Department of Statistics
Universitätsstraße 15, A-6020 Innsbruck, Austria,
stefan.lang@uibk.ac.at and nikolaus.umlauf@uibk.ac.at

Abstract. Models with structured additive predictor provide a very broad and rich framework for complex regression modeling. They can deal simultaneously with nonlinear covariate effects and time trends, unit- or cluster specific heterogeneity, spatial heterogeneity and complex interactions between covariates of different type. In this paper, we discuss a hierarchical version of regression models with structured additive predictor and its applications to insurance data. That is, the regression coefficients of a particular nonlinear term may obey another regression model with structured additive predictor. The proposed model may be regarded as a an extended version of a multilevel model with nonlinear covariate terms in every level of the hierarchy. We describe several highly efficient MCMC sampling schemes that allow to estimate complex models with several hierarchy levels and a large number of observations typically within a couple of minutes. We demonstrate the usefulness of the approach with applications to insurance data.

Keywords: Bayesian hierarchical models, multilevel models, P-splines, spatial heterogeneity

1 Introduction

The last 10 to 15 years have seen enormous progress in Bayesian semiparametric regression modeling based on MCMC simulation for inference. A particularly broad and rich framework is provided by generalized structured additive regression (STAR) models introduced in Fahrmeir et al. (2004) and Brezger and Lang (2006). STAR models assume that, given covariates, the distribution of response observations y_i, $i = 1, \ldots, n$, belongs to an exponential family. The conditional mean μ_i is linked to a semiparametric additive predictor η_i by $\mu_i = h(\eta_i)$ where $h(\cdot)$ is a known response function. The predictor η_i is of the form

$$\eta_i = f_1(z_{i1}) + \ldots + f_q(z_{iq}) + \mathbf{x}_i'\boldsymbol{\gamma}, \qquad i = 1, \ldots, n, \tag{1}$$

where $f_1, \ldots, f_q$ are possibly nonlinear functions of the covariates $z_1, \ldots, z_q$ and $\mathbf{x}_i'\boldsymbol{\gamma}$ is the usual linear part of the model. In contrast to pure additive models the nonlinear functions f_j are not necessarily smooth functions of

Y. Lechevallier, G. Saporta (eds.), *Proceedings of COMPSTAT'2010*,
DOI 10.1007/978-3-7908-2604-3_14, © Springer-Verlag Berlin Heidelberg 2010

some continuous (one-dimensional) covariates z_j. Instead, a particular covariate may for example indicate a time scale, a spatial index denoting the region or district a certain observation pertains to, or a unit- or cluster-index. Moreover, z_j may be two- or even three dimensional in order to model interactions between covariates. Summarizing, the functions f_j comprise usual nonlinear effects of continuous covariates, time trends and seasonal effects, two dimensional surfaces, varying coefficient terms, cluster- and spatial effects.

The nonlinear effects in (1) are modeled by a basis functions approach, i.e. a particular nonlinear function f of covariate z is approximated by a linear combination of basis or indicator functions

$$f(z) = \sum_{k=1}^{K} \beta_k B_k(z). \tag{2}$$

The B_k's are known basis functions and $\beta = (\beta_1, \ldots, \beta_K)'$ is a vector of unknown regression coefficients to be estimated. Defining the $n \times K$ design matrix $\mathbf{Z}$ with elements $\mathbf{Z}[i, k] = B_k(z_i)$, the vector $\mathbf{f} = (f(z_1), \ldots, f(z_n))'$ of function evaluations can be written in matrix notation as $\mathbf{f} = \mathbf{Z}\beta$. Accordingly, for the predictor (1) we obtain

$$\eta = \mathbf{Z}_1\beta_1 + \ldots + \mathbf{Z}_q\beta_q + \mathbf{X}\gamma. \tag{3}$$

In this paper we discuss a hierarchical or multilevel version of STAR models. That is the regression coefficients β_j of a term f_j may themselves obey a regression model with structured additive predictor, i.e.

$$\beta_j = \eta_j + \varepsilon_j = \mathbf{Z}_{j1}\beta_{j1} + \ldots + \mathbf{Z}_{jq_j}\beta_{jq_j} + \mathbf{X}_j\gamma_j + \varepsilon_j, \tag{4}$$

where the terms $\mathbf{Z}_{j1}\beta_{j1}, \ldots, \mathbf{Z}_{jq_j}\beta_{jq_j}$ correspond to additional nonlinear functions $f_{j1}, \ldots, f_{jq_j}$, $\mathbf{X}_j\gamma_j$ comprises additional linear effects, and $\varepsilon_j \sim N(\mathbf{0}, \tau_j^2 \mathbf{I})$ is a vector of i.i.d. Gaussian errors. A third or even higher levels in the hierarchy are possible by assuming that the second level regression parameters β_{jl}, $l = 1, \ldots, q_j$, obey again a STAR model. In that sense, the model is composed of a hierarchy of complex structured additive regression models.

The typical application for hierarchical STAR models are multilevel data where a hierarchy of units or clusters grouped at different levels is given. One of the main aspects of the paper are applications of multilevel STAR models to insurance data. In a first example, we apply our methods to analyze the amount of loss and claim frequency for car insurance data from a German insurance company. In our analysis in section 4.1 we will distinguish three levels: policyholders (level-1) are nested in districts (level-2) and districts are nested in counties (level-3). Our second example analyzes time-space trends for health insurance data.

2   Priors for the regression coefficient

We distinguish two types of priors: "direct" or "basic" priors for the regression coefficients β_j (or β_{jl} in a second level equation) and compound priors (4). We first briefly describe the general form of "basic" priors in the next subsection. Subsection 2.2 shows how the basic priors can be used as building blocks for the compound priors.

2.1   General form of basic priors

In a frequentist setting, overfitting of a particular function $\mathbf{f} = \mathbf{Z}\beta$ is avoided by defining a roughness penalty on the regression coefficients, see for instance Belitz and Lang (2008) in the context of structured additive regression. The standard quadratic penalties of the form $\lambda\beta'\mathbf{K}\beta$ where $\mathbf{K}$ is a penalty matrix. The penalty depends on the smoothing parameter λ that governs the amount of smoothness imposed on the function f.

In a Bayesian framework a standard smoothness prior is a (possibly improper) Gaussian prior of the form

$$p(\beta|\tau^2) \propto \left(\frac{1}{\tau^2}\right)^{rk(\mathbf{K})/2} \exp\left(-\frac{1}{2\tau^2}\beta'\mathbf{K}\beta\right) \cdot I(\mathbf{A}\beta = \mathbf{0}), \qquad (5)$$

where $I(\cdot)$ is the indicator function. The key components of the prior are the penalty matrix $\mathbf{K}$, the variance parameter τ^2 and the constraint $\mathbf{A}\beta = \mathbf{0}$.

The structure of the penalty or prior precision matrix $\mathbf{K}$ depends on the covariate type and on our prior assumptions about smoothness of f. Typically the penalty matrix in our examples is rank deficient, i.e. $rk(\mathbf{K}) < K$, resulting in a partially improper prior.

The amount of smoothness is governed by the variance parameter τ^2. A conjugate inverse Gamma prior is employed for τ^2 (as well as for the overall variance parameter σ^2 in models with Gaussian responses), i.e. $\tau^2 \sim IG(a, b)$ with small values such as $a = b = 0.001$ for the hyperparameters a and b resulting in an uninformative prior on the log scale. The smoothing parameter λ of the frequentist approach and the variance parameter τ^2 are connected by $\lambda = \sigma^2/\tau^2$.

The term $I(\mathbf{A}\beta = \mathbf{0})$ imposes required identifiability constraints on the parameter vector. A straightforward choice is $\mathbf{A} = (1, \ldots, 1)$, i.e. the regression coefficients are centered around zero. A better choice in terms of interpretability and mixing of the resulting Markov chains is to use a weighted average of regression coefficients, i.e. $\mathbf{A} = (c_1, \ldots, c_K)$. As a standard we use $c_k = \sum_{i=1}^n B_k(z_i)$ resulting in the more natural constraint $\sum_{i=1}^n f(z_i) = 0$.

Specific examples for modeling nonlinear terms are one or two dimensional P-splines for nonlinear effects of continuous covariates, or Gaussian Markov random fields and Gaussian fields (kriging) for modeling spatial heterogeneity, see Brezger and Lang (2006) for details.

2.2 Compound priors

In the vast majority of cases a compound prior is used if a covariate $z_j \in \{1, \ldots, K\}$ is a unit- or cluster index and z_{ij} indicates the cluster observation i pertains to. Then the design matrix $\mathbf{Z}_j$ is a $n \times K$ incidence matrix with $\mathbf{Z}_j[i, k] = 1$ if the i-th observation belongs to cluster k and zero else. The $K \times 1$ parameter vector $\boldsymbol{\beta}_j$ is the vector of regression parameters, i.e. the k-th element in $\boldsymbol{\beta}$ corresponds to the regression coefficient of the k-th cluster. Using the compound prior (4) we obtain an additive decomposition of the cluster specific effect. The covariates z_{jl}, $l = 1, \ldots, q_j$, in (4) are cluster specific covariates with possible nonlinear cluster effect. By allowing a full STAR predictor (as in the level-1 equation) a rather complex decomposition of the cluster effect $\boldsymbol{\beta}_j$ including interactions is possible. A special case arises if cluster specific covariates are not available. Then the prior for $\boldsymbol{\beta}_j$ collapses to $\boldsymbol{\beta}_j = \boldsymbol{\varepsilon}_j \sim N(\tau_j^2 \mathbf{I})$ and we obtain a simple i.i.d. Gaussian cluster specific random effect with variance parameter τ_j^2.

Another special situation arises if the data are grouped according to some discrete geographical grid and the cluster index z_{ij} denotes the geographical region observation i pertains to. For instance, in our applications on insurance data in section 4 for every observation the district of the policyholders residence is given. Then the compound prior (4) models a complex spatial heterogeneity effect with possibly nonlinear effects of region specific covariates z_{jl}.

In a number of applications geographical information and spatial covariates are given at different resolutions. For instance, in our case studies on insurance problems, the districts (level-2) are nested within counties (level-3). This allows to model a spatial effect over two levels of the form

$$
\boldsymbol{\beta}_j \ = \mathbf{Z}_{j1}\boldsymbol{\beta}_{j1} + \mathbf{Z}_{j2}\boldsymbol{\beta}_{j2} + \ldots + \boldsymbol{\varepsilon}_j,
$$
$$
\boldsymbol{\beta}_{j1} = \mathbf{Z}_{j11}\boldsymbol{\beta}_{j11} + \mathbf{Z}_{j12}\boldsymbol{\beta}_{j12} + \ldots + \boldsymbol{\varepsilon}_{j1}.
$$

Here, the first covariate z_{j1} in the district specific effect is another cluster indicator that indicates the county in which the districts are nested. Hence $\mathbf{Z}_{j1}$ is another incidence matrix and $\boldsymbol{\beta}_{j1}$ is the vector of county specific effects modeled through the level-3 equation.

Other possibilities for compound priors can be found in Lang et al. (2010).

3 Sketch of MCMC Inference

In the following, we will describe a Gibbs sampler for models with Gaussian errors. The non-Gaussian case can be either traced back to the Gaussian case via data augmentation, see e.g Frühwirth-Schnatter et al. (2008), or is technically similar (Brezger and Lang (2006)).

For the sake of simplicity we restrict the presentation to a two level hierarchical model with one level-2 equation for the regression coefficients of the first term $\mathbf{Z}_1\boldsymbol{\beta}_1$. That is, the level-1 equation is $\mathbf{y} = \boldsymbol{\eta} + \boldsymbol{\varepsilon}$ with predictor (3) and errors $\boldsymbol{\varepsilon} \sim N(\mathbf{0}, \sigma^2\mathbf{W}^{-1})$ with diagonal weight matrix $\mathbf{W} = diag(w_1, \ldots, w_n)$. The level-2 equation is of the form (4) with $j = 1$.

The parameters are updated in blocks where each vector of regression coefficients $\boldsymbol{\beta}_j$ ($\boldsymbol{\beta}_{1l}$ in a second level of the hierarchy) of a particular term is updated in one (possibly large) block followed by updating the regression coefficients $\boldsymbol{\gamma}$, $\boldsymbol{\gamma}_1$ of linear effects and the variance components τ_j^2, τ_{1l}^2, σ^2. The next subsection 3.1 sketches updates of regression coefficients $\boldsymbol{\beta}_j$, $\boldsymbol{\beta}_{1l}$ of nonlinear terms. Updates of the remaining parameters are straightforward.

3.1   Full conditionals for regression coefficients of nonlinear terms

The full conditionals for the regression coefficients $\boldsymbol{\beta}_1$ with the compound prior (4) and the coefficients $\boldsymbol{\beta}_j$, $j = 2, \ldots, q$, $\boldsymbol{\beta}_{1l}$, $l = 1, \ldots, q_1$ with the basic prior (5) are all multivariate Gaussian. The respective posterior precision $\boldsymbol{\Sigma}^{-1}$ and mean $\boldsymbol{\mu}$ is given by

$$\boldsymbol{\Sigma}^{-1} = \tfrac{1}{\sigma^2}\left(\mathbf{Z}_1'\mathbf{W}\mathbf{Z}_1 + \tfrac{\sigma^2}{\tau_1^2}\mathbf{I}\right), \quad \boldsymbol{\Sigma}^{-1}\boldsymbol{\mu} = \tfrac{1}{\sigma^2}\mathbf{Z}_1'\mathbf{W}\mathbf{r} + \tfrac{1}{\tau_1^2}\boldsymbol{\eta}_1, \; (\boldsymbol{\beta}_1),$$

$$\boldsymbol{\Sigma}^{-1} = \tfrac{1}{\sigma^2}\left(\mathbf{Z}_j'\mathbf{W}\mathbf{Z}_j + \tfrac{\sigma^2}{\tau_j^2}\mathbf{K}_j\right), \; \boldsymbol{\Sigma}^{-1}\boldsymbol{\mu} = \tfrac{1}{\sigma^2}\mathbf{Z}_j'\mathbf{W}\,\mathbf{r}, \qquad (\boldsymbol{\beta}_j), \qquad (6)$$

$$\boldsymbol{\Sigma}^{-1} = \tfrac{1}{\tau_1^2}\left(\mathbf{Z}_{1l}'\mathbf{Z}_{1l} + \tfrac{\tau_1^2}{\tau_{1l}^2}\mathbf{K}_{1l}\right), \; \boldsymbol{\Sigma}^{-1}\boldsymbol{\mu} = \tfrac{1}{\tau_1^2}\mathbf{Z}_{1l}'\,\mathbf{r}_1, \qquad (\boldsymbol{\beta}_{1l}),$$

where $\mathbf{r}$ is the current partial residual and $\mathbf{r}_1$ is the "partial residual" of the level-2 equation. More precisely, $\mathbf{r}_1 = \boldsymbol{\beta}_1 - \tilde{\boldsymbol{\eta}}_1$ and $\tilde{\boldsymbol{\eta}}_1$ is the predictor of the level-2 equation excluding the current effect of z_{1l}.

MCMC updates of the regression coefficients takes advantage of the following key features:

Sparsity: Design matrices $\mathbf{Z}_j$, $\mathbf{Z}_{1l}$ and penalty matrices $\mathbf{K}_j$, $\mathbf{K}_{1l}$ and with it cross products $\mathbf{Z}_j'\mathbf{W}\mathbf{Z}_j$, $\mathbf{Z}_{1l}'\mathbf{Z}_{1l}$ and posterior precision matrices in (6) are often sparse. The sparsity can be exploited for highly efficient computation of cross products, Cholesky decompositions of posterior precision matrices and for fast solving of relevant linear equation systems.

Reduced complexity in the second or third stage of the hierarchy: Updating the regression coefficients $\boldsymbol{\beta}_{1l}$, $l = 1, \ldots, q_1$, in the second (or third level) is done conditionally on the parameter vector $\boldsymbol{\beta}_1$. This facilitates updating the parameters for two reasons. First the number of "observations" in the level-2 equation is equal to the length of the vector $\boldsymbol{\beta}_1$ and therefore much less than the actual number of observations n. Second the full conditionals for $\boldsymbol{\beta}_{1l}$ are Gaussian regardless of the response distribution in the first level of the hierarchy.

Number of different observations smaller than sample size: In most cases the number m_j of different observations $z_{(1)}, \ldots, z_{(m_j)}$ in $\mathbf{Z}_j$ (or m_{1l} in $\mathbf{Z}_{1l}$ in the level-2 equation) is much smaller than the total number n of observations. The fact that $m_j \ll n$ may be utilized to considerably speed up computations of the cross products $\mathbf{Z}'_j \mathbf{W} \mathbf{Z}_j$, $\mathbf{Z}'_{1l} \mathbf{Z}_{1l}$, the vectors $\mathbf{Z}'_j \mathbf{W} \mathbf{r}$, $\mathbf{Z}'_{1l} \mathbf{r}_1$ and finally the updated vectors of function evaluations $\mathbf{f}_j = \mathbf{Z}_j \boldsymbol{\beta}_j$, $\mathbf{f}_{1l} = \mathbf{Z}_{1l} \boldsymbol{\beta}_{1l}$.

Full details of the MCMC techniques can be found in Lang et al. (2010).

3.2   Alternative sampling scheme based on a transformed parametrization

An alternative sampling scheme works with a transformed parametrization such that the cross product of the design matrix and the penalty matrix of a nonlinear term are diagonal resulting in a diagonal posterior precision matrix.

We describe the alternative parametrization for a particular nonlinear function f with design matrix $\mathbf{Z}$ and parameter vector $\boldsymbol{\beta}$ with general prior (5).

Let $\mathbf{Z}'\mathbf{W}\mathbf{Z} = \mathbf{R}\mathbf{R}'$ be the Cholesky decomposition of the cross product of the design matrix and let $\mathbf{Q}\mathbf{S}\mathbf{Q}'$ be the singular value decomposition of $\mathbf{R}^{-1}\mathbf{K}\mathbf{R}^{-T}$. The diagonal matrix $\mathbf{S} = diag(s_1, \ldots, s_K)$ contains the eigenvalues of $\mathbf{R}^{-1}\mathbf{K}\mathbf{R}^{-T}$ in ascending order. The columns of the orthogonal matrix $\mathbf{Q}$ contain the corresponding eigenvectors. Columns 1 through $rk(\mathbf{K})$ form a basis for the vector space spanned by the columns of $\mathbf{R}^{-1}\mathbf{K}\mathbf{R}^{-T}$. The remaining columns are a basis of the nullspace.

Then the decomposition $\boldsymbol{\beta} = \mathbf{R}^{-T}\mathbf{Q}\tilde{\boldsymbol{\beta}}$ yields

$$\mathbf{Z}\boldsymbol{\beta} = \mathbf{Z}\mathbf{R}^{-T}\mathbf{Q}\tilde{\boldsymbol{\beta}} = \tilde{\mathbf{Z}}\tilde{\boldsymbol{\beta}},$$

where the transformed design matrix $\tilde{\mathbf{Z}}$ is defined by $\tilde{\mathbf{Z}} = \mathbf{Z}\mathbf{R}^{-T}\mathbf{Q}$.

We now obtain for the cross product

$$\mathbf{Z}'\mathbf{W}\mathbf{Z} = \mathbf{Q}'\mathbf{R}^{-1}\mathbf{Z}'\mathbf{W}\mathbf{Z}\mathbf{R}^{-T}\mathbf{Q} = \mathbf{Q}'\mathbf{Q} = \mathbf{I}$$

and for the penalty

$$\boldsymbol{\beta}'\mathbf{K}\boldsymbol{\beta} = \tilde{\boldsymbol{\beta}}'\mathbf{Q}'\mathbf{R}^{-1}\mathbf{K}\mathbf{R}^{-T}\mathbf{Q}\tilde{\boldsymbol{\beta}} = \tilde{\boldsymbol{\beta}}'\mathbf{S}\tilde{\boldsymbol{\beta}}$$

with the new diagonal penalty matrix $\mathbf{S}$ given by the singular value decomposition of $\mathbf{R}^{-1}\mathbf{K}\mathbf{R}^{-T}$, see above.

Summarizing, we obtain the equivalent formulation $\mathbf{f} = \tilde{\mathbf{Z}}\tilde{\boldsymbol{\beta}}$ for the vector of function evaluations based on the transformed design matrix $\tilde{\mathbf{Z}}$ and the transformed parameter vector $\tilde{\boldsymbol{\beta}}$ with (possibly improper) Gaussian prior

$$\tilde{\boldsymbol{\beta}} \,|\, \tau^2 \sim N(\mathbf{0}, \tau^2 \mathbf{S}^-).$$

The result of the transformation is that the prior precision or penalty matrix $\mathbf{S}$ is diagonal resulting in a diagonal posterior precision matrix. More specifically, the full conditional for $\tilde{\boldsymbol{\beta}}$ is Gaussian with k-th element μ_k, $k = 1, \ldots, K$, of the mean vector $\boldsymbol{\mu}$ given by

$$\mu_k = \frac{1}{1 + \lambda s_k} \cdot u_k,$$

where $\lambda = \sigma^2/\tau^2$ and u_k is the k-th element of the vector $\mathbf{u} = \tilde{\mathbf{Z}}'\mathbf{W}\mathbf{r}$ with $\mathbf{r}$ the partial residual. The covariance matrix $\boldsymbol{\Sigma}$ is diagonal with diagonal elements

$$\boldsymbol{\Sigma}[k, k] = \frac{\sigma^2}{1 + \lambda s_k}.$$

More details on this alternative sampling scheme can be found in Lang et al. (2010).

The main advantage of the transformation is that it provides fast MCMC inference even in situations where the posterior precision is relatively dense as is the case for many surface estimators. The prime example is a Gaussian random field (kriging) which is almost intractable in the standard parametrization.

4 Applications to insurance data

4.1 Car insurance data

The analyzed data set contains individual observations for a sample of policyholders with full comprehensive car insurance for one year. Regression analyzes for claim probabilities and amount of loss were carried out separately for different types of damage: traffic accidents, breakage of glass and theft. Here we report only results for claim probabilities of one type (specific type not mentioned to guarantee anonymity of the data source).

Claim probabilities were analyzed with a multilevel structured additive probit model $y_i \sim B(\pi_i)$ with three hierarchy levels for the probability $\pi_i = \Phi(\eta_i)$ that a damage occurred:

$$
\begin{aligned}
\textbf{level-1} \quad \boldsymbol{\eta} \ &= \cdots + \mathbf{f}_1(nclaim) + \mathbf{f_2}(g) + \mathbf{f_3}(dist) \\
&= \cdots + \mathbf{Z}_1\boldsymbol{\beta}_1 + \mathbf{Z}_2\boldsymbol{\beta}_2 + \mathbf{Z}_3\boldsymbol{\beta}_3 \\
\textbf{level-2} \quad \boldsymbol{\beta}_2 \ &= \boldsymbol{\varepsilon}_2 \\
\textbf{level-2} \quad \boldsymbol{\beta}_3 \ &= \mathbf{f}_{31}(dist) + \mathbf{f}_{32}(county) + \mathbf{f}_{33}(dens) + \boldsymbol{\varepsilon}_3 \\
&= \mathbf{Z}_{31}\boldsymbol{\beta}_{31} + \mathbf{Z}_{32}\boldsymbol{\beta}_{32} + \mathbf{Z}_{33}\boldsymbol{\beta}_{33} + \boldsymbol{\varepsilon}_3 \\
\textbf{level-3} \quad \boldsymbol{\beta}_{32} \ &= \boldsymbol{\varepsilon}_{32}
\end{aligned}
$$

The level-1 equation consists of a nonlinear function f_1 of the covariate "no-claims bonus" ($nclaim$) and of nonlinear effects of three other continuous covariates (indicated through the dots, results not shown to guarantee anonymity of the data provider). All nonlinear effects are modeled using P-splines. Additionally a random effect of the "car classification" (g) measured by scores from 10-40 and a spatial random effect of the districts ($dist$) in Germany is included. For "car classification" a simple i.i.d random effect with $\varepsilon_2 \sim N(0, \sigma_2^2)$ is assumed, see the first level-2 equation. The spatial random effect is modeled through the other level-2 equation and is composed of a spatially correlated effect $\mathbf{f}_{31}$ using a Markov random fields prior, another spatial random effect of the counties, and a smooth nonlinear effect of the population density ($dens$). The "error term" in the district effect is a i.i.d random effect, i.e. $\varepsilon_3 \sim N(0, \sigma_3^2)$. For the county specific effect in the third level equation a simple i.i.d random effect without further covariates is assumed, i.e. $\varepsilon_{32} \sim N(0, \sigma_{32}^2)$. One of the advantages of our approach is that we are able to model spatial heterogeneity at different resolutions (here district and county level). This allows a very detailed modeling of spatial heterogeneity and provides further insight into the problem.

Results for the effects of "no-claims bonus" and "car classification" are given in figure 1 showing a monotonically decreasing effect for $nclaim$. Since higher scores for car classification roughly correspond to "bigger cars" the random effect for g is more or less increasing with scores (with notable exceptions for car groups 32 and 34).

A visualization of the spatial effect β_3 can be found in figure 3. It is composed of the spatially smooth district effect $\mathbf{f}_{31}(dist)$, the district i.i.d. random effect ε_3, the county random effect $\mathbf{f}_{32}(county)$ and the nonlinear effect $\mathbf{f}_{33}(dens)$ of population density. The i.i.d district random effect is very small while the other effects are considerably stronger and roughly of equal size (all effects not shown to save space). Inspecting the total spatial effect in figure 3 reveals a clear north south pattern with lower damage probabilities in the north, in particular the less densely populated north eastern part of Germany, and higher probabilities in the south. We nicely see the effect of the "population density" $dens$ as the most densely populated urban areas of Germany are mostly colored in dark grey or black indication higher damage probabilities as in the rural areas. The effect $\mathbf{f}_{33}(dens)$ itself is almost linearly increasing (not shown).

4.2   Health insurance data

In our second example we exemplify modeling of space-time interactions using data from a German private health insurance company. In a consulting case the main interest was on analyzing the dependence of treatment costs on covariates with a special emphasis on modeling the spatio-temporal development. We distinguish several types of treatment costs. In this demonstrating example, we present results for "treatment with operation" in hospital. We assumed a two level Gaussian model for the log treatment costs $C_{it} \sim N(\eta_{it}, \sigma^2)$ for policyholder i at time t and with predictor

$$\eta_{it} = \cdots + f_1(A_{it}) + f_2(t, county_{it}) + f_3(D_{it}),$$

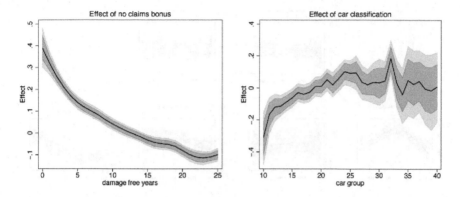

Fig. 1. Car insurance: Effect of "no claims bonus" and "car classification" random effect including 80% and 95% pointwise credible intervals.

Fig. 2. Car insurance: Visualization of the spatial random effect.

where f_1 is a nonlinear effect of the policyholders age modeled via P-splines, f_2 represents county specific nonlinear time trends modeled again using P-splines, and f_3 is a district specific spatial random effect modeled in a second level equation (not shown here). The time-space interaction f_2 is regularized by assuming a common variance parameter for the otherwise unrestricted curves.

Figure 4 displays the county specific time trends showing considerable variation from county to county. For comparison figure 3 shows for the counties in the last row of figure 4 the time trend if the different curves are *not* regularized through common variance parameters, i.e. *different* variance parameters are assumed for each curve. Obviously the curves are much more wiggled and the credible intervals show some instability.

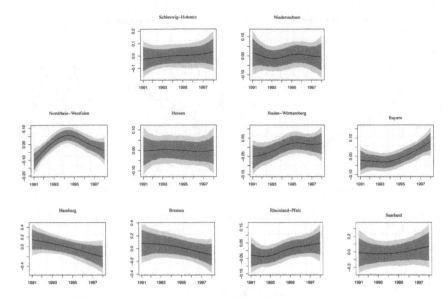

Fig. 3. Health insurance: Visualization of the space-time interaction $f_2(t, county_{it})$.

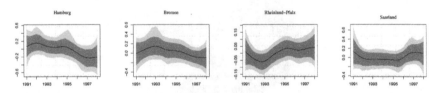

Fig. 4. Health insurance: Visualization of the space-time interaction for Hamburg, Bremen, Rheinland-Pfalz and Saarland if different variance parameters are used for the county specify time trends.

References

BELITZ, C. and LANG, S. (2008): Simultaneous selection of variables and smoothing parameters in structured additive regression models. *Computational Statistics and Data Analysis 53, 61-81.*

BREZGER, A. and LANG, S. (2006): Generalized structured additive regression based on Bayesian P-splines. *Computational Statistics and Data Analysis 50, 967-991.*

FAHRMEIR, L., KNEIB, T. and LANG, S. (2004): Penalized structured additive regression for space-time data: a Bayesian perspective. *Statistica Sinica 14, 731-761.*

FRÜHWIRTH-SCHNATTER, S., FRÜHWIRTH, R., HELD, L. and RUE, H. (2008): Improved Auxiliary Mixture Sampling for Hierarchical Models of Non-Gaussian Data. *IFAS, University of Linz.*

LANG, S., UMLAUF, N., KNEIB, T. and WECHSELBERGER, P. (2010): Multilevel Generalized Structured Additive Regression.

Part VII

Data Stream Mining

Temporally-Adaptive Linear Classification for Handling Population Drift in Credit Scoring

Niall M. Adams[1], Dimitris K. Tasoulis[1], Christoforos Anagnostopoulos[2], and David J. Hand[1,2]

[1] Department of Mathematics
Imperial College London, UK *[n.adams, d.tasoulis, d.j.hand]@imperial.ac.uk*
[2] The Institute for Mathematical Sciences
Imperial College London, UK *canagnos@imperial.ac.uk*

Abstract. Classification methods have proven effective for predicting the creditworthiness of credit applications. However, the tendency of the underlying populations to change over time, *population drift,* is a fundamental problem for such classifiers. The problem manifests as decreasing performance as the classifier ages and is typically handled by periodic classifier reconstruction. To maintain performance between rebuilds, we propose an adaptive and incremental linear classification rule that is updated on the arrival of new labeled data. We consider adapting this method to suit credit application classification and demonstrate, with real loan data, that the method outperforms static and periodically rebuilt linear classifiers.

Keywords: classification, credit scoring, population drift, forgetting factor

1 Introduction

An important application of credit scoring is classifying credit applicants as good or bad risk. In many situations, such as classifying unsecured personal loans (UPLs) in the UK, there is a legislative requirement to justify the rejection of applications. Such justifications are easier to make with some forms of statistical model than others. In particular, if a model is linear in the predictor variables then the coefficient of each variable can be regarded as a measure of its importance to the prediction. For this reason, logistic regression, and to a lesser extent linear discriminant analysis (LDA), are widely used (Hand and Henley (1997)).

There are a number of outstanding problems related to credit application classification (CAC), including reject inference (e.g. Hand (2001)) and population drift (e.g. Kelly et al. (1999)). The latter problem arises because the classifier is deployed on data arising from distributions different to the training data. These distributional changes can be gradual or abrupt, and can arise for many reasons, including changes in the economic climate and changing legislation. Population drift is a problem in many areas, including

Y. Lechevallier, G. Saporta (eds.), *Proceedings of COMPSTAT'2010*,
DOI 10.1007/978-3-7908-2604-3_15, © Springer-Verlag Berlin Heidelberg 2010

target tracking, spam filtering, user preference tracking, and telecommunications. There are various proposals for extending conventional classifiers to handle population drift; Anagnostopoulos et al. (2009) gives a brief review.

Population drift in particular leads to the operational performance of CAC degrading over time. When this degradation is sufficiently serious the classifier is rebuilt (Lucas (1992)). This classifier rebuilding exercise is expensive, and while effective, the operational classifier is still subject to performance degradation between rebuilds. In this paper, we extend a recently developed incremental and adaptive classifier (Anagnostopoulos et al. (2009)) to ameliorate the effect of population drift in CAC, by incorporating new data as they become available during the operational life of the classifier. We restrict attention to linear classifiers, in order to match the legacy systems used by banks, as well as explanatory legislative requirements.

In the next section, we describe how CAC can be treated in the framework of LDA. In Sec. 3, we employ the method of Anagnostopoulos et al. (2009) to derive adaptive and online updates for the classifier, with attention to specific aspects of CAC. The approach is demonstrated on real UPL data in Sec. 4.

2   Classification and credit scoring

CAC is typically a two-class problem, classifying applications as either good risk or bad risk. Vectors of predictor variables, $\mathbf{x}$, are derived from the loan application, including information related to applicant's address and background, and employment. Usually, components of these vectors are categorical, with continuous variables being divided into categories, and with a wide range of transformations begin explored (e.g. Siddiqi (2006, Ch. 6)).

The approach we consider is inspired by two-class LDA. Following Webb (2002, Ch.4), we begin with Fisher's criterion, which seeks a linear combination of the predictor variables, $\mathbf{w}$, to maximise

$$\frac{|\mathbf{w}^T(\hat{\boldsymbol{\mu}}^{(1)} - \hat{\boldsymbol{\mu}}^{(2)})|^2}{\mathbf{w}^T\hat{\boldsymbol{\Sigma}}_W\mathbf{w}} \tag{1}$$

where $\boldsymbol{\mu}^{(i)}$ is the sample mean vector of the ith class data, and $\hat{\boldsymbol{\Sigma}}_W$ is the *pooled within-group covariance matrix*:

$$\hat{\boldsymbol{\Sigma}}_W = \frac{1}{n-2}\left(n^{(1)}\hat{\boldsymbol{\Sigma}}_1 + n^{(2)}\hat{\boldsymbol{\Sigma}}_2\right).$$

Here, $\hat{\boldsymbol{\Sigma}}_i$ and $n^{(i)}$ are the sample covariance matrix and the sample size of the ith class data set, respectively, and $n = n^{(1)} + n^{(2)}$. These parameters are computed as

$$\hat{\boldsymbol{\mu}}^{(j)} = \frac{1}{n^{(j)}}\sum_{t=1}^{n^{(j)}}\mathbf{x}_t, \quad \hat{\boldsymbol{\Sigma}}^{(j)} = \frac{1}{n^{(j)}}\sum_{t=1}^{n^{(j)}}(\mathbf{x}_t-\hat{\boldsymbol{\mu}}^{(j)})(\mathbf{x}_t-\hat{\boldsymbol{\mu}}^{(j)})^T, \quad \hat{p}^{(j)} = \frac{n^{(j)}}{n^{(1)}+n^{(2)}} \tag{2}$$

Where we additionally compute the estimated prior probabilities, $p^{(i)}$, which contribute later to the classification threshold. The vector $\mathbf{w}$ which maximises Eq.(1) is proportional to $\hat{\boldsymbol{\Sigma}}_W^{-1}(\hat{\boldsymbol{\mu}}_1 - \hat{\boldsymbol{\mu}}_2)$. This provides a quite general formulation, which is simply concerned with the estimated first and second moments of each class distribution. By adding a threshold related to the prior probabilities (e.g. Webb (2002, Ch.4)), we obtain the linear discriminant function

$$g_j(\mathbf{x}) = \log(\hat{p}^{(j)}) - \frac{1}{2}(\hat{\boldsymbol{\mu}}^{(j)})^T \hat{\boldsymbol{\Sigma}}_W^{-1} \hat{\boldsymbol{\mu}}^{(j)} + \mathbf{x}^T \hat{\boldsymbol{\Sigma}}_W^{-1} \hat{\boldsymbol{\mu}}^{(j)}. \tag{3}$$

We briefly discuss the complex timing of credit application data. Predictor vectors, $\mathbf{x}$, arrive when applications are granted credit. Later, the associated class label arrives. Typical definitions of creditworthiness mean the bad risk label can often be assigned within a months of the loan commencing, whereas the good-risk label can only be assigned near the end. As such these populations may not be comparable. This is a fundamental and difficult point that is usually overlooked.

Credit application classifiers are built from sets of historic data. These sets consist of complete (predictor vector and label) observations in a time window. The timing of predictor vectors and associated class labels, and other aspects of temporal misalignment, are ignored. Missing data tools and information fusion are required for a complete treatment of CAC.

Our objective in this paper is to show that adaptive classifiers can improve performance between rebuilds by incorporating new data, during the operational life of the classifier. As with the conventional approach, we ignore other aspects of synchronisation.

3   Adaptive Linear Classifier

We outline an efficient and temporally adaptive mechanism for parametric estimation, which updates parameter estimates for each class when new labeled data is available. This updating is implemented in an adaptive way, involving *forgetting factors*, for each class. Such parameters control the extent of the contribution of historical data. Moreover, we develop an adaptive version that sets forgetting factors in response to changes in the data. This version provides a potentially useful monitoring tool. The generic approach is described in detail in Anagnostopoulos et al. (2009), where an adaptive quadratic discriminant rule is demonstrated to be effective for a variety of population drift scenarios. This framework is concerned with first and second moment estimates and is hence applicable in this case. Certain modifications are required in order to deal with important characteristics of the CAC problem. We explain these modifications in Sec. 3.2.

First, consider the problem of computing the sample mean vector and sample covariance matrix of t p-dimensional vectors $\mathbf{x}_i$, $i = 1, \ldots, t$. The sample estimates are given in Eq. (2). These estimates can be *updated* with the following recursions:

$$\mathbf{m}_{t+1} = \mathbf{m}_t + \mathbf{x}_{t+1}, \ \hat{\boldsymbol{\mu}}_{t+1} = \frac{\mathbf{m}_{t+1}}{t+1}, \ \mathbf{m}_0 = \mathbf{0},$$

$$\mathbf{S}_{t+1} = \mathbf{S}_t + (\mathbf{x}_{t+1} - \hat{\boldsymbol{\mu}}_{t+1})(\mathbf{x}_{t+1} - \hat{\boldsymbol{\mu}}_{t+1})^T, \ \hat{\boldsymbol{\Sigma}}_{t+1} = \frac{\mathbf{S}_{t+1}}{t+1}, \ \mathbf{S}_0 = \mathbf{0}.$$

This formulation is computationally efficient and requires no data storage. However, it assumes that the data are identically distributed. If the distribution is changing then this approach is clearly inadequate. To avoid using an *explicit* model for this change, we appeal to heuristics. Perhaps the simplest approach is to use a sliding window, and a simple refinement is variable window size. In either case, selecting the window size is non-trivial.

The more elegant approach developed by Anagnostopoulos et al. (2009), borrowing ideas from adaptive filter theory (Haykin (2001)), is to incorporate a *forgetting factor*, λ, which is responsible for down-weighting older data:

$$\mathbf{m}_{t+1} = \lambda\mathbf{m}_t + \mathbf{x}_{t+1}, \ \hat{\boldsymbol{\mu}}_{t+1} = \mathbf{m}_{t+1}/n_{t+1}, \ \mathbf{m}_0 = \mathbf{0} \tag{4}$$

$$\mathbf{S}_{t+1} = \lambda\mathbf{S}_t + (\mathbf{x}_{t+1} - \hat{\boldsymbol{\mu}}_{t+1})(\mathbf{x}_{t+1} - \hat{\boldsymbol{\mu}}_{t+1})^T, \ \hat{\boldsymbol{\Sigma}}_{t+1} = \mathbf{S}_{t+1}/n_{t+1}, \ \mathbf{S}_0 = \mathbf{0} \tag{5}$$

where $\mathbf{m}$ and $\mathbf{S}$ are not scaled by the number of datapoints, but rather by the quantity n_t, which represents the total amount of information currently employed, i.e., the *effective sample size*:

$$n_{t+1} = \lambda n_t + 1, \ n_0 = 0 \tag{6}$$

For $\lambda = 1$, $n_t = t$, and the entire data history is employed. However, for $\lambda < 1$, the effective sample size remains finite as t increases. This captures the fact that only a finite amount of the most recent information is employed, i.e., the algorithm has *finite memory*. Thus, the forgetting factor can be regarded as a smoother version of a fixed-size window. In this sense, setting λ is equivalent to choosing a window-size. However, the fact that this parameter interacts with the data in a continuous way may be exploited to devise efficient, data-adaptive tuning methods, as described next. Note that analogous recursive equations for a multinomial distribution, relevant for tracking the class prior, $\hat{p}^{(i)}$, are given in Anagnostopoulos et al. (2009).

3.1   Adaptive memory

Extending the above framework to handle a time-varying forgetting factor, λ_t, is straightforward. In particular, the effective sample size will be given by

$$n_t = \lambda_t n_{t-1} + 1,$$

which is analogous to a variable size sliding window.

The proposal of Haykin (2001) for tuning forgetting factors in recursive least squares is extended in Anagnostopoulos et al. (2009) to a general likelihood framework, which seeks to optimise the model with respect to the forgetting factor, yielding the following recursion:

$$\lambda_t = \lambda_{t-1} + \alpha \mathcal{L}'_t, \quad \text{where} \quad \mathcal{L}'_t := \frac{\mathcal{L}(\mathbf{x}_t; \hat{\theta}_{t-1})}{\partial \lambda}$$

is the partial derivative of the a-priori likelihood at time t wrt the forgetting factor λ, and α is a step-size parameter. Within this framework, the parameters $\hat{\Sigma}_W$, $\hat{\mu}^{(i)}$, and $\hat{p}^{(i)}$, in Eq.(3), can be handled in a fully adaptive manner.

Detailed calculations in Anagnostopoulos et al. (2009) provide recursions for both Gaussian and multinomial distributions, implementing the stochastic optimisation above. This framework is very efficient, with a complexity that may be reduced to $O(p^2)$ operations per timepoint. In the context of CAC, such efficiency may be unnecessary. For brevity, we defer the complete algorithmic description to Anagnostopoulos et al. (2009).

3.2   Building adaptive classifiers

The key to obtaining an adaptive linear classifier is to replace the parameter estimates in Eq.(3) with adaptive parameters computed using the framework above. We now discuss adapting this idea to the CAC, with particular attention to computation of the pooled covariance and the relaxation of the regular sampling frequency underlying the adaptive framework.

First, we consider how to construct the streaming equivalent of $\hat{\Sigma}_W$. In the static case, this matrix is obtained by an average of the class-conditional covariance matrices, weighted by the respective relative frequencies. These latter are tracked by the adaptive multinomial model in the streaming case. This analogy suggests that we should employ the estimated prior probabilities in order to form the weighted sum that constitutes the pooled covariance.

Another view of the static construction provides an alternative streaming formulation. The static $\hat{\Sigma}_W$ may be obtained by computing the class-conditional means, then centering all datapoints around their respective means and finally computing the sample covariance of this novel, zero mean dataset. Defining a streaming analogue of this procedure is straightforward in our framework: upon receiving a novel datapoint, we first use it to update the class-conditional mean vectors. These vectors are tracked via two adaptive models, one for each class, where the covariance is fixed to the identity matrix. We then subtract the respective mean estimate from the novel datapoint and input the residual to a third adaptive model that is responsible for tracking the within-group covariance, where the mean is fixed to zero.

The most significant difference in the latter approach is that the pooled covariance matrix has its own forgetting factor, tuned independently of all other parameters. Therefore, the objective of adaptive forgetting in the latter model is not to track the classes as well as possible, and subsequently form the decision rule, but rather to monitor changes in the parameters that directly affect the decision boundary, namely the means and pooled covariance.

In summary, we have two distinct streaming implementations of LDA

- **LDA-3**: (3 forgetting factors) adaptively estimate $\hat{p}^{(i)}$; adaptively estimate parameters for each class; construct $\hat{\Sigma}_W$ using $\hat{p}^{(i)}$.
- **LDA-4C**: (4 forgetting factors) adaptively estimate $\hat{p}^{(i)}$; adaptively estimate $\hat{\mu}_i$; adaptively estimate $\hat{\Sigma}_W$ on the Centered datapoints.

The second issue to resolve for CAC relates to sampling frequency. The adaptive methods in Sec. 3 are built on a constant sampling frequency model, which is certainly not correct for CAC. To deploy our methodology, we regard both predictor vector and class label as arriving when the class label arrives. We resort to two simple solutions, *immediate updating* and *periodic updating*, to handle the sampling frequency issue. The former updates every time a new labeled datum arrives – effectively treating the data sequence as if it were regularly sampled. Given the complicated structure of the labeling mechanism, this simple heuristic may not be appropriate. Alternatively, we may set a certain time period as our fundamental sampling unit. A reasonable choice would be a working day. In this case, on a given day, there are three possibilities: (a) a single labeled datum arrives, (b) multiple labeled data arrives or (c) no data arrives. Problems arise with (b) and (c). For (b), consider that r_t labelled accounts arrive on day t. In this case we simply update using the mean vector of these r_t data. In case (c) the corresponding estimated statistics are not updated. The main difference between immediate and daily updating is expected to lie in the behavior of the forgetting factors: in the former case they are meant to react to change between consecutive datapoints, whereas in the latter they should react to change over regular time periods.

4   Data and Experiments

We experiment with real data previously analysed in Kelly et al. (1999). This consists of 92258 UPL applications accepted between 1993 and 1997. The twenty predictor variables are standard for this application, including age, occupation, income, time at address, and details of the applicant's relationship with the lender. These were selected and transformed according to the data provider's standard procedures.

Population drifts may manifest differently across the predictor variables. Fig. 1 gives two examples of drift. The top left plot shows the weekly average value of a categorical indicator representing credit card ownership, with a smooth regression estimate. The top right plot of Fig. 1 shows the weekly average for a repayment method variable. The abrupt change in this plot

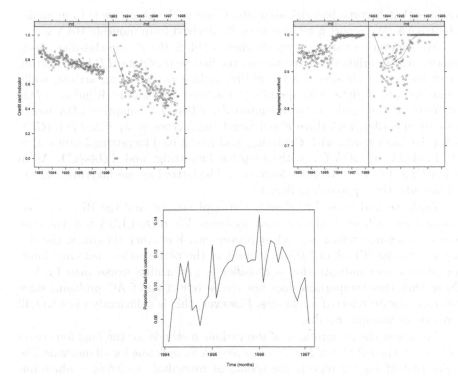

Fig. 1. Population drift examples. Top left and middle show applicants labelled as good risk and bad risk for two variables. Bottom shows monthly estimated class prior.

can be accounted for by a change in policy, to discourage non-automatic repayment.

The bottom plot of Fig. 1 demonstrates changing priors by plotting the monthly proportion of bad risk customers. The dataset is sufficiently large that these monthly differences are unlikely to be statistical fluctuations. Thus, it is reasonable to suppose that the prior for the bad risk class actually varied between 8% and 14% over the observation period. Note also clear jumps around the Christmas period each year in the right plot of Fig. 1.

Various modes of population drift are certainly evident in this data set. To determine its impact on any type of classifier requires an appropriate performance measure. Frequently, the area under the ROC curve (AUC) is used as a performance measure for assessing classifiers. For a variety of reasons (e.g. Adams and Hand (1999), Hand (2005), Hand (2009)), and for consistency with Kelly et al. (1999) we prefer to assess performance using the "bad rate among accepts". This measure proceeds by giving loans to a fixed proportion, π, of applications, over a fixed period. These should be the $100\pi\%$ of applications predicted as least likely to be bad risk. The performance measure, bad rate among accepts (BRAA) is then the proportion of these accepted applications that become bad risk accounts. Clearly, the objective is to minimise the BRAA. We report a relative measure derived from monthly BRAA.

We compare a variety of approaches: *LDA-S*, the *S*tatic classifier, never modified after original construction on the first year of data; *LDA-W*, starting with the static classifer, incrementally update as new data arrives, while removing oldest data, corresponding to a fixed size sliding *W*indow; *LDA-R*, *R*ebuild the model at yearly intervals; *LDA-3Fλ*, adaptive LDA model described earlier, with three *F*ixed forgetting factors, at $\lambda_t = \lambda$; *LDA-4CFλ*, adaptive LDA model with *C*entering, and four *F*ixed forgetting factors, $\lambda_t = \lambda$; *LDA-3A*, as LDA-Fλ, with *A*daptive forgetting; and *LDA-4CA*. As in LDA-CFλ, but with *A*daptive forgetting. The latter four methods are variants of the adaptive approach in Sec. 3.1.

Each method is used to classify the applications, and the BRAA is calculated for each method on a monthly basis. We regard LDA-S as the base classifier against which we seek improvement. For other classifiers, the difference to the BRAA of LDA-S, is used as the performance measure. Thus, negative values indicate that a classifier is performing worse than LDA-S. Note that this comparison does not really reflect the CAC problem, since we incorporate rejected applicants. However, this is sufficiently close to still provide meaningful results.

We assess the performance of the various methods for the final four years of data. In the left plot of Fig. 2, we employ *daily updating* for all methods.The right plot of Fig. 2 reports the results of *immediate updating* – which improves performance for all algorithms (note scale difference between plots), but interestingly does not affect the relative qualities of the algorithms.

The primary observation is that all streaming methods outperform the static classifier considerably, confirming the presence of drift in the data and the adaptive capacities of streaming methods. Note that 7867 and 6729 bads have been correctly identified by LDA-S, and the best-performing streaming classifier, LDA-3F0.9, respectively. Since bad customers are associated with higher costs, this reduction will be associated with increased profit.

The periodically rebuilt classifier LDA-R performs better than LDA-W, presumably since it has sufficient sample size to achieve stable estimates. Nevertheless, LDA-R still experiences long periods of negligible performance

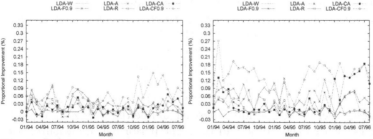

Fig. 2. Relative performance of various methods. Left: Daily update. Right: Immediate update.

improvement and is greatly outperformed by streaming methods. This is unsurprising since we would expect that, in the absence of strong prior knowledge, the updating period would in general fail to synchronise with the timing of the changes in the underlying distributions. This problem is also overcome with forgetting factors, either fixed or adaptive: the algorithm is capable of discounting information all the time.

We now compare different streaming methods. The centering approach, LDA-4C, demonstrates superior performance to LDA-3A, very visibly so in the case of fixed forgetting (LDA-4CF0.9 vs LDA-3F0.9), but also in the case of adaptive forgetting (LDA-C vs LDA-A). This confirms our claim that LDA-C is better suited to accurately track changes in the decision boundary than its counterpart. Note that fixed forgetting is preferable to adaptive tuning for both models in this experiment. However not all fixed forgetting factors perform as well as the best choice (not shown). Determining good fixed choices required offline experimentation. Thus, there is merit in the adaptive approach, since it requires no tuning from the user.

Another strength of adaptive forgetting is the capacity to reveal aspects of the drift structure. For example, the left plot in Fig. 3 displays λ_t for the two classes (for LDA-CAF) using daily updating. In the right plot of Fig. 3 the same results are shown for immediate updating, smoothed and further zoomed in. Note that the increased volatility of λ_t for immediate updating is expected: drift or changepoints are exacerbated by irregular sampling. In both plots $\lambda^{(1)}$ corresponds to the forgetting factor related to the non-defaulting class, $\lambda^{(2)}$ for the defaulting class and $\lambda^{(3)}$ corresponds to the pooled within-group sample covariance.

Both methods identify a change in January. However, the methodology yields further insight into how this change unfolds: just before the end of year the good risk class changes substantially, whereas the bad risk class shows changes in a relatively uniform manner. However the low values of $\lambda^{(3)}$ just after the end of year show that there is a need to change the decision surface at this point. This phenomenon is confirmed by either daily and immediate updating.

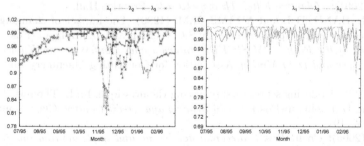

Fig. 3. Monitoring behaviour of adaptive forgetting factors, July 1995-March 1996, from LDA-CAF. Left: Daily updating. Right: Immediate updating.

5   Conclusion

We have shown how to adapt streaming classification technology to the CAC problem. In experiments, we have shown that some amount of temporal adaption yields improved performance. In particular, for this data set, changing class-priors and within-group covariance are important sources of population drift. Our approach is generic however, and can handle other sources of drift, in addition to providing a means of monitoring which is particularly useful for data exploration.

Of course, caution suggests that any automatically updated model should be monitored to check that it is behaving reasonably. For CAC, performance monitoring tools are in any case in routine use as a matter of course.

Acknowledgements: This work was supported by the ALADDIN project and is jointly funded by a BAE Systems and EPSRC (Engineering and Physical Research Council) strategic partnership, under EPSRC grant EP/C548051/1. We are grateful to the UK bank that provided the data. The work of David Hand was supported by a Royal Society Wolfson Research Merit Award.

References

ADAMS, N.M. and HAND, D.J. (1999): Comparing classifiers when the misallocation costs are uncertain. *Pattern Recognition 32, 1139–1147.*

ANAGNOSTOPOULOS, C., TASOULIS D.K., ADAMS, N.M., PAVLIDIS, N. G. and D.J. HAND, D.J. (2009): Streaming Gaussian classification using recursive maximum likelihood with adaptive forgetting *Machine Learning*, under review.

HAND, D.J. (2001): Reject inference in credit operations. In: E. Mays (Eds.): *Handbook of Credit Scoring*, Glenlake Publishing, Chicago, 225–240.

HAND, D.J. (2005): Good practice in retail credit scorecard assessment. *Journal of the Operational Research Society 56, 1109–1117.*

HAND, D.J. (2009): Measuring classifier performance: a coherent alternative to the area under the ROC curve. *Machine Learning 77, 103–123.*

HAND, D.J. and HENLEY, W.E. (1997): Statistical classification methods in consumer credit scoring: a review. *Journal of the Royal Statistical Society Series A, Statistics in Society 160(3), 523–541.*

HAYKIN, S. (2001): *Adaptive Filter Theory, 4th edn.* Prentice Hall.

KELLY, M. G., HAND, D.J. and ADAMS, N.M. (1999): The impact of changing populations on classifier performance. In: S.Chaudhuri and D. Madigan (Eds.), *Proceedings of the Fifth ACM SIGKDD International Conference on Knowledge Discovery and Data Mining*, Association for Computing Machinery, New York, 367–371.

LUCAS, A. (1992): Updating scorecards: removing the mystique. In: L. Thomas, J. Crook, and D. Edelman (Eds.), *Credit Scoring and Credit Control*, Clarendon: Oxford, 180–197.

SIDDIQI, N. (2006): *Credit Risk Scorecards: developing and implementing intelligent credit scoring.* Wiley.

WEBB, A. (2002): *Statistical Pattern Recognition, 2nd edn.* Wiley.

Large-Scale Machine Learning
with Stochastic Gradient Descent

Léon Bottou

NEC Labs America, Princeton NJ 08542, USA
leon@bottou.org

Abstract. During the last decade, the data sizes have grown faster than the speed of processors. In this context, the capabilities of statistical machine learning methods is limited by the computing time rather than the sample size. A more precise analysis uncovers qualitatively different tradeoffs for the case of small-scale and large-scale learning problems. The large-scale case involves the computational complexity of the underlying optimization algorithm in non-trivial ways. Unlikely optimization algorithms such as stochastic gradient descent show amazing performance for large-scale problems. In particular, second order stochastic gradient and averaged stochastic gradient are asymptotically efficient after a single pass on the training set.

Keywords: stochastic gradient descent, online learning, efficiency

1 Introduction

The computational complexity of learning algorithm becomes the critical limiting factor when one envisions very large datasets. This contribution advocates stochastic gradient algorithms for large scale machine learning problems. The first section describes the stochastic gradient algorithm. The second section presents an analysis that explains why stochastic gradient algorithms are attractive when the data is abundant. The third section discusses the asymptotic efficiency of estimates obtained after a single pass over the training set. The last section presents empirical evidence.

2 Learning with gradient descent

Let us first consider a simple supervised learning setup. Each example z is a pair (x, y) composed of an arbitrary input x and a scalar output y. We consider a *loss function* $\ell(\hat{y}, y)$ that measures the cost of predicting $\hat{y}$ when the actual answer is y, and we choose a family $\mathcal{F}$ of functions $f_w(x)$ parametrized by a weight vector w. We seek the function $f \in \mathcal{F}$ that minimizes the loss $Q(z, w) = \ell(f_w(x), y)$ averaged on the examples. Although we would like to average over the unknown distribution $dP(z)$ that embodies the Laws of

Y. Lechevallier, G. Saporta (eds.), *Proceedings of COMPSTAT'2010*,
DOI 10.1007/978-3-7908-2604-3_16, © Springer-Verlag Berlin Heidelberg 2010

Nature, we must often settle for computing the average on a sample $z_1 \ldots z_n$.

$$E(f) = \int \ell(f(x), y) \, dP(z) \qquad E_n(f) = \frac{1}{n} \sum_{i=1}^{n} \ell(f(x_i), y_i) \qquad (1)$$

The *empirical risk* $E_n(f)$ measures the training set performance. The *expected risk* $E(f)$ measures the generalization performance, that is, the expected performance on future examples. The statistical learning theory (Vapnik and Chervonenkis (1971)) justifies minimizing the empirical risk instead of the expected risk when the chosen family $\mathcal{F}$ is sufficiently restrictive.

2.1   Gradient descent

It has often been proposed (e.g., Rumelhart et al. (1986)) to minimize the empirical risk $E_n(f_w)$ using *gradient descent* (GD). Each iteration updates the weights w on the basis of the gradient of $E_n(f_w)$,

$$w_{t+1} = w_t - \gamma \frac{1}{n} \sum_{i=1}^{n} \nabla_w Q(z_i, w_t), \qquad (2)$$

where γ is an adequately chosen gain. Under sufficient regularity assumptions, when the initial estimate w_0 is close enough to the optimum, and when the gain γ is sufficiently small, this algorithm achieves *linear convergence* (Dennis and Schnabel (1983)), that is, $-\log \rho \sim t$, where ρ represents the residual error.

Much better optimization algorithms can be designed by replacing the scalar gain γ by a positive definite matrix Γ_t that approaches the inverse of the Hessian of the cost at the optimum:

$$w_{t+1} = w_t - \Gamma_t \frac{1}{n} \sum_{i=1}^{n} \nabla_w Q(z_i, w_t). \qquad (3)$$

This *second order gradient descent* (2GD) is a variant of the well known Newton algorithm. Under sufficiently optimistic regularity assumptions, and provided that w_0 is sufficiently close to the optimum, second order gradient descent achieves *quadratic convergence*. When the cost is quadratic and the scaling matrix Γ is exact, the algorithm reaches the optimum after a single iteration. Otherwise, assuming sufficient smoothness, we have $-\log \log \rho \sim t$.

2.2   Stochastic gradient descent

The *stochastic gradient descent* (SGD) algorithm is a drastic simplification. Instead of computing the gradient of $E_n(f_w)$ exactly, each iteration estimates this gradient on the basis of a single randomly picked example z_t:

$$w_{t+1} = w_t - \gamma_t \nabla_w Q(z_t, w_t). \qquad (4)$$

The stochastic process $\{\, w_t,\ t=1,\dots \}$ depends on the examples randomly picked at each iteration. It is hoped that (4) behaves like its expectation (2) despite the noise introduced by this simplified procedure.

Since the stochastic algorithm does not need to remember which examples were visited during the previous iterations, it can process examples on the fly in a deployed system. In such a situation, the stochastic gradient descent directly optimizes the expected risk, since the examples are randomly drawn from the ground truth distribution.

The convergence of stochastic gradient descent has been studied extensively in the stochastic approximation literature. Convergence results usually require decreasing gains satisfying the conditions $\sum_t \gamma_t^2 < \infty$ and $\sum_t \gamma_t = \infty$. The Robbins-Siegmund theorem (Robbins and Siegmund (1971)) provides the means to establish almost sure convergence under mild conditions (Bottou (1998)), including cases where the loss function is not everywhere differentiable.

The convergence speed of stochastic gradient descent is in fact limited by the noisy approximation of the true gradient. When the gains decrease too slowly, the variance of the parameter estimate w_t decreases equally slowly. When the gains decrease too quickly, the expectation of the parameter estimate w_t takes a very long time to approach the optimum. Under sufficient regularity conditions (e.g. Murata (1998)), the best convergence speed is achieved using gains $\gamma_t \sim t^{-1}$. The expectation of the residual error then decreases with similar speed, that is, $\mathbb{E}\,\rho \sim t^{-1}$.

The *second order stochastic gradient descent* (2SGD) multiplies the gradients by a positive definite matrix Γ_t approaching the inverse of the Hessian:

$$w_{t+1} \;=\; w_t - \gamma_t \Gamma_t \nabla_w\, Q(z_t, w_t). \tag{5}$$

Unfortunately, this modification does not reduce the stochastic noise and therefore does improve the variance of w_t. Although constants are improved, the expectation of the residual error still decreases like t^{-1}, that is, $\mathbb{E}\,\rho \sim t^{-1}$, (e.g. Bordes et al. (2009), appendix).

2.3   Stochastic gradient examples

Table 1 illustrates stochastic gradient descent algorithms for a number of classic machine learning schemes. The stochastic gradient descent for the Perceptron, for the Adaline, and for k-Means match the algorithms proposed in the original papers. The SVM and the Lasso were first described with traditional optimization techniques. Both Q_{svm} and Q_{lasso} include a regularization term controlled by the hyperparameter λ. The K-means algorithm converges to a local minimum because Q_{kmeans} is nonconvex. On the other hand, the proposed update rule uses second order gains that ensure a fast convergence. The proposed Lasso algorithm represents each weight as the difference of two positive variables. Applying the stochastic gradient rule to these variables and enforcing their positivity leads to sparser solutions.

Table 1. Stochastic gradient algorithms for various learning systems.

Loss	Stochastic gradient algorithm
Adaline (Widrow and Hoff, 1960) $Q_{\text{adaline}} = \frac{1}{2}\left(y - w^\top \Phi(x)\right)^2$ $\Phi(x) \in \mathbb{R}^d,\ y = \pm 1$	$w \leftarrow w + \gamma_t \left(y_t - w^\top \Phi(x_t)\right) \Phi(x_t)$
Perceptron (Rosenblatt, 1957) $Q_{\text{perceptron}} = \max\{0, -y\, w^\top \Phi(x)\}$ $\Phi(x) \in \mathbb{R}^d,\ y = \pm 1$	$w \leftarrow w + \gamma_t \begin{cases} y_t\, \Phi(x_t) & \text{if } y_t\, w^\top \Phi(x_t) \leq 0 \\ 0 & \text{otherwise} \end{cases}$
K-Means (MacQueen, 1967) $Q_{\text{kmeans}} = \min_k \frac{1}{2}(z - w_k)^2$ $z \in \mathbb{R}^d,\ w_1 \ldots w_k \in \mathbb{R}^d$ $n_1 \ldots n_k \in \mathbb{N}$, initially 0	$k^* = \arg\min_k (z_t - w_k)^2$ $n_{k^*} \leftarrow n_{k^*} + 1$ $w_{k^*} \leftarrow w_{k^*} + \frac{1}{n_{k^*}}(z_t - w_{k^*})$
SVM (Cortes and Vapnik, 1995) $Q_{\text{svm}} = \lambda w^2 + \max\{0, 1 - y\, w^\top \Phi(x)\}$ $\Phi(x) \in \mathbb{R}^d,\ y = \pm 1,\ \lambda > 0$	$w \leftarrow w - \gamma_t \begin{cases} \lambda w & \text{if } y_t\, w^\top \Phi(x_t) > 1, \\ \lambda w - y_t\, \Phi(x_t) & \text{otherwise.} \end{cases}$
Lasso (Tibshirani, 1996) $Q_{\text{lasso}} = \lambda\|w\|_1 + \frac{1}{2}\left(y - w^\top \Phi(x)\right)^2$ $w = (u_1 - v_1, \ldots, u_d - v_d)$ $\Phi(x) \in \mathbb{R}^d,\ y \in \mathbb{R},\ \lambda > 0$	$u_i \leftarrow \left[u_i - \gamma_t\left(\lambda - (y_t - w^\top \Phi(x_t))\Phi_i(x_t)\right)\right]_+$ $v_i \leftarrow \left[v_i - \gamma_t\left(\lambda + (y_t - w_t^\top \Phi(x_t))\Phi_i(x_t)\right)\right]_+$ with notation $[x]_+ = \max\{0, x\}$.

3   Learning with large training sets

Let $f^* = \arg\min_f E(f)$ be the best possible prediction function. Since we seek the prediction function from a parametrized family of functions $\mathcal{F}$, let $f_{\mathcal{F}}^* = \arg\min_{f \in \mathcal{F}} E(f)$ be the best function in this family. Since we optimize the empirical risk instead of the expected risk, let $f_n = \arg\min_{f \in \mathcal{F}} E_n(f)$ be the empirical optimum. Since this optimization can be costly, let us stop the algorithm when it reaches an solution $\tilde{f}_n$ that minimizes the objective function with a predefined accuracy $E_n(\tilde{f}_n) < E_n(f_n) + \rho$.

3.1   The tradeoffs of large scale learning

The excess error $\mathcal{E} = \mathbb{E}\big[E(\tilde{f}_n) - E(f^*)\big]$ can be decomposed in three terms (Bottou and Bousquet, 2008):

$$\mathcal{E} = \mathbb{E}\big[E(f_{\mathcal{F}}^*) - E(f^*)\big] + \mathbb{E}\big[E(f_n) - E(f_{\mathcal{F}}^*)\big] + \mathbb{E}\big[E(\tilde{f}_n) - E(f_n)\big]. \quad (6)$$

- The approximation error $\mathcal{E}_{\text{app}} = \mathbb{E}\big[E(f_{\mathcal{F}}^*) - E(f^*)\big]$ measures how closely functions in $\mathcal{F}$ can approximate the optimal solution f^*. The approximation error can be reduced by choosing a larger family of functions.

- The estimation error $\mathcal{E}_{\text{est}} = \mathbb{E}\big[E(f_n) - E(f_{\mathcal{F}}^*)\big]$ measures the effect of minimizing the empirical risk $E_n(f)$ instead of the expected risk $E(f)$.

The estimation error can be reduced by choosing a smaller family of functions or by increasing the size of the training set.

- The optimization error $\mathcal{E}_{\text{opt}} = E(\tilde{f}_n) - E(f_n)$ measures the impact of the approximate optimization on the expected risk. The optimization error can be reduced by running the optimizer longer. The additional computing time depends of course on the family of function and on the size of the training set.

Given constraints on the maximal computation time T_{max} and the maximal training set size n_{max}, this decomposition outlines a tradeoff involving the size of the family of functions $\mathcal{F}$, the optimization accuracy ρ, and the number of examples n effectively processed by the optimization algorithm.

$$\min_{\mathcal{F},\rho,n} \quad \mathcal{E} = \mathcal{E}_{\text{app}} + \mathcal{E}_{\text{est}} + \mathcal{E}_{\text{opt}} \quad \text{subject to} \begin{cases} n \leq n_{\text{max}} \\ T(\mathcal{F}, \rho, n) \leq T_{\text{max}} \end{cases} \quad (7)$$

Two cases should be distinguished:

- *Small-scale learning problems* are first constrained by the maximal number of examples. Since the computing time is not an issue, we can reduce the optimization error $\mathcal{E}_{\text{opt}}$ to insignificant levels by choosing ρ arbitrarily small, and we can minimize the estimation error by chosing $n = n_{\text{max}}$. We then recover the approximation-estimation tradeoff that has been widely studied in statistics and in learning theory.

- *Large-scale learning problems* are first constrained by the maximal computing time. Approximate optimization can achieve better expected risk because more training examples can be processed during the allowed time. The specifics depend on the computational properties of the chosen optimization algorithm.

3.2 Asymptotic analysis

Solving (7) in the asymptotic regime amounts to ensuring that the terms of the decomposition (6) decrease at similar rates. Since the asymptotic convergence rate of the excess error (6) is the convergence rate of its slowest term, the computational effort required to make a term decrease faster would be wasted.

For simplicity, we assume in this section that the Vapnik-Chervonenkis dimensions of the families of functions $\mathcal{F}$ are bounded by a common constant. We also assume that the optimization algorithms satisfy all the assumptions required to achieve the convergence rates discussed in section 2. Similar analyses can be carried out for specific algorithms under weaker assumptions (e.g. Shalev-Shwartz and Srebro (2008)).

A simple application of the uniform convergence results of (Vapnik and Chervonenkis (1971)) gives then the upper bound

$$\mathcal{E} = \mathcal{E}_{\text{app}} + \mathcal{E}_{\text{est}} + \mathcal{E}_{\text{opt}} = \mathcal{E}_{\text{app}} + \mathcal{O}\left(\sqrt{\frac{\log n}{n}} + \rho\right).$$

182   Léon Bottou

Table 2. Asymptotic equivalents for various optimization algorithms: gradient descent (GD, eq. 2), second order gradient descent (2GD, eq. 3), stochastic gradient descent (SGD, eq. 4), and second order stochastic gradient descent (2SGD, eq. 5). Although they are the worst optimization algorithms, SGD and 2SGD achieve the fastest convergence speed on the expected risk. They differ only by constant factors not shown in this table, such as condition numbers and weight vector dimension.

	GD	2GD	SGD	2SGD
Time per iteration:	n	n	1	1
Iterations to accuracy ρ:	$\log\frac{1}{\rho}$	$\log\log\frac{1}{\rho}$	$\frac{1}{\rho}$	$\frac{1}{\rho}$
Time to accuracy ρ:	$n\log\frac{1}{\rho}$	$n\log\log\frac{1}{\rho}$	$\frac{1}{\rho}$	$\frac{1}{\rho}$
Time to excess error ε:	$\frac{1}{\varepsilon^{1/\alpha}}\log^2\frac{1}{\varepsilon}$	$\frac{1}{\varepsilon^{1/\alpha}}\log\frac{1}{\varepsilon}\log\log\frac{1}{\varepsilon}$	$\frac{1}{\varepsilon}$	$\frac{1}{\varepsilon}$

Unfortunately the convergence rate of this bound is too pessimistic. Faster convergence occurs when the loss function has strong convexity properties (Lee et al. (2006)) or when the data distribution satisfies certain assumptions (Tsybakov (2004)). The equivalence

$$\mathcal{E} \;=\; \mathcal{E}_{\mathrm{app}}+\mathcal{E}_{\mathrm{est}}+\mathcal{E}_{\mathrm{opt}} \;\sim\; \mathcal{E}_{\mathrm{app}} + \left(\frac{\log n}{n}\right)^{\alpha} + \rho, \quad \text{for some } \alpha \in \left[\tfrac{1}{2},1\right], \quad (8)$$

provides a more realistic view of the asymptotic behavior of the excess error (e.g. Massart (2000), Bousquet (2002)). Since the three component of the excess error should decrease at the same rate, the solution of the tradeoff problem (7) must then obey the multiple asymptotic equivalences

$$\mathcal{E} \;\sim\; \mathcal{E}_{\mathrm{app}} \;\sim\; \mathcal{E}_{\mathrm{est}} \;\sim\; \mathcal{E}_{\mathrm{opt}} \;\sim\; \left(\frac{\log n}{n}\right)^{\alpha} \;\sim\; \rho. \qquad (9)$$

Table 2 summarizes the asymptotic behavior of the four gradient algorithm described in section 2. The first three rows list the computational cost of each iteration, the number of iterations required to reach an optimization accuracy ρ, and the corresponding computational cost. The last row provides a more interesting measure for large scale machine learning purposes. Assuming we operate at the optimum of the approximation-estimation-optimization tradeoff (7), this line indicates the computational cost necessary to reach a predefined value of the excess error, and therefore of the expected risk. This is computed by applying the equivalences (9) to eliminate n and ρ from the third row results.

Although the stochastic gradient algorithms, SGD and 2SGD, are clearly the worst optimization algorithms (third row), they need less time than the other algorithms to reach a predefined expected risk (fourth row). Therefore, in the large scale setup, that is, when the limiting factor is the computing time rather than the number of examples, the stochastic learning algorithms performs asymptotically better!

4   Efficient learning

Let us add an additional example z_t to a training set $z_1 \ldots z_{t-1}$. Since the new empirical risk $E_t(f)$ remains close to $E_{t-1}(f)$, the empirical minimum $w_{t+1}^* = \arg\min_w E_t(f_w)$ remains close to $w_t^* = \arg\min_w E_{t-1}(f_w)$. With sufficient regularity assumptions, a first order calculation gives the result

$$w_{t+1}^* = w_t^* - t^{-1} \Psi_t \nabla_w Q(z_t, w_t^*) + \mathcal{O}(t^{-2}), \qquad (10)$$

where Ψ_t is the inverse of the Hessian of $E_t(f_w)$ in w_t^*. The similarity between this expression and the second order stochastic gradient descent rule (5) has deep consequences. Let w_t be the sequence of weights obtained by performing a *single second order stochastic gradient pass* on the randomly shuffled training set. With adequate regularity and convexity assumptions, we can prove (e.g. Bottou and LeCun (2004))

$$\lim_{t\to\infty} t\left(E(f_{w_t}) - E(f_{\mathcal{F}}^*)\right) = \lim_{t\to\infty} t\left(E(f_{w_t^*}) - E(f_{\mathcal{F}}^*)\right) = \mathcal{I} > 0. \quad (11)$$

Therefore, a single pass of second order stochastic gradient provides a prediction function f_{w_t} that approaches the optimum $f_{\mathcal{F}}^*$ as efficiently as the empirical optimum $f_{w_t^*}$. In particular, when the loss function is the log likelihood, the empirical optimum is the asymptotically efficient maximum likelihood estimate, and the second order stochastic gradient estimate is also asymptotically efficient.

Unfortunately, second order stochastic gradient descent is computationally costly because each iteration (5) performs a computation that involves the large dense matrix Γ_t. Two approaches can work around this problem.

- Computationally efficient approximations of the inverse Hessian trade asymptotic optimality for computation speed. For instance, the SGDQN algorithm (Bordes et al. (2009)) achieves interesting speed using a diagonal approximation.

- The *averaged stochastic gradient descent* (ASGD) algorithm (Polyak and Juditsky (1992)) performs the normal stochastic gradient update (4) and recursively computes the average $\bar{w}_t = \frac{1}{t} \sum_{i=1}^t w_t$:

$$w_{t+1} = w_t - \gamma_t \nabla_w Q(z_t, w_t), \quad \bar{w}_{t+1} = \frac{t}{t+1} \bar{w}_t + \frac{1}{t+1} w_{t+1}. \quad (12)$$

When the gains γ_t decrease slower than t^{-1}, the $\bar{w}_t$ converges with the optimal asymptotic speed (11). Reaching this asymptotic regime can take a very long time in practice. A smart selection of the gains γ_t helps achieving the promised performance (Xu (2010)).

Algorithm	Time	Test Error
Hinge loss SVM, $\lambda = 10^{-4}$.		
SVMLIGHT	23,642 s.	6.02 %
SVMPERF	66 s.	6.03 %
SGD	**1.4** s.	6.02 %
Log loss SVM, $\lambda = 10^{-5}$.		
TRON (-e0.01)	30 s.	5.68 %
TRON (-e0.001)	44 s.	5.70 %
SGD	**2.3** s.	5.66 %

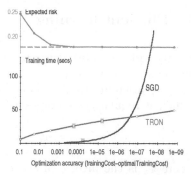

Fig. 1. Results achieved with a linear SVM on the RCV1 task. The lower half of the plot shows the time required by SGD and TRON to reach a predefined accuracy ρ on the log loss task. The upper half shows that the expected risk stops improving long before the superlinear TRON algorithm overcomes SGD.

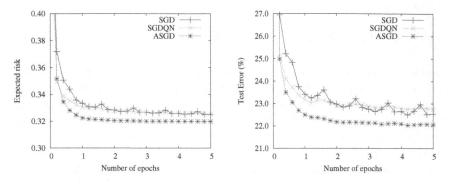

Fig. 2. Comparaison of the test set performance of SGD, SGDQN, and ASGD for a linear squared hinge SVM trained on the ALPHA task of the 2008 Pascal Large Scale Learning Challenge. ASGD nearly reaches the optimal expected risk after a single pass.

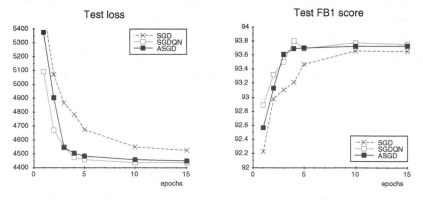

Fig. 3. Comparison of the test set performance of SGD, SGDQN, and ASGD on a CRF trained on the CONLL Chunking task. On this task, SGDQN appears more attractive because ASGD does not reach its asymptotic performance.

5 Experiments

This section briefly reports experimental results illustrating the actual performance of stochastic gradient algorithms on a variety of linear systems. We use gains $\gamma_t = \gamma_0(1 + \lambda\gamma_0 t)^{-1}$ for SGD and $\gamma_t = \gamma_0(1 + \lambda\gamma_0 t)^{-0.75}$ for ASGD. The initial gains γ_0 were set manually by observing the performance of each algorithm running on a subset of the training examples.

Figure 1 reports results achieved using SGD for a linear SVM trained for the recognition of the CCAT category in the RCV1 dataset (Lewis et al. (2004)) using both the hinge loss (Q_{svm} in table 1), and the log loss, ($Q_{logsvm} = \lambda w^2 + \log(1 + \exp(-y\, w^\top \Phi(x)))$). The training set contains 781,265 documents represented by 47,152 relatively sparse TF/IDF features. SGD runs considerably faster than either the standard SVM solvers SVMLIGHT and SVMPERF (Joachims (2006)) or the superlinear optimization algorithm TRON (Lin et al. (2007)).

Figure 2 reports results achieved using SGD, SGDQN, and ASGD for a linear SVM trained on the ALPHA task of the 2008 Pascal Large Scale Learning Challenge (see Bordes et al. (2009)) using the squared hinge loss ($Q_{sqsvm} = \lambda w^2 + \max\{0, 1 - y\, w^\top \Phi(x)\}^2$). The training set contains 100,000 patterns represented by 500 centered and normalized variables. Performances measured on a separate testing set are plotted against the number of passes over the training set. ASGD achieves near optimal results after one pass.

Figure 3 reports results achieved using SGD, SGDQN, and ASGD for a CRF (Lafferty et al. (2001)) trained on the CONLL 2000 Chunking task (Tjong Kim Sang and Buchholz (2000)). The training set contains 8936 sentences for a 1.68×10^6 dimensional parameter space. Performances measured on a separate testing set are plotted against the number of passes over the training set. SGDQN appears more attractive because ASGD does not reach its asymptotic performance. All three algorithms reach the best test set performance in a couple minutes. The standard CRF L-BFGS optimizer takes 72 minutes to compute an equivalent solution.

References

BORDES. A., BOTTOU, L., and GALLINARI, P. (2009): SGD-QN: Careful Quasi-Newton Stochastic Gradient Descent. *Journal of Machine Learning Research, 10:1737-1754.* With Erratum (to appear).

BOTTOU, L. and BOUSQUET, O. (2008): The Tradeoffs of Large Scale Learning, In *Advances in Neural Information Processing Systems*, vol.20, 161-168.

BOTTOU, L. and LECUN, Y. (2004): On-line Learning for Very Large Datasets. *Applied Stochastic Models in Business and Industry, 21(2):137-151*

BOUSQUET, O. (2002): Concentration Inequalities and Empirical Processes Theory Applied to the Analysis of Learning Algorithms. Thèse de doctorat, Ecole Polytechnique, Palaiseau, France.

CORTES, C. and VAPNIK, V. N. (1995): Support Vector Networks, *Machine Learning, 20:273-297.*

DENNIS, J. E., Jr., and SCHNABEL, R. B. (1983): *Numerical Methods For Un-constrained Optimization and Nonlinear Equations.* Prentice-Hall

JOACHIMS, T. (2006): Training Linear SVMs in Linear Time. In *Proceedings of the 12th ACM SIGKDD,* ACM Press.

LAFFERTY, J. D., MCCALLUM, A., and PEREIRA, F. (2001): Conditional Random Fields: Probabilistic Models for Segmenting and Labeling Sequence Data. In *Proceedings of ICML 2001,* 282-289, Morgan Kaufman.

LEE, W. S., BARTLETT, P. L., and WILLIAMSON, R. C. (1998): The Importance of Convexity in Learning with Squared Loss. *IEEE Transactions on Information Theory, 44(5):1974-1980.*

LEWIS, D. D., YANG, Y., ROSE, T. G., and LI, F. (2004): RCV1: A New Benchmark Collection for Text Categorization Research. *Journal of Machine Learning Research, 5:361-397.*

LIN, C. J., WENG, R. C., and KEERTHI, S. S. (2007): Trust region Newton methods for large-scale logistic regression. In *Proceedings of ICML 2007,* 561-568, ACM Press.

MACQUEEN, J. (1967): Some Methods for Classification and Analysis of Multivariate Observations. In *Fifth Berkeley Symposium on Mathematics, Statistics, and Probabilities,* vol.1, 281-297, University of California Press.

MASSART, P. (2000): Some applications of concentration inequalities to Statistics, *Annales de la Faculté des Sciences de Toulouse, series 6,9,(2):245-303.*

MURATA, N. (1998): A Statistical Study of On-line Learning. In *Online Learning and Neural Networks,* Cambridge University Press.

POLYAK, B. T. and JUDITSKY, A. B. (1992): Acceleration of stochastic approximation by averaging. *SIAM J. Control and Optimization, 30(4):838-855.*

ROSENBLATT, F. (1957): The Perceptron: A perceiving and recognizing automaton. Technical Report 85-460-1, Project PARA, Cornell Aeronautical Lab.

RUMELHART, D. E., HINTON, G. E., and WILLIAMS, R. J. (1986): Learning internal representations by error propagation. In *Parallel distributed processing: Explorations in the microstructure of cognition,* vol.I, 318-362, Bradford Books.

SHALEV-SHWARTZ, S. and SREBRO, N. (2008): SVM optimization: inverse dependence on training set size. In *Proceedings of the ICML 2008,* 928-935, ACM.

TIBSHIRANI, R. (1996): Regression shrinkage and selection via the Lasso. *Journal of the Royal Statistical Society, Series B, 58(1):267-288.*

TJONG KIM SANG E. F., and BUCHHOLZ, S. (2000): Introduction to the CoNLL-2000 Shared Task: Chunking. In *Proceedings of CoNLL-2000,* 127-132.

TSYBAKOV, A. B. (2004): Optimal aggregation of classifiers in statistical learning, *Annals of Statististics, 32(1).*

VAPNIK, V. N. and CHERVONENKIS, A. YA. (1971): On the Uniform Convergence of Relative Frequencies of Events to Their Probabilities. *Theory of Probability and its Applications, 16(2):264-280.*

WIDROW, B. and HOFF, M. E. (1960): Adaptive switching circuits. *IRE WESCON Conv. Record, Part 4., 96-104.*

XU, W. (2010): Towards Optimal One Pass Large Scale Learning with Averaged Stochastic Gradient Descent. *Journal of Machine Learning Research (to appear).*

Part VIII

Functional Data Analysis

Anticipated and Adaptive Prediction in Functional Discriminant Analysis

Cristian Preda[1], Gilbert Saporta[2], and Mohamed Hadj Mbarek[3]

[1] Ecole Polytehnique Universitaire de Lille & Laboratoire Painlevé, UMR 8524
Université des Sciences et Technologies de Lille, France,
cristian.preda@polytech-lille.fr
[2] Chaire de statistique appliquée & CEDRIC, CNAM
292 rue Saint Martin, Paris, France, *gilbert.saporta@cnam.fr*
[3] Institut Supérieur de Gestion de Sousse, Tunisie, *benmbarekmhedi@yahoo.fr*

Abstract. Linear discriminant analysis with binary response is considered when the predictor is a functional random variable $X = \{X_t, t \in [0, T]\}, T \in \mathbb{R}$. Motivated by a food industry problem, we develop a methodology to anticipate the prediction by determining the smallest T^*, $T^* \leq T$, such that $X^* = \{X_t, t \in [0, T^*]\}$ and X give similar predictions. The adaptive prediction concerns the observation of a new curve ω on $[0, T^*(\omega)]$ instead of $[0, T]$ and answers to the question "How long should we observe ω ($T^*(\omega) =?$) for having the same prediction as on $[0, T]$?". We answer to this question by defining a conservation measure with respect to the class the new curve is predicted.

Keywords: functional data, discriminant analysis, classification, adaptive prediction

1 Introduction

Statistical methods for data represented by curves (or functions) have received much interest in the last years. Random variables taking values into an infinite dimensional function space are called *functional random variables* (Ferraty and Vieu (2006)) and methods dealing with such variables define the *functional data analysis* (FDA) framework (Ramsay and Silverman (1997)). Examples of functional data can be found in several application domains such as medicine (patient evolution over time), economics (stock-exchange data), chemometrics (spectrometric data) and many others (for an overview, see Ramsay and Silverman (2002)).

A well accepted model for univariate functional data is to consider it as paths of a stochastic process $\mathbf{X} = \{X_t\}_{t \in \mathcal{T}}$ taking values into a Hilbert space of real-valued functions defined over some set $\mathcal{T}$. For example, if $\mathcal{T} = [0, T]$ with $T \in \mathbb{R}_+$, a second order stochastic process $\mathbf{X} = \{X_t\}_{t \in [0,T]}$ L_2-continuous with sample paths in $L_2([0, T])$ can be used as model for describing the behavior of some quantitative parameter associated to a process observed on a time interval of length T.

Y. Lechevallier, G. Saporta (eds.), *Proceedings of COMPSTAT'2010*,
DOI 10.1007/978-3-7908-2604-3_17, © Springer-Verlag Berlin Heidelberg 2010

Suppose that for each curve we have a single response variable Y. If Y is categorical we have a classification (or discrimination) problem and a regression one if Y is numerical.

In this paper we assume that Y is a binary response and all trajectories of X are observed continuously on $[0, T]$ and belong to $L_2([0, T])$. The main purpose of discriminant analysis (supervised classification) is to define a discriminant score $\Phi(X)$, $\Phi : L_2([0, T]) \to \mathbb{R}$, such that the prediction of Y using $\Phi(X)$ is as good as possible.

The linear discriminant analysis for functional data considers that

$$\Phi(X) = \int_0^T X_t \beta(t) dt, \quad \beta \in L_2([0, T]),$$

and has been addressed by James and Hastie (2001) and Preda et al. (2007). This problem is not new and comes back to Fisher (1924) who used the expression *integral regression*. It is well known that the estimation of this regression model by least squares criterion yields to an ill-posed problem. Regularization techniques such as principal component regression (PCR) and partial least squares regression (PLS) have been proposed in Preda and Saporta (2005).

An estimating procedure of the functional logistic model is proposed by Escabias et al. (2004, 2005) with environmental applications. Nonparametric models have been proposed by Ferraty and Vieu (2003), Biau et al. (2005) and Preda (2007). More details on nonparametric models for functional data can be found in the recent monograph of Ferraty and Vieu (2006).

In this paper we are firstly interested to the problem of *anticipated prediction* : find minimal T^*, $T^* < T$, such that the predictor X observed on $[0, T^*]$ gives "similar results"', in terms of prediction of Y, as considered on $[0, T]$. By "similar results" we mean, for example, not significantly different results with respect to some statistical test. This problem comes naturally from the following practical example : in Preda et al. (2007) we have developed functional discriminant models to predict the quality of cookies at Danone from curves representing the resistance of dough observed during the first 8 minutes of the kneading process (Lévéder et al. (2004)). The discriminant power of the linear model is satisfactory with a misclassified rate of about 11.2%. Then, the interest of reducing the observation time and take decision keeping the same discriminant power is evident.

Secondly, we address the problem of the prediction of Y from X for a new observation ω in an *adaptive* way. Usually, the new curve X_ω is observed on the whole interval $[0, T]$ and then the prediction is made using the score $\Phi(X_\omega)$. Provided the existence of a good prediction model of Y from X, in adaptive prediction we are interested to determine a time $T^*(\omega)$ such that the prediction of Y from the observation X on $[0, T^*\omega)]$ is similar to the prediction with X on $[0, T]$. In other words, to observe X after $T^*(\omega)$ will no change the prediction.

The paper is organized as follows. In section 2 we present some basics of the PLS approach for linear discriminant analysis with functional data. The anticipated and adapted prediction are introduced in Section 3. The Section 4 presents the results of the anticipated and adaptive prediction for the quality of cookies to Danone.

2 Linear discriminant analysis on functional data. The PLS approach

Let $X = \{X_t\}_{t \in [0,T]}$ be a second order stochastic process L_2-continuous with sample paths in $L_2[0,T]$ and Y a binary random variable, $Y \in \{0,1\}$. Without loss of generality we assume also that $\mathbb{E}(X_t) = 0$, $\forall t \in [0,T]$. As an extension of the classical multivariate approach, the aim of linear discriminant analysis (LDA) for functional data is to find linear combinations $\Phi(X) = \int_0^T X_t \beta(t)dt$, $\beta \in L_2([0,T])$ such that the between class variance is maximized with respect to the total variance, i.e.

$$\max_{\beta \in L_2[0,T]} \frac{\mathbb{V}(\mathbb{E}(\Phi(X)|Y))}{\mathbb{V}(\Phi(X))}. \tag{1}$$

Let $\{(x_i, y_i)\}_{i=1,\ldots,n}$ be n observations of random variables (X,Y) with $x_i = \{x_i(t), t \in [0,T]\}$ and $y_i \in \{0,1\}$, $i = 1, \ldots, n$. Due to infinite dimension of the predictor, the estimation of β is in general an ill–posed problem. In Preda and Saporta (2005) it is shown that the optimization problem (13) is equivalent to find the regression coefficients in the linear model which predicts Y (after a convenient encoding) by the stochastic process X under the least-squares criterion.

Without loss of generality, let us recode Y by : $0 \rightsquigarrow \sqrt{\frac{p_1}{p_0}}$ and $1 \rightsquigarrow -\sqrt{\frac{p_0}{p_1}}$, where $p_0 = \mathbb{P}(Y = 0)$ and $p_1 = \mathbb{P}(Y = 1)$. If β is a solution of (1) then β satisfies the Wiener-Hopf equation

$$\mathbb{E}(YX_t) = \int_0^T \mathbb{E}(X_t X_s)\beta(s)ds, \tag{2}$$

which is the equation giving, up to a constant, the regression coefficient function of the linear regression of Y on $X = \{X_t\}_{t \in [0,T]}$. Equation (14) has an unique solution under conditions of convergence of series implying the eigenvalues and eigenvectors of the covariance operator of the process X (Saporta (1981)). These conditions are rarely satisfied. Thus, in practice, the problem to find β is generally an ill-posed problem. However, if the aim is to find the discriminant variable (scores), then one can use the above relationship between LDA and linear regression.

Using this result, there are several ways to approximate the discriminant score $\Phi(X)$. Thus, $\Phi(X)$ can be approximate using the linear regression on the principal components of X. The choice of principal components used for regression is not easy and should be a trade off between the quality of the model and the quality of the representation of X. The PLS approach proposed in Preda and Saporta (2005) is an efficient alternative and provides generally better results. It allows to approximate $\Phi(X)$ by $\Phi_{PLS}(X) = \int_0^T \beta_{PLS}(t)X_t dt$ and thus, to compute for a new observation the discriminant score for further prediction.

2.1   The PLS approximation

The PLS regression is an iterative method. Let $X_{0,t} = X_t$, $\forall t \in [0,1]$ and $Y_0 = Y$. At step q, $q \geq 1$, of the PLS regression of Y on X, we define the qth PLS component, t_q, by the eigenvector associated to the largest eigenvalue of the operator $\mathbf{W}_{q-1}^X \mathbf{W}_{q-1}^Y$, where $\mathbf{W}_{q-1}^X$, respectively $\mathbf{W}_{q-1}^Y$, are the Escoufier's operators (Saporta (1981)) associated to X, respectively to Y_{q-1}. The PLS step is completed by the ordinary linear regression of $X_{q-1,t}$ and Y_{q-1} on t_q. Let $X_{q,t}$, $t \in [0,1]$ and Y_q be the random variables which represent the residual of these regressions : $X_{q,t} = X_{q-1,t} - p_q(t)t_q$ and $Y_q = Y_{q-1} - c_q t_q$. Then, for each $q \geq 1$, $\{t_q\}_{q \geq 1}$ forms an orthogonal system in $L_2(X)$ and the PLS approximation of Y by $\{X_t\}_{t \in [0,T]}$ at step q, $q \geq 1$, is given by :

$$\hat{Y}_{PLS(q)} = c_1 t_1 + \cdots + c_q t_q = \int_0^T \hat{\beta}_{PLS(q)}(t)X_t dt. \tag{3}$$

In practice, the number of PLS components used for regression is determined by cross-validation.

2.2   Quality criterion. The ROC curve

Let denote by $d_T = \Phi_{PLS}(X) = \int_0^T \beta_{PLS}(t)X_t dt$ the approximation for the discriminant score given by the PLS regression on the process $X = \{X_t\}_{t \in [0,T]}$. There are several criteria to evaluate the quality of the discriminant model, for example the error rate for a defined threshold, the squared correlation ration $\eta^2(d_T|Y) = \dfrac{\mathbb{V}(\mathbb{E}(d_T|Y))}{\mathbb{V}(d_T)}$, the ROC curve, etc.

For a binary target Y, the ROC curve is generally accepted as the best measure of the discriminating power of a discriminant score.

Let $d_T(x)$ be the score value for some unit x. Given a threshold r, x is classified into $Y = 1$ if $d_T(x) > r$. The true positive rate or "sensitivity" is $P(d_T > r|Y = 1)$ and the false positive rate or $1 -$ "specificity", $P(d_T > r|Y = 0)$. The ROC curve gives the true positive rate as a function of the false positive rate and is invariant under any monotonic increasing transformation of the score. In the case of an inefficient score, both conditional distributions of d_T given $Y = 1$ and $Y = 0$ are identical and the ROC curve is the diagonal line. In case of perfect discrimination, the ROC curve is confounded with the edges of the unit square.

The Area Under ROC Curve or AUC, is then a global measure of discrimination. It can be easily proved that $AUC = P(X_1 > X_0)$, where X_1 is a random variable distributed as d when $Y = 1$ and X_0 is independently distributed as d for $Y = 0$. Taking all pairs of observations, one in each group, AUC is thus estimated by the percentage of concordant pairs (Wilcoxon-Mann-Whitney statistic).

3 Anticipated and adaptive prediction

3.1 Anticipated prediction

Let denote by d_t the approximation for the discriminant score given by PLS regression on the process X considered on the interval time $[0, t]$, with $t \leq T$. The objective here is to find $T^* < T$ such that the discriminant function d_{T^*} performs quite as well as d_T.

The stochastic process $\{d_t\}_{t \in [0, T]}$ is such that :

- $d_t = Y - \varepsilon_t$, where Y is recoded by $0 \rightsquigarrow \sqrt{\frac{p_1}{p_0}}$ and $1 \rightsquigarrow -\sqrt{\frac{p_0}{p_1}}$. $\mathbb{E}(d_t) = 0$.
- $\mathbb{E}(\varepsilon_t, d_s) = 0$, $\forall s \leq t$,
- $\mathbb{E}(d_t d_s) = \mathbb{E}(d_s Y) = \sqrt{p_0 p_1}(\mathbb{E}(d_s | Y = 0) - \mathbb{E}(d_s | Y = 1))$, $\forall s \leq t$.

Once a quality measure Q_s is defined, a solution could be to define T^* as the smallest value of s such that Q_s is not significantly different from Q_T. Since Q_s and Q_T are dependent random variables, we will use a non parametric paired comparison test.

We will use in the following the AUC criterion for defining the quality of the discriminant model.

Since the distribution of AUC is not known, we will test the equality of $AUC(s)$ with $AUC(T)$, by using boostrap methodology: we resample M times the data, according to a stratified scheme in order to keep invariant the number of observations of each group. Let $AUC_m(s)$ and $AUC_m(T)$ be the resampled values of AUC for $m = 1$ to M, and δ_m their difference. Testing if $AUC(s) = AUC(T)$ is performed by using a paired t-test, or a Wilcoxon paired test, on the M values δ_m.

3.2 Adaptive prediction

Let $\Omega = \{\omega_1, \ldots, \omega_n\}$, $n \geq 1$, be a training sample and $\{(x_1, y_1), \ldots, (x_n, y_n)\}$ be the observation of (X, Y) on Ω, X being considered on $[0, T]$. Let also suppose that one has a good discriminant score d_T for the prediction of Y by $\{X\}_{t \in [0, T]}$ with respect to some criterion (misclassified rate, AUC, R^2, etc).

Let now consider a new data ω.

By *adaptive prediction* for ω we understand to find the smallest time $T^* = T^*(\omega)$ such that the prediction of $Y(\omega)$ on $[0, T^*]$ is similar to that on $[0, T]$. Let observe that T^* is here a random variable, whereas in the anticipated approach T^* is a constant.

Let h be the step of a convenient discretisation of $[0, T]$ and suppose that for ω the process X is observed until the time t, $t < T$. It is clear that the decision to continue the observation $X(\omega)$ at $t + h$ or to stop it $(T^* = t)$ depends on the similarity of $X(\omega)$ with $x_1, \ldots, x_n$ with respect to the prediction of Y. We define this similarity at the time t in the following way :

Let d_t be a discriminant score for Y using only the observation interval $[0, t]$ and denote by $\hat{Y}_t(\omega)$ and $\hat{Y}_{t,i}, i = 1, \ldots, n$ the predictions for ω, respectively Ω, with respect to d_t.

Denote by

$$\Omega_\omega(t) = \{\omega_i \in \Omega | \hat{Y}_t(\omega) = \hat{Y}_{t,i}\} \text{ and } \overline{\Omega}_\omega(t) = \Omega - \Omega_\omega(t)$$

the class of elements having the same prediction as ω, respectively its complement with respect to Ω.

Let

$$p_{0|\Omega_\omega(t)} = \frac{\left|\{\omega' \in \Omega | \hat{Y}_T(\omega') = 0\} \cap \Omega_\omega(t)\}\right|}{|\Omega_\omega(t)|} \tag{4}$$

be the observed rate of elements in $\Omega_\omega(t)$ predicted in the class $Y = 0$ at the time T. Similarly, let $p_{1|\Omega_\omega(t)}$, $p_{0|\overline{\Omega}_\omega(t)}$ and $p_{1|\overline{\Omega}_\omega(t)}$. Obviously,

$$p_{0|\Omega_\omega(t)} + p_{1|\Omega_\omega(t)} = 1 \text{ and } p_{0|\overline{\Omega}_\omega(t)} + p_{1|\overline{\Omega}_\omega(t)} = 1.$$

Let define $C_{\Omega_\omega(t)} = \max\{p_{0|\Omega_\omega(t)}, p_{1|\Omega_\omega(t)}\}$ and $C_{\overline{\Omega}_\omega(t)} = \max\{p_{0|\overline{\Omega}_\omega(t)}, p_{1|\overline{\Omega}_\omega(t)}\}$ the *conservation* rate of prediction group at the time t with respect to the time T for the elements of $\Omega_\omega(t)$, respectively of $\overline{\Omega}_\omega(t)$. As a global measure of conservation we consider

$$C_\Omega(\omega, t) = \min\{C_{\Omega_\omega(t)}, C_{\overline{\Omega}_\omega(t)}\}. \tag{5}$$

For each $t \in [0, T]$, $C_\Omega(\omega, t)$ is such that $0.5 \leq C_\Omega(\omega, t) \leq 1$ and $C_\Omega(\omega, T) = 1$.

Given a confidence conservation threshold $\gamma \in (0, 1)$, e.g. $\gamma = 0.90$, we define the following rule :

Adaptive prediction rule for ω and t :

(1) if $C_\Omega(\omega, t) \geq \gamma$ then the observation of X for ω on the time interval $[0, t]$ is sufficient for the prediction of $Y(\omega)$. $\hat{Y}(\omega)$ is then the same as the prediction at time T of the subgroup of $\Omega_\omega(t)$ corresponding to $C_{\Omega_\omega(t)}$.
(2) if $C_\Omega(\omega, t) < \gamma$ then the observation process of X for ω should continue after t. Put $t = t + h$ and repeat the adaptive prediction procedure.

Then, $T^*(\omega)$ is the smallest t such that the condition (1) of the adaptive prediction rule is satisfied.

An important role in the proposed adaptive prediction methodology is the observation of the discriminant score process d_t, $t \geq 0$ for the new data ω. We propose two approaches to define $d_t(\omega)$.

(M1) by *completion* : Use a functional regression model with functional response as in Preda and Saporta (2005) or Lian (2007) and predict $X(\omega)$ on $[t, T]$. Then, by completion one obtains a trajectory $X(\omega)$ on $[0, T]$ for which the score $d_T(\omega)$ provides a prediction for Y. Put $d_t(\omega) = d_T(\omega)$.

(M2) *sequential* : Construct the discriminant score d_t progressively for each time t and predict Y using d_t.

The first approach uses two regression models : one for the completion step, which is sequently performed for each t, and a second one for discrimination. The discrimination model concerns the training sample Ω for which X is considered on the whole interval $[0, T]$. The second approach, M2, involves the estimation of several discriminant models, one for each considered time t. However, our intuition is that the error associated to M1 is greater than that given by M2 since the first approach cumulates errors from both models. Moreover, even for t close to T, the prediction error given by the regression model used in the completion step of the trajectories in the training sample (PRESS) could be important and thus misleading for the discrimination step. For these reasons, we used the sequential approach in our application on kneading data.

4 Application

We use the anticipated approach for kneading data from Danone. The quality (Y) of cookies produced by a set of 90 flours for which one knows the dough resistance (X) during the first 480 seconds of the kneading process is evaluated. One obtains 50 flours yielding to good quality of cookies and 40 to a bad one. Because of large local variation, the curves are smoothed using cubic B-spline basis. Figure 1 shows the set of the 90 flours before and after smoothing.

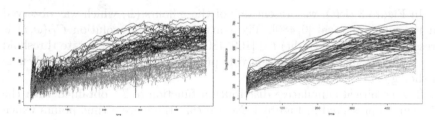

Fig. 1. Good (black) and bad (red) flours. Left : original data. Right : smoothed data

We use for prediction the smoothed curves that we consider as sample paths of a stochastic process $\{X_t\}_{t \in [0,480]}$. Considering $Y \in \{Bad, Good\}$, the PLS approach for discrimination of Y from $\{X_t\}_{t \in [0,480]}$ Preda et al. (2007) yields to a misclassification rate of about 11.2%. For a signification level of 5% and using the AUC criterion, the anticipated approach provides $T^* = 186$.

Thus, the predictive power of the dough curves for the cookies quality is resumed by the first 186 seconds of the kneading process. In the next paragraph we extend the anticipated prediction methodology by adapting the optimal time T^* to each new trajectory given its incoming measurements, in that sense that observation of the trajectory after the time T^* does not change the prediction of Y.

Adaptive prediction 25 new flours have been tested for adaptive prediction. These flours were classified by Danone as being of quality "adjustable", somewhere between "good" and "bad". 12 of these flours are predicted by the PLS discriminant analysis using the interval time [0, 480] into the "good" class. Using as training sample Ω the set of the 90 flours considered in the anticipated prediction approach, we perform for each one the adaptive prediction starting from $t = 100$.

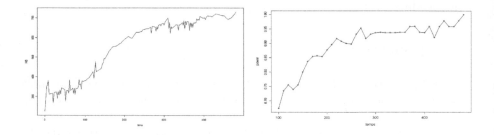

Fig. 2. Left : new flour ω.   Right : $C_\Omega(\omega, t)$, $t \in [100, 480]$, $\gamma = 0.90$.

In Figure 3 (left), we present one of these flours (ω) which was observed on the whole interval [0, 480]. The conservation rate evolution $C_\Omega(\omega, t)$ is presented in Figure 3 (right) $t \in [100, 480]$. For a conservation rate threshold $\gamma = 0.90$, the adaptive prediction rule provides $T^*(\omega) = 220$ and predicts ω in the "good" class of flours.

The empirical cumulative distribution function of T^* obtained with the 25 flours is presented in Figure 4. Notice that there are 5 time points which are earlier than the optimal time for anticipated prediction ($T^* = 186$). 10 flours are predicted in the "good" class.

5   Conclusions

In this paper we addressed the problem of the prediction of a binary response Y using as predictor data of functional type represented by paths

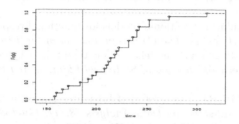

Fig. 3. Empirical cumulative distribution function of T^* (in red, the time point t=186).

of a continuous–time stochastic process $\{X_t\}_{t\in[0,T]}$. We faced the problem by means of the PLS approach for which forecasting the binary response is drawn as 'anticipated prediction' from the process $\{X_t\}_{t\in[0,T^*]}$ with $T^* < T$. Under the hypothesis of existence of an acceptable prediction model, we investigated the possibility of reducing the length of the observation period without loss of the quality prediction. We provided methodologies for anticipated and adaptive prediction for preserving the global quality model as well as the quality prediction of individual curves. An example is provided on kneading data from Danone.

References

BIAU, G., BUNEA, F. and WEGKAMP, M. (2005): Function classification in Hilbert spaces. *IEEE Transactions on Information Theory,* 51, 2162-2172.

ESCABIAS, M., AGUILERA, A.M. and VALDERAMA, M.J. (2004): Principal component estimation of functional logistic regression: discussion of two different approaches. *Journal of Nonparametric Statistics, 16 (3-4), 365-384.*

ESCABIAS, M., AGUILERA, A.M. and VALDERAMA, M.J. (2005): Modelling environmental data by functional principal component logistic regression. *Environmetrics, 16 (1), 95-107.*

FERRATY, F. and VIEU, P. (2006): *Nonparametric functional data analysis. Theory and practice,* Springer.

FERRATY, F. and VIEU, P. (2003): Curves discrimination: a nonparametric approach. *Computational Statistics & Data Analysis, 44, 161-173.*

FISHER, R.A. (1924): The Influence of Rainfall on the Yield of Wheat at Rothamsted. *Philosophical Transactions of the Royal Society, B 213, 89-142.*

FISHER, R.A. (1936):, The use of multiple measurement in taxonomic problems. *Ann. Eugen,* 7, 179-188.

JAMES, G.M. and HASTIE, T.J. (2001): Functional discriminant analysis for irregularly sampled curves. *Journal of the Royal Statistical Society, Series B,* 63,533-550.

LÉVÉDER, C., ABRAHAM, C., CORNILLON P. A., MATZNER-LOBER, E. and MOLINARI N. (2004): Discrimination de courbes de pétrissage. *Chimiométrie*, p. *37–43*.

LIAN, H. (2007): Nonlinear functional models for functional responses in reproducing kernel Hilbert spaces. *The Canadian Journal of Statistics, 35, 597-606*.

PREDA, C. (2007): Regression models for functional data by reproducing kernel Hilbert space methods. *Journal of Statistical Planning and Inference*, Vol. 137, 3, p. 829-840.

PREDA, C. and SAPORTA, G. (2005): PLS regression on a stochastic process. *Computational Statistics and Data Analysis 48 (1), 149-158*.

RAMSAY, J.O. and SILVERMAN, B.W. (1997): *Functional Data Analysis*, Springer Series in Statistics, Springer-Verlag, New York.

RAMSAY, J.O. and SILVERMAN, B.W. (2002): *Applied Functional Data Analysis: Methods and Case Studies*, Springer.

SAPORTA, G. (1981): Méthodes exploratoires d'analyse de données temporelles. *Cahiers du B.U.R.O, Université Pierre et Marie Curie*, 37-38, Paris.

Bootstrap Calibration in Functional Linear Regression Models with Applications

Wenceslao González-Manteiga[1] and Adela Martínez-Calvo[2]

[1] Departamento de Estadística e I.O., Universidad de Santiago de Compostela,
Facultad de Matemáticas, Campus Sur, 15782, Santiago de Compostela, Spain
wenceslao.gonzalez@usc.es
[2] Departamento de Estadística e I.O., Universidad de Santiago de Compostela,
Facultad de Matemáticas, Campus Sur, 15782, Santiago de Compostela, Spain
adela.martinez@usc.es

Abstract. Our work focuses on the functional linear model given by $Y = \langle \theta, X \rangle + \epsilon$, where Y and ϵ are real random variables, X is a zero-mean random variable valued in a Hilbert space $(\mathcal{H}, \langle \cdot, \cdot \rangle)$, and $\theta \in \mathcal{H}$ is the fixed model parameter. Using an initial sample $\{(X_i, Y_i)\}_{i=1}^{n}$, a bootstrap resampling $Y_i^* = \langle \hat{\theta}, X_i \rangle + \hat{\epsilon}_i^*$, $i = 1, \ldots, n$, is proposed, where $\hat{\theta}$ is a general pilot estimator, and $\hat{\epsilon}_i^*$ is a naive or wild bootstrap error. The obtained consistency of bootstrap allows us to calibrate distributions as $P_X\{\sqrt{n}(\langle \hat{\theta}, x \rangle - \langle \theta, x \rangle) \le y\}$ for a fixed x, where P_X is the probability conditionally on $\{X_i\}_{i=1}^{n}$. Different applications illustrate the usefulness of bootstrap for testing different hypotheses related with θ, and a brief simulation study is also presented.

Keywords: bootstrap, functional linear regression, functional principal components analysis, hypothesis test

1 Introduction

Nowadays, the Functional Data Analysis (FDA) has turned into one of the most interesting statistical fields. Particularly, the functional regression models have been studied from *parametric* point of view (see Ramsay and Silverman (2002, 2005)) and *non-parametric* one (see Ferraty and Vieu (2006)). Our work focuses on the first approach, specifically, on the functional linear regression model with scalar response given by

$$Y = \langle \theta, X \rangle + \epsilon, \tag{1}$$

where Y is a real random variable, X is a zero-mean random variable valued in a real separable Hilbert space $(\mathcal{H}, \langle \cdot, \cdot \rangle)$ such that $\mathbb{E}(\|X\|^4) < +\infty$ (being $\|\cdot\| = \langle \cdot, \cdot \rangle^{1/2}$), $\theta \in \mathcal{H}$ is the model parameter which verifies $\|\theta\|^2 < +\infty$, and ϵ is a real random variable satisfying that $\mathbb{E}(\epsilon) = 0$, $\mathbb{E}(\epsilon^2) = \sigma^2 < +\infty$, and $\mathbb{E}(\epsilon X) = 0$. Many authors have dealt with model (1) in recent papers, and methods based on functional principal components analysis (FPCA) are one of the most popular techniques in order to estimate the model parameter (see

Y. Lechevallier, G. Saporta (eds.), *Proceedings of COMPSTAT'2010*,
DOI 10.1007/978-3-7908-2604-3_18, © Springer-Verlag Berlin Heidelberg 2010

Cardot et al. (1999, 2003b), Cai and Hall (2006), Hall and Hosseini-Nasab (2006), or Hall and Horowitz (2007)). That is the reason why the FPCA approach has been considered here for estimating θ (see Section 2).

The main aim of this work is to present a general bootstrap resampling which, from an initial sample $\{(X_i, Y_i)\}_{i=1}^{n}$ of independent and identically distributed random variables drawn from (X, Y), builds

$$Y_i^* = \langle \hat{\theta}, X_i \rangle + \hat{\epsilon}_i^*, \text{ for } i = 1, \ldots, n,$$

where $\hat{\theta}$ is a FPCA-type pilot estimator, and $\hat{\epsilon}_i^*$ is obtained by means of a naive or wild bootstrap procedure. This kind of methodology allows us to approximate certain sampling distributions by means of the corresponding bootstrap distributions. Consequently, bootstrap becomes in an useful tool when the asymptotics are unknown or inaccurate due to sample size.

Since its introduction by Efron (1979), the bootstrap method resulted in a new distribution approximation applicable to a large number of situations as the calibration of pivotal quantities in the finite dimensional context (see Bickel and Freedman (1981) and Singh (1981)). As far as multivariate regression models are concerned, its validity for linear and nonparametric models was also stated (see Freedman (1981) and Cao-Abad (1991)).

Currently, the application of bootstrap techniques to more general functional fields has successfully started. For example, Cuevas et al. (2006) have proposed bootstrap confidence bands for several functional estimators as the sample functional mean or the trimmed functional mean. In the regression context, Ferraty et al. (2009) have shown the validity of the bootstrap in nonparametric functional regression, and they have constructed pointwise confidence intervals for the regression operator. Bootstrap can also be very helpful testing hypotheses, because it can be used to approximate the distribution of the statistic under the null hypothesis. For example, Cuevas et al. (2004) have developed a sort of parametric bootstrap to obtain quantiles for an anova test, and Hall and Vial (2006) have studied the finite dimensionality of functional data using a bootstrap approximation.

Refering to functional linear regression, the most of authors have proposed test methods for which they have derived an asymptotic distribution approximation: Cardot et al. (2003a) and Kokoszka et al. (2008) have tested the null hypothesis of lack of dependence between X and Y; an F-test for functional linear models with functional response and multivariate predictor was studied by Shen and Faraday (2004); and the existence of two different functional linear models was analysed by Horváth et al. (2009). On the other hand, Chiou and Müller (2007) have proposed a randomization test for regression diagnostics by means of the analysis of the residual processes.

In this paper, we present a bootstrap procedure to approximate the distribution of some statistics and decide if we accept or reject null hypotheses related with the model parameter. First of all, in Section 2 we introduce some notation and basic concepts about the linear model (1), and FPCA-type estimates. Section 3 is devoted to several applications of bootstrap calibration. Besides, the naive and wild bootstrap procedure for each case is described and the asymptotic validity is shown. Finally, a simulation study is compiled in Section 4. We should note that, due to space restrictions, the simulation results have been reduced and the real data applications have been removed.

2   FPCA-type estimates

A natural way to estimate θ in model (1) is to solve the next problem

$$\min_{\beta \in H} \mathbb{E}[(Y - \langle \beta, X \rangle)^2].$$

For that, the second moment operator Γ, and the cross second moment operator Δ must be defined. The former is a nuclear, self-adjoint, positive and linear operator such that $\Gamma(x) = \mathbb{E}(\langle X, x \rangle X)$, and the latter is defined as $\Delta(x) = \mathbb{E}(\langle X, x \rangle Y)$, for all $x \in H$. Moreover, $\{(\lambda_j, v_j)\}_j$ will denote the eigenvalues and eigenfunctions of Γ, assuming that $\lambda_1 > \lambda_2 > \ldots > 0$. Assuming that $\sum_{j=1}^{\infty} (\Delta(v_j)/\lambda_j)^2 < +\infty$ and $Ker(\Gamma) = \{x \in H / \Gamma(x) = 0\} = \{0\}$, there is an unique solution for the previous minimization problem (see Cardot et al. (2003b)) which can be expressed as

$$\theta = \sum_{j=1}^{\infty} \frac{\Delta(v_j)}{\lambda_j} v_j.$$

Given that there is no bounded inverse of Γ, Cardot et al. (1999) decided to project on the subspace spanned by the first k_n eigenfunctions of its empirical counterpart Γ_n, where $\Gamma_n(x) = n^{-1} \sum_{i=1}^{n} \langle X_i, x \rangle X_i$, and estimate θ by

$$\hat{\theta}_{k_n} = \sum_{j=1}^{k_n} \frac{\Delta_n(\hat{v}_j)}{\hat{\lambda}_j} \hat{v}_j, \tag{2}$$

where $\Delta_n(x) = n^{-1} \sum_{i=1}^{n} \langle X_i, x \rangle Y_i$, and $\{(\hat{\lambda}_j, \hat{v}_j)\}_{j=1}^{\infty}$ are the eigenvalues and the eigenfunctions of Γ_n.

Subsequently, the estimator (2) was generalized to a larger class of FPCA-type estimates by Cardot et al. (2007) who solved the ill-conditioned inverse problem by means of the next estimator

$$\hat{\theta}_c = \sum_{j=1}^{n} f_n^c(\hat{\lambda}_j) \Delta_n(\hat{v}_j) \hat{v}_j, \tag{3}$$

where $c = c_n$ is a strictly positive sequence such that $c \to 0$ and $c < \lambda_1$, and $\{f_n^c : [c, +\infty) \to \mathbb{R}\}_n$ is a sequence of positive functions, verifying certain conditions. Let us note that, when $f_n(x) = x^{-1} 1_{\{x \geq c\}}$, the estimator (3) is asymptotically equivalent to (2). Besides, when $f_n(x) = (x + \alpha_n)^{-1} 1_{\{x \geq c\}}$ for α_n a sequence of positive parameters, the estimator (3) is asymptotically equivalent to the ridge-type estimator proposed by Martínez-Calvo (2008).

3   Bootstrap calibration

The bootstrap techniques considered in this work are the adaptation of the multivariate naive and wild bootstrap procedures to the functional context defined by (1). They allow us to obtain as bootstrap resamples as we need in order to approximate sampling distributions in the next subsections. For wild bootstrap procedure, we will use $\{V_i\}_i$ i.i.d. random variables independent of $\{(X_i, Y_i)\}_{i=1}^n$, such that

$$\mathbb{E}(V_1) = 0, \quad \mathbb{E}(V_1^2) = 1. \tag{4}$$

3.1   Building confidence intervals for prediction

For a fixed x, one can be interested in obtain pointwise confidence intervals for the prediction with a certain confidence level α. When θ and/or x are very well approximated by the projection on the subspace spanned by the first k_n^c eigenfunctions of Γ_n, the Central Limit Theorem shown by Cardot et al. (2007) allows us to evaluate the following approximated asymptotic confidence interval for $\langle \theta, x \rangle$

$$I_{x,\alpha}^{asy} = [\langle \hat{\theta}_c, x \rangle - \hat{t}_{n,x}^c \hat{\sigma} n^{-1/2} z_{1-\alpha/2}, \langle \hat{\theta}_c, x \rangle + \hat{t}_{n,x}^c \hat{\sigma} n^{-1/2} z_{1-\alpha/2}], \tag{5}$$

with $\hat{t}_{n,x}^c = \sqrt{\sum_{j=1}^{k_n^c} \hat{\lambda}_j [f_n^c(\hat{\lambda}_j)]^2 \langle x, \hat{v}_j \rangle^2}$, $\hat{\sigma}^2$ a consistent estimate of σ^2, and z_α the quantile of order α of a Gaussian random variable $\mathcal{N}(0,1)$. The value k_n^c is determined by the eigenvalues of Γ, the distances among them, and the sequence c (see Cardot et al. (2007)), although it can be interpreted, in a way, as the number of eigenfunctions involved in the estimator (3).

Alternative confidence intervals can be built using bootstrap. The resampling procedure proceeds as follows (we consider Step 2 or Step 2' depending on which bootstrap procedure we have chosen).

Step 1. Obtain a pilot estimator $\hat{\theta}_d = \sum_{j=1}^n f_n^d(\hat{\lambda}_j) \Delta_n(\hat{v}_j) \hat{v}_j$, and the residuals $\hat{\epsilon}_i = Y_i - \langle \hat{\theta}_d, X_i \rangle$ for $i = 1, \ldots, n$.

Step 2. (Naive) Draw $\hat{\epsilon}_1^*, \ldots, \hat{\epsilon}_n^*$ i.i.d. random variables from the cumulative distribution of $\{\hat{\epsilon}_i - \bar{\hat{\epsilon}}\}_{i=1}^n$, where $\bar{\hat{\epsilon}} = n^{-1} \sum_{i=1}^n \hat{\epsilon}_i$.

Step 2'. (Wild) For $i = 1, \ldots, n$, define $\hat{\epsilon}_i^* = \hat{\epsilon}_i V_i$, with V_i satisfying (4).

Step 3. Construct $Y_i^* = \langle \hat{\theta}_d, X_i \rangle + \hat{\epsilon}_i^*$, for $i = 1, \ldots, n$.

Step 4. Build $\hat{\theta}_{c,d}^* = \sum_{j=1}^n f_n^c(\hat{\lambda}_j) \Delta_n^*(\hat{v}_j) \hat{v}_j$, where Δ_n^* is defined as $\Delta_n^*(x) = n^{-1} \sum_{i=1}^n \langle X_i, x \rangle Y_i^*$.

Theorem 1 ensures that the α-quantiles $q_\alpha(x)$ of the distribution of the true error $(\langle \hat{\theta}_c, x \rangle - \langle \theta, x \rangle)$ can be aproximated by the bootstrap α-quantiles $q_\alpha^*(x)$ of $(\langle \hat{\theta}_{c,d}^*, x \rangle - \langle \hat{\theta}_d, x \rangle)$. Hence, we can build the following confidence intervals

$$I_{x,\alpha}^* = [\langle \hat{\theta}_c, x \rangle - q_{1-\alpha/2}^*(x), \langle \hat{\theta}_c, x \rangle - q_{\alpha/2}^*(x)]. \tag{6}$$

Theorem 1. *Let $\hat{\Pi}_{k_n^c}$ be the projection on the first k_n^c eigenfunctions of Γ_n. Under certain hypotheses, for both the naive and the wild bootstrap,*

$$\sup_{y\in\mathbb{R}} |P_{XY}(\sqrt{n}\{\langle\hat{\theta}_{c,d}^*,x\rangle - \langle\hat{\theta}_d,x\rangle\} \leq y) - P_X(\sqrt{n}\{\langle\hat{\theta}_c,x\rangle - \langle\hat{\Pi}_{k_n^c}\theta,x\rangle\} \leq y)| \xrightarrow{P} 0,$$

where P_{XY} denotes probability conditionally on $\{(X_i,Y_i)\}_{i=1}^n$, and P_X denotes probability conditionally on $\{X_i\}_{i=1}^n$.

Lastly, let us remark that we have to fix the sequences d for $\hat{\theta}_d$ and c for $\hat{\theta}_{c,d}^*$. For consistency results, we need that $c \leq d$, so the number of principal components used for constructing $\hat{\theta}_{c,d}^*$ is larger than the number of components used for $\hat{\theta}_d$. Hence, in some way, we should *oversmooth* when we calculate the pilot estimator.

3.2   Testing for lack of dependence

Cardot et al. (2003) tested the null hypothesis

$$H_0: \quad \theta = 0,$$

being the alternative $H_1: \theta \neq 0$. The authors deduced that testing H_0 is equivalent to test $H_0: \Delta = 0$, so they analysed the cross second moment operator asymptotics, and proposed as test statistic

$$T_{1,n} = \frac{1}{\sqrt{k_n}} \left(\frac{1}{\hat{\sigma}^2}||\sqrt{n}\Delta_n\hat{A}_n||^2 - k_n \right)$$

where $\hat{\sigma}^2$ is a estimator of σ^2, and $\hat{A}_n(\cdot) = \sum_{j=1}^{k_n}\hat{\lambda}_j^{-1/2}\langle\cdot,\hat{v}_j\rangle\hat{v}_j$. They obtained that, under H_0, $T_{1,n}$ converges in distribution to a centered gaussian variable with variance equals to 2. Hence, H_0 is rejected if $|T_{1,n}| > \sqrt{2}z_\alpha$, and accepted otherwise. Besides, Cardot et al. (2003) also proposed another calibration of the statistic distribution based on a permutation mechanism.

Bootstrap can also be used to test the lack of dependence, considering

$$H_0: \quad ||\theta|| = 0.$$

Since $||\theta||^2 = \sum_{j=1}^\infty (\Delta(v_j))^2/\lambda_j^2$, we can use the statistic

$$T_{2,n} = \sum_{j=1}^{k_n} \frac{(\Delta_n(\hat{v}_j))^2}{\hat{\lambda}_j^2}.$$

Under the null hypothesis, the bootstrap becomes in a very simple algorithm.

Step 1. (Naive) Draw $\hat{\epsilon}_1^*,\ldots,\hat{\epsilon}_n^*$ i.i.d. random variables from the cumulative distribution of $\{Y_i - \bar{Y}\}_{i=1}^n$, where $\bar{Y} = n^{-1}\sum_{i=1}^n Y_i$.

Step 1'. (Wild) For $i = 1,\ldots,n$, define $\hat{\epsilon}_i^* = Y_iV_i$, with V_i satisfying (4).

Step 2. Build $\Delta_n^*(x) = n^{-1}\sum_{i=1}^n \langle X_i,x\rangle Y_i^*$ with $Y_i^* = \hat{\epsilon}_i^*$, for $i = 1,\ldots,n$.

As the distribution of $T_{2,n}$ can be approximated by the bootstrap distribution of $T_{2,n}^* = \sum_{j=1}^{k_n}(\Delta_n^*(\hat{v}_j))^2/\hat{\lambda}_j^2$, H_0 is accepted when $T_{2,n}$ belongs to the interval defined by the $\alpha/2$-quantile and $(1-\alpha/2)$-quantiles of $T_{2,n}^*$.

3.3 Testing for equality of model parameters

Let us assume that we have two samples $Y_{i_1}^1 = \langle \theta^1, X_{i_1}^1 \rangle + \epsilon_{i_1}^1$, $1 \leq i_1 \leq n_1$, and $Y_{i_2}^2 = \langle \theta^2, X_{i_2}^2 \rangle + \epsilon_{i_2}^2$ with $1 \leq i_2 \leq n_2$. Now the aim is to test

$$H_0: \quad ||\theta^1 - \theta^2|| = 0.$$

Horváth et al. (2009) proposed several statistics for different cases, even for the lineal model with functional response.

Let us assume that X^1 and X^2 have the same covariance operator Γ and $Var(\epsilon^1) = Var(\epsilon^2)$. Then $||\theta^1 - \theta^2||^2 = \sum_{j=1}^{\infty} ((\Delta^1 - \Delta^2)(v_j))^2 / \lambda_j^2$ where $\{(\lambda_j, v_j)\}_j$ are the eigenelements of Γ, and Δ^1 and Δ^2 are the cross second moment operator for each sample. Let us introduce the following notation: $\Gamma_n(x) = (n_1 + n_2)^{-1} \sum_{l=1}^{2} \sum_{i=1}^{n_l} \langle X_i^l, x \rangle X_i^l$; $\{(\hat{\lambda}_j, \hat{v}_j)\}_j$ are the eigenvalues and the eigenfunctions of Γ_n; $\Delta_n(x) = (n_1 + n_2)^{-1} \sum_{l=1}^{2} \sum_{i=1}^{n_l} \langle X_i^l, x \rangle Y_i^l$; and $\Delta_n^l(x) = n_l^{-1} \sum_{i=1}^{n_l} \langle X_i^l, x \rangle Y_i^l$ for $l \in \{1, 2\}$. Using this notation, one can think of considering the following statistic

$$T_{3,n} = \sum_{j=1}^{k_n} ((\Delta_n^1 - \Delta_n^2)(\hat{v}_j))^2 / \hat{\lambda}_j^2.$$

Under the null hypothesis, the resampling procedure is the following.

Step 1. Obtain $\hat{\theta}_d = \sum_{j=1}^{n_1+n_2} f_n^d(\hat{\lambda}_j) \Delta_n(\hat{v}_j) \hat{v}_j$. Calculate the residuals $\hat{\epsilon}_i^l = Y_i^l - \langle \hat{\theta}_d, X_i^l \rangle$ for all $i = 1, \ldots, n_l$, for $l \in \{1, 2\}$.

Step 2. (Naive) Draw $\hat{\epsilon}_1^{l,*}, \ldots, \hat{\epsilon}_{n_l}^{l,*}$ i.i.d. random variables from the cumulative distribution of $\{\hat{\epsilon}_i^l - \bar{\hat{\epsilon}}^l\}_{i=1}^{n_l}$, where $\bar{\hat{\epsilon}}^l = n_l^{-1} \sum_{i=1}^{n_l} \hat{\epsilon}_i^l$, for $l \in \{1, 2\}$.

Step 2'. (Wild) For $i = 1, \ldots, n_l$, define $\hat{\epsilon}_i^{l,*} = \hat{\epsilon}_i^l V_i$, with V_i satisfying (4), for $l \in \{1, 2\}$.

Step 3. Build $\Delta_n^{l,*}(x) = n_l^{-1} \sum_{i=1}^{n_l} \langle X_i^l, x \rangle Y_i^{l,*}$, where $Y_i^{l,*} = \langle \hat{\theta}_d, X_i^l \rangle + \hat{\epsilon}_i^{l,*}$, for all $i = 1, \ldots, n_l$, for $l \in \{1, 2\}$.

Then, H_0 is accepted when $T_{3,n}$ belongs to the interval defined by the $\alpha/2$ and $(1 - \alpha/2)$-quantiles of $T_{3,n}^* = \sum_{j=1}^{k_n} ((\Delta_n^{1,*} - \Delta_n^{2,*})(\hat{v}_j))^2 / \hat{\lambda}_j^2$.

4 Simulation study

To illustrate the behaviour of bootstrap calibration, we have consider the standard FPCA estimator (2), and we have compared asymptotic and bootstrap confidence intervals given by (5) and (6). For latter, 1000 bootstrap iterations were done and wild bootstrap was considered.

We have simulated $ns = 500$ samples, each being composed of $n \in \{50, 100\}$ observations from the model (1), being X a Brownian motion and $\epsilon \sim \mathcal{N}(0, \sigma^2)$ with signal-to-noise ratio $r = \sigma / \sqrt{\mathbb{E}(\langle X, \theta \rangle^2)} = 0.2$. The model parameter is $\theta(t) = \sin(4\pi t)$ for $t \in [0,1]$, and both X and θ were discretized to 100 design points. We have fixed six deterministic curves x

$$x_1 = \sin(\pi t/2),\; x_2 = \sin(3\pi t/2),\; x_3 = t,\; x_4 = t^2,\; x_5 = 2|t-0.5|,\; x_6 = 2I_{t>0.5},$$

for which we have obtained confidence intervals, empirical coverage rate and lenght for two confidence levels: $\alpha \in \{0.05, 0.10\}$. Let us remark that this simulation study repeats the conditions of simulations by Cardot et al. (2004).

To select k_n, we have used GCV technique. For the bootstrap intervals (6), we have considered different pilot values $\{\hat{k}_n - 5, \ldots, \hat{k}_n + 2\}$, where $\hat{k}_n$ is the number of principal components selected by GCV. Moreover, for asymptotic intervals (5) the estimation for the true variance σ^2 is the residual sum of squares where k_n is chosen by GCV.

The empirical coverage rate and the mean length of the intervals for the different sample size n (in brackets, and multiplied by 10^2) are presented in Table 1 and Table 2. To clarify the results, the boldface emphasizes the best empirical coverage rates for bootstrap intervals.

α	CI	x_1	x_2	x_3	x_4	x_5	x_6
5%	$I_{x,\alpha}^{asy}$	8.8 (1.15)	9.0 (3.44)	10.6 (1.02)	13.2 (1.15)	19.8 (3.83)	23.0 (5.46)
	$I_{x,\alpha}^* \hat{k}_n + 2$	10.6 (1.14)	10.8 (3.38)	11.4 (1.01)	13.4 (1.14)	14.4 (4.53)	17.0 (6.33)
	$I_{x,\alpha}^* \hat{k}_n + 1$	10.4 (1.15)	10.4 (3.41)	12.0 (1.02)	13.2 (1.14)	15.6 (4.45)	19.6 (6.27)
	$I_{x,\alpha}^* \hat{k}_n$	10.6 (1.15)	11.6 (3.43)	11.6 (1.02)	13.6 (1.15)	14.4 (4.41)	18.8 (6.23)
	$I_{x,\alpha}^* \hat{k}_n - 1$	6.4 (1.36)	8.8 (4.04)	8.0 (1.21)	10.2 (1.37)	11.2 (4.97)	15.2 (7.11)
	$I_{x,\alpha}^* \hat{k}_n - 2$	**5.4 (1.67)**	**5.4 (4.99)**	5.8 (1.48)	7.4 (1.67)	7.6 (5.95)	10.8 (8.69)
	$I_{x,\alpha}^* \hat{k}_n - 3$	4.4 (2.11)	3.2 (6.33)	**4.6 (1.88)**	**5.8 (2.11)**	6.4 (7.33)	9.8(10.97)
	$I_{x,\alpha}^* \hat{k}_n - 4$	3.2 (2.62)	2.2 (7.74)	3.8 (2.32)	**4.2 (2.59)**	**5.0 (8.75)**	7.2(13.59)
	$I_{x,\alpha}^* \hat{k}_n - 5$	2.2 (2.96)	1.8 (8.80)	2.8 (2.63)	2.4 (2.92)	4.2 (9.69)	**5.4(15.63)**
10%	$I_{x,\alpha}^{asy}$	17.4 (0.97)	15.2 (2.89)	18.0 (0.86)	19.2 (0.96)	26.0 (3.21)	29.8 (4.58)
	$I_{x,\alpha}^* \hat{k}_n + 2$	17.2 (0.96)	18.0 (2.87)	18.2 (0.86)	19.6 (0.97)	21.0 (3.77)	26.8 (5.29)
	$I_{x,\alpha}^* \hat{k}_n + 1$	17.2 (0.97)	18.0 (2.88)	18.8 (0.86)	19.4 (0.97)	20.6 (3.70)	26.2 (5.21)
	$I_{x,\alpha}^* \hat{k}_n$	17.4 (0.97)	17.6 (2.89)	18.4 (0.86)	19.2 (0.97)	21.8 (3.66)	27.6 (5.16)
	$I_{x,\alpha}^* \hat{k}_n - 1$	12.6 (1.15)	12.0 (3.42)	13.8 (1.03)	14.4 (1.16)	18.6 (4.08)	20.8 (5.87)
	$I_{x,\alpha}^* \hat{k}_n - 2$	**10.4 (1.41)**	**10.8 (4.22)**	**10.0 (1.26)**	12.4 (1.41)	14.8 (4.86)	18.2 (7.13)
	$I_{x,\alpha}^* \hat{k}_n - 3$	6.6 (1.78)	5.8 (5.35)	6.6 (1.59)	**8.0 (1.78)**	**10.8 (5.92)**	13.6 (8.93)
	$I_{x,\alpha}^* \hat{k}_n - 4$	5.6 (2.21)	4.6 (6.55)	5.4 (1.96)	5.6 (2.18)	8.0 (7.03)	**10.0(10.97)**
	$I_{x,\alpha}^* \hat{k}_n - 5$	3.8 (2.51)	2.6 (7.44)	4.0 (2.22)	4.8 (2.46)	7.0 (7.71)	7.2(12.58)

Table 1. Empirical coverage rate (lenght$\times 10^2$) for $n = 50$.

The conclusions that can be derived are the following. Firstly, with a correct pilot k_n selection, the empirical coverage rate of bootstrap intervals is closer theoretical α than the empirical coverage rate of asymptotic intervals. Hovewer, these *optimal* bootstrap intervals tend to be larger than the asymptotic ones. In fact, the asymptotic approach tends to give larger coverage rates and shorter intervals (it looks as if asymptotic intervals were decentered).

On the other hand, the deterministic curves x are ordered from greatest to least according to their *smoothness* level. This fact justifies that both asymptotic and bootstrap intervals give better results for $x_1, \ldots, x_4$ than for x_5 and x_6. Besides, the sample size affects asymptotic intervals seriously: their

α	CI	x_1	x_2	x_3	x_4	x_5	x_6
5%	$I_{x,\alpha}^{asy}$	6.0 (0.83)	6.8 (2.47)	6.0 (0.74)	6.6 (0.83)	14.6 (2.89)	14.2 (4.13)
	$I_{x,\alpha}^{*}\,\hat{k}_n+2$	7.0 (0.82)	7.8 (2.44)	7.6 (0.73)	8.0 (0.84)	8.4 (3.42)	7.4 (4.84)
	$I_{x,\alpha}^{*}\,\hat{k}_n+1$	7.4 (0.83)	7.2 (2.44)	8.2 (0.74)	7.8 (0.83)	9.2 (3.37)	8.6 (4.77)
	$I_{x,\alpha}^{*}\,\hat{k}_n$	7.2 (0.83)	7.6 (2.44)	7.8 (0.74)	8.0 (0.84)	9.0 (3.32)	9.4 (4.72)
	$I_{x,\alpha}^{*}\,\hat{k}_n-1$	6.0 (0.90)	6.8 (2.66)	6.2 (0.80)	6.2 (0.91)	8.2 (3.46)	8.8 (4.93)
	$I_{x,\alpha}^{*}\,\hat{k}_n-2$	**4.2 (1.09)**	**5.0 (3.20)**	**4.2 (0.97)**	**4.8 (1.09)**	7.4 (4.03)	7.8 (5.82)
	$I_{x,\alpha}^{*}\,\hat{k}_n-3$	1.8 (1.37)	3.0 (4.08)	2.8 (1.22)	3.6 (1.38)	5.8 (5.01)	**5.4 (7.41)**
	$I_{x,\alpha}^{*}\,\hat{k}_n-4$	2.2 (1.69)	2.6 (5.04)	1.6 (1.50)	2.4 (1.69)	**4.4 (5.96)**	4.4 (9.31)
	$I_{x,\alpha}^{*}\,\hat{k}_n-5$	1.4 (1.97)	2.2 (5.87)	1.2 (1.75)	1.4 (1.96)	3.4 (6.69)	3.0(10.94)
10%	$I_{x,\alpha}^{asy}$	13.4 (0.69)	12.8 (2.08)	13.0 (0.62)	15.0 (0.70)	22.0 (2.43)	22.6 (3.47)
	$I_{x,\alpha}^{*}\,\hat{k}_n+2$	14.2 (0.70)	13.4 (2.06)	14.4 (0.62)	15.2 (0.70)	14.2 (2.85)	16.0 (4.04)
	$I_{x,\alpha}^{*}\,\hat{k}_n+1$	14.6 (0.70)	14.0 (2.06)	14.8 (0.62)	15.8 (0.70)	16.4 (2.80)	18.2 (3.96)
	$I_{x,\alpha}^{*}\,\hat{k}_n$	13.8 (0.70)	14.0 (2.06)	14.8 (0.62)	15.8 (0.70)	17.0 (2.76)	18.2 (3.91)
	$I_{x,\alpha}^{*}\,\hat{k}_n-1$	**10.8 (0.76)**	12.2 (2.25)	11.8 (0.68)	12.0 (0.76)	16.4 (2.86)	17.4 (4.06)
	$I_{x,\alpha}^{*}\,\hat{k}_n-2$	8.6 (0.92)	**10.0 (2.70)**	**8.4 (0.82)**	**9.0 (0.92)**	13.6 (3.31)	14.0 (4.78)
	$I_{x,\alpha}^{*}\,\hat{k}_n-3$	6.8 (1.16)	5.8 (3.45)	5.8 (1.03)	6.8 (1.16)	**10.6 (4.09)**	10.2 (6.04)
	$I_{x,\alpha}^{*}\,\hat{k}_n-4$	5.4 (1.43)	4.4 (4.25)	4.2 (1.27)	5.2 (1.42)	8.6 (4.82)	7.4 (7.50)
	$I_{x,\alpha}^{*}\,\hat{k}_n-5$	3.6 (1.66)	3.2 (4.96)	3.2 (1.47)	3.6 (1.65)	5.6 (5.38)	4.8 (8.76)

Table 2. Empirical coverage rate (lenght$\times 10^2$) for $n = 100$.

empirical coverage is far from the nominal one when $n = 50$ (see Table 1). Nevertheless, bootstrap intervals behave properly for all sample sizes.

With regard to pilot k_n for bootstrap procedure, it is not easy to deduce from simulation which is the best choice of this parameter. However, the adequate pilot seems to be smaller than the value obtained by GCV and tends to increase in accordance with the smoothness of x. We must remark that there are other methods to select the principal components involved in the estimator construction. For example, one possibility could be to carry out a cross-validation criterio to choose the principal components with higher correlation with the response.

To sum up, we can say that bootstrap intervals can be an interesting alternative to the asymptotic confidence intervals, above all when sample size is small. However, the profit of bootstrap procedure is subject to a correct choice of pilot k_n. This adequate selection seems to be influenced by smoothness of θ and x, and sample size n, and it is still an open question.

Acknowledgements. The work of the authors was supported by Ministerio de Ciencia e Innovación (grant MTM2008-03010) and Consellería de Innovación e Industria, Xunta de Galicia (regional grant PGIDIT07PXIB207031PR).

References

BICKEL, P.J. and FREEDMAN, D.A. (1981): Some asymptotic theory for the bootstrap. *Annals of Statistics 9, 1196-1217.*

CAI, T.T. and HALL, P. (2006): Prediction in functional linear regression. *Annals of Statistics 34, 2159-2179.*

CAO-ABAD, R. (1991): Rate of convergence for the wild bootstrap in nonparametric regression. *Annals of Statistics 19, 2226-2231.*

CARDOT, H., FERRATY, F., MAS, A. and SARDA, P (2003a): Testing hypothesis in the functional linear model. *Scandinavian Journal of Statistics 30, 241-255.*

CARDOT, H., FERRATY, F. and SARDA, P. (1999): Functional linear model. *Statistics & Probability Letters 45, 11-22.*

CARDOT, H., FERRATY, F. and SARDA, P. (2003b): Spline estimators for the functional linear model. *Statistica Sinica 13, 571-591.*

CARDOT, H., MAS, A. and SARDA, P. (2004): CLT in functional linear regression models: application to confidence sets for prediction. *Technical Report.* University Montpellier II, Departament of Mathematics.

CARDOT, H., MAS, A. and SARDA, P. (2007): CLT in functional linear regression models. *Probability Theory and Related Fields 138, 325-361.*

CHIOU, J.M. and MÜLLER, H.G. (2007): Diagnostics for functional regression via residual processes. *Computational Statistics & Data Analysis 51, 4849-4863.*

CUEVAS, A., FEBRERO, M. and FRAIMAN, R. (2004): An Anova test for functional data. *Computational Statistics & Data Analysis 47, 111-122.*

CUEVAS, A., FEBRERO, M. and FRAIMAN, R. (2006): On the use of the bootstrap for estimating functions with functional data. *Computational Statistics & Data Analysis 51, 1063-1074.*

EFRON, B. (1979): Bootstrap methods: another look at the jackknife. *Annals of Statistics 7, 1-26.*

FERRATY, F., VAN KEILEGOM, I. and VIEU, P (2009): On the validity of the bootstrap in nonparametric functional regression. *Scandinavian Journal of Statistics* (to appear). doi: 10.1111/j.1467-9469.2009.00662.x.

FERRATY, F. and VIEU, P. (2006): *Nonparametric Functional Data Analysis: Theory and Practice.* Springer, New York.

FREEDMAN, D.A. (1981): Bootstrapping regression models. *Annals of Statistics 9, 1218-1228.*

HALL, P. and HOROWITZ, J.L. (2007): Methodology and convergence rates for functional linear regression. *Annals of Statistics 35, 70-91.*

HALL, P. and HOSSEINI-NASAB, M. (2006): On properties of functional principal components analysis. *Journal of the Royal Statistical Society Series B 68, 109-126.*

HALL, P. and VIAL, C. (2006): Assessing the finite dimensionality of functional data. *Journal of the Royal Statistical Society Series B 68, 689-705.*

HORVÁTH, L., KOKOSZKA, P. and REIMHERR, M. (2009): Two sample inference in functional linear models. *Canadian Journal of Statistics 37, 571-591*

KOKOSZKA, P., MASLOVA, I., SOJKA, J. and ZHU, L. (2006): Testing for lack of dependence in the functional linear model. *Journal of the Royal Statistical Society Series B 68, 689-705.*

MARTÍNEZ-CALVO, A. (2008): Presmoothing in functional linear regression. In: S. Dabo-Niang and F. Ferray (Eds.): *Functional and Operatorial Statistics.* Physica-Verlag, Heidelberg, 223-229.

RAMSAY, J.O. and SILVERMAN, B.W. (2002): *Applied Functional Data Analysis. Methods and Case Studies.* Springer, New York.

RAMSAY, J.O. and SILVERMAN, B.W. (2005): *Functional Data Analysis.* Second edition. Springer, New York.

SHEN, Q. and FARADAY, J. (2004): An F test for linear models with functional responses. *Statistica Sinica 14, 1239-1257.*

SINGH, K. (1981): On the asymptotic accuracy of Efron's bootstrap. *Annals of Statistics 9, 1187-1195.*

Empirical Dynamics and Functional Data Analysis

Hans-Georg Müller

Department of Statistics, University of California, Davis
One Shields Avenue, Davis, CA 95616, U.S.A. *mueller@wald.ucdavis.edu*

Abstract. We review some recent developments on modeling and estimation of dynamic phenomena within the framework of Functional Data Analysis (FDA). The focus is on longitudinal data which correspond to sparsely and irregularly sampled repeated measurements that are contaminated with noise and are available for a sample of subjects. A main modeling assumption is that the data are generated by underlying but unobservable smooth trajectories that are realizations of a Gaussian process. In this setting, with only a few measurements available per subject, classical methods of Functional Data Analysis that are based on presmoothing individual trajectories will not work. We review the estimation of derivatives for sparse data, the PACE package to implement these procedures, and an empirically derived stochastic differential equation that the processes satisfy and that consists of a linear deterministic component and a drift process.

Keywords: dynamics, Gaussian process, drift term

1   Introduction

Functional data analysis (FDA) is a collection of nonparametric statistical techniques to analyze data that include samples of random functions. In earlier versions of FDA (Gasser et al. (1984), Gasser and Kneip (1995)) fully observed or densely sampled functions were typically assumed. More recently, the analysis of sparsely observed samples of random curves, where observations may also be contaminated by noise, has found increasing interest, due to the need for nonparametric methods to analyze such data.

Consider for example longitudinal measurements of Body Mass Index (BMI) between ages 45 and 70 that were obtained in the Baltimore Longitudinal Study of Aging (BLSA) (Shock et al. (1984), Pearson et al. (1997)). As typical for many longitudinal data, the BMI measurements were made at irregular times and contain substantial measurement errors. For further details, we refer to Müller and Yang (2010). For eight out of a sample of $n = 507$ subjects, the longitudinal measurements are shown in Figure 1. As can be seen, the number of measurements per subject is often quite small and there is substantial variation across subjects.

A reasonable and often useful assumption is that these and similar types of data are generated by smooth underlying random trajectories that are

Y. Lechevallier, G. Saporta (eds.), *Proceedings of COMPSTAT'2010*,
DOI 10.1007/978-3-7908-2604-3_19, © Springer-Verlag Berlin Heidelberg 2010

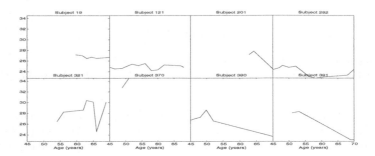

Fig. 1. Longitudinal measurements of Body Mass Index (BMI) for 8 randomly selected subjects

not directly observable, but which may be considered to be realizations of a Gaussian stochastic process, so that each subject is characterized by an underlying random function. This set-up is more realistic than the traditional "functional data" assumption of fully observed curves, which is often enforced through a presmoothing step (Ramsay and Silverman (2005)) that can lead to suboptimal performance and asymptotic consistency problems.

For an assessment of the underlying dynamics related to longitudinal trajectories such as BMI, a first step is to obtain the derivatives of the trajectories. Due to the sparseness of the data, this is a non-trivial task in the longitudinal settings we consider here, which requires to borrow strength from the entire sample, by pooling information across subjects. That this idea actually works was shown in Liu and Müller (2009) and the consequences of derivative estimation and linearity of relations between the levels assumed by Gaussian processes at pre-set times were explored in Müller and Yang (2010).

A more recent development that is based on derivative estimation is an empirical stochastic differential equation that governs longitudinal data under weak assumptions (Müller and Yao (2010)). For nonparametric statistical approaches in which derivatives of stochastic processes constitute central model components we use the term Empirical Dynamics. Empirical Dynamics draws on methodology from FDA, and aims at empirically learning the dynamics of temporal phenomena from a sample of trajectories that are realizations of an underlying stochastic process.

We provide here a review of these developments, focusing on the estimation of derivatives from sparse data, available software for this and related tasks, and first order empirical dynamics.

2   Estimating derivatives from sparsely sampled data

Statistical estimation of derivatives in sparsely sampled data situations cannot be based on smoothing difference quotients as in Gasser et al. (1984) or applying derivative kernels (Gasser and Müller (1984)) or similar kernel or spline based approaches. These methods rely on densely sampled data and break down if the sampling times have large gaps. Some of these difficulties can be overcome by pooling information across subjects and exploiting smoothness and differentiability of mean and covariance functions of the underlying stochastic process. This is the approach taken in Liu and Müller (2009) that we review in this section.

Consider a square integrable Gaussian stochastic process X with mean function $\mu(t) = EX(t)$ and covariance surface $G(t, s) = \text{cov}(X(t), X(s))$, defined on a domain T, which are smoothly differentiable to an order that depends on the specific context and may vary in the following. If the linear operator $(A_G f)(t) = \int_T G(t, s) f(s) ds$ possesses eigenvalues $\lambda_1 \geq \lambda_2 \geq \ldots \geq 0$ with corresponding orthonormal eigenfunctions $\phi_k(t)$, the process X has a Karhunen-Loève representation $X(t) = \mu(t) + \sum_{k=1}^{\infty} \xi_k \phi_k(t)$, where the functional principal components (FPCs) ξ_k are defined as inner products

$$\xi_k = \int_T (X(t) - \mu(t)) \phi_k(t) dt, \quad k = 1, 2, \ldots . \tag{1}$$

These are (in the Gaussian case) independent random variables with zero mean and variances $\text{var}(\xi_k) = \lambda_k$. Functional principal component analysis has been a focus of much research in FDA (Rice and Silverman (1991), Bosq (2000), Mas and Menneteau (2003)).

Differentiating the Karhunen-Loève representation, one obtains a corresponding representation for the ν-th derivative, $\nu \geq 0$,

$$X^{(\nu)}(t) = \mu^{(\nu)}(t) + \sum_{k=1}^{\infty} \xi_k \phi_k^{(\nu)}(t). \tag{2}$$

By taking the νth derivative on both sides of the eigen-equations that define the eigenfunctions, one obtains

$$\frac{d^\nu}{dt^\nu} \int_T G(t, s) \phi_k(s) ds = \lambda_k \frac{d^\nu}{dt^\nu} \phi_k(t). \tag{3}$$

This relationship can be utilized to obtain estimates for the derivatives of eigenfunctions, as it implies

$$\phi_k^{(\nu)}(t) = \frac{1}{\lambda_k} \int_T \frac{\partial^\nu}{\partial t^\nu} G(t, s) \phi_k(s) ds.$$

From this relation it emerges that if estimates with good properties can be constructed for the eigenvalues, eigenfunctions and the partial derivatives of the covariance surface, one obtains from these reasonable estimators for eigenfunction derivatives. Such estimators have been proposed in Liu and Müller (2009), modifying earlier approaches of Müller and Yao (2005a). In these developments, the following sparse sampling model was assumed: The j-th measurement for the i-th individual Y_{ij} pertains to an observation of the random trajectory X_i at a random time T_{ij}, where the number of available measurements N_i is also random and independent of the other random variables. The data model then is

$$Y_{ij} = Y_i(T_{ij}) = X_i(T_{ij}) + \varepsilon_{ij} = \mu(T_{ij}) + \sum_{k=1}^{\infty} \xi_{ik}\phi_k(T_{ij}) + \varepsilon_{ij}, \qquad (4)$$

with errors ε_{ij} that are i.i.d. Gaussian with mean zero and variance σ^2.

Within the framework of this model, improved rates of convergence for covariance surface and eigenfunction estimates, under a somewhat different set of assumptions regarding the sparse sampling of the random trajectories, have been derived recently in Müller and Yao (2010). To obtain estimates for the functional principal components, their definition as inner products in (1) cannot be directly employed, as due to the sparseness of the data these integrals cannot be well approximated. An alternative best linear unbiased prediction (BLUP) approach, developed in Yao et al. (2005a) and modified in Liu and Müller (2009), aims at estimating the conditional expectation $E(X_i^{(\nu)}(t)|Y_{i1},\ldots,Y_{iN_i})$, for which consistent estimators are available under Gaussianity assumptions.

These estimates are based on the principle of "Principal Analysis by Conditional Expectation" (PACE) (Yao et al. (2005a)). Letting $\mathbf{X}_i = (X_i(T_{i1}), \ldots, X_i(T_{iN_i}))^T$, $\mathbf{Y}_i = (Y_{i1}, \ldots, Y_{iN_i})^T$, $\mu_i = (\mu(T_{i1}), \ldots, \mu(T_{iN_i}))^T$, $\phi_{ik} = (\phi_k(T_{i1}), \ldots, \phi_k(T_{iN_i}))^T$, by Gaussianity

$$E[\xi_{ik}|\mathbf{Y}_i] = \lambda_k \phi_{ik}^T \Sigma_{\mathbf{Y}_i}^{-1}(\mathbf{Y}_i - \mu_i), \qquad (5)$$

where $\Sigma_{\mathbf{Y}_i} = \text{cov}(\mathbf{Y}_i, \mathbf{Y}_i) = \text{cov}(\mathbf{X}_i, \mathbf{X}_i) + \sigma^2 \mathbf{I}_{N_i}$.

This conditioning approach has been demonstrated to work well in practice. Estimates of trajectory derivatives are then obtained by plugging the estimators for eigenvalues, eigenfunction derivatives and functional principal components into equation (2). A particularly noteworthy feature is that the estimates obtained through (2) and those obtained by directly approximating integrals (1) are practically identical in densely sampled or fully observed functional designs, so that the PACE method (2) has the advantage that it always provides reasonable estimates, irrespective of whether the design is dense or not.

3   The PACE Package

This is a Matlab package that has been developed since 2005, starting with an initial version that was created by Fang Yao. In early 2010, version 2.11 is being released, along with a R version, which currently contains only a small subset of the procedures. The code and descriptions can be downloaded from http://anson.ucdavis.edu/~mueller/data/programs.html.

Due to superior precision and much faster run times, the Matlab version is preferable. The Principal Analysis by Conditional Expectation (PACE) code implements a number of core procedures for FDA. PACE refers to the conditioning step (2) on which the estimation of the functional principal components is based, and which is key to implement the BLUP estimators, as described in the previous section.

The FDA procedures implemented in PACE are based on functional principal component analysis, as described above. For each of a sample of subjects or experimental units, the *input* consists of the longitudinal measurements made for each of the subjects, which can be dense and regularly spaced or sparse and irregularly spaced. For each subject, one may have more than one kind of longitudinal data, and also non time-dependent subject-specific covariates. Basic *output* includes the mean functions $\hat{\mu}$ of the random trajectories and covariance surfaces $\hat{G}$, as well as the PACE estimates, derived from (2), for the functional principal components.

In order to obtain this basic output, two smoothing steps are needed, one for the mean function and one for the covariance surface, and for the case of derivatives also for partial derivatives of the covariance surface. These smoothing steps are implemented with local least squares, and the requisite smoothing bandwidths are selected by generalized cross-validation.

The smoothed covariance surfaces will be symmetric (as the input data, consisting of raw covariances, are symmetric and it is easy to see that the smoothed surfaces then also will be symmetric) but not necessarily non-negative definite. Therefore, after initial estimates of eigenvalues and eigenfunctions have been obtained by numerical linear algebra from the smoothed discretized covariance matrices, we project on the set of positive definite symmetric covariances by means of the projection

$$\hat{G}(s,t) = \sum_{k=1,\hat{\lambda}_k>0}^{\hat{K}} \hat{\lambda}_k \hat{\phi}_k(s) \hat{\phi}_k(t),$$

where $\hat{K}$ is the selected number of included components, for which various pseudo-likelihood criteria analogous to AIC and BIC have been studied (Yao et al. (2005a), Liu and Müller (2009)). Both smoothed and projected covariance surface are included in the output.

Basic output also includes the fitted subject-specific trajectories and their derivatives, based on (2). First and second order derivatives are particularly useful when one is interested in dynamics. This approach stands in contrast to usual FDA implementations, where one typically assumes densely sampled and nearly noise-free trajectory data as input, corresponding to fully observed functions. Where this is not the case, because the data are noisy or not densely sampled, such implementations will include an initial presmoothing step. The resulting smooth curves are then taken as fully observed sample of functions.

This approach can be problematic for data with large noise or subject to irregular and sparse sampling, as in the BMI example discussed in the Introduction. In such cases presmoothing and differentiation may introduce distortions; while the presmoothing step often has troublesome implications for the statistical properties of the subsequent FDA procedures, these are often ignored in the subsequent analysis. As pointed out above, the conditioning approach (2) implemented in PACE is robust with regard to the design and works across the common designs one encounters in repeated measurement situations.

Besides this basic output, PACE offers various results pertaining to the particular FDA procedure that one chooses. A requirement for this methodology to work properly is that the measurement times, pooled across all subjects, are dense on the domain and the pooled pairs of the locations of observations made for the same subject are dense on the domain squared (PACE outputs a two-dimensional design plot that enables a user to check whether these assumptions are satisfied; in case non-negligible gaps are found in these plots, the analysis can still proceed if one is willing to choose over-smoothing bandwidths for the smoothing steps, which may lead to increased bias).

The following approaches and outputs are included in the PACE package, among others:

- Fitting of both sparsely and densely sampled random functions and their derivatives, and spaghetti plots to view the sample of functions. Examples for such spaghetti plots are the graphs in Figure 1, which would be overlaid for all subjects in a typical output. This allows to make an initial assessment about extreme curves, outliers, the general variation across functions, functional clusters, and the signal-to-noise ratio.

- A variant of interest in many longitudinal studies from the life and social sciences pertains to the case when the repeated responses correspond to series of generalized (binary, Poisson etc.) variables. These are modeled by a latent Gaussian process, the trajectories of which are the underlying functions that generate the responses (Hall et al. (2008)).

- Time-synchronization based on pairwise warping, as proposed in Tang and Müller (2008). This method aims to align (register) curves that are subject to random time deformations, as is typically observed for growth curves, movement and other biological data, where each individual follows its own internal clock or "eigenzeit".

- A generalized functional distance for the case of sparse data, where the usual L^2 distance in function space is not useful, as integration methods cannot be adapted to the sparse case. This distance has various applications, including functional clustering, as demonstrated for online auction data in Peng and Müller (2008).

- Functional linear regression, fitting functional linear regression models for both sparsely or densely sampled random trajectories, for cases where the predictor is a random function and the response is a scalar or a random function. The details of the implementation are based on the methods in Yao et al. (2005b) and the version that is implemented is described in Müller et al. (2008).
- Diagnostic plots based on a residual process, leverage plots and bootstrap inference for functional linear regression (see Chiou and Müller (2007)).
- Functional quadratic regression, a more flexible model than functional linear regression, that can lead to substantially improved fitting, as described in Yao and Müller (2010).
- Generalized Functional Linear Regression (GFLM), which is an extension of Generalized Linear Models (GLM) to the functional case. Here the predictor is a random function and the response is a scalar generalized variable, such as binary or Poisson. The binary GFLM can be used for classification of functional data (Müller and Stadtmüller (2005)).
- Functional Additive Modeling (FAM), an additive generalization of functional linear regression, for the case of functional predictors and both functional and scalar responses; this is a flexible model that easily adapts to many shapes of the regression relation and efficiently addresses the curse-of-dimension problem for the case of infinite-dimensional predictors, in analogy to additive models with nonparametric components for regression with high-dimensional predictors (Müller and Yao, 2008).
- Fitting of the functional variance process, an extension of nonparametric variance function estimation. This process is based on the assumption that the random variation in the errors in itself is governed by the realization of a random process, which can then be characterized by its functional components (Müller et al. (2006)).

These methods include a variety of options that the user can specify. For the purposes of empirical dynamics, derivative estimation as provided by PACE is of central interest.

4 Empirical dynamics

In the Gaussian case, the values of trajectories and of their derivatives at a fixed time t are jointly normal. As was observed in Müller and Yao (2010), this implies a pointwise relationship between derivative and level that is given by

$$X^{(1)}(t) - \mu^{(1)}(t) = \beta(t)\{X(t) - \mu(t)\} + Z(t). \qquad (6)$$

Here the varying coefficient function β, which determines the relationship at each time t, is found to correspond to

$$\beta(t) = \frac{\sum_{k=1}^{\infty} \lambda_k \phi_k^{(1)}(t)\phi_k(t)}{\sum_{k=1}^{\infty} \lambda_k \phi_k(t)^2}, \qquad (7)$$

and Z is a Gaussian drift process that is independent of X.

This is a first order stochastic differential equation that is "empirical" in the sense that beyond Gaussianity and smoothness of trajectories no further assumptions are needed for its derivation. Dynamic relationships, that similar to the above equation are the consequence of basic general assumptions but are not in any way pre-specified, constitute "Empirical Dynamics".

To study the implications of the dynamic equation (6), it is paramount to quantify the variance of the drift process Z and to estimate the varying coefficient function β from the data. The latter can be easily achieved by truncating the expansion at (7) at an increasing sequence K and to substitute estimates for eigenvalues, eigenfunctions and eingefunction derivatives. This procedure is shown to be consistent in Müller and Yao (2010).

The fraction of variance of $X^{(1)}(t)$ that is explained by the fixed part of the differential equation (6) can be quantified by

$$R^2(t) = 1 - \mathrm{var}(Z(t))/\mathrm{var}(X^{(1)}(t)).$$

Further calculations lead to more detailed representations and to the derivation of consistent estimates for $R^2(t)$.

If we apply Empirical Dynamics to the BMI data that were described in the Introduction, the trajectories are found to display sizeable variation but no clear overall trend. The function $R^2(t)$ is large in the beginning and near the end of the domain, which means that the deterministic part of the equation is dominant in these areas, while the stochastic drift process is the main driver in the mid-age range, where also the varying coefficient function β is seen to hover around relatively small values.

Near both ends the function β is negative, which indicates that for subjects with BMI values away from (either above or below) the overall mean BMI level, BMI levels at these ages tend to decline if they are above, and tend to increase if they are below the mean level. It may indicate that there exist stabilizing mechanisms built into the physiological processes that control BMI over the age range covered by these data. This phenomenon has been characterized as "dynamic regression to the mean".

Acknowledgments

This research was supported by NSF grant DMS08-06199. Thanks are due to Wenjing Yang for creating the plots for the figures.

References

BOSQ, D. (2000): *Linear Processes in Function Spaces: Theory and Applications.* Springer-Verlag, New York.

CHIOU, J.-M. and MÜLLER, H.-G. (2007): Diagnostics for functional regression via residual processes. *Computational Statistics & Data Analysis 51, 4849–4863.*

GASSER, T. and KNEIP, A. (1995): Searching for structure in curve samples. *Journal of the American Statistical Association 90, 1179–1188.*

GASSER, T. and MÜLLER, H.-G. (1984): Estimating regression functions and their derivatives by the kernel method. *Scandinavian Journal of Statistics. Theory and Applications 11, 171–185.*

GASSER, T., MÜLLER, H.-G., KÖHLER, W., MOLINARI, L. and PRADER, A. (1984): Nonparametric regression analysis of growth curves. *The Annals of Statistics 12, 210–229.*

HALL, P., MÜLLER, H.-G. and YAO, F. (2008): Modeling sparse generalized longitudinal observations with latent Gaussian processes. *Journal of the Royal Statistical Society: Series B (Statistical Methodology) 70, 730–723.*

LIU, B. and MÜLLER, H.-G. (2009): Estimating derivatives for samples of sparsely observed functions, with application to on-line auction dynamics. *Journal of the American Statistical Association 104, 704–714.*

MAS, A. and MENNETEAU, L. (2003): Perturbation approach applied to the asymptotic study of random operators. In *High dimensional probability, III (Sandjberg, 2002)*, vol. 55 of *Progr. Probab.* Birkhäuser, Basel, 127–134.

MÜLLER, H.-G., CHIOU, J.-M. and LENG, X. (2008): Inferring gene expression dynamics via functional regression analysis. *BMC Bioinformatics 9, 60.*

MÜLLER, H.-G. and STADTMÜLLER, U. (2005): Generalized functional linear models. *The Annals of Statistics 33, 774–805.*

MÜLLER, H.-G., STADTMÜLLER, U. and YAO, F. (2006): Functional variance processes. *Journal of the American Statistical Association 101, 1007–1018.*

MÜLLER, H.-G. and YANG, W. (2010): Dynamic relations for sparsely sampled Gaussian processes. *Test 19, in press.*

MÜLLER, H.-G. and YAO, F. (2008): Functional additive models. *Journal of the American Statistical Association 103, 1534–1544.*

MÜLLER, H.-G. and YAO, F. (2010): Empirical dynamics for longitudinal data. *The Annals of Statistics 38, in press.*

PEARSON, J. D., MORRELL, C. H., BRANT, L. J. and LANDIS, P. K. (1997): Gender differences in a longitudinal study of age associated changes in blood pressure. *Journal of Gerontology - Biological Sciences and Medical Sciences 52, 177–183.*

PENG, J. and MÜLLER, H.-G. (2008): Distance-based clustering of sparsely observed stochastic processes, with applications to online auctions. *Annals of Applied Statistics 2, 1056–1077.*

RAMSAY, J. O. and SILVERMAN, B. W. (2005): *Functional Data Analysis.* 2nd ed. Springer Series in Statistics, Springer, New York.

RICE, J. A. and SILVERMAN, B. W. (1991): Estimating the mean and covariance structure nonparametrically when the data are curves. *Journal of the Royal Statistical Society: Series B (Statistical Methodology) 53, 233–243.*

SHOCK, N. W., GREULICH, R. C., ANDRES, R., LAKATTA, E. G., ARENBERG, D. and TOBIN, J. D. (1984): Normal human aging: The Baltimore Longitudinal Study of Aging. In *NIH Publication No. 84-2450.* U.S. Government Printing Office, Washington, D.C.

TANG, R. and MÜLLER, H.-G. (2008): Pairwise curve synchronization for functional data. *Biometrika 95, 875–889.*

YAO, F. and MÜLLER, H.-G. (2010): Functional quadratic regression. *Biometrika* *97, in press.*

YAO, F., MÜLLER, H.-G. and WANG, J.-L. (2005a): Functional data analysis for sparse longitudinal data. *Journal of the American Statistical Association 100, 577–590.*

YAO, F., MÜLLER, H.-G. and WANG, J.-L. (2005b): Functional linear regression analysis for longitudinal data. *The Annals of Statistics 33, 2873–2903.*

Part IX

Kernel Methods

Indefinite Kernel Discriminant Analysis

Bernard Haasdonk[1] and Elżbieta Pękalska[2]

[1] Institute of Applied Analysis and Numerical Simulation
University of Stuttgart, Germany, *haasdonk@mathematik.uni-stuttgart.de*
[2] School of Computer Science
University of Manchester, United Kingdom, *pekalska@cs.man.ac.uk*

Abstract. Kernel methods for data analysis are frequently considered to be restricted to positive definite kernels. In practice, however, indefinite kernels arise e.g. from problem-specific kernel construction or optimized similarity measures. We, therefore, present formal extensions of some kernel discriminant analysis methods which can be used with indefinite kernels. In particular these are the multi-class kernel Fisher discriminant and the kernel Mahalanobis distance. The approaches are empirically evaluated in classification scenarios on indefinite multi-class datasets.

Keywords: kernel methods, indefinite kernels, Mahalanobis distance, Fisher Discriminant Analysis

1 Introduction

Kernel methods are powerful statistical learning techniques, widely applied to various data analysis scenarios thanks to their flexibility and good performance, e.g. the support vector machine, kernel principal component analysis (KPCA), kernel Fisher discriminant (KFD), kernel k-means, etc. We refer to the monographs of Schölkopf and Smola (2002) and Shawe-Taylor and Cristianini (2004) for extensive presentations. The class of permissible kernels is often, and frequently wrongly, considered to be limited due to their requirement of being positive definite (pd). In practice, however, many non-pd similarity measures arise, e.g. when invariance or robustness is incorporated into the measure. Naturally, indefinite (dis-)similarities arise from non-Euclidean or non-metric dissimilarities, such as modified Hausdorff distances, or non-pd similarities, such as Kullback-Leibler divergence between probability distributions. Consequently, there is a practical need to handle these measures properly. Apart from embedding into Banach spaces or regularizing indefinite kernels, more general approaches are of high interest. A natural extension of Mercer kernels leads to indefinite kernels and the corresponding learning methods, cf. Ong et al. (2004), Pekalska and Duin (2005), Haasdonk (2005), Pekalska and Haasdonk (2009) and references therein.

In the current presentation, we extend two kernel discriminant methods, known from the positive definite case, to their indefinite counterparts. First, we focus on the generalized discriminant analysis (Baudat and Anouar

Y. Lechevallier, G. Saporta (eds.), *Proceedings of COMPSTAT'2010*,
DOI 10.1007/978-3-7908-2604-3_20, © Springer-Verlag Berlin Heidelberg 2010

(2000)), which is a kernel version of the standard linear discriminant analysis for feature extraction (Duda et al. (2001)). Secondly, we consider the Mahalanobis distance for indefinite kernels, which is an extensions of the pd case of Haasdonk and Pekalska (2008). For completeness, we also want to mention other existing approaches for pd kernels of Ruiz and Lopez-de Teruel (2001) and Wang et al. (2008).

The structure of the paper is as follows. In the next section we provide the basic notation and background on indefinite kernel spaces, which are the geometric framework for indefinite kernels. We derive the kernelized versions of the Fisher discriminant and two versions of the Mahalanobis distance for indefinite kernels in Sec. 3. We perform classification experiments in Sec. 4 and conclude in Sec. 5.

2   Kernels and Feature Space Embedding

The proper frame for indefinite kernel functions, to be used in the sequel, are indefinite vector spaces such as pseudo-Euclidean (Goldfarb (1985), Pekalska and Duin (2005)) or more general Kreĭn spaces (Bognar (1974), Rovnyak (2002)). A *Kreĭn space* over $\mathbb{R}$ is a vector space $\mathcal{K}$ equipped with a nondegenerate indefinite inner product $\langle \cdot, \cdot \rangle_{\mathcal{K}} \colon \mathcal{K} \times \mathcal{K} \to \mathbb{R}$ such that $\mathcal{K}$ admits an orthogonal decomposition as a direct sum, $\mathcal{K} = \mathcal{K}_+ \oplus \mathcal{K}_-$, where $(\mathcal{K}_+, \langle \cdot, \cdot \rangle_+)$ and $(\mathcal{K}_-, \langle \cdot, \cdot \rangle_-)$ are separable Hilbert spaces with their corresponding pd inner products. The inner product of $\mathcal{K}$, however, is the difference of $\langle \cdot, \cdot \rangle_+$ and $\langle \cdot, \cdot \rangle_-$, i.e. for any $\xi_+, \xi'_+ \in \mathcal{K}_+$ and any $\xi_-, \xi'_- \in \mathcal{K}_-$ holds

$$\langle \xi_+ + \xi_-, \xi'_+ + \xi'_- \rangle_{\mathcal{K}} := \langle \xi_+, \xi'_+ \rangle_+ - \langle \xi_-, \xi'_- \rangle_- \, .$$

The natural projections P_+ onto $\mathcal{K}_+$ and P_- onto $\mathcal{K}_-$ are *fundamental projections*. Any $\xi \in \mathcal{K}$ can be represented as $\xi = P_+\, \xi + P_-\, \xi$, while $I_{\mathcal{K}} = P_+ + P_-$ is the identity operator. The linear operator $\mathcal{J} = P_+ - P_-$ is called the *fundamental symmetry* and is the basic characteristic of a Kreĭn space $\mathcal{K}$, satisfying $\mathcal{J} = \mathcal{J}^{-1}$. The space $\mathcal{K}$ can be turned into its *associated Hilbert space* $|\mathcal{K}|$ by using the positive definite inner product $\langle \xi, \xi' \rangle_{|\mathcal{K}|} := \langle \xi, \mathcal{J}\xi' \rangle_{\mathcal{K}}$. We use the "transposition" abbreviation $\xi^T \xi' := \langle \xi, \xi' \rangle_{|\mathcal{K}|}$ for vectors and now additionally (motivated by $\mathcal{J}$ operating as a sort of "conjugation") a "conjugate-transposition" notation $\xi^* \xi' := \langle \xi, \xi' \rangle_{\mathcal{K}} = \langle \mathcal{J}\xi, \xi' \rangle_{|\mathcal{K}|} = (\mathcal{J}\xi)^T \xi' = \xi^T \mathcal{J} \xi'$.

Finite-dimensional Kreĭn spaces with $\mathcal{K}_+ = \mathbb{R}^p$ and $\mathcal{K}_- = \mathbb{R}^q$ are denoted by $\mathbb{R}^{(p,q)}$ and called *pseudo-Euclidean spaces*. They are characterized by the so-called *signature* $(p,q) \in \mathbb{N}^2$. $\mathcal{J}$ becomes the matrix $\mathcal{J} = \mathrm{diag}(1_p, -1_q)$ with respect to an orthonormal basis in $\mathbb{R}^{(p,q)}$. Kreĭn spaces are important as they provide feature-space representations of dissimilarity data (Goldfarb (1985)) or indefinite kernels. In analogy to the pd case, an indefinite kernel represents an inner product in an implicitly defined Kreĭn space. Hence algorithms working with indefinite kernels have a geometric interpretation in these spaces.

We assume a c-class problem with n training samples $X := \{x_i\}_{i=1}^n \subset \mathcal{X}$ and integer class labels $\{y_i\}_{i=1}^n \subset \{1,\ldots,c\} \subset \mathbb{N}$, where $\mathcal{X}$ denotes a general set of objects. The class labels induce a partition of the training data $X = \cup_{j=1}^c X^{[j]}$ with $X^{[j]} = \{x_i^{[j]}\}_{i=1}^{n^{[j]}}$, i.e. $n^{[j]}$ denoting the number of samples per class satisfying $\sum_{j=1}^c n^{[j]} = n$. Let $\psi \colon \mathcal{X} \to \mathcal{K}$ be an embedding of the sample set $\mathcal{X}$ into a Kreĭn space $\mathcal{K}$ and $\Psi := [\psi(x_1),\ldots,\psi(x_n)]$ be a sequence of embedded samples. We use natural "sequence-vector-products" to abbreviate linear combinations, so the empirical mean is defined as $\psi_\mu := \frac{1}{n}\sum_{i=1}^n \psi(x_i) = \frac{1}{n}\Psi\mathbf{1}_n$ with $\mathbf{1}_n \in \mathbb{R}^n$ being the vector of all ones. Similarly, we adopt "sequence-sequence-product" notation for expressing matrices, e.g. $K := \Psi^*\Psi = \Psi^T \mathcal{J}\Psi \in \mathbb{R}^{n\times n}$ being the kernel-matrix with respect to the kernel $k(x,x') := \langle \psi(x),\psi(x')\rangle_\mathcal{K}$. If $\Psi^{[j]} = [\psi(x_1^{[j]}),\ldots,\psi(x_{n^{[j]}}^{[j]})]$ denotes the sequence of class-wise embedded data, we define the class mean as $\psi_\mu^{[j]} := \frac{1}{n^{[j]}}\Psi^{[j]}\mathbf{1}_{n^{[j]}}$ and we abbreviate the column-blocks of the kernel matrix as $K^{[j]} := \Psi^*\Psi^{[j]} \in \mathbb{R}^{n\times n^{[j]}}$. We finally introduce the kernel-quantities $\mathbf{k}_x := (\psi(x_i)^*\psi(x))_{i=1}^n$. In practice, the embedding ψ will not be given for defining the kernel k. Instead a symmetric kernel function $k(x,x')$ will be chosen in a problem-specific way, which then implicitly represents the inner-product in some Kreĭn space obtained via a suitable embedding ψ. The strength of kernel methods relies in the fact that the computation of this embedding ψ can mostly be avoided, if the analysis algorithm only requires inner-products between embedded samples, as these are provided by the given function k.

3   Kernel Discriminant Analysis

3.1   Indefinite Kernel Fisher Discriminant Analysis

We demonstrated in (Haasdonk and Pekalska (2008b)) how the two-class indefinite Kernel Fisher discriminant classifier can be rigorously derived. This represents an extension of the KFD (Mika et al. (1999)) to indefinite kernels. Here, we generalize this further to multicategory Fisher Discriminant Analysis for feature extraction (Duda et. al. (2001)). The within-class scatter operator $\Sigma_W^{[j]} : \mathcal{K} \to \mathcal{K}$ for the j-th class is defined by

$$\Sigma_W^{[j]}\varphi := \sum_{i=1}^{n^{[j]}} \left(\psi(x_i^{[j]}) - \psi_\mu^{[j]}\right)\left(\psi(x_i^{[j]}) - \psi_\mu^{[j]}\right)^*\varphi, \quad \varphi \in \mathcal{K} \tag{1}$$

which results in the (normalized) overall within-class scatter $\Sigma_W := \frac{1}{n}\sum_{j=1}^c \Sigma_W^{[j]}$. Similarly, the (normalized) between-class scatter operator is defined by

$$\Sigma_B\varphi := \sum_{j=1}^c \frac{n^{[j]}}{n}\left(\psi_\mu^{[j]} - \psi_\mu\right)\left(\psi_\mu^{[j]} - \psi_\mu\right)^*\varphi, \quad \varphi \in \mathcal{K}. \tag{2}$$

The multiple discriminant analysis problem is then solved by searching a sequence of vectors $W = [w_1, \ldots, w_{c-1}] \in \mathcal{K}^{c-1}$ such that

$$J(W) := \frac{\det(W^* \Sigma_B W)}{\det(W^* \Sigma_W W)} = \frac{\det(W^T \mathcal{J} \Sigma_B W)}{\det(W^T \mathcal{J} \Sigma_W W)} \tag{3}$$

is maximized. This is obtained by solving the generalized eigenvalue problem

$$\mathcal{J} \Sigma_B w_j = \lambda_j \mathcal{J} \Sigma_W w_j \tag{4}$$

for the $c-1$ largest eigenvalues λ_j. The practical computation can now be kernelized similarly to Baudat and Anouar (2000) or Haasdonk and Pekalska (2008b). First, we note from the eigenvalue equation (4) that the range of both scatter operators is spanned by embedded training examples, implying $w_j \in \text{span}\{\psi(x_i)\}_{i=1}^n$. Hence, there exists a matrix $\boldsymbol{\alpha} \in \mathbb{R}^{n \times (c-1)}$ such that $W = \boldsymbol{\Psi \alpha}$ and the discriminant quotient (3) becomes

$$J(W) := \frac{\det(\boldsymbol{\alpha}^T \boldsymbol{\Psi}^T \mathcal{J} \Sigma_B \boldsymbol{\Psi \alpha})}{\det(\boldsymbol{\alpha}^T \boldsymbol{\Psi}^T \mathcal{J} \Sigma_W \boldsymbol{\Psi \alpha})} =: \frac{\det(\boldsymbol{\alpha}^T M \boldsymbol{\alpha})}{\det(\boldsymbol{\alpha}^T N \boldsymbol{\alpha})}. \tag{5}$$

The matrices M, N can now be computed based on the kernel data. We define $\mathbf{c} := \frac{1}{n} \mathbf{1}_n$ and $\mathbf{c}^{[j]} := (c_i^{[j]})_{i=1}^n$ with $c_i^{[j]} := 1/n^{[j]}$ for $x_i \in X^{[j]}$ and $c_i^{[j]} := 0$ otherwise. Then the between-class scatter is rewritten as $\Sigma_B = \sum_{j=1}^c \frac{n^{[j]}}{n} \boldsymbol{\Psi}(\mathbf{c}^{[j]} - \mathbf{c})(\mathbf{c}^{[j]} - \mathbf{c})^T \boldsymbol{\Psi}^*$. Setting $D := \sum_{j=1}^c \frac{n^{[j]}}{n} (\mathbf{c}^{[j]} - \mathbf{c})(\mathbf{c}^{[j]} - \mathbf{c})^T$, we obtain

$$M = \boldsymbol{\Psi}^T \mathcal{J} \Sigma_B \boldsymbol{\Psi} = \boldsymbol{\Psi}^T \mathcal{J} \boldsymbol{\Psi} D \boldsymbol{\Psi}^T \mathcal{J} \boldsymbol{\Psi} = KDK. \tag{6}$$

Note that both D and M are positive semidefnite by construction. Further, we introduce the centering matrix $H^{[j]} := I_{n^{[j]}} - \frac{1}{n^{[j]}} \mathbf{1}_{n^{[j]}} \mathbf{1}_{n^{[j]}}^T \in \mathbb{R}^{n^{[j]} \times n^{[j]}}$ and obtain for the class-specific within-class scatter operator $\Sigma_W^{[j]} = \frac{1}{n^{[j]}} \boldsymbol{\Psi}^{[j]} H^{[j]} \boldsymbol{\Psi}^{[j]} \mathcal{J}$. Consequently, $\Sigma_W = \sum_{j=1}^c \frac{n^{[j]}}{n} \Sigma_W^{[j]} = \frac{1}{n} \sum_{j=1}^c \boldsymbol{\Psi}^{[j]} H^{[j]} \boldsymbol{\Psi}^{[j]} \mathcal{J}$. Hence, the denominator matrix of (5) is expressed as

$$N = \boldsymbol{\Psi}^T \mathcal{J} \Sigma_W \boldsymbol{\Psi} = \frac{1}{n} \sum_{j=1}^c K^{[j]} H^{[j]} (K^{[j]})^T. \tag{7}$$

N is positive semidefinite irrespectively of the definiteness of $K^{[j]}$. To see this, it is sufficient to remark that $K^{[j]} H^{[j]} (K^{[j]})^T = (K^{[j]} H^{[j]})(K^{[j]} H^{[j]})^T$ is positive semidefinite as $H^{[j]}$ is idempotent, and N is a positive linear combination of such matrices. Identical to the pd case, the matrix N will be singular and maximizing (5) is not well defined. Therefore, the matrix N is regularized, e.g. by $N_\beta = N + \beta I_{n \times n}$ with $\beta > 0$. The coefficient matrix $\boldsymbol{\alpha} = [\boldsymbol{\alpha}_1, \ldots, \boldsymbol{\alpha}_{c-1}]$ is then obtained columnwise by solving the following eigenvalue problem

$$(N_\beta^{-1} M) \boldsymbol{\alpha}_j = \lambda_j \boldsymbol{\alpha}_j,$$

Obviously, thanks to the positive semidefiniteness of $N_\beta^{-1} M$, the eigenvalues λ_j are nonnegative. The normalized eigenvectors $\boldsymbol{\alpha}_j$ define the indefinite kernel Fisher (IKF) feature extractors by suitable projections via the indefinite inner product as follows:

$$f_{IKF}(x) := [\langle w_1, \psi(x) \rangle_\mathcal{K}, .., \langle w_{c-1}, \psi(x) \rangle_\mathcal{K}]^T = W^* \psi(x) = \boldsymbol{\alpha}^T \Psi^* \psi(x) = \boldsymbol{\alpha}^T \mathbf{k}_x.$$

The above formulation is equivalent to the kernel Fisher discriminant analysis for pd kernels; here, however, K is indefinite.

We now want to note an interesting theoretical fact of the IKF feature extractor: it is equivalent to embedding the data in the associated Hilbert space $|\mathcal{K}|$ and performing a positive definite kernel Fisher discriminant analysis. The latter approach would be in the spirit of "regularizing" the indefinite kernel matrix to a pd matrix, but is algorithmically quite cumbersome. After an eigenvalue decomposition of the possibly huge indefinite kernel matrix the negative eigenvalues are flipped yielding an explicit feature space embedding, which enables the traditional discriminant analysis. If we show the equivalence of IKF to this procedure, then IKF is a simple algorithmical alternative to this regularizing approach. To see this equivalence, we first note with view on (1) and (2) that the between-class and within-class scatter operators in the associated Hilbert space are given by $\Sigma_B^{|\mathcal{K}|} = \Sigma_B \mathcal{J}$ and $\Sigma_W^{|\mathcal{K}|} = \Sigma_W \mathcal{J}$. Then, the corresponding positive definite Fisher discriminant eigenvalue problem $\Sigma_B^{|\mathcal{K}|} w_j^{|\mathcal{K}|} = \lambda_j^{|\mathcal{K}|} \Sigma_W^{|\mathcal{K}|} w_j^{|\mathcal{K}|}$ is solved by $\lambda_j^{|\mathcal{K}|} = \lambda_j$ and $w_j^{|\mathcal{K}|} = \mathcal{J} w_j$ as can be seen by (4). Setting $W^{|\mathcal{K}|} := [w_1^{|\mathcal{K}|}, \dots, w_{c-1}^{|\mathcal{K}|}]$ allows to define the Fisher discriminant in the associated Hilbert space and gives the equivalence to f_{IKF}:

$$f_{IKF}^{|\mathcal{K}|}(x) := (W^{|\mathcal{K}|})^T \psi(x) = (\mathcal{J}W)^T \psi(x) = W^T \mathcal{J} \psi(x) = W^* \psi(x) = f_{IKM}(x).$$

3.2   Indefinite Kernel Mahalanobis Distances

For simplicity of presentation we describe the computation of the Mahalanobis distance for the complete dataset and assume that it is centered in the embedded Kreĭn space. This can be obtained by explicit centering operations, cf. Shawe-Taylor and Cristianini (2004). As a result, $K = \Psi^* \Psi$ is now a centered kernel matrix. Then, the empirical covariance operator $C \colon \mathcal{K} \to \mathcal{K}$ acts on $\phi \in \mathcal{K}$ as $C\phi := \frac{1}{n} \sum_{i=1}^{n} \psi(x_i) \langle \psi(x_i), \phi \rangle_\mathcal{K} = \frac{1}{n} \Psi \Psi^* \phi$. We will therefore identify the empirical covariance operator as

$$C = \frac{1}{n} \Psi \Psi^* = \frac{1}{n} \Psi \Psi^T \mathcal{J} = C^{|\mathcal{K}|} \mathcal{J},$$

where $C^{|\mathcal{K}|} = \frac{1}{n} \Psi \Psi^T$ is the empirical covariance operator in $|\mathcal{K}|$. The operator C is not pd in the Hilbert sense, but it is pd in the Kreĭn sense. It means that $\langle \xi, C\xi \rangle_\mathcal{K} \geq 0$ for $\xi \neq 0$ in agreement with the inner product of that space. In (Haasdonk and Pekalska (2008)) we presented a kernelized version of the

Mahalanobis distance for pd kernels. In the case of an invertible covariance (IC) operator, the derivation directly extends to indefinite kernels resulting in

$$d_{IC}^2(x) := \psi(x)^* C^{-1} \psi(x) = n(\mathbf{k}_x)^T (K^-)^2 \mathbf{k}_x$$

where the superscript $\cdot^- = \mathrm{pinv}(\cdot, \alpha)$ denotes the pseudo-inverse with a threshold $\alpha > 0$. This means that in the computation of the inverse singular values smaller than α are set to zero.

The above distance is evaluated per class and does not involve between-class information. Hence, alternatively, we also proposed a kernel Mahalanobis distance in a full kernel (FK) space, determined via KPCA (Pekalska and Haasdonk (2009)). This distance for class j is obtained as

$$(d_{FK}^{[j]}(x))^2 := \frac{n^{[j]}}{2} (\tilde{\mathbf{k}}_x^{[j]})^T (\tilde{K}_{\mathrm{reg}}^{[j]})^{-1} \tilde{\mathbf{k}}_x^{[j]}, \tag{8}$$

where $\tilde{\mathbf{k}}_x^{[j]} := \mathbf{k}_x - \frac{1}{n^{[j]}} K^{[j]} \mathbf{1}_{n^{[j]}}$ and $\tilde{K}_{\mathrm{reg}}^{[j]} := \tilde{K}^{[j]} + \alpha_j I_n$ for some $\alpha_j > 0$ with $\tilde{K}^{[j]} := K^{[j]} H^{[j]} (K^{[j]})^T \in \mathbb{R}^{n \times n}$. The extension to indefinite kernels is straightforward as the kernel matrices $\tilde{K}^{[j]} := K^{[j]} H^{[j]} (K^{[j]})^T$ still are positive semidefinite. As a result, the indefinite kernel Mahalanobis distance using the full kernel matrix is identical to (8), but based on an indefinite kernel. See Appendix of Pekalska and Haasdonk (2009) for details.

Since we compute kernel Mahalanobis distances per class, we can now define the feature representations of a sample x as a c-dimensional vector by the indefinite kernel Mahalanobis distance with invertible covariance (IKM-IC) as $f_{IKM-IC}(x) := [d_{IC}^{[1]}(x), \ldots, d_{IC}^{[c]}(x)]^T$ and similarly f_{IKM-FK} using the full kernel distance $d_{FK}^{[j]}$.

4   Classification Experiments

Multi-class problems characterized by indefinite proximity data can now be approached via the feature representations f_{IKF}, f_{IKM-IC} and f_{IKM-FK} defined in the previous section. Although the features are extracted from indefinite kernels, the resulting either c- or $(c-1)$-dimensional feature vector spaces are assumed to be equipped with the traditional inner product and Euclidean metric. As a result, different classifiers can now be trained there.

Table 4 lists basic properties of eight multi-class datasets, i.e. the type of dissimilarity measure, the class names and sizes and the fraction of data used for training in the hold-out experiments. Some measures of indefiniteness of the resulting training kernel matrices are also provided: $r_{\mathrm{neg}} \in [0, 1]$ denotes the ratio of negative to overall variance of the centered training kernel matrix and (p, q) indicates the signature of the embedding Krein space. These quantities are averaged over 25 runs based on random drawings of a training subset. For detailed descriptions and references to the single datasets, we refer to Appendix of (Pekalska and Haasdonk (2009)).

Table 1. Characteristics of indefinite datasets, cf. Pekalska and Haasdonk (2009) for details and references.

	Dissimilarity	Kernel	c $(n^{[j]})$	β	$r_{neg}(p,q)$
Cat-cortex	Prior knowl.	$-d^2$	4 (10–19)	0.80	0.19 (35, 18)
Protein	Evolutionary	$-d^2$	4 (30–77)	0.80	0.00 (167, 3)
News-COR	Correlation	$-d^2$	4 (102–203)	0.60	0.19 (127,208)
ProDom	Structural	s	4 (271–1051)	0.25	0.01 (518, 90)
Chicken29	Edit-dist.	$-d^2$	5 (61–117)	0.80	0.31 (192,166)
Files	Compression	$-d^2$	5 (60–255)	0.50	0.02 (392, 63)
Pen-ANG	Edit-dist.	$-d^2$	10 (334–363)	0.15	0.24 (261,269)
Zongker	Shape-match.	s	10 (200)	0.25	0.36 (274,226)

In our hold-out experiments, each data set is split into the training and test set of suitable sizes as reported in Table 1. The dissimilarity data set is first scaled such that the average dissimilarity is 1 on the training set. This is done in order to have a consistent choice over a range of crossvalidated parameters. The training kernel matrix based on the kernel $k = -d^2$ is then centered and used to extract features either by f_{IKF}, f_{IKM-IC} or f_{IKM-FK}. Next, four classifiers are constructed in the derived feature spaces, namely the nearest mean classifier (NM), Fisher discriminant (FD), quadratic discriminant (QD) and k-nearest neighbour (KNN) rule. Since we use the same training data both to extract the features and train the classifiers, simple classifiers are preferred to avoid the overuse of the data. The classifiers are then applied to suitably projected test data. This is repeated 20 times and the results are averaged.

As a reference, we use classifiers that directly work with original proximity measures as kernels. These are the indefinite kernel Fisher discriminant (IKFD), indefinite support vector machine (ISVM) and indefinite kernel nearest neighbour (IKNN) classifier. In particular, FD, IKFD and ISVM are binary classifiers, which solve the multi-class problems by the one-versus-all approach. The remaining classifiers are inherently multi-class classifiers.

The free parameters of both feature extractors and classifiers are determined via a (nested, if necessary) 10-fold crossvalidation. The regularization parameters of the kernel discriminant feature extractors are selected from $\{10^{-6}, 10^{-4}, 10^{-3}, 10^{-2}, 0.05, 0.1, 0.5, 1, 10, 10^2, 10^3\}$. The number of nearest neighbors is found from 1 to 15. The parameter C for ISVM is found within $\{0.01, 0.1, 0.5, 1, 5, 10, 10^2, 10^3, 10^4, 10^6, 10^8\}$.

The classification results are reported in Table 2. Although strong conclusions cannot be drawn due to high standard deviations, the following observations can be made. The features obtained by f_{IKM-IC} are performing much worse than all other extracted features. This may be due to two facts. First, the assumption of an invertible covariance matrix may be wrong, leading to a degeneration in classification accuracy. Second, this Mahalanobis distance

Table 2. Average classification errors (and standard deviation) over 20 hold-out repetitions of data drawing and cross-validated parameter selection.

Classifier+Features	Cat-cortex	Protein	News-COR	ProDom
NM+IKM-IC	45.5 (13.2)	21.2 (7.7)	38.6 (2.4)	15.0 (3.5)
NM+IKM-FK	10.9 (6.3)	2.1 (2.6)	24.9 (2.5)	6.4 (2.4)
NM+IKF	12.6 (5.7)	0.1 (0.4)	24.1 (1.8)	2.0 (0.6)
FD+IKM-IC	42.2 (11.3)	25.9 (5.5)	39.7 (2.6)	9.4 (3.0)
FD+IKM-FK	10.3 (5.4)	1.1 (2.0)	24.2 (2.0)	1.7 (0.6)
FD+IKF	11.2 (5.2)	0.2 (0.5)	24.2 (3.1)	1.6 (0.6)
QD+IKM-IC	48.5 (12.4)	11.9 (4.5)	41.4 (3.0)	3.6 (0.9)
QD+IKM-FK	22.7 (6.7)	0.5 (0.8)	25.5 (2.7)	2.0 (0.7)
QD+IKF	18.4 (7.4)	0.5 (1.3)	24.4 (3.1)	1.5 (0.5)
KNN+IKM-IC	43.9 (8.6)	19.8 (7.4)	42.9 (3.1)	5.0 (1.6)
KNN+IKM-FK	11.3 (6.5)	0.6 (1.7)	25.7 (1.7)	2.2 (0.9)
KNN+IKF	11.7 (6.5)	0.2 (0.5)	24.7 (2.2)	1.6 (0.7)
IKFD	10.6 (5.6)	0.3 (0.7)	23.6 (2.4)	2.0 (0.6)
ISVM	16.5 (5.7)	0.5 (0.8)	24.4 (2.3)	1.6 (0.6)
IKNN	15.6 (5.8)	4.7 (5.2)	29.6 (2.3)	3.1 (0.8)
	Chicken29	Files	Pen-ANG	Zongker
NM+IKM-IC	36.1 (5.4)	53.1 (4.4)	32.9 (1.9)	37.6 (2.1)
NM+IKM-FK	20.4 (3.2)	44.4 (3.6)	33.0 (1.6)	14.5 (0.8)
NM+IKF	6.6 (2.3)	5.3 (1.5)	1.3 (0.5)	5.9 (0.6)
FD+IKM-IC	36.9 (2.9)	50.4 (5.1)	11.5 (1.1)	33.5 (1.3)
FD+IKM-FK	8.9 (4.0)	22.3 (3.3)	3.2 (0.9)	6.3 (0.9)
FD+IKF	5.9 (2.3)	5.4 (1.5)	1.5 (0.4)	7.1 (0.8)
QD+IKM-IC	30.1 (3.4)	29.3 (4.5)	4.9 (0.9)	39.3 (2.1)
QD+IKM-FK	6.9 (2.8)	7.7 (2.7)	1.2 (0.3)	6.5 (0.9)
QD+IKF	5.0 (1.5)	6.7 (1.4)	1.5 (0.4)	5.8 (0.6)
KNN+IKM-IC	31.8 (5.0)	30.1 (4.6)	5.7 (0.7)	33.9 (1.6)
KNN+IKM-FK	4.2 (1.3)	8.0 (2.4)	1.8 (0.3)	4.8 (0.5)
KNN+IKF	5.1 (2.2)	4.9 (1.3)	1.2 (0.3)	5.5 (0.8)
IKFD	6.4 (2.2)	5.5 (1.4)	1.4 (0.4)	6.3 (0.7)
ISVM	6.5 (2.2)	11.6 (2.7)	5.0 (0.5)	7.0 (0.5)
IKNN	5.1 (2.0)	36.7 (2.8)	0.9 (0.3)	11.4 (1.4)

misses the between-class correlations of the datasets, which is increasingly important with higher number of classes. Hence, the full-kernel Mahalanobis distances f_{IKM-FK} are clearly preferable to the former. Still, the $(c-1)$-dimensional feature spaces f_{IKF} mostly lead to better results than the c-dimensional feature spaces obtained by the IKM approaches, hence the IKF-features are overall preferable. Among the chosen classifiers on the extracted features, KNN is overall the best classifier which suggests that these spaces benefit from non-linear classifiers. Among the reference classifiers, IKFD is frequently the best, closely followed by ISVM, but occasionally outperformed by IKNN. Overall, the extracted features f_{IKM-FK} and f_{IKF} in combination with the chosen simple classifiers consistently yield classification results in the range of the reference classifiers.

5 Conclusion

We presented extensions of kernel Fisher discriminant analysis and kernel Mahalanobis distances to indefinite kernels. The natural framework for indefinite kernels are Kreĭn spaces, which give a geometrical interpretation of these indefinite methods. An interesting theoretical finding for the IKF feature extractor is that it correspond to its counterpart in the associated Hilbert space. This implies that the indefinite kernel Fisher discriminant analysis saves the unnecessary preprocessing step of embedding the data, flipping the negative eigenvalues and performing an explicit Fisher discriminant in the embedded space. In particular, the f_{IKF} feature extractor is a real kernel method avoiding the explicit embedding. For the indefinite kernel Mahalanobis distance, we proposed to use two formulations from the pd case for indefinite kernels. We performed experiments on indefinite multi-class classification problems, that demonstrate the applicability of the f_{IKF} and f_{IKM-FK} methods, but clearly discarded the f_{IKM-IC} features. In particular, the successful features yield results comparable to standard indefinite kernel classifiers such as IKFD and ISVM.

6 Acknowledgements

The authors acknowledge funding by the German Research Foundation (DFG) within the Cluster of Excellence in Simulation Technology (EXC 310/1) at the University of Stuttgart and by the Engineering and Physical Science Research Council in the UK, project no. EP/D066883/1.

References

BAUDAT, G. and ANOUAR, F. (2000): Generalized discriminant analysis using a kernel approach. *Neural Computation*, 12(10):2385–2404.

BOGNAR, J. (1974): *Indefinite Inner Product Spaces*. Springer Verlag.

DUDA, R.O., HART, P.E. and STORK, D.G. (2001): *Pattern Classification*. John Wiley & Sons, Inc., 2nd edition.

GOLDFARB, L. (1985): A new approach to pattern recognition. In L. Kanal and A. Rosenfeld, editors, *Progress in Pattern Recognition*, volume 2, pages 241–402. Elsevier Science Publishers BV.

HAASDONK, B. (2005): Feature space interpretation of SVMs with indefinite kernels. *IEEE TPAMI*, 27(4):482–492, 2005.

HAASDONK, B. and PEKALSKA, E. (2008): Classification with kernel Mahalanobis distances. In *Proc. of 32nd. GfKl Conference, Advances in Data Analysis, Data Handling and Business Intelligence*.

HAASDONK, B. and PEKALSKA, E. (2008b): Indefinite kernel Fisher discriminant. In *Proc. of ICPR 2008, International Conference on Pattern Recognition.*

MIKA, S., RÄTSCH, G., WESTON, J., SCHÖLKOPF and MÜLLER, K.R. (1999): Fisher discriminant analysis with kernels. In *Neural Networks for Signal Processing,* pages 41–48.

ONG, C.S., MARY, X., CANU, S. and SMOLA, A.J. (2004): Learning with non-positive kernels. In *ICML,* pages 639–646. ACM Press.

PEKALSKA, E. and DUIN, R.P.W. (2005): *The Dissimilarity Representation for Pattern Recognition. Foundations and Applications.* World Scientific.

PEKALSKA, E. and HAASDONK, B. (2009): Kernel discriminant analysis with positive definite and indefinite kernels. *IEEE Transactions on Pattern Analysis and Machine Intelligence.* 31(6):1017–1032.

ROVNYAK, J. (2002): Methods of Krein space operator theory *Operator Theory: Advances and Applications,* 134:31–66.

RUIZ, A. and LOPEZ-DE TERUEL, P.E. (2001): Nonlinear kernel-based statistical pattern analysis. *IEEE Transactions on Neural Networks,* 12(1):16–32.

SCHÖLKOPF, B. and SMOLA, A.J. (2002): *Learning with Kernels.* MIT Press, Cambridge.

SHAWE-TAYLOR, J. and CRISTIANINI, N. (2004): *Kernel Methods for Pattern Analysis.* Cambridge University Press, UK.

WANG, J., PLATANIOTIS, K.N., LU, J. and VENETSANOPOULOS, A.N. (2008): Kernel quadratic discriminant analysis for small sample size problem. *Pattern Recognition,* 41(5):1528–1538.

Data Dependent Priors in PAC-Bayes Bounds

John Shawe-Taylor[1], Emilio Parrado-Hernández[2], and Amiran Ambroladze

[1] Dept. of Computer Science & CSML, University College London
London, WC1E 6BT, UK, *jst@cs.ucl.ac.uk*
[2] Dept. of Signal Processing and Communications, University Carlos III of
Madrid
Leganés, 28911, Spain, *emipar@tsc.uc3m.es*

Abstract. One of the central aims of Statistical Learning Theory is the bounding
of the test set performance of classifiers trained with i.i.d. data. For Support Vector
Machines the tightest technique for assessing this so-called generalisation error is
known as the PAC-Bayes theorem. The bound holds independently of the choice of
prior, but better priors lead to sharper bounds. The priors leading to the tightest
bounds to date are spherical Gaussian distributions whose means are determined
from a separate subset of data. This paper gives another turn of the screw by
introducing a further data dependence on the shape of the prior: the separate data
set determines a direction along which the covariance matrix of the prior is stretched
in order to sharpen the bound. In addition, we present a classification algorithm
that aims at minimizing the bound as a design criterion and whose generalisation
can be easily analysed in terms of the new bound.

The experimental work includes a set of classification tasks preceded by a
bound-driven model selection. These experiments illustrate how the new bound acting on the new classifier can be much tighter than the original PAC-Bayes Bound
applied to an SVM, and lead to more accurate classifiers.

Keywords: PAC Bayes Bound, Support Vector Machines, generalization prediction, model selection

1 Introduction

Support vector machines (SVM) (Boser (1992)) are accepted among practitioners as one of the most accurate automatic classification techniques. They
implement linear classifiers in a high-dimensional feature space using the
kernel trick to enable a dual representation and efficient computation. The
danger of overfitting in such high-dimensional spaces is countered by max-
imising the margin of the classifier on the training examples. For this reason
there has been considerable interest in bounds on the generalisation in terms
of the margin.

In fact, a main drawback that restrains engineers from using these advanced machine learning techniques is the lack of reliable predictions of generalisation, especially in what concerns worse-case performance. In this sense,
the widely used cross-validation generalization measures say little about the

Y. Lechevallier, G. Saporta (eds.), *Proceedings of COMPSTAT'2010*,
DOI 10.1007/978-3-7908-2604-3_21, © Springer-Verlag Berlin Heidelberg 2010

worst case performance of the algorithms. The error of the classifier on a set of samples follows a binomial distribution whose mean is the true error of the classifier. Cross-validation is a sample mean estimation of the true error, and worst case performance estimations concern the estimation of the tail of the distribution of the error of these sets of samples. One could then employ Statistical Learning Theory (SLT) tools to bound the tail of the distribution of errors. Early bounds have relied on covering number computations (Shawe-Taylor et al. (1998)), while later bounds have considered Rademacher complexity. The tightest bounds for practical applications appear to be the PAC-Bayes bound (Langford and Shawe-Taylor (2002)) and in particular the one given in (Ambroladze et al. (2007)), with a data dependent prior.

Another issue affected by the ability to predict the generalisation capability of a classifier is the selection of the hyperparameters that define the training. In the SVM case, these parameters are the trade-off between maximum margin and minimum training error, C, and the kernel parameters. Again, the more standard method of cross-validation has proved more reliable in most experiments, despite the fact that it is statistically poorly justified and relatively expensive.

The PAC-Bayes Bounds (overviewed in Section 2) use a Gaussian prior with zero mean and identity covariance matrix. The Prior PAC-Bayes Bound (Ambroladze et al. (2007)) tightens the prediction of the generalisation error of an SVM by using a separate subset of the training data to learn the mean of the Gaussian prior. The key to the new bound introduced in this work to come up with even more informative priors by using the separate data to also learn a stretching of the covariance matrix. Then section 4 presents a classification algorithm, named η−Prior SVM, that introduces a regularization term that tries to optimise a PAC-Bayes Bound.

The new bounds and algorithms are evaluated in some classification tasks after parameters selection in Section 5. The experiments illustrate the capabilities of the Prior PAC-Bayes Bound to (i) select an acceptable model (hyperparameter estimation) for an SVM and (ii) to provide tighter predictions of the generalisation of the resulting classifier.

Finally, the main conclusions of this work and some ongoing related research are outlined in Section 6.

2   PAC-Bayes bound for SVM

This section is devoted to a brief review of the PAC-Bayes Bound of Langford (2005) and the Prior PAC-Bayes Bound of Ambroladze (2006). Let us consider a distribution $\mathcal{D}$ of patterns $\mathbf{x}$ lying in a certain input space $\mathcal{X}$, with their corresponding output labels y, $y \in \{-1, 1\}$. In addition, let us also consider a distribution Q over the classifiers c. For every classifier c, one can define the *True error*, as the probability of misclassifying a pair pattern-label $(\mathbf{x}, y)$ selected at random from $\mathcal{D}$, $c_{\mathcal{D}} \equiv \Pr_{(\mathbf{x},y)\sim\mathcal{D}}(c(\mathbf{x}) \neq y)$. In addition, the

Empirical error $\hat{c}_S$ of a classifier c on a sample S of size m is defined as the error rate on S, $\hat{c}_S \equiv \Pr_{(\mathbf{x},y)\sim S}(c(\mathbf{x}) \neq y) = \frac{1}{m}\sum_{i=1}^{m} I(c(\mathbf{x}_i) \neq y_i)$, where $I(\cdot)$ is a function equal to 1 if the argument is true and equal to 0 if the argument is false.

Now we can define two error measures on the distribution of classifiers: the true error, $Q_{\mathcal{D}} \equiv \mathbb{E}_{c\sim Q} c_{\mathcal{D}}$, as the probability of misclassifying an instance $\mathbf{x}$ chosen uniformly from $\mathcal{D}$ with a classifier c chosen according to Q; and the empirical error $\hat{Q}_S \equiv \mathbb{E}_{c\sim Q}\hat{c}_S$, as the probability of classifier c chosen according to Q misclassifying an instance $\mathbf{x}$ chosen from a sample S.

For these two quantities we can derive the PAC-Bayes Bound on the true error of the distribution of classifiers:

Theorem 1. (PAC-Bayes Bound) *For all prior distributions $P(c)$ over the classifiers c, and for any $\delta \in (0,1]$*

$$Pr_{S\sim\mathcal{D}^m}\left(\forall Q(c) : KL(\hat{Q}_S||Q_{\mathcal{D}}) \leq \frac{KL(Q(c)||P(c)) + \ln(\frac{m+1}{\delta})}{m}\right) \geq 1 - \delta,$$

where KL is the Kullback-Leibler divergence, $KL(p||q) = q\ln\frac{q}{p} + (1-q)\ln\frac{1-q}{1-p}$ and $KL(Q(c)||P(c)) = \mathbb{E}_{c\sim Q}\ln\frac{Q(c)}{P(c)}$.

The proof of the theorem can be found in Langford (2005).

This bound can be particularised for the case of linear classifiers in the following way. The m training patterns define a linear classifier that can be represented by the following equation[1]:

$$c(\mathbf{x}) = \text{sign}(\mathbf{w}^T\phi(\mathbf{x})) \tag{1}$$

where $\phi(\mathbf{x})$ is a nonlinear projection to a certain feature space[2] where the linear classification actually takes place, and $\mathbf{w}$ is a vector from that feature space that determines the separating hyperplane.

For any vector $\mathbf{w}$ we can define a stochastic classifier in the following way: we choose the distribution $Q = Q(\mathbf{w}, \mu)$ to be a spherical Gaussian with identity covariance matrix centred on the direction given by $\mathbf{w}$ at a distance μ from the origin. Moreover, we can choose the prior $P(c)$ to be a spherical Gaussian with identity covariance matrix centred on the origin. Then, for classifiers of the form in equation (1) performance can be bounded by

Corollary 1. (PAC-Bayes Bound for margin classifiers (Langford (2005))) *For all distributions $\mathcal{D}$, for all $\delta \in (0,1]$, we have*

$$Pr_{S\sim\mathcal{D}^m}\left(\forall \mathbf{w}, \mu : KL(\hat{Q}_S(\mathbf{w},\mu)||Q_{\mathcal{D}}(\mathbf{w},\mu)) \leq \frac{\frac{\mu^2}{2} + \ln(\frac{m+1}{\delta})}{m}\right) \geq 1 - \delta.$$

---

[1] We are considering here unbiased classifiers, i.e., with $b = 0$.

[2] This projection is induced by a kernel $\kappa(\cdot)$ satisfying $\kappa(\mathbf{x},\mathbf{y}) = \langle\phi(\mathbf{x}),\phi(\mathbf{y})\rangle$

It can be shown (see Langford (2005)) that

$$\hat{Q}_S(\mathbf{w}, \mu) = \mathbb{E}_m[\tilde{F}(\mu\gamma(\mathbf{x}, y))] \tag{2}$$

where $\mathbb{E}_m$ is the average over the m training examples, $\gamma(\mathbf{x}, y)$ is the normalised margin of the training patterns

$$\gamma(\mathbf{x}, y) = \frac{y\mathbf{w}^T \phi(\mathbf{x})}{\|\phi(\mathbf{x})\|\|\mathbf{w}\|} \tag{3}$$

and $\tilde{F} = 1 - F$, where F is the cumulative normal distribution

$$F(x) = \int_{-\infty}^{x} \frac{1}{\sqrt{2\pi}} e^{-x^2/2} \mathrm{d}x. \tag{4}$$

Note that the SVM is a thresholded linear classifier expressed as (1) computed by means of the kernel trick (Boser et al. (1992)). The generalisation error of such a classifier can be bounded by at most twice the true (stochastic) error $Q_D(\mathbf{w}, \mu)$ in Corollary 1, (see Langford and Shawne-Taylor (2002));

$$\Pr_{(\mathbf{x}, y) \sim \mathcal{D}} \left(\operatorname{sign}(\mathbf{w}^T \phi(\mathbf{x})) \neq y \right) \leq 2Q_D(\mathbf{w}, \mu)$$

for all μ.

These bounds where further refined in Ambroladze et al. (2006) by the introduction of data dependent priors.

Theorem 2. (Multiple Prior PAC-Bayes Bound) *Let* $\{P_j(c)\}_{j=1}^J$ *be a set of possible priors that can be selected with positive weights* $\{\pi_j\}_{j=1}^J$ *so that* $\sum_{j=1}^J \pi_j = 1$. *Then, for all* $\delta \in (0, 1]$,

$$Pr_{S \sim \mathcal{D}^m} \left(\begin{array}{c} \forall Q(c) : KL(\hat{Q}_S \| Q_D) \leq \\[2mm] \min_j \dfrac{KL(Q(c) \| P_j(c)) + \ln \frac{m+1}{\delta} + \ln \frac{1}{\pi_j}}{m} \end{array} \right) \geq 1 - \delta,$$

In the standard application of the bound the prior is chosen to be a spherical Gaussian centred at the origin. We now consider learning a different prior based on training an SVM on a subset R of the training set comprising r training patterns and labels. In the experiments this is taken as a random subset but for simplicity of the presentation we will assume these to be the last r examples $\{\mathbf{x}_k, y_k\}_{k=m-r+1}^m$ in the description below. With these left-out r examples we can determine an SVM classifier, $\mathbf{w}_r$ and form a set of potential priors $P_j(\mathbf{w}|\mathbf{w}_r)$ by centering spherical Gaussian distributions along $\mathbf{w}_r$, at distances $\{\eta_j\}$ from the origin, where $\{\eta_j\}_{j=1}^J$ are positive real numbers. In such a case, we obtain

Corollary 2. (Multiple Prior based PAC-Bayes Bound for margin classifiers) *Let us consider a set $\{P_j(\mathbf{w}|\mathbf{w}_r, \eta_j)\}_{j=1}^J$ of prior distributions of classifiers consisting in spherical Gaussian distributions with identity covariance matrix centered on $\eta_j \tilde{\mathbf{w}}_r$, where $\{\eta_j\}_{j=1}^J$ are real numbers. Then, for all distributions $\mathcal{D}$, for all $\delta \in (0,1]$, we have*

$$
Pr_{S \sim \mathcal{D}^m} \left(\begin{array}{c} \forall \mathbf{w}, \mu : KL(\hat{Q}_{S \backslash R}(\mathbf{w}, \mu) \| Q_{\mathcal{D}}(\mathbf{w}, \mu)) \leq \\[2mm] min_j \dfrac{\frac{\|\eta_j \tilde{\mathbf{w}}_r - \mu \hat{\mathbf{w}}\|^2}{2} + \ln(\frac{m-r+1}{\delta}) + \ln J}{m-r} \end{array} \right) \geq 1 - \delta \qquad (5)
$$

3 Stretched Prior PAC-Bayes Bound

The first contribution of this paper consists in a new data dependent PAC-Bayes Bound where not only the mean, but the covariance matrix of the Gaussian prior can be shaped by the data distribution. Rather than take a spherically symmetric prior distribution we choose the variance in the direction of the prior vector to be $\tau > 1$. As with the Prior PAC-Bayes Bound the mean of the prior distribution is also shifted from the original in the direction $\tilde{\mathbf{w}}_r$.

We introduce notation for the norms of projections for unit vector $\mathbf{u}$, $P_{\mathbf{u}}^{\|}(\mathbf{v}) = \langle \mathbf{u}, \mathbf{v} \rangle$ and $P_{\mathbf{u}}^{\perp}(\mathbf{v})^2 = \|\mathbf{v}\|^2 - P_{\mathbf{u}}^{\|}(\mathbf{v})^2$.

Theorem 3. (τ-Prior PAC-Bayes Bound for linear classifiers) *Let us consider a prior $P(\mathbf{w}|\mathbf{w}_r, \tau, \eta)$ distribution of classifiers consisting of a Gaussian distribution centred on $\eta \tilde{\mathbf{w}}_r$, with identity covariance matrix in all directions except $\tilde{\mathbf{w}}_r$ in which the variance is τ^2. Then, for all distributions $\mathcal{D}$, for all $\delta \in (0,1]$, for all posteriors ($\mathbf{w}$, μ) we have that with probability greater or equal than $1 - \delta$*

$$
KL(\hat{Q}_{S \backslash R}(\mathbf{w}, \mu) \| Q_{\mathcal{D}}(\mathbf{w}, \mu)) \leq \qquad (6)
$$

$$
\frac{0.5(\ln(\tau^2) + \tau^{-2} - 1 + P_{\mathbf{w}_r}^{\|}(\mu \mathbf{w} - \eta \tilde{\mathbf{w}}_r)^2 / \tau^2 + P_{\mathbf{w}_r}^{\perp}(\mu \mathbf{w})^2) + \ln(\frac{m-r+1}{\delta})}{m-r}
$$

Proof. The application of the PAC-Bayes theorem follows that of Langford (2005) except that we must recompute the KL divergence. Note that the quantity

$$
\hat{Q}_{S \backslash R}(\mathbf{w}, \mu) = \mathbb{E}_{m-r}[\tilde{F}(\mu \gamma(\mathbf{x}, y))] \qquad (7)
$$

remains unchanged as the posterior distribution is still a spherical Gaussian centred at $\mathbf{w}$. Using the expression for the KL divergence between two Gaussians

$$
KL(\mathcal{NN}(\mu_0, \Sigma_0) \| \mathcal{NN}(\mu_1, \Sigma_1)) =
$$
$$
\frac{1}{2} \left(\ln \left(\frac{\det \Sigma_1}{\det \Sigma_0} \right) + \operatorname{tr}(\Sigma_1^{-1} \Sigma_0) + (\mu_1 - \mu_0)^T \Sigma_1^{-1}(\mu_1 - \mu_0) - N \right), \qquad (8)
$$

we obtain

$$KL(Q(\mathbf{w}, \mu) \| P(\mathbf{w}|\mathbf{w}_r, \tau, \eta)) =$$
$$\frac{1}{2} \left(\ln(\tau^2) + \left(\frac{1}{\tau^2} - 1 \right) + \frac{P_{\mathbf{w}_r}^{\|}(\mu\mathbf{w} - \eta\tilde{\mathbf{w}}_r)^2}{\tau^2} + P_{\mathbf{w}_r}^{\perp}(\mu\mathbf{w})^2 \right)$$

and the result follows.

In order to apply the bound we need to consider the range of priors that are needed to cover the data in our application. The experiments with the Prior PAC-Bayes Bound required a range of scalings of $\tilde{\mathbf{w}}_r$ from 1 to 100. For this we can choose $\eta = 50$ and $\tau = 50$, giving an increase in the bound over the factor $P_{\mathbf{w}_r}^{\perp}(\mu\mathbf{w})^2$ directly optimised in the algorithm of

$$\frac{0.5(\ln(\tau^2) + \tau^{-2} - 1 + P_{\tilde{\mathbf{w}}_r}^{\|}(\mu\mathbf{w} - \eta\tilde{\mathbf{w}}_r)^2/\tau^2}{m - r} \leq \frac{\ln(\tau) + 0.5\tau^{-2}}{m - r} \approx \frac{3.912}{m - r}. \tag{9}$$

4 η-Prior SVM

The good performance of the Prior PAC-Bayes bound as a means to select good hyperparameters for SVMs reported in Ambroladze et al. (2006) motivates the exploration of new classifiers that incorporate the optimisation of the bound as a design criterion.

The Prior PAC-Bayes Bound defined the prior distribution as mixture of Gaussians along the direction given by $\mathbf{w}_r$ and searched for the component in the mixture that yielded the tightest bound. The τ-Prior PAC-Bayes Bound presented above replaces the covering of the prior direction with a mixture of Gaussians by a stretching of the prior along $\mathbf{w}_r$. This motivates the introduction of the following classifier, termed η-Prior SVM. The η-Prior SVM is a combination of a prior classifier, $\mathbf{w}_r$ and a posterior one, $\mathbf{v}$: $\mathbf{w} = \mathbf{v} + \eta\tilde{\mathbf{w}}_r$. The prior $\mathbf{w}_r$ is determined as in the Prior PAC-Bayes framework, running an SVM on a subset of r training patterns. The posterior part $\mathbf{v}$ and the scaling of the prior η come out of the following optimisation problem:

$$\min_{\mathbf{v}, \eta, \xi_i} \left[\frac{1}{2} \|\mathbf{v}\|^2 + C \sum_{i=1}^{m-r} \xi_i \right] \tag{10}$$

subject to

$$y_i(\mathbf{v} + \eta\bar{\mathbf{w}}_r)^T \phi(\mathbf{x}_i) \geq 1 - \xi_i \ i = 1, \dots, m - r \tag{11}$$

$$\xi_i \geq 0 \ i = 1, \dots, m - r \tag{12}$$

Since the tightness of the bound depend on the KL divergence between the prior and posterior distribution, the proposed minimisation of the norm of $\mathbf{v}$

brings the posterior classifier $\mathbf{w}$ close to the prior $\mathbf{w}_r$. Besides, the constraints push towards a reduced stochastic training error on the samples used to learn the posterior. Therefore, these two factors pursue an optimisation of the PAC-Bayes bound.

The statistical analysis of the η-Prior SVM can be performed in two ways. On the one hand, one could envisage making a sequence of applications of the PAC-Bayes bound with spherical priors using the union bound and applying the result with the nearest prior. On the other hand, the analysis can be performed based on the τ-Prior PAC-Bayes Bound.

5   Experimental Work

This section is devoted to an experimental analysis of the bounds and algorithms introduced in the paper. The comparison of the algorithms is carried out on a classification preceded by model selection task using some UCI (Blake and Merz (1998)) datasets: handwritten digits, waveform, pima, ringnorm and spam filtering.

For every dataset, we prepare 10 different training/test set partitions where 80% of the samples form the training set and the remaining 20% form the test set. With each of the partitions we learn a classifier with Gaussian RBF kernels preceded by a model selection. The model selection consists in the determination of an optimal pair of hyperparameters (C, σ). C is the SVM trade-off between the maximisation of the margin and the minimisation of the number of misclassified training samples; σ is the width of the Gaussian kernel, $\kappa(\mathbf{x}, \mathbf{y}) = \exp(-\|\mathbf{x} - \mathbf{y}\|^2/(2\sigma^2))$. The best pair is sought in a 5×5 grid of parameters where $C \in \{1, 10, 100, 1000, 10000\}$ and $\sigma \in \{\frac{1}{4}\sqrt{d}, \frac{1}{2}\sqrt{d}, \sqrt{d}, 2\sqrt{d}, 4\sqrt{d}\}$, where d is the input space dimension. With respect to the parameters needed by the Prior PAC-Bayes bounds, the experiments reported in Ambroladze (2007) suggest that $J = 10$ priors and leaving half of the training set to learn the prior direction lead to reasonable results.

The results presented in the sequel correspond to the combination of a model selection method plus a classification algorithm. Model selection methods refer to the fitness function (usually a bound) used in the grid search for the optimal pair of hyperparameters. The studied combinations are:

- Using the regular SVM as classifier:
  PAC-SVM Regular SVM with model selection driven by the PAC-Bayes bound of Langford (2005).
  Prior-PAC Regular SVM and Multiple Prior PAC-Bayes Bound.
  2FCV Regular SVM with the model selection made through two fold cross-validation. This setting involves a computational burden similar to the bound based ones, where half of the training data are used to learn the prior and the other half to learn the posterior).
- Using the η-Prior SVM as classifier we have the following two configurations:

Prior-PAC-η-PSVM η-Prior SVM and Multiple Prior PAC-Bayes Bound considering η comes from a multiple prior setting of $J = 50$ priors $\eta_j \mathbf{w}_r / \|\mathbf{w}_r\|$ with the η_j equally spaced between $\eta_1 = 1$ and $\eta_{50} = 100$. This setting minimises the penalty term in the Prior PAC-Bayes Bound as we are not actually using these priors to learn the posterior.

τ-**PriorPAC** η-**PSVM** η-Prior SVM and the new τ-Prior PAC-Bayes Bound.

The displayed values of training set bounds (PAC-Bayes and (Multiple) Prior PAC-Bayes) are obtained according to the following setup. For each one of the 10 partitions we train an instance of the corresponding classifier for each position of the grid of hyperparameters and compute the bound. For that partition we select the classifier with the minimum value of the bound found through the whole grid and compute its test error rate. Then we display the sample average and standard deviation of the 10 values of the bound and of the test error. Note that proceeding this way we select a (possibly) different pair of parameters for every partition. That is the reason why we name this task as model selection plus classification.

Moreover, the reported values of the PAC-Bayes and the Multiple Prior PAC-Bayes bounds correspond to the mean of the true error over the distribution of classifiers Q_D. The real true error c_D could then bounded by twice this value assuming a Gaussian distribution of variance equal to one.

Table 1 displays values of the bounds for the studied configurations of bound plus classifier. Notice that most of the configurations involving the new bounds achieve a significant cut in the value of the PAC-Bayes Bound, which indicates that learning the prior distribution helps to improve the PAC-Bayes bound. The tightest values of the bound correspond to the η-Prior SVM, it was expected since this algorithm aims at optimising the bound as well as at reducing the classification error. However, for the explored datasets and range of hyperparameters, the tightness of the bound presented in this paper acting on the η-Prior SVM is very close to the Multiple Prior PAC Bayes Bound one.

Table 1 also displays the test error rates averaged over the 10 partitions plus the sample standard deviation. The results illustrate that although cross-validation seems to be the safest model selection option, the PAC-Bayes bounds are catching up. It is remarkable how the η-Prior SVM achieves a fairly good trade-off between good model selection (reduced test error) and tightness of the generalisation error prediction (low bound).

6   Concluding remarks

We have presented a new bound (the τ Prior PAC-Bayes Bound) on the performance of SVMs based on the estimation of a Gaussian prior with an

Problem			Classifier				
			SVM			ηPrior SVM	
		2FCV	PAC	PrPAC	PrPAC	τ-PrPAC
digits	Bound	−	0.175	0.107	0.050	0.047
		−	± 0.001	± 0.004	± 0.006	± 0.006
	CE	0.007	0.007	0.014	0.010	0.009
		± 0.003	± 0.002	± 0.003	± 0.005	± 0.004
waveform	Bound	−	0.203	0.185	0.178	0.176
		−	± 0.001	± 0.005	± 0.005	± 0.005
	CE	0.090	0.084	0.088	0.087	0.086
		± 0.008	± 0.007	± 0.007	± 0.006	± 0.006
pima	Bound	−	0.424	0.420	0.428	0.416
		−	± 0.003	± 0.015	± 0.018	± 0.020
	CE	0.244	0.229	0.229	0.233	0.233
		± 0.025	± 0.027	± 0.026	± 0.027	± 0.028
ringnorm	Bound	−	0.203	0.110	0.053	0.050
		−	± 0.000	± 0.004	± 0.004	± 0.004
	CE	0.016	0.018	0.018	0.016	0.016
		± 0.003	± 0.003	± 0.003	± 0.003	± 0.003
spam	Bound	−	0.254	0.198	0.186	0.178
		−	± 0.001	± 0.006	± 0.008	± 0.008
	CE	0.066	0.067	0.077	0.070	0.072
		± 0.006	± 0.007	± 0.011	± 0.009	± 0.010

Table 1. Values of the bounds and Test Classification Error Rates (CE) for various settings.

stretched covariance matrix of the distribution of classifiers given a particular dataset, and the use of this prior in the PAC-Bayes generalisation bound.

The new bound has motivated the development of a classification algorithm (η−Prior SVM), that automatically determines the position of the mean of the prior as part of the optimisation. Empirical results show that the statistical analysis of this new algorithms yields tighter values of the Multiple Prior PAC-Bayes Bound, even when compared to this bound applied to a regular SVM. Moreover, if we use the bounds to guide the model selection (we select the values of C and σ that yield a minimum value of the bound), the new algorithms combined with the bound arrive at better models in terms of classification error that the original SVM and PAC-Bayes Bound. In fact, the performance of the Multiple Prior PAC-Bayes Bound model selection plus η−Prior SVM is comparable to that of a regular SVM using cross-validation for model selection.

The work presented in this paper is being continued in two main directions. On the one hand, we are studying new structures for the prior along the lines of the bound of equation (6), based on multivariate Gaussian distributions with more sophisticate covariance matrices that help tighten the bounds. On the other hand, we are envisaging the implementation of a meta-classifier consisting in a series of prior and posterior classifiers within a dynamic programming framework. This second line of research aims at the application of these ideas in incremental learning scenarios.

Acknowledgments

This work was partially supported by the IST Programme of the European Community under the PASCAL2 Network of Excellence IST-2007-216886. E. P-H. acknowledges support from Spain CICYT grant TEC2008-02473/TEC. This publication only reflects the authors' views.

References

AMBROLADZE, A., PARRADO-HERNANDEZ, E. and SHAWE-TAYLOR, J. (2007): Tighter PAC-Bayes bounds. In Scholkopf B., Platt J. and Homan T. (Eds.): *Advances in Neural Information Processing Systems 19*, 9-16, MIT Press, Cambridge MA.

BLAKE, L. and MERZ, C. J. (1998): *UCI Repository of machine learning databases.* University of California, Irvine, Dept. of Information and Computer Sciences, http://www.ics.edu/mlearn/MLRepository.hml

BOSER B., E., GUYON, I. and VAPNIK, V. (1992): A training algorithm for optimal margin classifiers. *Computational Learning Theory: 144-152.*

LANGFORD, J. (2005): Tutorial on practical prediction theory for classification. *Journal of Machine Learning Research, 6: 273-306.*

LANGFORD, J. and SHAWE-TAYLOR, J. (2002): PAC-Bayes & Margins. In Scholkopf B., Platt J. and Homan T. editors, *Advances in Neural Information Processing Systems 14*, MIT Press, Cambridge MA.

SHAWE-TAYLOR, J., BARTLETT, P. L., WILLIAMSON ,R. C. and ANTHONY, M. (1998): Structural risk minimization over data-dependent hierarchies, *IEEE Trans. Information Theory, 44(5): 1926-1940.*

Part X

Monte Carlo Methods in System Safety,
Reliability and Risk Analysis

Some Algorithms to Fit some Reliability Mixture Models under Censoring

Laurent Bordes[1] and Didier Chauveau[2]

[1] Université de Pau et des Pays de l'Adour
   Laboratoire de Mathématiques et de leurs Applications
   UMR CNRS 5142 - Avenue de l'Université - BP 1155
   64013 Pau Cedex, France *laurent.bordes@univ-pau.fr*
[2] Université d'Orléans
   UMR CNRS 6628 - MAPMO - BP 6759
   45067 Orléans Cedex 2, France *didier.chauveau@univ-orleans.fr*

Abstract. Estimating the unknown parameters of a reliability mixture model may be a more or less intricate problem, especially if durations are censored. We present several iterative methods based on Monte Carlo simulation that allow to fit parametric or semiparametric mixture models provided they are identifiable. We show for example that the well-known data augmentation algorithm may be used successfully to fit semiparametric mixture models under right censoring. Our methods are illustrated by a reliability example.

Keywords: reliability, mixture models, stochastic EM algorithm, censored data

1 The latent data model

Let $\mathcal{F}$ be a parametric family of density functions on $\mathbb{R}$, indexed by $\xi \in \Xi \subset \mathbb{R}^{\ell}$; $f \in \mathcal{F}$ means that there exists $\xi \in \Xi$ such that $f \equiv f(\cdot|\xi)$. Let Z be a multinomial distributed random variable with parameters 1 and $\boldsymbol{\lambda} = (\lambda_1, \ldots, \lambda_p) \in [0,1]^p$ with $\sum_{j=1}^{p} \lambda_j = 1$; we write $Z \sim \mathcal{M}ult(1, \boldsymbol{\lambda})$. Let $Y_1, \ldots, Y_p$ be p random variables with $Y_i \sim f(\cdot|\xi_i)$ where $\xi_i \in \Xi$ for $1 \leq i \leq p$.

Let us consider the random variable $X = Y_Z$ distributed according to the distribution function

$$G(x|\boldsymbol{\theta}) = \sum_{j=1}^{p} \lambda_j F(x|\xi_j),$$

where $F(\cdot|\xi_j)$ is the distribution function corresponding to the density function $f(\cdot|\xi_j)$, $\boldsymbol{\theta} = (\boldsymbol{\lambda}, \boldsymbol{\xi})$ where $\boldsymbol{\xi} = (\xi_1, \ldots, \xi_p)$. Note that the density function of X is

$$g(x|\boldsymbol{\theta}) = \sum_{j=1}^{p} \lambda_j f(x|\xi_j). \tag{1}$$

Y. Lechevallier, G. Saporta (eds.), *Proceedings of COMPSTAT'2010*,
DOI 10.1007/978-3-7908-2604-3_22, © Springer-Verlag Berlin Heidelberg 2010

Estimating the unknown parameter $\boldsymbol{\theta}$ from n i.i.d. values $x_1, \ldots, x_n$ having the same parent distribution as X is known as the finite (parametric) mixture model problem (see e.g. McLachlan and Peel (2000)).

However estimating unknown parameters of a reliability mixture model may be a more or less intricate problem, especially if durations are censored. In the parametric framework one approach consists in minimizing the distance between a parametric distribution and its nonparametric estimate. Several distances may be chosen: e.g. Hellinger in Karunamuni and Wu (2009) or Cramèr-von Mises in Bordes and Beutner (2009). These methods fail to account semiparametric mixture models without training data. There are many iterative algorithms to reach mixture models maximum likelihood estimates, mostly in the well-known class of EM algorithms, but few of them integrate the additional problem of censoring. Chauveau (1995) proposed an extention of the Stochastic EM algorithm (Celeux and Diebolt (1986)) to handle Type-I deterministic right censoring. One advantage of the Stochastic EM algorithm is that it can be extended easily to some semiparametric mixture models provided they are identifiable (see e.g. Bordes et al. (2007)). We present several iterative methods based on Monte Carlo simulation that allow to fit identifiable (semi-)parametric right censored reliability mixture models.

Let C be a random variable with density function q and distribution function Q. Consider n i.i.d. values $c_1, \ldots, c_n$ having the same parent distribution as C. In the right censoring setup the only available information is

$$(T, D) = (\min(X, C), 1(X \leq C)).$$

Therefore our n i.i.d. observations are $(t_i, d_i)_{1 \leq i \leq n}$ where $t_i = \min(x_i, c_i)$ and $d_i = 1(x_i \leq c_i)$.

The joint distribution of (T, D, Z) is defined by

$$f_{T,D,Z}(t, d, z|\boldsymbol{\theta}) = (\lambda_z f(t|\xi_z) \bar{Q}(t))^d (\lambda_z q(t) \bar{F}(t|\xi_z))^{1-d},$$

where $z \in \{1, \ldots, p\}, d \in \{0, 1\}, t \geq 0$, $\bar{F}(\cdot|\xi_j)$ denotes the survival function of Y_j and $\bar{Q}$ is the survival function of the censoring time. As a consequence we can compute the "posterior" probability that an observed or censored observation belongs to component z, which is an essential ingredient of any EM algorithm:

$$\begin{aligned} \eta_z(t, d|\boldsymbol{\theta}) &= P(Z = z|(T, D) = (t, d), \boldsymbol{\theta}) \\ &= \left(\frac{\lambda_z f(t|\xi_z)}{\sum_{j=1}^p \lambda_j f(t|\xi_j)}\right)^d \left(\frac{\lambda_z \bar{F}(t|\xi_z)}{\sum_{j=1}^p \lambda_j \bar{F}(t|\xi_j)}\right)^{1-d} \\ &= \lambda_z \bar{F}(t|\xi_z) \left(\frac{\alpha(t|\xi_z)}{\sum_{j=1}^p \lambda_j f(t|\xi_j)}\right)^d \left(\sum_{j=1}^p \lambda_j \bar{F}(t|\xi_j)\right)^{d-1}, \end{aligned}$$

where $\alpha(\cdot|\xi_j) = f(\cdot|\xi_j)/\bar{F}(\cdot|\xi_j)$ is the hazard rate function of Y_j.

Remark: This conditional probability does not depend on the censoring distribution.

Remark: Under parameters identifiability, one can consider that one or several components are nonparametrically unknown.

2 Parametric Stochastic-EM algorithm for model (1)

Let us define by $\boldsymbol{\theta}_0$ and $\boldsymbol{\theta}^k$ the initial and current value of $\boldsymbol{\theta}$. Let $\bar{\boldsymbol{\theta}}^1, \ldots, \bar{\boldsymbol{\theta}}^k$ be the first k estimates of $\boldsymbol{\theta}$; we write $\bar{\boldsymbol{\theta}}^k = k^{-1} \sum_{u=1}^{k} \boldsymbol{\theta}^u$.

Step 1. For each individual $i \in \{1, \ldots, n\}$ calculate

$$\boldsymbol{\eta}(t_i, d_i|\bar{\boldsymbol{\theta}}^k) = (\eta_1(t_i, d_i|\bar{\boldsymbol{\theta}}^k), \ldots, \eta_p(t_i, d_i|\bar{\boldsymbol{\theta}}^k)),$$

then simulate

$$Z_i^k \sim \mathcal{M}ult(1, \boldsymbol{\eta}(t_i, d_i|\bar{\boldsymbol{\theta}}^k)).$$

Step 2. For each component $j \in \{1, \ldots, p\}$ define the subsets

$$\chi_j^k = \{i \in \{1, \ldots, n\}; Z_i^k = j\}. \tag{2}$$

Step 3. For each component $j \in \{1, \ldots, p\}$

$$\lambda_j^{k+1} = \mathrm{Card}(\chi_j^k)/n,$$

and

$$\xi_j^{k+1} = \arg\max_{\xi \in \Xi} L_j(\xi)$$

where

$$L_j(\xi) = \prod_{i \in \chi_j^k} (f(t_i|\xi))^{d_i} (\bar{F}(t_i|\xi))^{1-d_i}.$$

Remark: The main advantage of this iterative method is that it does not require to use some numerical optimization routine; standard maximum likelihood programs may be used on each subsample. As a consequence this method easily handles mixtures of various parametric families of distributions.

Remark: In Step 1 we can use $\boldsymbol{\theta}^k$ produced by Step 3 instead of $\bar{\boldsymbol{\theta}}^k$. Hence the sequence $(\boldsymbol{\theta}^k)$ is a Markov chain and the final estimate is the ergodic mean.

3   Nonparametric estimation under censoring

Let us introduce the two counting processes N and Y defined by

$$N(t) = \sum_{i=1}^{n} 1(t_i \leq t, d_i = 1) \quad \text{and} \quad Y(t) = \sum_{i=1}^{n} 1(t_i \geq t) \quad t \geq 0,$$

counting respectively the number of failures in $[0, t]$ and the set of items at risk at time t^-. The Nelson-Aalen estimator of the cumulative hazard rate function A is defined by

$$\hat{A}(t) = \int_0^t \frac{dN(s)}{Y(s)} = \sum_{\{i; t_i \leq t\}} \frac{\Delta N(t_i)}{Y(t_i)} \quad t \geq 0,$$

where $\Delta N(s) = N(s) - N(s-)$. The Kaplan-Meier estimator of the survival (reliability) function $\bar{F}$ is defined by

$$\hat{\bar{F}}(t) = \prod_{s \leq t} \left(1 - \Delta \hat{A}(s)\right) = \prod_{s \leq t} \left(1 - \frac{\Delta N(s)}{Y(s)}\right) \quad t \geq 0.$$

Let $\mathcal{K}$ be a kernel function and h_n a window size satisfying $h_n \searrow 0$ and $nh_n \nearrow +\infty$, it is well known that the hazard rate function α can be estimated nonparametrically by

$$\hat{\alpha}(t) = \int_0^{+\infty} \mathcal{K}_{h_n}(t - s) d\hat{A}(s) = \sum_{i=1}^{n} \mathcal{K}_{h_n}(t - t_i) \frac{\Delta N(t_i)}{Y(t_i)},$$

where $\mathcal{K}_{h_n} = h_n^{-1} \mathcal{K}(\cdot / h_n)$. Because $f = \alpha \times \bar{F}$ it can be estimated by $\hat{f}(t) = \hat{\alpha}(t) \times \hat{\bar{F}}(t)$.

Since we considered that the unknown distribution is absolutely continuous with respect to the Lebesgue measure we have $t_i \neq t_j$ for $i \neq j$ with probability 1. Let us denote by $t_{(1)} < \cdots < t_{(n)}$ the ordered durations, and write $d_{(i)}$ the corresponding censoring indicators ($d_{(i)} = d_j$ if $t_{(i)} = t_j$). The estimates can be written

$$\hat{A}(t) = \sum_{\{i; t_{(i)} \leq t\}} \frac{d_{(i)}}{n - i + 1},$$

$$\hat{\bar{F}}(t) = \sum_{\{i; t_{(i)} \leq t\}} \left(1 - \frac{d_{(i)}}{n - i + 1}\right),$$

and

$$\hat{\alpha}(t) = \sum_{i=1}^{n} \frac{1}{h_n} \mathcal{K}\left(\frac{t - t_{(i)}}{h_n}\right) \frac{d_{(i)}}{n - i + 1}.$$

For more properties about these estimators see, e.g., Andersen et al. (1993).

4 Semiparametric mixture models

4.1 Identifiability

We say that the density function f is exp-symmetric if $f(x; \mu) = x^{-1}s(\ln x - \mu)$ for all $x > 0$ where s is an even density function. Log-normal distributions are exp-symmetric. More generally if X has a symmetric distribution, $\exp(X)$ has an exp-symmetric distribution. In Bordes et al. (2006) it is shown that s, $\mu_1 \in \mathbb{R}$, $\mu_2 \in \mathbb{R}$ and $\lambda \in (0,1)$ are identifiable for the following two-component mixture model:

$$g(x|\lambda, \mu_1, \mu_2, s) = \lambda f(x; \mu_1) + (1 - \lambda) f(x; \mu_2),$$

whenever $\mu_1 \neq \mu_2$. Other semiparametric mixture models have identifiable parameters; see, e.g., Hall and Zhou (2003), Bordes et al. (2007), Benaglia et al. (2009). In the next example we consider the following mixture of accelerated lifetime model. It means that we consider a model where two lifetime populations are mixed with lifetimes distribution equal up to a scale parameter. It leads to the following two-component mixture model:

$$g(x|\lambda, \xi, f) = \lambda f(x) + (1 - \lambda) \xi f(\xi x) \quad x > 0. \tag{3}$$

From a latent variable point of view this model is obtained by considering the random variable $X = UV$ where $V \sim f$ is independent of the $\{1, 1/\xi\}$-valued random variable U that satisfies $P(U = 1) = \lambda$.

4.2 Semiparametric Stochastic-EM algorithm for model (3)

Without censoring. The unknown parameter is $\theta = (\lambda, \xi, f) \in (0,1) \times \mathbb{R}_*^+ \times \mathcal{F}$ where $\mathcal{F}$ is a set of density functions. Let us define by $\theta_0 = (\lambda^0, \xi^0, f^0)$ and $\theta^k = (\lambda^k, \xi^k, f^k)$ the initial and current values of θ.

Step 1. For each item $i \in \{1, \dots, n\}$ calculate

$$\eta(x_i|\theta^k) = \frac{\lambda^k f^k(x_i)}{\lambda^k f^k(x_i) + (1 - \lambda^k)\xi^k f^k(\xi^k x_i)},$$

then for $\boldsymbol{\eta}(x_i|\theta^k) = (\eta(x_i|\theta^k), 1 - \eta(x_i|\theta^k))$ simulate

$$Z_i^k \sim Mult(1, \boldsymbol{\eta}(x_i|\theta^k)).$$

Step 2. For each component $j \in \{1, 2\}$ define the subsets χ_j^k is as in (2).
Step 3. Update parameters:

$$\lambda^{k+1} = n_1/n \quad \text{where } n_1 = \text{Card}(\chi_1^k),$$

$$\xi^{k+1} = \frac{n - n_1}{n_1} \frac{\sum_{i \in \chi_1^k} x_i}{\sum_{i \in \chi_2^k} x_i}$$

$$f^{k+1}(x) = \frac{1}{nh}\left(\sum_{i \in \chi_1^k} \mathcal{K}\left(\frac{x - t_i}{h}\right) + \sum_{i \in \chi_2^k} \mathcal{K}\left(\frac{x - \xi^k t_i}{h}\right) \right),$$

where $\mathcal{K}$ is a kernel function and h a bandwidth.

Remark: Note that at the third step ξ^k is updated using a moment estimation method instead of a maximum likelihood principle. This later method is hard to use here since it requires to estimate nonparametrically the first derivative of f which generally leads to unstable estimates.

Final estimators for λ and ξ are obtained taking the ergodic mean of $(\lambda^k)_{1 \le k \le K}$ and $(\xi^k)_{1 \le t \le K}$:

$$\hat{\lambda} = \frac{\lambda^1 + \cdots + \lambda^K}{K} \quad \text{and} \quad \hat{\xi} = \frac{\xi^1 + \cdots + \xi^K}{K}.$$

Accounting censoring. Steps 1 and 3 of the above algorithm needs to be modified in the following way:

Step 1C. Computation of $\boldsymbol{\eta}(t_i, d_i | \boldsymbol{\theta}^k)$ for $i \in \{1, \ldots, n\}$:
If $d_i = 0$ then

$$\eta(t_i, d_i | \boldsymbol{\theta}^k) = \frac{\lambda^k \bar{F}^k(t_i)}{\lambda^k \bar{F}^k(t_i) + (1 - \lambda^k) \bar{F}^k(\xi^k t_i)},$$

else

$$\eta(t_i, d_i | \boldsymbol{\theta}^k) = \frac{\lambda^k \alpha^k(t_i) \bar{F}^k(t_i)}{\lambda^k \alpha^k(t_i) \bar{F}^k(t_i) + (1 - \lambda^k) \xi^k \alpha^k(\xi^k t_i) \bar{F}^k(\xi^k t_i)},$$

then set $\boldsymbol{\eta}(t_i, d_i | \boldsymbol{\theta}^k) = (\eta(t_i, d_i | \boldsymbol{\theta}^k), 1 - \eta(t_i, d_i | \boldsymbol{\theta}^k))$.

Step 3C. Calculation of new estimates of α and $\bar{F}$: Let $\boldsymbol{t}^k = (t_1^k, \ldots, t_n^k)$ be the order statistic of $\{t_i; i \in \chi_1^k\} \cup \{\xi^k t_i; i \in \chi_2^k\}$, so that $t_1^k \le \cdots \le t_n^k$. Then we have

$$\alpha^{k+1}(x) = \sum_{i=1}^{n} \frac{1}{h} \mathcal{K} \left(\frac{x - t_i^k}{h} \right) \frac{1}{n - i + 1},$$

and

$$\bar{F}^{k+1}(x) = \prod_{\{i : t_i^k \le x\}} \frac{n - i + 1 - d_{(i)}}{n - i + 1}.$$

Remark: For the above algorithms several choices have to be made. To chose the initial values of $\boldsymbol{\theta}$ we can start to fit a parametric model where f belongs, e.g., to the Weibull family of distributions. Concerning the choice of the bandwidth h we used the usual formula $h = \sigma_{t^k} (4/3n)^{1/5}$ where σ_{t^k} is the standard deviation of $\boldsymbol{t}^k$.

5 Illustrative examples

5.1 A parametric example

We consider lifetimes distributed according to the density function

$$g(x) = \lambda_1 \xi_1 \exp(-\xi_1 x) + \lambda_2 \xi_2 \exp(-\xi_2 x) \quad x > 0,$$

where $\lambda_1 = 1/3$, $\xi_1 = 1$ and $\xi_2 = 0.2$. We assume that C is uniformly distributed on $[0, 10]$. The censoring rate is about 35%.

Updating at Step 3 is easy since we have

$$\xi_j^{t+1} = \frac{\sum_{i \in \chi_j^t} d_i}{\sum_{i \in \chi_j^t} x_i} \quad \text{for } j = 1, \ldots, p.$$

Hereafter are two simulations. Fig. 1 shows that starting from the good initial values the algorithm is very stable for moderate sample size ($n = 200$). Fig. 2 shows empirical evidence of convergence for large sample size ($n = 1000$) even if the initial values are not well chosen.

5.2 A semiparametric example

We consider lifetimes distributed on $\mathbb{R}^+$ according to the density function

$$g(x) = \lambda f(x) + (1 - \lambda)\xi f(\xi x)$$

where $\lambda = 0.3$, $\xi = 0.1$ and f is the density of a lognormal distribution with parameters $(1,0.5)$ (denoted by $\mathcal{LN}(1, 0.5)$ in the sequel). The number of observations is fixed to $n = 100$ and the number of iteration is equal to $K = 100$. This example does not include censoring, and the algorithm we used is that of Section 4.2. As we can see on Fig. 3, estimation results based on ergodic mean are very stable for this example where the mixture components are well separated. Note that we used the quadratic kernel $\mathcal{K}(x) = (1 - x^2)1(|x| \leq 1)$ with adaptive bandwidth in the neighborhood of 0.

References

ANDERSEN, P.K., BORGAN, O. GILL, R.D., and KEIDING, N. (1993): *Statistical Models Based on Counting Processes*. Springer, New York.

BENAGLIA, T., CHAUVEAU, D., and HUNTER, D. R. (2009): An EM-like algorithm for semi- and non-parametric estimation in multivariate mixtures. *Journal of Computational and Graphical Statistics 18 (2), 505-526.*

BORDES, L., MOTTELET, S., and VANDEKERKHOVE, P. (2006): Semiparametric estimation of a two-component mixture model. *Annals of Statistics 34, 1204-1232.*

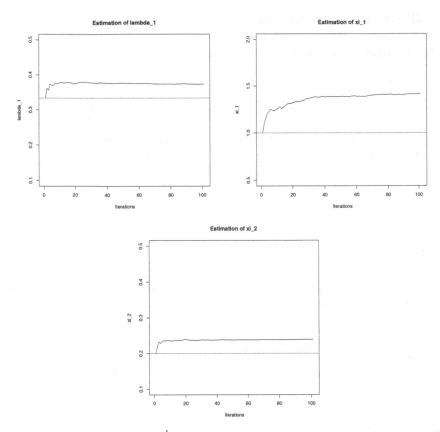

Fig. 1. Ergodic means $k \mapsto \bar{\theta}^k$ ($1 \le k \le 100$) for $\theta = (1/3, 2/3, 1, 0.2)$ and $n = 200$.

BORDES, L., CHAUVEAU, D., and VANDEKERKHOVE, P. (2007): A stochastic EM algorithm for a semiparametric mixture model. *Computational Statistics and Data Analysis 51 (11), 5429-5443.*

BORDES, L., DELMAS, C., and VANDEKERKHOVE, P. (2007): Semiparametric estimation of a two-component mixture model when a component is known. *Scandinavian Journal of Statistics 33, 733-752.*

BORDES, L., and BEUTNER, E. (2009): Estimators based on data-driven generalized weighted Cramer-von Mises distances under censoring - with applications to mixture models. *Submitted paper.*

CELEUX, G., and DIEBOLT, J. (1986): The SEM algorithm: A probabilistic teacher algorithm derived from the EM algorithm for the mixture problem. *Computational Statistics Quarterly 2, 73-82.*

CHAUVEAU, D. (1995): A stochastic EM algorithm for mixtures with censored data. *Journal of Statistical Planning and Inference 46 (1), 1-25.*

HALL, P., and ZHOU, X. (2003): Nonparametric estimation of component distributions in a multivariate mixture. *Annals of Statistics 31, 201-224.*

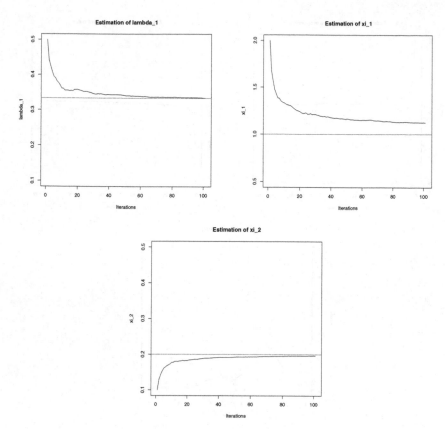

Fig. 2. Ergodic means $k \mapsto \bar{\theta}^k$ $(1 \leq k \leq 100)$ for $\theta = (0.5, 0.5, 2, 0.1)$ and $n = 1000$.

KARUNAMUNI, R.J., and WU, J. (2009): Minimum Hellinger distance estimation in a nonparametric mixture model. *Journal of Statistical Planning and Inference 139 (3), 1118-1133.*

MCLACHLAN, G.J., and PEEL, D. (2000): *Finite Mixture Models.* Wiley.

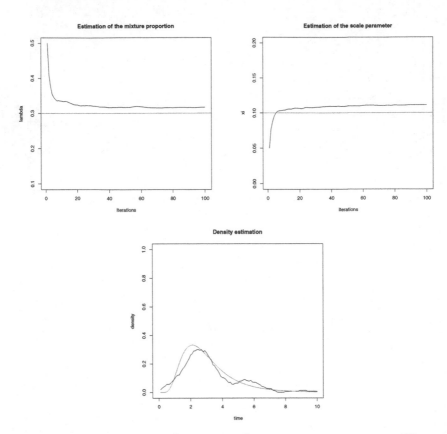

Fig. 3. Ergodic means $k \mapsto \bar{\lambda}^k$ and $k \mapsto \bar{\xi}^k$ $(1 \leq k \leq 100)$, and $x \mapsto f^{100}(x)$ for $\theta = (0.3, 0.1, \mathcal{L}N(1, 0.5))$ and $n = 100$.

Computational and Monte-Carlo Aspects of Systems for Monitoring Reliability Data

Emmanuel Yashchin[1]

IBM, Thomas J. Watson Research Ctr., Box 218,
Yorktown Heights, NY 10598, USA, *yashchi@us.ibm.com*

Abstract. Monitoring plays a key role in today's business environment, as large volumes of data are collected and processed on a regular basis. Ability to detect onset of new data regimes and patterns quickly is considered an important competitive advantage. Of special importance is the area of monitoring product reliability, where timely detection of unfavorable trends typically offers considerable opportunities of cost avoidance. We will discuss detection systems for reliability issues built by combining Monte-Carlo techniques with modern statistical methods rooted in the theory of Sequential Analysis, Change-point theory and Likelihood Ratio tests. We will illustrate applications of these methods in computer industry.

Keywords: SPC, lifetime data, wearout, warranty

1 Introduction

This paper will focus on problems of data monitoring related to so-called time-managed lifetime data streams that are frequently encountered in reliability applications. Specifically, consider a sequence of lifetime tests corresponding to points in time t = 1,2,.., T. In what follows we will refer to these points as "vintages". They could, for example, correspond to dates at which batches of items were produced; as time goes by, these batches generate lifetime data. In other words, data corresponding to a given vintage can be viewed as an outcome of a lifetime test (Fig. 1). The results pertain to a specific point in time (typically, time at which the table has been compiled). For example, in Fig. 1 the table was compiled on 2007-08-02; however, the most recent vintage for which data is available is 2009-07-21. The lifetime tests corresponding to a given vintage typically have a Type-I censoring structure. For example, for the first vintage the number of items on test is 120; of these, 6 items failed, 2 items got right-censored in midstream, and the remaining 112 items survived till the present point in time and thus are type-1 censored. The table shows a distinct triangular structure due to the fact that for very recent vintages only results for relatively short time horizons are available.

In many applications the key problem is one of detection: one is interested in statistical methodology that enables rapid detection of unfavorable process conditions that manifest themselves through the data of type shown in Fig. 1. In essence, the situation here is similar to one handled by conventional

Y. Lechevallier, G. Saporta (eds.), *Proceedings of COMPSTAT'2010*,
DOI 10.1007/978-3-7908-2604-3_23, © Springer-Verlag Berlin Heidelberg 2010

254   Yashchin, E.

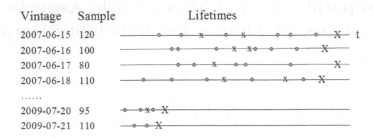

x – individually right-censored lifetimes

X – globally right-censored

Fig. 1. A sequence of lifetime tests corresponding to range of vintages (2007-06-15, 2009-07-21), as compiled on 2009-08-02.

Statistical Process Control (SPC) methods: one would like to detect rapidly unfavorable changes in parameters of the process driving lifetime data, while keeping the rate of false alarms at some fixed low level. However, the conventional SPC performance measures are not applicable in situations of type described in Fig. 1 because the central premise of the SPC setup (that requires the observations corresponding to a given time to remain unchanged as the data is compiled for subsequent points in time) is no longer valid. For example, for the first vintage in Fig. 1 one could expect to see additional failures and censored points as we compile data for subsequent points in time. So, if a given characteristics of a vintage is represented as a point on a control chart, then this point will continue to change as the new points on the control chart are coming online. Furthermore, this point will continue to change even if there are no new data points (vintages) coming online. For example, if we recompile the data in Fig.1 on the next day (2007-08-03), we could end up with a situation where the last vintage for which the data is available is the same as before, i.e., 2009-07-21 (yet, the data for every vintage would need to be adjusted). Therefore, the concept of Run Length would not be suitable for assessing the performance of this type of control charts. We call such setup as "control charting with *dynamically changing observations (DCO)*" to emphasize the fact that the previous data points on a control chart would continue to change as the new data comes in.

Another practical aspect one has to deal with is the "time-management" of the lifetime data: the data corresponding to older vintages is likely to become either gradually underpopulated (especially with respect to items with longer lifetimes) or become unavailable altogether because of the administrative constraints of the data management. For example, if a machine carrying a 3-year warranty is introduced into the field at some point in time (corresponding to its "vintage"), then one could expect to find in the database only lifetimes occurring in the first 3 years of service. Information on subsequent failures would typically be either unavailable or unreliable, in light of missing infrastructure for keeping track of censoring and failure events beyond a 3-year horizon. As the vintage becomes too "old", it could also disappear from the "rolling" database completely - another artifact of a standard warranty data management policy. For example, after recompiling the data in Fig.1 on the next day (2007-08-03), one could find that the data for the first vintage 2007-06-15 is no longer available.

The computational challenges in the phases of design, analysis and implementation of this type of control schemes are substantial. In conventional control charting one can typically convert the sequence of observations to a sequence of control schemes (e.g., Cusum or EWMA) that obey some form of a Markov property. This enables one to design and analyze monitoring procedures by taking advantage of the theory of Markov Chains (though more complex cases still require Monte Carlo approach). In contrast, in the case of schemes with DCO, no such Markovian representation is apparent and we have to rely almost exclusively on simulation.

A number of articles and books have been published that deal with various aspects of monitoring lifetime data. For example, likelihood ratio methods for monitoring parameters of lifetime distributions in non-DCO setting were discussed in Olteanu and Vining (2009) and Sego et al. (2009). Several methods for monitoring warranty data by using Shewhart-type procedures are discussed in Dubois et al. (2008), Wu and Meeker (2002). Steiner and McKay (2000, 2001) discuss methods and applications related to monitoring of type I censored data. This type of data (in conjunction with an EWMA monitoring procedure and Weibull observations) was considered in Zhang and Chen (2004). Analysis of warranty claims data is discussed in Blischke and Murthy (2000), Doganaksoy et al. (2006), Kalbfleisch et al. (1991), Lawless (1998) and Lawless and Kalbfleisch (1992). Methods for analysis of failure data based on marginal counts of warranty claim (and under incomplete information about items introduced into the field) are discussed in Karim et al. (2001). Finally, methods based on change-point analysis for hazard curves have also be considered by a number of authors, e.g., Patra and Dey (2002).

In the next section we will present the basic approach to design and analysis of non-DCO control schemes. In Sec. 3 we will focus on computational and Monte-carlo issues. In Sec. 4 we discuss the problem of detecting wearout conditions.

2   Basic Approach

The base methodology is based on using a version of the weighted Cusum approach, e.g. see Yashchin (1993). The key steps are as follows:

1. Sort data in accordance with vintages of interest. This will make sure that the control scheme is tuned to detect unfavorable changes that happen on

the time scale of these vintages. Typically, several representations of type shown in Fig. 1 are available for the same data collection. For example, a given component of a PC can be associated with a component manufacturing vintage, machine ship vintage or calendar time vintage. If one is interested, for example, in detection of a problem at the component manufacturer's then the vintages in Fig. 1 should correspond to component manufacturing dates. If one is interested in detection of problems at the PC assembly plant then one should organize Fig. 1 so that the vintages correspond to machine ship dates. To detect changes related to introduction of a new version of an operating system one should construct Fig. 1 data with vintages corresponding to calendar time (i.e., a row in Fig. 1 represents machines that were in the field at the respective date).

2. Introduce time scale transformation that corresponds to *reference hazard* behavior, so as to reduce the number of monitored parameters. For example, let us suppose that one anticipates a hazard curve that is proportional to some known function $h_0(t)$ exhibiting complex behaviour (for example, U-shaped). Then it may be beneficial to switch from the natural time scale t to a scale determined by $\int_0^t h_0(z)dz$. Data presented on such a scale would generally be easier to model parametrically: for example, if the anticipated hazard pattern indeed holds exactly then the lifetimes on the transformed scale are exponentially distributed. If, on the other hand, the anticipated pattern holds only approximately then there is a good possibility that one could model lifetimes through one of numerous extensions of the exponential law, e.g., Weibull family. In what follows we will assume that we are already working on a scale where a relatively simple parametric model applies. For the sake of simplicity, we will assume that the lifetime distribution is Weibull.

3. For every lifetime distribution parameter (or a function of parameters of interest, say, λ), establish a sequence of statistics $X_i, i = 1, 2, \ldots$ to serve as a basis of monitoring scheme. In general, one should try to use control sequences that represent unbiased estimates of the underlying parameters. For example, such a parameter could represent the expected lifetime or an expected rate of failures. Another parameter of interest could be a measure of wearout (for example, under the Weibull assumption one can use the shape parameter as such a measure). Yet another one could be the scale parameter of the lifetime distribution. One will generally choose parameters that are meaningful to the users and facilitate problem diagnostics.

4. For control sequences of interest, obtain corresponding weights. These weights determine the impact of individual vintages based on inherent properties of control sequence members (such as number of failures observed for the vintages or number of Machine-Months (MM) for the vintages; we will refer to such weights as $w_i, i = 1, 2, \ldots$) or based on desired properties of the monitoring scheme (such as weights that enhance the importance of more recent vintages).

5. For every parameter establish acceptable and unacceptable regions. For example, if λ represents the expected failure rate (say, expected number of fails per 1000 MM of service), then we could set the acceptable level of failure rate to λ_0 and the unacceptable rate to $\lambda_1 > \lambda_0$.

6. For every parameter establish the acceptable rate of false alarms. As noted earlier, in the context of schemes with DCO we cannot use the criteria related to Run Length (such as ARL); one reasonable criterion appears to be related to the *probability of flagging* of a parameter. One can control the rate of false alarms in the monitoring system by setting this probability to a low level that reflects the desirable degree of trade-off between false alarms and sensitivity.

7. Deploy the designed scheme to every relevant data set; flag this data set if out-of-control conditions are present. For some monitoring systems the deployment will involve massive re-computing of control sequences, thresholds and control schemes on a regular basis. For example, for PC manufacturing operation it was considered suitable to activate the system on a weekly basis (note, however, that the vintages in Fig. 1 were still being summarized on a daily basis). For other systems re-computing could be, at least in part, event-driven.

3   Computational and Monte-Carlo Aspects

For every monitored parameter we convert the control sequence $X_i, i = 1, 2, \ldots, N$ to the values of a control scheme $S_i, i = 1, 2, \ldots, N$ via the weighed Cusum algorithm. For example, for a parameter λ we can use the *Weighted Geometric Cusum* defined by

$$S_0 = 0, S_i = max[0, \gamma S_{i-1} + w_i(X_i - k)], i = 1, 2, \ldots, N, \qquad (1)$$

where γ is typically chosen in $[0.7, 1]$ and the *reference value* $k \approx (\lambda_0 + \lambda_1)/2$ ("optimal" values for k are obtained based on behavior of likelihood ratios for X_i, see Hawkins and Olwell (1998).

For schemes with DCO we define $S = max[S_1, S_2, \ldots, S_N]$ and refer to the current point in time as T. The data set (i.e., sequence of lifetime tests) is flagged at time T if $S > h$, where the threshold h is chosen based on

$$Prob[S > h | N, \lambda = \lambda_0] = \alpha_0, \qquad (2)$$

where typically $\alpha_0 < 0.01$. Thus, test(1) is a series of repeated Cusum tests in the sense that at every new point in time the whole sequence (1) is re-computed from scratch.

We should note immediately that in many cases the scheme (1) alone is not sufficient for efficient detection of change in the process level, and so supplemental tests may be needed. For example, consider the situation where X_i is the replacement rate (number of replacements per 1000 MM for parts of vintage i) and w_i is the number of MM accumulated by parts of vintage i. As data for new vintages continues to come in, the value of the threshold h will be moving up (note that threshold violation could occur not only at the last vintage, but for some earlier vintages as well) - and this could desensitize the scheme with respect to more recent vintages, especially given the fact that weights w_i will tend to be large for early vintages and small for recent vintages. Use of $\gamma < 1$ will typically help somewhat to ameliorate the extreme manifestations of this problem - however, supplemental tests specifically geared towards detection of unfavorable events for later vintages are sometimes needed. Such tests will be discussed later in the section. Analogously to the case of conventional (non-DCO) schemes, use of $\gamma < 1$ is advisable when the primary mode of change in the process level is in the form of drifts rather than shifts.

The immediate computational problem spawned by (1) is related to obtaining h by solving (2). The algorithm needs to be efficient because in massive data monitoring systems (such as a warranty data system) the number of schemes run in parallel can easily reach 100,000 - and the computing operation typically needs to complete within a narrow time window. For procedures of type (1) Monte Carlo methods have proven to be effective, provided that certain measures be taken to enhance their efficiency. For example:

- Use parallel computation and elemental procedures (i.e., procedures designed to be applied to every element of an array simultaneously). In the PC warranty data application we use a set of K (typically, about 2000) replications of the trajectory (1). For every replication a value of S is computed and h is obtained by solving (2) based on the empirical distribution of the K values of S. To reduce the computing time, the values of K replications for a given point in time are treated as a K-dimensional vector; its values are computed for $i = 1, 2, \ldots, N$, and the corresponding vector of S values is computed progressively in time. This is much more efficient than computing the statistics for every trajectory (1) and repeating the process K times. What helps us here is that the characteristics S of every trajectory (1) can be computed recursively in time i.
  A key element enhancing the efficiency of this vector-based operation is also related to generation of random variables X_i. Special algorithms of random variable generation, optimized for simultaneous production of K variables simultaneously, enable one to complete the computation of trajectories for each time i in an efficient manner.
- Take advantage of asymptotic properties of statistics S that can be derived on the basis of theory of stochastic processes. For example, one can expect that for distributions of X_i that have first two moments, the distribution of S can be approximated based on the tail property

$$Prob[S > h | \lambda = \lambda_0] \sim A \times exp[-ah], h \to \infty, \qquad (3)$$

where A is a constant and a is a function of the first two moments and γ. When $\gamma = 1$, relations of type (3) can typically be justified (for analysis of in-control situations only) based on the approximation of (1) by a Brownian motion with reflecting barrier at zero (e.g., see Cox and Miller (1977), Bagshaw and Johnson (1975)). Our experience suggests that (3) continues to hold even when $\gamma < 1$, though we have no proof of it at this time.

If for a given in-control situation it is known a-priori that (3) holds, one can reduce substantially the number of replications K that is needed to achieve the required level of accuracy. In particular, one can use a relatively low K, obtain the replications and obtain a non-parametric estimate of the upper 25-th percentile $\hat{q}_{75}$ of S. Subsequently, one can fit an exponential distribution to the excess points above $\hat{q}_{75}$, taking advantage of (3). Finally, the equation (2) is solved by using the pair of estimates $(\hat{q}_{75}, \hat{a})$. This approach can be used not only for threshold derivation, but also for computing the *severity* of an observed trajectory, expressed in terms of a *p-value* corresponding to S observed for the data set at hand. Note that test based on (1) effectively triggers an alarm if the p-value of the test falls below α_0.

- When *ancillary* statistics are available, try to *condition* on them in the course of Monte-Carlo replications, in line with usual recommendations of statistical theory. For example, suppose that X_i are rates per 1000 MM. Then the overall MM observed for a vintage, though a random quantity, can typically be assumed to have a distribution that does not depend on λ. It is, therefore, advisable to resample X_i based on the MM in period i that was actually observed in the data.

Supplemental Tests. As noted above, tests based on (1)-(2) could turn out to be insensitive to recent unfavorable changes - and such changes could be of high importance to the users. In the PC warranty data system we introduce the concept of *active component*. In particular, we set a threshold of, say, D_a days; a part is considered active if there are vintages present in the data within the last D_a days from the current point in time T. A warranty system will typically contain many inactive parts that are no longer produced (even though failures related to older parts of this type are still in the field, continue to contribute data and could present a risk to the manufacturer). For inactive parts there is little benefit from emphasis on recent vintages because all the parts are anyway out of manufacturer's reach and so there is no longer an opportunity to prevent an escape of unreliable parts into the field. In contrast, for *active* parts such an opportunity does exist. Therefore, supplemental tests are applied to active parts only.

The first supplemental criterion for currently active part calls for testing the hypothesis that the collection of X_i observed within the last D_a days correspond to the in-control parameter not exceeding λ_0. The corresponding p-value can sometimes be computed numerically. The criterion triggers an alarm if this p-value is smaller than a pre-specified threshold.

The second supplemental criterion is based on the final value S_N of the scheme (1). The corresponding p-value is computed via Monte-Carlo method, by using the same runs that were used for the analysis of (1). Techniques described earlier for enhancing efficiency of the computations fully apply to this criterion; in many situations the relationship of type (3) can also shown to be relevant for it.

The overall severity (p-value) of the battery of (1) and two supplemental tests can be approximated by a function of the individual p-values $\psi(p_1, p_2, p_3)$ of these tests. Typically, correlation between the supplemental test statistics and S is negligible and can be ignored. However, the supplemental tests do tend to be correlated - and, therefore, one important issue here is obtaining a suitable form for ψ.

4   Monitoring of Wearout

One of issues of primary concern to engineers is onset of wearout. Such an event can substantially damage the reputation of a company - but when wearout occurs within the warranty period, this could lead to substantial additional losses and even to loss of the whole operation. Organizing an effective system for lifetime data monitoring that detects onset of wearout should, therefore, be a key priority for many manufacturing operations, especially those involved in mass manufacturing.

The computational strategy for wearout monitoring could be developed along the lines of that in Sec. 2. It is important to note, however, that in many situations it is unpractical to compute the wearout indicator for every vintage, for example, because of issues of parameter estimability. Therefore, data is typically grouped by vintages: for example, the rows of Fig. 1 are consolidated so as to yield just one row per month.

One can use several characteristics that are sensitive to wearout; any given characteristic can be used as a basis for a monitoring scheme of type (1). Given that (possibly after time scale transformation as mentioned in Sec. 1) the data under acceptable conditions is likely to show behavior that is "similar" to exponential, we could select an index that represents the estimate of the Weibull shape parameter. Note that we do not really have to believe that the data is Weibull: the estimated shape parameter can be used as a form of "wearout index" even in many situations where the lifetime distribution is non-Weibull, as it retains a substantial graphical and analytical appeal.

Denoting by c the shape parameter of the Weibull distribution we can specify the acceptable and unacceptable levels as c_0 and $c_1 > c_0$ (in many practical situations, $c_0 = 1$ is a good choice). One way to proceed is to compute consecutive *unbiased* estimates $\hat{c}_1, \hat{c}_2, \ldots, \hat{c}_M$, where M is the number of months for which data is available. These values are then used in the Cusum test:

$$S_{0w} = 0, S_{iw} = max[0, \gamma_w S_{i-1,w} + w_{iw}(\hat{c}_{iw} - k_w)], i = 1, 2, \ldots, M, \qquad (4)$$

where γ_w is the geometric parameter (typically close to 1) and $k_w \approx (c_0 + c_1)/2$. The weight w_{iw} is the number of failures observed in the period i (and not the overall number of MM for period i, as in (1)). This is because a period with large MM but very few failures does not contain much information about c). Now we can see why we want the sequence of estimates $\hat{c}_i$ to be bias-corrected: with such a choice we can use the same reference value k_w for every period. Since we operate under the DCO conditions, the decision statistics is $S_w = max[S_{1w}, S_{2w}, \ldots, S_{Mw}]$ and we flag the data set at time T if $S_w > h_w$, where h_w is chosen from the equation:

$$Prob[S_w > h_w | M, c_0] = \alpha_0. \qquad (5)$$

As before, Monte-Carlo approach is used to derive the threshold h_w and p-value of the test. In the course of replications we assume that the scale parameter β of the Weibull law can change from period to period, and we focus our attention entirely on c. Under such an assumption the number of fails w_{iw} in period i can be treated as an ancillary statistic for c and we condition the replications for this period on the number of fails being equal to w_{iw}. For period i we then estimate the scale parameter $\hat{\beta}_i$ under the hypothesized assumption $c = c_0$ and produce replications of w_{iw} failures under the assumption that lifetimes for this period are distributed Weibull $(\hat{\beta}_i, c_0)$, taking into account the censoring times. Processing such replications for our collection of periods enables one to evaluate the null distribution of S_w and obtain the corresponding threshold h_w and a p-value for the observed value of S_w.

Note that a process similar to that described above can also be used to deploy schemes for monitoring the scale parameter β.

5   Conclusions

Design and analysis of systems for monitoring reliability, especially in the DCO environment is a highly complex task, both from the methodological and computational points of view. The main technical challenges include (a) establishing "on the fly" the thresholds for a large number of tests and efficient use of Monte Carlo techniques (b) establishing "newsworthiness" of the detected conditions based on p-values and similar indices of severity and (c) deployment in the field that satisfies the requirements for low rate of false alarms, detection capability, user interface and report generation. In this article we discuss a possible approach that was deployed several years ago at the IBM PC company. Our impression, based on user feedback, was that this approach can lead to usable and powerful system for monitoring massive streams of reliability and warranty data.

References

BAGSHAW, M. and JOHNSON, R. (1975): The Effect of Serial Correlation on the Performance of CUSUM TESTS II, *Technometrics, 17, 73-80.*

BLISCHKE, W.R. and MURTHY, D.N.P. (2000): *Reliability Modeling, Prediction and Optimization.* Wiley, New York.

COX, D. and MILLER, H. (1977): *The Theory of Stochastic Processes.* Chapman and Hall/CRC, New York.

DOGANAKSOY, N., HAHN, G.J. and MEEKER, W.Q. (2006): Improving reliability through warranty data analysis. *Quality Progress, November, 63-67.*

DUBOIS, A., EVANS, V.R., JENSEN, D., KHABIBRAKHMANOV, I., RESTIVO, S. ROSS, C. and YASHCHIN, E. (2008): System and method for early detection of system component failure. *US Patent 7401263,* US Patent Office.

HAWKINS, D. and OLWELL, D. (1998): *Cumulative Sum Charts and Charting for Quality Improvement.* Springer, New York.

KALBFLEISCH, J.D., LAWLESS, J.F. and ROBINSON, J.A. (1991): Methods for the analysis and prediction of warranty claims. *Technometrics 33, 273-285.*

KARIM, M.R., YAMAMOTO, W. and SUZUKI, K (2001): Statistical analysis of of marginal count failure data. *Lifetime Data Analysis, 7, 173-186.*

LAWLESS, J.F. (1998): Statistical Analysis of Product Warranty Data. *International Statistical Review 66, 41-60.*

LAWLESS, J.F. and KALBFLEISCH, J.D. (1992): Some issues in the collection and analysis of field reliability data. *Survival Analysis: State of the Art, J.P. Klein and P.K. Goel (eds.). Kluwer Academic Publishers, Netherlands, 141-152.*

OLTEANU, D. and VINING, G.G. (2009): CUSUM Charts for Censored Lifetime Data. *Paper at the 2009 Joint Statistical Meetings, Washington, DC.*

PATRA, K. and DEY, D.K. (2002): A general class of change point and change curve modeling for lifetime data. *Ann. Inst. Statist. Math., 54(3) 517-530.*

SEGO, L., REYNOLDS, M. and WOODALL, W. (2009): Risk-adjusted monitoring of survival times. *Statist. Med., 28, 1386-1401.*

STEINER, S.H. and MACKAY, R.J. (2000): Monitoring processes with highly censored data. *J. Qual. Technol., 32, 199-208.*

STEINER, S.H. and MACKAY, R.J. (2001): Detecting Changes in the Mean from Censored Lifetime Data. *Frontiers in Statistical Quality Control 6, H.J. Lenz and P.T. Wilrich eds., Physica-Verlag, 275-289.*

WU, H. and MEEKER, W.Q. (2002): Early detection of reliability problems using information from warranty databases. *Technometrics 44(2), 120-133.*

YASHCHIN, E. (1993): Statistical control schemes: methods, applications and generalizations. *International Statistical Review 61, 41-66.*

ZHANG, L. and CHEN, G. (2004): EWMA charts for monitoring the mean of censored Weibull lifetimes *J. of Quality Technology 36(3), 321-328.*

Part XI

Optimization Heuristics in Statistical
Modelling

Evolutionary Computation for Modelling and Optimization in Finance

Sandra Paterlini[1,2]

[1] Department of Economics, CEFIN and RECent, University of Modena and Reggio E., Viale Berengario 51, Modena, Italy, *sandra.paterlini@unimore.it*
[2] CEQURA, Center for Quantitative Risk Analysis, Akademiestr. 1/I, Munich, Germany

Abstract. In the last decades, there has been a tendency to move away from mathematically tractable, but simplistic models towards more sophisticated and real-world models in finance. However, the consequence of the improved sophistication is that the model specification and analysis is no longer mathematically tractable. Instead solutions need to be numerically approximated. For this task, evolutionary computation heuristics are the appropriate means, because they do not require any rigid mathematical properties of the model. Evolutionary algorithms are search heuristics, usually inspired by Darwinian evolution and Mendelian inheritance, which aim to determine the optimal solution to a given problem by competition and alteration of candidate solutions of a population. In this work, we focus on credit risk modelling and financial portfolio optimization to point out how evolutionary algorithms can easily provide reliable and accurate solutions to challenging financial problems.

Keywords: population-based algorithms, multi-objective optimization, clustering, credit risk modelling, financial portfolio optimization.

1 Introduction

Quantitative finance has been a rapidly developing field in the last decades. The recent financial crises, the new regulations for banks and insurances and the increasing development of complex financial products have prompted intermediaries to promote the use of quantitative tools inside their organizations in many different sectors, such as risk management, pricing and provisioning of financial products, derivatives accounting. New models have been developed for portfolio selection, pricing and risk management. Often these models, even if easily tractable, turn out to be too simplistic and inadequate as tools to analyze real-world settings (e.g. the Markowitz mean-variance model for portfolio selection). Hence, they cannot be reliable as decision-support system for managers. Nowadays, the financial and econometric academic literature shows a tendency to move towards more complex models (e.g. Zhao (2008)) that represent the real-world dynamics better. However, this development poses new challenges. The models become often extremely

Y. Lechevallier, G. Saporta (eds.), *Proceedings of COMPSTAT'2010*,
DOI 10.1007/978-3-7908-2604-3_24, © Springer-Verlag Berlin Heidelberg 2010

difficult to accurately specify and estimate. There is the need of robust model selection and estimation methodologies which can provide reliable information even when the problem is multivariate and the variables involved are highly correlated.

Optimization search heuristics have already found application in statistical modelling and estimation problems (Winker and Gilli (2004) and references). Search heuristics, such as trajectory methods (e.g., simulated annealing, threshold accepting, tabu search), evolutionary algorithms (e.g. genetic algorithms, differential evolution) or hybrid methods (e.g., memetic algorithms), take inspiration from biological processes (Corne at al. (1999), Michalewich and Fogel (2002)). Their main advantage, compared to standard optimization approaches, is that they do not require rigid properties of the optimization problem, such as continuity, linearity, monotonicity or convexity of the objective functions and constraints. Basically, they can tackle a whole range of problems for which most other optimization methods are not applicable. Most financial practitioners are not familiar with such methodologies, as they have been developed mainly in non-financial research areas. Nevertheless, their use can lead to impressive results in a number of financial and econometric applications (see Gilli et al. (2008), Schlottmann and Seese (2004) for reviews).

In this paper, we plan to provide some insights about using evolutionary algorithms (EAs), a type of search heuristics, for financial modelling and optimization. In particular, Section 2 shortly describes EAs, while Sections 3 and 4 discuss their application in credit risk modelling and portfolio optimization, respectively. Finally, Section 5 concludes.

2   Evolutionary Computation

Stochastic search heuristics work by probabilistic stepwise refinement of solutions. Their main advantages, compared to conventional techniques, are related to their high generality which allows them to tackle problems as complex as they are: they can easily deal with plateaus, ridges, multimodal problems avoiding to get trapped in local optima, they do not require any rigid assumption about the problem or auxiliary information (e.g. gradient), they can produce meaningful results if the run is prematurely terminated and their easy implementation can work for a wide range of problems. On the other hand, they have been mainly criticized because solutions are not guaranteed to be optimal, are inferior to conventional techniques for simple problems and sometimes they require expensive parameter tuning, which however often allows to better control the trade-off between exploitation and exploration of the search space and to avoid convergence to local optima. Evolutionary Algorithms (EAs) are a type of stochastic search heuristics, which work evolving a population of candidate solutions using operators inspired by Darwinian evolution and Mendelian inheritance. The first step to implement an EA for a single-objective optimization problem is to decide a coding scheme in order to represent a candidate solution to the optimization problem in a binary or real-world string. Each string corresponds to a single individual of the EA population. The algorithm usually starts with a randomly generated population and each individual's fitness value is computed. The fitness value quantifies the goodness of the candidate solution to the optimization problem at hand. Then, until a given termination criterion is satisfied, the population is iteratively altered by means of biologically-ispired operators, such as selection, mutation, crossover and elitism in order to promote the survival of the fittest. At the end of the run, the string with highest fitness value encodes the optimal solution of the problem at hand. Figure 1 shows the pseudo-code of a simple evolutionary algorithm.

```
void EvolutionaryAlgorithm()
{
  t = 0;
  initialize population P(t);    // create random solutions
  evaluate population P(t);    // calculate fitnesses
  while (not termination condition) {
    t = t + 1;
    select next generation P(t) from P(t-1);
    alter P(t);    // mutate and recombine genes
    evaluate population P(t);    // calculate fitnesses
  }
}
```

Fig. 1. Pseudo code of an evolutionary algorithm.

Many different EAs and their variants have been proposed in the literature (see Corne et al. (1999), Michalewich and Fogel (2002)). Genetic Algorithms (Holland (1975)), Particle Swarm Optimization (Kennedy and Eberhart (1995)) and Differential Evolution (Storn and Price (1997)) are probably the most known and used in scientific literature. Compared to single-individual search heuristics, one of their main advantages is that they work by evolving simultaneously a population of candidate solutions and not a single individual, which result in more efficient runs if implemented in parallel system and also provides a more natural way of tackling multi-objective optimization problems, given that the whole population at the end of the run can be used to determine the Pareto front of optimal solutions. This is one of the most promising field of research in recent years (Deb (2001)). Section 3 focuses on a single-objective optimization problem in credit risk modelling, while Section 4 describes an application of EAs in multi-objective financial portfolio optimization.

3   Clustering in Credit Risk Bucketing

The recent financial crises have pointed out the relevance of credit risk products and their impact on real economy. Basel II requires banks to measure the probability of default (PD) of single obligors and then to group them in at least 7 rating classes or buckets $(PD$ buckets$)$, to assign clients in the same bucket the same PD (i.e. the mean of individual PDs) and to compute capital charges against the buckets' PDs. The problem of bucketing clients can be formulated as a clustering problem with the target of determining a cluster structure which minimizes the loss in precision when replacing the PD of each single client by the bucket PD. The partition must also be consistent with Basel II guidelines regarding the minimum value of each bucket pooled $\overline{PD}_b$ and avoiding the presence of too large buckets in terms of exposure and too small buckets in terms of number of obligors for ex-post validation. One simple approach, proposed by Krink et al. (2007, 2008), is then to determine the buckets by solving the following optimization problem

$$\min \sum_b \sum_{i \in b} (\overline{PD}_b - PD_i)^2 \tag{1}$$

such that

- $\overline{PD}_b \geq 0.03\%$
- $N_j > 0$
- $N_j/N \geq k, k \in]0,1]$
- $\sum_{i=1}^{N_j} E_{ij}/E_{Total} \leq 0.35\%$

$\forall j = 1,..,b$, where b is the number of buckets, $\overline{PD}_b$ is the pooled PD for the b-th bucket, PD_i is the individual PD for obligor i, N_j is the number of clients in bucket j such that $\sum_{j=1}^{b} N_j = N$, E_{ji} is the exposure of the i-th client in bucket j, E_{Total} is the sum of the exposures of all clients.

Given the presence of many plateaus in the search space (see Figure 3 Krink

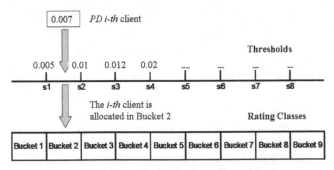

Fig. 2. PD bucketing allocation

et al. (2007)) and of the constraints, Krink et al. (2007, 2008) propose to use EAs to tackle the PD bucketing problem. In particular, as Figure 2 shows, each individual of an EA could encode the bucket thresholds (i.e. $s_1,...,s_8$ for b=9), which determine in which bucket each obligor should be allocated depending on the value of her PD. Krink et al. (2007) compare the performance of genetic algorithm, particle swarm optimization and differential evolution in tackling the PD bucketing problem and show that EAs outperform k-means clustering and two other naive approaches, especially when the problem becomes more challenging (i.e. increase the number of buckets, use more sophisticated error functions). Furthermore, their analysis suggests that differential evolution, which is known for little parameter tuning, is superior to genetic algorithms and particle swarm optimization. Recently, Lyra et al. (in press) have extended the investigation by introducing new methods to determine not only the bucketing structure but also the optimal number of buckets and have also shown that threshold accepting, an individual-based search heuristic which exploits the inherent discrete nature of the clustering problem, could outperform differential evolution in this single-objective optimization problem.

Other recent studies further show that EAs can be effectively employed in other credit risk modelling applications, such as in estimating transition probability matrices (Zhang et al. (2009)) and in multi-objective optimization of credit portfolios (Schlottmann and Seese (2004b)).

4   Financial Portfolio Optimization

Financial portfolio selection consists of deciding how much of an investor's wealth to allocate to different investment opportunities. The problem can be formulated as an optimization problem, with a single objective (e.g. maximize the investor's utility) or more often multi-objective, as the following Markowitz mean-variance model

$$\min f_1(\mathbf{w}) = \sum_{i=1}^{N}\sum_{j=1}^{N} w_i w_j \sigma_{ij}^2 \tag{2a}$$

$$\max f_2(\mathbf{w}) = \sum_{i=1}^{N} w_i \mu_i \tag{2b}$$

subject to

$$\sum_{i=1}^{N} w_i = 1, 0 \le w_i \le 1 \tag{3}$$

where w_i is the portfolio weight of the i-th asset (i=1,...,N) with $\mathbf{w} = [w_1,..,w_N]$, μ_i the expected return of i-th asset and σ_{ij} is the expected covariance between the i-th and the j-th assets.

The choice of the optimization algorithm depends on the characteristics of the objective functions and of the constraints. Hence, while the mean-variance optimization problem can be easily solved by quadratic programming, this is hardly true when considering real-world portfolio optimization settings. In particular, the main challenges are usually due to the need to replace the objective function $f_1(\mathbf{w})$ by more realistic but multimodal and non-convex risk measures, such as Value-at-Risk or Omega, and to the presence of real-world non linear constraints, such as the cardinality or turnover constraints. Stochastic search heuristics can then provide a valid alternative to classic optimization methods for financial portfolio selection, as also shown by the fast development in the field in the last decade (Chang et al. (2000), Maringer (2005)). One of the most promising research field in financial modelling is evolutionary multi-objective portfolio optimization, where the EAs can better exploit the fact that it is a population-based algorithm (see Deb (2001), Coello Coello et al. (2002), Coello Coello (1999) for surveys and http://www.lania.mx/ ccoello/EMOO/EMOObib.html for a repository of EAs for multi-objective optimization problems). In fact, in most multi-objective evolutionary algorithms, the population of candidate solutions is used to search (simultaneously) for a set of solutions that represents the entire Pareto front, i.e. the set of optimal solutions. The EAs allow to determine the Pareto set in a single run of the algorithm, instead of having to perform a series of separate runs as in the case of the traditional mathematical programming techniques. Furthermore, EAs can better deal with discontinuous and concave Pareto fronts.

The main challenges when using EAs for multi-objective problems are related to the mechanism to determine the *non-dominated* solutions and to keep *diversity* among them, that is to avoid the convergence of the EA population into a single area of the Pareto front instead of covering all of it.

Let F be a multi-objective minimization problem with p objectives f_k with $k = 1,..., p$. A candidate solution x_i dominates x_j if and only if

$$\forall k, f_k(x_i) = f_k(x_j)$$
$$\exists l, f_l(x_i) < f_l(x_j)$$

Then, one can assign a rank to each candidate solution according to how much it is dominated by others. As Figure 3 shows, solutions that are non-dominated by any others will receive rank one and then solutions will be ranked iteratively depending by how many other fronts dominate them. The EAs selection operator will then prefer the individuals which have a lower rank and in case they have the same rank, diversity drives the selection process. This definition of dominance can also be easily extended to include constraints and penalize solutions that violates more constraints (Deb et al. (2002), Krink and Paterlini (in press)).

Diversity preservation is the other operator that drives the selection and the convergence of the EA population to the Pareto front. Furthermore, diversity preservation is important not only in multi-objective optimization in order to

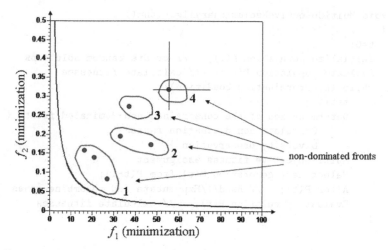

Fig. 3. Determination of non-dominated fronts in a 2-dimensional problem

cover the whole Pareto front, but also in multimodal optimization (to identify more than one optimum), in constraint optimization (to cover all feasible
regions) and in standard optimization (to prevent premature convergence to
local optima). The main techniques to keep diversity are *sharing* which works
by punishing individuals for crowding close together by scaling the fitness according to the proximity among individuals, and *crowding*, where each new
candidate solution replaces the most similar solution in the current population if it is better. Given that scaling the fitness in the sharing approach can
be difficult, crowding seem to be nowadays preferred within the community,
given that it only requires the definition of a distance measure (see Deb et al.
(2002), Krink and Paterlini (in press)) for examples of EAs using the cuboid
distance measure). Then, if competing solutions have the same rank, the ones
with largest distance to their nearest neighbours are preferred.
Summing up, the algorithm works by first rewarding candidate solutions
that are closer to the Pareto front and then by rewarding solutions that
allow a good coverage of the Pareto front. Figure 4 shows the pseudo-code
of a multi-objective evolutionary algorithm. Recent investigations (Anagnostopoulos and Mamanis, in press, Krink and Paterlini, in press) have shown
that multi-objective evolutionary algorithms are efficient and robust strategies to deal with typical real-world multi-objective financial portfolio problems, which so far have been a major challenge for financial practitioners and
researchers. We believe research in financial multi-objective optimization by
means of EAs and other stochastic search heuristics is just at the beginning
and surely will contribute to the development of fast and reliable quantitative
tools for investment decisions.

```
void MultiObjectiveEvolutionaryAlgorithm()
{
  t=0;
  Initialize population P(t);   // create random solutions
  Evaluate population P(t);   // calculate fitnesses
  while (not termination condition){
      t=t+1
      Determination of the constrained non-dominated fronts {
          Calculate non-domination ranks
          Diversity preservation }
      Multi-objective fitness assignment
      Select next generation P(t) from P(t-1);
      Alter P(t);   // Rand/1/Exp-mutate and recombine genes
      Evaluate population P(t);   // calculate fitnesses
  }
}
```

Fig. 4. Pseudo code of a multi-objective evolutionary algorithm.

5   Conclusion and Further Research

This paper aims to introduce EAs and to show that challenging optimization problems in financial modelling could be easily and reliably tackled by them. By using two simple examples, PD bucketing in credit risk modelling and portfolio selection, which typically require optimizing complex functions (i.e. non-convex, multimodal, non-differentiable) with hard constraints (i.e. non-linear, non-continuous), we describe the general idea behind the implementation of two simple EAs to tackle them. In particular, we underline the difference between an EA to tackle a single-objective optimization problem, as the PD bucketing, where the fittest solution at the end of the run encodes the optimal solution, and one to tackle a multi-objective optimization problem, as the portfolio optimization, where the whole population at the end of the run identifies the set of optimal solutions (the so-called Pareto front). EAs usually allow an easy encoding of the problem at hand no matter how complex it is, without requiring any rigid assumption about the model. Hence, compared to conventional methods, they are general in their scope of application and capable of dealing with challenging optimization set-ups. Despite they have been criticized because of their speed of convergence, the recent developments in computing hardware and the possibility of running them in parallel suggest that the issue is becoming less relevant. Furthermore, even the parameter tuning issue is becoming more an advantage of EAs rather than a shortcoming, given the fact that it betters allows to tackle the trade-off between exploration and exploitation and avoid premature convergence. While using EAs in financial modelling is still at an early stage, the increasing complexity of financial optimization and modelling problems and the development of the scientific literature in the last decades seem to point out that EAs and other stochastic search heuristics will become standard optimization tools in the very near future.

6   Acknowledgement

The author would like to thank Roberto Baragona, Francesco Battaglia, Manfred Gilli, Thiemo Krink, Dietmar Maringer, Tommaso Minerva, Irene Poli and Peter Winker for many interesting and inspiring discussions on EAs and stochastic search heuristics. Financial support from MIUR PRIN 20077P5AWA005 and from Fondazione Cassa di Risparmio di Modena for ASBE Project is gratefully acknowledged.

References

ANAGNOSTOPOULOS, K.P. and MAMANIS, G. (in press): Multiobjective evolutionary algorithms for complex portfolio optimization problems. *Computational Management Science, 10.1007/s10287-009-0113-8*

BRUSCH, M. and BAIER, D. (2002): Conjoint analysis and stimulus representation: a comparison of alternative methods. In: K. Jajuga, A. Sokołowski and H.H. Bock (Eds.): *Classification, Clustering, and Data Analysis.* Springer, Berlin, 203–210.

CHANG, T.-J., MEADE, N., BEASLEY, J.E. and SHARAIHA, Y.M. (2000): Heuristics for Cardinality Constrained Portfolio Optimization. *Computers and Operations Research, 27, 1271—1302.*

COELLO COELLO, C.A., 1999. A Comprehensive Survey of Evolutionary-Based Multiobjective Optimization Techniques. *Knowledge and Information Systems, An International Journal, 1, 3, 269–308.*

COELLO COELLO, C.A., DAVID, A.V.V., and GARY, B.L. (2002): *Evolutionary Algorithms for Solving Multi-Objective Problems.* Kluwer Academic/Plenum, New York.

CORNE, D., DORIGO, M. and GLOVER, F. (1999): *New Ideas in Optimization.* McGraw-Hill.

DEB, K. (2001): *Multi-Objective Optimization using Evolutionary Algorithms.* WILEY.

DEB, K., PRATAP, A., AGARWAL, S., and MEYARIVAN, T., (2002): A Fast and Elitist Multiobjective Genetic Algorithm. *IEEE Transactions on Evolutionary Computation, 6, 2, 182–197.*

GILLI, M., MARINGER, D. and WINKER, P. (2008): Applications of Heuristics in Finance. In: D. Seese, C. Weinhardt and F. Schlottmann (Eds.): *Handbook on Information Technology in Finance.* Springer.

HOLLAND, J., (1975): *Adaptation in Natural and Artificial Systems.* University of Michigan Press, Ann Harbor.

KENNEDY, J. and EBERHART, R.C., (1995): Particle swarm optimization. *Proceedings of the 1995 IEEE International Conference on Neural Networks* IEEE Press, Piscataway, NJ, 4, 1942–1948.

KRINK, T. and PATERLINI, S. (in press): Multiobjective Optimization using Differential Evolution for Real-World Portfolio Optimization. *Computational Management, doi: 10.1007/s10287-009-0107-6.*

KRINK, T., MITTNIK, S. and PATERLINI, S. (2009): Differential Evolution and Combinatorial Search for Constrained Index Tracking. *Annals of Operations Research, 172, 153–176.*

KRINK, T., RESTI, A. and PATERLINI, S. (2008): The optimal structure of PD buckets. *Journal of Banking and Finance, 32, 10, 2275–2286.*

KRINK, T., RESTI, A. and PATERLINI, S. (2007): Using Differential Evolution to improve the accuracy of bank rating systems. *Computational Statistics & Data Analysis, Elsevier, 52/1, 68–87.*

LYRA, M., PAHA, J., PATERLINI, S. and WINKER, P. (in press): Optimization Heuristics for Determining Internal Rating Grading Scales. *Computational Statistics & Data Analysis, doi: 10.1016/j.csda.2009.03.004.*

MARINGER, D. (2005): *Portfolio Management with Heuristic Optimization.* Springer.

MICHALEWICH, Z. and FOGEL, D. (2002): *How to Solve It: Modern Heuristics.* Springer.

SCHLOTTMANN, F. and SEESE, D. (2004): Modern Heuristics for Finance Problems: A Survey of Selected Methods and Applications. In: S. T. Rachev(Eds.): *Handbook of Computational and Numerical Methods in Finance.* Birkhäuser.

SCHLOTTMANN, F. and SEESE, D. (2004b): A hybrid heuristic approach to discrete multi-objective optimization of credit portfolios. *Computational Statistics & Data Analysis, 47, 373–399.*

STORN, R. and PRICE, K. (1997): Differential evolution: a simple and efficient adaptive scheme for global optimization over continuous spaces. *J. Global Optimization, 11, 341–359*

ZHANG, J., AVASARALA, V. and SUBBU, E. (2009): Evolutionary Optimization of transition probability matrices for credit decision-making. *European Journal of Operational Research, doi: 10.1016/j.ejor.2009.01.020.*

ZHAO, Z. (2008): Parametric and nonparametric models and methods in financial econometrics. *Statistical Surveys, 2, 1–42.*

WINKER, P. and GILLI, M. (2004): Applications of optimization heuristics to estimation and modelling problems. *Computational Statistics & Data Analysis, 47, 211–223.*

Part XII

Spatial Statistics / Spatial Epidemiology

Examining the Association between Deprivation Profiles and Air Pollution in Greater London using Bayesian Dirichlet Process Mixture Models

John Molitor, Léa Fortunato, Nuoo-Ting Molitor, Sylvia Richardson

MRC-HPA Centre for Environment and Health and Department of Epidemiology and Biostatistics, Imperial College, London

Abstract. Standard regression analyses are often plagued with problems encountered when one tries to make inference going beyond main effects, using datasets that contain dozens of variables that are potentially correlated. This situation arises, for example, in environmental deprivation studies, where a large number of deprivation scores are used as covariates, yielding a potentially unwieldy set of inter-related data from which teasing out the joint effect of multiple deprivation indices is difficult. We propose a method, based on Dirichlet-process mixture models that addresses these problems by using, as its basic unit of inference, a profile formed from a sequence of continuous deprivation measures. These deprivation profiles are clustered into groups and associated via a regression model to an air pollution outcome. The Bayesian clustering aspect of the proposed modeling framework has a number of advantages over traditional clustering approaches in that it allows the number of groups to vary, uncovers clusters and examines their association with an outcome of interest and fits the model as a unit, allowing a region's outcome potentially to influence cluster membership. The method is demonstrated with an analysis UK Indices of Deprivation and PM10 exposure measures corresponding to super output areas (SOA's) in greater London.

Keywords: Bayesian analysis, Dirichlet processes, mixture models, MCMC, environmental justice

1 Introduction

Many early studies in the USA have highlighted the apparent clustering of hazardous and polluting sites in areas dominated by ethnic minorities of lower SES. (See, for example Brown et al. (1998).) A large body of research has resulted, suggesting that people who are socially disadvantaged become subject to a more polluted and hazardous living environment (Briggs et al. (2008)). However, SES is a complex concept (Abellan et al. (2007)) and the highly inter-correlated nature of deprivation metrics makes it difficult to examine their combined associations with measures of air pollution. As such, epidemiological studies have often focused on models that employ single measures

Y. Lechevallier, G. Saporta (eds.), *Proceedings of COMPSTAT'2010*,
DOI 10.1007/978-3-7908-2604-3_25, © Springer-Verlag Berlin Heidelberg 2010

of deprivation or on a combined deprivation score. Such combined scores are useful, but information is lost when an entire pattern of deprivation indices is reduced to a single number. Thus, the highly correlated nature of measures of deprivation makes marginal, single deprivation models inadequate.

2   Materials and Methods

Our overall approach is to cluster joint patterns of deprivation, denoted as a deprivation profile, and relate these clusters to the air pollution exposure, PM10. The methods proposed will utilize recently developed powerful Bayesian dimension-reduction and clustering techniques that will characterize the patterns of deprivation. The multi-deprivation profile approach proposed adopts a global point of view, where inference is based on the joint pattern of deprivation scores. The methodology consists of the following two key components. First, a *Deprivation profile assignment sub-model* assigns multi-deprivation profiles to clusters, and second, an *Association sub-model* links clusters of deprivation profiles to measures of air pollution exposure via a regression model. Since the model is fit in a unified Bayesian manner, the deprivation cluster assignments will also be informed by the exposure outcome. Further, all components of the modeling framework will be fitted jointly using Markov chain Monte Carlo (MCMC) methods (Gilks et al. (1996)). Some of these methodologies have been developed in a recent paper by Molitor et al. (2010), where the method was illustrated on an analysis of epidemiological profiles using data from a children's health survey, and these profiles were used to predict the mental health status of the child.

2.1   Deprivation Profile Assignment Sub-Model

Our basic data structure consists of, for each region, a covariate profile, $\mathbf{x}_i = (x_1, x_2, \ldots, x_P)$ where each covariate x_p, $p = 1, \ldots, P$, within each profile denotes a measure of deprivation p in area i. We first construct an allocation sub-model of the probability that a region is assigned to a particular cluster. The basic model we use to cluster profiles is a standard discrete mixture model, the kind described in Neal (1998). Our mixture model incorporates a Dirichlet process prior on the mixing distribution. For further background information regarding mixture models with Dirichlet process priors, see Green and Richardson (2001). Profiles of areas are grouped into clusters, and an allocation variable, z_i indicates the cth cluster to which area, i, belongs.

Measures of deprivation will be characterized using a multivariate normal mixture distribution. Our basic mixture model for assignment is

$$f(\mathbf{x}_i) = \sum_{c=1}^{C} \psi_c f(\mathbf{x}_i | \boldsymbol{\mu}_c, \Sigma_c), \tag{1}$$

where $f(\mathbf{x}_i|\boldsymbol{\mu}_c, \Sigma_c)$ denotes a multivariate normal distribution with location parameters $\boldsymbol{\mu}_c = (\mu_c^1, \ldots, \mu_c^P)$ and covariance matrix Σ_c. The mixture weights ψ_c, $c = 1, \ldots, C$ will be given a "stick-breaking prior" (Green et al. (2001)) using the following construction. We define a series of independent random variables, $V_1, V_2, \ldots, V_{C-1}$, each having distribution $V_c \sim Beta(1, \alpha)$. Since we have little *a priori* information regarding the specification of α, we place a uniform prior on the interval $(0.3, 10)$. By considering a maximum number of clusters, C, we have approximated the infinite cluster model with a finite one. This formulation allows for straightforward parameter estimation while retaining the flexibility of discovering a variable number of clusters. Note that for all analyses in this paper, we define $C = 20$, which we found be be sufficiently large for our applications.

Since it is possible that a cluster will be empty, we cannot assign non-informative, "flat" priors to cluster parameters. Therefore, we adopt an empirical Bayes approach and assign a prior for the mean of each deprivation score, p, across SOA's in cluster c as, $\mu_c^p \sim N(\nu^p, \phi^p)$, where each ϕ^p is assigned a vague prior but each ν^p is set to the observed empirical average, $\bar{x}^p$. Similarly, we assign a prior of $\Sigma_c \sim Wish(R, \rho)$, where $\rho = P + 1$, which sets a uniform prior on within cluster correlation parameters and sets $E(\Sigma_c) = R$, which is set to equal the empirical covariance matrix. Note that in our model formulation, cluster hyper-parameters are assumed to come from distributions centered on empirical averages. Thus cluster specific parameters are used to represent clusters that deviate from a single empirically derived "center" population.

2.2   Deprivation Sub-Model

Here, as above, we define for each region, i, an allocation variable, $z_i = c$, $c = 1, \ldots, C$ which indicates the cluster to which region i belongs. The cth cluster is assigned a random-effects parameter that measures the cluster's influence on the outcome, denoted as θ_c, which is given a non-informative prior. Our association sub-model, which links the deprivation clusters with measures of PM10 exposure is,

$$y_i = \theta_{z_i} + \epsilon_i, \tag{2}$$

where $\epsilon_i \sim N(0, \sigma^2)$.

In order to examine the level of association between each deprivation cluster and the deprivation outcome, we rewrite equation (2) using centered random-effects terms, $\theta_c^* = \theta_c - \bar{\theta}$ and define $\alpha = \bar{\theta}$, yielding,

$$y_i = \alpha + \theta_{z_i}^* + \epsilon_i, \tag{3}$$

where, $\sum_{c=1}^{C} \theta_c^* = 0$. For each deprivation cluster, c, we can obtain posterior credible intervals for the corresponding centered random-effects terms, θ_c^*. If both endpoints of this interval are away from zero, we conclude that the cluster is associated with deprivation in a statistically significant manner.

2.3   Finding the Clustering That Best Fits the Data

One important aspect of our flexible Bayesian modelling framework is that our model implementation allows the number of deprivation clusters to change from iteration to iteration of the sampler. We therefore wish to find the "typical" manner that the algorithm groups profiles into clusters, and then process this best partition of the data using modern Bayesian model-averaing tecniques that utilize the entire output of the MCMC sampler. The problem of find a "typical" clustering or partition of the data has been addressed in the literature by many authors in the context of mixture models; see, for example, Medvedovic et al. (2002) and Dahl (2006). The basic procedure, is to construct, at each iteration of the sampler, a score matrix with each element of the matrix set equal to 1 if regions i and j belong to the same cluster, and zero otherwise. At the end of the estimation process, a probability matrix, $\mathbf{S}$, is formed by averaging the score matrices obtained at each iteration, so element S_{ij} denotes the probability that regions i and j belong to the same cluster. The task is then to find the partition, z_{best}, that best represents the final average probability matrix, $\mathbf{S}$. Dahl (2006) suggests an approach to finding the best partition by choosing among all the partitions generated by the sampler the one which minimizes the least-squared distance to the matrix . We have found this approach useful, however, it requires one to choose one of the observed partitions as optimal, resulting in a choice that is somewhat susceptible to Monte-Carlo error. We find that a more robust approach is to process the similarity matrix, $\mathbf{S}$, through a deterministic clustering procedure such as the Partitioning Around Medoids (PAM) (Kaufman et al. (2005)), a deterministic clustering method available in R (R Development Core Team (2006)), where an optimal number of clusters can be chosen by maximizing an associated clustering score.

One the best partition is obtained, we wish to find posterior distributions for cluster parameters corresponding to each cluster in z_{best}. We do this by simply computing, at each iteration of the sampler, the average of value for, say θ^* (equation 3), for all regions within a particular cluster, k, of the best partition. This average random effect for cluster k is computed as

$$\bar{\theta}^*_c = \frac{1}{n_c} \sum_{i:z_i^{best}=c} \theta^*_{z_i}, \tag{4}$$

where n_c denotes the number of SOA's in cluster k of $\mathbf{z}^{best}$. Posterior distributions for cluster parameter values corresponding to μ_c^p in equation (1) can be computed similarly.

3   Example - Association between Deprivation Profiles and Air Pollution Exposure

Here, we examine the joint effects of multiple measures of deprivation corresponding to 4,742 Super Output Areas (SOA's) across Greater London with exposure to PM10 measured in Tonnes/km2/year as our outcome of inter-est. Deprivation measures utilize data in the UK based on relatively new Indices of Deprivation 2004 (Nobel et al. (2004)), which contains measures of deprivation relating to Income, Employment, Health, Education, Housing, Crime and living Environment. Values for Income and Employment were log-transformed to satisfy normality modeling assumptions. In order to facility comparison across deprivation scores, posterior distributions for deprivation parameters were standardized. This was achieved for each cluster by sub-tracting, for deprivation p, the mean of the clusters scores divided by their standard deviation at each iteration of the sampler.

Results from our analysis are depicted in Table 1 and Figure 1, with clusters sorted by association with PM10 (θ^* in equation 3). The "typical" clustering revealed 6 clusters, each containing several hundred SOA's except for the very small cluster 6. (See comments below.) We first note from Figure 1 that the deprivation clusters exhibit a high level of spatial dependency, with exposure levels increasing as one moves more towards the center of London, though no explicit spatial structure was included in the model. Table 1 demonstrates a general tendency for more deprived regions to be associated with higher levels of PM10 exposure, as the largest cluster, cluster 4 ($n_4 = 1421$) is associated with higher than average exposure levels with $\theta_4^* = 0.03$ and consistently positive deprivation scores. Also, the second largest cluster, cluster 3 ($n_3 = 1229$) is associated with lower than average exposure, with $\theta_3^* = -0.04$ and generally negative deprivation scores. Further, cluster 1 has the lowest exposure of all clusters, $\theta_1^* = -0.11$, and consistently has the lowest deprivation scores.

Nevertheless, clusters 2 and 5 exhibit contrasting patterns of exposure and deprivation. For example, cluster 2 ($n_2 = 963$) has lower than average exposure, $\theta_2^* = -0.06$, but is associated with many deprivation scores that are higher than average. Further, cluster 5 ($n_5 = 320$) is associated with higher than average exposure, $\theta_5^* = 0.05$, and is associated with many deprivation scores that are lower than average. This cluster corresponds geographically to SOA's around Heathrow Airport, which represent an anomaly in regards to exposure/deprivation exposure patters. Finally cluster 6 ($n_6 = 6$) is a tiny cluster in the centre of London which has the highest exposure, $\theta_6^* = 0.13$, but also is associated with the least deprivation as could be expected for high-income central London areas.

Clearly there may be a general tendency for more deprived regions to be more exposed to PM10, as is the case for the largest clusters of SOA's depicted in Table 1. However, people living in smaller clusters of SOA's as-sociated with wealthier individuals living in the centre of the city also suffer from pollution exposure, due to the high level of traffic present in expensive central London locations. Further work is necessary to fully examine the com-plex associations between deprivation and air pollution exposure in London, suggesting further analyses using other outcomes, such as NO_2. Nevertheless, it is clear that analyses conducted using simple, additive linear models will mask the complex deprivation/exposure associations to be discovered.

Table 1. Association Between Deprivation Profiles and PM10 Exposure

	C1 ($n_1 = 803$)	C2 ($n_2 = 963$)	C3 ($n_3 = 1229$)	C4 ($n_4 = 1421$)	C5 ($n_5 = 320$)	C6 ($n_6 = 6$)
PM10[1]	-0.11	-0.06	-0.04	0.03	0.05	0.13
95% C.I.	(-0.12,-0.11)	(-0.07,-0.05)	(-0.05,-0.04)	(0.03,0.04)	(0.04,0.06)	(0.09,0.17)
IncomeD[2]	-1.46	0.56	-0.42	1.33	-0.51	-0.50
95% C.I.	(-1.54,-1.36)	(0.37,0.72)	(-0.52,-0.31)	(1.05,1.51)	(-0.66,-0.33)	(-0.63,1.06)
EmployD[2]	-1.24	0.45	-0.49	1.36	-0.78	-0.70
95% C.I.	(-1.33,-1.15)	(0.28,0.58)	(-0.58,-0.40)	(1.09,1.56)	(-0.92,-0.62)	(0.21,1.15)
HealthD[2]	-1.40	0.21	-0.49	1.27	-0.48	0.90
95% C.I.	(-1.49,-1.30)	(0.07,0.37)	(-0.58,-0.41)	(1.00,1.53)	(-0.64,-0.31)	(0.38,1.30)
EducatD[2]	-0.87	1.44	-0.94	0.94	-0.43	-0.14
95% C.I.	(-1.04,-0.65)	(1.19,1.54)	(-1.09,-0.72)	(0.72,1.07)	(-0.60,-0.23)	(-0.84,-0.70)
HousingD[2]	-1.27	-0.48	-0.77	0.72	0.47	1.33
95% C.I.	(-1.36,-1.17)	(-0.56,-0.40)	(-0.84,-0.71)	(0.53,0.91)	(0.28,0.67)	(1.06,1.55)
CrimeD[2]	-0.41	0.33	0.28	1.16	0.39	-1.75
95% C.I.	(-0.89,-0.18)	(0.20,0.39)	(0.17,0.35)	(0.97,1.50)	(0.25,0.48)	(-1.90,-1.32)
EnvironD[2]	-1.46	-0.67	-0.33	0.53	0.72	1.21
95% C.I.	(-1.54,-1.38)	(-0.71,-0.63)	(-0.39,-0.28)	(0.41,0.66)	(0.57,0.89)	(0.96,1.42)

[1]Represents values for θ^* in equation (3).
[2]Values have been standardized.

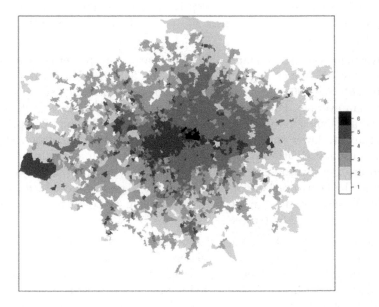

Fig. 1. Deprivation clusters in London sorted by θ_c^* (equation 3).

References

ABELLAN, J. J., FECHT, D., BEST, N., RICHARDSON, S. and BRIGGS, D. (2007): Bayesian analysis of the multivariate geographical distribution of the socio-economic environment in england. *Environmetrics, 18(7):745–758.* 10.1002/env.872.

BRIGGS, D., ABELLAN, J.J. and FECHT, D. (2008): Environmental inequity in england: small area associations between socio-economic status and environmental pollution. *Soc Sci Med, 67(10):1612–29.*

BROWN, P. (1995): Race, class, and environmental health: a review and systematization of the literature. *Environ Res, 69(1):15–30.*

DAHL, D. (2006): *Bayesian Inference for Gene Expression and Proteomics,* chapter Model-Based Clustering for Expression Data via a Dirichlet Process Mixture Model. Cambridge University Press.

GILKS, W., RICHARDSON, S. and SPIEGELHALTER, D. (1996): *Markov chain Monte Carlo in practice.* Chapman and Hall.

GREEN, P.J. and RICHARDSON, S. (2001): Modelling heterogeneity with and without the Dirichlet process. *Scandinavian Journal of Statistics, 28(2):355–375.*

ISHWARAN, H. and JAMES, L. (2001): Gibbs sampling methods for stick-breaking priors. *J. Amer. Statist. Assoc., 96:161–173.*

KAUFMAN, L. and ROUSSEEUW, P.J. (2005): *Finding groups in data : an introduction to cluster analysis.* Wiley series in probability and mathematical statistics. Wiley-Interscience, Hoboken, N.J..

MEDVEDOVIC, M. and SIVAGANESAN, S. (2002): Bayesian infinite mixture model based clustering of gene expression profiles. *Bioinformatics, 18(9):1194–206.*

MOLITOR, J., PAPATHOMAS, M., JERRETT, M. and RICHARDSON, S. (accepted): Bayesian profile regression with an application to the national survey of children's health.

NEAL, R.M. (2000): Markov chain sampling methods for Dirichlet process mixture models. *Journal of Computational and Graphical Statistics, 9(2):249–265.*

NOBLE, M. WRIGHT, G, DIBBEN, C., SMITH, G., MCLENNAN, D., ANTTILA, G. and SDRC TEAM (2004): *The English Indices of Deprivation.* Office of the Deputy Prime Minister, Neighbourhood Renewal Unit.

R DEVELOPMENT CORE TEAM (2006): *R: A Language and Environment for Statistical Computing.* R Foundation for Statistical Computing, Vienna, Austria. URL http://www.R-project.org.

References

Assessing the Association between Environmental Exposures and Human Health

Linda J. Young[1], Carol A. Gotway[2], Kenneth K. Lopiano[1], Greg Kearney[2], and Chris DuClos[3]

[1] Department of Statistics, IFAS, University of Florida,
   Gainesville FL 32611-0339 USA, *LJYoung@ufl.edu, klopiano@ufl.edu*
[2] U.S. Centers for Disease Control & Prevention
   Atlanta, GA USA *cdg7@cdc.gov, irr8cdc.gov*

Abstract. In environmental health studies, health effects, environmental exposures, and potential confounders are seldom collected during the study on the same set of units. Some, if not all of the variables, are often obtained from existing programs and databases. Suppose environmental exposure is measured at points, but health effects are recorded on areal units. Further assume that a regression analysis the explores the association between health and environmental exposure is to be conducted at the areal level. Prior to analysis, the information collected on exposure at points is used to predict exposure at the areal level, introducing uncertainty in exposure for the analysis units. Estimation of the regression coefficient associated with exposure and its standard error is considered here. A simulation study is used to provide insight into the effects of predicting exposure. Open issues are discussed.

Keywords: modified areal unit problem, change of support, errors in variables

1 Introduction

The U.S. Centers for Disease Control's (CDC's) Environmental Public Health Tracking (EPHT) program uses data from existing databases and on-going programs to relate public health to environmental exposures and hazards. The data used in any one study generally come from multiple sources. The original studies giving rise to the data may have used different observational units, each of which is different from the one of interest. The process of linking data on a common spatial scale and then performing a regression to assess the association between public health and environmental exposures or hazards presents numerous statistical challenges. Here we focus on the proper measure of uncertainty associated with the regression coefficient corresponding to the environmental exposure when that exposure is observed at points (monitors) but health effects are recorded for areal units (counties) and analysis is to be conducted at the areal level.

Here we use data collected in support of the EPHT program to motivate our work. In section 2, a motivating study, typical of those in the EPHT

Y. Lechevallier, G. Saporta (eds.), *Proceedings of COMPSTAT'2010*,
DOI 10.1007/978-3-7908-2604-3_26, © Springer-Verlag Berlin Heidelberg 2010

program, is presented. A review of the change-of-support problem is given in Section 3 followed by the resulting analytical challenges it presents in Section 4. Based on a small simulation study of the estimation of the regression coefficient associated with environmental exposure and its standard error, some of the statistical issues arising when using environmental data collected at points to draw inference about the association between health and environmental exposure at the areal level are highlighted in Section 5. In the final section, some of the issues that must be resolved before we can reliably present such analyses as part of EPHT are discussed. Although our focus is on data collected in support of the EPHT program, the methodology, concepts, and key ideas we present pertain to most studies linking health with environmental factors.

2   The Study and Supporting Data

Two of the core measures of the EPHT program are ozone and myocardial infarction (MI). Working with the data from August, 2005, we focus on modeling the association between ozone (environmental exposure) and MI (health outcome) at the county level. When assessing the potential association between ozone and MI, care must be taken to account for potential confounders. The ozone, MI, and socio-demographic data used in this effort have been gathered from five different sources.

Ozone measurements, recorded from a network of air monitors placed throughout the state, were obtained from Floridas Department of Environmental Protection (FDEP). During the study period of August 2005, ozone data were available from 56 monitors. Thus, some of the 67 counties have one or more ozone monitors; others have none. The maximum of the daily maximum 8-hour average ozone values during a month is used as the monthly data value for a particular monitor.

Florida's Department of Health (FDOH) has a data-sharing agreement (DSA) with Florida's Agency for Health Care Administration (AHCA), providing us with access to two data sources: confidential hospitalization records and emergency room records. The hospitalization records contain all admissions to Florida's public and private hospitals where either the primary or secondary cause of admission was MI (ICD-10 codes 410.0–414.0). Non-Florida residents were excluded from the analysis. Consistent with our DSA, AHCA provided both the zip code and county of residence for each patients record. Selected patient demographic information is also recorded, including sex, age, and race/ethnicity.

Meteorological data, such as relative humidity, temperature, and pressure, were available from the EPA's space-time Bayesian fusion model (McMillan, et al. (2009). This model predicts the daily minimum, maximum, and average value for each variable on a 12-km grid across the U.S.

Selected sociodemographic data were obtained from two sources: the U.S. Census Bureau and CDC's Behavioral Risk Factor Surveillance System (BRFSS). Census estimates at the state and county level are available on an annual basis. BRFSS is a state-based system of health surveys that collect annual information on health risk behaviors, preventive health practices, and health-care access, primarily related to chronic disease and injury.

Florida's population was used as the comparison standard to calculate the number of expected MI cases. This gave an MI standardized event ratio (MI SER), defined as the ratio of the number of observed MI cases to that expected among the Florida population, for each county and each month. The goal of the analysis is to evaluate the association between public health (MI SER) and environmental exposure (ozone) at the county level, adjusting for potential confounders. The first step is to link all data at the county level, a change of support problem as discussed in the next section.

3 Change of Support

As with our motivating study, health data collected for EPHT are routinely reported for counties so that confidentiality is maintained. Whenever grouped (or *ecological*) data are used in an analysis, the assumption made is that the observed relationships in the aggregated data hold at the individual level. In numerous epidemiological studies, ecological analyses have proven useful. Early ecological analyses included works by Snow (1855) who related the incidence of cholera to groundwater and Dean (1938) who studied the association between dental caries and endemic fluorosis. In 1950, Robinson illustrated the potential *ecological fallacy* of assuming that inferences for grouped data hold for individual data. In exploring the association between being born in a foreign country and illiteracy, he found a correlation of 0.118 at the individual level, but a correlation of −0.526 when working with state-level data, leading him to question the use of ecological data for inferential purposes.

The broader challenge of drawing inference on one set of units given data that are collected on another set of units has been discovered by researchers in numerous disciplines (Gotway and Young (2002)). This problem is prevalent in the study of human populations, leading geographers Openshaw and Taylor (1979) to coin the term: the Modifiable Areal Unit Problem (MAUP). Because our approach is a geostatistical one, we will refer to it as the Change of Support (COS) problem.

COS has two aspects. The first, called the "scale effect" or the "aggregation effect," is that different results and inferences are obtained when the same set of data is grouped into increasingly larger areal units. The second, known as the "zoning effect" or the "grouping effect," is the variability in results and inference that is due to alternative formations of the areal units. We will encounter the aggregation effect as we move from points to counties, but we must also recognize that the inference could differ if the county boundaries changed.

4   Spatial regression models with misaligned data

Let $\boldsymbol{x} = (x(\boldsymbol{s}_1), x(\boldsymbol{s}_2), \ldots x(\boldsymbol{s}_n))'$, be the vector of exposure measurements (ozone) observed at point spatial locations $\boldsymbol{s}_1, \boldsymbol{s}_2, \ldots \boldsymbol{s}_n$, (air quality monitors) and let $\boldsymbol{y} = (y(\mathrm{B}_1), y(\mathrm{B}_2), \ldots y(\mathrm{B}_m))'$ be the vector of health observations associated with counties $\mathrm{B}_1, \mathrm{B}_2, \ldots \mathrm{B}_m$.

Spatial statistical methods assume that the environmental exposure (ozone) is a realization of a random spatial process: $\{X(s)|s \in D \subset \Re^2\}$, where $X(\boldsymbol{s})$ is a random variable at a known location $\boldsymbol{s}$, and $\boldsymbol{s}$ varies smoothly over region D, which is the state of Florida for the motivating study. Assume the following spatial model for the exposure variable (ozone):

$$x(\boldsymbol{s}) = \boldsymbol{\mu_x}(\boldsymbol{s}) + \boldsymbol{e_x}(\boldsymbol{s}) = \boldsymbol{T}(\boldsymbol{s})\boldsymbol{\gamma} + \boldsymbol{e_x}(\boldsymbol{s}), \tag{1}$$

where $\boldsymbol{T}(\boldsymbol{s})$ is the $(n \times p)$ matrix of covariates that depend on spatial locations $\boldsymbol{s}$, $\boldsymbol{\gamma}$ is a $(p \times 1)$ vector of parameters, and $\boldsymbol{e_x}$ is an $(n \times 1)$ vector of errors. Whereas Madsen, et al. (2008), Gryparis, et al. (2008), and Szpiro, et al. (2009) assumed that that $\boldsymbol{x}$ has a constant mean in the spatial domain ($\mu_{\boldsymbol{x}}(\boldsymbol{s}) = \mu, \boldsymbol{s} \in D$), we assume that $\mu_{\boldsymbol{x}}(\boldsymbol{s})$ is a linear combination of explanatory covariates. Because environmental exposure is measured on the point scale, but inference is to be conducted for areal units, environmental exposure must be predicted for the areal units.

This change-of-support problem can be addressed via block kriging (Schabenberger and Gotway (2004)), and has been used in relating public health to environmental exposures (Gotway and Young (2007), Young and Gotway (2007), Young, et al. (2009a), and Young, et al. (2009)). In this setting, the inferential goal in universal block kriging is the prediction of the spatial average of environmental exposure

$$x_i(\mathrm{B}) = \frac{1}{|\mathrm{B}_i|} \int_{\mathrm{B}_i} x(\boldsymbol{s}) d\boldsymbol{s} \tag{2}$$

from the point-support (monitor) measurements $x(\boldsymbol{s}_1), x(\boldsymbol{s}_2), \ldots, x(\boldsymbol{s}_n)$, where $|\mathrm{B}_i|$ is the volume of the areal regions (counties) $\mathrm{B}_i \subset \mathrm{D}, i = 1, 2, \ldots, m$, that form the spatial support of $x(\mathrm{B}_1), x(\mathrm{B}_2), \ldots, x(\mathrm{B}_m)$.

The moments of $x(\mathrm{B})$ can be derived from the underlying process. Thus, because $E(x(\boldsymbol{s})) = \boldsymbol{T}(\boldsymbol{s})\boldsymbol{\gamma}$,

$$E(x(\mathrm{B})) = \boldsymbol{T}(\mathrm{B})'\boldsymbol{\gamma},$$

and

$$T_j(\mathrm{B}) = \frac{1}{|\mathrm{B}|} \int_{\mathrm{B}} T_j(\boldsymbol{u}) d\boldsymbol{u}, j = 1, 2, \ldots, m.$$

Note that the regression coefficients $\gamma = (\gamma_1, \gamma_2, \ldots \gamma_p)'$ are invariant to the change of support if it is also reflected in the explanatory variables (Arbia (2009), Cressie (1996)). The $\text{cov}(x(\mathrm{B}_i), x(\mathrm{B}_j))$ may be written as

$$\text{cov}(x(\mathrm{B}_i), x(\mathrm{B}_j)) = \bar{C}(\mathrm{B}_i, \mathrm{B}_j) = \frac{1}{|\mathrm{B}_i \| \mathrm{B}_i|} \int_{\mathrm{B}_j} \int_{\mathrm{B}_i} C(u, v) du dv$$

(see Schabenberger and Gotway (2004)). Note that the behavior of the covariances depends not only on the point suppot covariance, but also on the specific size, shape, and orientation of the blocks considered.

To predict environmental exposure $x(\mathrm{B})$ from the point samples $x(s_1)$, $x(s_2), \ldots, x(s_n)$, we use the spatial predictor:

$$\hat{x}(\mathrm{B}) = \sum_{k=1}^{n} \lambda_k x(s_k). \tag{3}$$

Minimizing prediction mean-squared error subject to unbiasedness constraints, the optimal weights $\{\lambda_i\}$ are obtained by solving

$$\sum_{k=1}^{n} \lambda_k C(s_i, s_k) - \sum_{j=1}^{p} m_j x_j(s_i) = \bar{C}(\mathrm{B}, s_i), i = 1, 2, \ldots, n \tag{4}$$

and

$$\sum_{i=1}^{n} \lambda_i x_j(s_i) = x_j(\mathrm{B}), j = 1, 2, \ldots, p. \tag{5}$$

The m_j are Lagrange multipliers from the constrained minimization, and $\bar{C}(\mathrm{B}, s_i)$ is the point-to-block covariance given by

$$\bar{C}(\mathrm{B}, s_i) = \text{cov}(x(\mathrm{B}), x(s_i)) = \frac{1}{|B|} \int_{\mathrm{B}} C(u, v) du dv \tag{6}$$

The point-to-point covariance function, $C(.)$, is assumed known for theoretical derivations, but is then estimated and modeled with a valid positive definite function based on the data. Thus, given environmental exposure observations at locations (monitors) with point support, block kriging can be used to predict the average value $\hat{x}(\mathrm{B})$ of the process at a larger scale, accounting for not only the size, bust also the shape of the orientation of the blocks (counties).

In EPHT and many other programs, the prediction of environmental exposure is only one step toward the final goal. Suppose that for the vector of observed environmental exposures x, there is a corresponding vector of health observations, $y = (y(s_1), y(s_2), \ldots y(s_n))'$ associated with spatial locations $s_1, s_2, \ldots s_n$. For simplicity, we assume a simple linear regression model for the relationship between environmental exposure and the health outcome:

$$y(s) = \beta_0 j + \beta_1 x(s) + e(s) \tag{7}$$

where j is a vector of ones, β_0 and β_1 are unknown regression parameters to be estimated, and $e(s) \sim N(0, \Sigma_e)$ is the error of the model. However, because health has been observed for counties and analysis is to be conducted at the county level, we have

$$y(B) = \beta_0 j + \beta_1 x(B) + e(B) \tag{8}$$

where $e(B) = \frac{1}{|B|} \int_{|B|} e(s)ds$. Although, as Robinson (1950) noted, the correlation coefficient tends to increase with aggregation, the regression coefficients β_0 and β_1 are invariant under change of support.

Because $x(B)$ is unknown and thus predicted using $\hat{x}(B)$ from observations at points, the resulting predicted values are generally smoother than the true ones. Recently, when working with misaligned point data, several (Madsen, et al. (2008), Gryparis, et al. (2009), Szpiro, et al. (2009)) have found that this smoothing can lead to bias and impact proper uncertainty assessment when the predicted values are used to estimate the association between health effects and environmental exposure. Here we build on the work by Young, et al. (2009a), which considers the effect of predicting environmental exposure for areal units based on point support.

Because the environmental exposure $x(B)$ in (8) is more variable than its smoothed predictor $\hat{x}(B)$, we have $x(B) = \hat{x}(B) + u(B)$, where $u(B) = x(B) - \hat{x}(B)$ is the error associated with predicting exposure. We assume that $u(B) \sim N(0, \Sigma_{u(B)})$ and is independent of $e_{x(B)}$. Thus the use of $\hat{x}(B)$ for $x(B)$ in model (8) results in Berkson error (Grpyaris, et al. (2008)). Covariates are typically used in the regression relating the health outcome values y to the predicted environmental exposure, thereby adjusting for confounders. However, a simpler model without covariates is considered for the simulation:

$$
\begin{aligned}
y(B) &= \beta_0 j + \beta_1 x(B) + e(B) \\
&= \beta_0 j + \beta_1 (\hat{x}(B) + u(B)) + e(B) \\
&= \beta_0 j + \beta_1 \hat{x}(B) + \beta_1 u(B) + e(B) \\
&= \beta_0 j + \beta_1 \hat{x}(B) + \eta(B)
\end{aligned}
\tag{9}
$$

where $\eta(B) = \beta_1 u(B) + e(B)$. Let $\hat{X} = (j\ \hat{x}(B))$ and $\beta = (\beta_0, \beta_1)$. If $\hat{x}(B)$ is an unbiased predictor of x, then

$$\hat{\beta}_{ols} = (\hat{X}'\hat{X})^{-1}\hat{X}'y, \tag{10}$$

the ordinary least squares (OLS) estimator of β, is unbiased. However, as described in Madsen, et al. (2008) and Gryparis, et al. (2009), substituting predicted environmental exposures for the true values in the regression expression leads to a correlated error structure,

$$\text{var}(\eta(B)) = \beta_1^2 \Sigma_{u(B)} \Sigma_{e(B)}. \tag{11}$$

Thus, the OLS variance of $\hat{\beta}_1$ is incorrect because it does not utilize the proper covariance matrix in equation (11) that results from the additional uncertainty induced by predicting the unknown x values. How important is it to account for this additional uncertainty? Because our ultimate goal is to have these methods adopted by state health departments with widely varying technological capacity, we would prefer to continue to use simple methods. Here we consider the two methods most commonly used today.

4.1   Traditional Krige and Regress (KR)

This is a common approach in analyses today. Assuming $\boldsymbol{\Sigma}_e = \sigma^2 \boldsymbol{I}$, the predicted values, $\hat{\boldsymbol{x}}$, of the unknown exposure values $\boldsymbol{x}$ are used in model (8) as if they were the true values, resulting in the OLS estimates of β_1 and its standard error. No adjustment for the additional uncertainty due to spatial prediction of $\boldsymbol{x}$ is made.

4.2   Traditional Krige and Regress with a General Covariance Structure (KRGC)

Using the predicted values $\hat{\boldsymbol{x}}$ instead of the true environmental exposure values $\boldsymbol{x}$ leads to a more complex covariance structure as in equation (11). Perhaps geostatistics and variography can be used to to model the spatial structure in the error term. Thus, this approach uses generalized least squares with a general variance-covariance matrix inferred through geostatistical techniques (Schabenberger and Gotway (2004)).

In KR, an assumption is that all of the spatial variability in $\boldsymbol{y}$ can be explained by the spatial variability in $\boldsymbol{x}$ so that, conditional on $\boldsymbol{x}$, the y's are independent, i.e., $\boldsymbol{\Sigma}_e = \sigma^2 \boldsymbol{I}$. Often researchers are unwilling to make that assumption and choose to use a general covariance structure, such as the exponential or spherical, to account for any additional spatial variability in the y's. Notice that this is equivalent to the KRGC. Whether attempting to account for errors in $\boldsymbol{x}$ or for additional spatial variability in $\boldsymbol{y}$, the KRGC is the same, and the cause of the more complex error structure cannot be attributed to either potential source. Further, because β_1 is the unknown parameter to be estimated and is part of the error structure, proper modeling of the error structure may be challenging.

KR and KRGC were used to analyze the Florida data discussed in Section 2 (see Table 1). A 12-km grid was used for block kriging.

Table 1. Estimates of $\hat{\beta}_1$ and the Standard Error of $\hat{\beta}_1$ for Florida

Estimation Method	$\hat{\beta}_1$	$s_{\hat{\beta}_1}$
KR	0.025	0.015
KRGC	0.038	0.017

5 Simulation Study

A simulation study was conducted to gain insight into the effect of moving from the point to the areal scale, with emphasis on the application at hand. When exploring the ozone data described in Section 2, a quadratic trend surface was estimated so that the estimated mean function based on equation (1) is

$$\hat{\mu}(s) = -747.71 + 53.77 * l - 0.911 l^2. \tag{12}$$

where l is the latitude of an exposure measurement. The error associated with fitting the trend surface was estimated to have an exponential covariance function with a scale of 50.1 and a range of 1. To link the MI SER with the ozone data, block kriging was conducted by predicting ozone onto a 12-km grid and then the predictions were averaged within each county to obtain an average maximum ozone value for that county. Then, the natural logarithm of MI SER, denoted by ln(SER), was modeled. The covariates used in the analysis were the average monthly temperature, average monthly relative humidity, percent of county residents who smoke, percent of county residents with less than a high school education, and an indicator variable of whether or not the median income for the family was above the median income for the state. Adjusting for the covariates, the regression of ln(SER) on ozone produced estimates of the intercept and slope of -0.8 and 0.02, respectively. Assuming an independent error structure, the variance associated with the regression was estimated to be 2.3^2. This analysis and the resulting parameter estimates serve as the foundation for the simulation study below.

To explore the effect of change of support, the same 12-km grid used for block kriging was laid over the state of Florida. For each of 1000 simulations, a realization of ozone at the monitors and grid points was generated assuming that the estimated parameters were in fact the true values of the parameters, with one exception. Because the estimated coefficient on ozone, $\hat{\beta}_1$ was only 0.02, we used 0.2 for that coefficient in the simulation study. Given a realization of ozone, the health effects for the areal (county) units were generated in four different ways. In the first two, data were simulated for environmental exposure. Then, given a realization of ozone, the health effects were generated for each grid point according to model (7) with $\beta_0 = -0.8$, $\beta_1 = 0.2$, and normally distributed independent errors, each with a mean of zero and a variance of (1) 2.3^2 and (2) 3.2^2. To move from points to areas, the response y and the predicted environmental exposures $\hat{x}$ were block kriged as in equation (2) to obtain the areal health effects, y_B and the areal environmental exposures, $\hat{x}_B$, respectively. Then y_B was regressed on $\hat{x}_B$.

For the other two approaches, the true exposure values x were block-kriged to the areal level, and y_B was generated by conditioning on (1) the areal value for environmental exposure and (2) the exposure value at the centroid of the county. Then, for each approach, all but the monitor values of true exposure values were deleted, ozone was predicted at the areal level using block kriging, and y_B was regressed on $\hat{x}_B$.

When simulating the data, the true exposure model did not converge for about 4% of the data sets. We generated simulated data sets until 1000 sets for which the true exposure model did converge were obtained. For each of the data sets, we predicted environmental exposure (1) by block kriging and (2) by predicting exposure at the areal centroid. Then KR and KRGC were used for each data set. Because the results of KR and KRGC did not differ appreciably, we include only the results for KR in Table 1.

Table 2. Average $\bar{\hat{\beta}}_1$ and Variance $\hat{\sigma}^2_{\hat{\beta}_1}$ of the Estimates of β_1 and Average of the Estimated Variance $\bar{s}^2_{\hat{\beta}_1}$ of $\hat{\beta}_1$ for Areal Simulated Data Sets using KR

Model	Prediction	$\bar{\hat{\beta}}_1$	$\hat{\sigma}^2_{\hat{\beta}_1}$	$\bar{s}^2_{\hat{\beta}_1}$
Conditioning at Points and	Kriging	0.198	0.00101	0.000459
Averaging to Areal Level, $\sigma^2 = 2.3$	Centroid	0.180	0.000901	0.000438
Conditioning at Points and	Kriging	0.197	0.00116	0.000678
Averaging to Areal Level, $\sigma^2 = 3.2$	Centroid	0.179	0.00107	0.000638
Conditioning on Average	Kriging	0.197	0.00380	0.00334
Ozone	Centroid	0.180	0.00336	0.00304
Conditioning on Ozone	Kriging	0.206	0.00832	0.00757
at Centroid	Centroid	0.197	0.00670	0.00586

6   Discussion

Regardless of the manner in which y was modeled, the estimates of β_1 are slightly below the true parameter value $\beta_1 = 0.2$ when block kriging is used to estimate exposure. This may be the result of classical measurement error induced by the estimation of the parameters of the environmental exposure model (1), resulting in an attenuation towards zero (Carroll, et al. (2006), Szpiro, et al. (2009)). Here the bias is not of practical concern, regardless of the method by which health is modeled.

Because it is less computationally intensive to predict exposure at the areal centroid than it is to block krige to predict exposure as the average for the areal unit, analyses based on centroids are commonly conducted. From Table 2, it is evident that this is problematic because, unless health effects are conditional on exposure at the centroids, a downward bias of about 10% is observed. Thus, it is important to average exposure over the areas and to not use the simpler method of kriging at centroids.

Whether block kriging or using centroids to predict environmental exposure, the variances, and hence the standard errors of $\hat{\beta}_1$ exhibit a strong downward bias. Methods have been proposed for correcting this bias when exposure and health are observed at misaligned points. These methods need to be extended for the case where health is observed for area units and trend is present in exposure.

References

ARBIA, G. (1986): The modifiable areal unit problem and the spatial autocorrelation problem: Towards a joint approach. *Metron 44: 391-407.*

CRESSIE, N. (1996): Change of support and the modifiable areal unit problem. *Geographical Systems 3: 159-180.*

DEAN, H.T. (1938): Endemic fluorosis and its relation to dental caries. *Public Health Reports 53: 1443-52.*

CARROLL, R.J., RUPPERT, D., STEFANSKI, L.A., and CRAINICEANU, C.M. (2006): *Measurement Error in Nonlinear Models: A Modern Perspective,* 2nd Ed. Chapman & Hall/CRC: Boca Raton, Florida.

GOTWAY, C.A. and YOUNG, L.J. (2002): Combining incompatible spatial data. *Journal of the American Statistical Association 97: 632-648.*

GOTWAY, C.A. and YOUNG L.J. (2004): A spatial view of the ecological inference problem. In *Ecological Inference: New Methodological Strategies,* King G, Tanner M, Rasen O (eds). Cambridge University Press: New York. Pp. 233-244.

GRYPARIS, A., PACIOREK, C.J., ZEKA, A., SCHWARTZ, J. and COULL, B. (2009): Measurement error caused by spatial misalignment in environmental epidemiology. *Biostatistics 10:258-274; doi:10.1093/biostatistics/kxn033.*

MADSEN, L., RUPPERT, D. and ALTMAN, N.S. (2008): Regression with Spatially Misaligned Data. *Environmetrics 19, 453-467*

McMILLAN, N.J., HOLLAND, D.M., MORARA, M. and FENG, J. (2009): Combining numerical model output and particulate data using Bayesian space-time modeling. *Environmetrics DOI: 10.1002/env.984.*

OPENSHAW, S. and TAYLOR, P. (1979): A million or so correlation coefficients. In *Statistical Methods in the Spatial Sciences,* Wrigley N (ed.). Pion: London. Pp. 127-144.

ROBINSON, W.S. (1950):. Ecological correlations and the behavior of individuals. *American Sociological Review 15: 351-357.*

SCHABENBERGER, O. and GOTWAY, C.A. (2004): *Statistical Methods for Spatial Data Analysis.* Chapman & Hall/CRC: Boca Raton, Florida.

SNOW, J. (1855): *On the Mode of Communication of Cholera.* Churchill, London. Reprinted by Hafner, New York, 1965.

SZPIRO, A.A., SHEPPARD, L., and LUMLEY, T. (2009): Efficient measurement error correction with spatially misaligned data. *University of Washington Biostatistics Working Paper Series.* Paper 350.

YOUNG, L.J. and GOTWAY, C.A. (2007): Linking spatial data from different sources: The effect of change of support. *Stochastic Environmental Research and Risk Assessment 21: 589-600.*

YOUNG, L.J., GOTWAY, C.A., KEARNEY, G., and DUCLOS, C. (2009A): Assessing uncertainty in support-adjusted spatial misalignment problems. *Communications in Statistics - Theory and Methods 38:1-16.*

YOUNG, L.J., GOTWAY, C.A., YANG, J., KEARNEY, G., and DUCLOS, C. (2009B): Linking health and environmental data in geographical analysis: Its so much more than centroids. *Spatial and Spatio-temporal Epidemiology 1: 73-84.*

Part XIII

ARS Session (Financial) Time Series

Semiparametric Seasonal Cointegrating Rank Selection

Byeongchan Seong[1], Sung K. Ahn[2], and Sinsup Cho[3]

[1] Department of Statistics, Chung-Ang University,
   221, Heukseok-dong, Dongjak-gu, Seoul 156-756, Korea, *bcseong@cau.ac.kr*
[2] Department of Management and Operations, Washington State University,
   Pullman, WA 99164-4736, USA, *ahn@wsu.edu*
[3] Department of Statistics, Seoul National University,
   Seoul 151-747, Korea, *sinsup@snu.ac.kr*

Abstract. This paper considers the issue of seasonal cointegrating rank selection by information criteria as the extension of Cheng and Phillips (The Econometrics Journal (2009), Vol. 12, pp. S83–S104). The method does not require the specification of lag length in vector autoregression, is convenient in empirical work, and is in a semiparametric context because it allows for a general short memory error component in the model with only lags related to error correction terms. Some limit properties of usual information criteria are given for the rank selection and small Monte Carlo simulations are conducted to evaluate the performances of the criteria.

Keywords: seasonal cointegrating rank, information criteria, nonparametric, model selection

1 Introduction

Various procedures have been proposed to determine cointegrating (CI) ranks in nonseasonal and seasonal models. They are mostly the likelihood ratio type of tests, considered by Johansen (1996) for nonseasonal cointegration, Johansen and Schaumburg (1999), Cubadda (2001), and Seong et al. (2006) for seasonal cointegration, among others. However, these procedures are based on parametric models which require the specification of a full model such as lag length in vector autoregression and can occur the misspecification of CI rank possibly through an inappropriate specification of the lag length. Recently, the works by Phillips (2008), and Cheng and Phillips (2008, 2009) consider semiparametric models as alternatives to parametric ones in determining CI rank. They regard CI rank as an order parameter for which information criteria are particularly well suited since there are only a finite number of possible choices.

In this paper, we extend the issue of cointegrating rank selection by information criteria to seasonal models, by using Gaussian reduced rank (GRR) procedure of Ahn and Reinsel (1994). The GRR estimation has a special

Y. Lechevallier, G. Saporta (eds.), *Proceedings of COMPSTAT'2010*,
DOI 10.1007/978-3-7908-2604-3_27, © Springer-Verlag Berlin Heidelberg 2010

characteristic that it simultaneously imposes rank conditions at all existing
seasonal unit roots (Seong and Yi (2008)). If we use a partial regression procedure, often used by the previous literature such as Johansen and Schaumburg
(1999), it is impossible to construct the simultaneous estimation because it
ignores the constraints of reduced ranks (i.e., cointegrated structures) of the
other unit roots except one unit root focused by the partial regression. Note
that seasonal CI rank tests, performed independently by focusing on one unit
root at a time, can result in a seriously inflated Type I error in terms of multiple hypothesis testing (Seong (2009)). Therefore, this paper combines three
advantages: (i) simultaneous estimation from the GRR, (ii) semiparametric
model without the specification of complete form, and (iii) convenience for
practical implementation.

The paper is organized as follows. In section 2, the semiparametric error
correction model (ECM) is presented for seasonal cointegration. The asymptotic results are given in section 3. In section 4, small Monte Carlo simulations are conducted to evaluate performances of the proposed methods.
Conclusions are drawn in section 5.

2   The semiparametric seasonal ECM

We consider the following semiparametric seasonal ECM:

$$
\begin{aligned}
Z_t =& A_1 B_1 U_{t-1} + A_2 B_2 V_{t-1} + (A_3 B_4 + A_4 B_3) W_{t-1} \\
&+ (A_4 B_4 - A_3 B_3) W_{t-2} + e_t,
\end{aligned}
\tag{1}
$$

where X_t is an m-vector time series with $Z_t = (1 - L^4) X_t$ stationary,

$$
U_t = (1 + L)(1 + L^2) X_t, V_t = (1 - L)(1 + L^2) X_t, W_t = (1 - L^2) X_t,
$$

and A_j and B_j are $m \times r_{0j}$ and $r_{0j} \times m$ matrices, respectively, with rank
equal to r_{0j} for $j = 1, \cdots, 4$, and $r_{03} = r_{04}$. The error term e_t is weakly
dependent stationary time series with zero mean and continuous spectral
density matrix $f_e(\lambda)$. We assume that the initial value X_0 is fixed and, for
brevity, X_t is observed on a quarterly basis. Models with the other seasonal
periods, e.g., monthly, can be easily implemented as in Ahn et al. (2004). Note
that r_{01}, r_{02}, and $r_{03}(r_{04})$ denote the CI ranks at seasonal unit roots 1, -1,
and $i(-i)$, respectively, (i.e., frequencies 0, π, and $\pi/2(3\pi/2)$, respectively),
and $B_1 U_t$, $B_2 V_t$, $(B_3 + B_4 L) W_t$, and $(B_4 - B_3 L) W_t$ are stationary processes,
i.e., CI relationships.

As in Phillips (2008) and Cheng and Phillips (2009), we treat model (1)
semiparametrically with regard to e_t and identify the seasonal CI ranks r_{01},
r_{02}, and $r_{03}(r_{04})$ directly and simultaneously in model (1) by information criteria and the GRR estimation. Specifically, we identify the ranks as follows:
model (1) is estimated by the GRR for all combinations of $\mathbf{r} = (r_1, r_2, r_3)$
with $r_j = 0, 1, \cdots, m$ $(j = 1, 2, 3)$ just as if e_t were a martingale difference,

and the combination of $\mathbf{r} = (r_1, r_2, r_3)$ is chosen to minimize the corresponding information criteria as if model (1) were a correctly specified parametric framework up to the ranks parameter $\mathbf{r}$. Thus, the selection method is convenient for practical implementation in empirical work because no explicit account is taken of the weak dependence structure of e_t in the process. The criterion used to evaluate the seasonal CI ranks takes the following form:

$$IC(\mathbf{r}) = \log\left|\hat{\Sigma}(\mathbf{r})\right| + C_n n^{-1}\{(2mr_1 - r_1^2) + (2mr_2 - r_2^2) + 2(2mr_3 - r_3^2)\}, \quad (2)$$

where $\hat{\Sigma}(\mathbf{r})$ denotes the residual covariance matrix from the GRR and coefficient $C_n = \log n$, $2\log\log n$, or 2 corresponds to the BIC (Schwarz (1978)), HQ (Hannan and Quinn (1979)), and AIC (Akaike (1973)) penalties, respectively. Note that, in equation (2), the degrees of freedom terms $2mr_1 - r_1^2$, $2mr_2 - r_2^2$, and $2(2mr_3 - r_3^2)$ account for the $2mr_j (j = 1, 2, 3, 4)$ elements of the matrices A_j and B_j that have to be estimated, adjusted for the r_j^2 restrictions on B_j that ensure a unique parameterization.

For each combination $\mathbf{r} = (r_1, r_2, r_3)$ with $r_j = 0, 1, \cdots, m$ $(j = 1, 2, 3)$, we estimate the $m \times r_j$ matrices A_j and B_j by the GRR estimation, denoted by $\hat{A}_j$ and $\hat{B}_j$, and, for use in equation (2), we form the corresponding residual covariance matrices

$$\hat{\Sigma}(\mathbf{r}) = n^{-1}\sum_{t=4}^{n}\hat{e}_t\hat{e}_t' \text{ for } r_j = 0, 1, \cdots, m \ (j = 1, 2, 3),$$

where

$$\begin{aligned}\hat{e}_t =& Z_t - \hat{A}_1\hat{B}_1 U_{t-1} - \hat{A}_2\hat{B}_2 V_{t-1} \\ & - (\hat{A}_3\hat{B}_4 + \hat{A}_4\hat{B}_3)W_{t-1} - (\hat{A}_4\hat{B}_4 - \hat{A}_3\hat{B}_3)W_{t-2}\end{aligned}$$

and $r_j = 0$ and $r_j = m$ imply that $A_j B_j' = O_m$ and $B_j = I_m$, respectively. Model evaluation based on $IC(\mathbf{r})$ then leads to the seasonal CI ranks selection criterion

$$\hat{\mathbf{r}} = \underset{0 \le r_1, r_2, r_3 \le m}{\arg\min} \ IC(\mathbf{r}). \quad (3)$$

Similarly in the Cheng and Phillips (2009), the information criterion $IC(\mathbf{r})$ is expected to be weakly consistent for selecting the CI ranks $\mathbf{r} = (r_1, r_2, r_3)$ provided that the penalty term in equation (2) satisfies the weak requirements that $C_n \to \infty$ and $C_n/n \to 0$ as $n \to \infty$. No minimum expansion rate for C_n such as $\log\log n$ is required and no more complex parametric model needs to be estimated. The approach is therefore quite straightforward for practical implementation.

3 Asymptotic results

We consider the weak consistency of the information criteria for selecting the true seasonal CI ranks $\mathbf{r}_0 = (r_{01}, r_{02}, r_{03})$ under suitable regular conditions which are standard in the study of linear process condition of the innovations, and seasonal cointegration. The following theorem can be conjectured from that of Cheng and Phillips (2009).

Theorem 1. *Under suitable assumptions,*
(a) the criterion $IC(\mathbf{r})$ is weakly consistent for selecting the seasonal CI ranks provided $C_n \to \infty$ and $C_n/n \to 0$ as $n \to \infty$;
(b) the asymptotic distribution of the AIC criterion is given by

$$\lim_{n\to\infty} P(\hat{\mathbf{r}}_{AIC} = \mathbf{r}_0) = \xi_1 > 0,$$

$$\lim_{n\to\infty} P(\hat{\mathbf{r}}_{AIC} = \mathbf{r}|\mathbf{r} \succ \mathbf{r}_0) = \xi_2 > 0,$$

$$and \lim_{n\to\infty} P(\hat{\mathbf{r}}_{AIC} = \mathbf{r}|\mathbf{r} \prec \mathbf{r}_0) = 0,$$

where $\mathbf{r}_1 \succ \mathbf{r}_2$ and $\mathbf{r}_1 \prec \mathbf{r}_2$ denote that all components of the vector $\mathbf{r}_1 - \mathbf{r}_2$ and $\mathbf{r}_2 - \mathbf{r}_1$, respectively, are positive.

Part (a) of theorem implies that all information criteria with $C_n \to \infty$ and $C_n/n \to 0$, such as BIC and HQ, are consistent for the selection of seasonal CI rank with semiparametric estimation approach, i.e., without the specification of a full model. Part (b) implies that AIC is inconsistent in that it asymptotically never underestimates CI ranks and, instead, asymptotically overestimates them. This outcome is analogous to the well-known overestimation tendency of AIC or the result of Cheng and Phillips (2009).

4   Monte Carlo simulations

Monte Carlo simulations are conducted to evaluate the performances of the information criteria in identifying seasonal CI ranks.

The first data generating process (DGP I) considered is the bivariate quarterly process modified from that of Ahn and Reinsel (1994):

$$(1 - L^4)X_t = A_1 B_1 U_{t-1} + A_2 B_2 V_{t-1} + A_4 B_2 W_{t-1} - A_3 B_2 W_{t-2} + e_t,$$

where

$A_1 = (0.6, 0.6)'$, $A_2 = (-0.4, 0.6)'$, $A_3 = (0.6, -0.6)'$, $A_4 = (0.4, -0.8)'$,
$B_1 = (1, -0.7)$, $B_2 = (1, 0.4)$.

Note that the characteristic roots are ± 1, $\pm i$, $0.9715 \pm 0.7328i$, and $-1.3508 \pm 0.3406i$ when e_t is regarded as a martingale difference and, then, X_t is seasonally cointegrated with CI rank of one at unit roots 1, -1, and i each.

In the second data generating process (DGP II), we consider the case without cointegration at any seasonal unit root,

$$(1 - L^4)X_t = e_t.$$

In both DGPs, the error process e_t is assumed, as in Cheng and Phillips (2008), to be AR(1), MA(1), and ARMA(1,1) errors, corresponding to the models

$$e_t = \psi I_m e_{t-1} + \eta_t, e_t = \eta_t + \phi I_m \eta_{t-1}, \text{ and } e_t = \psi I_m e_{t-1} + \eta_t + \phi I_m \eta_{t-1},$$

where $|\psi| < 1$, $|\phi| < 1$, and η_t are i.i.d. $N(0, \Sigma)$ with $\Sigma = \text{diag}\{1 + \theta, 1 - \theta\}$. The parameters are set to $\psi = \phi = 0.4$, and $\theta = 0.25$.

Table 1. Seasonal CI rank selection when DGP I with $e_t \sim AR(1)$

	BIC		HQ		AIC	
(r_1, r_2, r_3)	$T = 100$	$T = 400$	$T = 100$	$T = 400$	$T = 100$	$T = 400$
(0,0,0)	0	0	0	0	0	0
(0,1,0)	0	0	0	0	0	0
(0,2,0)	0	0	0	0	0	0
(0,0,1)	0	0	0	0	0	0
(0,1,1)	0	0	0	0	0	0
(0,2,1)	0	0	0	0	0	0
(0,0,2)	0	0	0	0	0	0
(0,1,2)	0	0	0	0	0	0
(0,2,2)	0	0	0	0	0	0
(1,0,0)	0	0	0	0	0	0
(1,1,0)	0	0	0	0	0	0
(1,2,0)	0	0	0	0	0	0
(1,0,1)	0	0	0	0	0	0
(1,1,1)	8688	9342	7228	7942	5194	5334
(1,2,1)	177	59	550	358	1050	1059
(1,0,2)	0	0	0	0	0	0
(1,1,2)	605	332	1154	979	1656	1692
(1,2,2)	12	2	83	37	336	319
(2,0,0)	0	0	0	0	0	0
(2,1,0)	0	0	0	0	0	0
(2,2,0)	0	0	0	0	0	0
(2,0,1)	0	0	0	0	0	0
(2,1,1)	474	253	801	589	1145	980
(2,2,1)	14	3	64	21	243	214
(2,0,2)	0	0	0	0	0	0
(2,1,2)	30	9	108	73	293	333
(2,2,2)	0	0	12	1	83	69
Total	10000	10000	10000	10000	10000	10000

We generate 10,000 replications of the sample sizes with $T = 100$ and 400. We use initial values that are set to zero, but discard the first 50 observations in order to eliminate dependence on the starting conditions. The performances of the criteria BIC, HQ, and AIC are investigated for the samples sizes and the results are summarized in Tables 1 and 2 which show the results for DGP I and DGP II, respectively. The tables display the results for the model with AR(1) error. We omit the tables for that with the other errors because similar results are observed.

From Tables 1, as expected from Theorem 1, all the information criteria are generally minimized when selected seasonal CI ranks coincide with true ranks, i.e., $(r_1, r_2, r_3) = (1, 1, 1)$. An interesting thing is that they never select the case that at least one rank among CI ranks is underestimated and, then, the criteria have a tendency to overestimate ranks. The tendency is strengthened when only one rank is overestimated, such as $(r_1, r_2, r_3) = (1, 1, 2)$, $(1,2,1)$, and $(2,1,1)$. Nevertheless, BIC performs better than HQ and AIC which show a strong tendency to overestimate CI ranks.

Table 2. Seasonal CI rank selection when DGP II with $e_t \sim AR(1)$

	BIC		HQ		AIC	
(r_1, r_2, r_3)	$T = 100$	$T = 400$	$T = 100$	$T = 400$	$T = 100$	$T = 400$
(0,0,0)	6568	8508	2736	4233	526	522
(0,1,0)	543	160	1423	1091	1035	1005
(0,2,0)	5	0	58	38	116	125
(0,0,1)	1540	798	2051	1984	1063	1070
(0,1,1)	64	9	718	464	1819	1865
(0,2,1)	0	0	29	16	197	217
(0,0,2)	127	42	274	217	209	239
(0,1,2)	4	0	76	45	357	406
(0,2,2)	0	0	2	1	30	44
(1,0,0)	824	380	935	878	378	318
(1,1,0)	36	9	425	200	770	660
(1,2,0)	1	0	13	5	92	80
(1,0,1)	133	42	592	352	754	632
(1,1,1)	1	0	152	80	1150	1096
(1,2,1)	0	0	10	0	122	109
(1,0,2)	8	1	71	46	142	129
(1,1,2)	0	0	18	7	230	240
(1,2,2)	0	0	0	0	22	24
(2,0,0)	120	48	191	188	122	131
(2,1,0)	6	2	82	46	213	257
(2,2,0)	0	0	4	1	22	36
(2,0,1)	19	1	90	81	204	225
(2,1,1)	0	0	27	16	278	391
(2,2,1)	0	0	1	0	42	32
(2,0,2)	1	0	16	8	40	47
(2,1,2)	0	0	6	3	62	94
(2,2,2)	0	0	0	0	5	6
Total	10000	10000	10000	10000	10000	10000

As underestimation of CI ranks cannot occur in DGP II, we can analysis overestimation better than in DGP I. From Table 2, we observe similar results to Table 1 but the overestimation by AIC is noticeably strong, especially, in that AIC selects $(r_1, r_2, r_3) = (0, 1, 0)$, $(0, 0, 1)$, $(0, 1, 1)$, and $(1,1,1)$ comparatively often, instead of true ranks $(r_1, r_2, r_3) = (0, 0, 0)$. This tendency is noticeably attenuated when CI rank is overestimated at unit root 1.

Note that, from Tables 1 and 2, we can conjecture the results that the information criteria will give when we use the partial regression procedure by Johansen and Schaumburg (1999) instead of the GRR. As the partial regression is performed by focusing on one unit root by regarding the ranks of the other unit roots as full ranks, the selection frequencies at the cases $(r_1, r_2, r_3) = (0, 2, 2)$, $(1,2,2)$, and $(2,2,2)$ can show the conjecture.

5   Conclusions

In this paper, we show that information criteria can consistently select seasonal CI ranks if they satisfy weak conditions on the expansion rate of the penalty coefficient, as extension of nonseasonal model in Cheng and Phillips (2009) to seasonal. The method by the criteria offers substantial convenience to the empirical researcher because it is robust to weak dependence of error term.

References

AHN, S. K., CHO, S., and SEONG, B. C. (2004): Inference of seasonal cointegration: Gaussian reduced rank estimation and tests for various types of cointegration. *Oxford Bulletin of Economics and Statistics 66, 261–284.*

AHN, S. K., and REINSEL, G. C. (1994): Estimation of partially nonstationary vector autoregressive models with seasonal behavior. *Journal of Econometrics 62, 317–350.*

AKAIKE, H. (1973): Information theory and an extension of the maximum likelihood principle. In B. N. Petrov and F. Csaki (Eds.): *Second International Symposium on Information Theory.* Budapest: Akademiai Kiado.

CHENG, X. and PHILLIPS, P. C. B. (2008): Cointegrating rank selection in models with time-varying variance. *Cowles Foundation Discussion Paper No. 1688.*

CHENG, X. and PHILLIPS, P. C. B. (2009): Semiparametric cointegrating rank selection. *The Econometrics Journal 12, S83–S104.*

CUBADDA, G. (2001): Complex reduced rank models for seasonally cointegrated time series. *Oxford Bulletin of Economics and Statistics 63, 497–511.*

HANNAN, E. J. and QUINN, B. G. (1979): The determination of the order of an autoregression. *Journal of the Royal Statistical Society, Series B, 41, 190–195.*

JOHANSEN, S. (1996): *Likelihood-based inference in cointegrated vector autoregressive models, 2nd ed..* Oxford University Press, Oxford.

JOHANSEN, S., and SCHAUMBURG, E. (1999): Likelihood analysis of seasonal cointegration. *Journal of Econometrics 88, 301–339.*

PHILLIPS, P. C. B. (2008): Unit root model selection. *Journal of the Japan Statistical Society 38, 65–74.*

SCHWARZ, G. (1978): Estimating the dimension of a model. *Annals of Statistics 6, 461–464.*

SEONG, B. (2009): Bonferroni Correction for Seasonal Cointegrating Ranks. *Economics Letters 103, 42–44.*

SEONG, B., CHO, S., and AHN, S. K. (2006): Maximum eigenvalue test for seasonal cointegrating ranks. *Oxford Bulletin of Economics and Statistics 68, 497–514.*

SEONG, B., and YI, Y. J. (2008): Joint Test for Seasonal Cointegrating Ranks. *Communications of the Korean Statistical Society 15, 719–726.*

Estimating Factor Models for Multivariate Volatilities: An Innovation Expansion Method

Jiazhu Pan[1], Wolfgang Polonik[2], and Qiwei Yao[3]

[1] Department of Mathematics and Statistics, University of Strathclyde
   26 Richmond Street, Glasgow, G1 1XH, UK, *jiazhu.pan@strath.ac.uk*
[2] Division of Statistics, University of California at Davis
   Davis, CA 95616, USA, *wpolonik@ucdavis.edu*
[3] Department of Statistics, London School of Economics
   London WC2A 2AE, UK, *q.yao@lse.ac.uk*

Abstract. We introduce an innovation expansion method for estimation of factor models for conditional variance (volatility) of a multivariate time series. We estimate the factor loading space and the number of factors by a stepwise optimization algorithm on expanding the "white noise space". Simulation and a real data example are given for illustration.

Keywords: dimension reduction, factor models, multivariate volatility

1 Introduction

Factor modelling plays an important role in the analysis of high-dimensional multivariate time series(see Sargent and Sims (1977); Geweke (1977)) because it is both flexible and parsimonious. Most of factor analysis in the literature is for the mean and conditional mean of a multivariate time series and panel data, see Pan and Yao (2008) and a series of papers of article by Forni, Hallin, Lippi and Reichlin (2000,2004), and Hallin and Liška (2007).

For the conditional variance, which is so-called volatility, the multivariate generalized autoregressive conditional heteroskedastic (GARCH) models are commonly used, see Engle and Kroner (1995), Engle (2002), Engle & Sheppard (2001). But a multivariate GARCH model often has too many parameters so that it is difficult to estimate the model, which is a high-dimensional optimization problem. Factor models for volatility are useful tools to overcome the overparametrisation problem, e.g. Factor-ARCH (Engle, Ng and Rothschild 1990).

In this paper, we consider a frame work of factor analysis for the multivariate volatility, including factor ARCH as a special case. We introduce a innovation expansion method for the estimation of the factor loading space and the number of factors. Our method can change a high-dimensional optimization problem to a stepwise optimization algorithm by expanding the "white noise space" (innovation space) one step each time.

Y. Lechevallier, G. Saporta (eds.), *Proceedings of COMPSTAT'2010*,
DOI 10.1007/978-3-7908-2604-3_28, © Springer-Verlag Berlin Heidelberg 2010

2   Models and methodology

Let $\{Y_t\}$ be a $d \times 1$ time series, and $E(Y_t|\mathcal{F}_{t-1}) = 0$, where $\mathcal{F}_t = \sigma(Y_t, Y_{t-1}, \cdots)$. Assume that $E(Y_t Y_t^\tau)$ exists, and we use the notation $\Sigma_y(t) = var(Y_t|\mathcal{F}_{t-1})$. Pan et al. (2009) consider a common factor model

$$Y_t = AX_t + \varepsilon_t, \tag{1}$$

where X_t is a $r \times 1$ time series, $r < d$ is unknown, A is a $d \times r$ unknown constant matrix, $\{\varepsilon_t\}$ is a sequence of i.i.d. innovations with mean 0 and covariance matrix Σ_ε, and ε_t is independent of X_t and $\mathcal{F}_{t-1}$. This assumes that the volatility dynamics of Y is determined effectively by a lower dimensional volatility dynamics of X_t plus the static variation of ε_t, as

$$\Sigma_y(t) = A\Sigma_x(t)A^\tau + \Sigma_\varepsilon, \tag{2}$$

where $\Sigma_x(t) = var(X_t|\mathcal{F}_{t-1})$. The component variables of X_t are called the factors. There is no loss of generality in assuming $\mathrm{rk}(A) = r$ and requiring the column vectors of $A = (a_1, \cdots, a_r)$ to be orthonormal, i.e. $A^\tau A = I_r$, where I_r denotes the $r \times r$ identity matrix.

We are concerned with the estimation for the factor loading space $\mathcal{M}(A)$, which is uniquely defined by the model, rather than the matrix A itself. This is equivalent to the estimation for orthogonal complement $\mathcal{M}(B)$, where B is a $d \times (d-r)$ matrix for which (A, B) forms a $d \times d$ orthogonal matrix, i.e. $B^\tau A = 0$ and $B^\tau B = I_{d-r}$. Now it follows from (1) that

$$B^\tau Y_t = B^\tau \varepsilon_t. \tag{3}$$

Hence $B^\tau Y_t$ are homoscedastic components since

$$E\{B^\tau Y_t Y_t^\tau B|\mathcal{F}_{t-1}\} = E\{B^\tau \varepsilon_t \varepsilon_t^\tau B\} = E\{B^\tau Y_t Y_t^\tau B\} = B^\tau var(Y_t)B.$$

This implies that

$$B^\tau E[\{Y_t Y_t^\tau - var(Y_t)\}I(Y_{t-k} \in C)]B = 0, \tag{4}$$

for any $t, k \geq 1$ and any measurable $C \subset R^d$.

For matrix $H = (h_{ij})$, let $||H|| = \{tr(H^\tau H)\}^{1/2}$ denote its norm. Then (4) implies that

$$\sum_{k=1}^{k_0} \sum_{C \in \mathcal{B}} w(C) || \sum_{t=k_0+1}^{n} E[B^\tau \{Y_t Y_t^\tau - var(Y_t)\}BI(Y_{t-k} \in C)]||^2 = 0 \tag{5}$$

where $k_0 \geq 1$ is a prescribed integer, $\mathcal{B}$ is a finite or countable collection of measurable sets, and the weight function $w(\cdot)$ ensures the sum on the right-hand side finite. In fact we may assume that $\sum_{C \in \mathcal{B}} w(C) = 1$. Even without the stationarity on Y_t, $var(Y_t)$ in (5) may be replaced by $\hat{\Sigma}_y \equiv$

$(n - k_0)^{-1} \sum_{k_0 < t \leq n} Y_t Y_t^\tau$. This is due to the fact $B^\tau var(Y_t)B = B^\tau \Sigma_\varepsilon B$, and

$$(n - k_0)^{-1} \sum_{t=k_0+1}^{n} B^\tau Y_t Y_t^\tau B = (n - k_0)^{-1} \sum_{t=k_0+1}^{n} B^\tau \varepsilon_t \varepsilon_t^\tau B \overset{a.s.}{\to} B^\tau \Sigma_\varepsilon B,$$

see (3). Therefore $B^\tau \hat{\Sigma}_y B$ is a consistent estimator for $B^\tau var(Y_t)B$ for all t. Denote

$$D_k(C) = (n - k_0)^{-1} \sum_{t=k_0+1}^{n} (Y_t Y_t^\tau - \hat{\Sigma}_y)I(Y_{t-k} \in C).$$

Now (5) suggests to estimate $B \equiv (b_1, \cdots, b_{d-r})$ by minimizing

$$\Phi_n(B) = \sum_{k=1}^{k_0} \sum_{C \in \mathcal{B}} w(C) \left\| B^\tau D_k(C)B \right\|^2 \tag{6}$$

$$= \sum_{k=1}^{k_0} \sum_{1 \leq i,j \leq d-r} \sum_{C \in \mathcal{B}} w(C) \{b_i^\tau D_k(C)b_j\}^2$$

subject to the condition $B^\tau B = I_{d-r}$. This is a high-dimensional optimization problem. Further it does not explicitly address the issue how to determine the number of factors r. We present an algorithm which expands the innovation space step by step and which also takes care of these two concerns. Note for any $b^\tau A = 0$, $Z_t \equiv b^\tau Y_t (= b^\tau \varepsilon_t)$ is a sequence of independent random variables, and therefore, exhibits no conditional heterosedasticity. The determination of the r is based on the likelihood ratio test for the null hypothesis that the conditional variance of Z_t given its lagged valued is a constant against the alternative that it follows a GARCH(1,1) model with normal innovations. See also Remark 1(vii) below.

Put

$$\Psi(b) = \sum_{k=1}^{k_0} \sum_{C \in \mathcal{B}} w(C)[b^\tau D_k(C)b]^2,$$

$$\Psi_m(b) = \sum_{k=1}^{k_0} \left\{ 2 \sum_{i=1}^{m-1} \sum_{C \in \mathcal{B}} w(C)[\hat{b}_i^\tau D_k(C)\, b]^2 + \sum_{C \in \mathcal{B}} w(C)[b^\tau D_k(C)b]^2 \right\}.$$

An Innovation Expansion Algorithm for estimating B and r: let p be an integer between 1 and k_0 and $\alpha \in (0,1)$ specify the level of significance test.

Step 1. Compute $\hat{b}_1$ which minimises $\Psi(b)$ subject to the constraint $b^\tau b = 1$. Let $Z_t = \hat{b}_1^\tau Y_t$. Compute the 2log-likelihood ratio test statistic

$$T = (n-k_0)\left\{1+\log\left(\frac{1}{n - k_0} \sum_{t=k_0+1}^{n} Z_t^2\right)\right\} - \min \sum_{t=k_0+1}^{n} \left\{\frac{Z_t^2}{\sigma_t^2} + \log(\sigma_t^2)\right\}, \tag{7}$$

where $\sigma_t^2 = \alpha + \beta Z_{t-1}^2 + \gamma \sigma_{t-1}^2$, and the minimisation is taken over $\alpha > 0$, $\beta, \gamma \geq 0$ and $\beta + \gamma < 1$. Terminate the algorithm with $\hat{r} = d$ and $\hat{B} = 0$ if T is greater than the top α-point of the χ_2^2-distribution. Otherwise proceed to Step 2.

Step 2. For $m = 2, \cdots, d$, compute $\hat{b}_m$ which minimizes $\Psi_m(b)$ subject to the constraint

$$b^\tau b = 1, \quad b^\tau \hat{b}_i = 0 \quad \text{for } i = 1, \cdots, m-1. \tag{8}$$

Terminate the algorithm with $\hat{r} = d-m+1$ and $\hat{B} = (\hat{b}_1, \cdots, \hat{b}_{m-1})$ if T, calculated as in (7) but with $Z_t = |\hat{b}_m^\tau Y_t|$ now, is greater than the top α-point of the χ_2^2-distribution.

Step 3. In the event that T_p never exceeds the critical value for all $1 \leq m \leq d$, let $r = 0$ and $\hat{B} = I_d$.

Remark 1. (i) The algorithm grows the dimension of $\mathcal{M}(B)$ by 1 each time until a newly selected direction $\hat{b}_m$ being relevant to the volatility dynamics of Y_t. This effectively reduces the number of the factors in model (1) as much as possible without losing significant information.

(ii) The minimization problem in Step 2 is a d-dimensional subject to constraint (8). It has only $(d - m + 1)$ free variables. In fact, the vector b satisfying (8) is of the form

$$b = A_m u, \tag{9}$$

where u is any $(d-m+1) \times 1$ unit vector, A_m is a $d \times (d-m+1)$ matrix with the columns being the $(d - m + 1)$ unit eigenvectors, corresponding to the $(d-m+1)$-fold eigenvalue 1, of matrix $I_d - B_m B_m^\tau$, and $B_m = (\hat{b}_1, \cdots, \hat{b}_{m-1})$. Note that the other $(m - 1)$ eigenvalues of $I_d - B_m B_m^\tau$ are all 0.

(iii) We may let $\hat{A}$ consist of the $\hat{r}$ (orthogonal) unit eigenvectors, corresponding to the common eigenvalue 1, of matrix $I_d - \hat{B}\hat{B}^\tau$ (i.e. $\hat{A} = A_{d-\hat{r}+1}$). Note that $\hat{A}^\tau \hat{A} = I_{\hat{r}}$.

(iv) A general formal $d \times 1$ unit vector is of the form $b^\tau = (b_1, \cdots, b_d)$, where

$$b_1 = \prod_{j=1}^{d-1} \cos \theta_j, \quad b_i = \sin \theta_{i-1} \prod_{j=i}^{d-1} \cos \theta_j \ (i = 2, \cdots, d-1), \quad b_d = \sin \theta_{d-1},$$

where $\theta_1, \cdots, \theta_{d-1}$ are $(d-1)$ free parameters.

(v) We may choose $\mathcal{B}$ consisting of the balls centered at the origin in R^d. Note that $EY_{t-k} = 0$. When the underlying distribution of Y_{t-k} is symmetric and unimodal, such a $\mathcal{B}$ is the collection of the minimum volume sets of the distribution of Y_{t-k}, and this $\mathcal{B}$ determines the distribution of Y_{t-k} (Polonik 1997). In numerical implementation we simply use $w(C) = 1/K$, where K is the number the balls in $\mathcal{B}$.

(vi) Under the additional condition that

$$c^\tau A \{E(X_t X_t^\tau | \mathcal{F}_{t-1}) - E(X_t X_t^\tau)\} A^\tau c = 0 \tag{10}$$

if and only if $A^\tau c = 0$, (4) is equivalent to

$$E\{(b_i^\tau Y_t Y_t^\tau b_i - 1)I(Y_{t-k} \in C)\} = 0, \quad 1 \le i \le d - r, \quad k \ge 1 \text{ and } C \in \mathcal{B}.$$

See model (1). In this case, we may simply use $\Psi(\cdot)$ instead of $\Psi_m(\cdot)$ in Step 2 above. Note that for b satisfying constraint (8), (9) implies

$$\Psi(b) = \sum_{k=1}^{k_0} \sum_{C \in \mathcal{B}} w(C) \left(u^\tau A_m^\tau D_k(C) A_m u\right)^2. \tag{11}$$

Condition (10) means that all the linear combinations of AX_t are genuinely (conditionally) heteroscadastic.

(vii) When the number of factors r is given, we may skip all the test steps, and stop the algorithm after obtaining $\hat{b}_1, \cdots, \hat{b}_r$ from solving the r optimization problems.

Remark 2. The estimation of A leads to a dynamic model for $\Sigma_y(t)$ as follow:

$$\hat{\Sigma}_y(t) = \hat{A}\hat{\Sigma}_z(t)\hat{A}^\tau + \hat{A}\hat{A}^\tau \hat{\Sigma}_y \hat{B}\hat{B}^\tau + \hat{B}\hat{B}^\tau \hat{\Sigma}_y,$$

where $\hat{\Sigma}_y = n^{-1} \sum_{1 \le t \le n} Y_t Y_t^\tau$, and $\hat{\Sigma}_z(t)$ is obtained by fitting the data $\{\hat{A}^\tau Y_t, 1 \le t \le n\}$ with, for example, the dynamic correlation model of Engle (2002).

3 Consistency of the estimator

For $r < d$, let $\mathcal{H}$ be the set consisting of all $d \times (d-r)$ matrices H satisfying the condition $H^\tau H = I_{d-r}$. For $H_1, H_2 \in \mathcal{H}$, define

$$D(H_1, H_2) = \|(I_d - H_1 H_1^\tau)H_2\| = \{d - r - tr(H_1 H_1^\tau H_2 H_2^\tau)\}^{1/2}. \tag{12}$$

Denote our estimator by $\hat{B} = argmin_{B \in \mathcal{H}_D} \Phi_n(B)$.

Theorem 1. Let $\mathcal{C}$ denote the class of closed convex sets in $\mathcal{R}^d$. Under some mild assumptions (see Pan et al. (2009)), if the collection $\mathcal{B}$ is a countable subclass of $\mathcal{C}$, then $D(\hat{B}, B_0) \xrightarrow{P} 0$.

4 Numerical properties

We always set $k_0 = 30$, $\alpha = 5\%$, and the weight function $C(\cdot) \equiv 1$. Let $\mathcal{B}$ consist of all the balls centered at the origin.

4.1   Simulated examples

Consider model (1) with $r = 3$ factors, and $d \times 3$ matrix A with $(1, 0, 0)$, $(0, 0.5, 0.866)$ $(0, -0.866, 0.5)$ as its first 3 rows, and $(0, 0, 0)$ as all the other $(d - 3)$ rows. We consider 3 different settings for $X_t = (X_{t1}, X_{t2}, X_{t3})^\tau$, namely, two sets of GARCH(1,1) factors $X_{ti} = \sigma_{ti} e_{ti}$ and $\sigma_{ti}^2 = \alpha_i + \beta_i X_{t-1,i}^2 + \gamma_i \sigma_{t-1,i}^2$, where $(\alpha_i, \beta_i, \gamma_i)$, for $i = 1, 2, 3$, are

$$(1,\ 0.45,\ 0.45), \qquad (0.9,\ 0.425,\ 0.425), \qquad (1.1,\ 0.4,\ 0.4), \qquad (13)$$

or

$$(1,\ 0.1,\ 0.8), \qquad (0.9,\ 0.15,\ 0.7), \qquad (1.1,\ 0.2,\ 0.6), \qquad (14)$$

and one mixing setting with two ARCH(2) factors and one stochastic volatility factor:

$$X_{t1} = \sigma_{t1} e_{t1}, \qquad \sigma_{t1}^2 = 1 + 0.6 X_{t-1,1}^2 + 0.3 X_{t-2,1}^2, \qquad (15)$$
$$X_{t2} = \sigma_{t2} e_{t2}, \qquad \sigma_{t2}^2 = 0.9 + 0.5 X_{t-1,2}^2 + 0.35 X_{t-2,2}^2,$$
$$X_{t3} = \exp(h_t/2) e_{t3}, \qquad h_t = 0.22 + 0.7 h_{t-1} + u_t.$$

We let $\{\varepsilon_{ti}\}$, $\{e_{ti}\}$ and $\{u_t\}$ be sequences of independent $N(0, 1)$ random variables. Note that the (unconditional) variance of X_{ti}, for each i, remains unchanged under the above three different settings. We set the sample size $n = 300, 600$ or 1000. For each setting we repeat simulation 500 times.

Table 1. Relative frequency estimates of r with $d = 5$ and normal innovations

Factors	n	0	1	2	**3**	4	5
GARCH(1,1) with	300	.000	.046	.266	**.666**	.014	.008
coefficients (13)	600	.000	.002	.022	**.926**	.032	.018
	1000	.000	.000	.000	**.950**	.004	.001
GARCH(1,1) with	300	.272	.236	.270	**.200**	.022	.004
coefficients (14)	600	.004	.118	.312	**.500**	.018	.012
	1000	.006	.022	.174	**.778**	.014	.006
Mixture (15)	300	.002	.030	.166	**.772**	.026	.004
	600	.000	.001	.022	**.928**	.034	.014
	1000	.000	.000	.000	**.942**	.046	.012

We conducted the simulation with $d = 5, 10, 20$. To measure the difference between $\mathcal{M}(A)$ and $\mathcal{M}(\hat{A})$, we define

$$D(A, \hat{A}) = \{|(I_d - AA^\tau)\hat{A}|_1 + |AA^\tau \hat{B}|_1\}/d^2, \qquad (16)$$

where $|A|_1$ is the sum of the absolute values of all the elements in matrix A.

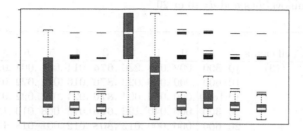

Fig. 1. Boxplots of $D(A, \hat{A})$ with two sets of GARCH(1,1) factors specified, respectively, by (13) and (14), and mixing factors (15). Innovations are Gaussian and $d = 5$.

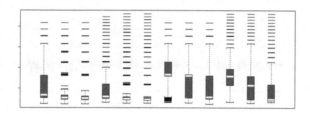

Fig. 2. Boxplots of $D(A, \hat{A})$ with two sets of GARCH(1,1) factors specified in (13) and (14), normal innovations and $d = 10$ or 20.

We report the results with $d = 5$ first. Table 1 lists for the relative frequency estimates for r in the 500 replications. When sample size n increases, the relative frequency for $\hat{r} = 3$ (i.e. the true value) also increases. Even for $n = 600$, the estimation is already very accurate for GARCH(1,1) factors (13) and mixing factors (14), less so for the persistent GARCH(1,1) factors (14). For $n = 300$, the relative frequencies for $\hat{r} = 2$ were non-negligible, indicating the tendency of underestimating of r, although this tendency disappears when n increases to 600 or 1000. Figure 1 displays the boxplots of $D(A, \hat{A})$. The estimation was pretty accurate with GARCH factors (13) and mixing factors (15), especially with correctly estimated r. Note with $n = 600$ or 1000, those outliers (lying above the range connected by dashed lines) typically correspond to the estimates $\hat{r} \neq 3$.

When $d = 10$ and 20, comparing with Table 1, the estimation of r is only marginally worse than that with $d = 5$. Indeed the difference with $d = 10$ and 20 is not big either. Note the D-measures for different d are not comparable; see (16). Nevertheless, Figure 2 shows that the estimation for A becomes more

Table 2. Relative frequency estimates of r with GARCH(1,1) factors, normal innovations and d=10 or 20

Coefficients	d	n	$\hat{r}$ 0	1	2	**3**	4	5	6	≥ 7
(13)	10	300	.002	.048	.226	**.674**	.014	.001	.004	.022
	10	600	.000	.000	.022	**.876**	.016	.012	.022	.052
	10	1000	.000	.000	.004	**.876**	.024	.022	.022	.052
	20	300	.000	.040	.196	**.626**	.012	.008	.010	.138
	20	600	.000	.000	.012	**.808**	.012	.001	.018	.149
	20	1000	.000	.000	.000	**.776**	.024	.012	.008	.180
(14)	10	300	.198	.212	.280	**.248**	.016	.008	.014	.015
	10	600	.032	.110	.292	**.464**	.018	.026	.012	.046
	10	1000	.006	.032	.128	**.726**	.032	.020	.016	.040
	20	300	.166	.266	.222	**.244**	.012	.004	.001	.107
	20	600	.022	.092	.220	**.472**	.001	.001	.012	.180
	20	1000	.006	.016	.092	**.666**	.018	.016	.014	.172

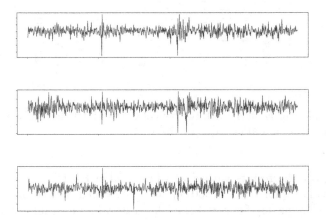

Fig. 3. Time plots of the daily log-returns of S&P 500 index, Cisco System and Intel Coprporation stock prices.

accurate when n increases, and the estimation with the persistent factors (14) is less accurate than that with (13).

4.2   A real data example

Figure 3 displays the daily log-returns of the S&P 500 index, the stock prices of Cisco System and Intel Corporation in 2 January 1997 – 31 December 1999. For this data set, $n = 758$ and $d = 3$. The estimated number of factors

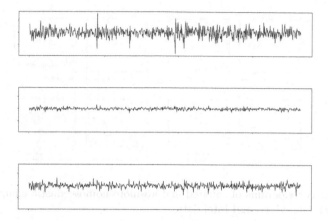

Fig. 4. Time plots of the estimated factor and two homoscedastic compoments for the S&P 500, Cisco and Intel data.

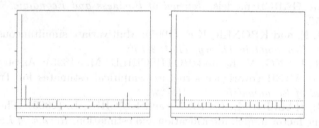

Fig. 5. The correlograms of squared and absulote factor for the the S&P 500, Cisco and Intel data

is $\hat{r} = 1$ with $\hat{A}^{\tau} = (0.310, 0.687, 0.658)$. The time plots of the estimated factor $Z_t \equiv \hat{A}^{\tau} Y_t$ and the two homoscedastic components $\hat{B}^{\tau} Y_t$ are displayed in Figure 4. The P-value of the Gaussian-GARCH(1,1) based likelihood ratio test for the null hypothesis of the constant conditional variance for Z_t is 0.000. The correlograms of the squared and the absolute factor are depicted in Figure 5 which indicates the existence of heteroscedasticity in Z_t. The fitted GARCH(1,1) model for Z_t is $\hat{\sigma}_t^2 = 2.5874 + 0.1416 Z_{t-1}^2 + 0.6509 \hat{\sigma}_{t-1}^2$. In contrast, Figure 6 shows that there is little autocorrelation in squared or absolute components of $\hat{B}^{\tau} Y_t$. The estimated constant covariance matrix is

$$\hat{\Sigma}_0 = \begin{pmatrix} 1.594 & & \\ 0.070 & 4.142 & \\ -1.008 & -0.561 & 4.885 \end{pmatrix}.$$

The overall fitted conditional variance process is given with $\hat{\Sigma}_z(t) = \hat{\sigma}_t^2$.

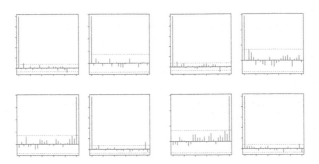

Fig. 6. The correlograms of squared and absulote homoscedastic compoments for the the S&P 500, Cisco and Intel data

References

ENGLE, R. F. (2002): Dynamic conditional correlation - a simple class of multivariate GARCH models. *Journal of Business and Economic Statistics, 20, 339-350.*

ENGLE, R. F. and KRONER, K.F. (1995): Multivariate simultaneous generalised ARCH. *Econometric Theory, 11, 122-150.*

ENGLE, R. F., NG, V. K. and ROTHSCHILD, M. (1990): Asset pricing with a factor ARCH covariance structure: empirical estimates for Treasury bills. *Journal of Econometrics, 45, 213-238.*

FORNI, M., HALLIN, M., LIPPI, M. and REICHIN, L. (2000): The generalized dynamic factor model: Identification and estimation. *Review of Economics and Statistics,82, 540-554.*

FORNI, M., HALLIN, M. LIPPI, M. and REICHIN, L. (2004): The generalized dynamic factor model: Consistency and rates. *Journal of Econometrics,119, 231-255.*

GEWEKE, J. (1977): The dynamic factor analysis of economic time series. In: D.J. Aigner and A.S. Goldberger (eds.): *Latent Variables in Socio-Economic Models*, Amsterdam: North-Holland, 365-383.

HALLIN, M. and LIŠKA, R. (2007): Determining the number of factors in the general dynamic factor model. *Journal of the American Statistical Association, 102, 603-617.*

LIN, W.-L. (1992): Alternative estimators for factor GARCH models – a Monte Carlo comparison. *Journal of Applied Econometrics, 7, 259-279.*

PAN, J., POLONIK,W., YAO,Q., and ZIEGELMANN,F. (2009): Modelling multivariate volatilities by common factors.*Research Report*, Department of Statistics, London School of Economics.

PAN, J. and YAO, Q. (2008). Modelling multiple time series via common factors. *Biometrika, 95, 365-379.*

SARGENT,T. J. and SIMS, C.A. (1977): Business cycle modelling without pretending to have too much a priori economic theory. In: C. A. Sims (ed.): *New Methods in Business Cycle Research*, Minneapolis: Federal Reserve Bank of Minneapolis, 45-109.

Multivariate Stochastic Volatility Model with Cross Leverage

Tsunehiro Ishihara[1] and Yasuhiro Omori[2]

[1] Graduate School of Economics, University of Tokyo. 7-3-1 Hongo, Bunkyo-Ku, Tokyo 113-0033, Japan.
[2] Faculty of Economics, University of Tokyo. 7-3-1 Hongo, Bunkyo-Ku, Tokyo 113-0033, Japan. Tel: +81-3-5841-5516. *omori@e.u-tokyo.ac.jp*

Abstract. The Bayesian estimation method using Markov chain Monte Carlo is proposed for a multivariate stochastic volatility model that is a natural extension of the univariate stochastic volatility model with leverage, where we further incorporate cross leverage effects among stock returns.

Keywords: asymmetry, Bayesian analysis, leverage effect, Markov chain Monte Carlo, multi-move sampler, multivariate stochastic volatility, stock returns

1 Introduction

The univariate stochastic volatility (SV) models have been well known and successful to account for the time-varying variance in financial time series (e.g. Broto and Ruiz (2004)). Extending these models to the multivariate SV (MSV) model has become recently a major concern to investigate the correlation structure of multivariate financial time series for the purpose of the portfolio optimisation, the risk management, and the derivative pricing. Multivariate factor modelling of stochastic volatilities has been widely introduced to describe the complex dynamic structure of the high dimensional stock returns data (Aguilar and West (2000), Jacquier, Polson and Rossi (1999), Liesenfeld and Richard (2003), Pitt and Shephard (1999), Lopes and Carvalho (2006), and several efficient MCMC algorithms have been proposed (So and Choi (2009), Chib, Nardari and Shephard (2006)). On the other hand, efficient estimation methods for MSV models with cross leverage (non-zero correlation between the i-th asset return at time t and the j-th log volatility at time $t+1$ for all i,j) or asymmetry have not been well investigated in the literature except for simple bivariate models (see surveys by Asai, McAleer and Yu (2006) and Chib, Omori and Asai (2009)). Chan, Kohn and Kirby (2006) considered the Bayesian estimation of MSV models with correlations between measurement errors and state errors, but their setup did not exactly correspond to the leverage effects. Asai and McAleer (2006) simplified the MSV model with leverage by assuming no cross leverage effects (no correlation between the i-th asset return at time t and the j-th log volatility at time $t+1$ for $i \neq j$) and describe the Monte Carlo likelihood estimation method.

Y. Lechevallier, G. Saporta (eds.), *Proceedings of COMPSTAT'2010*,
DOI 10.1007/978-3-7908-2604-3_29, © Springer-Verlag Berlin Heidelberg 2010

In this paper, we consider a general MSV model with cross leverage, and propose a novel efficient MCMC algorithm using a multi-move sampler which samples a block of many latent volatility vectors simultaneously. In the MCMC implementation for the SV models, it is critical to sample the latent volatility (or state) variables from their full conditional posterior distributions efficiently. The single-move sampler that draws a single volatility variable at a time given the rest of the volatility variables and other parameters is easy to implement, but obtained MCMC samples are known to have high autocorrelations. This implies we need to iterate the MCMC algorithm a huge number of times to obtain accurate estimates when we use a single-move sampler. Thus we propose a fast and efficient state sampling algorithm based on the approximate linear and Gaussian state space model.

The rest of the paper is organised as follows. Section 2 discusses a Bayesian estimation of the MSV model using a multi-move sampler for the latent state variables. Section 3 concludes the paper.

2   MSV model with cross leverage

2.1   Model

Let y_t denote a stock return at time t. The univariate SV model with leverage is given by

$$y_t = \exp(\alpha_t/2)\varepsilon_t, \quad t = 1, \ldots, n, \tag{1}$$

$$\alpha_{t+1} = \phi\alpha_t + \eta_t, \quad t = 1, \ldots, n-1, \tag{2}$$

$$\alpha_1 \sim \mathcal{N}(0, \sigma_\eta^2/(1-\phi^2)), \tag{3}$$

where

$$\begin{pmatrix} \varepsilon_t \\ \eta_t \end{pmatrix} \sim \mathcal{N}_2(\mathbf{0}, \boldsymbol{\Sigma}), \quad \boldsymbol{\Sigma} = \begin{pmatrix} \sigma_\varepsilon^2 & \rho\sigma_\varepsilon\sigma_\eta \\ \rho\sigma_\varepsilon\sigma_\eta & \sigma_\eta^2 \end{pmatrix}, \tag{4}$$

α_t is a latent variable for the log-volatility, and $\mathcal{N}_m(\mu, \boldsymbol{\Sigma})$ denotes an m-variate normal distribution with mean μ and covariance matrix $\boldsymbol{\Sigma}$. To extend it to the MSV model, we let $\mathbf{y}_t = (y_{1t}, \ldots, y_{pt})'$ denote a p dimensional stock returns vector and $\alpha_t = (\alpha_{1t}, \ldots, \alpha_{pt})'$ denote their corresponding log volatility vectors, respectively. We consider the MSV model given by

$$\mathbf{y}_t = \mathbf{V}_t^{1/2}\varepsilon_t, \quad t = 1, \ldots, n, \tag{5}$$

$$\alpha_{t+1} = \boldsymbol{\Phi}\alpha_t + \eta_t, \quad t = 1, \ldots, n-1, \tag{6}$$

$$\alpha_1 \sim \mathcal{N}_p(\mathbf{0}, \boldsymbol{\Sigma}_0), \tag{7}$$

where

$$\mathbf{V}_t = \mathrm{diag}\left(\exp(\alpha_{1t}), \ldots, \exp(\alpha_{pt})\right), \tag{8}$$

$$\boldsymbol{\Phi} = \mathrm{diag}(\phi_1, \ldots, \phi_p), \tag{9}$$

$$\begin{pmatrix} \varepsilon_t \\ \eta_t \end{pmatrix} \sim \mathcal{N}_{2p}(\mathbf{0}, \boldsymbol{\Sigma}), \quad \boldsymbol{\Sigma} = \begin{pmatrix} \boldsymbol{\Sigma}_{\varepsilon\varepsilon} & \boldsymbol{\Sigma}_{\varepsilon\eta} \\ \boldsymbol{\Sigma}_{\eta\varepsilon} & \boldsymbol{\Sigma}_{\eta\eta} \end{pmatrix}. \tag{10}$$

The (i, j)-th element of $\boldsymbol{\Sigma}_0$ is the (i, j)-th element of $\boldsymbol{\Sigma}_{\eta\eta}$ divided by $1 - \phi_i\phi_j$ to satisfy a stationarity condition $\boldsymbol{\Sigma}_0 = \boldsymbol{\Phi}\boldsymbol{\Sigma}_0\boldsymbol{\Phi} + \boldsymbol{\Sigma}_{\eta\eta}$ such that

$$\mathrm{vec}(\boldsymbol{\Sigma}_0) = \left(\mathbf{I}_{p^2} - \boldsymbol{\Phi} \otimes \boldsymbol{\Phi}\right)^{-1} \mathrm{vec}(\boldsymbol{\Sigma}_{\eta\eta}).$$

The expected value of the volatility evolution processes α_t is set equal to $\mathbf{0}$ for the identifiability. Let $\theta = (\phi, \boldsymbol{\Sigma})$ where $\phi = (\phi_1, \ldots, \phi_p)'$ and $\mathbf{1}_p$ denote a $p \times 1$ vector with all elements equal to one. Then the likelihood function of the MSV model (5)–(7) is given by

$$f(\alpha_1|\theta) \prod_{t=1}^{n-1} f(\mathbf{y}_t, \alpha_{t+1}|\alpha_t, \theta)f(\mathbf{y}_n|\alpha_n, \theta)$$

$$\propto \exp\left\{\sum_{t=1}^{n} l_t - \frac{1}{2}\alpha_1'\boldsymbol{\Sigma}_0^{-1}\alpha_1 - \frac{1}{2}\sum_{t=1}^{n-1}(\alpha_{t+1} - \boldsymbol{\Phi}\alpha_t)'\boldsymbol{\Sigma}_{\eta\eta}^{-1}(\alpha_{t+1} - \boldsymbol{\Phi}\alpha_t)\right\}$$

$$\times |\boldsymbol{\Sigma}_0|^{-\frac{1}{2}}|\boldsymbol{\Sigma}|^{-\frac{n-1}{2}}|\boldsymbol{\Sigma}_{\varepsilon\varepsilon}|^{-\frac{1}{2}}, \tag{11}$$

where

$$l_t = \mathrm{const} - \frac{1}{2}\mathbf{1}_p'\alpha_t - \frac{1}{2}(\mathbf{y}_t - \mu_t)'\boldsymbol{\Sigma}_t^{-1}(\mathbf{y}_t - \mu_t), \tag{12}$$

$$\mu_t = \mathbf{V}_t^{1/2}\mathbf{m}_t, \quad \boldsymbol{\Sigma}_t = \mathbf{V}_t^{1/2}\mathbf{S}_t\mathbf{V}_t^{1/2}, \tag{13}$$

and

$$\mathbf{m}_t = \begin{cases} \boldsymbol{\Sigma}_{\varepsilon\eta}\boldsymbol{\Sigma}_{\eta\eta}^{-1}(\alpha_{t+1} - \boldsymbol{\Phi}\alpha_t), & t < n, \\ \mathbf{0} & t = n, \end{cases} \tag{14}$$

$$\mathbf{S}_t = \begin{cases} \boldsymbol{\Sigma}_{\varepsilon\varepsilon} - \boldsymbol{\Sigma}_{\varepsilon\eta}\boldsymbol{\Sigma}_{\eta\eta}^{-1}\boldsymbol{\Sigma}_{\eta\varepsilon}, & t < n, \\ \boldsymbol{\Sigma}_{\varepsilon\varepsilon} & t = n. \end{cases} \tag{15}$$

2.2 MCMC implementation

Since there are many latent volatility vectors α_t's, it is difficult to integrate them out to evaluate the likelihood function of θ analytically or using a high dimensional numerical integration. In this paper, by taking a Bayesian approach, we employ a simulation method, the MCMC method, to generate samples from the posterior distribution to conduct a statistical inference regarding the model parameters.

For prior distributions of θ, we assume

$$\frac{\phi_j + 1}{2} \sim \mathcal{B}(a_j, b_j), \quad j = 1, \ldots, p, \quad \boldsymbol{\Sigma} \sim \mathcal{IW}(n_0, \mathbf{R}_0),$$

where $\mathcal{B}(a_j, b_j)$ and $\mathcal{IW}(n_0, \mathbf{R}_0)$ denote Beta and inverse Wishart distributions with probability density functions

$$\pi(\phi_j) \propto (1 + \phi_j)^{a_j - 1}(1 - \phi_j)^{b_j - 1}, \quad j = 1, 2, \ldots, p, \tag{16}$$

$$\pi(\boldsymbol{\Sigma}) \propto |\boldsymbol{\Sigma}|^{-\frac{n_0 + p + 1}{2}} \exp\left\{-\frac{1}{2}\mathrm{tr}\left(\mathbf{R}_0^{-1}\boldsymbol{\Sigma}^{-1}\right)\right\}. \tag{17}$$

Using Equations (11), (16) and (17), we obtain the joint posterior density function of (θ, α) given $Y_n = \{\mathbf{y}_t\}_{t=1}^n$ is

$$\pi(\theta, \alpha | Y_n) \propto f(\alpha_1 | \theta) \prod_{t=1}^{n-1} f(\mathbf{y}_t, \alpha_{t+1} | \alpha_t, \theta) f(\mathbf{y}_n | \alpha_n, \theta) \prod_{j=1}^{p} \pi(\phi_j) \pi(\Sigma), \quad (18)$$

where $\alpha = (\alpha_1', \ldots, \alpha_n')'$. We implement the MCMC algorithm in three blocks:

1. Generate $\alpha | \phi, \Sigma, Y_n$.
2. Generate $\Sigma | \phi, \alpha, Y_n$.
3. Generate $\phi | \Sigma, \alpha, Y_n$.

First we discuss two methods to sample α from its conditional posterior distribution in Step 1. One is a so-called single-move sampler which samples one α_t at a time given other α_j's, while the other method is a multi-move sampler which samples a block of state vectors, say, $(\alpha_t, \ldots, \alpha_{t+k})$ given the rest of state vectors.

Generation of α We propose an efficient block sampler for α to sample a block of α_t's from the posterior distribution extending Omori and Watanabe (2008) who considered the univariate SV model with leverage (see also Takahashi, Omori and Watanabe (2009)). First we divide $\alpha = (\alpha_1', \ldots, \alpha_n')'$ into $K+1$ blocks $(\alpha_{k_{i-1}+1}', \ldots, \alpha_{k_i}')'$ using $i = 1, \ldots, K+1$ with $k_0 = 0$, $k_{K+1} = n$ and $k_i - k_{i-1} \geq 2$. The K knots $(k_1, \ldots, k_K)$ are generated randomly using

$$k_i = \text{int}[n \times (i + U_i)/(K + 2)], \quad i = 1, \ldots, K,$$

where U_i's are independent uniform random variable on $(0, 1)$ (see e.g., Shephard and Pitt (1997)). These stochastic knots have an advantage to allow the points of conditioning to change over the MCMC iterations where K is a tuning parameter to obtain less autocorrelated MCMC samples.

Suppose that $k_{i-1} = s$ and $k_i = s + m$ for the i-th block and consider sampling this block from its conditional posterior distribution given other state vectors and parameters. Let $\xi_t = \mathbf{R}_t^{-1} \eta_t$, where the matrix $\mathbf{R}_t$ denotes a Choleski decomposition of $\Sigma_{\eta\eta} = \mathbf{R}_t \mathbf{R}_t'$ for $t = s, s+1, \ldots, s+m$, and $\Sigma_0 = \mathbf{R}_0 \mathbf{R}_0'$ for $t = s = 0$. To construct a proposal distribution for MH algorithm, we focus on the distribution of the disturbance $\xi \equiv (\xi_s', \ldots, \xi_{s+m-1}')'$ which is fundamental in the sense that it derives the distribution of $\alpha \equiv (\alpha_{s+1}', \ldots, \alpha_{s+m}')'$. Then, the logarithm of the full conditional joint density distribution of ξ excluding constant terms is given by

$$\log f(\xi | \alpha_s, \alpha_{s+m+1}, \mathbf{y}_s, \ldots, \mathbf{y}_{s+m}) = -\frac{1}{2} \sum_{t=s}^{s+m-1} \xi_s' \xi_s + L, \quad (19)$$

where

$$L = \sum_{t=s}^{s+m} l_s - \frac{1}{2}(\alpha_{s+m+1} - \Phi\alpha_{s+m})' \Sigma_{\eta\eta}^{-1}(\alpha_{s+m+1} - \Phi\alpha_{s+m}) I(s + m < n). \quad (20)$$

Then using the second order Taylor expansion of (19) around the mode $\hat{\xi}$, we obtain approximating normal density f^* to be used for the MH algorithm as follows

$$\log f(\underline{\xi}|\alpha_s, \alpha_{s+m+1}, \mathbf{y}_s, \ldots, \mathbf{y}_{s+m})$$

$$\approx \text{const.} - \frac{1}{2} \sum_{t=s}^{s+m-1} \xi_t'\xi_t + \hat{L} + \left.\frac{\partial L}{\partial \underline{\xi}'}\right|_{\underline{\xi}=\hat{\underline{\xi}}} (\underline{\xi} - \hat{\underline{\xi}}) + \frac{1}{2}(\underline{\xi} - \hat{\underline{\xi}})'\mathbb{E}\left(\frac{\partial^2 L}{\partial \underline{\xi}\partial \underline{\xi}'}\right)(\underline{\xi} - \hat{\underline{\xi}})$$

$$= \text{const.} - \frac{1}{2} \sum_{t=s}^{s+m-1} \xi_t'\xi_t + \hat{L} + \hat{\mathbf{d}}'(\underline{\alpha} - \hat{\underline{\alpha}}) - \frac{1}{2}(\underline{\alpha} - \hat{\underline{\alpha}})'\hat{\mathbf{Q}}(\underline{\alpha} - \hat{\underline{\alpha}}), \tag{21}$$

$$= \text{const.} + \log f^*(\underline{\xi}|\alpha_s, \alpha_{s+m+1}, \mathbf{y}_s, \ldots, \mathbf{y}_{s+m}) \tag{22}$$

where $\hat{\mathbf{Q}}$ and $\hat{\mathbf{d}}$ are $\mathbf{Q} = -E(\partial^2 L/\partial\underline{\alpha}\partial\underline{\alpha}')$ and $\mathbf{d} = \partial L/\partial\underline{\alpha}$ evaluated at $\underline{\alpha} = \hat{\underline{\alpha}}$ (*i.e.*, $\underline{\xi} = \hat{\underline{\xi}}$). Note that $\mathbf{Q}$ is positive definite and invertible. However, when m is large, it is time consuming to invert the $mp \times mp$ Hessian matrix to obtain the covariance matrix of the mp-variate multivariate normal distribution. To overcome this difficulty, we interpret the equation (22) as the posterior probability density derived from an auxiliary state space model so that we only need to invert $p \times p$ matrices by using the Kalman filter and the disturbance smoother. It can be shown that f^* is a posterior probability density function of $\underline{\xi}$ obtained from the state space model:

$$\hat{\mathbf{y}}_t = \mathbf{Z}_t\alpha_t + \mathbf{G}_t\mathbf{u}_t, \quad t = s+1, \ldots, s+m, \tag{23}$$

$$\alpha_{t+1} = \mathbf{\Phi}\alpha_t + \mathbf{H}_t\mathbf{u}_t, \quad t = s+1, \ldots, s+m-1, \tag{24}$$

$$\mathbf{u}_t \sim \mathcal{N}_{2p}(\mathbf{0}, \mathbf{I}_{2p}),$$

where $\hat{\mathbf{y}}_t$, $\mathbf{Z}_t$, $\mathbf{G}_t$ are functions of $\hat{\underline{\alpha}}$ (see Appendix), and $\mathbf{H}_t = [\mathbf{O}, \mathbf{R}_t]$. To find a mode $\hat{\xi}$, we repeat following steps until it converges,

a. Compute $\hat{\underline{\alpha}}$ at $\underline{\xi} = \hat{\xi}$ using (6).
b. Obtain the approximating linear Gaussian state-space model given by (23) and (24).
c. Applying the disturbance smoother by Koopman (1993) to the approximating linear Gaussian state-space model in Step 2, compute the posterior mode $\hat{\xi}$.

since these steps are equivalent to the method of scoring to find a maximiser of the conditional posterior density. As an initial value of $\hat{\xi}$, the current sample of $\underline{\xi}$ may be used in the MCMC implementation. If the approximate linear Gaussian state-space model is obtained using a mode $\hat{\xi}$, then we draw a sample $\underline{\xi}$ from the conditional posterior distribution by MH algorithm as follows.

1. Propose a candidate $\xi^{\dagger}$ by sampling from $q(\underline{\xi}^{\dagger}) \propto \min(f(\underline{\xi}^{\dagger}), cf^*(\underline{\xi}^{\dagger}))$ using the Acceptance-Rejection algorithm where c can be constructed from a constant term and $\hat{L}$ of (21):

(a) Generate $\underline{\xi}^\dagger \sim f^*$ using a simulation smoother (e.g. de Jong and Shephard (1995), Durbin and Koopman (2002)) based on the approximating linear Gaussian state-space model (23) - (24).

(b) Accept $\underline{\xi}^\dagger$ with probability $\min\{f(\underline{\xi}^\dagger)/cf^*(\underline{\xi}^\dagger), 1\}$. If it is rejected, go back to (a).

2. Given the current value $\underline{\xi}$, accept $\underline{\xi}^\dagger$ with probability

$$\min\left\{1, \frac{f(\underline{\xi}^\dagger)\min(f(\underline{\xi}), cf^*(\underline{\xi}))}{f(\underline{\xi})\min(f(\underline{\xi}^\dagger), cf^*(\underline{\xi}^\dagger))}\right\}$$

if rejected, accept the current $\underline{\xi}$ as a sample.

Generation of Σ and ϕ The sampling method for Σ and ϕ is rather straightforward as we discuss below.

Generation of Σ. The conditional posterior probability density function of Σ is

$$\pi(\Sigma|\phi, \alpha, Y_n) \propto |\Sigma|^{-\frac{n_1+2p+1}{2}} \exp\left\{-\frac{1}{2}\mathrm{tr}\left(\mathbf{R}_1^{-1}\Sigma^{-1}\right)\right\} \times g(\Sigma),$$

$$g(\Sigma) = |\Sigma_0|^{-\frac{1}{2}}|\Sigma_{\varepsilon\varepsilon}|^{-\frac{1}{2}} \exp\left\{-\frac{1}{2}\left(\alpha_1'\Sigma_0^{-1}\alpha_1 + \mathbf{y}_n'\mathbf{V}_n^{-1/2}\Sigma_{\varepsilon\varepsilon}^{-1}\mathbf{V}_n^{-1/2}\mathbf{y}_n\right)\right\},$$

where $n_1 = n_0 + n - 1$, $\mathbf{R}_1^{-1} = \mathbf{R}_0^{-1} + \sum_{t=1}^{n-1}\mathbf{v}_t\mathbf{v}_t'$ and

$$\mathbf{v}_t = \begin{pmatrix} \mathbf{V}_t^{-1/2}\mathbf{y}_t \\ \alpha_{t+1} - \mathbf{\Phi}\alpha_t \end{pmatrix}.$$

Then, using MH algorithm, we propose a candidate $\Sigma^\dagger \sim \mathcal{IW}(n_1, \mathbf{R}_1)$ and accept it with probability $\min\{g(\Sigma^\dagger)/g(\Sigma), 1\}$.

Generation of ϕ. Let Σ^{ij} be a $p \times p$ matrix and denote the (i,j)-th block of Σ^{-1}. Further, let $\mathbf{A} = \sum_{t=1}^{n-1}\alpha_t\alpha_t'$, $\mathbf{B} = \sum_{t=1}^{n-1}\{\alpha_t\mathbf{y}_t'\mathbf{V}_t^{-1/2}\Sigma^{12} + \alpha_t\alpha_{t+1}'\Sigma^{22}\}$ and $\mathbf{b}$ denote a vector whose i-th element is equal to the (i,i)-th element of $\mathbf{B}$. Then the conditional posterior probability density function of ϕ is

$$\pi(\phi|\Sigma, \alpha, Y_n) \propto h(\phi) \times \exp\left\{-\frac{1}{2}\mathrm{tr}(\mathbf{\Phi}\Sigma^{22}\mathbf{\Phi}\mathbf{A}) - 2\mathrm{tr}(\mathbf{\Phi}\mathbf{B})\right\}$$

$$\propto h(\phi) \times \exp\left\{-\frac{1}{2}(\phi - \mu_\phi)'\Sigma_\phi(\phi - \mu_\phi)\right\},$$

$$h(\phi) = |\Sigma_0|^{-\frac{1}{2}}\prod_{j=1}^{p}(1 + \phi_j)^{a_j-1}(1 - \phi_j)^{b_j-1}\exp\left\{-\frac{1}{2}\alpha_1'\Sigma_0^{-1}\alpha_1\right\},$$

where $\mu_\phi = \Sigma_\phi\mathbf{b}$, $\Sigma_\phi^{-1} = \Sigma^{22} \odot \mathbf{A}$ and $\odot$ denotes a Hadamard product. To sample ϕ from its conditional posterior distribution using MH algorithm, we generate a candidate from a truncated normal distribution over the region R, $\phi^\dagger \sim \mathcal{TN}_R(\mu_\phi, \Sigma_\phi)$, $R = \{\phi : |\phi_j| < 1, j = 1, \ldots, p\}$ and accept it with probability $\min\{h(\phi^\dagger)/h(\phi), 1\}$.

3   Conclusion

This paper proposes efficient MCMC algorithms using a multi-move sampler for the latent volatility vectors for MSV models with cross leverage. To sample a block of such state vectors, we construct a proposal density for MH algorithm based on the normal approximation using Taylor expansion of the logarithm of the target likelihood and exploit the sampling algorithms which are developed for the linear and Gaussian state space model.

Acknowledgement

The authors are grateful to Siddhartha Chib, Mike K P So and Boris Choy, for helpful comments and discussions. This work is supported by the Research Fellowship (DC1) from the Japan Society for the Promotion of Science and the Grants-in-Aid for Scientific Research (A) 21243018 from the Japanese Ministry of Education, Science, Sports, Culture and Technology. The computational results are generated using Ox (Doornik (2006)).

Appendix

A   Derivation of the approximating state space model

First, noting that $E[\partial^2 L/\partial \alpha_t \partial \alpha'_{t+k}] = \mathbf{O}$ $(k \geq 2)$, define $\mathbf{A}_t$ and $\mathbf{B}_t$ as

$$\mathbf{A}_t = -E\left[\frac{\partial^2 L}{\partial \alpha_t \partial \alpha'_t}\right], \quad t = s+1, \ldots, s+m, \tag{25}$$

$$\mathbf{B}_t = -E\left[\frac{\partial^2 L}{\partial \alpha_t \partial \alpha'_{t-1}}\right], \quad t = s+2, \ldots, s+m, \quad \mathbf{B}_{s+1} = \mathbf{O}, \tag{26}$$

and let $\mathbf{d}_t = \partial L/\partial \alpha_t$ for $t = s+1, \ldots, s+m$. Using $\mathbf{d}_t, \mathbf{A}_t$ and $\mathbf{B}_t$ (see Ishihara and Omori (2009) for details), we obtain the approximating state space model as follows. First evaluate $\mathbf{d}_t, \mathbf{A}_t$ and $\mathbf{B}_t$ at the current mode, $\underline{\alpha} = \underline{\hat{\alpha}}$. Using $\hat{\mathbf{d}}_t, \hat{\mathbf{A}}_t$ and $\hat{\mathbf{B}}_t$,

a. Set $\mathbf{b}_s = \mathbf{0}$ and $\hat{\mathbf{B}}_{s+m+1} = \mathbf{O}$. Compute

$$\mathbf{D}_t = \hat{\mathbf{A}}_t - \hat{\mathbf{B}}_t \mathbf{D}_{t-1}^{-1}\hat{\mathbf{B}}'_t, \quad \mathbf{b}_t = \hat{\mathbf{d}}_t - \hat{\mathbf{B}}_t \mathbf{D}_{t-1}^{-1}\mathbf{b}_{t-1}, \quad \hat{\gamma}_t = \hat{\alpha}_t + \mathbf{D}_t^{-1}\hat{\mathbf{B}}'_{t+1}\hat{\alpha}_{t+1},$$

for $t = s+1, \ldots, s+m$, recursively where $\mathbf{K}_t$ denotes a Choleski decomposition of $\mathbf{D}_t$ such that $\mathbf{D}_t = \mathbf{K}_t\mathbf{K}'_t$.
b. Define auxiliary vectors and matrices

$$\hat{\mathbf{y}}_t = \hat{\gamma}_t + \mathbf{D}_t^{-1}\mathbf{b}_t, \quad \mathbf{Z}_t = \mathbf{I}_p + \mathbf{D}_t^{-1}\hat{\mathbf{B}}'_{t+1}\mathbf{\Phi}, \quad \mathbf{G}_t = [\mathbf{K}_t'^{-1}, \mathbf{D}_t^{-1}\hat{\mathbf{B}}'_{t+1}\mathbf{R}_t],$$

for $t = s+1, \ldots, s+m$.

Then, we obtain the approximating linear Gaussian state-space model given by (23) and (24).

References

ASAI, M. and MCALEER, M. (2006): Asymmetric multivariate stochastic volatility. *Econometric Reviews* 25, *453–473*.

BROTO, C. and RUIZ, E. (2004): Estimation methods for stochastic volatility models: a survey. *Journal of Economic Survey* 18, *613–649*.

CHAN, D., KOHN, R. and KIRBY, C. (2006): Multivariate stochastic volatility models with correlated errors. *Econometric Reviews* 25, *245–274*.

CHIB, S., NARDARI, F. and SHEPHARD, N. (2006): Analysis of high dimensional multivariate stochastic volatility models. *Journal of Econometrics* 134, *341–371*.

CHIB, S., OMORI, Y. and ASAI, M. (2009): Multivariate stochastic volatility. In T. G. Andersen, R. A. Davis, J. P. Kreiss, and T. Mikosch (Eds.), *Handbook of Financial Time Series*, pp. 365–400. New York: Springer-Verlag.

DE JONG, P. and SHEPHARD, N. (1995): The simulation smoother for time series models. *Biometrika* 82, *339–350*.

DOORNIK, J. (2006): *Ox: Object Oriented Matrix Programming*. London: Timberlake Consultants Press.

DURBIN, J. and KOOPMAN S.J. (2002): A simple and efficient simulation smoother for state space time series analysis. *Biometrika* 89, *603–616*.

ISHIHARA, T. and OMORI, Y. (2009): Efficient Bayesian estimation of a multivariate stochastic volatility model with cross leverage and heavy-tailed errors. Discussion paper series, CIRJE-F-700, Faculty of Economics, University of Tokyo.

JACQUIER, E., N. G. POLSON, and P. E. ROSSI (1999): Stochastic volatility: Univariate and multivariate extensions. CIRANO Working paper 99s–26, Montreal.

KOOPMAN, S. J. (1993): Disturbance smoother for state space models. *Biometrika 80*, 117–126.

LIESENFELD, R. and RICHARD, J.F. (2003): Univariate and multivariate stochastic volatility models: Estimation and diagnostics. *Journal of Empirical Finance* 10, *505–531*.

LOPES, H.F. and CARVALHO C.M. (2007): Factor stochastic volatility with time varying loadings and Markov switching regimes. *Journal of Statistical Planning and Inference* 137, *3082–3091*.

OMORI, Y. and WATANABE, T. (2008): Block sampler and posterior mode estimation for asymmetric stochastic volatility models. *Computational Statistics and Data Analysis* 52-6, *2892–2910*.

PITT, M.K. and SHEPHARD, N. (1999): Time varying covariances: a factor stochastic volatility approach. In J. M. Bernardo, J. O. Berger, A. P. Dawid, and A. F. M. Smith (Eds.), *Bayesian Statistics*, Volume 6, pp. 547–570. Oxford: Oxford University Press.

SHEPHARD, N. and PITT, M.K. (1997): Likelihood analysis of non-Gaussian measurement time series. *Biometrika 84, 653–667.*

SO, M.K.P. and CHOI, C.Y. (2009): A threshold factor multivariate stochastic volatility model. *Journal of Forecasting* 28-8, *712–735*.

TAKAHASHI, M., OMORI, Y. and WATANABE, T. (2009): Estimating stochastic volatility models using daily returns and realized volatility simultaneously. *Computational Statistics and Data Analysis* 53-6, *2404–2426*.

Part XIV

KDD Session: Topological Learning

Bag of Pursuits and Neural Gas for Improved Sparse Coding

Kai Labusch, Erhardt Barth, and Thomas Martinetz

University of Lübeck
Institute for Neuro- and Bioinformatics
Ratzeburger Allee 160
23562 Lübeck, Germany {*labusch,barth,martinetz*} *@inb.uni-luebeck.de*

Abstract. Sparse coding employs low-dimensional subspaces in order to encode high-dimensional signals. Finding the optimal subspaces is a difficult optimization task. We show that stochastic gradient descent is superior in finding the optimal subspaces compared to MOD and K-SVD, which are both state-of-the art methods. The improvement is most significant in the difficult setting of highly overlapping subspaces. We introduce the so-called "Bag of Pursuits" that is derived from Orthogonal Matching Pursuit. It provides an improved approximation of the optimal sparse coefficients, which, in turn, significantly improves the performance of the gradient descent approach as well as MOD and K-SVD. In addition, the "Bag of Pursuits" allows to employ a generalized version of the Neural Gas algorithm for sparse coding, which finally leads to an even more powerful method.

Keywords: sparse coding, neural gas, dictionary learning, matching pursuit

1 Introduction

Many tasks in signal processing and machine learning can be simplified by choosing an appropriate representation of given data. There are a number of desirable properties one wants to achieve, e.g., coding-efficiency, resistance against noise, or invariance against certain transformations. In machine learning, finding a good representation of given data is an important first step in order to solve classification or regression tasks.

Suppose that we are given data $X = (\mathbf{x}_1, \ldots, \mathbf{x}_L)$, $\mathbf{x}_i \in \mathbb{R}^N$. We want to represent X as a linear combination of some dictionary C, i.e., $\mathbf{x}_i = C\mathbf{a}_i$, where $C = (\mathbf{c}_1, \ldots, \mathbf{c}_M)$, $\mathbf{c}_l \in \mathbb{R}^N$. In case of $M > N$, the dictionary is overcomplete.

In this work, we consider the following framework for dictionary design: We are looking for a dictionary C that minimizes the representation error

$$E_h = \frac{1}{L} \sum_{i=1}^{L} \|\mathbf{x}_i - C\mathbf{a}_i\|_2^2 \qquad (1)$$

Y. Lechevallier, G. Saporta (eds.), *Proceedings of COMPSTAT'2010*,
DOI 10.1007/978-3-7908-2604-3_30, © Springer-Verlag Berlin Heidelberg 2010

where $\mathbf{x}_i^{\mathrm{opt}} = C\mathbf{a}_i$ with $\mathbf{a}_i = \arg\min_{\mathbf{a}} \|\mathbf{x}_i - C\mathbf{a}\|$, $\|\mathbf{a}\|_0 \leq k$ denotes the best k-term representation of $\mathbf{x}_i$ in terms of C. The number of dictionary elements M and the maximum number of non-zero entries k are user-defined model parameters.

It has been shown that finding $\mathbf{a}_i$ is in general NP-hard (Davis et al. (1997)). Methods such as Orthogonal Matching Pursuit (OMP) (Pati et al. 1993) or Optimized Orthogonal Matching Pursuit (OOMP, Rebollo-Neira and Lowe (2002)) can be used in order to find an approximation of the coefficients of the best k-term representation. The Method of Optimal Directions (MOD, Engan et al. (1999)) and the K-SVD algorithm (Aharon et al. (2006)) can employ an arbitrary approximation method for the coefficients in order to learn a dictionary from the data. First, the coefficients are determined, then they are considered fixed in order to update the dictionary.

Using data that actually was generated as a sparse linear combination of some given dictionary, it has been shown (Aharon et al. (2006)) that methods such as MOD or K-SVD can be used in order to reconstruct the dictionary only from the data even in highly overcomplete settings under the presence of strong noise. However, our experiments show that even K-SVD which performed best in (Aharon et al. (2006)) requires highly sparse linear combinations for good dictionary reconstruction performance. The SCNG algorithm does not possess this deficiency (Labusch et al. (2009)), but, unlike MOD or K-SVD, it is bound to a specific approximation method for the coefficients, i.e., OOMP.

Here, we propose a new method for designing overcomplete dictionaries that performs well even if the linear combinations are less sparse. Like MOD or K-SVD, it can employ an arbitrary approximation method for the coefficients. In order to demonstrate the performance of the method, we test it on synthetically generated overcomplete linear combinations of known dictionaries and compare the obtained performance against MOD and K-SVD.

2   From vector quantization to sparse coding

Vector quantization learns a representation of given data in terms of so-called codebook vectors. Each given sample is encoded by the closest codebook vector. Vector quantization can be understood as a special case of sparse coding where the coefficients are constrained by $\|\mathbf{a}_i\|_0 = 1$ and $\|\mathbf{a}_i\|_2 = 1$, i.e., vector quantization looks for a codebook C that minimizes (1) choosing the coefficients according to

$$(\mathbf{a}_i)_m = 1, \ (\mathbf{a}_i)_l = 0 \ \forall l \neq m \quad \text{where} \quad m = \arg\min_l \|\mathbf{c}_l - \mathbf{x}_i\|_2^2 . \quad (2)$$

In order to learn a good codebook, many vector quantization algorithms consider only the winner for learning, i.e., the codebook vector $\mathbf{c}_m$ for which $(\mathbf{a}_i)_m = 1$ holds. As a consequence of that type of hard-competitive learning scheme, problems such as bad quantization, initialization sensitivity, or slow convergence can arise.

In order to remedy these problems soft-competitive vector quantization methods such as the NG algorithm (Martinetz et al. (1993)) have been proposed. In the NG algorithm all possible encodings are considered in each learning step, i.e., $\mathbf{a}_i^1, \ldots, \mathbf{a}_i^M$ with $(\mathbf{a}_i^j)_j = 1$. Then, the encodings are sorted according to their reconstruction error

$$\|\mathbf{x}_i - C\mathbf{a}_i^{j_0}\| \leq \|\mathbf{x}_i - C\mathbf{a}_i^{j_1}\| \leq \cdots \leq \|\mathbf{x}_i - C\mathbf{a}_i^{j_p}\| \leq \cdots \leq \|\mathbf{x}_i - C\mathbf{a}_i^{j_M}\| . \quad (3)$$

In contrast to the hard-competitive approaches, in each learning iteration, every codebook vector $\mathbf{c}_l$ is updated. The update is weighted according to the rank of the encoding that uses the codebook vector $\mathbf{c}_l$. It has been shown in (Martinetz et al. (1993)) that this type of update is equivalent to a gradient descent on a well-defined cost function. Due to the soft-competitive learning scheme the NG algorithm shows robust convergence to close to optimal distributions of the codebook vectors over the data manifold.

Here we want to apply this ranking approach to the learning of sparse codes. Similar to the NG algorithm, for each given sample $\mathbf{x}_i$, we consider all K possible coefficient vectors $\mathbf{a}_i^j$, i.e., encodings that have at most k non-zero entries. The elements of each $\mathbf{a}_i^j$ are chosen such that $\|\mathbf{x}_i - C\mathbf{a}_i^j\|$ is minimal. We order the coefficients according to the representation error that is obtained by using them to approximate the sample $\mathbf{x}_i$

$$\|\mathbf{x}_i - C\mathbf{a}_i^{j_0}\| < \|\mathbf{x}_i - C\mathbf{a}_i^{j_1}\| < \cdots < \|\mathbf{x}_i - C\mathbf{a}_i^{j_p}\| < \cdots < \|\mathbf{x}_i - C\mathbf{a}_i^{j_K}\| . \quad (4)$$

If there are coefficient vectors that lead to the same reconstruction error

$$\|\mathbf{x}_i - C\mathbf{a}_i^{m_1}\| = \|\mathbf{x}_i - C\mathbf{a}_i^{m_2}\| = \cdots = \|\mathbf{x}_i - C\mathbf{a}_i^{m_V}\| , \quad (5)$$

we randomly pick one of them and do not consider the others. Note that we need this due to theoretical considerations while in practice this situation almost never occurs. Let $\mathrm{rank}(\mathbf{x}_i, \mathbf{a}_i^j, C) = p$ denote the number of coefficient vectors $\mathbf{a}_i^m$ with $\|\mathbf{x}_i - C\mathbf{a}_i^m\| < \|\mathbf{x}_i - C\mathbf{a}_i^j\|$. Introducing the neighborhood $h_{\lambda_t}(v) = e^{-v/\lambda_t}$, we consider the following modified error function

$$E_s = \sum_{i=1}^{L} \sum_{j=1}^{K} h_{\lambda_t}(\mathrm{rank}(\mathbf{x}_i, \mathbf{a}_i^j, C)) \|\mathbf{x}_i - C\mathbf{a}_i^j\|_2^2 \quad (6)$$

which becomes equal to (1) for $\lambda_t \to 0$. In order to minimize (6), we consider the gradient of E_s with respect to C, which is

$$\frac{\partial E_s}{\partial C} = -2 \sum_{i=1}^{L} \sum_{j=1}^{K} h_{\lambda_t}(\mathrm{rank}(\mathbf{x}_i, \mathbf{a}_i^j, C))(\mathbf{x}_i - C\mathbf{a}_i^j){\mathbf{a}_i^j}^T + R \quad (7)$$

with

$$R = \sum_{i=1}^{L} \sum_{j=1}^{K} h'_{\lambda_t}(\mathrm{rank}(\mathbf{x}_i, \mathbf{a}_i^j, C)) \frac{\partial \mathrm{rank}(\mathbf{x}_i, \mathbf{a}_i^j, C)}{\partial C} \|\mathbf{x}_i - C\mathbf{a}_i^j\|_2^2. \qquad (8)$$

In order to show that $R = 0$, we adopt the proof given in (Martinetz et al. (1993)) to our setting. With $\mathbf{e}_i^j = \mathbf{x}_i - C\mathbf{a}_i^j$, we write $\mathrm{rank}(\mathbf{x}_i, \mathbf{a}_i^j, C)$ as

$$\mathrm{rank}(\mathbf{x}_i, \mathbf{a}_i^j, C) = \sum_{m=1}^{K} \theta((\mathbf{e}_i^j)^2 - (\mathbf{e}_i^m)^2) \qquad (9)$$

where $\theta(x)$ is the heaviside step function. The derivative of the heaviside step function is the delta distribution $\delta(x)$ with $\delta(x) = 0$ for $x \neq 0$ and $\int \delta(x)dx = 1$. Therefore, we can write

$$R = \sum_{i=1}^{L} \sum_{j=1}^{K} h'_{\lambda_t}(\mathrm{rank}(\mathbf{x}_i, \mathbf{a}_i^j, C))(\mathbf{e}_i^j)^2 \sum_{m=1}^{T} ((\mathbf{a}_i^j)^T - (\mathbf{a}_i^m)^T) \delta((\mathbf{e}_i^j)^2 - (\mathbf{e}_i^m)^2) \quad (10)$$

Each term of (10) is non-vanishing only for those $\mathbf{a}_i^j$ for which $(\mathbf{e}_i^j)^2 = (\mathbf{e}_i^m)^2$ is valid. Since we explicitly excluded this case, we obtain $R = 0$. Hence, we can perform a stochastic gradient descent on (6) with respect to C by applying $t = 0, \ldots, t_{\max}$ updates of C using the gradient based learning rule

$$\Delta C = \alpha_t \sum_{j=1}^{K} h_{\lambda_t}(\mathrm{rank}(\mathbf{x}_i, \mathbf{a}_i^j, C))(\mathbf{x}_i - C\mathbf{a}_i^j)\mathbf{a}_j^{i T} \qquad (11)$$

for a randomly chosen $\mathbf{x}_i \in X$ where $\lambda_t = \lambda_0 (\lambda_{\mathrm{final}}/\lambda_0)^{\frac{t}{t_{\max}}}$ is an exponentially decreasing neighborhood-size and $\alpha_t = \alpha_0 (\alpha_{\mathrm{final}}/\alpha_0)^{\frac{t}{t_{\max}}}$ an exponentially decreasing learning rate. After each update has been applied, the column vectors of C are renormalized to one. Then the $\mathbf{a}_i^j$ are re-determined and the next update for C can be performed.

3   A bag of orthogonal matching pursuits

So far, for each training sample $\mathbf{x}_i$, all possible coefficient vectors $\mathbf{a}_i^j$, $j = 1, \ldots, K$ with $\|\mathbf{a}_i^j\|_0 \leq k$ have been considered. K grows exponentially with M and k. Therefore, this approach is not applicable in practice. However, since in (6) all those contributions in the sum for which the rank is larger than the neighborhood-size λ_t can be neglected, we actually do not need all possible coefficient vectors. We only need the first best ones with respect to the reconstruction error.

There are a number of approaches, which try to find the best coefficient vector, e.g., OMP or OOMP. It has been shown that in well-behaved cases they can find at least good approximations (Tropp (2004)). In the following, we extend OOMP such that not only the best but the first K_{user} best coefficients are determined, at least approximately.

OOMP is a greedy method that iteratively constructs a given sample $\mathbf{x}$ out of the columns of the dictionary C. The algorithm starts with $U_n^j = \emptyset$,

$R_0^j = (\mathbf{r}_1^{0,j}, \ldots, \mathbf{r}_M^{0,j}) = C$ and $\epsilon_0^j = \mathbf{x}$. The set U_n^j contains the indices of those columns of C that have been used during the j-th pursuit with respect to $\mathbf{x}$ up to the n-th iteration. R_n^j is a temporary matrix that has been orthogonalized with respect to the columns of C that are indexed by U_n^j. $\mathbf{r}_l^{n,j}$ is the l-th column of R_n^j. ϵ_n^j is the residual in the n-th iteration of the j-th pursuit with respect to $\mathbf{x}$.

In iteration n, the algorithm looks for that column of R_n^j whose inclusion in the linear combination leads to the smallest residual ϵ_{n+1}^j in the next iteration of the algorithm, i.e., that has the maximum overlap with respect to the current residual. Hence, with

$$\mathbf{y}_n^j = \left((\mathbf{r}_1^{n,j}{}^T \epsilon_n^j)/\|\mathbf{r}_1^{n,j}\|, \ldots, (\mathbf{r}_l^{n,j}{}^T \epsilon_n^j)/\|\mathbf{r}_l^{n,j}\|, \ldots, (\mathbf{r}_M^{n,j}{}^T \epsilon_n^j)/\|\mathbf{r}_M^{n,j}\| \right) \quad (12)$$

it looks for $l_{\mathrm{win}}(n,j) = \arg\max_{l, l \notin U_n^j} (\mathbf{y}_n^j)_l$. Then, the orthogonal projection of R_n^j to $\mathbf{r}_{l_{\mathrm{win}}(n,j)}^{n,j}$ is removed from R_n^j

$$R_{n+1}^j = R_n^j - (\mathbf{r}_{l_{\mathrm{win}}(n,j)}^{n,j}(R_n^j{}^T \mathbf{r}_{l_{\mathrm{win}}(n,j)}^{n,j})^T)/(\mathbf{r}_{l_{\mathrm{win}}(n,j)}^{n,j}{}^T \mathbf{r}_{l_{\mathrm{win}}(n,j)}^{n,j}) . \quad (13)$$

Furthermore, the orthogonal projection of ϵ_n^j to $\mathbf{r}_{l_{\mathrm{win}}(n,j)}^{n,j}$ is removed from ϵ_n^j

$$\epsilon_{n+1}^j = \epsilon_n^j - \left((\epsilon_n^j{}^T \mathbf{r}_{l_{\mathrm{win}}(n,j)}^{n,j})/(\mathbf{r}_{l_{\mathrm{win}}(n,j)}^{n,j}{}^T \mathbf{r}_{l_{\mathrm{win}}(n,j)}^{n,j}) \right) \mathbf{r}_{l_{\mathrm{win}}(n,j)}^{n,j} . \quad (14)$$

The algorithm stops if $\|\epsilon_n^j\| = 0$ or $n = k$. The j-th approximation of the coefficients of the best k-term approximation, i.e., $\mathbf{a}^j$, can be obtained by recursively tracking the contribution of each column of C that has been used during the iterations of pursuit j. In order to obtain a set of approximations $\mathbf{a}^1, \ldots, \mathbf{a}^{K_{\mathrm{user}}}$, where K_{user} is chosen by the user, we want to conduct K_{user} matching pursuits. To obtain K_{user} different pursuits, we implement the following function:

$$Q(l, n, j) = \begin{cases} 0 : & \begin{array}{l}\text{If there is no pursuit among all pursuits that have} \\ \text{been performed with respect to } \mathbf{x} \text{ that is equal to} \\ \text{the } j\text{-th pursuit up to the } n\text{-th iteration where in} \\ \text{that iteration column } l \text{ has been selected}\end{array} \\ 1 : & \text{else .} \end{cases} \quad (15)$$

Then, while a pursuit is performed, we track all overlaps $\mathbf{y}_n^j$ that have been computed during that pursuit. For instance if $\mathbf{a}^1$ has been determined, we have $\mathbf{y}_0^1, \ldots, \mathbf{y}_n^1, \ldots, \mathbf{y}_{s_1-1}^1$ where s_1 is the number of iterations of the 1st pursuit with respect to $\mathbf{x}$. In order to find $\mathbf{a}^2$, we now look for the largest overlap in the previous pursuit that has not been used so far

$$n_{\mathrm{target}} = \arg \max_{n=0,\ldots,s_1-1} \max_{l, Q(l,n,j)=0} (\mathbf{y}_n^1)_l \quad (16)$$

$$l_{\mathrm{target}} = \arg \max_l (\mathbf{y}_{n_{\mathrm{target}}}^1)_l . \quad (17)$$

We replay the 1st pursuit up to iteration n_{target}. In that iteration, we select column l_{target} instead of the previous winner and continue with the pursuit until the stopping criterion has been reached. If m pursuits have been performed, among all previous pursuits, we look for the largest overlap that has not been used so far:

$$j_{\text{target}} = \arg \max_{j=1,\dots,m} \max_{n=0,\dots,s_j-1} \max_{l,Q(l,n,j)=0} (\mathbf{y}_n^j)_l \qquad (18)$$

$$n_{\text{target}} = \arg \max_{n=0,\dots,s_{j_{\text{target}}}-1} \max_{l,Q(l,n,j_{\text{target}})=0} (\mathbf{y}_n^{j_{\text{target}}})_l \qquad (19)$$

$$l_{\text{target}} = \arg \max_{l,Q(l,n_{\text{target}},j_{\text{target}})=0} (\mathbf{y}_{n_{\text{target}}}^{j_{\text{target}}})_l . \qquad (20)$$

We replay pursuit j_{target} up to iteration n_{target}. In that iteration, we select column l_{target} instead of the previous winner and continue with the pursuit until the stopping criterion has been reached. We repeat this procedure until K_{user} pursuits have been performed.

4   Experiments

In the experiments we use synthetic data that actually can be represented as sparse linear combinations of some dictionary. We perform the experiments in order to asses two questions: (i) How good is the target function (1) minimized? (ii) Is it possible to obtain the generating dictionary only from the given data?

In the following $C^{\text{true}} = (\mathbf{c}_1^{\text{true}}, \dots, \mathbf{c}_{50}^{\text{true}}) \in \mathbb{R}^{20 \times 50}$ denotes a synthetic dictionary. Each entry of C^{true} is uniformly chosen in the interval $[-0.5, 0.5]$. Furthermore, we set $\|\mathbf{c}_l^{\text{true}}\| = 1$. Using such a dictionary, we create a training set $X = (\mathbf{x}_1, \dots, \mathbf{x}_{1500})$, $\mathbf{x}_i \in \mathbb{R}^{20}$ where each training sample $\mathbf{x}_i$ is a sparse linear combination of the columns of the dictionary:

$$\mathbf{x}_i = C^{\text{true}}\mathbf{b}_i . \qquad (21)$$

We choose the coefficient vectors $\mathbf{b}_i \in \mathbb{R}^{50}$ such that they contain k non-zero entries. The selection of the position of the non-zero entries in the coefficient vectors is performed according to three different data generation scenarios:

Random dictionary elements: In this scenario all combinations of k dictionary elements are possible. Hence, the position of the non-zero entries in each coefficient vector $\mathbf{b}_i$ is uniformly chosen in the interval $[1, \dots, 50]$.

Independent Subspaces: In this case the training samples are located in a small number of k-dimensional subspaces. We achieve this by defining $\lfloor 50/k \rfloor$ groups of dictionary elements, each group containing k randomly selected dictionary elements. The groups do not intersect, i.e., each dictionary element is at most member of one group. In order to generate a training sample, we uniformly choose one group of dictionary elements and obtain the training sample as a linear combination of the dictionary elements that belong to the selected group.

Dependent subspaces: In this case, similar to the previous scenario, the training samples are located in a small number of k-dimensional subspaces. In contrast to the previous scenario, the subspaces do highly intersect, i.e., the subspaces share basis vectors. In order to achieve this, we uniformly select $k-1$ dictionary elements. Then, we use $50-k+1$ groups of dictionary elements where each group consists of the $k-1$ selected dictionary elements plus one further dictionary element. Again, in order to generate a training sample, we uniformly choose one group of dictionary elements and obtain the training sample as a linear combination of the dictionary elements that belong to the selected group.

The value of the non-zero entries is always chosen uniformly in the interval $[-0.5, 0.5]$.

We apply MOD, K-SVD and the stochastic gradient descent method that is proposed in this paper to the training data. Let $C^{\text{learned}} = (\mathbf{c}_1^{\text{learned}}, \ldots, \mathbf{c}_{50}^{\text{learned}})$ denote the dictionary that has been learned by one of these methods on the basis of the training samples. In order to measure the performance of the methods with respect to the minimization of the target function, we consider

$$E_h = \frac{1}{1500} \sum_{i=1}^{1500} \|\mathbf{x}_i - C^{\text{learned}} \mathbf{a}_i\|_2^2 \qquad (22)$$

where $\mathbf{a}_i$ is obtained from the best pursuit out of $K_{\text{user}} = 20$ pursuits that have been performed according to the approach described in section 3. In order to asses if the true dictionary can be reconstructed from the training data, we consider the mean maximum overlap between each element of the true dictionary and the learned dictionary:

$$MMO = \frac{1}{50} \sum_{l=1}^{50} \max_{k=1,\ldots,50} |\mathbf{c}_l^{\text{true}} \mathbf{c}_k^{\text{learned}}| . \qquad (23)$$

k, the number of non-zero entries is varied from 1 to 11. For the stochastic gradient descent method, we perform 100×1500 update steps, i.e., 100 learning epochs. For MOD and K-SVD, we perform 100 learning iterations each iteration using 1500 training samples. We repeat all experiments 50 times and report the mean result over all experiments.

In the first set of experiments, for all dictionary learning methods, i.e., MOD, K-SVD, and stochastic gradient descent, a single orthogonal matching pursuit is used in order to obtain the dictionary coefficients during learning. Furthermore, the stochastic gradient descent is performed in hard-competitive mode, which uses a neighborhood-size that is practically zero, i.e., $\lambda_0 = \lambda_{\text{final}} = 10^{-10}$. The results of this experiment are depicted in table 1 (a)-(c) and (j)-(l). In case of the random dictionary elements scenario (see (a) and (j)) the stochastic gradient approach clearly outperforms MOD and K-SVD. From the mean maximum overlap it can be seen that almost all dictionary elements are well reconstructed with up to 6 non-zero coefficients in the linear

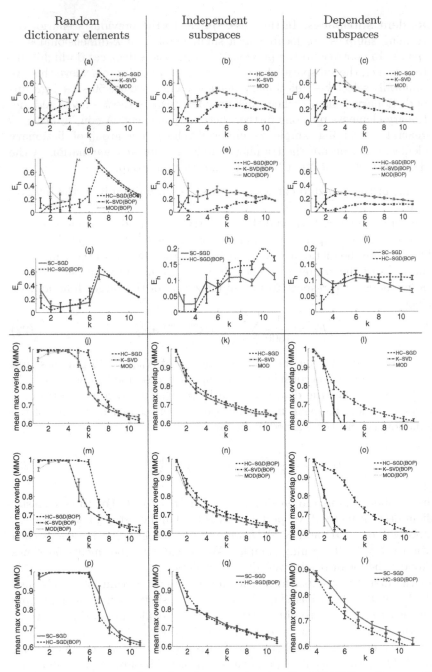

Table 1. Experimental results. See text for details. SC-SGD: soft-competitive stochastic gradient descent ($\lambda_0 = 20, \lambda_{\text{final}} = 0.65$). HC-SGD: hard-competitive stochastic gradient descent ($\lambda_0 = \lambda_{\text{final}} = 10^{-10}$).

combinations. If the dictionary elements cannot be reconstructed any more, i.e., for $k > 6$, the mean representation error E_h starts to grow. In case of the independent subspaces and dependent subspaces scenario the stochastic gradient method also outperforms MOD and K-SVD in terms of minimization of the representation error (see (b) and (c)) whereas in terms of dictionary reconstruction performance only in the intersecting subspaces scenario a clear performance gain compared to MOD and K-SVD can be seen ((k) and (l)). This might be caused by the fact that in case of the independent subspaces scenario it is sufficient to find dictionary elements that span the subspaces where the data is located in order to minimize the target function, i.e., the scenario does not force the method to find the true dictionary elements in order to minimize the target function.

In the second experiment for all methods the dictionary coefficients were obtained from the best pursuit out of $K_{user} = 20$ pursuits that were performed according to the "Bag of Pursuits" approach described in section 3. The results of this experiment are depicted in table 1 (d)-(f) and (m)-(o). Compared to the results of the first experiment (see (a)-(c)) it can be seen that the computationally more demanding method for the approximation of the best coefficients leads to a significantly improved performance of MOD, K-SVD and the stochastic gradient descent with respect to the minimization of the representation error E_h (see (d)-(f)). The most obvious improvement can be seen in case of the dependent subspaces scenario where also the dictionary reconstruction performance significantly improves (see (l) and (o)). In the random dictionary elements (see (j) and (m)) and independent subspaces scenario (see (k) and (n)) there are only small improvements with respect to the reconstruction of the true dictionary.

In the third experiment, we employed soft-competitive learning in the stochastic gradient descend, i.e., the coefficients corresponding to each of the $K_{user} = 20$ pursuits were used in the update step according to (11) with $\lambda_0 = 20$ and $\lambda_{final} = 0.65$. The results of this experiment are depicted in table 1 (g)-(i) and (p)-(r). It can be seen that for less sparse scenarios, i.e. $k > 6$, the soft-competitive learning further improves the performance. Particularly in case of the dependent subspaces scenario a significant improvement in terms dictionary reconstruction performance can be seen for $k > 4$ (see (r)). For very sparse settings, i.e. $k \leq 4$, the hard-competitive approach seems to perform better than the soft-competitive variant. Again, in case of the independent subspaces only the representation error decreases (see (h)) whereas no performance gain for the dictionary reconstruction can be seen (see (q)). Again this might be caused by the fact that in case of the subspace scenario learning of dictionary elements that span the subspaces is sufficient in order to minimize the target function.

5 Conclusion

We proposed a stochastic gradient descent method that can be used either for hard-competitive or soft-competitive learning of sparse codes. We introduced the so-called "bag of pursuits" in order to compute a better estimation of the best k-term approximation of given data. This method can be used together with a generalization of the neural gas approach to perform soft-competitive stochastic gradient learning of (overcomplete) dictionaries for sparse coding.

Our experiments on synthetic data show that compared to other state-of-the-art methods such as MOD or K-SVD a significant performance improvement in terms of minimization of the representation error as well as in terms of reconstruction of the true dictionary elements that were used to generate the data can be observed. While a significant performance gain is already obtained by hard-competitive stochastic gradient descend an even better performance is obtained by using the "bag of pursuits" and soft-competitive learning. In particular, as a function of decreasing sparseness, the performance of the method described in this paper degrades much slower than that of MOD and K-SVD. This should improve the design of overcomplete dictionaries also in more complex settings.

References

AHARON, M., ELAD, M. and BRUCKSTEIN. A. (2006): K-SVD: An Algorithm for Designing Overcomplete Dictionaries for Sparse Representation. *IEEE Transactions on Signal Processing,[see also IEEE Transactions on Acoustics, Speech, and Signal Processing]*, 54(11):4311–4322.

DAVIS, G., MALLAT, S. and AVELLANEDA. M. (1997): Greedy adaptive approximation. *J. Constr. Approx.*, 13:57–89.

K. ENGAN, K., AASE, S. O. and HAKON HUSOY., J. (1999): Method of optimal directions for frame design. In *ICASSP '99: Proceedings of the IEEE International Conference on Acoustics, Speech, and Signal Processing*, pages 2443–2446, Washington, DC, USA, 1999. IEEE Computer Society.

LABUSCH, K., BARTH, E. and MARTINETZ. T. (2009): Sparse Coding Neural Gas: Learning of Overcomplete Data Representations. *Neurocomputing, 72(7-9):1547–1555*.

MARTINETZ, T., BERKOVICH, S. and SCHULTEN. K. (1993): "Neural-gas" Network for Vector Quantization and its Application to Time-Series Prediction. *IEEE-Transactions on Neural Networks, 4(4):558–569*.

PATI, Y., REZAIIFAR, R. and KRISHNAPRASAD. P. (1993): Orthogonal Matching Pursuit: Recursive Function Approximation with Applications to Wavelet Decomposition. *Proceedings of the 27 th Annual Asilomar Conference on Signals, Systems, and Computers.*

REBOLLO-NEIRA, L. and LOWE. D. (2002): Optimized orthogonal matching pursuit approach. *IEEE Signal Processing Letters, 9(4):137–140*.

TROPP. J. A. (2004): Greed is good: algorithmic results for sparse approximation. *IEEE Transactions on Information Theory, 50(10):2231–2242*.

On the Role and Impact of the Metaparameters in t-distributed Stochastic Neighbor Embedding

John A. Lee[1] and Michel Verleysen[2]

[1] Imagerie Moléculaire et Radiothérapie Expérimentale
Avenue Hippocrate 54, B-1200 Brussels, Belgium *john.lee@uclouvain.be*
[2] Machine Learning Group - DICE, Place du Levant 3, B-1348 Louvain-la-Neuve,
Belgium *michel.verleysen@uclouvain.be*

Abstract. Similarity-based embedding is a paradigm that recently gained interest in the field of nonlinear dimensionality reduction. It provides an elegant framework that naturally emphasizes the preservation of the local structure of the data set. An emblematic method in this trend is *t*-distributed stochastic neighbor embedding (t-SNE), which is acknowledged to be an efficient method in the recent literature. This paper aims at analyzing the reasons of this success, together with the impact of the two metaparameters embedded in the method. Moreover, the paper shows that t-SNE can be interpreted as a distance-preserving method with a specific distance transformation, making the link with existing methods. Experiments on artificial data support the theoretical discussion.

Keywords: similarity-based embedding, dimensionality reduction, nonlinear projection, manifold learning, t-SNE

1 Introduction

Dimensionality reduction is the task of finding faithful, low-dimensional representations of high-dimensional data. Although the case of clustered data can be considered too, dimensionality reduction usually relies on the assumption that the data are sampled from a smooth manifold. Methods such as principal component analysis (PCA) or classical metric multidimensional scaling (MDS) (Young and Householder (1938)) can be successfully applied when the manifold is a linear subspace. However, when the manifold is curved or folded (Tenenbaum et al. (2000)), one should use adapted nonlinear dimensionality reduction (Lee and Verleysen (2007)) (NLDR). Nonmetric MDS (Shepard (1962), Kruskal (1964)) and Sammon's nonlinear mapping (SNLM) (Sammon (1969)) are early methods generalizing MDS, based on the principle of distance preservation. Spectral embedding (Saul et al. (2006)) has emerged since the seminal paper describing kernel PCA (Scholkopf et al. (1998)). Isomap (Tenenbaum et al. (2000)), locally linear embedding (Roweis and Saul (2000)), Laplacian eigenmaps (Belkin and Niyogi (2002)), and maximum variance unfolding (MVU) (Weinberger and Saul (2006)) are among

Y. Lechevallier, G. Saporta (eds.), *Proceedings of COMPSTAT'2010*,
DOI 10.1007/978-3-7908-2604-3_31, © Springer-Verlag Berlin Heidelberg 2010

the most representative methods in this category. Spectral methods provide the guarantee of finding the global optimum of their cost function. In contrast, methods based on other optimization techniques generally do not offer this advantage. However, they usually compensate for this drawback by the capability of handling a broader range of cost functions. Successful nonspectral methods are among others curvilinear component analysis (CCA) (Demartines and Herault (1997)), stochastic neighbor embedding (SNE) (Hinton and Roweis (2003)), and its variant t-SNE (Van der Maaten and Hinton (2008)). CCA has long been considered to be a distance-preserving method that can be related to SNLM. In contrast, SNE and t-SNE seek to match similarities, which are basically decreasing functions of the pairwise distances. This reformulation provides a more natural way to formalise the importance of preserving the local structure of data. t-SNE is nowadays considered as an efficient method for visualizing high-dimensional data (see for example Erhan et al. (2009), Parviainen and Vehtari (2009)).

This paper aims at analysing the behavior of t-SNE and the key influence of its two metaparameters, namely the so-called perplexity and the number of degrees of freedom. It addition, it shows that t-SNE can be cast within the framework of distance preservation, by means of a distance tranformation; we identify this transformation, and compare it to other methods.

The remainder of this paper is organized as follows. Section 2 briefly reviews SNE and t-SNE. Section 3 weaves the connection between distance preservation and similarity matching. Sections 4 and 5 provide and discuss the experimental results. Finally, Section 6 draws the conclusions.

2   Stochastic Neighbor Embedding

Let $\Xi = [\xi_i]_{1 \leq i \leq N}$ denote a data set of N vectors picked in an M dimensional space. Symbol δ_{ij} denotes the pairwise distance between data vectors ξ_i and ξ_j. The similarity between ξ_i and ξ_j is defined in SNE as:

$$p_{j|i}(\lambda_i) \doteq \begin{cases} 0 & \text{if } i = j \\ g(\delta_{ij}/\lambda_i) \Big/ \sum_{k \neq i} g(\delta_{ik}/\lambda_i) & \text{otherwise} \end{cases},$$

where $g(u) = \exp(-u^2/2)$. In Hinton and Roweis (2003), $p_{j|i}$ is referred to as a conditional probability and represents the empirical probability of ξ_j to be a neighbor of ξ_i. The softmax denominator indeed guarantees that $\sum_{j=1}^{N} p_{i|j} = 1$. Probabilities $p_{j|i}(\lambda_i)$ and $p_{i|j}(\lambda_j)$ are not equal since they involve kernels with individual widths. A user-defined metaparameter, the perplexity PPXT, induces all widths λ_i through the equation $2^{H(p_{j|i})} = \text{PPXT}$, where $H(p_{j|i}) \doteq \sum_{j=1}^{N} p_{j|i} \log_2 p_{j|i}$ is the entropy of $p_{j|i}$. Intuitively, the perplexity allows the Gaussian kernels to adapt their width to the local density of data points.

Within this framework, a symmetric similarity function between ξ_i and ξ_j can be defined by $p_{ij}(\lambda) \doteq \frac{1}{2N}\left(p_{j|i}(\lambda_i) + p_{i|j}(\lambda_j)\right)$, where $\lambda = [\lambda_i]_{1 \leq i \leq N}$

and p_{ij} is referred to as a joint probability. As for the conditional probability, we have $p_{ii}(\boldsymbol{\lambda}) = 0$ and $\sum_{i,j=1}^{N} p_{ij}(\boldsymbol{\lambda}) = 1$.

In the low-dimensional space, let $\mathbf{X} = [\mathbf{x}_i]_{1 \leq i \leq N}$ denote the embedding to be found by SNE. If d_{ij} is the Euclidean distance $\|\mathbf{x}_i - \mathbf{x}_j\|_2$, then pairwise similarities in the low-dimensional space can be written as

$$
q_{ij}(n) \doteq \begin{cases} 0 & \text{if } i = j \\ t(d_{ij}, n) \big/ \sum_{k \neq l} t(d_{kl}, n) & \text{otherwise} \end{cases} , \tag{1}
$$

where $t(u, n) = (1 + u^2/n)^{-(n+1)/2}$. Function $t(u, n)$ is proportional to the probability density of a Student's t-distributed variable with n degrees of freedom; n controls the tail thickness of the similarity kernel. It is noteworthy that $\lim_{n \to \infty} t(u, n) = g(u)$. Hence, SNE (Hinton and Roweis (2003) corresponds to the case $n \to \infty$ whereas t-SNE (Van der Maaten and Hinton (2008), Van der Maaten (2009)) turns out to be the case $n = 1$. Like $p_{ij}(\boldsymbol{\lambda})$, $q_{ij}(n)$ is referred to as a joint probability, although it is differently defined. Two important differences are the kernel shape and the absence of scaling parameter. Another difference is that $q_{ij}(n)$ can be interpreted as a (non-conditional) probability, thanks to the single softmax denominator.

The t-SNE method compares $p_{ij}(\boldsymbol{\lambda})$ and $q_{ij}(n)$ by means of a (discrete) Kullback-Leibler divergence:

$$
E(\boldsymbol{\Xi}, \mathbf{X}, \boldsymbol{\lambda}, n) = D_{\mathrm{KL}}(p\|q) \doteq \sum_{i,j=1}^{N} p_{ij}(\boldsymbol{\lambda}) \log \frac{p_{ij}(\boldsymbol{\lambda})}{q_{ij}(n)} .
$$

The minimization of E can be achieved by gradient descent. In t-SNE, the gradient of $E(\boldsymbol{\Xi}, \mathbf{X}, \boldsymbol{\lambda}, n)$ with respect to $\mathbf{x}_i$ can be written as (Van der Maaten and Hinton (2008), Van der Maaten (2009))

$$
\frac{\partial E}{\partial \mathbf{x}_i} = \frac{2n+2}{n} \sum_{j=1}^{N} \frac{p_{ij}(\boldsymbol{\lambda}) - q_{ij}(n)}{1 + d_{ij}^2/n} (\mathbf{x}_i - \mathbf{x}_j) . \tag{2}
$$

It is easy to verify that

$$
\lim_{n \to \infty} \frac{\partial E}{\partial \mathbf{x}_i} = 2 \sum_{j=1}^{N} (p_{ij}(\boldsymbol{\lambda}) - q_{ij}(n))(\mathbf{x}_i - \mathbf{x}_j) ,
$$

which corresponds to the gradient of SNE. In the context of a gradient descent, three factors can be identified in each term of (2). Factor $(\mathbf{x}_i - \mathbf{x}_j)$ is a vector that allows $\mathbf{x}_i$ to move towards $\mathbf{x}_j$. Factor $(p_{ij}(\boldsymbol{\lambda}) - q_{ij}(n))$ varies between -1 and $+1$; it is proportional to the similarity error and adjusts the length and direction (inwards/outwards) of the movement. Finally, factor $(1 + d_{ij}^2/n)^{-1}$ varies between 0 and 1 and damps the movement, especially if $\mathbf{x}_i$ lies far away from $\mathbf{x}_j$. A similar factor can be found in the gradient of CCA

(Demartines and Herault (1997)). It provides the capability of 'tearing' the manifold to be embedded. Additional details about t-SNE and the gradient descent of E can be found in van der Maaten and Hinton (2008).

The discrepancy between the kernels in the high- and low-dimensional spaces is intended to address the curse of dimensionality. Let us take the exemple of a curved P-dimensional manifold embedded in an M-dimensional space (with $M > P$). It is easy to see that the Euclidean distance between any two manifold points shrinks as the curvature increases, especially if they lie far away from each other. Hence, a strict isometry will not succeed in embedding the manifold in a low-dimensional space: a poor unfording with several regions superimposed would result (Hinton and Roweis (2003)). Based on this observation, the similarity kernels in t-SNE have heavier tails in the embedding space, to force large distances to grow in order to attain the same similarity value as in the data space.

3 Connection between similarity and distance preservation

Let us assume that t-SNE finds an embedding that cancels the gradient of its objective function. A sufficient condition to obtain such a solution is that one of the terms in (2) vanishes. A trivial (useless) solution is when $d_{ij} = 0$ for all i and j. Another trivial solution is $d_{ij} \to \infty$ for all i and j, because the damping factor tends to zero. The useful solution consists in satisfying $p_{ij}(\boldsymbol{\lambda}) = q_{ij}(n)$. In this last case, let us approximate the above definition of $p_{ij}(\boldsymbol{\lambda})$ with $p_{ij} \approx p_{j|i}/N$. Using this approximation in conjunction with the definition of $q_{ij}(n)$ in (1) allows us to write

$$d_{ij} \approx f(\delta_{ij}) \doteq \sqrt{nR_i^{\frac{2}{n+1}} \exp\left(\frac{\delta_{ij}^2}{(n+1)\lambda_i^2}\right) - n}, \qquad (3)$$

where $R_i = N \sum_{k \neq i} g(\delta_{ik}/\lambda_i) / \sum_{k \neq l} t(d_{kl}, n)$ is the ratio of the softmax denominators. If we get rid of the difficulty raised by the softmax denominators, namely if we assume that $R_i \approx 1$, then we can see SNE and t-SNE as NLDR methods that preserve transformed distances. The transformation has an exponentially increasing shape; its key properties are

- $f(0) = 0$ and f is monotonically increasing on $\mathbb{R}_+$,
- $\lim_{n \to \infty} f(\delta_{ij}) = \delta_{ij}/\lambda_i$,
- if $\delta_{ij} \ll \lambda_i$, then $d_{ij} = f(\delta_{ij}) \approx \delta_{ij}/(\lambda_i\sqrt{n+1})$.

Intuitively, t-SNE tries to preserve stretched distances; the stretch is exponential. In the case of SNE, the transformation degenerates and distances are merely locally scaled by λ_i. The second property shows that a similar scaling occurs when $\delta_{ij} \ll \lambda_i$. What is important to note is that λ_i and n act more or less in the same way in transformation (3), namely they modulate the exponential growth. However, the differences are that (i) n is global whereas the λ_i can fluctuate locally, (ii) changing the perplexity (which approximately amounts to multiplying all λ_i with approximately the same factor) impacts the scale of the embedding, while changing n does not have this effect.

The relationship between n and the intrinsic dimensionality of the manifold that is put forward in Van der Maaten (2009) is questioned by the above analysis. First, because n and the perplexity cannot be studied separately and, second, because n depends neither on the embedding dimensionality nor on the data dimensionality. In addition, the optimal distance transformation depends on the manifold shape: in the above example, changing the curvature of the manifold should have an impact on the required stretch, hence on n. This motivates the experiments described in the next section.

4   Experiments

The experiments rely on the widely used Swiss roll (Tenenbaum et al. (2000)) benchmark manifold. A dataset of 750 noisefree vectors is sampled from $\xi = [\sqrt{u}\cos(3\pi\sqrt{u}), \ \sqrt{u}\sin(3\pi\sqrt{u}), \ \pi v]^T$, where u and v have uniform distributions in $[0, 1]$. Two reasons justify using the Swiss roll. First, it is a widespread benchmark that has however not been used in (Van der Maaten and Hinton (2008), Van der Maaten (2009)). Second, it is a Euclidean manifold, which implies that a linear projection (such as in metric MDS) suffices to obtain a perfect embedding of the Swiss roll, provided geodesic distances are used (Tenenbaum et al. (2000), Lee and Verleysen (2007)).

The experiments compare t-SNE, CCA, SNLM, and classical metric MDS, whose result serves as baseline. Each method is used with both Euclidean and geodesic distances. The latter are approximated with graph distances, that is, with shortest paths in a Euclidean graph that stems from 6-ary neighborhoods around each data point. MDS is equivalent to PCA with Euclidean distances, and to Isomap (Tenenbaum et al. (2000)) with geodesic distances. CCA with geodesic distances is known as Curvilinear Distances Analysis (Lee and Verleysen (2004)). The implementation of t-SNE is provided by the authors of Van der Maaten and Hinton (2008); the only extension concerns the possibility to vary the number of degrees of freedom.

Performance assessment is achieved by means of the criteria proposed in (Lee and Verleysen (2009). These criteria look at K-ary neighborhoods around each vector in the data space as well as in the embedding space. Criterion $Q_{NX}(K)$ reflects the overall quality of the embedding; its value corresponds to the average percentage of identical neighbors in both spaces. Criterion $B_{NX}(K)$ measures to what extend a NLDR method can be 'intrusive' or 'extrusive'. A positive $B_{NX}(K)$ corresponds to an intrusive embedding, wherein many distant points are embedded close to each other; a negative value corresponds to many extrusions, i.e. to close neighbors em-

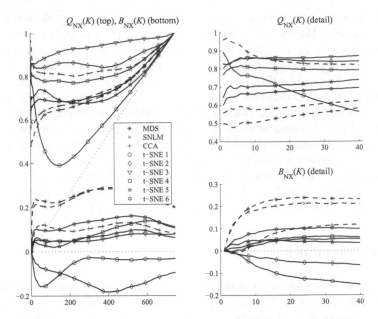

Fig. 1. Quality assessment of the embeddings using Euclidean distances. The numbered curves for t-SNE refer to perplexity values equal to 4, 25, 64, 121, 196, and 289 respectively. See text for details.

bedded far away from each other. Both $Q_{\mathrm{NX}}(K)$ and $B_{\mathrm{NX}}(K)$ are shown in specific diagrams that consist of three panels. The first one spans the interval $1 \leq K \leq N - 1$, whereas the small ones on the right focus on small values of K, for each criterion separately. The quality and behavior of the various methods are depicted in Figs. 1 and 2. Figure 3 shows the evolution of $Q_{\mathrm{NX}}(K)$ with respect to the perplexity, for $K = \{5, 15, 50, 150\}$.

5   Discussion

Unfolding the Swiss roll with Euclidean distances is a difficult task, as shown by the low values of $Q_{\mathrm{NX}}(K)$ produced by MDS, SNLM, and CCA in Fig. 1. The result of t-SNE largely depends on the value of the perplexity; it ranges from poorer than MDS to excellent. Looking at the curves for $B_{\mathrm{NX}}(K)$ shows that t-SNE tends to be extrusive or intrusive, depending on the perplexity, whereas all other methods are rather intrusive. An illustration of the embeddings provided by t-SNE with different perplexity values is given in Fig. 4.

   Replacing Euclidean distances with geodesic ones obviously facilitates the task. All methods achieve good results in Fig. 2, the best being CCA. The variability in t-SNE's results remains, but one sees that increasing the perplexity leads to better performances (see also Fig. 3). As expected, geodesic

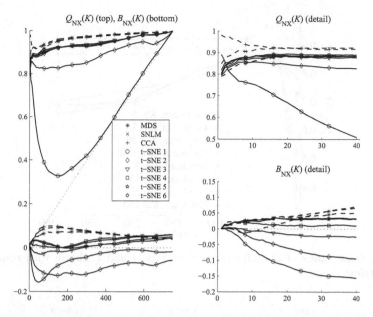

Fig. 2. Quality assessment of the embeddings using geodesic distances. The numbered curves for t-SNE refer to perplexity values equal to 4, 25, 64, 121, 196, and 289 respectively. See text for details.

distances do not need to be stretched, what can be achieved with a high (infinite) perplexity. For Euclidean distances, we observe a peak in $Q_{NX}(K)$: there exist an optimal value of the perplexity, such that the transformed distances approximate as closely as possible the geodesic distances.

At this point, we can state that the distance transformation that is implicitly achieved by t-SNE is not always optimal and that its parameters must be carefully tuned. More specifically, the perplexity controls the way distances are stretched. If stretching distances is fundamentally a pertinent idea when one wishes to unfold a manifold, t-SNE cannot always approximate the optimal transformation, which can be much more complex than in the Swiss roll. A positive point for t-SNE is that its gradient includes a damping factor that diminishes the importance of large distances, whose transformed value could be inappropriate. Nevertheless, this does not address the issue raised by non-Euclidean manifolds, such as an half (hollow) sphere. Near the pole, small distances should shrink or remain unchanged, whereas a stronger and stronger stretch is required when moving away from the pole. The situation gets obviously much more favorable with clustered data, as stretching large distances improves the separation between the clusters; examples can be found in Van der Maaten and Hinton (2008) and in Van der Maaten (2009). There is a risk however that too small a value of the perplexity could lead to an embedding with spurious clusters.

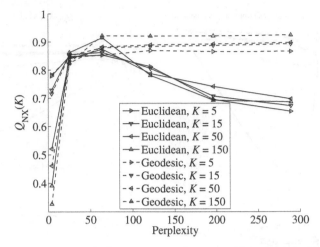

Fig. 3. Some values of $Q_{NX}(K)$ taken from Figs. 1 and 2, shown with respect to the perplexity.

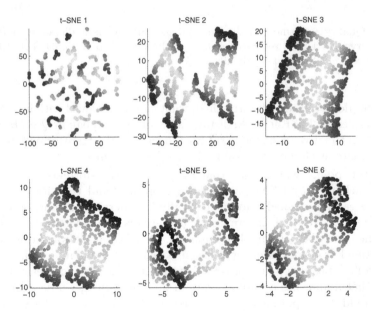

Fig. 4. Embeddings provided by t-SNE with Euclidean distances, for perplexity values equal to 4, 25, 64, 121, 196, and 289 (from top left to bottom right).

Finally, the paradigm of distance preservation can be used to compare t-SNE to other NLDR methods. The comparison is straightforward for many spectral methods that explicitly use distances, like Isomap and MVU. For other methods, such as those involving the bottom eigenvectors of some Gram matrix, duality (Xiao et al. (2006)) can be invoked in order to first build a virtual matrix of pairwise distances, on which classical MDS (isometric embedding) is applied. For example, Laplacian eigenmaps and related methods can be shown to involve commute time distances or random walks in a graph (Saerens et al. (2004)). Focusing on the transformation we see for instance that Isomap, MVU, and t-SNE all stretch distances. In this respect however, MVU proves to be more powerful than Isomap, which in turn is superior to t-SNE. The transformations in Isomap and MVU are indeed data-driven: any distance value depends on the shape of the underlying manifold. Moreover, the semidefinite programming step in MVU adjusts long distances in order to minimize the embedding dimensionality. In contrast, the transformation achieved by t-SNE marginally depends on the data density (when the individualized widths in λ are computed from the perplexity), not on the manifold shape. Apart from this and a minor impact of the softmax normalizations, t-SNE achieves an 'a priori' distance transformation, which is not data driven.

6   Conclusions

Many methods of nonlinear dimensionality reduction rely on distance preservation. Recent works reveal however a growing interest in similarity matching; an emblematic method that follows this trend is undoubtedly t-SNE. This contribution aims at analyzing t-SNE's properties. Casting t-SNE within the framework of distance preservation allows a better understanding of its behaviour. Specifically, it has been shown that t-SNE can be considered to preserve transformed distance and the transformation has been identified to be an exponential stretch. The slope of the transformation turns out to be controlled by the main two metaparameters of t-SNE, namely the perplexity and the number of degrees of freedom in the Student similarity functions. Such an exponential stretch increases the separation between clusters and this explains why t-SNE performs so well with clustered data. On the other hand, the transformation shape can be suboptimal for manifold data. Experiments are performed on the Swiss roll, a manifold for which an optimal distance transformation is known and consists in replacing Euclidean distances with geodesic distances. In this case, t-SNE requires a careful parameter adjustment and cannot outperform basic methods that preserve geodesic distances.

References

BELKIN, M. and NIYOGI, P. (2002): Laplacian eigenmaps and spectral techniques for embedding and clustering. In: T.G. Dietterich, S. Becker, Z. Ghahramani (Eds.): *NIPS 2001 proc., 14.* MIT Press, 585-591.

DEMARTINES, P. and HERAULT, J. (1997): Curvilinear component analysis: A self-organizing neural network for nonlinear mapping of data sets. *IEEE Transactions on Neural Networks, 8 (1), 148-154.*

ERHANY D., MANZAGOL P.-A., BENGIO Y., BENGIO S. and VINCENT P. (2009): The Difficulty of Training Deep Architectures and the Effect of Unsupervised Pre-Training *Journal of Machine Learning Research Proc., 5, 153-160.*

HINTON, G. and ROWEIS, S.T. (2003): Stochastic Neighbor Embedding. In: S. Becker, S. Thrun and K. Obermayer (Eds.): *Advances in NeuralInformation Processing Systems (NIPS 2002), 15.* MIT Press, 833-840.

KRUSKAL, J.B. (1964): Multidimensional scaling by optimizing goodness of fit to a nonmetric hypothesis. *Psychometrika, 29, 1-28.*

LEE, J.A. and VERLEYSEN, M. (2004): Curvilinear Distance Analysis versus Isomap. *Neurocomputing, 57, 49-76.*

LEE, J.A. and VERLEYSEN, M. (2007): *Nonlinear dimensionality reduction.* Springer, New York.

LEE, J.A. and VERLEYSEN, M. (2009): Quality assessment of dimensionality reduction: Rank-based criteria. *Neurocomputing, 72 (7-9), 1431-1443.*

PARVIAINEN E. and VEHTARI A. (2009): Features and metric from a classifier improve visualizations with dimension reduction In: C. Alippi, M. Polycarpou, C. Panayiotou, G. Ellinas (Eds.): *ICANN 2009 proc.* Springer, LNCS 5769, 225-234.

ROWEIS, S.T. and SAUL, L.K. (2000): Nonlinear dimensionality reduction by locally linear embedding. *Science, 290 (5500), 2323-2326.*

SAERENS, M., FOUSS, F., YEN, L. and DUPONT, P. (2004): The principal components analysis of a graph, and its relationships to spectral clustering. In: J.-F. Boulicaut, F. Esposito, F. Giannotti, D. Pedreschi (Eds.): *ECML 2004 proc..* Springer, LNCS 3201, 371-383.

SAMMON, J.W. (1969) A nonlinear mapping algorithm for data structure analysis. *IEEE Transactions on Computers, CC-18 (5), 401-409.*

SAUL, L.K., WEINBERGER, K.Q., HAM, J.H., SHA, F. and LEE, D.D. (2006): Spectral methods for dimensionality reduction. In: O. Chapelle, B. Schoelkopf, B. and A. Zien, A. (Eds.): *Semisupervised Learning.* MIT Press, 293-308.

SCHOLKOPF, B., SMOLA, A. and MULLER, K.-R. (1998): Nonlinear component analysis as a kernel eigenvalue problem. *Neural Computation, 10 ,1299–1319.*

SHEPARD, R.N. (1962): The analysis of proximities: Multidimensional scaling with an unknown distance function (1 - 2). *Psychometrika, 27, 125-140 and 219-249.*

TENENBAUM, J.B., DE SILVA, V. and LANGFORD, J.C. (2000): A Global Geometric Framework for Nonlinear Dimensionality Reduction. *Science, 290 (5500), 2319-2323.*

VAN DER MAATEN, L. and HINTON, G. (2008): Visualizing Data using t-SNE. *Journal of Machine Learning Research, 9, 2579-2605.*

VAN DER MAATEN, L.J.P. (2009): Learning a Parametric Embedding by Preserving Local Structure. In: D. van Dyk and M. Welling (Eds.): *Proc. 12th Int. Conf. on Artificial Intel. and Statistics, Clearwater Beach, FL.* JMLR Proceedings 5, 384-391.

XIAO, L. , SUN, J. and BOYD, S. (2006): A Duality View of Spectral Methods for Dimensionality Reduction. In: W. Cohen and A. Moore (Eds.): *ICML proc., Pittsburg (PA).* Omni Press, 1041-1048.

WEINBERGER K.Q. and SAUL, L.K. (2006): Unsupervised Learning of Image Manifolds by Semidefinite Programming. *International Journal of Computer Vision, 70 (1), 77-90.*

Part XV

IFCS Session: New Developments in Two or
Highermode Clustering; Model Based
Clustering and Reduction for High
Dimensional Data

Multiple Nested Reductions of Single Data Modes as a Tool to Deal with Large Data Sets

Iven Van Mechelen and Katrijn Van Deun

Center for Computational Systems Biology (SymBioSys), KULeuven
Tiensestraat 102 - box 3713, 3000 Leuven, Belgium,
Iven.VanMechelen@psy.kuleuven.be

Abstract. The increased accessibility and concerted use of novel measurement technologies give rise to a data tsunami with matrices that comprise both a high number of variables and a high number of objects. As an example, one may think of transcriptomics data pertaining to the expression of a large number of genes in a large number of samples or tissues (as included in various compendia). The analysis of such data typically implies ill-conditioned optimization problems, as well as major challenges on both a computational and an interpretational level.

In the present paper, we develop a generic method to deal with these problems. This method was originally briefly proposed by Van Mechelen and Schepers (2007). It implies that single data modes (i.e., the set of objects or the set of variables under study) are subjected to multiple (discrete and/or dimensional) nested reductions.

We first formally introduce the generic multiple nested reductions method. Next, we show how a few recently proposed modeling approaches fit within the framework of this method. Subsequently, we briefly introduce a novel instantiation of the generic method, which simultaneously includes a two-mode partitioning of the objects and variables under study (Van Mechelen et al. (2004)) and a low-dimensional, principal component-type dimensional reduction of the two-mode cluster centroids. We illustrate this novel instantiation with an application on transcriptomics data for normal and tumourous colon tissues.

In the discussion, we highlight multiple nested mode reductions as a key feature of the novel method. Furthermore, we contrast the novel method with other approaches that imply different reductions for different modes, and approaches that imply a hybrid dimensional/discrete reduction of a single mode. Finally, we show in which way the multiple reductions method allows a researcher to deal with the challenges implied by the analyis of large data sets as outlined above.

Keywords: high dimensional data, clustering, dimension reduction

1 Introduction

Nowadays many research areas witness an increased accessibility of novel measurement technologies. This typically gives rise to a data tsunami with matrices that comprise a high number of variables. Examples include various types of 'omics' data as collected in systems biology research, such as transcriptomics data pertaining to the expression of large sets of genes in a

Y. Lechevallier, G. Saporta (eds.), *Proceedings of COMPSTAT'2010*,
DOI 10.1007/978-3-7908-2604-3_32, © Springer-Verlag Berlin Heidelberg 2010

number of tissues or conditions, and metabolomics data pertaining to the concentration of hundreds of metabolites. Moreover, the concerted use of those technologies in different settings or laboratories may yield data matrices that comprise a very large number of experimental units as well. As an example, one may think of transcriptomics data pertaining to the genome of some microbial organism as contained in many compendia that have been collected by numerous research teams using a broad range of experimental conditions.

The analysis of such data implies at least three groups of major problems. Firstly, highdimensional data typically suffer from various kinds of between-variable redundancies and dependencies (e.g., between probes of a single probe set in transcriptomics research). These redundancies and dependencies may further imply that optimization problems as included in the data analysis become ill-conditioned (e.g., because of severe (near-)multicollinearities). Secondly, the analysis of highdimensional data implies major algorithmic challenges, both in terms of data handling and memory management, and in terms of computational aspects (e.g., operations such as matrix inversions are no longer feasible - see, e.g., Drineas et al. (2004)). Thirdly, dealing with the output of the analysis of large data sets is in may cases prohibitive. For example, standard lowdimensional graphical representations will look like dense clouds at best, and like inkblots if one is somewhat less fortunate; parameter estimates will typically show up in very large tables that can no longer be simply read or subjected to standard interpretational techniques.

To deal with the problems as outlined above, one might consider to apply classical reduction methods to the set of variables (and possibly also to the set of objects or experimental units), such as various kinds of clustering or dimension reduction. The problems as implied by the analysis of large data are often that severe, however, that they lead to a breakdown of classical (categorical or dimensional) reduction methods.

As a way out, quite a lot of recent research has been devoted to a rescue mission for classical reduction methods through calling in novel aids, such as variable selection methods and sparseness constraints. In the present paper, however, we propose a different approach to deal with the breakdown as outlined above. Our proposal elaborates a suggestion launched earlier by Van Mechelen and Schepers (2007). This proposal, which is generic in nature, reads that one or two single data modes (i.e., the variable mode or both variables and objects) are subjected to multiple nested reductions. To get an intuitive idea of what this is about, one may think of a large set of variables (e.g., genes) that are clustered into a number of partition classes (outer reduction, which in this example is categorical in nature); in their turn, the cluster centroids are subject to a dimension reduction (inner reduction, which in this example is continuous in nature, and which is 'nested' in the outer reduction). To avoid misunderstandings, it is important to emphasize that in our proposal the different nested reductions are part of a global, simultaneous optimization procedure within the framework of fitting a global model to the data at hand. (Such an approach is to be distinguished from a sequential application of different reduction techniques to one and the same data mode.)

The remainder of this paper is organized as follows. In Section (2), we will outline the principles of our generic proposal. Subsequently, we will illustrate in Section (3), both by means of two already existing methods subsumed by the generic approach, and by means of a novel extension of an existing method; moreover, we will also illustrate this extension making use of an analysis of transcriptomics data. Finally, in Section (4), we will highlight the key feature of our novel method, and contrast it with other approaches that imply different types of reductions of the data modes; also, we will show in which way the multiple reductions method allows a researcher to deal with the challenges implied by the analyis of large data sets as outlined above.

2 Principles

We assume a real-valued $I \times J$ object by variable data matrix $\mathbf{D}$ with entries d_{ij}. If the set of objects is denoted by O (with elements $o_i, i = 1, \ldots, I$) and the set of variables by V (with elements $v_j, j = 1, \ldots, J$), such data can also be formalized as a mapping from the Cartesian product $O \times V$ to $\mathbb{R}$. The sets O and V are further called the *modes* of the data.

To introduce the concept of multiple nested reductions, we go back to a unifying decomposition model as introduced by Van Mechelen and Schepers (2007). This model has a deterministic core, which optionally can be stochastically extended. In the special case of two-mode data as described above, the deterministic core of the unifying model first implies a (categorical or dimensional) reduction of each of the two modes as involved in the data. For the objects, such a reduction can be formalized by means of an $I \times P$ quantification matrix $\mathbf{A}$ that is either binary or real-valued. In case of a binary quantification matrix, the reduction is categorical in nature, and involves P different clusters (which in the unconstrained case are allowed to overlap); in particular, a_{ip} denotes whether the ith object o_i belongs to the pth cluster or not ($p = 1, \ldots, P$); special instances of constrained binary quantification matrices include partitionings and nested clusterings. In case of a real-valued quantification matrix, the reduction is dimensional in nature, with a_{ip} ($p = 1, \ldots, P$) denoting a representation of the ith object as a point in a lowdimensional (viz., P-dimensional) space. Similarly, a (categorical or dimensional) reduction of the variables can be formalized through a $J \times Q$ quantification matrix $\mathbf{B}$ (with possibly $P \neq Q$). One may note that the unifying model allows for some mode not to be reduced; in that case, the corresponding quantification matrix is put equal to an identity matrix.

To complete the recapitulation of the unifying model, we further need a $P \times Q$ core matrix $\mathbf{W}$ and a mapping f, which are such that:

$$\mathbf{D} = f(\mathbf{A}, \mathbf{B}, \mathbf{W}) + \mathbf{E}, \tag{1}$$

with $\mathbf{E}$ denoting an $I \times J$ array with error entries, and with $f(\mathbf{A}, \mathbf{B}, \mathbf{W})_{ij}$ not depending on other rows of $\mathbf{A}$ than the ith one, nor on other rows of $\mathbf{B}$ than the jth one. The latter means that for each data mode, it holds that all distinctive information on each element of that mode is contained in its corresponding row in the mode-specific quantification matrix (which means that this matrix does represent a reduction of the mode in question, indeed).

To clarify the above, we illustrate with two special cases. The first one pertains to a situation in which both $\mathbf{A}$ and $\mathbf{B}$ are binary, and in which f is an additive function. Equation (1) then reduces to:

$$f(\mathbf{A}, \mathbf{B}, \mathbf{W})_{ij} = \sum_{p=1}^{P} \sum_{q=1}^{Q} a_{ip} b_{jq} w_{pq}, \tag{2}$$

which yields a general biclustering model (Van Mechelen et al. (2004); Van Mechelen and Schepers (2006)).

The second special case involves two real-valued quantification matrices $\mathbf{A}$ and $\mathbf{B}$ and a distance-like mapping f:

$$f(\mathbf{A}, \mathbf{B}, \mathbf{W})_{ij} = \left[\sum_{p=1}^{P} \sum_{q=1}^{Q} (a_{ip} - b_{jq})^2 w_{pq} \right]^{\frac{1}{2}}. \tag{3}$$

In case $\mathbf{W}$ is an identity matrix, Equation (3) reduces to:

$$f(\mathbf{A}, \mathbf{B}, \mathbf{W})_{ij} = \left[\sum_{p=1}^{P} (a_{ip} - b_{jp})^2 \right]^{\frac{1}{2}}. \tag{4}$$

This formalizes a model that in the psychological literature is known as multidimensional unfolding (for a custom-made algorithm to fit this model to highdimensional data, see Van Deun et al. (2007)).

We are now ready to introduce the concept of multiple nested reductions. This recursive concept implies that the core matrix $\mathbf{W}$ as included in Equation (1) in its turn is subjected to a decomposition:

$$\mathbf{W} = f^*(\mathbf{A}^*, \mathbf{B}^*, \mathbf{W}^*), \tag{5}$$

with f^* denoting a mapping, $\mathbf{A}^*$ a $P \times P^*$ quantification matrix, $\mathbf{B}^*$ a $Q \times Q^*$ quantification matrix, and $\mathbf{W}^*$ a $P^* \times Q^*$ core matrix. Furthermore, $f^*(\mathbf{A}^*, \mathbf{B}^*, \mathbf{W}^*)_{pq}$ is not allowed to depend on other rows of $\mathbf{A}^*$ than the pth one, nor on other rows of $\mathbf{B}^*$ than the qth one. Substitution of (5) in (1) then yields:

$$\mathbf{D} = f(\mathbf{A}, \mathbf{B}, f^*(\mathbf{A}^*, \mathbf{B}^*, \mathbf{W}^*)) + \mathbf{E}. \tag{6}$$

When looking at our general multiple nested reductions model (6), two important remarks are in order. First, each of the quantification matrices involved (i.e., $\mathbf{A}$, $\mathbf{B}$, $\mathbf{A}^*$, and $\mathbf{B}^*$) can be an identity matrix (no reduction), a general binary matrix (categorical reduction into a number of clusters), or a real-valued matrix (dimensional reduction), with the possibility that different choices are made for different matrices; this gives room to a broad range of possible reduction patterns (including different reduction types for the outer and inner reduction, and even hybrid or mixed categorical-dimensional reductions within a certain reduction level). Second, although Model (6) is recursive or two-layered in nature, it is to be estimated as a whole, making use of one overall objective or loss function (that may, e.g., be of a least squares or a maximum likelihood type).

3   Examples

In this section we will illustrate the generic multiple nested reductions model by means of a few specific models subsumed by it. We will start with two existing models. Subsequently, we will turn to a novel expansion of one of those models, which we will also illustrate with a short empirical application.

3.1   Existing models

- Van Mechelen and Schepers (2007) briefly introduced a two-mode unfolding clustering model. The outer reduction as implied by this model is categorical in nature, both for the objects and the variables, whereas the inner reduction is dimensional. In particular, the outer reduction is a two-mode partitioning, which can be formalized by means of Equation (2); the inner reduction, from its part, is of the unfolding type, as formalized by Equation (4). Together, this yields the following model equation:

$$d_{ij} = \left[\sum_{p=1}^{P} \sum_{q=1}^{Q} a_{ip} b_{jq} \left[\sum_{p^*=1}^{P^*} (a_{pp^*}^* - b_{qp^*}^*)^2 \right]^{\frac{1}{2}} \right] + e_{ij}, \qquad (7)$$

with $\mathbf{A}$ and $\mathbf{B}$ binary partition matrices, and $\mathbf{A}^*$ as well as $\mathbf{B}^*$ real-valued. A stochastic variant of this model, in which the outer two-mode partitioning is captured by means of a double mixture model, has been introduced by Vera et al. (2009) under the name of dual latent class unfolding. Before, the special case that involved an outer reduction of the objects only (i.e., a mixture version of Model (7) with $\mathbf{B}$ being an identity matrix) was proposed by De Soete and Heiser (1993).
A nice feature of the two-mode unfolding clustering model and its stochastic extension is that they go with an insightful graphical representation, with both object and variable cluster centroids figuring as points in a lowdimensional Euclidean space.

- Recently, Van Mechelen and Van Deun (2010) have proposed principal component clustering as a family of methods to deal with data sets that comprise a large number of variables. We limit ourselves here to presenting one method from this family. When using this method, one may first wish to preprocess the data in terms of centering (or standardizing) each of the variables. The outer reduction of the method then involves a partitioning of the variables only, whereas the inner reduction is of the principal component type. Together, this yields the following model equation:

$$d_{ij} = \left[\sum_{p=1}^{P} \sum_{q=1}^{Q} a_{ip} b_{jq} \left[\sum_{p^*=1}^{P^*} (a_{pp^*}^* b_{qp^*}^*) \right] \right] + e_{ij}, \tag{8}$$

with $\mathbf{A}$ an identity matrix, $\mathbf{B}$ a binary partition matrix, and $\mathbf{A}^*$ as well as $\mathbf{B}^*$ real-valued. Taking into account that $\mathbf{A}$ is an identity matrix, Equation (8) can be further simplified to:

$$d_{ij} = \left[\sum_{q=1}^{Q} b_{jq} \left[\sum_{p^*=1}^{P^*} (a_{ip^*}^* b_{qp^*}^*) \right] \right] + e_{ij}. \tag{9}$$

Without loss of generality, $\mathbf{A}^*$ can be assumed to be columnwise orthonormal; this matrix can further be considered to comprise component scores, whereas $\mathbf{B}^*$ can be considered a matrix of component loadings. As argued by Van Mechelen and Van Deun (2010), the principal component clustering family bears interesting relationships with higher order component or factor-analytic models. Moreover, the methods of the family also go with very insightful graphical biplot representations.

3.2   Novel extension of existing model

The principal component clustering model as described above could be extended by turning the outer reduction into a two-mode partitioning, that is, a simultaneous partitioning of objects and variables, rather than a partitioning of the variables only. Assuming data that have been centered variablewise, the model equation of the resulting two-mode principal component clustering model is again Equation (8), but now with both $\mathbf{A}$ and $\mathbf{B}$ being partition matrices. In matrix notation this becomes:

$$\mathbf{D} = \mathbf{A}\,\mathbf{A}^*\,\mathbf{B}^{*T}\,\mathbf{B}^T + \mathbf{E}, \tag{10}$$

with ^{T} denoting transpose.

In a deterministic scenario, to fit the two-mode principal component clustering model to a data matrix at hand, we may rely on a least squares objective function,

$$\min_{\mathbf{A},\mathbf{B},\mathbf{A}^*,\mathbf{B}^*} \left\| \mathbf{D} - \mathbf{A}\,\mathbf{A}^*\,\mathbf{B}^{*T}\,\mathbf{B}^T \right\|^2, \tag{11}$$

with $\|.\|$ denoting the Frobenius norm. $\mathbf{A}^*$, which can be restricted to be columnwise orthonormal, contains the component scores of the object cluster centroids, and $\mathbf{B}^*$ the loadings of the variable cluster centroids.

For the optimization of Loss function (11) we may rely on an alternating least squares approach. Conditionally optimal estimates of $\mathbf{A}$ (resp. $\mathbf{B}$) can be obtained in a straightforward way. Indeed, the conditional loss functions for these matrices are rowwise quasi-separable (see Van Mechelen and Schepers (2007) for a more indepth discussion of this issue); as a consequence, updating can be pursued row by row (using for each row an enumerative strategy). Regarding the updating of $\mathbf{A}^*$ and $\mathbf{B}^*$, it can be shown that this can be achieved through a generalized singular value decomposition (GSVD) in the metrics $\left[\mathrm{diag}(\mathbf{A}^T \mathbf{A})\right]^{-1}$ and $\left[\mathrm{diag}(\mathbf{B}^T \mathbf{B})\right]^{-1}$ of the matrix of the two-mode centroids,

$$\left[\mathrm{diag}(\mathbf{A}^T \mathbf{A})\right]^{-1} \mathbf{A}^T \mathbf{D} \mathbf{B} \left[\mathrm{diag}(\mathbf{B}^T \mathbf{B})\right]^{-1}$$

(for more background on the generalized Eckart-Young theorem in two metrics, see, e.g., Appendix A in Gower and Hand (1996)). Three further remarks are in order. First, the procedure as outlined above may converge to a local minimum only, and therefore a multistart strategy is needed; for the initialization, one may, for instance, start from $\mathbf{A}$ and $\mathbf{B}$ matrices resulting from randomly started k-means analyses on the rows and the columns of $\mathbf{D}$. Second, from a computational perspective, the initial estimation and updating of the score and loading matrices $\mathbf{A}^*$ and $\mathbf{B}^*$ is not too expensive, as the GSVD involves a matrix of size $P \times Q$ only. Third, to satisfy the contraint of $\mathbf{A}^*$ to be columnwise orthonormal, one may wish to postprocess the score matrix resulting from the GSVD by subjecting it to a regular SVD (as the GSVD score matrix is orthonormal in the corresponding metric only).

To illustrate the two-mode principal component clustering model, we apply it to gene expression data in 40 tumor and 22 normal tissues as collected by Alon et al. (1999). For this application we retained data on the 400 genes that maximally differentiated cancer from normal tissues (in terms of correlations). Data were standardized per gene over the tissues. The alternating least squares algorithm was applied with 500 starts (pertaining to k-means seeds randomly drawn from the data). We selected a model with 4 tissue clusters, 5 gene clusters and 2 components; this accounted for 44% of the variance in the data. Two out of the 4 object clusters largely pertained to tumor tissues and two to normal ones. Figure 1 contains a biplot representation of the selected solution. From the figure, it appears that Gene clusters 2 and 5 differentiate most strongly between normal and tumor tissues. Those clusters appeared to contain several genes involved in an elevated cellular metabolism, including several serine/threonine protein kinase genes, the expression of which has been shown to be frequently altered in human cancers. Interestingly, the normal tissue cluster No1, the centroid of which lies closest to the tumor cluster centroids in terms of Gene clusters 2 and 5, appeared to pertain to tissues stemming from patients in a metastatic stage.

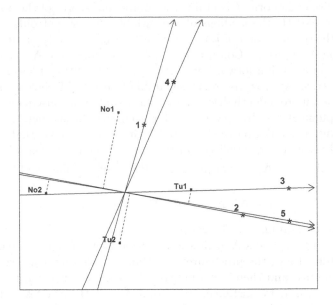

Fig. 1. Biplot representation of two-mode principal component clustering of gene expression data in tumor and normal colon tissues from a study of Alon et al. (1999). Tissue cluster centroids are labeled Tu (tumourous tissue) and No (normal tissue) as a function of the predominant nature of the tissues belonging to the corresponding cluster. Gene cluster centroids are labeled by numbered asterisks, and the corresponding biplot axes point at higher expression levels. Also shown are the predicted expression levels of the tissue clusters for Gene cluster 2 (which includes, amongst others, several serine/threonine protein kinase genes).

4   Discussion

In this paper we presented a generic modeling approach to deal with large data sets. The models in question involve a decomposition of the (recon-structed) data, and the key feature of the proposed approach is that of mul-tiple nested reductions of one and the same data mode. This feature is nicely clarified by the matrix form of the model equation of one of the instances of the generic model (viz., Equation (10)), which renders the idea of inner and outer reductions immediately visible. From a substantive point of view, reductions on different levels could fulfill different functions. One possibility in this regard is that outer reductions could primarily capture redundancies, whereas inner reductions could capture the core substantive mechanisms underlying the data. Otherwise, the recursive principle of multiple reductions can obviously be generalized to more than two reduction levels.

The approach of multiple nested reductions as taken in this paper is to be clearly distinguished from other reduction approaches that are seemingly related to ours, but that are in fact quite different. One such an approach implies several simultaneous reductions, yet with each reduction being applied to a different mode. As an example, one may think of k-means clustering in a low-dimensional Euclidean space (De Soete and Carroll (1994)), which implies a simultaneous partitioning of the objects and a dimension reduction of the variables. As a second example, one may think of a broad range of two-mode clustering methods that involve a simultaneous clustering of both objects and variables (Van Mechelen et al. (2004)). Another approach that is to be distinguished from ours involves a hybrid dimensional/discrete reduction of a single mode, rather than multiple nested reductions. As an example, one may think of disjoint principal component analysis as proposed by Vichi and Saporta (2009). This method implies a component-like dimensional reduction of the variables under study along with a partitioning of the variables, which are such that each component is a linear combination of variables that belong to a single partition class only. Our generic nested reductions model does not subsume disjoint principal component analysis, because in that method: (a) the partitioning of the variables does not imply a full reduction of the variable mode in the sense that variables are replaced by cluster centroids, and (b) partitioning and dimension reduction are interwoven rather than nested reductions.

Finally, it is useful to note that our multiple reductions method allows a researcher to deal with the challenges implied by the analyis of large data sets as outlined in the introduction to this paper. Firstly, it allows the researcher to deal with redundancies and strong dependencies, in particular through the outer reduction level. Moreover, it can do so without having to discard information like in variable selection methods. Also, it does not involve many of the arbitrarities as implied by methods based on sparseness constraints (although, admittedly, our approach, too, implies quite a few model selection issues and data-analytic choices that are to be dealt with). Secondly, our approach allows to deal with some of the computational challenges as implied by large data. This is exemplified by the algorithm we proposed in Section 3.2 to estimate the two-mode principal component clustering model. In particular, whereas in case of large data performing an SVD may be prohibitive, this is no longer the case for the GSVD that is to be applied on the two-mode cluster centroids. Thirdly, our method also provides a nice way out to deal with the output of the analysis of large data sets. This is nicely illustrated by the insightful (and substantively meaningful) biplot representation of the output of our analysis of the colon cancer data as displayed in Figure 1.

Acknowledgement footnote

The research reported in this paper was supported in part by the Research Fund of KU Leuven (EF/05/007 SymBioSys and GOA/10/02).

References

ALON, U., BARKAI, N., NOTTERMAN, D.A., GISH, K., YBARRA, S., MACK, D. and LEVINE, A.J. (1999): Broad patterns of gene expression revealed by clustering analysis of tumor and normal colon tissues probed by oligonucleotide arrays. *Proc. Natl. Acad. Sci. USA 96,6745-50.*

DE SOETE, G. and CARROLL, J.D. (1994): K-means clustering in a low-dimensional Euclidean space. In E. Diday, Y. Lechevallier, M. Schader, P. Bertrand and B. Burtschy (Eds.): *New Approaches in Classification and Data Analysis.* Springer, Heidelberg, 212–219.

DE SOETE, G. and HEISER, W. (1993): A latent class unfolding model for analyzing single stimulus preference ratings. *Psychometrika 58, 545-565.*

DRINEAS, P., FRIEZE, A., KANNAN, R., VEMPALA, S. and VINAY, V. (2004): Clustering large graphs via the singular value decomposition. *Machine Learning 56(1-3), 9-33.*

GOWER, J.C. and HAND, D.J. (1996): *Biplots.* Chapman & Hall, London.

VAN DEUN, K., MARCHAL, K., HEISER, W., ENGELEN, K. and VAN MECHELEN, I. (2007): Joint mapping of genes and conditions via multidimensional unfolding analysis. *BMC Bioinformatics 8, 181.*

VAN MECHELEN, I., BOCK, H.-H. and DE BOECK, P. (2004): Two-mode clustering methods: A structural overview. *Statistical Methods in Medical Research 13, 363-394.*

VAN MECHELEN, I. and SCHEPERS, J. (2006): A unifying model for biclustering. In A. Rizzi and M. Vichi (Eds.): *COMPSTAT 2006 - Proceedings in Computational Statistics.* Physica Verlag, Heidelberg, 81–88.

VAN MECHELEN, I. and SCHEPERS, J. (2007): A unifying model involving a categorical and/or dimensional reduction for multimode data. *Computational Statistics and Data Analysis 52, 537-549.*

VAN MECHELEN, I. and VAN DEUN, K. (2010): Principal component clustering. *Manuscript submitted for publication.*

VERA, J.F., MACÍAS, R. and HEISER, W.J. (2009): A dual latent class unfolding model for two-way two-mode preference rating data. *Computational Statistics and Data Analysis 53, 3231-3244.*

VICHI, M. and SAPORTA, G. (2009): Clustering and disjoint principal component analysis. *Computational Statistics and Data Analysis 53, 3194-3208.*

The Generic Subspace Clustering Model

Marieke E. Timmerman[1] and Eva Ceulemans[2]

[1] Heymans Institute for Psychology, University of Groningen
Grote Kruisstraat 2/1, 9712TS Groningen, the Netherlands,
m.e.timmerman@rug.nl
[2] Centre for Methodology of Educational Research, Catholic University of Leuven
A. Vesaliusstraat 2, BE-3000 Leuven, Belgium, *Eva.Ceulemans@ped.kuleuven.be*

Abstract. In this paper we present an overview of methods for clustering high dimensional data in which the objects are assigned to mutually exclusive classes in low dimensional spaces. To this end, we will introduce the generic subspace clustering model. This model will be shown to encompass a range of existing clustering techniques as special cases. As such, further insight is obtained into the characteristics of these techniques and into their mutual relationships. This knowledge facilitates selecting the most appropriate model variant in empirical practice.

Keywords: reduced k-means, common and distinctive cluster model, mixture model

1 Introduction

In a partitioning model, objects are assigned to a limited number of mutually exclusive clusters. Often, the partitioning takes place on the basis of high dimensional data, i.e., the objects' scores on multiple variables. Traditional partitioning approaches, like the well-known k-means clustering (MacQueen (1967)), perform the clustering in the entire space of the high-dimensional data. However, this approach may fail to yield a correct partition. A first problem is that the sample size needed to achieve a proper recovery increases strongly with increasing dimensionality. This phenomenon relates to the curse of dimensionality (Bellman (1957)). Secondly, the inclusion of variables in a cluster analysis that hardly reflect the clustering structure may hinder or even obscure the recovery of this cluster structure (e.g., Milligan (1996)). The recovery problems exacerbate when different clusters reside in different subspaces of the high dimensional data.

To deal with these problems, various approaches have been proposed. The variable importance approach differentially weights the variables in the cluster analysis, where the weights are determined on the basis of observed data (e.g., DeSarbo, Carroll, Clark & Green (1984); De Soete (1986); see also Milligan & Cooper (1988)). The variable selection approach aims at determining the subset of variables that define the clustering (see e.g., Steinley & Brusco (2008)). In this paper, we focus on the subspace clustering approach, which

Y. Lechevallier, G. Saporta (eds.), *Proceedings of COMPSTAT'2010*,
DOI 10.1007/978-3-7908-2604-3_33, © Springer-Verlag Berlin Heidelberg 2010

rests on the assumption that the clusters are located in some subspace of the variables.

The subspace clustering approach has been taken in both deterministic models (e.g., Bock (1987)) and stochastic models (e.g., Banfield & Raftery (1993)). Moreover, subspace clustering has been put forward in different model variants, of which the mutual relationships are not evident. To clarify this issue, we will introduce in this paper the generic subspace clustering model. This model will be shown to encompass a series of clustering models proposed so far.

2 Generic subspace clustering model

The generic subspace clustering model is a deterministic model. In this model, I objects are partitioned into C mutually exclusive clusters on the basis of their observed multivariate data.

The generic subspace clustering model is founded on a decomposition of the observed scores of each participant into an off-set term, a between-cluster part and a within-cluster part, analogously to the decomposition in analysis of variance. Specifically, the observed scores $\mathbf{x}_i$ ($J \times 1$) of the ith object ($i = 1, ..., I$) on J variables can be written as

$$\mathbf{x}_i = \mathbf{m} + \sum_{c=1}^{C} u_{ic}(\mathbf{b}^c + \mathbf{w}_i^c), \tag{1}$$

where $\mathbf{m}$ ($J \times 1$) denotes a vector containing off-set terms, u_{ic} denotes the entries of the binary cluster membership matrix $\mathbf{U}$, which specifies to which cluster each of the objects belongs (i.e., $u_{ic} = 1$ if object i belongs to cluster c, and $u_{ic} = 0$ otherwise, with $\sum_{c=1}^{C} u_{ic} = 1$); $\mathbf{b}^c$($J \times 1$) contains the centroids of cluster c, with constraint $\sum_{i=1}^{I} \sum_{c=1}^{C} u_{ic}\mathbf{b}^c = \mathbf{0}$; $\mathbf{w}_i^c$ ($J \times 1$) contains the within-cluster residuals of object i in cluster c, with constraint $\sum_{i=1}^{I} \sum_{c=1}^{C} u_{ic}\mathbf{w}_i^c = \mathbf{0}$ and $\mathbf{w}_i^c = \mathbf{0}$ if $u_{ic} = 0$. For any arbitrary cluster membership matrix $\mathbf{U}$, the decomposition in (1) perfectly applies. Therefore, a least squares loss function for (1) has no unique solution. Unique solutions can be achieved by imposing constraints on (1), of which different possibilities will be discussed in the next sections.

The essential feature of the generic subspace clustering model is that the cluster centroids and the within-cluster residuals may be located in subspaces of the data, where those subspaces may differ from each other. Thus, in the model, both the centroids ($\mathbf{b}^c$) and the within-cluster residuals ($\mathbf{w}_i^c$) may be represented by a low rank approximation. Furthermore, the models for the within-cluster residuals may differ across clusters.

The generic subspace clustering model can be written as

$$\mathbf{x}_i = \mathbf{m} + \sum_{c=1}^{C} u_{ic}(\mathbf{A}\mathbf{b}\,\mathbf{fb}^c + \mathbf{A}\mathbf{w}^c\mathbf{fw}_i^c) + \mathbf{e}_i^c, \tag{2}$$

where $\mathbf{fb}^c$ ($Qb \times 1$) denotes a vector with between-component scores of cluster c, $\mathbf{Ab}$ ($J \times Qb$) a between-loading matrix, and Qb the number of between-components; $\mathbf{fw}_i^c$ ($Qw^c \times 1$) denotes a vector with within-component scores of the ith object, with i being a member of cluster c, $\mathbf{Aw}^c$ ($J \times Qw^c$) a within-loading matrix of cluster c, and Qw^c the number of within-components for cluster c; $\mathbf{e}_i^c$ ($J \times 1$) is the error of the ith object (which is a member of cluster c). To partly identify the model, the between- and within-loading matrices are constrained to be columnwise orthonormal, i.e., $\mathbf{Ab}'\mathbf{Ab} = \mathbf{I}_{Qb}$ and $\mathbf{Aw}^{c'}\mathbf{Aw}^c = \mathbf{I}_{Qw^c}$; furthermore, the means of the component scores are constrained as $\sum_{i=1}^{I}\sum_{c=1}^{C} u_{ic}\mathbf{fb}^c = \mathbf{0}$ and $\sum_{i=1}^{I}\sum_{c=1}^{C} u_{ic}\mathbf{fw}_i^c = \mathbf{0}$ with $\mathbf{fw}_i^c = \mathbf{0}$ if $u_{ic} = 0$. Those constraints ensure that $\mathbf{Ab}\ \mathbf{fb}^c$ provide a model for the centroids of cluster c, and that $\mathbf{Aw}^c\ \mathbf{fw}_i^c$ provide a model for the within-cluster residuals of object i in cluster c.

2.1   Loss function of the generic subspace clustering model

To fit the generic subspace clustering model to observed data $\mathbf{X}$ ($I \times J$), the following least squares loss function is to be minimized, given specific values of C, Qb and Qw^c (numbers of clusters, and between- and within-components, respectively):

$$G(\mathbf{m}, \mathbf{U}, \mathbf{Fb}, \mathbf{Ab}, \mathbf{Fw}^c, \mathbf{Aw}^c) = \sum_{i=1}^{I} \|\mathbf{x}_i - \mathbf{m} - \sum_{c=1}^{C} u_{ic}(\mathbf{Ab}\ \mathbf{fb}^c + \mathbf{Aw}^c\mathbf{fw}_i^c)\|^2,$$

(3)

where $\mathbf{U}$ ($I \times C$) is the binary cluster membership matrix; the matrix $\mathbf{Fb}$ ($C \times Qb$) the between-component scores matrix, which rows are $\mathbf{fb}^{c'}$ ($c = 1,..,C$); the matrix $\mathbf{Fw}^c$ ($n_c \times Qw^c$) is the within-component matrix of cluster c, which rows are $\mathbf{fw}_{i'}^c$ ($i = 1,..,n_c$) with n_c the number of objects in cluster c. To satisfy the constraints on the means of the component scores, it is required that $\mathbf{1}_C'\ \text{diag}(\mathbf{n})\ \mathbf{Fb} = \mathbf{0}$ and $\mathbf{1}_{n_c}'\ \mathbf{Fw}^c = \mathbf{0}$, with $\mathbf{1}_C$ a ($C \times 1$) vector consisting of ones, and $\text{diag}(\mathbf{n})$ a diagonal matrix with as diagonal elements $\mathbf{n} = [n_1,...,n_C]$.

Because of the constraints on the means of the component matrices, the optimal offset vector $\mathbf{m}$ equals $I^{-1}\mathbf{1}_I'\mathbf{X}$. The remaining parameters could be estimated with some iterative algorithm that alternatingly updates $\mathbf{U}$, $\mathbf{Fb}$, $\mathbf{Ab}$, $\mathbf{Fw}^c$, $\mathbf{Aw}^c$.

It is important to note that for a given cluster membership matrix $\mathbf{U}$, the offset part, the between-part and the within-part of the data matrix $\mathbf{X}$ are orthogonal to each other (see Timmerman (2006), for a proof, in a slightly different context), and can therefore be separately updated. That is, for a given $\mathbf{U}$, the observed scores of each object i can be uniquely decomposed as in Equation (1).

Then, the between-part can be updated by minimizing

$$g_1(\mathbf{Fb}, \mathbf{Ab}) = \|\mathbf{W}(\mathbf{B} - \mathbf{Fb}\ \mathbf{Ab}')\|^2,$$

(4)

subject to $\mathbf{Ab'Ab} = \mathbf{I}_{Qb}$, with $\mathbf{W}$ ($C \times C$) a diagonal cluster size weight matrix, with $w_{i_i} = \sqrt{n_c}$ and $\mathbf{B} = [\mathbf{b}^1|...|\mathbf{b}^C]'$ ($C \times J$).

The within-part can be updated by minimizing

$$g_2(\mathbf{Fw}^c, \mathbf{Aw}^c) = \sum_{c=1}^{C} \|\mathbf{W}^c - \mathbf{Fw}^c \mathbf{Aw}^{c'}\|^2, \tag{5}$$

subject to $\mathbf{Aw}^{c'}\mathbf{Aw}^c = \mathbf{I}_{Qw^c}$, and where $\mathbf{W}^c = [\mathbf{w}_1^c|...|\mathbf{w}_{n_c}^c]'$ ($n_c \times J$) denotes the matrix containing the within-cluster residuals of the objects in cluster c. Different types of iterative algorithms could be proposed for minimizing (3), but they are beyond the scope of this paper.

3   Positioning of existing subspace clustering approaches into the generic framework

In this section, it will be shown that a number of clustering models that have been proposed in the literature, are special cases of the generic subspace clustering model. Specific model variants appear when a full space rather than a subspace is used at the between- or within-level, as will be discussed in Section 3.1. Furthermore, other model variants arise when specific features of the models for the within-cluster residuals are constrained to be equal across clusters, to be treated in Section 3.2.

3.1   Model variants: Reduced space at the between-level or within-level

In the generic subspace clustering model, the centroids and the within-cluster residuals may be modelled in subspaces of the observed data. However, in the literature, model variants have been proposed in which the centroids or within-residuals are modeled in the full space rather than the reduced space. For the centroids, the full centroid space is used when Qb is taken equal to $\min(C,J)$. For the within-part of cluster c, the full within-residual space of cluster c is used when Qw^c is taken equal to $\min(n_c,J)$. When the full within-residual space is used for all clusters, they are, obviously, depicted in the same space.

The generic subspace clustering model variant with centroids constrained to be in a subspace, while the within-residuals are set to zero, is proposed twice, namely as Projection Pursuit Clustering (Bock (1987)) and Reduced k-means analysis (De Soete & Carroll (1994)). The loss function associated with those analyses boils down to

$$g_3(\mathbf{m}, \mathbf{U}, \mathbf{Fb}, \mathbf{Ab}) = \sum_{i=1}^{I} \|\mathbf{x}_i - \mathbf{m} - \sum_{c=1}^{C} u_{ic}(\mathbf{Ab}\ \mathbf{fb}^c)\|^2. \tag{6}$$

The variant with centroids in the full space, and the within-residuals in reduced spaces is proposed by Bock (1987). He put forward the specific case with $Qw^c = Qw$ (i.e., the number of within components is equal across clusters) as PCA-based clustering with class-specific hyperplanes. The algorithm proposed differs from Equation (3) in that the between-part is in full space, and hence boils down to

$$g_4(\mathbf{m}, \mathbf{U}, \mathbf{b}^c, \mathbf{Fw}^c, \mathbf{Aw}^c) = \sum_{i=1}^{I} \|\mathbf{x}_i - \mathbf{m} - \sum_{c=1}^{C} u_{ic}\mathbf{b}^c + \sum_{c=1}^{C} u_{ic}(\mathbf{Aw}^c\mathbf{fw}_i^c)\|^2. \quad (7)$$

An even less constrained variant is obtained when the centroids are modelled in full space, and the within-residuals are zero. When the sum of squared within-residuals is to be minimized, the following loss function results

$$g_5(\mathbf{m}, \mathbf{U}, \mathbf{b}^c,) = \sum_{i=1}^{I} \|\mathbf{x}_i - \mathbf{m} - \sum_{c=1}^{C} u_{ic}\mathbf{b}^c\|^2. \quad (8)$$

This function is well-known, as it is the one associated with k-means clustering (MacQueen (1967)).

3.2   Model variants: Common and distinctive models of the within-residuals

In the models for the within-residuals of each cluster, one may restrict some or all model features to be the same across clusters. As a result, those models consist of a common and a distinctive part. In a deterministic model, like our general subspace model, the common part is modelled by imposing specific constraints on the model estimates of the within-part. In a stochastic model, this is approached via assumptions at the population level. In what follows, we discuss deterministic and stochastic models with common and distinctive features across the clusters.

Bock (1987) proposed a deterministic model that he referred to as 'PCA-clustering with common and class-specific dimensions'. In this model, each cluster is located in a common subspace and a cluster specific subspace, where the total sizes of the subspaces are equal across clusters. Thus, in terms of the general subspace model, the within-loading matrix of cluster c is $\mathbf{Aw}^c = [\mathbf{Aw}|\mathbf{Aw}^{c^*}]$, with $\mathbf{Aw}$ ($J \times Qw$) the common loading matrix, and $\mathbf{Aw}^{c^*}$ ($J \times Qw^{c^*}$) the class-specific loading matrix, and $Qw^c = Qw + Qw^{c^*}$. Restricting some features of the within-cluster models to be equal is more common in stochastic clustering than in deterministic clustering. Stochastic clustering models are known as mixture models. In those models, the observed data $\mathbf{x}_i$ are assumed to be a random sample from a mixture of C populations, with mean μ^c and (within-cluster) covariance matrix Σ^c. Furthermore, multivariate normality is commonly assumed, because of the use of maximum likelihood estimators.

In mixture modelling, different types of restrictions on the covariance matrices Σ^c, $c=1,...,C$ have been proposed. A rather stringent restriction is equality of covariance matrices across clusters, i.e., $\Sigma^c = \Sigma$ (Friedman & Rubin (1967); see also Gordon (1981, p. 51)). This implies that the sizes and shapes of within-cluster residuals are assumed to be equal across clusters.

A more general approach was taken by Banfield and Raftery (1993), who proposed a class of possible restrictions on Σ^c. In particular, they proposed a reparametrization of Σ^c in terms of its eigenvalue decomposition, namely as $\Sigma^c = \mathbf{K}^c \Lambda^c \mathbf{K}^{c'}$, with $\mathbf{K}^c$ the matrix of eigenvectors of Σ^c, and $\Lambda^c = (\lambda^c \mathbf{H}^c)$ the matrix with eigenvalues of Σ^c; λ^c is the first eigenvalue of Σ^c and $\mathbf{H}^c = \mathrm{diag}(\mathbf{h})$, with $\mathbf{h} = [h^{1c}, ..., h^{Jc}]$, and $1 = h^{1c} \geq ... \geq h^{Jc} \geq 0$. The matrix $\mathbf{K}^c$ expresses the subspace of cluster c, λ^c its size and $\mathbf{H}^c$ its shape. Each of those parameters ($\mathbf{K}^c$, λ^c and $\mathbf{H}^c$) may be assumed to be equal across clusters. This implies a series of models, which are associated with different optimization criteria (Banfield & Raftery (1993)). For example, the assumption of equality of covariance matrices across clusters (i.e., $\Sigma^c = \Sigma$) is attained by the assumption of equality of eigenvectors and eigenvalues across clusters (i.e., $\mathbf{K}^c = \mathbf{K}$, $\lambda^c = \lambda$ and $\mathbf{H}^c = \mathbf{H}$).

In the mixtures of factor analyzers model (McLachlan & Peel (2000); McLachlan, Peel & Bean (2003)), the covariance matrix of each cluster is assumed to comply with a common factor model. That is, $\Sigma^c = \mathbf{A}^c \mathbf{A}^{c'} + \mathbf{U}^c$, with $\mathbf{A}^c$ ($J \times q$) a factor loading matrix, $\mathbf{U}^c$ ($J \times J$) a diagonal matrix with unique variances of cluster c, and q the number of factors. Note that although the loadings and unique variances may differ across clusters, the number of factors is assumed to be equal. Finally, a hybrid variant of mixtures of factor analyzers and the reparametrization approach (Banfield & Raftery (1993)) is proposed by Bouveyron, Girard and Schmid (2007). Their models accommodate for differences and similarities of common factors in orientations, sizes and shapes across clusters.

An interesting question is whether the principles behind the various mixture models for the cluster covariance matrices could be usefully applied in the general subspace model as well. Whereas the reparametrization approach (Banfield & Raftery (1993)) is naturally covered in the generic subspace model, this is much less the case for the mixture of factor analyzers approaches, because of the unique variances involved.

To see how the reparametrization approach (Banfield & Raftery (1993)) could be adopted in the generic subspace clustering model, we first note that the within-part of the generic subspace clustering model (see 5) can be reparametrized in terms of $\mathbf{S}^c = n_c^{-1} \mathbf{W}^{c'} \mathbf{W}^c$, the within-cluster covariance matrix. Then, rather than minimizing (5), the within-loading matrices $\mathbf{A}\mathbf{w}^c$ and the within-component covariance matrices $\mathbf{S}_{\mathbf{Fw}}^c = n_c^{-1} \mathbf{F}\mathbf{w}^{c'} \mathbf{F}\mathbf{w}^c$ can be updated by minimizing

$$g_6(\mathbf{Aw}^c, \mathbf{S}_{\mathbf{Fw}}^c) = \sum_{c=1}^{C} \|\mathbf{S}^c - \mathbf{Aw}^c\, \mathbf{S}_{\mathbf{Fw}}^c\, \mathbf{Aw}^{c'}\|^2. \qquad (9)$$

The natural relationship between the generic subspace clustering model and the reparametrization approach can be seen by noting that the solution for $\mathbf{Aw}^c$ is found as the first Qw^c eigenvectors of $\mathbf{S}^c$. In the model for the within-cluster covariance matrices, the subspaces could be constrained to be equal across clusters by imposing $\mathbf{Aw}^c = \mathbf{Aw}$ for each cluster c, $c=1,...,C$. Then, the within-component covariance matrix $\mathbf{S}_{\mathbf{Fw}}^c$ could be either unconstrained, or required to be a diagonal matrix. The latter is in analogy with Banfield and Raftery. Equality constraints on the size and shape of the clusters can be imposed by requiring that the elements of the diagonal within-component covariance matrices $\mathbf{S}_{\mathbf{Fw}}^c$ would have equal λ^c and/or $\mathbf{H}^c$, i.e., $\lambda^c = \lambda$ and/or $\mathbf{H}^c = \mathbf{H}$, respectively.

4   Discussion and conclusion

In this paper, we have presented the generic subspace clustering model. In this deterministic model, the cluster centroids and the within-cluster residuals may be located in subspaces of the data. It has been shown that the generic subspace clustering model encompasses a variety of clustering models as special cases, which allows to gain insight into the mutual relationships between those models. In particular, specific model variants appear when a full space rather than a subspace is used at the between- or within-level. Furthermore, in the models for the within-cluster residuals, one may restrict some or all model features - subspace, size, and/or shape - to be equal across clusters.

An important question is how the generic subspace clustering model can be sensibly used in empirical practice. Herewith, the central issue to resolve boils down to a model selection problem: The key question in each empirical analysis is which model variant is most appropriate to reflect structural differences between clusters. Herewith, it is important to note that different models may capture other types of structural differences between the clusters. This implies that when these models are fitted to the same empirical data, different clusterings of the objects may be obtained. For example, objects may be clustered such that the cluster centroids are optimally separated, like in k-means clustering (MacQueen (1967)), or such that the clusters are of equal size and shape (using the reparametrization approach; Banfield & Raftery (1993)).

Fitting cluster models to empirical data can be burdensome. It might be tempting to impose constraints on the models to reduce the number of estimated parameters and hence relieve the estimation problems. However, as different constraints may yield a different clustering, the choice of the imposed constraints should be motivated from a substantive point of view. It is important to carefully consider the distinctive features of the empirical problem at hand. The generic subspace clustering model can be of help, as it clarifies the different features relevant in clustering objects. Besides the substantive, subject-matter related considerations also statistical considerations, like model fit and stability of solutions, should play an important role to avoid overfitting and overinterpretation. The real challenge apears to be not so much in defining model variants, but to select in a well-founded way a sensible model variant for the empirical data at hand.

References

BANFIELD, J.D. and RAFTERY, A.E. (1993): Model-based Gaussian and Non-Gaussian Clustering. *Biometrics, 49, 803-821.*

BOUVEYRON, C., GIRARD, S. and SCHMID, C. (2007): High-Dimensional Data Clustering. *Computational Statistics and Data Analysis, 52, 502-519.*

BELLMAN, R. (1957): *Dynamic programming.* Princeton University Press, Princeton, NJ.

BOCK, H.H. (1987). On the interface between cluster analysis, principal component analysis, and multidimensional scaling. In: H. Bozdogan and A.K. Gupta (Eds). *Multivariate Statistical Modeling and Data Analysis.* Dordrecht: D. Reidel Publishing Company. pp. 17-34.

DESARBO, W.S., CARROLL, J.D., CLARK, L.A. and GREEN, P.E. (1984): Synthesized clustering: A method for amalgating alternative clustering bases with differential weighting of variables. *Psychometrika, 49, 57-78.*

DE SOETE, G. (1986). Optimal variable weighting for ultrametric and additive tree clustering. *Quality and Quantity, 20, 169-180.*

DE SOETE, G. and CARROLL, J.D. (1994): K-means clustering in a low-dimensional Euclidean space. In: E. Diday et al. (Eds). *New Approaches in Classification and Data Analysis.* Springer: Heidelberg, pp. 212-219.

FRIEDMAN, H.P. and RUBIN, J. (1967): On some invariant criteria for grouping data. *Journal of the American Statistical Association, 62, 1159-1178.*

GORDON, A.D. (1981): *Classification.* London: Chapman and Hall.

MACQUEEN, J. (1967): Some methods for classification and analysis of multivariate observations. In: L.M. LeCarn and J. Neyman (Eds). *5th Berkeley Symposium on Mathematics, Statistics and Probability.* University of California Press, Berkeley, 1, 281-296.

MCLACHLAN, G.J. and PEEL, D. (2000): *Finite Mixture Models.* New York: Wiley.

MCLACHLAN, G.J., PEEL, D. and BEAN, R.W. (2003): Modelling high-dimensional data by mixtures of factor analyzers. *Computational Statistics and Data Analysis, 41, 379-388.*

MILLIGAN, G.W. (1996): Clustering validation: Results and implications for applied analysis. In: P. Arabie, L.J. Hubert and G. De Soete (Eds.). *Clustering and Classification.* River Edge: World Scientific Publishing, pp. 341-375.

MILLIGAN, G.W. and COOPER, M.C. (1988): A Study of Standardization of Variables in Cluster Analysis. *Journal of Classification, 5, 181-204.*

TIMMERMAN, M.E. (2006): Multilevel Component Analysis. *British Journal of Mathematical and Statistical Psychology, 59, 301-320.*

VICHI, M. and KIERS, H.A.L. (2001): Factorial k-means analysis for two-way data. *Computational Statistics and Data Analysis, 37, 49-64.*

Clustering Discrete Choice Data

Donatella Vicari[1] and Marco Alfò[1]

Dipartimento di Statistica, Probabilità e Statistiche Applicate
Sapienza Università di Roma, Italy, *donatella.vicari@uniroma1.it*

Abstract. When clustering discrete choice (e.g. customers by products) data, we may be interested in partitioning individuals in disjoint classes which are homogeneous with respect to product choices and, given the availability of individual- or outcome-specific covariates, in investigating on how these affect the likelihood to be in certain categories (i.e. to choose certain products). Here, a model for joint clustering of statistical units (e.g. consumers) and variables (e.g. products) is proposed in a mixture modeling framework, and the corresponding (modified) EM algorithm is sketched. The proposed model can be easily linked to similar proposals appeared in various contexts, such as in co-clustering gene expression data or in clustering words and documents in webmining data analysis.

Keywords: discrete choice, conditional logit, multinomial logit, co-clustering

1 Motivation

Let $\mathbf{Y}_i$, $i = 1, \ldots, n$, be a p-dimensional random vector and let $\mathbf{y}_i$, $i = 1, \ldots, n$ represent the corresponding realization in a sample of size n; furthermore, let $\mathbf{Y} = (\mathbf{Y}_1, \ldots, \mathbf{Y}_n)^{\mathsf{T}}$ be the (n, p) matrix containing the values y_{ij}, $i = 1, \ldots, n$, $j = 1, \ldots, p$, which represent the observed values (outcomes). Just to give and example, we may suppose to consider n customers and p products, where y_{ij} represents the number of items of the j-th product bought by the i-th customer.

In addition, a set of outcome-specific (i.e. characteristics of the products such as price, weight, type of package, etc.) and individual-specific (for example, age, gender, education level, income, etc.) covariates, influencing customers' choices, may be available. Let $\mathbf{x}_i$ be a K-dimensional vector containing the characteristics of the i-th individual, $i = 1, \ldots, n$ and $\mathbf{z}_j$ be an m-dimensional vector containing the characteristics of the j-th product, $j = 1, \ldots, p$.

In this context, we look for a partition of individuals in disjoint classes which are homogeneous with respect to product choices; the prior (conditional) probability for an individual to belong to a given class is assumed to be a function of individual-specific covariates, and we may be interested in knowing how these characteristics affect the class membership. Furthermore, we can reasonably imagine that, conditional on the individual-specific class

Y. Lechevallier, G. Saporta (eds.), *Proceedings of COMPSTAT'2010*,
DOI 10.1007/978-3-7908-2604-3_34, © Springer-Verlag Berlin Heidelberg 2010

(i.e. a class of customers), a partition of the outcomes (products) could also be identified based on their different characteristics. For example, some individuals may prefer a certain class of products due to products' observed characteristics, and these preferences may vary across classes of customers. Hence, we are interested in how the individual and product-specific characteristics affect the likelihood to choose certain categories of products.

Here, we are interested in a simultaneous partition of customers and products to investigate about the determinants of customers' choices. A similar purpose can be found when looking for a joint partition of genes and tissues (or experimental conditions) in microarray data analysis (see e.g. Martella et al. (2008)), of words and documents in web data analysis (see e.g. Li and Zha (2006)), or, in general, when latent block-based clustering is pursued (see e.g. Govaert and Nadif (2007)). Further interesting links can be established with multi-layer mixture, see e.g. Li (2005), and with hierarchical mixture of experts models, see e.g. Titsias and Likas (2002).

The plan of the paper is as follows. In section 2 the proposed model is introduced in a general setting. In section 3 a modified EM algorithm for ML estimation of model parameters is discussed. In section 4 the proposed model is detailed to analyze the empirical cases where the outcome y_{ij} represents the number of times the i-th individual buys the j-th product, ie a non negative integer (count) variable. In section 5 the analysis of a benchmark dataset is described. Concluding remarks and future research agenda are focused on in the last section.

2   The Model

We adopt a mixture model framework by assuming that the population consists of G classes in proportions $\pi_1, \ldots, \pi_G$, $\sum_{g=1}^{G} \pi_g = 1$, $\pi_g \geq 0, \forall g = 1, \ldots, G$. An unobservable G-dimensional component indicator vector $\mathbf{u}_i = (u_{i1}, \ldots, u_{iG})$ is associated to each unit with a unique non null element, denoting whether the i-th unit belongs to class g or not, $i = 1, \ldots, n$, $g = 1, \ldots, G$. Thus, the unobservable class-specific labels u_{ig} are defined to be 1 or 0 whether or not the i-th unit belongs to the g-th class, $g = 1, \ldots, G$, see e.g. Titterington et al. (1985). In such a mixture sampling scheme, the sample is obtained by first drawing, independently for each unit, its membership class label, u_{ig}, $g = 1, \ldots, G$ from the population with p.d.f. $h(\mathbf{u}_i; \pi)$; then, values of the outcome variables are drawn from the population with p.d.f.

$$f(\mathbf{y}_i; \theta_g, \mid u_{ig} = 1) = f_g(\mathbf{y}_i \mid \theta_g) \tag{1}$$

where $f_g(\mathbf{y}_i \mid \theta_g)$ is the g-th class-specific density with indexing parameter vector given by θ_g.

In this context, as usual, the individual (class-specific) component indicators $\mathbf{u}_i = (u_{i1}, \ldots, u_{iG})$ are assumed to be independent multinomial random variables with probabilities given by $\pi = (\pi_1, \ldots, \pi_G)$. Thus, each observation $\mathbf{y}_i$, $i = 1, \ldots, n$, is sampled from the finite mixture density

$$f(\mathbf{y}_i \mid \pi, \theta_1, \ldots, \theta_G) = \sum_{g=1}^{G} \pi_g f_g(\mathbf{y}_i \mid \theta_g) \qquad (2)$$

where $\pi = (\pi_1, \ldots, \pi_G)$ is the prior probability vector, with elements $\pi_g \geq 0$, $g = 1, \ldots, G$, $\sum_{g=1}^{G} \pi_g = 1$. Let $(\mathbf{y}_i, \mathbf{u}_i)$, $i = 1, \ldots, n$ be a sample drawn under the above sampling scheme; the (complete data) joint probability density function is given by:

$$f(\mathbf{y}_i, \mathbf{u}_i \mid \theta, \pi) = f(\mathbf{y}_i \mid \theta, \mathbf{u}_i) g(\mathbf{u}_i \mid \pi) = \prod_{g=1}^{G} [\pi_g f_g(\mathbf{y}_i \mid \theta_g)]^{u_{ig}} \qquad (3)$$

and the resulting *complete-data log-likelihood* is expressed by

$$\ell_c(\theta_1, \ldots, \theta_G, \pi) = \sum_{i=1}^{n} \sum_{g=1}^{G} u_{ig} \log[\pi_g f_g(y_i \mid \theta_g)] \qquad (4)$$

As usual in finite mixture modeling, the estimation of class-specific parameters θg, $g = 1, \ldots, G$ and class-specific priors, π is based on an EM-type algorithm that allows to identify the class densities and, as a byproduct, to assign each individual to a class, for instance through a maximum a posteriori (MAP) rule.

In the present context, however, we may use the available covariates to model choice behavior, where the explanatory variables may include attributes of the choice alternatives (for example cost) as well as characteristics of the individuals making the choices (such as income, age, etc.). Let us assume that, within the g-th individual-specific class ($g = 1, \ldots, G$), we can identify a partition of the outcomes (products) in K_g classes.

For example, we may assume that different classes of individuals present different propensities towards products and that their choices are influenced by individual characteristics as well as by the attributes of such products. It follows that individuals that are similar (belonging to the same g-th class) make different choices of products, i.e. they behave differently with respect to such products, defining K_g different classes of products. Let us define an unobservable K_g-dimensional product-specific component indicator $\mathbf{v}_{ij|g} = (v_{ij1|g}, \ldots, v_{ijK_g|g})$ indicating the product-specific cluster the j-th product belongs to, conditional on the i-th individual belonging to the g-th individual-specific class. Furthermore, let $\pi_{k|g} = \mathrm{Pr}(v_{ijk|g} = 1) = \mathrm{Pr}(v_{ijk} = 1 \mid u_{ig} = 1)$, $i = 1, \ldots, n$, $j = 1, \ldots, p$, $k = 1, \ldots, K_g$, $g = 1, \ldots, G$, denote the prior probability that the j-th product belongs to the k-th product class conditionally on the i-th individual belonging to the g-th individual-specific class.

We also denote with $\pi_{kg} = \Pr\left(u_{ig}v_{ijk|g} = 1\right) = \pi_g\pi_{k|g}$, $j = 1,\ldots,p$ the prior (joint) probability for individual i in class g and product j in class k within class g. However, due to covariates availability, we do not define directly the terms π_g, $g = 1,\ldots,G$, but rather their conditional counterpart τ_{ig}, given the observed individual-specific vector $\mathbf{x}_i$, $i = 1,\ldots,n$:

$$\tau_{ig} = \Pr\left(u_{ig} = 1 \mid \mathbf{x}_i\right) \propto \exp\left(\mathbf{x}_i^\mathsf{T}\beta_g\right) \quad i = 1,\ldots,n,\ g = 1,\ldots,G \quad (5)$$

where β_g is a class-specific vector of regression coefficients , with $\beta_G = 0$ to ensure model identifiability. Furthermore, let

$$\tau_{ijk|g} = \Pr\left(v_{ijk|g} = 1 \mid u_{ig} = 1, \mathbf{z}_j\right) \propto \exp\left(\mathbf{z}_j^\mathsf{T}\gamma_{k|g}\right) \quad j = 1,\ldots,p,\ k = 1,\ldots,K_g \quad (6)$$

denote the conditional counterpart of $\pi_{k|g}$, $\mathbf{z}_j$ be the observed product-specific covariates vector and $\gamma_{k|g}$ be the product class-specific vector of regression coefficients, given the class of individuals. The joint probability for the i-th individual and the j-th product follows: $\tau_{ijkg} = \Pr\left(u_{ig}v_{ijk|g} = 1 \mid \mathbf{x}_i, \mathbf{z}_j\right) = \tau_{ig}\tau_{ijk|g}$, $i = 1,\ldots,n$, $j = 1,\ldots,p$, $k = 1,\ldots,K_g$.

Given such modeling assumptions, the conditional probabilities may be written as

$$\log(\tau_{ig}) \propto \mathbf{x}_i^\mathsf{T}\beta_g$$
$$\log(\tau_{ijk|g}) \propto \mathbf{z}_j^\mathsf{T}\gamma_{k|g}$$
$$\log(\tau_{ijcr}) \propto \mathbf{x}_i^\mathsf{T}\beta_g + \mathbf{z}_j^\mathsf{T}\gamma_{k|g}$$

Expressions above define multinomial logit models that incorporate both types of covariates (individual- and product- specific) in order to study how they affect the probability of the i-th individual and the j-th product to belong to a certain class (defined by the couple $[g,(k \mid g)]$ from the whole set of $\sum_{g=1}^{G} K_g$ classes. Since each observation is sampled from a finite mixture density, the marginal density of $\mathbf{y}_i$ can be written as follows:

$$f\left(\mathbf{y}_i \mid \pi, \theta\right) = \sum_{g=1}^{G} \pi_g \sum_{k=1}^{K_g} \pi_{k|g} f_{k|g}\left(\mathbf{y}_i \mid \theta_{k|g}\right) = \sum_{g=1}^{G} \sum_{k=1}^{K_g} \pi_{gk} f_{k|g}\left(\mathbf{y}_i \mid \theta_{k|g}\right) \quad (7)$$

where $\theta_{k|g}$, $g = 1,\ldots,G$, $k = 1,\ldots,K_g$, is a class-specific parameter set (indexing the class-specific distribution $f_{k|g}$), and represents the *propensity* that an individual in the g-th class "chooses" a product in the k-th class, while $\theta = \{\theta_{k|g}, g = 1,\ldots,G, k = 1,\ldots,K_g\}$ shortly denotes the whole model parameter set. Thus, the marginal density, if the p products are assumed to be independent, can be written as follows:

$$f\left(\mathbf{y}_i \mid \mathbf{x}_i, \mathbf{z}_j, \theta\right) =$$

$$= \sum_{g=1}^{G} \tau_{ig} f_g\left(\mathbf{y}_i \mid u_{ig} = 1, \mathbf{x}_i, \theta\right) = \sum_{g=1}^{G} \tau_{ig}\left[\prod_{j=1}^{p} f_g\left(y_{ij} \mid u_{ig} = 1, \mathbf{x}_i, \theta_g\right)\right] =$$

$$= \sum_{g=1}^{G} \tau_{ig}\left[\prod_{j=1}^{p}\left[\sum_{k=1}^{K_g} \tau_{ijk|g} f_{k|g}\left(y_{ij} \mid u_{ig} = 1, v_{ijk|g} = 1, \mathbf{x}_i, \mathbf{z}_j, \theta_{k|g}\right)\right]\right]$$

while the log-likelihood has the following form:

$$\ell(\cdot) = \sum_{i=1}^{n} \log\left[\sum_{g=1}^{G} \tau_{ig} \prod_{j=1}^{p} \sum_{k=1}^{K_g} \tau_{ijk|g} f_{k|g}\left(y_{ij} \mid \theta_{jk|g}\right)\right]$$

3   ML Parameter Estimation

As usual, the component indicator labels $u_{ig}, v_{ijk|g}, i = 1, \ldots, n, j = 1, \ldots, p,$ $g = 1, \ldots, G, k = 1, \ldots, K_g$ are unobservable; thus, they can be considered as missing data and, naturally, an EM algorithm for parameter estimation can be adopted. The space of the complete data is given by $(y_{ij}, \mathbf{u}_i, \mathbf{v}_j),$ $i = 1, \ldots, n, j = 1, \ldots, p.$ Assuming multinomial distributions for both the $\mathbf{u}_i$'s and the $\mathbf{v}_j$'s, the log-likelihood for the *complete data* can be written as:

$$\ell_c(\cdot) \propto \sum_{i=1}^{n} \sum_{g=1}^{G} u_{ig} \log\left(\tau_{ig}\right) + \sum_{i=1}^{n} \sum_{g=1}^{G} \sum_{k=1}^{K_g} \sum_{j=1}^{p} u_{ig} v_{ijk|g}\left\{\log\left(\tau_{ijk|g}\right) + \log\left[f_{k|g}\left(y_{ij} \mid \theta_{k|g}\right)\right]\right\}$$

In the t-th step of the EM algorithm, we define the log-likelihood for the observed data by taking the expectation of the log-likelihood for complete data over the unobservable class label vectors $\mathbf{u}_i$ and $\mathbf{v}_j$ given the observed data $\mathbf{y}$ and the current maximum likelihood estimates of model parameters $\mathbf{\Phi}^{(t-1)} = \left\{\mathbf{\Theta}^{(t-1)}, \tau^{(t-1)}\right\}.$

Let $\tilde{u}_{ig}^{(t)} = \Pr(u_{ir} = 1 \mid \mathbf{y}_i, \theta_g^{(t-1)})$ and $\tilde{v}_{ijk|g} = \Pr(v_{ijk} = 1 \mid u_{ig} = 1, \mathbf{y}_i, \theta_{k|g})$ denote the posterior probabilities that the i-th individual belongs to the g-th class *and* that the j-th product belongs to the k-th class of products nested within the g-th class of individuals, conditional on the observed data and the current parameter estimates. Note that $\tilde{w}_{ijkg}^{(t)} = \tilde{u}_{ig}^{(t)} \tilde{v}_{ijk|g}^{(t)} = \Pr(u_{ig} v_{ijk|g} = 1 \mid \mathbf{y}_i, \theta_{k|g})$ holds, where $w_{ijkg} = u_{ig} v_{ijk|g}.$ Thus, computation of the expected value of the complete data log-likelihood (in the E step of the EM algorithm) involves computing these sets of posterior probabilities by considering an Upward/Downward-type algorithm which takes into account that product memberships are independent given the memberships of the individuals within class g, due to local independence assumption within class g.

Specifically, conditionally on the g-th class, the j-th product is independent of the other products.

At the t-th step, by replacing u_{ig} and $v_{ijk|g}$ with their conditional expectations we may define the conditional expectation of the complete data log-likelihood given the observed data and the current parameter estimates as:

$$Q^{(t)}(\cdot) = \mathrm{E}_{\Phi^{(t-1)}}\left[\ell(\cdot) \mid y, \theta^{(t-1)}\right] \propto \sum_{i=1}^{n} \sum_{g=1}^{G} \tilde{u}_{ig}^{(t)} \log\left[\frac{\exp(\mathbf{x}_i^\mathsf{T} \beta_g)}{1 + \sum_{s=1}^{G-1} \exp(\mathbf{x}_i^\mathsf{T} \beta_s)}\right] +$$

$$\sum_{i=1}^{n} \sum_{g=1}^{G} \sum_{k=1}^{K_g} \sum_{j=1}^{p} \tilde{u}_{ig}^{(t)} \tilde{v}_{ijk|g}^{(t)} \left\{\log\left[\frac{\exp(\mathbf{z}_j^\mathsf{T} \gamma_{k|g})}{1 + \sum_{l=1}^{K_g-1} \exp(\mathbf{z}_j^\mathsf{T} \gamma_{l|g})}\right] + \log\left[f_{k|g}\left(y_{ij} \mid \theta_{k|g}\right)\right]\right\}$$

Maximizing $Q^{(t)}(\cdot)$ with respect to $\Phi = \{\theta_{k|g}, \beta_g, \gamma_{k|g}\}$, $g = 1, \ldots, G$, $k = 1, \ldots, K_g$, the ML estimates for the class-specific and regression model parameters may be derived.

3.1   The EM algorithm

The adopted Expectation-Maximization (EM) algorithm requires a special implementation of the Expectation (E) step where an Upward/Downward-type algorithm, see e.g. Vermunt (2007, 2008), is used at the t-th step to first calculate $\tilde{u}_{ig}^{(t)}$, $i = 1, \ldots, n$, $g = 1, \ldots, G$ and $\tilde{v}_{ijk|g}^{(t)}$, $j = 1, \ldots, p$, $k = 1, \ldots, K_g$ within each class g.

E-Step   Given current model parameters estimates, calculate

$$\tilde{v}_{ijk|g}^{(t)} = \frac{\tau_{ijk|g}^{(t-1)} f_{k|g}\left(y_{ij} \mid \theta_{k|g}^{(t-1)}\right)}{\sum_{l=1}^{K_g} \tau_{ijl|g}^{(t-1)} f_{l|g}\left(y_{ij} \mid \theta_{l|g}^{(t-1)}\right)} = \frac{h_{ijk|g}}{h_{ij|g}}$$

and

$$\tilde{u}_{ig}^{(t)} = \frac{\tau_{ig}^{(t-1)} f_g\left(\mathbf{y}_i \mid \theta_g^{(t-1)}\right)}{\sum_{s=1}^{G} \tau_{is}^{(t-1)} f_s\left(\mathbf{y}_i \mid \theta_s^{(t-1)}\right)} = \frac{\tau_{ig} \prod_{j=1}^{p} h_{ij|g}}{\sum_{s=1}^{G} \tau_{ig} \prod_{j=1}^{p} h_{ij|g}}$$

Secondly, the joint posterior of u_{ig} and $v_{ijk|g}$, the term that enters in the expected complete data log-likelihood, is computed:

$$\tilde{w}_{ijkg}^{(t)} = \tilde{u}_{ig}^{(t)} \tilde{v}_{ijk|g}^{(t)} = \mathrm{Pr}\left(u_{ig} v_{ijk|g} = 1 \mid \mathbf{y}_i, \theta_{k|g}\right)$$

M-Step Given the current values of posterior probabilities, find the ML estimates for model parameters by solving the following *score* equations

$$\frac{\partial Q\left(\cdot\right)}{\partial \beta_g} = \sum_{i=1}^{n} \tilde{u}_{ig}^{(t)} \frac{\partial \tau_{ig}(\mathbf{x}_i)}{\partial \beta_g} = 0$$

$$\frac{\partial Q\left(\cdot\right)}{\partial \gamma_{k|g}} = \sum_{i=1}^{n} \tilde{u}_{ig}^{(t)} \sum_{j=1}^{p} \tilde{v}_{ijk|g}^{(t)} \frac{\partial \tau_{ijk|g}(\mathbf{z}_j)}{\partial \gamma_{k|g}} = \sum_{i=1}^{n} \sum_{j=1}^{p} \tilde{w}_{ijkg}^{(t)} \frac{\partial \tau_{ijk|g}(\mathbf{z}_j)}{\partial \gamma_{k|g}} = 0$$

$$\frac{\partial Q\left(\cdot\right)}{\partial \theta_{k|g}} = 0$$

$$g = 1, \ldots, G,\, k = 1, \ldots, K_g = 0.$$

4   Discrete Choice Count Data

In the case of count data (for example counts of different products bought by each consumer), the responses y_{ij} are assumed to be (conditionally) independent Poisson random variables

$$y_{ij} \mid u_{ig}, v_{ijk|g} \sim \mathrm{Poi}(\theta_{k|g})$$

in class k of products within class g of consumers. By solving the corresponding M-step equations, at the t-th step the class-specific parameter estimates are defined by:

$$\hat{\theta}_{jk|g}^{(t)} = \frac{\sum_{i=1}^{n} y_{ij} \tilde{w}_{ijkg}^{(t)}}{\sum_{i=1}^{n} \tilde{w}_{ijkg}^{(t)}} \qquad j = 1, \ldots, p, g = 1, \ldots, G, k = 1, \ldots, K_g$$

A more parsimonious model can be defined by assuming that the class-specific parameters are equal, up to a scale product-specific parameter, $\theta_{jk|g} = \theta_j \theta_{k|g}$, $j = 1, \ldots, p$, $g = 1, \ldots, G$, $k = 1, \ldots, K_g$. Under such an assumption, at the t-th step the corresponding parameter estimates are calculated, by adopting an ECM (Expectation-Conditional Maximization) algorithm, as follows:

$$\hat{\theta}_{k|g}^{(t)} = \frac{\sum_{i=1}^{n} \sum_{j=1}^{p} \tilde{w}_{ijkg}^{(t)} y_{ij}}{\sum_{i=1}^{n} \sum_{j=1}^{p} \tilde{w}_{ijkg}^{(t)} \hat{\theta}_j^{(t-1)}} \qquad g = 1, \ldots, G, k = 1, \ldots, K_g$$

and, respectively,

$$\hat{\theta}_j^{(t)} = \frac{\sum_{i=1}^{n} \sum_{g=1}^{G} \sum_{k=1}^{K_g} \tilde{w}_{ijkg}^{(t)} y_{ij}}{\sum_{i=1}^{n} \sum_{g=1}^{G} \sum_{k=1}^{K_g} \tilde{w}_{ijkg}^{(t)} \hat{\theta}_{k|g}^{(t)}}, \qquad j = 1, \ldots, p$$

5   Example: crackers data

We consider an optical scanner panel data set on purchases of four brands
of saltine crackers in the Rome (Georgia) market, collected by Information
Resources Incorporated. The data set contains information on purchases of
crackers made by $n = 136$ households over about two years (Franses and
Paap (2001). The brands were Nabisco, Sunshine, Keebler and a collection
of private labels. The total number of purchases (3292) has been synthesized
to get the number of purchases of each brand made by each household. The
average actual price (in US$) of the purchased brand and the shelf price of
other brands is available as product-specific covariate. Additionally, we know
whether there was a display and/or newspaper feature of the four brands
at the time of purchase. Hence, we use 3 product-specific covariates, namely
price, newspaper featured only, display and newspaper featured dummies.

We fitted the proposed model for a varying number of individual-specific
(i.e. row-specific) components, $G = 1, \ldots, 6$ and, for each choice of G, for
varying number of product-specific (i.e. column-specific) components, $K_g \equiv
K = 1, 2$. It is worth noting that, in the present context, no individual-
specific covariates have been used; for this reasons, we have covariates-free
prior estimates for the partition of units. The *optimal* number of components
can be selected by using penalized likelihood criteria, such as AIC or BIC.
Table 1 synthesizes obtained results in terms of row- and column-specific
partitions; moreover, the maximized log-likelihood value ℓ, the number of
estimated parameters d and the penalized likelihood criteria are reported.

$K = 1$						
G	1	2	3	4	5	6
ℓ	-2915.6	-2835.4	-2824.2	-2819.9	-2814.9	-2813.8
d	6	9	12	15	18	21
AIC	5843.2	5688.8	5672.4	5669.8	5665.8	5669.6
BIC	5860.7	5715.0	5707.4	5713.5	5718.2	5730.8
$K = 2$						
G	1	2	3	4	5	6
ℓ	-1533.9	-1366	-1329.4	-1308.1	-1308.1	-1308.1
d	10	17	24	31	38	45
AIC	3087.8	2766	2706.8	2678.2	2692.2	2706.2
BIC	3116.9	2815.5	2776.7	2768.5	2802.9	2837.3

Table 1. Penalized Likelihood Criteria for the crackers dataset

As can be easily observed by looking at the table above, both penalized
likelihood criteria suggest the use of a solution with $G = 4$ individual-specific
components and $K_g = 2$ product components. Component priors can be
interpreted by looking at the model parameter estimates, say β_g and $\gamma_{k|g}$,

$g = 1, \ldots, G$, $k = 1, \ldots, K_g$ or by looking at averaged $\hat{\tau}$ estimates. As far as the individual partition is concerned, by using a MAP allocation rule we have that the size of each component are $(n_1, n_2, n_3, n_4) = (32, 46, 37, 21)$, with estimated priors $(\hat{\tau}_1, \hat{\tau}_2, \hat{\tau}_3, \hat{\tau}_4) = (0.24, 0.34, 0.27, 0.15)$. The estimated column partition is, roughly speaking, composed of two classes: the first includes Nabisco, the second all the remaining brand. However, posterior product-specific component memberships vary across individual-specific classes, with a higher entropy associated to Nabisco and Private, while a smaller entropy is associated to Keebler and Sunshine. In the following table, we denote with P_g, $g = 1, \ldots, 4$, the household-specific components (i.e. row-specific clusters), and with $P_{k|g}$, $k = 1, 2$ the product-specific components (i.e. column-specific clusters).

	Nabisco		Private		Sunshine		Keebler	
Comp	$P_{1|g}$	$P_{2|g}$	$P_{1|g}$	$P_{2|g}$	$P_{1|g}$	$P_{2|g}$	$P_{1|g}$	$P_{2|g}$
P_1	0.36	0.64	0.68	0.32	0.90	0.10	0.92	0.08
P_2	0.75	0.25	0.35	0.65	0.18	0.82	0.17	0.83
P_3	0.43	0.57	0.71	0.29	0.90	0.10	0.92	0.08
P_4	0.81	0.19	0.35	0.65	0.26	0.74	0.31	0.69

Table 2. Prior estimates for product-specific partition for the crackers dataset

As far as column-specific partition is concerned, one of the two components (which vary according to row-specific components, showing some *label switching* phenomenon), is mainly linked to brand Nabisco, while the other component is associated to remaining brands. By a simple descriptive analysis, Nabisco is clearly the market leader (with a 54% share), while private labels represent a good second (31 % share). Nabisco is also associated to a medium-high price and with a higher sample mean for the dummies indicating whether the brand was on display and newspaper featured, or newspaper featured only; these covariates, therefore, tend to be significantly associated to the column-specific components the brand Nabisco belongs to. By looking at the components specific parameter estimates $\theta_{k|g}$ (not reported here for sake of brevity), we can notice that households in component 1 tend to purchase more products from the second class (ie Sunshine, Kleeber and Private brands), while households in components 2 and 3 tend to significantly favor Nabisco, especially in the 2nd column-specific component within the 3rd row-specific component. Row-component 4 mean purchase values are not far from the whole sample average. The obtained partition could be further explored, should household-specific covariates be available; this would help us understand whether the observed component-specific behaviors can be, at least partially, associated to observed, household-specific, heterogeneity.

6 Concluding remarks

In this paper, we have proposed a two-level finite mixture model for the clustering of rows (units) and columns (variables) of a data matrix. The proposal has been sketched in the field of consumers' behavior, but can be easily extended to other research context, such as gene expression and text mining analyses, where a partition of objects and features is of interest. The model has been proposed in a maximum likelihood framework and the corresponding (modified) EM algorithm has been outlined. Further extensions of this model can be proposed by looking at different combinations for individual and product-specific covariates, and by adopting different representations for component-specific distribution parameters.

References

FRANSES, P.H and PAAP, R. (2001): *Quantitative models in marketing research*. Cambridge University Press, Cambridge.

GOVAERT G. and NADIF M. (2003): Clustering with block mixture models. *Pattern Recognition 36(2), 463-473*.

LI J. (2005): Clustering based on a multi-layer mixture model. *Journal of Computational and Graphical Statistics 14(3), 547-568*

LI J. and ZHA H. (2006): Two-way Poisson mixture models for simultaneous document classification and word clustering. *Computational Statistics and Data Analysis 50(1), 163-180*.

MARTELLA, F., ALFÒ, M., VICHI, M. (2008): Biclustering of gene expression data by an extension of mixtures of factor analyzers. *The International Journal of Biostatistics 4(1), art. 3*.

TITTERINGTON, D.M., SMITH, A.F.M. and MAKOV, U.E. (1985): *Statistical Analysis of Finite Mixture Distributions*. John Wiley & Sons, Chichester.

TITSIAS K. and LIKAS A. (2002): Mixture of Experts Classification Using a Hierarchical Mixture Model. *Neural Computation 14(9), 2221-2244*.

VERMUNT, J.K. (2007): A hierarchical mixture model for clustering three-way data sets. *Computational Statistics and Data Analysis 51, 5368-5376*.

VERMUNT, J.K. (2008): Latent class and finite mixture models for multilevel data sets. *Statistical Methods in Medical Research 17, 33-51*.

Part XVI

Selected Contributed Papers

Application of Local Influence Diagnostics to the Buckley-James Model

Nazrina Aziz[1] and Dong Qian Wang[2]

[1] Universiti Utara Malaysia
O6010, Sintok, Kedah Darul Aman,
Malaysia, *nazrina@uum.edu.my*
[2] Victoria University Of Wellington
New Zealand

Abstract. This article reports the development of local influence diagnostics of Buckley-James model consisting of variance perturbation, response variable perturbation and independent variables perturbation. The proposed diagnostics improves the previous ones by taking into account both censored and uncensored data to have a possibility to become an influential observation. Note that, in the previous diagnostics of Buckley-James model, influential observations merely come from uncensored observations in the data set. An example based on the Stanford heart transplant data is used for illustration. The data set with three covariates is considered in an attempt to show how the proposed diagnostics is able to handle more than one covariate, which is a concern to us as it is more difficult to identify peculiar observations in a multiple covariates.

Keywords: Buckley-James model, censored data, diagnostic analysis, local influence, product-limit estimator

1 Introduction

Considering that researchers normally deal with data sets that contain more than one covariate, the multivariate censored regression emerges and can be defined as below

$$\mathbf{Y} = \mathbf{X}\beta + \varepsilon, \quad \varepsilon \sim F$$

where

- $\mathbf{Y}$ is a $n \times 1$ vector of response variable, which is right censored;
- $\mathbf{X}$ is a known $n \times (p+1)$ matrix as the first column of 1's to provide an intercept;
- β is a $(p+1) \times 1$ vector of parameters where it is estimated by $\mathbf{b^T} = (b_0, b_1, \ldots, b_p)$;
- ε is $n \times 1$ vector of errors and the distribution has an unknown survival function, $S = 1 - F$.

Y. Lechevallier, G. Saporta (eds.), *Proceedings of COMPSTAT'2010*,
DOI 10.1007/978-3-7908-2604-3_35, © Springer-Verlag Berlin Heidelberg 2010

If the matrix, $\mathbf{X}$ contains only uncensored observations, then the regression parameters can be estimated as

$$\mathbf{b} = (\mathbf{X^T X})^{-1} \mathbf{X^T Y}. \tag{1}$$

However, if $\mathbf{X}$ contains censored observations, then the regression parameters cannot be estimated directly as (1). Firstly, one needs to renovate the response variable for multivariate censored regression based on the censor indicator, $\delta^{\mathbf{T}} = (\delta_1, \delta_2, \ldots, \delta_n)$ as the following equation

$$\mathbf{Y^*(b)} = \mathbf{Xb} + \mathbf{Q(b)e(b)}, \tag{2}$$

where $Q(\mathbf{b}) = \text{diag}(\delta) + q_{ik}(\mathbf{b})$, is the upper triangle Renovation Weight Matrix containing censored status on the main diagonal (Smith (2002)) and $\mathbf{e(b)} = \mathbf{Z}\text{-}\mathbf{Xb}$ where $\mathbf{Z^T} = (Z_1, Z_2, \ldots, Z_n)$ are the observed responses subject to censoring indicator, δ and q_{ik} is

$$q_{ik}(\mathbf{b}) = \begin{cases} \dfrac{d\hat{F}(e_k(\mathbf{b}))\delta_k(1 - \delta_i)}{\hat{S}(e_i(\mathbf{b}))} & \text{if} \quad k > i, \\ 0 & \text{if} \quad \text{otherwise,} \end{cases} \tag{3}$$

where $d\hat{F}(e_k(\mathbf{b}))$ is the probability mass assigned by $\hat{F}$ to e_k and $\hat{S}(e_i(\mathbf{b}))$ is the Kaplan-Meier estimator applied to the $e_k(\mathbf{b})$.

In multivariate censored regression, the iteration concept is applied to develop the Buckley-James estimators:

$$b_{m+1} = (X^T X)^{-1} X^T (X b_m + Q(b_m)(Z - X b_m)). \tag{4}$$

Note that $m = 1, 2, \ldots$ refers to the number of iterations. The solution of (4) can be obtained as the norm of the left side is small (James and Smith (1984)) and (Lin and Wei (1992)). Nevertheless if the iteration fails to converge, one can solve this problem by taking the average of all possible solutions of β (Wu and Zubovic (1995)). Note that where there is an exact solution, the Buckley-James estimators are given as below

$$\hat{\beta} = (\mathbf{X^T Q X})^{-1} \mathbf{X^T Q Z}. \tag{5}$$

Since $QY^* = QZ$, therefore (5) can be rewritten as the following equation

$$\hat{\beta} = (\mathbf{X^T Q X})^{-1} \mathbf{X^T Q Y^*}. \tag{6}$$

2   Local Influence Diagnostics for the Buckley-James model

Local influence diagnostics can be used to discover influential observations in a data set. Local influence was proposed by Cook in 1986 and it was based on likelihood displacement. It is an alternative method to the global influence, i.e. deletion case, which suffers from a form of the masking effect. Details regarding diagnostics based on case deletion can be found in Andrews and Pregibon (1978) and Atkinson (1981).

Even though the local influence approach has been applied mostly to regression models, it also works well in other statistical areas. As an example, Shi (1997) studied local influence in a multivariate model. He presented the idea of combining a general influence function and generalised Cook statistic as a new concept of local influence. This concept is easier to apply without considering a likelihood assumption.

In a censored regression, most diagnostic studies based on local influence have been done for the Cox model and the Kaplan-Meier model (see, Reid (1981); Pettitt and Daud (1989); Weissfeld (1990)). Studies on influence observations for the Cox model using the local influence method can be found in Pettitt and Daud (1989) and Weissfeld (1990). Pettitt and Daud (1989) proposed an overall measure of influence that uses the asymptotic covariance matrix, where this measure approximates the change in likelihood displacement if the individual observation is deleted.

The local influence approach proposed by Weissfeld (1990) was different from Pettitt and Daud (1989) since it was based on perturbation of the likelihood function and perturbation of covariates included in the model.

To evaluate the local change of small perturbation on some issues, firstly, one needs to define the general influence function and generalised Cook statistics proposed by Shi (1997). The general influence function of $T \in R^{p+1}$, can be displayed as

$$GIF(T, h) = \lim_{\varepsilon \to 0} \frac{T(w_o + \epsilon h) - T(w_o)}{\epsilon}$$

where $w = w_o + \epsilon h \in R^n$ describes a perturbation with the null perturbation, w_o fulfils $T(w_o) = T$ and $h \in R^n$ refers to a unit-length vector. Next, one can specify generalised Cook statistics to measure the influence of the perturbations on T as

$$GC(T, h) = \frac{\{GIF(T, h)\}^T M \{GIF(T, h)\}}{c},$$

where M is a $p \times p$ positive-definite matrix and c is a scalar. One may find a direction of $h_{max}(T)$ to perturb a datum and maximize local change in T. The direction of $h_{max}(T)$ can be derived by maximizing the absolute value of $GC(T, h)$ with respect to h. The serious local influence appears if maximum value $GC_{max}(T) = GC(T, h_{max}(T))$. Next following sections will present the local influence diagnostics for the Buckley-James model, which consist of

- variance perturbation;
- response variable perturbation;
- independent variables perturbation.

2.1   Perturbing the variance for censored regression

By using the Buckley-James estimators as follows

$$b = (X^T Q X)^{-1} X^T Q Y^* \qquad (7)$$

perturb the variance of the error in (7), by replacing ϵ as $\epsilon_w \sim N(0, \sigma^2 W^{-1})$.

Let W be diagonal matrix

$$W = \begin{pmatrix} w_1 & 0 & \cdots & 0 \\ 0 & w_2 & \cdots & 0 \\ \vdots & \vdots & \ddots & \vdots \\ 0 & 0 & \cdots & w_n \end{pmatrix}$$

and vector $w^T = (w_1, w_2, \ldots, w_n)$ and w is given by $w = w_\circ + \epsilon h$, where $w_\circ^T = (1, 1, \ldots, 1)$, the n-vector of ones and $h^T = (h_1, h_2, \ldots, h_n)$ refers to a unit-length vector. Hence, W can be written as

$$W = \mathbf{I}_n + \epsilon D(h), \qquad (8)$$

where $I_n = \begin{pmatrix} 1 & 0 & \cdots & 0 \\ 0 & 1 & \cdots & 0 \\ \vdots & \vdots & \ddots & \vdots \\ 0 & 0 & \cdots & 1 \end{pmatrix}$ and $D(h) = \begin{pmatrix} h_1 & 0 & \cdots & 0 \\ 0 & h_2 & \cdots & 0 \\ \vdots & \vdots & \ddots & \vdots \\ 0 & 0 & \cdots & h_n \end{pmatrix}$.

Now (7) becomes

$$b(w) = (X^T W Q X)^{-1} X^T W Q Y^*. \qquad (9)$$

By replacing $W = \mathrm{diag}(w_1, w_2, \ldots, w_n)$ in (9), $b(w)$ can be rewritten as below

$$b(w) = (X^T \{\mathbf{I}_n + \epsilon D(h)\} Q X)^{-1} X^T W Q Y^*$$
$$= [(X^T Q X)^{-1} - \epsilon \{(X^T Q X)^{-1} X^T Q D(h) X (X^T Q X)^{-1}\}] \times X^T W Q Y^*,$$

where $X^T W Q Y^* = X^T \{\mathbf{I}_n + \epsilon D(h)\} Q Y^* = X^T Q Y^* + \epsilon X^T Q D(h) Y^*$.

Therefore, $b(w)$ is given by

$$b(w) = [(X^T Q X)^{-1} - \epsilon \{(X^T Q X)^{-1} X^T Q D(h) X (X^T Q X)^{-1}\}] \times X^T W Q Y^*$$
$$= b + \epsilon \{(X^T Q X)^{-1} (X^T Q D(h) e^*)\} + O(\epsilon^2). \qquad (10)$$

where $e^* = Y^* - Xb$. From (10), the general influence function of b under the perturbation is obtained as $GIF(b, h) = (X^T Q X)^{-1} X^T Q D(e^*) h$. Next, the generalised Cook statistic of b is developed. It is scaled by $M = X^T \triangle X$ in censored regression following that $cov(b) = (X^T \triangle X)^{-1} \sigma_{BJ}^2$, where $\triangle = \mathrm{diag}(\delta_1, \delta_2, \ldots, \delta_n)$. Therefore

$$GC_1(b, h) = \frac{h^T D(e^*)(H^*)^2 \triangle D(e^*) h}{p s^2}, \qquad (11)$$

where $H^* = X(X^TQX)^{-1}X^TQ$ is renovated leverage for censored regression and s^2 is the estimate variance.

By applying $M = X^TX$ to the scaled generalised Cook statistic, which is based on least square regression framework $cov(b) = (X^TX)^{-1}\sigma^2$, one can find $GC_2(b, h)$ as follows

$$GC_2(b, h) = \frac{h^T D(e^*)(H^*)^2 D(e^*)h}{ps^2}. \tag{12}$$

The diagnostic direction h_{max} can be obtained by calculating the eigenvector correpsonding to the largest eigen value of matrices $D(e^*)(H^*)^2 \triangle D(e^*)$ and $D(e^*)(H^*)^2D(e^*)$ from (11) and (12) respectively.

2.2   Perturbing response variables for censored regression

The response variable can be perturbed as $Y_w^* = Y^* + \varepsilon h$, where $h \in R^n$ refers to a unit-length vector. Let equation $(X^TQX)^{-1}X^TQY^*$ become

$$(X^TQX)^{-1}X^TQY_w^* = (X^TQX)^{-1}X^TQ(Y^* + \varepsilon h)$$
$$= b + \varepsilon(X^TQX)^{-1}X^TQh. \tag{13}$$

Therefore, the general influence function of b under the perturbation can be shown as

$$GIF(b, h) = (X^TQX)^{-1}X^TQh. \tag{14}$$

Now two generalised Cook statistics can be developed by using the scale $M = X^T \triangle X$ and $M = X^TX$ based on censored regression and the least square regression framework (LSR), which are

$$cov(b) = \begin{cases} (X^T \triangle X)^{-1}\sigma_{BJ}^2 & \text{if (censored regression)}, \\ (X^TX)^{-1}\sigma^2 & \text{if (LSR).} \end{cases} \tag{15}$$

respectively, where $\triangle = \text{diag}(\delta_1, \delta_2, \ldots, \delta_n)$. Hence, $GC_1(b, h) = \dfrac{h^T(H^*)^2 \triangle h}{ps^2}$ and $GC_2(b, h) = \dfrac{h^T(H^*)^2h}{ps^2}$.

2.3   Perturbing independent variables for censored regression

In global influence, the *ith* case can be considered as influential on independent variables if deleting it from the data set will change the estimated regression function. This crisis can be seen in local influence by introducing small perturbations to independent variables. If one perturbs the *ith* column of X as

$$X_w = X + \epsilon l_i h d_i^T,$$

where

- l_i represents the scale factor, this accounts for the different measurement units associated with the columns of X. Normally l_i is the standard deviation of the ith coefficient (Weissfeld (1990));
- $i = 1, 2, \ldots, p$ and
- d_i is a $p \times 1$ vector with one in the ith position and zeroes elsewhere.

Therefore,

$$
\begin{aligned}
(X_w^T Q X_w)^{-1} &= \left\{ (X + \epsilon l_i h d_i^T)^T Q (X + \epsilon l_i h d_i^T) \right\}^{-1} \\
&= (X^T Q X)^{-1} - \epsilon l_i (X^T Q X)^{-1} \times \\
&\quad (X^T Q h d_i^T + d_i h^T Q X + d_i h^T h d_i^T)(X^T Q X)^{-1} + O(\epsilon^2)
\end{aligned}
$$

and $X_w^T Q Y^* = (X + \epsilon l_i h d_i^T)^T Q Y^* = X^T Q Y^* + \epsilon l_i d_i h^T Q Y^*$. Later, one can find $(X_w^T Q X_w)^{-1}(X_w^T Q Y^*)$ as

$$
(X_w^T Q X_w)^{-1}(X_w^T Q Y^*) = b + \epsilon l_i (X^T Q X)^{-1} \left\{ d_i h^T Q(e^*) - X^T Q h d_i^T b \right\} + O(\epsilon^2).
$$

Thus the general influence function of b under the perturbation can be shown as

$$
GIF(b, h) = l_i (X^T Q X)^{-1}[d_i h^T Q(e^*) - X^T Q h d_i^T b].
$$

One can replace the ith element of b, therefore $d_i^T b = b_i$ and now one has

$$
GIF(b, h) = l_i (X^T Q X)^{-1}[d_i (e^*)^T - b_i X^T] Q h. \tag{16}
$$

Then two generalised Cook statistics for b are constructed as:

$$
GC_1(b, h) = \frac{l_i^2 h^T H^* \triangle \left\{ e^* d_i^T - b_i X \right\} (X^T Q X)^{-1} \left\{ d_i (e^*)^T - b_i X^T \right\} Q h}{p s^2}, \tag{17}
$$

whereas

$$
GC_2(b, h) = \frac{l_i^2 h^T H^* \left\{ e^* d_i^T - b_i X \right\} (X^T Q X)^{-1} \left\{ d_i (e^*)^T - b_i X^T \right\} Q h}{p s^2}. \tag{18}
$$

It is noted that (17) and (18) were developed using similar scales as §2.2 and $\triangle = \mathrm{diag}(\delta_1, \delta_2, \ldots, \delta_n)$. One can obtain the diagnostic direction h_{max} by computing the eigenvector corresponding to the largest eigenvalue of the following matrice

$$
H^* \triangle \left\{ e^* d_i^T - b_i X \right\} (X^T Q X)^{-1} \left\{ d_i (e^*)^T - b_i X^T \right\} Q,
$$

or

$$
H^* \left\{ e^* d_i^T - b_i X \right\} (X^T Q X)^{-1} \left\{ d_i (e^*)^T - b_i X^T \right\} Q
$$

from (17) and (18) respectively.

3   Illustration

This Stanford heart transplant data contains 184 patients with variables such as survival time(days), censored status, age at time of first transplant (in years) and T5 mismatch score. The mismatch score refers to the continuous score derived from antibody responses of pregnant women by Charles Bieber of Stanford University (Crowley and Hu (1977)). In this article, only 152 patients are considered, corresponding to a survival time equal to at least 10 days and with complete records. From 152 patients, 55 were deceased, i.e. were uncensored and 97 were alive, i.e. were censored. The Buckley-James model for this data set was developed as

$$Y = \beta_0 + \beta_1 AGE + \beta_2 AGE^2 + \beta_3 T5.$$

First, consider the variance perturbation. The index plot of $|h_{max}|$ in Figure 1 shows patients aged below 20 years as the most influential cases. The plot denote the censored observations as solid circles and uncensored observations as hollow triangles.This finding agrees well with Reid and Crepeau (1985), and Pettitt and Daud (1989) where patients aged 13, 15 and 12 years in order have the greatest influence on variance. Note that the patient aged 15 years old is a censored observation. Next, consider the perturbation of response variable and individual independent variables. It is obvious that the most influential patients are aged below 20 years and two patients aged above 60 years. Removal of the patients aged 12 and 13 decreases $\hat{\beta}_1$ by 0.010 and 0.030 respectively, while removal of the patient aged 15 increases $\hat{\beta}_1$ by 0.015. There is no impact on the estimator values in the Buckley-James model when deleting those observations (one at a time) since the maximum eigenvalues

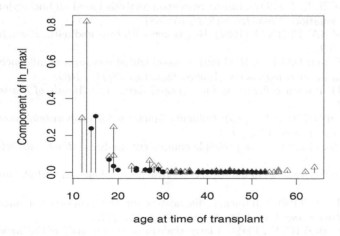

Fig. 1. Index plots of $|h_{max}|$ for perturbing variance for Stanford heart transplant data ($n = 152$).

for the perturbation of the variance, response variable, x_1 and x_2 are small at 0.142, 0.021, -0.002 and 1.000 respectively. However, when the p-value is scrutinized, one can find the p-value for x_1 is roughly five times larger when deleting case 1, and triple when deleting case 4, whereas deleting case 2 has a large effect on the p-value of x_2 where the value becomes fourteen times larger. No attention is given to x_3 since this variable is not strongly associated with survival time.

4   Conclusion

The proposed local influence diagnostics for the Buckley-James model performs very well for identifying influential cases and for assessing the effects that perturbations to the assumed data would have on inferences. It should also be noted that the proposed diagnostics is able to easily detects influential observations from both groups i.e. censored and uncensored observations in the data set as opposed to the previous diagnostics for Buckley-James model.

References

ANDREWS, D. F. and PREGIBON, D. (1978). Finding the outliers that matter. *Journal of Royal Statist. Soc. B 40: 85-93.*

ATKINSON, A. C. (1981): Robustness, transformations and two graphical displays for outlying and influential observations in regression. *Biometrika 68: 13-20.*

COOK, R. D. (1986): Assessment of local influence. *Journal of Royal Statist. Soc. B 48(2), 133-169.*

CROWLEY, J. and HU, M. (1977): Covariance analysis of heart transplant survival data. *Journal of the American Statistical Association 72(357), 27-36.*

JAMES, I. R. and SMITH, P. J. (1984): Consistency results for linear regression with censored data. *The Annals of Statistics 12(2), 590-600.*

LIN, J. S. and WEI, L. J. (1992): Linear regression analysis based on buckleyjames estimating equation. *Biometrics 48(3), 679-681.*

MILLER, R. and HALPERN, J. (1982): Regression with censored data. *Biometrika 69(3), 521-531.*

PETTITT, A. N. and DAUD, I. B. (1989): Case-weighted measures of influence for proportional hazards regression. *Applied Statistics 38(1), 51-67.*

REID, N. (1981): Influence functions for censored data. *The Annals of Statistics 9(1), 78-92.*

REID, N. and CREPEAU, H. (1985): Influence functions for proportional hazards regression. *Biometrika 72(1), 1-9.*

SHI, L. (1997): Local influence in principle component analysis. *Biometrika 84(1), 175-186.*

SMITH, P. J. (2002): Analysis of failure and survival data, Chapman & Hall, United States.

WEISSFELD, L. A. (1990): Influence diagnostics for the proportional hazards model. *Statistics and Probability Letters 10(5): 411-417.*

WU, C. P. and ZUBOVIC, Y. (1995): A large-scale monte carlo study of the buckley-james estimator with censored data. *Journal of Statistical Computation and Simulation 51: 97-119.*

Multiblock Method for Categorical Variables. Application to the Study of Antibiotic Resistance

Stéphanie Bougeard[1], El Mostafa Qannari[2] and Claire Chauvin[1]

[1] AFSSA (French Agency for Food Safety), Department of Epidemiology, Zoopole, BP53, 22440 Ploufragan, France, *s.bougeard@afssa.fr,* *c.chauvin@afssa.fr*

[2] ONIRIS (Nantes-Atlantic National College of Veterinary Medicine, Food Science and Engineering), Department of Sensometrics and Chemometrics, Rue de la Géraudière, BP82225, 44322 Nantes Cedex, France, *elmostafa.qannari@oniris-nantes.fr*

Abstract. We address the problem of describing several categorical variables with a prediction purpose. We focus on methods in the multiblock modelling framework, each block being formed of the indicator matrix associated with each qualitative variable. We propose a method, called categorical multiblock Redundancy Analysis, based on a well-identified global optimization criterion which leads to an eigensolution. In comparison with usual procedures, such as logistic regression, the method is well-adapted to the case of a large number of redundant explanatory variables. Practical uses of the proposed method are illustrated using an empirical example in the field of epidemiology.

Keywords: supervised classification, discriminant analysis, multiblock redundancy analysis, multiblock *PLS*, categorical variables

1 Introduction

Research in veterinary epidemiology is concerned with assessing risk factors of animal health issues, usually manifested as binary variable (uninfected/infected) or categorical variable with more than two categories which cover a spectrum of categories rangin from unapparent to fatal. Explanatory variables, *i.e.* potential risk factors for the disease, consist in data gathered from animal characteristics, farm structure, management practices and laboratory results, among others. These variables are usually measured or coded as qualitative variables. In a more formal way, we address the problem of explaining a qualitative variable y with respect to K other qualitative explanatory variables $(x_1, \ldots, x_K)$. All these variables are measured on the same epidemiological unit, *i.e.* animals or farms. This problem is related to discriminant analysis or supervised classification on categorical data. The statistical procedures usually performed are particular cases of Generalized Linear Models, especially complex models of logistic regression. These models

Y. Lechevallier, G. Saporta (eds.), *Proceedings of COMPSTAT'2010,*
DOI 10.1007/978-3-7908-2604-3_36, © Springer-Verlag Berlin Heidelberg 2010

have appealing advantages that justified their wide use. However, all the potential explanatory variables can usually not be included in a single model. Moreover, all the potential explanatory variables cannot be included in a single model because they are usually plagued by redundancy. It is known that in these circumstances, the relevance and the stability of the results are impaired. As a consequence, alternative non-parametric procedures, such as recursive partitioning (decision trees) or artificial neural networks, are also applied to veterinary epidemiological data. But the performance of such specific techniques is highly dependent on sample size assumptions. They do not perform well on veterinary data. Other discrimination methods, such as Boosting, Bagging or Support Vector Machine can also be applied. Although their misclassification error rate is small, they do not provide a link between dependent and explanatory variables to assess the significant risk factors. Therefore, they are not used for veterinary data, except when no risk factor assessment is needed, *e.g.* molecular epidemiology or gene ranking.

Considering the aim and the specificity of veterinary data, our research work focus on methods related to the multiblock modelling framework, each block being formed of the indicator matrix associated with each qualitative variable. The well-known conceptual model is the Structural Equation Modelling (SEM), also known as $LISREL$. It is extended to categorical data (Skrondal and Rabe-Hesketh (2005)). As an alternative to $LISREL$, PLS Path Modelling is a distribution-free data analysis approach and appears to be more adapted to biological data. It requires neither distributional nor sample size assumptions, but lacks a well-identified global optimization criterion. Moreover, the iterative algorithm convergence is only proven in few particular cases (Hanafi (2007)). This method is also extended to categorical data (Lohmöller (1989); Jakobowicz and Derquenne (2007)). For our purpose of exploring and modelling the relationships between categorical variables, these problems can be circumvented while using simpler procedures, such as multiblock $(K + 1)-$methods. Multiblock Partial Least Squares (Wold (1984)) is a multiblock modelling technique which is widely used in the field of chemometrics. It is not originally designed as a discrimination tool but it is used routinely for this purposes in the two-block case (Sjöström et al. (1986); Barker and Rayens (2003)). We propose a categorical extension of an alternative method to multiblock PLS, which gives results more oriented towards the Y explanation (Bougeard et al. (2008)) and shall refer to it as categorical multiblock Redundancy Analysis ($Cat - mRA$).

2 Method

We denote by y the dependent categorical variable measured on N individuals, each belonging to one of the classes associated with the Q categories of y. The associated indicator matrix Y is characterized by a $(N \times Q)$ dummy matrix. Let $(x_1, \ldots, x_K)$ be the K explanatory categorical variables measured on the same N individuals. Each variable x_k has P_k categories and is transformed into a $(N \times P_k)$ indicator matrix X_k for $k = (1, \ldots, K)$. The overall explanatory dataset, segmented into K blocks, is defined as $X = [X_1 | \ldots | X_K]$ and, thus, consists of an $(N \times P)$ matrix, where $P = \sum_k P_k$. Furthermore, let $D_k = X'_k X_k$ (resp. $D_Y = Y'Y$) the diagonal matrix whose diagonal elements are the class size associated with the x_k (resp. y) modalities. We denote by $P_{X_k} = X_k D_k^{-1} X'_k$ (resp. $P_Y = Y D_Y^{-1} Y'$) the projector onto the subspace spanned by the dummy variables associated with x_k (resp. y). We consider $\tilde{Y} = Y D_Y^{-1/2}$. It is well-known that this standardization restricts the effect of the class size.

The main idea is that each indicator matrix, $\tilde{Y}$ and X_k for $k = (1, \ldots, K)$, is summed up with a latent variable, resp. $u = \tilde{Y}v$ and $t_k = X_k w_k$, which represents the coding of the categorical variable, resp. y and x_k. This can be related to the measurement model of SEM, which relates observed indicators to latent variables. In addition, the structural model which specifies the relations among latent variables is given by the maximization problem (1):

$$\sum_{k=1}^{K} cov^2(u^{(1)}, t_k^{(1)}) \text{ with } t_k^{(1)} = X_k w_k^{(1)}, \ u^{(1)} = \tilde{Y}v^{(1)}, \ ||t_k^{(1)}|| = ||v^{(1)}|| = 1$$

(1)

We prove that the solution is given by $v^{(1)}$ the eigenvector of $\sum_k \tilde{Y}'P_{X_k}\tilde{Y}$ associated with the largest eigenvalue, and that $t_k = P_{X_k} u^{(1)} / ||P_{X_k} u^{(1)}||$ (Bougeard et al. (2008)). Actually, the first order solution is proportional to the constant vector $\mathbf{1}$ and is therefore removed as it is deemed to correspond to a trivial solution. From these results, the criterion (1) can be written as the equivalent maximization problem (2).

$$\sum_{k-1}^{K} ||P_{X_k} u^{(1)}||^2 \text{ with } t_k^{(1)} = X_k w_k^{(1)}, \ u^{(1)} = \tilde{Y}v^{(1)}, \ ||t_k^{(1)}|| = ||v^{(1)}|| = 1 \ (2)$$

As the latent variable $u^{(1)}$ is centered, $||P_{X_k} u^{(1)}||^2$ is the inter-group variance of the component $u^{(1)}$, the groups being associated with the modalities of the variable x_k. We recall that $u^{(1)}$ represents the coding of y. Therefore, it follows that $Cat - mRA$ discriminates the groups associated with the y modalities on the one hand, and of each x_k modalities on the other hand.

As a way to extract a more overall and interpretable information, $Cat - mRA$ seeks a compromise component $t^{(1)}$ which sums up all the partial codings $(t_1^{(1)}, \ldots, t_K^{(1)})$ associated with the categorical variables $(x_1, \ldots, x_K)$, are summed up. This global component is sought such as $t^{(1)} = \sum_k a_k^{(1)} t_k^{(1)}$ and $\sum_k a_k^{(1)2} = 1$. This leads to Eq. (3):

$$t^{(1)} = \sum_{k=1}^{K} \frac{||P_{X_k}u^{(1)}||}{\sqrt{\sum_l ||P_{X_l}u^{(1)}||^2}} t_k^{(1)} = \frac{\sum_k P_{X_k}u^{(1)}}{\sqrt{\sum_l ||P_{X_l}u^{(1)}||^2}} \qquad (3)$$

It follows that $t^{(1)}$ can directly be related to the partial codings $(t_1^{(1)}, \ldots, t_K^{(1)})$ on the one hand, and with the coding of the dependent variable y on the other hand. According to the first equality of Eq. (3), the overall coding $t^{(1)}$ is all the more related to the codings $t_k^{(1)}$ since the normalized squared root of the inter-group variance is large. In addition, the second equality of Eq. (3) shows that $t^{(1)}$ is proportional to the average projection of the dependent variable coding $u^{(1)}$ onto each subspace spanned by the indicator matrix columns of x_k. Moreover, we prove that the overall coding $t^{(1)}$ is also optimum in the sense that it maximizes the criterion (4), which is equivalent to the previous criteria (1) and (2).

$$cov^2(u^{(1)}, t^{(1)}) \text{ with } t^{(1)} = \sum_{k=1}^{K} a_k^{(1)} t_k^{(1)}, \ t_k^{(1)} = X_k w_k^{(1)}, \ u^{(1)} = \tilde{Y} v^{(1)}, \quad (4)$$

$$\sum_{k=1}^{K} a_k^{(1)^2} = 1, \ ||t_k^{(1)}|| = ||v^{(1)}|| = 1$$

As complex biological issues, such as veterinary epidemiological surveys, are on the whole not one-dimensional, higher order solutions are provided by considering the residuals of the orthogonal projections of the indicator matrices $(X_1, \ldots, X_K)$ onto the subspace spanned by the first global component $t^{(1)}$. The same maximization is then performed by replacing the matrices with their residuals. This process is reiterated in order to determine subsequent components. Moreover, these orthogonal latent variables $(t^{(1)}, \ldots, t^{(H)})$ allow orthogonalised regressions which take in account all the explanatory variables without any redundancy problem. They also provide the link between dependent and explanatory variables. Bootstrapping simulations ($m_{bt} = 500$) are performed to assess standard deviations and tolerance intervals associated with the regression coefficient matrix. An explanatory variable is considered to be significantly associated with the dependent variable if the 95% tolerance interval does not contain 0.

Categorical multiblock Redundancy Analysis can be firstly compared to logistic regression. Moreover, another usual procedure for categorical discrimination, called *Disqual*, is also of paramount interest (Saporta, & Niang (2006)). $Cat - mRA$ can be compared to the categorical extension of multiblock PLS, called $Cat - mPLS$, that can be related to PLS path modelling $(PLS - PM)$ associated with a A mode and a structural scheme. Indeed, norm constraints and criteria of multiblock methods can respectively be related to modes and schemes of $PLS - PM$, although equivalences are proven for some specific cases only (Krämer (2007) ; Tenenhaus and Hanafi (2007)). First of all, the optimal number of components to introduce in the model of $Cat - mRA$, $Disqual$ and $Cat - mPLS$ is assessed on the basis of a two-fold cross-validation procedure ($m_{cv} = 500$) (Stone (1974)). This led us to provide fitting and prediction abilities as functions of the number $h = (1, \ldots, H)$ of latent variables $(t^{(1)}, \ldots, t^{(H)})$ used in the model. Then, all the methods are compared on the basis of their ROC (=Receiver Operating Characteristic) curves, plots of the sensitivity *versus* (1-specificity) for a two-class prediction problem, as the discrimination threshold is varied from 0 to 1. It depicts relative trade-offs between benefits (true positives) and costs (false negatives).

3   Application

3.1   Epidemiological data and objectives

Data are collected as part of the French antimicrobial resistance monitoring program. They allow the study of the relationships between antibiotic consumption on farms and antibiotic resistance in healthy slaughtered poultry. The population consists in a cohort of ($N = 554$) broiler chickens, randomly selected from the main slaughterhouses from 1999 to 2002. From each broiler, *Escherichia coli* are isolated from pooled cæca and screened for antimicrobial resistances. The variable of interest ($RNAL$), *i.e.* the Nalidixic Acid resistance, is expressed by two classes: $RNAL = 0$ corresponding to susceptible *E.Coli* ($n_0 = 405$) and $RNAL = 1$ to resistant ($n_1 = 149$). The antimicrobial resistance is studied in the light of 14 potential explanatory variables, related to the chicken production type (one variable coded in three categories: light, standard, free-range), the previous antimicrobial treatments (7 dichotomous variables: exposed *vs* non-exposed, to the different antimicrobials) and the co-resistances observed (6 dichotomous variables: resistant *vs* susceptible, towards the different antimicrobials). Links between explanatory variables are checked using χ^2 tests: 35% of the associations are significant ($pvalue_{\chi^2} \leq 5\%$); all the variables are involved.

3.2   Selection of the optimal models

The two-fold cross-validation procedure provides fitting and prediction abilities for $Cat - mRA$, $Cat - mPLS$ and $Disqual$, as illustrated in Fig. 1. For all the methods under consideration, best models are obtained with ($h = 2$) latent variables. $Disqual$ and $Cat - mPLS$ have comparable abilities, whereas $Cat - mRA$ outperforms both these methods, especially by its ability to predict susceptible *E.Coli* (non-presented results).

3.3   Risk factors obtained from $Cat - mRA$

All the 14 putative explanatory variables are included in the categorical multiblock Redundancy Analysis. Significant risk factors of the Nalidixic Acid re-

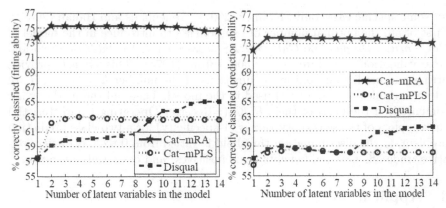

Fig. 1. Fitting and prediction abilities assessed by a two-fold cross-validation procedure. Comparison of the results obtained from categorical multiblock Redundancy Analysis, categorical multiblock *PLS* and *Disqual* procedure.

sistance are given in Table 1. Chicken exposure to quinolones is found to increase the risk of isolating a resistant *E. Coli* strain to the Nalidixic Acid rather than a susceptible one. Nevertheless, the unrelated antimicrobial usage would also play a role in selecting resistant *E. Coli* strains, as other resistances to chloramphenicol and neomycin are found to be related to the resistance under study. Moreover, graphical displays of the variable loadings associated with the first global components may highlight the relationships among the variable modalities (non-presented results).

3.4   Method comparison

Finally, all the methods are compared on the basis of their *ROC* curves (Fig. 2). The logistic regression appears to be the less accurate method, both in terms of sensibility and specificity. The redundancy between explanatory variables seems to affect the result stability. The categorical applications of multiblock methods, *i.e.* $Cat - mRA$ and $Cat - mPLS$, give comparable and correct results. The *Disqual* procedure provides intermediate results between logistic regression and multiblock methods, especially for low values of sensibility and specificity.

4   Concluding remarks

We discuss methods for the analysis of several categorical variables with a prediction purpose. The key feature is to focus on methods in the multiblock modelling framework, each block being formed of the indicator matrix of each qualitative variable. We propose a relevant method, called categorical multiblock Redundancy Analysis, based on a well-identified global optimization criterion with an eigensolution. In comparison with the logistic regression

Explanatory variables	Number of cases	Nalidixic Acid resistance
Treatments during rearing:		
Tetracyclin	153/554 (27.6%)	NS
Beta-lactams	75/554 (13.5%)	NS
Quinolones	93/554 (16.8%)	0.0058 [0.0015 ; 0.0101]
Peptids	48/554 (8.7%)	NS
Sulfonamides	38/554 (6.9%)	NS
Lincomycin	33/554 (6.0%)	NS
Neomycin	26/554 (4.7%)	NS
Observed co-resistances:		
Ampicillin	278/554 (50.2%)	NS
Tetracyclin	462/554 (83.4%)	NS
Trimethoprim	284/554 (51.3%)	NS
Chloramphenicol	86/554 (15.5%)	0.0066 [0.0012 ; 0.0119]
Neomycin	62/554 (11.2%)	0.0094 [0.0037 ; 0.0151]
Streptomycin	297/554 (53.6%)	NS
Production:		
Export	192/554 (34.6%)	NS
Free-range	63/554 (11.4%)	NS
Light	299/554 (54.0%)	NS

Table 1. Significant contributions of the 14 explanatory variables to the explanation of the Nalidixic Acid resistance, through regression coefficients with their 95% tolerance intervals. Results obtained from categorical multiblock Redundancy Analysis with ($h = 2$) latent variables.

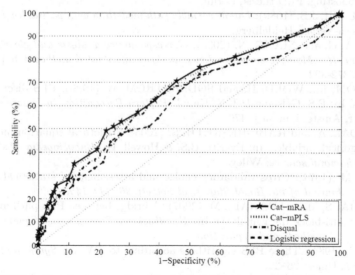

Fig. 2. ROC (=Receiver Operating Characteristic) curves of logistic regression, categorical multiblock Redundancy Analysis, categorical multiblock *PLS* and *Disqual*. The three last methods are based on a model with ($h = 2$) latent variables.

procedure, this method is well-adapted to the case of a large number of redundant explanatory variables. Moreover, all the interpretation tools developed in the multiblock framework can be adapted to enhance the interpretation of categorical data. Statistical procedures are performed using code programs developed in Matlab® and also made available in R. Needless to mention that multiblock methods can be directly adapted to more complex data, *e.g.* several blocks of variables to be explained, thus extending the strategy of analysis to the prediction of several categorical variables.

References

BARKER, M. and RAYENS, W. (2003): Partial least squares for discrimination. *Journal of Chemometrics 17, 166-173.*

BOUGEARD, S., HANAFI, M., LUPO, C. and QANNARI, E.M. (2008): From multiblock Partial Least Squares to multiblock redundancy analysis. A continuum approach. In: *International Conference on Computational Statistics.* Porto, 607–616

HANAFI, M. (2007): PLS path modelling: computation of latent variables with the estimation mode B. *Computational Statistics and Data Analysis 22, 275-292.*

JAKOBOWICZ, E. and DERQUENNE, C. (2007): A modified PLS path modeling algorithm handling reflective categorical variables and a new model building strategy. *Computational Statistics and Data Analysis 51, 3666-3678.*

KRÄMER, N. (2007): Analysis of high-dimensional data with Partial Least Squares and boosting. PhD thesis, Berlin.

LOHMÖLLER, J.B. (1989): *Latent variable path modelling with partial least square.* Physica-Verlag, Heidelberg.

SAPORTA, G. and NIANG, N. (2006): *Correspondence analysis and classification (Chap. 16). Multiple correspondence analysis and related method.* Chapman & Hall, 372-392.

SJÖSTRÖM, M., WOLD, H. and SÖDERSTRÖM, B. (1986): PLS discriminant plots. In: E.S. Gelsema & L.N. Kanal, *Pattern Recognition in Practice II*, Elsevier, Amsterdam, 461–470.

SKRONDAL, A. and RABE-HESKETH, S. (2005): Structural equation modeling: categorical variables. In: Everitt, B.S. & Howell, D., *Encyclopedia of statistics in behavioral science.* Wiley.

STONE, M. (1974): Cross-validatory choice and assessment of statistical predictions. *Journal of the Royal Statistical Society 36, 111-147.*

TENENHAUS, M. and HANAFI, M. (2007): A bridge between PLS path modeling and multi-block data analysis. In: *Handbook on Partial Least Square (PLS): concepts, methods and applications.*

WOLD, S. (1984): Three PLS algorithms according to SW. In: *Symposium MULDAST*, Umea, 26–30.

A Flexible IRT Model for Health Questionnaire: an Application to HRQoL

Serena Broccoli and Giulia Cavrini

Faculty of Statistics
Via delle Belle Arti 41, Bologna, Italy, E-mail: *serena.broccoli@unibo.it*

Abstract. The aim of this study is to formulate a suitable Item Response Theory (IRT) based model to measure HRQoL (as latent variable) using a mixed responses questionnaire and relaxing the hypothesis of normal distributed latent variable. The new model is a combination of two models, that is a latent trait model for mixed responses and an IRT model for Skew Normal latent variable. It is developed in a Bayesian framework. The proposed model was tested on a questionnaire composed by 5 discrete items and one continuous to measure HRQoL in children. The new model has better performances, in term of Deviance Information Criterion, Monte Carlo Markov chain convergence times and precision of the estimates.

Keywords: IRT model, skew normal distribution, health-related quality of life.

1 Introduction

Quality of Life (QoL) is an ill-defined term. Although it is not difficult to intuitively understanding the meaning of quality of life and most people are familiar with the expression "quality of life" and have an intuitive understanding of what it comprises, there is not still an uniform opinion about it. The most commonly accepted definition was proposed by the World Health Organization (WHO) in 1995 (WHOQOL (1995)). They defined QoL as "individuals' perceptions of their position in life, in the context of the culture and value systems in which they live, and in relation to their goals, expectations, standards and concerns". A special aspect of quality of life is Health-Related Quality of life (HRQoL). The HRQoL is the way, which according to health of a person, influences his/her capacity to lead with physical and social "normal" activities. It is generally accepted that HRQoL is a multidimensional construct incorporating at least three broad domains: physical, psychological and social functioning. Clinicians and policymakers are recognizing the importance of measuring HRQol to inform patient management and policy decisions. The advantage of using HRQoL respect to (or in association with) conventional clinical measurements is the self-perceived point of few. Since 1990 the measurement of HRQoL in adults has seen rapid advances, with the development of many questionnaires. Two basic approaches to quality of life measurement are available: generic instruments that provide a summary

Y. Lechevallier, G. Saporta (eds.), *Proceedings of COMPSTAT'2010*,
DOI 10.1007/978-3-7908-2604-3_37, © Springer-Verlag Berlin Heidelberg 2010

of HRQoL; and specific instruments that focus on problems associated with single disease states, patient groups, or areas of function. One of the most commonly used generic measure of HRQoL in the European community is the EQ-5D. This questionnaire has been advanced by a collaborative group from Western Europe known as the EuroQol group. The group, originally formed in 1987, comprises a network of international, multi-disciplinary researchers, originally from seven centers in England, Finland, the Netherlands, Norway, and Sweden. More recently, researchers from Spain as well as researchers from Germany, Greece, Canada, the US, Japan and Italy have joined the group. The intention of this effort is to develop a generic currency for health that could be used commonly across Europe (and in other Countries in the World). It was concurrently developed in many languages by an interdisciplinary team of European researchers (the EuroQol Group) and published in 1990 (Euro-Qol Group (1990)). There are official translations in many languages and more are awaiting official status. The EQ-5D is a brief, standardized, generic measure of HRQoL that provides a profile of patient function and a global health state rating (Kind et al. (1998)). The EQ-5D questionnaire was designed for self-administration and simplicity was an important component of the design. It is intended for use in population health surveys or in combination with a condition-specific instrument for assessment to a specific condition. It has good reliability and validity and contains five dimensions (mobility, self-care, usual activity, pain/discomfort and anxiety/depression) rated on three levels ("no problem," "some problem" or "extreme problem"). It defines the perceived health status according to five dimensions: mobility, self care, usual activities, pain/discomfort, and anxiety/ depression. Each dimension is described by one specific level of adequacy: no problem, moderate problems or severe problems. The EQ-5D questionnaire also includes a Visual Analogue Scale (VAS), by which respondents can attribute their perceived health status a grade ranging from 0 (the worst possible health status) to 100 (the best possible health status). The responses are classified into one of 243 possible health state profiles determined by the combinations of the 5 items answers. Each profile can be transformed into the corresponding preference-based EQ-5D Index, if a valuation study of key health states has been conducted (Dolan (1997)). The purpose of the study is to use psychometric scaling models (or Item Response Theory models) as an alternative to preference-based methods to derive HRQoL scores relative to different health states. IRT models are usually based on the assumption that the observed items are measuring an underlying (latent) construct, i.e. manifest responses are assumed to reflect the location of a given subject on a continuum which is not directly observable (such as intelligence, depressed mood or health-related quality of life). The parameters of these psychometric measurement models are estimated by using statistical techniques derived from the specific assumptions that constitute a particular model. The HRQoL scores are called person parameters, and the tariffs associated with each level of a given item are called item parameters. Item parameters are mathematically treated such as real parameters of a latent trait model in which person parameters are the latent trait. The advantage of using psychometric models is that, in contrast to the techniques used for obtaining preference-based valuations, psychometric scores can be estimated from existing data without requiring the conduct of extensive interview studies. However, while preference-based valuations are measured on a "natural" scale ranging from perfect health (HRQoL=1) to death (HRQoL=0) the origin and spread of psychometric category quantifications are generally defined by suitable but arbitrary scaling parameters. In this thesis an Item Response Theory (IRT) model for mixed responses (5 polytomous items and the VAS) is proposed to analyzed Italian EQ-5D-Y questionnaire. The model is developed under the Bayesian framework and it includes the possibility to suppose Normal or Skew Normal distributions for the HRQoL latent variable.

2   Material and methods

Item Response Theory (IRT) is usually used as an alternative to Classical Response Theory (CTT) for analyzing the results of a questionnaire and improve the instrument. It overcomes the limits of CTT and provides more information. In this paper, the interest is focused on an aspect of IRT that usually receives less attention. IRT is explored as a possible alternative to "conventional" summative scale for the EQ-5D-Y questionnaire answers. The results of the analysis will furnish also information on the quality of the measurement, but since the validation procedure is finished in 2007 and it gave satisfying results, the attention will focused on the ranking ability of the IRT model. An extensive bibliography is available in this field. IRT originated in the 1960s (Lord and Novick (1968); Rasch (1960)) and over the years a large number of researchers have contributed further to the subject. The general idea is that the probability of a certain answer is a function of a latent trait value θ, the HRQoL in this case, plus one or more parameters characterizing the particular item. For each item the probability of a certain answer as a function of the latent trait is called Item Characteristic Curve (ICC) or Item Response Function (IRF). The simplest IRT logistic models for binary items will be presented as a basic introduction. Afterwards, the dichotomous model is generalized to the Partial Credit Model for polytomous items, which will be used to analyzed the EQ-5D-Y questionnaire. Estimation procedures are presented with particular attention to Bayesian techniques. Let' θ a latent variable be defined on a scale of minus infinity to plus infinity. It might be a cognitive ability, a physical ability, a skill, knowledge, attitude, satisfaction or, more generally, any unobservable variable that describes a state or condition of a person. The probability of a "correct response", or more generally the answer coded as 1, for subject i on a dichotomous item j, given the latent trait (usually called person parameter) is equal to

$$P(y_{ij} = 1|\theta_i) = P_{ij}(\theta_i) = c_j + (1 - c_j)\frac{exp[a_j(\theta_i - b_j)]}{1 + exp[a_j(\theta_i - b_j)]} \qquad (1)$$

where a_j, b_j and c_j are the *item parameters*.

b_j represents the *item difficulty*, that is the value of the latent trait for which the probability of a correct answer is equal to the probability of an incorrect answer. If an high number of subjects answer an item correctly it is considered easier than an item to which only a small number of subjects answer correctly.

a_j is the *discrimination parameter* of item j. In fact, in many tests the item does not differ only in respect to difficulty but also in respect to discriminating power. It indicates the degree to which an item distinguishes between the different levels of latent variable across the continuum.

c_j is the *pseudo-chance level parameter*. It is the probability of answering correctly when the latent trait level is very low, that is, the probability of guessing. This parameter is specific for cognitive tests, where there is the possibility that a student answers item correctly because he/she guesses; in the context of HrQoL it is more difficult to imagine the use of this kind of parameter.

The 2 parameter logistic model (2-PLM) is a special case of the 3 parameter logistic model (3-PLM) with $c_j = 0$ for all items. The 1 parameter logistic model (1-PLM or Rasch Model) is a special case of the 2 parameter logistic model with $a_j = 1$ for all items. Because of its special properties, it is not usually considered to be a particular IRT model, but a different kind of model. The logistic model presented in the previous section is valid only for tests composed of dichotomous items. Also, the items of a questionnaire frequently have a polytomous form, that is, more than two possible answers. The advantage of polytomous items is that, by virtue of their greater number of response categories, they are able to provide more information over a wider range of the latent variables than dichotomous items. From the several existing types of generalized Rasch models for polytomous response categories, our attention is focused on the Partial Credit Model (PCM), because it will be used in further parts of the work. The PCM was presented in 1982 by Master. It can be applied in any situation in which performances on an item are recorded in two or more ordered categories and there is an intention to combine results across items to obtain measures on some underlying variable. The mathematical formulation of the PCM comes from an extension of the 1-PLM. The interpretation of the parameters is similar to the interpretation of the 1-PLM parameters, except for the fact that in the case of the PCM the number of item parameters for each item is greater than one. In fact, an item parameter is obtained for each step (threshold) from a modality to the one that follows. The total number of thresholds for each item is given by the number of responses minus 1. The probability of each level answer can be plotted as function of the latent variable. One curve for every level will be obtained and they are called Category Characteristic Curves (CCCs). The item parameter is the latent variable level at which two consecutive CCCs intersect. The main procedures used to estimate the parameters of IRT models are the Joint Maximum Likelihood (JML) estimation, the Conditional Maximum Likelihood (CML) estimation and the Marginal Maximum (MML) Likelihood estimation (Baker (1992)). Further to the methods based on the maximization of the likelihood function, Bayesian estimation methods are frequently used.

A more flexible statistical model then the IRT models already presented is to theorize to obtain a synthetic score of quality of life (latent variable) from the EQ-5D-Y questionnaire. Firstly, the model must allow for the analysis of continuous responses, because the information of the VAS scale could be included. Secondly, the assumption of normal distribution of the quality of life score must be relaxed in favour of a skew normal distribution. In fact, few children coming from a school population are expected to exhibit low values of quality of life, thus the latent variable is supposed to be skewed to the right.

Supposing there is a questionnaire composed of r continuous items, s dichotomous items and c polytomous items, where $r + s + c = q$ (total number of items). Letting w_{ij} with $j=1...r$ be the answer of subject i to the continuous item j, v_{ij} with $j=1...s$ being the answer of subject i to the dichotomous item j and t_{ij} with $j=1...c$ being the answer of subject i to the polytomous item j.

$w_{ij} \sim N(\mu_{ij}, \sigma^2)$ $j=1...r$ $i=1...N$ $v_{ij} \sim Ber(\mu_{ij})$ $j=1...s$ $i=1...N$

$t_{ij} \sim Multinomial(\mu_{ij}, 1)$ $j=1...c$ $i=1...N$

We assumed the existence of a latent variable θ_i such that $\mu_{ij} = a_j \theta_i - b_j$ $j=1...r$

$$\mu_{ij} = P(v_{ij} = 1) = \frac{exp[a_j(\theta_i - b_j)]}{1 + exp[a_j(\theta_i - b_j)]} j=1...s \tag{2}$$

$$\mu_{ij} = [\mu_{ijx} = \frac{exp\Sigma_{t=0}^{x}[a_j(\theta_i - b_{jt})]}{1 + exp\Sigma_{k=0}^{k_j}[a_j(\theta_i - b_j)]}, x=1...k_j and \Sigma_{t=0}^{0}(\theta_i - b_{jt}) = 0] \tag{3}$$

It is assumed that θ comes from a generalized normal distribution, the skew normal distribution $\theta_{ij} \sim SN(\alpha, \beta, \delta)$ $i=1...N$. The marginal distribution of the observed variables y_{ij} (w_{ij}, t_{ij} and v_{ij}) is the same as expressed by Moustaky (1996) and discussed previously, with the difference that the $h(\theta_{ij})$, the prior distribution of the latent variable, is now the Skew Normal distribution function. Consequently, the log-likelihood can be expressed as

$$logL = \Sigma_{i=1}^{n} log f(\mathbf{y}_j) = \Sigma_{i=1}^{n} log \int_{-\infty}^{+\infty} g(\mathbf{y}_j|\theta) SN(\theta) d(\theta) \tag{4}$$

Considering the likelihood function in equation 4, it is possible to implement a Bayesian estimation procedure. In fact, having defined priors and hyperpriors it is possible to write the posterior distribution of the parameters of the model as

$$p(\omega_i|\mathbf{y}_i) \propto \prod_{j=1}^{n} g(w_{ij}|\omega_i)h(\sigma_j) \prod_{j=1}^{s} g(v_{ij}|\omega_i) \prod_{j=1}^{c} g(t_{ij}|\omega_i) \prod_{j=1}^{q} h(a_j)h(b_j)h(\theta_j) (5)$$

With Gibbs sampling procedures, random samples of person and item parameters can be drawn from the full conditionals derived from the posterior distribution specified in equation 5 for this hierarchical model. The validated Italian EQ-5D-Y questionnaire was included for the first time in a cross-sectional regional nutritional surveillance study (So.N.I.A) aimed assessing eating habits in a population of children. Data on HRQoL, nutritional habits and BMI (calculated from measured weight and height) were collected referring to a subsample of 13-year old children. The flexible IRT model discussed above is used principally to obtain a continuum synthetic quality of life score for each child who compiled the EQ-5D-Y questionnaire. As the item parameters are also estimates, information on the severity of the items are also furnished. A Bayesian approach was adopted to obtain the estimates, and the analyses were carried out using the software WinBUGS 1.4. The results of the IRT model for mixed items with skew latent variables were compared with the results obtained using a PCM (only polytomous items) or the IRT model for mixed items, but not skewed a priori for the latent variable.

3   Results

The posterior estimates for the three models were obtained as the average of the Gibbs samples. As a rule of thumb, the simulation should be run until the Monte Carlo error for each parameter of interest is less than about 5% of the sample standard deviation (Spiegelhalter et al. (2003)). The person parameters are reported as example for four subjects, three of which have the same pattern of answers (11111) and different VAS score ($\theta_1 = 11111$, 85; $\theta_6 = 11111$, 50; $\theta_{43} = 11111$, 100) and one with a more serious pattern of answers (31122) and VAS equal to 65 ($\theta_{29} = 31122$, 65). It is interesting to consider that Model 1 the HRQoL estimated for the three children with same pattern but different VAS scores is very similar ($\theta_{43} = 1.162$, $\theta_1 = 1.146$ and $\theta_6 = 1.164$), indeed in this case the VAS information is not used. On the contrary, Model 2 and Model 3 are able to distinguish between the three children 1, 6, and 43 and they are ranked according to their VAS score values. This result is particularly interesting because it demonstrated that the use of the VAS score permits to distinguish between the large number of children 11111-responders, but with different VAS values. The difference in their HRQoL is probably due to health problems not covered or not so severe as to be caught by the items included in the questionnaire. The VAS score could be thought as a latent domain, directly measured by the responders, that contributes together with the five questions in building the main latent variable measure HRQoL. As concern the HRQoL estimated for the fourth subject, it is lower for all the three models and it demonstrates that the PCM is also ranking between subjects if they have different patterns of answers. Moreover, in Model 3 the distance between child 43 and child 49 is lower than for the other two models. This is probably due to the fact that for Model 3 the variance of the latent variable a priori distribution is constrained equal to 1, and in Model 1 and Model 2 it is estimated by the data. In conclusion, Model 2 and Model 3 are able to distinguish between children in terms of HRQoL better than the PCM and they should be preferred when analyzing data from the EQ-5D-Y questionnaire, especially when a large number of children answer "No problem" in all the items. Still, some other aspects must be taken in account when choosing between the three models, particularly between Model 2 and Model 3 which seem to perform similarly in terms of subject ranking. The performance in chain convergence is one of these aspects. The convergence times could be quite long if a lot of children are in the sample, because an increase in one unit in the sample increases by one unit the number of parameters to be estimated. Model 2 takes a substantially longer time to reach convergence than Model 3. The misspecification of the a priori for the latent variable (assumed to be normal) might be the cause of the Model 2 delay. Secondly, as introduced at the beginning of this section, the DIC measure for the fit of the model has been used. Since the lower the DIC value, the higher the performance of the model, the best is Model 3, but the difference between Model 2 and Model 3 is lower than 5 and it could be misleading just to report the model with the lowest DIC (Spiegelhalter et al. (2002)). In short, the several aspects evaluated in this section suggest Model 3 as the best of one between the three studied models for analyzing the EQ-5D-Y questionnaire.

4 Conclusion

In this paper the attention was focused on the measurement and the analysis of HRQoL in children. The increasing importance acquired in the last years by HrQoL needs a special attention toward suitable statistical tools for its measurement. In particular, the attention was paid on the potentialities of IRT models as an alternative to preference-based methods to derive HRQoL scores relative to different health states. The EQ-5D-Y questionnaire has been used as instrument to measure HRQoL in children. Some methodological aspects and possible extension of the known IRT models, strongly related with the applied problem, were studied in-depth. Above all, the problem of the skewness of the latent variable and the treatment of mixed responses were investigated. In Chapter 3 an IRT model that combines the possibility of analyzing different types of responses at one time and latent variables assumed to be skewed is developed. It arises from the combination in a Bayesian framework of two different IRT models already known in literature (Moustaki (1996); Bazan et al. (2004)). The combined model furnishes the estimates of HRQoL for every child in a sample, taking in account all the items of a questionnaire independently of their nature, in this context the five questions of the EQ-5D-Y and the VAS score. Furthermore, the hypothesis of normal distribution of the latent variable is relaxed, allowing the analysis of typical asymmetric and skewed phenomenon like that the HRQoL in a population of young students. The model was formulated as WINBUGS code and the estimates of the parameters were obtained using a Bayesian procedure, more flexible than the likelihood methods and similarly in the results. A comparison between 3 different models showed the qualities of the flexible model proposed.

References

BAKER, F. (1992): *Item response theory: parameter estimation techniques*. New York: Dekker.

BAZAN, J., BOLFARINE and H., BRANCO, D. M. (2004): *A new family of asymmetric models for item response theory: A skew normal IRT family*. Technical report (RT-MAE-2004-17). Department of Statistics. University of Sao Paulo.

DOLAN, P. (1997): Modelling valuations for EuroQol health states. *Med. Care, 35:1095-1108*.

KIND, P., DOLAN, P., GUDEX, C. and WILLIAMS, A. (1998): Variations in population health status: results from United Kingdom national questionnaire survey. *BMJ, 316:736-741*.

LORD, F., NOVICK, M. (1968): *Statistical theories of mental test scores*. MA: Adisson-Wesley.

MOUSTAKI, I., KNOTT, M. (2000): Generalized latent trait model. *Psychometrika, 65(3), 391-411*.

RASCH, G. (1960): *Probabilistic models for some intelligence and attainment tests*. Copenhagen: Denmarks Paedagogiske Institut (Reprinted by University of Chicago Press, 1980).

SPIEGELHALTER, D. J., BEST, N. G., CARLIN, B. P. and VAN DER LINDE, A. (2002): Bayesian measures of model complexity and fit. *Journal of the Royal Statistical Society Series B-Statistical Methodology , 64:583-616*.

THE EUROQOL GROUP (1990): EuroQol- a new facility for the measurement of health-related quality of life. *Health Policy, 16:199-208*.

WHOQOL (1995): The world health organization quality of life assessment (WHOQOL): position paper from the World Health Organization. *Social Science and Medicine , 41:1403-1409*.

Multidimensional Exploratory Analysis of a Structural Model Using a Class of Generalized Covariance Criteria

Xavier Bry[1], Thomas Verron[2], and Patrick Redont[1]

[1] I3M, UM2, Place Eugène Bataillon, 34095 Montpellier, France
[2] SEITA-ITG, SCR, 4 rue André Dessaux, 45404 Fleury les Aubrais, France

Abstract. Our aim is to explore a structural model: several variable groups describing the same observations are assumed to be structured around latent dimensions that are linked through a linear model that may have several equations. This type of model is commonly dealt with by methods assuming that the latent dimension in each group is unique. However, conceptual models generally link concepts which are multidimensional. We propose a general class of criteria suitable to measure the quality of a Structural Equation Model (SEM). This class contains the covariance criteria used in PLS Regression and the Multiple Covariance criterion of the SEER method. It also contains quartimax-related criteria. All criteria in the class must be maximized under a unit norm constraint. We give an equivalent unconstrained maximization program, and algorithms to solve it. This maximization is used within a general algorithm named THEME (Thematic Equation Model Exploration), which allows to search the structures of groups for all dimensions useful to the model. THEME extracts locally nested structural component models.

Keywords: path modeling, PLS, SEER, SEM, THEME

Introduction

The framework is that of SEM's: R variable groups $X_1, \ldots, X_R$ describing the same n observations are assumed structured around few dimensions linked together through a linear model. SEM´s are usually dealt with according to the Latent Variable (LV) paradigm: each group X_r is assumed to be the output of one single LV that is to be estimated. Two approaches are currently available: the first one, PLS Path Modeling (Lohmöller (1989); Chin and Newsted (1999); Tenenhaus (2005)), being based on no global criterion optimization, remains very empirical. The second one consists in optimizing an interpretable global criterion. According to the chosen criterion, several methods have been proposed (Jöreskog and Wold (1982); Smilde et al. (2000)). This more rigorous approach is often paid for by some difficulty to deal with small samples. So far, these methods have assumed that each group is structured around a single underlying dimension. One could object that if this is the case, all variables in the group being strongly correlated, this dimension could simply be estimated by the group´s 1st PC. Mark that this

Y. Lechevallier, G. Saporta (eds.), *Proceedings of COMPSTAT'2010*,
DOI 10.1007/978-3-7908-2604-3_38, © Springer-Verlag Berlin Heidelberg 2010

solution would not take into account the structural model, and so could not be considered as a proper SEM estimation. The linear model would then merely link these PC's. The problem of identifying the dimensions useful to the conceptual model really arises when variable groups measure out truly multidimensional concepts; a case most modelers are currently confronted with, without knowing how many dimensions have to play a role, nor which. It is then essential to explore the structure of these groups in relation to the model, so as to extract dimensions useful to it. Such methods as Multiblock PLS (Wangen and Kowalski (1988); Westerhuis et al. (1998)) try to achieve that; but, for want of a criterion reflecting properly partial relations between each explanatory group and the corresponding dependent one, they have to include recurring deflation steps which remain empirical and arbitrary. In order to extend PLS Regression to the case where a dependent group is related to several predictor groups, we proposed in Bry et al. (2009) to maximize what we called a multiple covariance criterion. This maximization is the basis of a single dependent group model exploration method: Structural Equation Exploratory Regression (SEER). SEER extracts as many components per group as wanted, ranked in a clearly interpretable way through a local nesting principle. The use of a global criterion makes backward component selection possible. Here, we extend the multiple covariance criterion in two ways: 1) The criterion is generalized so as to take into account the structural strength of a component in a more flexible way, including multiple covariance, but also variable-bundle-oriented measures; 2) It is also extended to models having any number of dependent /predictor groups. We then give algorithms to maximize the criterion.

1   Model and problem:

1.1   Thematic model

Conceptually, any variable group $X_r = \left(x_r^1, \ldots, x_r^{J_r}\right)$ may depend on other groups, or contribute to model other groups. This dependency pattern is the *thematic model* (cf. fig. 1). A group may have several models; let E_r^h be model h for dependent group X_r. In fact, such dependencies concern (unknown) dimensions underlying in groups. We expect such dimensions to be revealed in X_r through K_r components $f_r^1, \ldots, f_r^{K_r}$, where $\forall r, k : f_r^k = X_r v_r^k$.

1.2   Problem

Components are wanted to give their model a good fit, and also to have some structural strength in their group (i.e. account for a non-residual part of observation discrepancies as coded by the group), so that the final model be robust and easier to interpret. Let P be the weighting matrix of the observations. To each group X_r, we associate metric matrix M_r. The structural

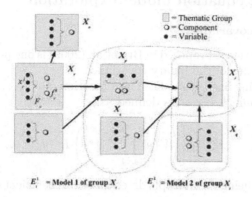

Fig. 1. Thematic model.

strength of component $f_r^k = X_r v_r^k$ will be measured by a function of the form: $S(v_r^k) = \sum_{t=1}^{T} (v_r^{k'} A_{rt} v_r^k)^a$ with matrices A_{rt} symmetric positive (s.p.) and $a > 0$. Generally, v_r^k has to be constrained by: $v_r^{k'} D_r v_r^k = 1$, where D_r is an appropriate definite s.p. matrix. As particular instances, we have:

- Component variance: $S(v_r^k) = V(f_r^k) = v_r^{k'} X_r' P X_r v_r^k$; $a = 1$; $T = 1$; $A_r = X_r' P X_r$; $D_r = M_r^{-1}$.
- Group variance explained by component. All variables being standardized, we consider:

$$S(v_r^k) = \sum_{x_r^j \in X_r} \rho^2(f_r^k, x_r^j) = \sum_{x_r^j \in X_r} \langle f_r^k | x_r^j \rangle_P^2 = v_r^{k'} (X_r' P X_r)^2 v_r^k$$

with $D_r = X_r' P X_r$, so that $\|f_r^k\|_P^2 = 1$; $a = 1$, $T = 1$, $A_r = (X_r P X_r)^2$.

- The previous criterion can be extended to:

$$S(v_r^k) = \sum_{x_r^j \in X_r} a_j \rho^{2a}(f_r^k, x_r^j) = \sum_{j=1}^{J_r} a_j (v_r^{k'} X_r' P x_r^j x_r^{j'} P X_r v_r^k)^a$$

with $D_r = X_r' P X_r$. Then: $T = J_r$, $A_{rj} = a_j^{1/a} w_j w_j'$ where $w_j = X_r' P x_r^j$.

The motivation of such a criterion is the same as Quartimax rotation of PC's: to make components point to variable bundles instead of original PC's. Tuning parameter a allows to draw components more (greater a) or less (lower a) towards local variable bundles.

Group X_r depending on other groups $X_s, \ldots, X_t$ in some model E_r^h, every component f_r^k in X_r will be linearly modeled through components of these groups $\{f_s^l, s \in P_r^h, l \leq K_s\}$, where P_r^h is the index-set of predictor groups in E_r^h. Goodness of fit of $f_r^{k'}$s model will simply be measured by its R^2 coefficient, denoted $R^2(f_r^k | \{f_s^l, s \in P_r^h, l \leq K_s\})$ or $R^2(E_r^h)$.

2   Thematic equation model exploration

2.1   Multiple covariance.

The multiple covariance proposed in Bry et al. (2009) is one possible extension of the absolute value of the binary covariance.

Definition: y being linearly modeled as a function of $x^1, \ldots, x^S$, the *Multiple Covariance of y on $x^1, \ldots, x^S$* is defined as:

$$MC(y|x^1, \ldots, x^S) = \left[\left(V(y) \prod_{s=1}^{S} V(x^s) \right) R^2(y|x^1, \ldots, x^S) \right]^{1/2}$$

$R^2(y|x^1, \ldots, x^S)$ being the multiple determination coefficient of y on $\{x^1, \ldots, x^S\}$.

2.2   Multiple co-structure

Given some measure of structural strength $S(v)$ of any component $f = Xv$, and given the linear component model: $f_d = \sum_{p \in P(d)} b_p f_p + \varepsilon$, $P(d)$ being the index set of predictor components of f_d, we term Multiple Co-Structure (MCS) of f_d onto $\{f_p, p \in P(d)\}$:

$$MCS(f_d|\{f_p, p \in P(d)\}) = \left[S(v_d) \left(\prod_{p \in P(d)} S(v_p) \right) R^2(f_d|\{f_p, p \in P(d)\}) \right]^{1/2}$$

2.3   THEME criterion for rank 1 components.

Let E_r be the set of models involving f_r, and e_r their number. The first criterion we propose to be maximized by rank 1 components is:

$$C_1 = \prod_{r=1}^{R} (S(v_r))^{e_r} \prod_{d,h} R^2(f_d|\{f_s, s \in P_d^h\})$$

C_1 compounds the structural strength of components with the goodness of fit of component-based regression models.

2.4   Beyond 1 component per group.

When we want to extract K_r components in group X_r, we must account for the fact that predictor components of model E_d^h: $\{f_p^k; p \in P_d^h, \forall p : k = 1, K_p\}$ must predict K_d components $\{f_d^k; k = 1, K_d\}$ in dependent group X_d. Then, the search for explanatory components should be based on some optimization including some compound MCS. Let $CM_d^k(h)$ be the component model of f_d^k in thematic equation h:

$$CM_d^k(h) = f_d^k|\{f_p^l|p \in P_d^h, l \leq K_p\} \quad \text{and}$$

$$\sum_{k=1}^{K_d} MCS^2(\mathcal{CM}_d^k(h)) = \prod_{\substack{p \in P_d^h \\ l \le K_p}} S(v_p^l) \left(\sum_{k=1}^{K_d} S(v_d^k) R^2(\mathcal{CM}_d^k(h)) \right)$$

Let us define a nesting principle that makes component ranking interpretable.

2.5 The local nesting principle.

Our Local Nesting Principle (LNP) states that:

- Rank k component in $X_r : f_r^k$, should help best predict - with respect to MCS - *all* components of X_d dependent on it in some model E_d^h, when associated to *all* components predicting this group in E_d^h except X_r's higher rank components, which are considered not yet available, i.e.:

$$\{f_r^l; l < k\} \cup \{f_t^l; r \in P_d^h, t \in P_d^h, t \neq r, l \le K_t\}$$

- Rank k component in $X_r : f_r^k$, should be best predictable - with respect to the criterion - by all components from groups explanatory of X_r in some model, under the orthogonality constraint:

$$\forall l < k : f_r^{k'} P f_r^l = 0$$

This sequential principle is not a priori compatible with a global criterion that the set of all components would maximize. Indeed, the R^2 coefficients in MCS's change from one rank to another. But it is easy to define, for each f_r^k component, the criterion it should maximize, according to the LNP:

$$\left(S(v_r^k) \right)^{e_r} \left(\prod_{h | P_r^h \neq \emptyset} R^2(\mathcal{CM}_r^k(h)) \right) \prod_{(s,h)|r \in P_s^h} \left(\sum_{l=1}^{K_s} S(v_s^l) R^2(\mathcal{CM}_s^k(h)) \right) \quad (1)$$

2.6 Generic form of the criterion

Let g be a numeric variable and $F = \{f_1, \dots, f_q\}$ the set of its predictors in a linear model. For any $f_s \in F$, let $F_{-s} = F \backslash \{f_s\}$. In Bry et al. (2009), we have shown that, $\forall f_s \in F$, we can write:

$$R^2(g|F) = \frac{f_s' A_s(g) f_s}{f_s' B_s f_s} \quad (2)$$

with: $B_s = P\Pi_{F_{-s}^\perp}$ and $A_s(g) = \frac{1}{\|g\|_P^2} \left[(g' P\Pi_{F_{-s}} g) B_s + B_s' gg' B_s \right]$

where, E being any space, Π_E denotes the orthogonal projector onto E. It follows that, if $g_1, \dots, g_K$ are numeric variables linearly modeled using the same F, we have :

$$\sum_{k=1}^K \omega_k R^2(g_k|F) = \frac{f_s' A_s f_s}{f_s' B_s f_s} \quad (3)$$

with: $A_s = P\Pi_{F^{\perp}_{-s}} tr(G\Omega G' P\Pi_{F_{-s}}) + \Pi_{F^{\perp}_{-s}}' P (G\Omega G') P\Pi_{F^{\perp}_{-s}}$, $\Omega = diag(\omega_k)_k$, $G = [g_1, \ldots, g_K]$. Besides, we have that:

$$R^2(g|F) = \frac{g'(P\Pi_F)g}{g'Pg} \tag{4}$$

It follows from (1) to (4) that the criterion in (1), to be currently maximized by component f_r^k, may be written under the generic form:

$$\left(\sum_{t=1}^{T}(v_r^{k'} A_{rkt} v_r^k)^a\right)^{e_r} \prod_{l=1}^{e_r} \frac{f_r^{k'} C_{rkl} f_r^k}{f_r^{k'} D_{rkl} f_r^k}$$

To ensure orthogonality constraint: $\forall l < k$: $f_r^{k'} P f_r^l = 0$, we choose to take $f_r^k = X_r^{k-1} v_r^k$, where $X_r^0 = X_r$ and $X_r^k = \Pi_{\langle f_r^k \rangle^{\perp}} X_r^{k-1}$.

So, we end up with the following program yielding current component f_r^k:

$$\mathbf{P}: \max_{v_r^{k'} D_r v_r^k = 1} C(v_r^k) \text{ where } C(v_r^k) = \left(\sum_{t=1}^{T}(v_r^{k'} A_{rkt} v_r^k)^a\right)^{e_r} \prod_{l=1}^{e_r} \frac{v_r^{k'} T_{rkl} v_r^k}{v_r^{k'} W_{rkl} v_r^k}$$

2.7 Equivalent unconstrained minimization program.

We can show that, taking:

$$C(v) = \left(\sum_{t=1}^{T}(v' A_t v)^a\right)^e \prod_{l=1}^{e} \frac{v' T_l v}{v' W_l v} \text{ and } \varphi(v) = \frac{1}{2}[ae(v' Dv) - \ln C(v)],$$

$\mathbf{P}: \max_{v' Dv = 1} C(v)$ is equivalent to the unconstrained minimization problem:

$$\mathbf{S}: \min_{v \neq 0} \varphi(v)$$

General minimization software can, and should, be used to solve $\mathbf{S}$.

2.8 An alternative algorithm.

In case no minimization routine is available, we propose the algorithm:

$$v(t+1) = v(t) - h(t)\left[aeD + \sum_{l=1}^{e} \frac{W_l}{v(t)' W_l v(t)}\right]^{-1} \nabla\varphi(v(t)) \tag{5}$$

where $h(t)$ is a positive parameter to be specified later. Algorithm (5) is nothing but a descent method to minimize φ, with:

$$d(t) = -\left[aeD + \sum_{l=1}^{e} \frac{W_l}{v(t)' W_l v(t)}\right]^{-1} \nabla\varphi(v(t))$$

as a descent direction at point $v(t)$.

General minimization methods (see Bonnans et al. (1997); Nocedal and Wright (1999); Absil et al. (2005)) grant that: if $h(t)$ is chosen according to the Wolfe, or Goldstein-Price, rule, then for any initial $v(0)$, algorithm (5) generates a sequence $v(t)$ that converges to a point $\bar{v}$ satisfying:

$$\|\bar{v}\|_D = 1, \ \nabla\varphi(\bar{v}) = 0$$

Numerous simulations have shown that (5) always yields a local minimum for problem **S** (hence a local maximum for **P**).

Although we do not have theoretical arguments for preferring (5) to the plain gradient iteration:

$$v(t+1) = v(t) - h(t)\nabla\varphi(v(t))$$

we have checked that (5) is numerically faster. The reason for choosing $d(t)$ as a descent direction is the following. A way of expressing $\nabla\varphi(\bar{v}) = 0$ is:

$$\underbrace{\left[aeD + \sum_{l=1}^{e} \frac{W_l}{\bar{v}'W_l\bar{v}} \right]}_{T_1} \bar{v} = \underbrace{\left[ae\frac{\sum_{t=1}^{T}(\bar{v}'A_t\bar{v})^{a-1}A_t}{\sum_{t=1}^{T}(\bar{v}'A_t\bar{v})^a} + \sum_{l=1}^{e}\frac{T_l}{\bar{v}'T_l\bar{v}} \right]}_{T_2} \bar{v}$$

This suggests the following fixed point iterative procedure:

$$v(t+1) = T_1^{-1}T_2 v(t) \tag{6}$$

which is (5) with $h(t) \equiv 1$. Indeed for $a = 1$, iterations (6) have always proved numerically convergent ; but to enforce convergence, theoretically and for $a \geq 1$, $h(t)$ has to be chosen according to some adequate rule.

From (5), an iterative process on the unit sphere $v'Dv = 1$ may be designed. Suppose $\|v(t)\|_D = 1$ and let $\delta(t) = d(t) - v(t)(d(t)'Dv(t))$ be the projection of $d(t)$ onto the plane tangent to the sphere at point $v(t)$. Use $\delta(t)$ as a descent direction to decrease function φ on the sphere; i.e., $q(\theta) = \varphi(v(t)cos(\theta) + w(t)sin(\theta))$, with $w(t) = \delta(t)/\|\delta(t)\|_D$, is to be minimized for $\theta > 0$. Let:

$$v(t+1) = v(t)cos(\theta(t)) + w(t)sin(\theta(t)) \tag{7}$$

where $\theta(t)$ is chosen according to the Wolfe, or Goldstein-Price, rule to decrease q. General results (see Lageman (2007)) state that algorithm (7) generates a sequence that converges to a point $\bar{v}$ of the sphere verifying $\nabla\varphi(\bar{v}) = 0$. Numerical experiments showed that iterations (7) are slightly faster than (5).

3   Chemometrical application

We have applied THEME to model the production of Hoffmann compounds from 52 physical and chemical variables describing n=19 cigarettes. The variables were partitioned by chemists into 7 thematic groups, linked through 2 component models: one for the combustion process, and the other for the filter ventilation process. THEME allowed to separate the complementary roles, on Hoffmann Compounds, of: tobacco quality, tobacco type, combustion chemical enhancers or inhibitors, filter retention and ventilation powers. It yielded a complete and robust model having accuracy within reproducibility limits.

4   Conclusion and perspectives:

Thematic partitioning allows to interpret components conceptually, and also to analyze the complementarity of thematic aspects. Compared to other multi-group techniques, THEME: 1) solves the problem of group-weighting; 2) extends PLSR; 3) uses a criterion grounding component backward selection; 4) allows various measures of component structural strength. Current research is being carried out to extend THEME to GLM.

References

ABSIL, P.-A., MAHOMY, R. and ANDREWS, B. (2005): Convergence of the Iterates of Descent Methods for Analytic Cost Functions, *SIAM J. OPTIM.*, *Vol. 16, No. 2, pp. 531-547.*

BONNANS, J. F., GILBERT, J. C, LEMARÉCHAL, C. and SAGASTIZÁBAL, C. (1997): Optimisation Numérique, *Springer, Mathématiques et Applications, 27.*

BRY X., VERRON T.and CAZES P. (2009): Exploring a physico-chemical multiarray explanatory model with a new multiple covariance-based technique: Structural equation exploratory regression, *Anal. Chim. Acta, 642, 45–58.*

CHIN, W.W., NEWSTED, P.R., (1999): Structural equation modeling analysis with small samples using partial least squares. *In: Statistical Strategies for Small Sample Research. Sage, 307–341.*

HWANG, H., and TAKANE, Y. (2004): Generalized structured component analysis. *Psychometrika, 69, 81-99.*

JÖRESKOG, K. G. and WOLD, H. (1982): The ML and PLS techniques for modeling with latent variables: historical and competitive aspects, *in Systems under indirect observation, Part 1, 263-270.*

LAGEMAN, Ch. (2007): Pointwise convergence of gradient-like systems, Math. Nachr. *280, No. 13-14, 1543-1558.*

LOHMÖLLER J.-B. (1989): Latent Variables Path Modeling with Partial Least Squares, *Physica-Verlag, Heidelberg.*

NOCEDAL, J., WRIGHT, S. J. (1999): Numerical Optimization, *Springer, Series in Operations Research.*

SMILDE, A.K., WESTERHUIS, J.A. and BOQUÉE, R., (2000): Multiway multiblock component and covariates regression models. *J. Chem. 14, 301–331.*

TENENHAUS M., VINZI V.E., CHATELIN Y-M. and LAURO C. (2005): PLS path modeling - *CSDA, 48, 159-205.*

WANGEN L., KOWALSKI B. (1988): A multiblock partial least squares algorithm for investigating complex chemical systems. *J. Chem.; 3: 3-20.*

WESTERHUIS, J.A., KOURTI and K., MACGREGOR, J.F., (1998): Analysis of multiblock and hierarchical PCA and PLS models. *J. Chem. 12, 301-321.*

Semiparametric Models with Functional Responses in a Model Assisted Survey Sampling Setting : Model Assisted Estimation of Electricity Consumption Curves

Hervé Cardot[1], Alain Dessertaine[2], and Etienne Josserand[1]

[1] Institut de Mathématiques de Bourgogne, UMR 5584 CNRS,
Université de Bourgogne, 9, Av. A. Savary - B.P. 47 870, 21078 Dijon, France
herve.cardot@u-bourgogne.fr, etienne.josserand@u-bourgogne.fr
[2] EDF, R&D, ICAME - SOAD
1, Av. du Général de Gaulle, 92141 Clamart , France
alain.dessertaine@edf.fr

Abstract. This work adopts a survey sampling point of view to estimate the mean curve of large databases of functional data. When storage capacities are limited, selecting, with survey techniques a small fraction of the observations is an interesting alternative to signal compression techniques. We propose here to take account of real or multivariate auxiliary information available at a low cost for the whole population, with semiparametric model assisted approaches, in order to improve the accuracy of Horvitz-Thompson estimators of the mean curve. We first estimate the functional principal components with a design based point of view in order to reduce the dimension of the signals and then propose semiparametric models to get estimations of the curves that are not observed. This technique is shown to be really effective on a real dataset of 18902 electricity meters measuring every half an hour electricity consumption during two weeks.

Keywords: design-based estimation, functional principal components, electricity consumption, Horvitz-Thompson estimator

1 Introduction

With the development of distributed sensors one can have access of potentially huge databases of signals evolving along fine time scales. Collecting in an exhaustive way such data would require very high investments both for transmission of the signals through networks as well as for storage. As noticed in Chiky and Hébrail (2009) survey sampling procedures on the sensors, which allow a trade off between limited storage capacities and accuracy of the data, can be relevant approaches compared to signal compression in order to get accurate approximations to simple estimates such as mean or total trajectories. Our study is motivated, in such a context of distributed data streams, by the estimation of the temporal evolution of electricity consumption curves.

Y. Lechevallier, G. Saporta (eds.), *Proceedings of COMPSTAT'2010*,
DOI 10.1007/978-3-7908-2604-3_39, © Springer-Verlag Berlin Heidelberg 2010

The French operator EDF has planned to install in a few years more than 30 millions electricity meters, in each firm and household, that will be able to send individual electricity consumptions at very fine time scales. Collecting, saving and analysing all this information which can be seen as functional would be very expensive and survey sampling strategies are interesting to get accurate estimations at reasonable costs (Dessertaine (2006)). It is well known that consumption profiles strongly depend on covariates such as past consumptions, meteorological characteristics (temperature, nebulosity, etc) or geographical information (altitude, latitude and longitude). Taking this information into account at an individual level ($i.e$ for each electricity meter) is not trivial.

We have a test population of $N = 18902$ electricity meters that have collected electricity consumptions every half an hour during a period of two weeks, so that we have $d = 336$ time points. We are interested in estimating the mean consumption curve during the second week and we suppose that we know the mean consumption, $\bar{Y}_k = \frac{1}{336} \sum_{j=1}^{336} Y_k(t_j)$, for each meter k of the population during the first week. This mean consumption will play the role of auxiliary information. Note that meteorological variables are not available in this preliminary study.

One way to achieve this consists in reducing first the high dimension of the data by performing a functional principal components analysis in a survey sampling framework with a design based approach (Cardot $et\ al.$ (2010)). It is then possible to build models, parametric or nonparametric, on the principal component scores in order to incorporate the auxiliary variables effects and correct our estimator with model assisted approaches (Särndal $et\ al.$ (1992)). Note that this strategy based on modeling the principal components instead of the original signal has already been proposed, with a frequentist point of view, by Chiou $et\ al.$ (2003) with singel index models and Müller and Yao (2008) with additive models.

We present in section 2 the Horvitz-Thomposon estimator of the mean consumption profile as well as the functional principal components analysis. We develop, in section 3, model assisted approaches based on statistical modeling of the principal components scores and derive an approximated variance that can be useful to build global confidence bands. Finally, we illustrate, in section 4, the effectiveness of this methodology which allows to improve significantly more basic approaches on a population of 18902 electricity consumption curves measured every half an hour during one week.

2   Functional data in a finite population

Let us consider a finite population $U = \{1, \ldots, k, \ldots, N\}$ of size N, and suppose we can observe, for each element k of the population U, a deterministic curve $Y_k = (Y_k(t))_{t \in [0,1]}$ that is supposed to belong to $L^2[0,1]$, the space of square integrable functions defined on the closed interval $[0, 1]$ equipped with

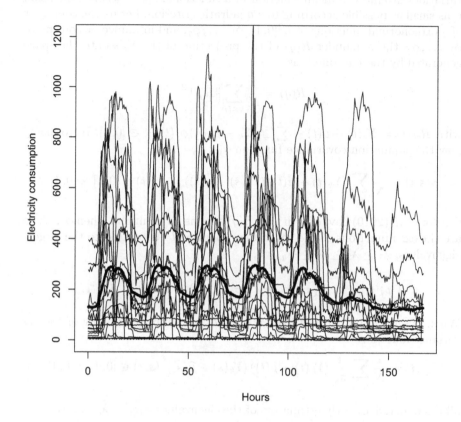

Fig. 1. Mean curve and sample of individual electricity consumption curves.

its usual inner product $\langle \cdot, \cdot \rangle$ and norm denoted by $\| \cdot \|$. Let us define the mean population curve $\mu \in L^2[0,1]$ by

$$\mu(t) = \frac{1}{N} \sum_{k \in U} Y_k(t), \quad t \in [0,1]. \tag{1}$$

Consider now a sample s, *i.e.* a subset $s \subset U$, with known size n, chosen randomly according to a known probability distribution p defined on all the subsets of U. We suppose that all the individuals in the population can be selected, with probabilities that may be unequal, $\pi_k = \Pr(k \in s) > 0$ for all $k \in U$ and $\pi_{kl} = \Pr(k \,\&\, l \in s) > 0$ for all $k, l \in U$, $k \neq l$. The Horvitz-Thompson estimator of the mean curve, which is unbiased, is given by

$$\widehat{\mu}(t) = \frac{1}{N} \sum_{k \in s} \frac{Y_k(t)}{\pi_k} = \frac{1}{N} \sum_{k \in U} \frac{Y_k(t)}{\pi_k} \mathbf{1}_{k \in s}, \quad t \in [0,1]. \tag{2}$$

As in Cardot *et al.* (2010) we would like to describe now the individual variations around the mean function in a functional space whose dimension is as small as possible according to a quadratic criterion. Let us consider a set of q orthonormal functions of $L^2[0,1]$, $\phi_1, \ldots, \phi_q$, and minimize, according to $\phi_1, \ldots, \phi_q$, the remainder $R(q)$ of the projection of the Y_k's onto the space generated by these q functions

$$R(q) = \frac{1}{N} \sum_{k \in U} \|R_{qk}\|^2$$

with $R_{qk}(t) = Y_k(t) - \mu(t) - \sum_{j=1}^{q} \langle Y_k - \mu, \phi_j \rangle \phi_j(t)$, $t \in [0,1]$. Introducing now the population covariance function $\gamma(s,t)$,

$$\gamma(s,t) = \frac{1}{N} \sum_{k \in U} (Y_k(t) - \mu(t)) (Y_k(s) - \mu(s)), \quad (s,t) \in [0,1] \times [0,1],$$

Cardot *et al.* (2010) have shown that $R(q)$ attains its minimum when $\phi_1, \ldots, \phi_q$ are the eigenfunctions of the covariance operator Γ associated to the largest eigenvalues, $\lambda_1 \geq \lambda_2 \geq \cdots \geq \lambda_q \geq 0$,

$$\Gamma \phi_j(t) = \int_0^1 \gamma(s,t) \phi_j(s) ds = \lambda_j \phi_j(t), \quad t \in [0,1], j \geq 1.$$

When observing individuals from a sample s, a simple estimator of the covariance function

$$\widehat{\gamma}(s,t) = \frac{1}{N} \sum_{k \in s} \frac{1}{\pi_k} (Y_k(t) - \widehat{\mu}(t)) (Y_k(s) - \widehat{\mu}(s)) \quad (s,t) \in [0,1] \times [0,1], \quad (3)$$

allows to derive directly estimators of the eigenvalues $\widehat{\lambda}_1, \ldots, \widehat{\lambda}_q$ and the corresponding eigenfuctions $\widehat{\phi}_1, \ldots, \widehat{\phi}_q$.

Remark: *with real data, one only gets discretized trajectories of the Y_k at d points, $t_1, \ldots, t_d$, so that we observe $\mathbf{Y}_k = (Y_k(t_1), \ldots, Y_k(t_d)) \in \mathbb{R}^d$. When observations are not corrupted by noise, linear interpolation allows to get accurate approximations to the true trajectories,*

$$\widetilde{Y}_k(t) = Y_k(t_j) + \frac{Y_k(t_{j+1}) - Y_k(t_j)}{t_{j+1} - t_j} (t - t_j), \quad t \in [t_j, t_{j+1}]$$

and to build consistent estimates of the mean function provided the grid of time points is dense enough (Cardot and Josserand (2009)).

3 Semiparametric estimation with auxiliary information

Suppose now we have access to m auxiliary variables $X_1, \ldots, X_m$ that are supposed to be linked to the individual curves Y_k and we are able to observe these variables, at a low cost, for every individual k in the population. Taking this additional information into account would certainly be helpful to improve the accuracy of the basic estimator $\widehat{\mu}$. Going back to the decomposition of the individual trajectories Y_k on the eigenfunctions,

$$Y_k(t) = \mu(t) + \sum_{j=1}^{q} \langle Y_k - \mu, \phi_j \rangle \phi_j(t) + R_{qk}(t), \quad t \in [0,1],$$

and borrowing ideas from Chiou et al. (2003) and Müller and Yao (2008), an interesting approach consists in modeling the population principal components scores $\langle Y_k - \mu, \phi_j \rangle$ with respect to auxiliary variables at each level j of the decomposition on the eigenfunctions, $\langle Y_k - \mu, \phi_j \rangle \approx f_j(x_{k1}, \ldots, x_{km})$ where the regression function f_j can be parametric or not and $(x_{k1}, \ldots, x_{km})$ is the vector of observations of the m auxiliary variables for individual k.

It is possible to estimate the principal component scores

$$\widehat{C}_{kj} = \langle Y_k - \widehat{\mu}, \widehat{\phi}_j \rangle,$$

for $j = 1, \ldots, q$ and all $k \in s$. Then, a design based least squares estimator for the functions f_j

$$\widehat{f}_j = \arg\min_{g_j} \sum_{k \in s} \frac{1}{\pi_k} \left(\widehat{C}_{kj} - g_j(x_{k1}, \ldots, x_{km}) \right)^2, \tag{4}$$

is useful to construct the following model-assisted estimator $\widehat{\mu}_X$ of μ,

$$\widehat{\mu}_x(t) = \widehat{\mu}(t) - \frac{1}{N} \left(\sum_{k \in s} \frac{\widehat{Y}_k(t)}{\pi_k} - \sum_{k \in U} \widehat{Y}_k(t) \right) \tag{5}$$

where the predicted curves $\widehat{Y}_k$ are estimated for all the individuals of the population U thanks to the m auxiliary variables,

$$\widehat{Y}_k(t) = \widehat{\mu}(t) + \sum_{j=1}^{q} \widehat{f}_j(x_{k1}, \ldots, x_{km}) \, \widehat{v}_j(t), \quad t \in [0,1].$$

4   Estimation of electricity consumption curves

We consider now the population consisting in the $N = 18902$ electricity consumption curves measured during the second week very half an hour. We have $d = 336$ time points. Note that meteorological variables are not available in this preliminary study and our auxiliary information is the mean consumption, for each meter k, during the first week.

We first perform a simple random sampling without replacement (SR-SWR) with fixed size of $n = 2000$ electricity meters during the second week

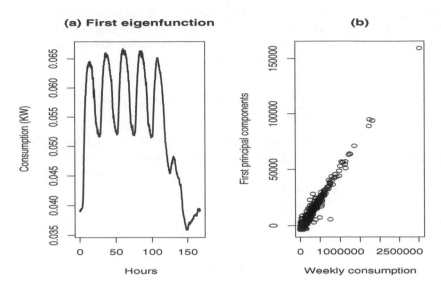

Fig. 2. Mean curve and sample of individual electricity consumption curves.

in order to get $\widehat{\mu}$ and perform the functional principal components analysis (FPCA). The true mean consumption curve $\mu(t)$ during this period is drawn in Figure 1 whereas Figure 3 (a) present the result of the FPCA. The first principal component explains more than 80% of the total variance telling us that there is a strong temporal structure in these data. The associated estimated eigenfunction $\widehat{\phi}_1$ presents strong daily periodicity. Looking now at the relationship between the estimated first principal components and the auxiliary variable, we can notice that there is a strong linear relationship between these two variables and thus considering a linear regression model for estimating f_1 seems to be appropriate.

To evaluate the accuracy of estimator (5) we made 500 replications of the following scheme

- Draw a sample of size $n = 2000$ in population U with SRSWR and estimate $\widehat{\mu}, \widehat{\phi}_1$ and $\widehat{C}_{k1}$, for $k \in s$, during the second week.
- Estimate a linear relationship between X_k and $\widehat{C}_{k1}$, for $k \in s$ where $X_k = \frac{1}{336} \sum_{j=1}^{336} Y_k(t_j)$ is the mean consumption during the first week, and predict the principal component using the estimated relation $\widehat{C}_{k1} \approx \widehat{\beta}_0 + \widehat{\beta}_1 X_k$.
- Estimate $\widehat{\mu}_X$ taking the auxiliary information into account with equation (5).

The following loss criterion $\int |\mu(t) - \widehat{\mu}(t)| dt$ has been considered to evaluate the accuracy of the estimators $\widehat{\mu}$ and $\widehat{\mu}_X$. We also compare the estimation error with an optimal stratification sampling scheme in which strata are built

	SAS	OPTIM	MA1
Mean	4.245	1.687	1.866
Median	3.348	1.613	1.813
First quartile	2.213	1.343	1.499
Third quartile	5.525	1.944	2.097

Table 1. Comparison of mean absolute deviation from the true mean curve for SRSWR, optimal allocation for stratification (OPTIM) and model assisted (MA1) estimation procedures.

on the curves of the population observed during the first week. As in Cardot and Josserand (2009), the population is partitioned into $K = 7$ strata thanks to a k-means algorithm. It is then possible to determine the optimal allocation weights, according to a mean variance criterion, in each stratum for the stratified sampling procedure during the second week.

The estimation errors are presented in Table 4 for the three estimators. We first remark that considering optimal stratification (OPTIM) or model assisted estimators (MA1) lead to a significant improvement compared to the basic SRSWR approach. Secondly, the performances of the stratification and the model assisted approaches are very similar in terms of accuracy but they do not need the same amount of information. The optimal stratification approach necessitates to know the cluster of each individual of the population and the covariance function within each cluster whereas the model assisted estimator only needs the past mean consumption for each element of the population.

Looking now at the empirical variance, at each instant, of these estimators, we see in Figure (3) that the simple SRSWR has much larger variances, in which we recognize the first eigenfunction of the covariance operator, than the more sophisticated OPTIM and MA1. Among these two estimators the model assisted estimator has a smaller pointwise variance, indicating that it is certainly more reliable.

Acknowledgment. Etienne Josserand thanks the Conseil Régional de Bourgogne, France, for its financial support (FABER PhD grant).

References

CARDOT, H., CHAOUCH, M., GOGA, C. and C. LABRUÈRE (2010): Properties of Design-Based Functional Principal Components Analysis, *J. Statist. Planning and Inference.*, **140**, 75-91.

CARDOT, H., JOSSERAND, E. (2009): Horvitz-Thompson Estimators for Functional Data: Asymptotic Confidence Bands and Optimal Allocation for Stratified Sampling. http://arxiv.org/abs/0912.3891.

CHIKY, R., HEBRAIL, G. (2009): Spatio-temporal sampling of distributed data streams. *J. of Computing Science and Engineering*, to appear.

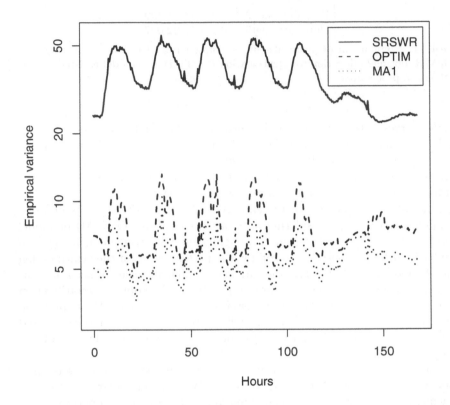

Fig. 3. Comparison of the empirical pointwise variance for SRSWR, optimal allocation for stratification (OPTIM) and model assisted (MA1) estimation procedures.

CHIOU, J-M., MÜLLER, H.G. and WANG, J.L. (2003): Functional quasi-likelihood regression models with smooth random effects. *J.Roy. Statist. Soc., Ser. B*, **65**, *405-423*.

DESSERTAINE, A. (2006): Sampling and Data-Stream : some ideas to built balanced sampling using auxiliary hilbertian informations. *56th ISI Conference*, Lisboa, Portugal, 22-29 August 2007.

MÜLLER, H-G., YAO, F. (2008): Functional Additive Model. *J. Am. Statist. Ass.* **103**, *1534-1544*.

SÄRNDAL, C.E., SWENSSON, B. and J. WRETMAN, J. (1992): *Model Assisted Survey Sampling*. Springer-Verlag.

SKINNER, C.J, HOLMES, D.J, SMITH and T.M.F. (1986): The Effect of Sample Design on Principal Components Analysis. *J. Am. Statist. Ass.* **81**, *789-798*.

Stochastic Approximation for Multivariate and Functional Median

Hervé Cardot[1], Peggy Cénac[1], and Mohamed Chaouch[2]

[1] Institut de Mathématiques de Bourgogne, UMR 5584 CNRS,
Université de Bourgogne, 9, Av. A. Savary - B.P. 47 870, 21078 Dijon, France
herve.cardot@u-bourgogne.fr, peggy.cenac@u-bourgogne.fr
[2] EDF - Recherche et Développement, ICAME-SOAD
1 Av. Général de Gaulle, 92141 Clamart, France
mohamed.chaouch@edf.fr

Abstract. We propose a very simple algorithm in order to estimate the geometric median, also called spatial median, of multivariate (Small (1990)) or functional data (Gervini (2008)) when the sample size is large. A simple and fast iterative approach based on the Robbins-Monro algorithm (Duflo (1997)) as well as its averaged version (Polyak and Juditsky (1992)) are shown to be effective for large samples of high dimension data. They are very fast and only require $O(Nd)$ elementary operations, where N is the sample size and d is the dimension of data. The averaged approach is shown to be more effective and less sensitive to the tuning parameter. The ability of this new estimator to estimate accurately and rapidly (about thirty times faster than the classical estimator) the geometric median is illustrated on a large sample of 18902 electricity consumption curves measured every half an hour during one week.

Keywords: geometric quantiles, high dimension data, online estimation algorithm, robustness, Robbins-Monro, spatial median, stochastic gradient averaging

1 Introduction

Estimation of the median of univariate and multivariate data has given rise to many publications in robust statistics, data mining, signal processing and information theory. For instance, the volume of data treated and analyzed by "Electricité De France" (E.D.F.) is getting increasingly important. The installation of systems of measurement becoming more and more efficient, will increase consequently this volume. Our aim will be to have a lighting on these data and information delivered in a current way for a better reactivity about some decision-makings. Then, for example, a rise in competence on the use and modelling of structured data stream should allow the computation and the analysis of monitoring indicators and performances of the power stations of production in real time, with a data stream environment. Most of the data will be functional data, like load curves for example. Thus, there is

Y. Lechevallier, G. Saporta (eds.), *Proceedings of COMPSTAT'2010*,
DOI 10.1007/978-3-7908-2604-3_40, © Springer-Verlag Berlin Heidelberg 2010

a need to have fast and robust algorithms to analyse these functional data. In this context purposes are various, estimation of multivariate central point in a robust way, clustering data around their median, *etc.*

Our work is motivated by the estimation of median profiles with online observations of numerous individual electricity consumption curves which are measured every days at fine time scale for a large sample of electricity meters. The median temporal profile is then a robust indicator of habit of consumption which can be useful for instance for unsupervised classification of the individual electricity demand.

In a multivariate setting different extensions of the median have been proposed in the literature (see for instance Small (1990) and Koenker (2005) for reviews) which lead to different indicators. We focus here on the spatial median, also named geometric median which is probably the most popular one and can be easily defined in a functional framework (Kemperman (1987), Cadre (2001), Gervini (2008)). The median m of a random variable X taking values in some space H ($H = \mathbb{R}^d$, with $d \geq 2$, or a separable Hilbert space) is

$$m =: \arg\min_{u \in H} \mathbb{E}\left(\|X - u\|\right) \tag{1}$$

where the norm in H, which is the euclidean norm if $H = \mathbb{R}^d$, is denoted by $\|.\|$. The median m is uniquely defined unless the support of the distribution of X is concentrated on a one dimensional subspace of H. Note also that it is translation invariant. The median $m \in H$ defined in (1) is completely characterized by the following gradient equation (Kemperman (1987),

$$\Phi(m) = -\mathbb{EEE}\left(\frac{X - m}{\|X - m\|}\right) = 0. \tag{2}$$

When observing a sample $X_1, X_2, \ldots, X_N$ of N (not necessarily independent) realizations of X, a natural estimator of m is the solution $\widehat{m}$ of the empirical version of (2),

$$\sum_{i=1}^{N} \frac{X_i - \widehat{m}}{\|X_i - \widehat{m}\|} = 0. \tag{3}$$

Algorithms have been proposed to solve this equation (Gower (1974), Vardi and Zhang (2000) or Gervini (2008)). They are needing important computational efforts and can not be adapted directly when data arrive online. For example, the algorithm proposed by Gervini (2008) which is a variant of Gower's approach requires first the computation of the Gram matrix of the data and has a computational cost of $O(N^2 d)$. This also means that a great amount of memory is needed when the sample size N is large. Furthermore it can not be updated simply if the data arrive online. We propose here an estimation algorithm that can be simply updated and only requires $O(d)$ operations at each step in the multivariate setting. Let us also note that when the data are functional they are generally observed on a common grid of d design points, $\mathbf{X}_i = (X_i(t_1), \ldots, X_i(t_d))$ and then the algorithm will require only $O(d)$ operations at each step, so that it has a global computational cost $O(Nd)$. Let us note that our algorithm is not adapted when one has sparsely and irregularly distributed functional data and this issue deserves further investigation. Note also that in such a large samples context, survey sampling approaches are interesting alternatives (Chaouch and Goga (2010)).

We present in section 2 the stochastic approximation algorithm which is based on the Robbins-Monro procedure. Note that it is very simple and it can be extended directly to the estimation of geometric quantiles (Chaudhuri (1996)). In section 3 a simulation study confirms that this estimation procedure is effective and robust even for moderate sample size (a few thousands). We also remark averaging produces even more efficient estimations. We finally present in section 4 a real study in which we have a sample of $N = 18902$ electricity meters giving every half and hour, during one week, individual electricity consumption and we aim at estimating the temporal median profile.

2   A stochastic algorithm for online estimation of the median

We propose a stochastic iterative estimation procedure which is a Robbins-Monro algorithm (Duflo (1997), Kushner and Yin (2003)) in order to find the minimum of (1). It is based on a stochastic approximation to the gradient of the objective function and leads to the simple iterative procedure

$$\widehat{m}_{n+1} = \widehat{m}_n + \gamma_n \frac{X_{n+1} - \widehat{m}_n}{\|X_{n+1} - \widehat{m}_n\|}, \qquad (4)$$

where the sequence of steps γ_n satisfies, $\gamma_n > 0$ for all $n \geq 1$, $\sum_{n \geq 1} \gamma_n = \infty$ and $\sum_{n \geq 1} \gamma_n^2 < \infty$. Classical choices for γ_n are $\gamma_n = g(n+1)^{-\alpha}$, with $0.5 < \alpha \leq 1$. The starting point, m_0 is arbitrarily chosen to be zero.

When α is close to 1, better rates of convergence can be attained at the expense of a larger instability of the procedure so that averaging approaches (Polyak and Juditsky (1992), Kushner and Yin (2003), Dippon and Walk (2006)) have been proposed to get more effective estimators which are less sensitive to the selected values for α and g. When the value of g is a bit too large, averaging also stabilizes the estimator and can reduce significantly its variance. Thus, we also consider an averaged estimator defined as follows

$$\widetilde{m} = \frac{1}{N - n_0} \sum_{n=n_0}^{N} \widehat{m}_n, \qquad (5)$$

where n_0 is chosen so that averaging is made on the last ten percent iterations.

Remark 1. Note that this approach can be extended directly to get stochastic approximations to geometric quantiles which are defined as follows by Chaudhuri (1996). Consider a vector $u \in H$, such that $\|u\| < 1$, the geometric quantile of X, say m^u, corresponding to direction u, is defined, uniquely under previous assumptions, by

$$m^u = arg \min_{Q \in H} \mathbb{E}\left(\|X - Q\| + \langle X - Q, u \rangle\right).$$

It is characterized by $\Phi_u(m^u) = \Phi(m^u) - u = 0$, so that one can propose the following stochastic approximation

$$\widehat{m}_{n+1}^u = \widehat{m}_n^u + \gamma_n \left(\frac{X_{n+1} - \widehat{m}_n^u}{\|X_{n+1} - \widehat{m}_n^u\|} + u\right). \tag{6}$$

Remark 2. It can be shown, under classical hypotheses on the distribution of X and the sequence γ_n, that these estimators of the population median and quantiles are consistent. Rates of convergence can also be obtained in the multivariate setting as well as the functional one when H is a separable Hilbert space.

3   A simulation study

We perform simulations in order to check the effectiveness of the algorithm and to evaluate its sensitivity to the tuning parameter g. We have simulated samples of $N = 5000$ brownian motions discretized at $d = 100$ equispaced points in the interval $[0, 1]$. We then added the mean function $m(t) = \sin(2\pi t)$, $t \in [0, 1]$, which is also the median curve for gaussian processes.

Our estimators are defined according (4) and (5) and we take the averaged estimators $\widetilde{m}$ with parameter $n_0 = 500$. They depend on the sequence γ_n. We consider, as it is usually done in stochastic approximation, a sequence defined as follows

$$\gamma_n = \frac{g}{(n+1)^{3/4}}$$

for few different values of $g \in \{0.1, 0.5, 1, 2, 5, 10\}$. The estimation procedure is very fast and computing the geometric median estimator takes less than one second on a PC with the $\mathbb{R}$ language.

We made 100 simulations and evaluate the estimation error with the loss criterion $L(\widehat{m}) = \sqrt{\frac{1}{d}\sum_{j=1}^d (m(t_j) - \widehat{m}(t_j))^2}$, with $t_j = (j-1)/(d-1)$. We first present in Figure (1) the estimation error for $\widehat{m}_N$ for different values of g and compare it to the error of the empirical mean curve. The iterative estimators are always less effective than the mean curve and their performances depend on the value of the tuning parameter g. In Figure (2) we clearly see that the averaged estimators $\widetilde{m}$ perform really better than the simple ones, with performances which are now comparable to the empirical mean, and do not really depend on g provided that g is not too small.

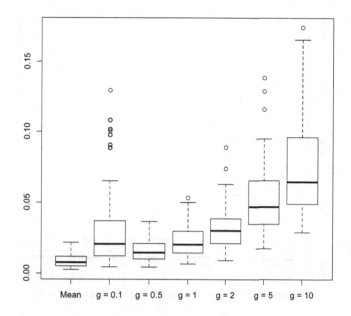

Fig. 1. Approximation error for the mean and the Robbins-Monro estimator of the median for different values of the tuning parameter g, when $\alpha = 0.75$.

We also considered the case of a contaminated distribution in which 5% of the observations are also realizations of a brownian with mean function which is now $\mu_c(t) = 5\mu(t)$. The estimation error are presented in Figure (3) and we clearly see that the empirical mean is affected by contamination or outliers whereas the performances of the averaged iterative estimators are still interesting.

As a conclusion of this simulation study, the averaged Robbins-Monro procedure appears to be effective to estimate the geometric median of high dimension data when the sample size is large enough and is not really sensitive to the choice of the tuning parameter g.

4   Estimation of the median electricity consumption curve

We have a sample of $N = 18902$ electricity meters that are able to send electricity consumptions every half an hour during a period of one week, so that we have $d = 336$ time points. We are interested in estimating the median consumption curve. We present in Figure (4) the estimated geometric

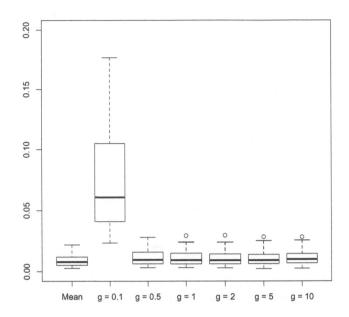

Fig. 2. Approximation error for the mean and the averaged Robbins-Monro estimator of the median for different values of the tuning g when $\alpha = 0.75$.

median profile for $g = 5$ obtained by averaging the 1000 last iterations and compare it with the mean profile and the pointwise median curve which is obtained by estimating the median value at each instant $t_j, j = 1, \ldots, 336$. The Robbins-Monro estimators are very similar, when averaging, for $g \in [1, 10]$, and different starting points m_0 and are not presented here.

We first remark that there is an important difference between the mean curve and the geometric median curve that is probably due to a small fraction of consumers which have high demands in electricity. There is also a difference, even if it is less important, between the pointwise median and the geometric median and this clearly means that pointwise estimation does not produce the center of our functional distribution according to criterion (1) which takes the following empirical values, 184.3 for the mean function, 173.3 for the pointwise median and 171.7 for the geometric median. The multivariate median was also estimated with the algorithm proposed by Vardi and Zhang (2000) thanks to the function `spatial.median` from the $\mathbb{R}$ package `ICSNP`. The estimated median curve is exactly the same as our but the computation time is much longer (130 seconds versus 3 seconds on the same computer).

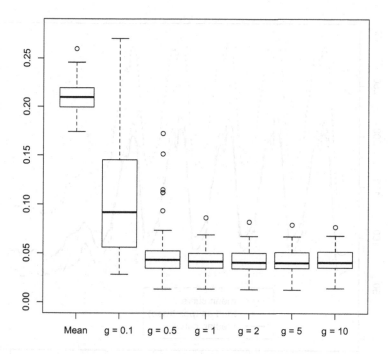

Fig. 3. Estimation error for the mean and the averaged Robbins-Monro estimator of the median for different values of the tuning parameter g when 5% of the data are contaminated.

References

CADRE, B. (2001): Convergent estimators for the L_1-median of Banach valued random variable. *Statistics, 35, 509-521.*

CHAOUCH, M., GOGA, C. (2010): Design-Based Estimation for Geometric Quantiles. Accepted for publication in *Comput. Statist. and Data Analysis.*

CHAUDHURI, P. (1996): On a geometric notion of quantiles for multivariate data. *J. Amer. Statist. Assoc., 91, 862-871.*

DIPPON, J., WALK, H. (2006): The averaged Robbins-Monro method for linear problems in a Banach space. *J. Theoret. Probab. 19, (2006), 166-189.*

DUFLO, M. (1997): *Random Iterative Models.* Springer Verlag, Heidelberg.

GERVINI, D. (2008): Robust functional estimation using the spatial median and spherical principal components. *Biometrika, 95, 587-600.*

GOWER, J.C. (1974): The mediancentre. *Applied Statistics, 23, 466-470.*

HUBER, P.J., RONCHETTI, E.M. (2009): *Robust Statistics.* John Wiley & Sons, second edition.

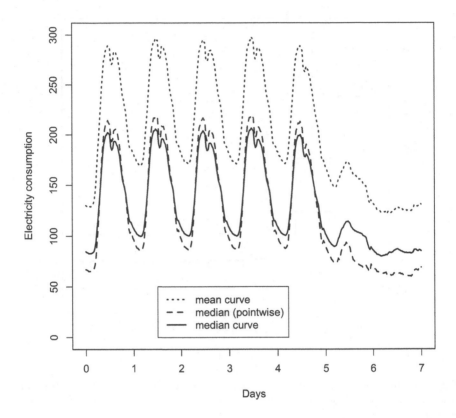

Fig. 4. Comparison of the estimated geometric median profile with the mean electricity consumption curve and the pointwise medians.

KEMPERMAN, J.H.D. (1987): The median of finite measure of a Banach space. In *Statistical data analysis based on the L_1-norm and related methods*, eds Y. Dodge, North-Holland, Amsterdam, 217-230.

KUSHNER, H.J, YIN, G.G. (2003): *Stochastic Approximation and Recursive Algorithms and Applications*. Springer Verlag, New York.

KOENKER, R. (2005). *Quantile regression*. Cambridge University Press.

POLYAK, B.T., JUDITSKY, A.B. (1992): Acceleration of Stochastic Approximation. *SIAM J. Control and Optimization, 30, 838-855.*

SMALL, C.G. (1990): A survey of multidimensional medians. *Int. Statist. Inst. Rev.*, **58**, 263-277.

VARDI, Y., ZHANG, C.H. (2000): The multivariate L_1-median and associated data depth. *Proc. Natl. Acad. Sci. USA*, **97**, *1423-1426.*

A Markov Switching Re-evaluation
of Event-Study Methodology

Rosella Castellano[1] and Luisa Scaccia[2]

[1] Dip. di Istituzioni Economiche e Finanziarie, Università di Macerata
via Crescimbeni 20, 62100 Macerata, Italy, *castellano@unimc.it*
[2] Dip. di Istituzioni Economiche e Finanziarie, Università di Macerata
via Crescimbeni 20, 62100 Macerata, Italy, *scaccia@unimc.it*

Abstract. This paper reconsiders event-study methodology in light of evidences showing that Cumulative Abnormal Return (CAR) can result in misleading inferences about financial market efficiency and pre(post)-event behavior. In particular, CAR can be biased downward, due to the increased volatility on the event day and within event windows. We propose the use of Markov Switching Models to capture the effect of an event on security prices. The proposed methodology is applied to a set of 45 historical series on Credit Default Swap (CDS) quotes subject to multiple credit events, such as reviews for downgrading. Since CDSs provide insurance against the default of a particular company or sovereign entity, this study checks if market anticipates reviews for downgrading and evaluates the time period the announcements lag behind the market.

Keywords: hierarchical Bayes, Markov switching models, credit default swaps, event-study

1 Introduction

An event-study is the name given to the empirical investigation of the relationship between security prices and economic events. It allows to estimate and draw inferences about the impact of an event in a particular period or over several periods. The most common approach involves four steps: 1) identification of the event dates for a sample of securities subject to the disclosure item of interest (i.e. rating announcements) and creation of equally sized event windows around each event date; 2) selection of an appropriate reference period preceding each event window (the so-called *estimation period*), used to estimate the mean and standard deviation of the returns of each security, under normal market conditions; 3) computation of Abnormal Returns (ARs) on each security supposed to be influenced by the event and for each event window around the announcement date; 4) computation of the mean ARs across securities in the sample, possibly cumulated over the event windows, and comparison with the mean returns estimated under normal market conditions, through parametric and non parametric test statistics (Brown and Warner (1985); Kothari and Warner (1997)).

Y. Lechevallier, G. Saporta (eds.), *Proceedings of COMPSTAT'2010*,
DOI 10.1007/978-3-7908-2604-3_41, © Springer-Verlag Berlin Heidelberg 2010

In most situations, event-study tests relying on the Cumulated Abnormal Return (CAR) methodology may provide misleading results because of the kurtosis and volatility clustering characterizing financial time series. Therefore, we propose to incorporate into the classical event-study methodology the ability of Markov Switching Models, also known as Hidden Markov Models (HMMs), to model state-dependent means and variances of the ARs. In practice, instead of performing the hypothesis testing described in the fourth step of the above illustrated methodology, we model the ARs in each event window through an HMM characterized by two states, normal and abnormal market conditions, and look at the probability that the generating process is in each of the two states, at any time in the event window. In this way, we explicitly account for the kurtosis and the volatility clustering commonly observed in financial time series. We adopt a Bayesian perspective and rely on the flexibility of hierarchical modeling. It is worth to notice that HMMs have been successfully applied to financial time series. For instance, segmented time-trends in the US dollar exchange rates (Engel and Hamilton (1990), Castellano and Scaccia (2010), Otranto and Gallo (2002)), stylized facts about daily returns (Rydén et al. (1998)), option prices and stochastic volatilities (Rossi and Gallo (2006)), temporal behavior of daily volatility on commodity returns (Haldrup and Nielsen (2006)) have been modeled via HMMs.

In this paper we apply the proposed methodology to study the reactions of Credit Default Swap (CDS) quotes to reviews for downgrading announced by three major credit rating agencies (Moody's, Fitch and Standard&Poor's), in order to examine if and to what extent this market responds to these announcements which should reflect the latest available information. The focal idea is to analyze if rating agencies have access to non-public information, implying that their announcements can be viewed as conveying extra information to the market, and if the size and variance of ARs may provide information about the creditworthiness of a specific company. Basically, if reviews for downgrading convey new information to the market, CDS quotes should react after the announcement and a significant increase in market volatility should be expected at the event day or after the announcements. Otherwise, it might be possible that reviews for downgrading only reflect information already discounted by the market, implying that CDS quotes do not react to watchlisting and abnormal performances are observed before the announcements.

Data over the period 2004 - 2009 for 45 international companies belonging to different credit grades are taken into consideration and the effects of reviews for downgrading on CDS quote generating process are investigated.

The paper proceeds as follows: the Markov Switching re-evaluation of the classical event-study methodology and the priors on model parameters are illustrated in Section 7; Section 3 deals with computational implementation;

Section 4 discusses the application on CDS quotes; conclusions are reported in Section 5.

2   The revised event-study methodology

The approach proposed in this paper to investigate the above mentioned hypotheses is based on the Markov Switching re-evaluation of event-study methodology. In this context, the event window is set equal to almost three months, starting 60 business days before a review for downgrading and ending 20 business days after the announcement, thus the series considered will be indexed by $t \in [-60, +20]$. In the following, we will use t_0 and T to indicate, respectively the starting day and the ending day of the event window, so that $t_0 = -60$ and $T = 20$. If the announcement is fully anticipated, then the CDS quote generating process should adjust prior to $t = 0$, the day of the announcement. If the rating announcement has a new informational content, it should have an effect on price at $t = 0$ and, in the case of post-announcement effect, the impact of the review for downgrading might be delayed after $t = 0$. This choice of the event window aims at analyzing the reactions of the markets before and around the day of the announcement, the period in which a potential market reaction is expected, as many studies have shown (Kliger and Sarig (2000); Steiner and Heinke (2001); Norden and Weber (2004); Hull et al. (2004); Heinke (2006)).

To examine the impact of reviews for downgrading on the generating process of CDS quotes, we focus on the daily returns of each CDS, defined as:

$$R_t = P_t - P_{t-1},$$

where P_t is the market value of the CDS at time t. Daily returns are then used to calculate standardized ARs as:

$$y_t = \frac{R_t - \overline{R}}{s_R},$$

where the sample mean and standard deviation of the returns for each CDS subject to review for downgrading are estimated over an estimation period of 100-day preceding each event window, so that $\overline{R} = \sum_{t=-160}^{-61} R_t/100$ and $s_R^2 = \sum_{t=-160}^{-61}(R_t - \overline{R})^2/99$.

In a HMM formulation, the distribution of each standardized AR, y_t, is assumed to depend on an unobserved (hidden) variable, denoted by s_t, that takes on values from 1 to k. The vector of hidden variables $\boldsymbol{s} = (s_t)_{t=t_0}^{T}$ characterizes the "state" or "regime" in which the AR generating process is at any time t. The y_t are assumed to be independent, conditional on the s_t's:

$$y_t|s_t \sim f_{s_t}(y_t) \qquad \text{for} \quad t = t_0, t_0 + 1, \ldots, T, \tag{1}$$

with $f_{s_t}(\cdot)$ being a specified density function. We further postulate that the dynamics of $\boldsymbol{s}$ are described by a Markov Chain with transition matrix $\Lambda =$

$(\lambda_{ij})_{i,j=1}^k$, implying that s_t is presumed to depend on the past realizations of $\boldsymbol{y}$ and $\boldsymbol{s}$, only through s_{t-1}:

$$p(s_t = j|s_{t-1} = i) = \lambda_{ij} \ .$$

Since we apply the HMM to ARs of CDSs, we implicitly assume y_t to be normally distributed, so that the model in (1) becomes

$$y_t|\boldsymbol{s}, \boldsymbol{\mu}, \boldsymbol{\sigma} \sim \phi(\cdot; \mu_{s_t}, \sigma_{s_t}^2) \qquad (2)$$

conditional on means $\boldsymbol{\mu} = (\mu_i)_{i=1}^k$ and standard deviations $\boldsymbol{\sigma} = (\sigma_i)_{i=1}^k$, where $\phi(\cdot; \mu_i, \sigma_i^2)$ is the density of the $N(\mu_i, \sigma_i^2)$. Thus, if $s_t = i$, y_t is assumed to be drawn from a $N(\mu_i, \sigma_i^2)$. Notice that, if we let $\boldsymbol{\pi}$ being the stationary vector of the transition matrix, so that $\boldsymbol{\pi}'\boldsymbol{\Lambda} = \boldsymbol{\pi}'$, and we integrate out s_t in (2) using its stationary distribution, the model in (2) can be analogously formalized as

$$y_t|\boldsymbol{\pi}, \boldsymbol{\mu}, \boldsymbol{\sigma} \sim \sum_{i=1}^k \pi_i\phi(\cdot; \mu_i, \sigma_i^2) \qquad \text{for} \quad t = t_0, t_0 + 1, \ldots, T \ .$$

In this paper the number of states, k, is assumed equal to 2, as briefly explained in Section 4. In a forthcoming paper, k will be considered unknown and subject to inference, as well as the other parameters of the model.

In a Bayesian context, the uncertainty on the parameters of the model is formalized using appropriate prior distributions. Weakly informative priors are chosen, by introducing an hyperprior structure. We assume:

a) $\mu_i|\sigma_i^2 \sim \mathcal{N}(\xi, \kappa\sigma_i^2)$, independently for each $i = 1, \ldots, k$.
b) $\sigma_i^{-2} \sim \mathcal{G}(\eta, \zeta)$, independently for each $i = 1, \ldots, k$, with the mean and the variance of the Gamma distribution being η/ζ and η/ζ^2.
c) $\kappa \sim \mathcal{IG}(q, r)$, with $\mathcal{IG}$ denoting the Inverse Gamma distribution.
d) $\zeta \sim \mathcal{G}(f, h)$.
e) $\lambda_{ij} \sim \mathcal{D}(\boldsymbol{\delta}_j)$, for $i = 1, \ldots, k$ where $\mathcal{D}$ denotes the Dirichlet distribution and $\boldsymbol{\delta}_j = (\delta_{ij})_{i=1}^k$.

3   Computational implementation

In order to approximate the posterior joint distribution of all the parameters of the above HMM, we apply Markov Chain Monte Carlo (MCMC) methods and exploit the natural conditional independence structure of the model so that the joint distribution of all variables, conditional to the fixed values of the hyperparameters, is:

$$p(\boldsymbol{y}, \boldsymbol{\mu}, \boldsymbol{\sigma}, \boldsymbol{s}, \boldsymbol{\Lambda}, \zeta, \kappa|\boldsymbol{\delta}, f, h, q, r, \xi, \eta, k)$$
$$= p(\boldsymbol{y}|\boldsymbol{s}, \boldsymbol{\mu}, \boldsymbol{\sigma})p(\boldsymbol{s}|\boldsymbol{\Lambda})p(\boldsymbol{\Lambda}|\boldsymbol{\delta}, k)p(\boldsymbol{\mu}|\boldsymbol{\sigma}, \xi, \kappa, k)p(\kappa|r, q)p(\boldsymbol{\sigma}|\eta, \zeta, k)p(\zeta|f, h).$$

To generate realizations from the posterior joint distribution, the parameters of the model are in turn updated, by means of Gibbs sampler. At each sweep of the MCMC algorithm, the following steps are performed:

Updating Λ. The i-th row of Λ is sampled from $D(\delta_{i1}+n_{i1},\ldots,\delta_{ik}+n_{ik})$, where $n_{ij} = \sum_{t=t_0}^{T-1} I\{s_t = i, s_{t+1} = j\}$ is the number of transitions from regime i to regime j and $I\{\cdot\}$ denotes the indicator function.

Updating s. The standard solution for updating s would be to sample $s_{t_0},\ldots,s_T$ one at a time from $t = t_0$ to $t = T$, drawing values from their full conditional distribution $p(s_t = i|\cdots) \propto \lambda_{s_{t-1}i}\phi(y_t;\mu_i,\sigma_i^2)\lambda_{is_{t+1}}$ where '$\cdots$' denotes 'all other variables'. For a faster mixing algorithm (Scott (2002)), we instead sample s from $p(s|y,\Lambda)$ through a stochastic version of the forward–backward recursion. The forward recursion produces matrices $P_{t_0+1}, P_{t_0+2},\ldots,P_T$, where $P_t = (p_{tij})$ and $p_{tij} = p(s_{t-1} = i, s_t = j|y_1,\ldots,y_t,\Lambda)$. In words, P_t is the joint distribution of $(s_{t-1} = i, s_t = j)$ given parameters and observed data up to time t. P_t is computed from P_{t-1} as $p_{tij} \propto p(s_{t-1} = i, s_t = j, y_t|y_1,\ldots,y_{t-1},\Lambda) = p(s_{t-1} = i|y_1,\ldots,y_{t-1},\Lambda)\lambda_{ij}\phi(y_t;\mu_j,\sigma_j^2)$ with proportionality reconciled by $\sum_i \sum_j p_{tij} = 1$, where $p(s_{t-1} = i|y_1,\ldots,y_{t-1},\Lambda) = \sum_j p_{t-1,i,j}$ can be computed once P_{t-1} is known. The recursion starts computing $p(s_{t_0} = i|y_{t_0},\Lambda) \propto \phi(y_{t_0};\mu_i,\sigma_i^2)\pi_i$ and thus P_{t_0+1}. The stochastic backward recursion begins by drawing s_T from $p(s_T|y,\Lambda)$, then recursively drawing s_t from the distribution proportional to column s_{t+1} of P_{t+1}. In this way, the stochastic backward recursion samples from $p(s|y,\Lambda)$, factorizing this as $p(s|y,\Lambda) = p(s_T|y,\Lambda)\prod_{t=t_0}^{T-1} p(s_{T-t}|s_T,\ldots,s_{T-t+1},y,\Lambda)$ where $p(s_{T-t} = i|s_T,\ldots,s_{T-t+1},y,\Lambda) = p(s_{T-t} = i|s_{T-t+1},y_{t_0},\ldots,y_{T-t+1},\Lambda) \propto p_{T-t+1,i,s_{T-t+1}}$.

Updating μ. Letting n_i being the number of observations currently allocated in regime i, the μ_i can be updated by drawing them independently from

$$\mu_i|\cdots \sim \mathcal{N}\left(\frac{\kappa\sum_{t:s_t=i} y_t + \xi}{1+\kappa n_i}, \frac{\sigma_i^2\kappa}{1+\kappa n_i}\right).$$

Updating κ. We sample κ^{-1} from $\kappa^{-1}|\cdots \sim \mathcal{G}\left(q + \frac{k}{2}, r + \frac{1}{2}\sum_{i=1}^k \frac{(\mu_i-\xi)^2}{\sigma_i^2}\right)$.

Updating σ. For identifiability purpose, we adopt a unique labeling in which the σ_i's are in increasing numerical order. Hence, their joint prior distribution is $k!$ times the product of the individual $\mathcal{IG}$ densities, restricted to the set $\sigma_1 < \sigma_2 < \ldots < \sigma_k$. The σ_i can be drawn independently from

$$\sigma_i^{-2}|\cdots \sim \mathcal{G}\left(\eta + \frac{1}{2}(n_i+1), \zeta + \frac{1}{2}\sum_{t:s_t=i}(y_t-\mu_i)^2 + \frac{1}{2\kappa}(\mu_i-\xi)^2\right). \text{ The}$$

move is accepted, provided the invariance of the order.

Updating ζ. We sample ζ from $\zeta|\cdots \sim \mathcal{G}\left(f + k\eta, h + \sum_{i=1}^k \sigma_i^{-2}\right)$.

4   An Application

To estimate the parameters of the model and the posterior probabilities of y_t being in each of the states, at any time $t \in [-60,+20]$, we performed 100,000 sweeps of the MCMC algorithm, allowing for a burn-in of 10,000 sweeps. Notice that our data set considers 45 historical series of CDSs and related reviews for downgrading, leading to 57 non-overlapping events (in the sense that we only analyze subsequent event time windows including one event) and, thus, to 57 different ARs series. The MCMC algorithm was run independently for each of the 57 series of ARs. Since most of the ARs in the events windows are well represented by two regimes, characterized by high and low volatility respectively, we set $k = 2$.

Performing a preliminary analysis, we find that the probability of being in the high volatility state in each event window of the data base, is characterized by different patterns. As a consequence, cluster analysis is performed by applying the k-means algorithm to the event windows. Using the Schwarz criterion, five clusters were selected.

Figure 1 shows the averaged posterior probabilities of being in the high volatility regime for the event windows belonging to the first four clusters. Cluster (a) highlights that reviews for downgrading are fully anticipated by the market. In this cluster the probability of being in the high volatility regime is larger than 0.5 almost fifty days before the announcement occurs and it is relevant the absence of announcement and post-announcement effects. This cluster is the most interesting among those under consideration, because it shows that reviews for downgrading announced by rating agencies, which should reflect the latest available information, are largely anticipated by an increase in the volatility of ARs and announcements do not convey new information to the market.

Cluster (b) groups event windows for which the volatility of the abnormal returns is drawn from the high volatility state almost twenty days before the event occurrence. This implies that CDS market anticipates the announcements. At the same time, the ARs of the event windows belonging to this cluster show that volatility remains in the high state also around $t = 0$ and for twenty days after the announcements, highlighting also the presence of announcement and post-announcement effects. From a financial point of view, it may be useful to note that this behavior is probably due to the specific nature of the events under consideration, which represent only reviews for possible downgrades and not effective downgrades, meaning that announcements are not always followed by a reduction in the effective creditworthiness of the reference entity. Persistence of the high volatility state after $t = 0$ may be interpreted as a measure of the market's expectation regarding the future effective downgrading (in the data base under consideration the 65% of reviews for downgrading is followed by effective downgrading in an average period of 80 days).

The ARs of the event windows belonging to cluster (c) show that market volatility anticipates the reviews for downgrading by almost ten days and decreases very quickly about ten days after the event. For the ARs of the event windows belonging to this cluster, we can conclude that nevertheless the rating announcement is anticipated by the market via an increase in volatility, it is still present an announcement effect, while the post announcement effect

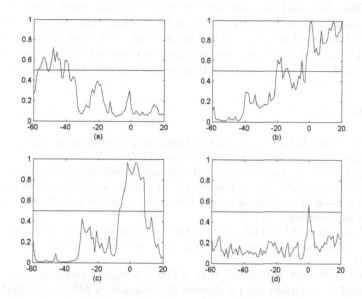

Fig. 1. Estimated mean posterior probabilities of being in the high volatility regime for series belonging to four different clusters.

is largely reduced. The fourth cluster (d) collects event windows for which the mean posterior probability of being in a high volatility state exceeds 0.5 only at $t = 0$, implying the existence of an announcement effect.

The fifth cluster, not shown here, is a residual cluster which collects event windows characterized by a higher degree of heterogeneity than those in the other clusters. In this case, the mean posterior probability of being in a high volatility regime is not particularly meaningful.

5   Conclusions

This study was conducted to answer fundamental questions about the effectiveness of event-study methodology in capturing the effect of events on financial asset behavior. We used a data set on CDS quotes and credit rating data. It covers the period from June, 2004 to October, 2009. We choose the five-year CDS quotes since this is the benchmark maturity in the CDS market. We collected the reviews for downgrading (watchlistings) announced by three major rating agencies (Fitch, Moody's and Standard&Poor's) for the sample firms in order to verify whether announcements carry new information to the CDS market or not. At the end of the sampling period, we selected 57 non-overlapping events.

Since the estimated effect of events on security behavior investigated by classic event-study methodology may be biased downward, because of the averaging effect and the increased volatility around events, we re-evaluate the classical approach by introducing a HMM characterized by two volatility regimes (high and low) to model the ARs of each event window. We find that CDS market anticipates reviews for downgrading and we show, through cluster analysis, that the anticipation period can follows different patterns.

References

BROWN, S. and WARNER, J. (1985): Using daily stock returns: The case of event studies. *Journal of Financial Economics 14 (1), 3-31.*

CASTELLANO, R. and SCACCIA, L. (2010): Bayesian hidden Markov models for financial data. In: F. Palumbo, C.N. Lauro and M.J. Greenacre (Eds.): *Data Analysis and Classification: From Exploration to Confirmation.* Springer, Berlin-Heidelberg, 453–461.

ENGEL, C. and HAMILTON, J.D. (1990): Long swings in the dollar: Are they in the data and do markets know it? *The American Economic Review 80 (4), 689-713.*

HALDRUP, N. and NIELSEN, M.O. (2006): A regime switching long memory model for electricity prices. *Journal of econometrics 135 (1-2), 349-376*

HEINKE, V.G. (2006): Credit spread volatility, bond ratings and the risk reduction effect of watchlistings. *International Journal of Finance and Economics 11 (4), 293-303.*

HULL, J., PREDESCU, M. and WHITE, A. (2004): The relationship between credit default swap spreads, bond yields, and credit rating announcements. *Journal of Banking and Finance 28 (11), 2789-2811.*

KLIGER, D. and Sarig, O. (2000): The information value of bond ratings. *The Journal of Finance 55 (6), 2879-2902.*

KOTHARI, S. and WARNER, J. (1997): Measuring long-horizon security price performance. *Journal of Financial Economics 43 (3), 301-339.*

NORDEN, L. and WEBER, M. (2004): Informational efficiency of credit default swap and stock markets: The impact of credit rating announcements. *Journal of Banking and Finance 28 (11), 2813-2843.*

OTRANTO, E. and GALLO, G.(2002): A nonparametric Bayesian approach to detect the number of regimes in Markov switching models. *Econometric Reviews 21 (4), 477-496.*

ROSSI, A. and GALLO, G. (2006): Volatility estimation via hidden Markov models. *Journal of Empirical Finance 13 (2), 203-230.*

RYDÉN, T., TERÄSVIRTA, T. and rASBRINK, S. (1998): Stylized facts of daily return series and the hidden Markov model. *Journal of Applied Econometrics 13 (3), 217-244.*

STEINER, M. and HEINKE, V.G. (2001): Event study concerning international bond price effects of credit rating actions. *International Journal of Finance and Economics 6 (2), 139-157.*

Evaluation of DNA Mixtures Accounting for Sampling Variability

Yuk-Ka Chung[1], Yue-Qing Hu[2], De-Gang Zhu[3], and Wing K. Fung[4]

[1] Department of Statistics and Actuarial Science, The University of Hong Kong, Pokfulam Road, Hong Kong, China, *yukchung@hku.hk*
[2] Department of Statistics and Actuarial Science, The University of Hong Kong, Pokfulam Road, Hong Kong, China, *yqhu@hku.hk*
[3] Nanjing Forestry University, Nanjing, China,
[4] Department of Statistics and Actuarial Science, The University of Hong Kong, Pokfulam Road, Hong Kong, China, *wingfung@hku.hk*

Abstract. In the conventional evaluation of DNA mixtures, the allele frequencies are often taken as constants. But they are in fact estimated from a sample taken from a population and thus the variability of the estimates has to be taken into account. Within a Bayesian framework, the evaluation of DNA mixtures accounting for sampling variability in the population database of allele frequencies are discussed in this paper. The concise and general formulae are provided for calculating the likelihood ratio when the people involved are biologically related. The implementation of the formula is demonstrated on the analysis of a real example. The resulting formulae are shown to be more conservative, which is generally more favorable to the defendant.

Keywords: Bayesian inference, Hardy-Weinberg equilibrium, relatedness coefficient, likelihood ratio, mixed stain, relative

1 Introduction

Deoxyribonucleic acid (DNA) profiling is widely known as an important tool for the identification of perpetrator in a crime investigation. The mixed stain found in the crime scene often contains DNA from more than one contributor. This kind of mixture complicates the evaluation of weight of DNA evidence presented in the court. The problem of how to assess the strength of evidence that connects the offender to the crime case became a challenging task and attracted a great deal of attention from statisticians over the past decade or so (Weir et al. (1997), Curran et al. (1999), Fukshansky and Bär (2000), Hu and Fung (2003, 2005), Cowell et al. (2007), Dawid et al. (2007)). Usually, the strength of evidence is quantified by the likelihood ratio (LR) of two probability values under different hypotheses that explain who contribute to the DNA mixture. Weir et al. (1997) considered the interpretation of DNA mixtures and derived a general formula for the evaluation of the LR which was extended by Curran et al. (1999) and Fung and Hu (2000) to allow

Y. Lechevallier, G. Saporta (eds.), *Proceedings of COMPSTAT'2010*,
DOI 10.1007/978-3-7908-2604-3_42, © Springer-Verlag Berlin Heidelberg 2010

for population substructure. Fukshansky and Bär (1999) also considered the situation when the contributors of the mixed stains are of different ethnic origins. Some further contributions have been presented for the evaluation of DNA mixtures with complicated features. For example, Fukshansky and Bär (2000) constructed a formula for the evaluation of the LR when the suspect is not tested but his/her relatives are. Hu and Fung (2003, 2005) developed general formulae for the calculation of the LR when there are one or two pairs of related persons involved in determining the source contributors. Mortera et al. (2003), Dawid et al. (2007) and Cowell et al. (2007) demonstrated the use of probabilistic expert systems or object-oriented Bayesian network for evaluating DNA mixtures in complex identification problems involving unknown number of contributors, missing individuals and unobserved alleles.

In these evaluations of the DNA evidences, the allele frequencies are often taken as constants. However, they are in fact estimated from a sample and the uncertainty arises due to sampling error. Ignoring this uncertainty may lead to unconservative estimates (Balding (1995)) that are not desirable in analyzing forensic evidence. Balding (1995), Balding and Donnelly (1995) and Foreman et al. (1997) advocated the use of Bayesian methods modeling the probability distributions of the relative frequencies of alleles. Their works dealt with simple identification cases and have demonstrated how the sample size of the database affects the weight of evidence. In Corradi et al. (2003), the allele frequency distribution was modeled under a Bayesian hierarchical framework in their application of the graphical approach to the evaluation of DNA evidences on various cases including paternity test and missing person identification. In practical crime cases, there can be many possible alleles found in the mixed stain with several unknown contributors. This adds complexity to the calculation of the LR under the Bayesian hierarchical approach, especially when related persons are involved in the hypotheses. This paper therefore describes how the formulae used in the plug-in approach for general identification problems can be modified for calculating the LR within a Bayesian framework.

In section 2, we present a concise and general formula that can meet most needs. With the aid of this formula, the plug-in approach for calculating the LR can be easily transformed into the Bayesian framework without increasing the computational complexity. Section 3 presents the results when the modified formulae are used on the analysis of a real example in which relatives are considered. Finally, section 4 summarizes our findings and discusses their implications.

2   Likelihood ratio

Suppose in a crime case two competing hypotheses, the prosecution hypothesis H_p and the defense proposition H_d, about who contribute to the mixture are raised. In addition to the alleles found in the mixture, some involved persons are usually typed, *e.g.* the victim and the suspect(s). Denote M the set of alleles present in the mixture and K the set of genotypes typed, then the evidence can be simply written as (M, K). The likelihood ratio is usually used to evaluate the weight of the evidence and can be expressed as

$$LR = \frac{P(\text{Evidence}|H_p)}{P(\text{Evidence}|H_d)} = \frac{P(M, K|H_p)}{P(M, K|H_d)}. \tag{1}$$

Usually, the known contributors and the number of unknown contributors are specified in the following general hypothesis:

H : some typed persons and x unknowns are contributors of the mixture.

The issue of calculating $P(M, K|H)$ was discussed by many researchers. See Weir et al. (1997), Fukshansky and Bär (1998, 2000) and Hu and Fung (2003, 2005) among many others.

In the evaluation of the evidence using equation (1), the allele frequencies are treated as constants. But they are in fact estimated from a sample D with size n taken from a population θ. The uncertainty is naturally raised in the process of estimating allele frequencies as the sample size n is usually not very large. By intuition, the uncertainty of the estimated allele frequencies will decrease when the sample size n increases. Ignoring this uncertainty is unfair to the defendant. In order to take account of this uncertainty, suppose that there are l alleles $\{1, 2, \ldots, l\}$ at an autosomal locus and the corresponding allele frequencies $x_\theta = (x_{\theta,1}, x_{\theta,2}, \ldots, x_{\theta,l})$ ($\sum_{i=1}^{l} x_{\theta,i} = 1$) has the Dirichlet prior distribution with parameter $\alpha = (\alpha_1, \alpha_2, \ldots, \alpha_l)$, *i.e.* the corresponding probability density function is

$$\text{Dir}(x_\theta|\alpha) = \frac{\Gamma(\alpha_.)}{\prod_{i=1}^{l} \Gamma(\alpha_i)} \prod_{i=1}^{l} x_{\theta,i}^{\alpha_i - 1}, \quad x_{\theta,i} \geq 0, i = 1, \ldots, l, \quad \sum_{i=1}^{l} x_{\theta,i} = 1,$$

where $\alpha_. = \sum_{i=1}^{l} \alpha_i$. In this situation, the LR is assessed as

$$LR = \frac{\int_{\mathcal{X}_\theta} P(M, K, D|x_\theta, H_p)\text{Dir}(x_\theta|\alpha)\, dx_\theta}{\int_{\mathcal{X}_\theta} P(M, K, D|x_\theta, H_d)\text{Dir}(x_\theta|\alpha)\, dx_\theta},$$

where $\mathcal{X}_\theta$ is the sample space of parameter x_θ. This version of LR is often more conservative and thus favorable to the defendant. In order to find the LR, it suffices to calculate

$$P(M, K, D|H) = \int_{\mathcal{X}_\theta} P(M, K, D|x_\theta, H)\text{Dir}(x_\theta|\alpha)\, dx_\theta \tag{2}$$

for the hypothesis H about who the contributors of the mixture are. Since given x_θ, M is independent of D and the probability of observing K and D does not depend on the hypothesis H, equation (2) can be written as

$$P(M, K, D|H) = \int_{\mathcal{X}_\theta} P(M|x_\theta, K, H)P(K, D|x_\theta)\text{Dir}(x_\theta|\alpha)\, dx_\theta. \tag{3}$$

In the general situation with presumably known allele frequencies, the quantity of $P(M|x_\theta, K, H)$ is in fact a particular value of the Q-function (Hu and Fung (2005)):

$$Q(j, B|x_\theta) = \sum_{M \backslash B \subset C \subset M} (-1)^{|M \backslash C|} \left(\sum_{i \in C} x_{\theta,i} \right)^j, \qquad (4)$$

where B is any subset of M; j is a non-negative integer; and $|.|$ is the cardinality of a set. This function can be interpreted as the probability of j alleles taken from the set M that explain all the alleles in the set B. Based on equations (3) and (4), we introduce the following modified Q-function for any non-negative integer j and subset B of M:

$$Q^*(j, B) = \int_{\mathcal{X}_\theta} Q(j, B|x_\theta) P(K, D|x_\theta) \mathrm{Dir}(x_\theta|\alpha) \, dx_\theta. \qquad (5)$$

For convenience, let z denote an individual taken from the population θ and $n_{i,z}$ denote the count of allele i of this individual, $1 \le i \le l$. Obviously, $n_{i,z}$ can take on only values of 0, 1, and 2. Let $n_{i,K \cup D} = \sum_{z \in K \cup D} n_{i,z}$, $\alpha_C = \sum_{i \in C} \alpha_i$ and $n_{C,K \cup D} = \sum_{i \in C} n_{i,K \cup D}$ for any $C \subset \{1, 2, \ldots, l\}$. It follows that $\sum_{i=1}^{l} n_{i,K \cup D} = 2(k+n)$, where k is the number of typed persons whose genotypes comprise K, and n is the number of individuals in the sample D. For arbitrary $j \ge 0$ and $B \subset M$, the following formula is resulted from equation (5) and the proof is sketched in the Appendix:

$$Q^*(j, B) = \frac{\kappa}{\alpha^{(2k+2n+j)}} \sum_{M \backslash B \subset C \subset M} (-1)^{|M \backslash C|} (\alpha_C + n_{C,K \cup D})^{(j)}, \qquad (6)$$

where

$$\kappa = \prod_{i=1}^{l} \frac{\Gamma(\alpha_i + n_{i,K \cup D})}{\Gamma(\alpha_i)} \prod_{z \in K \cup D} \frac{2!}{\prod_{i=1}^{l} n_{i,z}!},$$

$r^{(j)} = \Gamma(r+j)/\Gamma(r) = r(r+1) \cdots (r+j-1)$ for any real r and $r^{(0)} = 1$. Note that $Q^*(0, \phi) = \kappa/\alpha^{(2k+2n)}$ and $Q^*(j, B) = 0$ for $|B| > j$. Also note that κ does not depend on the hypothesis H and hence can be omitted in the calculation of LR. Throughout all the calculations, the Hardy-Weinberg equilibrium (p.23, Fung and Hu (2008)) is assumed in the population θ.

In the next section, concise formulae for calculating $P(M, K, D|H)$ in a real example is presented using the modified Q-function.

3   Case Study

In this section, we demonstrate the application of formula (6) to a rape case that happened in Hong Kong (Fung and Hu (2000)) where the victim and the suspect were typed at three loci D3S1358, vWA and FGA in the Profiler PCR-STR system. Table 1 shows the alleles detected from the mixed stain and the two typed persons, as well as the corresponding allele frequencies estimated from a Chinese population database (Wong et al. (2001)). Note that for illustrative purpose the genotypes of the victim and the suspect are slightly modified while the mixture alleles are unchanged. A prosecution hypothesis and two defense propositions are proposed as follows:

H_p : the victim and the suspect were contributors of the mixture;
H_{d_1}: the victim and one unknown were contributors;
H_{d_2}: the victim and one relative of the suspect were contributors.

Table 1. Alleles (modified) detected in a rape case in Hong Kong (Fung and Hu (2000)).

Locus	Mixture (M)	Victim (V)	Suspect (S)	Frequency
D3S1358	14		14	0.033
	15	15		0.331
	17	17		0.239
	18		18	0.056
vWA	16		16	0.156
	18	18		0.160
FGA	20		20	0.044
	24	24		0.166
	25	25		0.110

Let us consider the locus FGA for demonstration, where the mixture is $M = \{20, 24, 25\}$, the genotypes of the victim and the suspect are respectively 24/25 and 20/20. Using equation (7.5) in Fung and Hu (2008) and formula (6), the $P(M, K, D|H)$ under H_p, H_{d_1} and H_{d_2} are respectively

$$P(M, K, D|H_p) = Q^*(0, \phi),$$
$$P(M, K, D|H_{d_1}) = Q^*(2, \{20\}),$$
$$P(M, K, D|H_{d_2}) = k_0 Q^*(2, \{20\}) + 2k_1 Q^*(1, \phi) + k_2 Q^*(0, \phi),$$

where $(k_0, 2k_1, k_2)$ are the relatedness coefficients between the suspect and his/her relative. The formulae for the calculation of $P(M, K, D|H)$ for the other loci can be determined similarly. Based on uniform Dirichlet prior of the allele frequencies, the LRs for various relationships at all the three loci are computed and summarized in Table 2. Note that the last row is corresponding to H_{d_1} while the other rows are corresponding to H_{d_2}. As can be seen, there is a moderate reduction in the individual and overall LRs when the sample size is changed from 1000 to 100. For example, at locus D3S1358, the value of $LR_1 = 193.31$ based on $n = 100$ is only 74% of 260.46, which is the one based on $n = 1000$, and the overall LR_1 based on $n = 100$ is only one half of that based on $n = 1000$. Also noted is that the effect of the kinship relationship between R and S on the evaluation of DNA mixture is remarkable. The smallest LR always goes to the one corresponding to full siblings relationship. The overall LR_2 in the case of full siblings is less than 0.1% of that in the case of second cousins. Moreover, LR_2 does not constitute a substantial change, especially when a close relationship is considered in H_{d_2}. This is due to the fact that the suspect is homozygous in loci vWA and FGA, so that the same allele is highly probable to be found in a close relative, $e.g.$ full sibling.

Table 2. The effect of sample size n on the likelihood ratio in a rape case (Fung and Hu (2000)), where the prosecution proposition is H_p: contributors were the victim and the suspect and the defense proposition is H_{d_2}: contributors were the victim and a relative R of suspect S.

		Likelihood ratios			
(R, S)	n	D3S1358	vWA	FGA	Overall
Parent-child	100	19.17	2.99	2.93	168
	1000	22.08	3.15	3.10	216
Full siblings	100	3.61	2.28	2.33	19
	1000	3.66	2.34	2.39	20
Half siblings	100	34.89	4.79	5.31	886
	1000	40.70	5.09	5.73	1186
First cousins	100	59.11	6.84	8.93	3607
	1000	70.41	7.36	9.91	5135
Second cousins	100	123.32	10.08	18.27	22710
	1000	155.51	11.07	21.93	37740
Unrelated	100	193.31	11.97	28.08	64960
	1000	260.46	13.30	36.82	127536

4   Discussion

In this paper we present a general formula for DNA mixture analysis within a Bayesian framework, taking into account the uncertainty arise from estimating allele frequencies in a population database. Based on the modified Q-function $Q^*(.,.)$, the existing plug-in approach can be easily modified to compute the weight of evidence under various prosecution or defense propositions, in which related persons may be involved. The calculation of $Q^*(.,.)$ does not increase the computational complexity and can be easily implemented. Moreover, our approach asymptotically gives the same results as the plug-in approach as n, the sample size of the database from which the allele frequencies are estimated, goes to infinity.

The case study shows the importance of taking into account the uncertainty in allele frequency estimates. The sample size does affect the likelihood ratio, especially when rare alleles found in the DNA mixture are included in the set of alleles with unknown contributors. Using the Bayesian approach, substantial reduction in the likelihood ratio can be found in some situations even when a close relationship is considered in the defense proposition. It is concluded that the Bayesian approach provides a conservative evaluation of the evidence which would be more desirable in some crime cases.

In this study, all the people involved are assumed to be from the same population. In practical crime cases, it is not uncommon that the contributors of the mixed stain may come from different ethnic groups. To handle this, subpopulation models as suggested by Balding and Nichols (1994) should be incorporated into the calculation of the weight of evidence. Further extension of our current approach in this direction constitutes our future work.

Appendix

Proof of equation (6). First consider

$$\left(\sum_{i\in C} x_{\theta,i}\right)^j P(K,D|x_\theta)\mathrm{Dir}(x_\theta|\alpha)$$

$$= \left(\sum_{i\in C} x_{\theta,i}\right)^j \left\{\prod_{z\in K\cup D}\frac{2!}{\prod_{i=1}^l n_{i,z}!}\prod_{i=1}^l x_{\theta,i}^{n_{i,z}}\right\}\frac{\Gamma(\alpha.)}{\prod_{i=1}^l \Gamma(\alpha_i)}\prod_{i=1}^l x_{\theta,i}^{\alpha_i-1}$$

$$= \left\{\prod_{z\in K\cup D}\frac{2!}{\prod_{i=1}^l n_{i,z}!}\frac{\Gamma(\alpha.)}{\prod_{i=1}^l \Gamma(\alpha_i)}\right\}\left\{\left(\sum_{i\in C} x_{\theta,i}\right)^j\prod_{i=1}^l x_{\theta,i}^{n_{i,K\cup D}+\alpha_i-1}\right\}.$$

From the properties of the Dirichlet distribution, $\sum_{i\in C} x_{\theta,i} \sim \mathrm{Beta}(\alpha_C, \alpha. - \alpha_C)$ and $E\left(\sum_{i\in C} x_{\theta,i}\right)^j = \alpha_C^{(j)}/\alpha^{(j)}$. It follows that

$$\int_{\mathcal{X}_\theta} (\sum_{i\in C} x_{\theta,i})^j P(K,D|x_\theta)\mathrm{Dir}(x_\theta|\alpha)\,dx_\theta$$

$$= \prod_{z\in K\cup D}\frac{2!}{\prod_{i=1}^l n_{i,z}!}\frac{\Gamma(\alpha.)}{\prod_{i=1}^l \Gamma(\alpha_i)}\int_{\mathcal{X}_\theta}(\sum_{i\in C} x_{\theta,i})^j\prod_{i=1}^l x_{\theta,i}^{n_{i,K\cup D}+\alpha_i-1}\,dx_\theta$$

$$= \prod_{z\in K\cup D}\frac{2!}{\prod_{i=1}^l n_{i,z}!}\frac{\Gamma(\alpha.)}{\prod_{i=1}^l \Gamma(\alpha_i)}\frac{\prod_{i=1}^l \Gamma(\alpha_i+n_{i,K\cup D})}{\Gamma(\alpha.+2k+2n)}\frac{(\alpha_C+n_{C,K\cup D})^{(j)}}{(\alpha.+2k+2n)^{(j)}}$$

$$= \frac{\kappa}{\alpha.^{(2k+2n+j)}}(\alpha_C+n_{C,K\cup D})^{(j)}. \tag{7}$$

Substituting equation (7) into equation (5) and using equation (4) yields equation (6) immediately.

References

BALDING, D. J. (1995): Estimating products in forensic identification using DNA profiles. *J. Am. Statist. Ass. 90, 839-844.*

BALDING, D. J. and DONNELLY, P. (1995): Inference in forensic identification (with discussion). *J. R. Statist. Soc. A 158, 21-53.*

BALDING, D. J. and NICHOLS, R. A. (1994) DNA profile match probability calculations: how to allow for population stratification, relatedness, data base selection and single bands. *Forens. Sci. Int. 64, 125-140.*

CORRADI, F., LAGO, G. and STEFANINI, F. M. (2003) The evaluation of DNA evidence in pedigrees requiring population inference. *J. R. Statist. Soc. A 166, 425-440.*

COWELL, R. G., LAURITZEN, S. L. and MORTERA, J. (2007) A gamma model for DNA mixture analyses. *Bayesian Analysis 2, 333-348.*

CURRAN, J. M., TRIGGS, C. M., BUCKLETON, J. and WEIR, B. S. (1999) Interpreting DNA mixtures in structured populations. *J. Forens. Sci. 44, 987-995.*

DAWID, A. P., MORTERA, J. and VICARD, P. (2007): Object-oriented Bayesian networks for forensic DNA profiling, allowing for missing subjects, mutation and silent alleles. *Forens. Sci. Int. 169, 195-205.*

FOREMAN, L. A., SMITH, A. F. M. and EVETT, I. W. (1997): Bayesian analysis of DNA profiling data in forensic identification applications (with discussion). *J. R. Statist. Soc. A 160, 429-469.*

FUKSHANSKY, N. and BÄR, W. (1998): Interpreting forensic DNA evidence on the basis of hypotheses testing. *Int. J. Legal Med. 111, 62-66.*

FUKSHANSKY, N. and BÄR, W. (1999): Biostatistical evaluation of mixed stains with contributors of different ethnic origin. *Int. J. Legal Med. 112, 383-387.*

FUKSHANSKY, N. and BÄR, W. (2000): Biostatistical for mixed stains: the case of tested relatives of a non-tested suspect. *Int. J. Legal Med. 114, 78-82.*

FUNG, W. K. and HU, Y. Q. (2000): Interpreting forensic DNA mixtures: allowing for uncertainty in population substructure and dependence. *J. R. Statist. Soc. A 163, 241-254.*

FUNG, W. K. and HU, Y. Q. (2008): *Statistical DNA Forensics: Theory, Methods and Computation.* Chichester: Wiley.

HU, Y. Q. and FUNG, W. K. (2003): Interpreting DNA mixtures with the presence of relatives. *Int. J. Legal Med. 117, 39-45.*

HU, Y. Q. and FUNG, W. K. (2005): Evaluation of DNA mixtures involving two pairs of relatives. *Int. J. Legal Med. 119, 251-259.*

MORTERA, J., DAWID, A. P. and LAURITZEN, S. L. (2003): Probabilistic expert systems for DNA mixture profiling. *Theor. Popul. Biol. 63, 191-205.*

WEIR, B. S., TRIGGS, C. M., STARLING, L., STOWELL, L. I., WALSH, K. A. J. and BUCKLETON, J. S. (1997): Interpreting DNA mixtures. *J. Forens. Sci. 42, 113-122.*

WONG, D. M., LAW, M. Y., FUNG, W. K., CHAN, K. L., LI, C., LUN, T. S., LAI, K. M., CHEUNG, K. Y. and CHIU, C. T. (2001): Population data for 12 STR loci in Hong Kong Chinese. *Int. J. Legal Med. 114, 281-284.*

Monotone Graphical Multivariate Markov Chains

Roberto Colombi[1] and Sabrina Giordano[2]

[1] Dept. of Information Technology and Math. Methods, University of Bergamo
viale Marconi, 5, 24044 Dalmine (BG), Italy, *colombi@unibg.it*
[2] Dept. of Economics and Statistics, University of Calabria
via Bucci, 87036 Arcavacata di Rende (CS), Italy, *sabrina.giordano@unical.it*

Abstract. In this paper, we show that a deeper insight into the relations among marginal processes of a multivariate Markov chain can be gained by testing hypotheses of Granger non-causality, contemporaneous independence and monotone dependence coherent with a stochastic ordering. The tested hypotheses associated to a multi edge graph are proven to be equivalent to equality and inequality constraints on interactions of a multivariate logistic model parameterizing the transition probabilities. As the null hypothesis is specified by inequality constraints, the likelihood ratio statistic has chi-bar-square asymptotic distribution whose tail probabilities can be computed by simulation. The introduced hypotheses are tested on real categorical time series.

Keywords: graphical models, Granger causality, stochastic orderings, chi-bar-square distribution

1 Introduction

When multivariate categorical data are collected over time, the dynamic character of their association must be taken into account. This aspect plays an important role in modelling discrete time-homogeneous multivariate Markov chains (MMCs). To investigate the underlying dynamic relations among the marginal processes of a multivariate Markov chain, we employ the multi edge graph (ME graph, Colombi and Giordano (2009)) which encodes Granger non-causality and contemporaneous independence conditions among the components of an MMC. Moreover, we specify the nature of the dependence, if any, of the present of a marginal process of the MMC on the past of another, in terms of stochastic dominance criteria. Our approach enables us to establish whether the dependence of a component of the MMC on its parents - according to the graph terminology - satisfies an appropriate stochastic ordering by testing equality and inequality constraints on certain parameters. We start by defining the conditions which specify when an MMC is graphical and monotone in Sections 2 and 3. In Sections 4 and 5, we illustrate how to test these hypotheses through equality and inequality constraints on parameters. The given methodology is applied to real data in the final Section.

Y. Lechevallier, G. Saporta (eds.), *Proceedings of COMPSTAT'2010*,
DOI 10.1007/978-3-7908-2604-3_43, © Springer-Verlag Berlin Heidelberg 2010

2   Basic notation

Given a set of integers $\mathcal{V} = \{1, ..., q\}$, let $\mathbf{A}_{\mathcal{V}} = \{A_{\mathcal{V}}(t) : t \in \mathcal{Z}\} = \{A_j(t) : t \in \mathcal{Z}, j \in \mathcal{V}\}$ be a time-homogeneous first order q−variate Markov chain in a discrete time interval $\mathcal{Z} = \{0, 1, 2, ..., T\}$. For all $t \in \mathcal{Z}$, $A_{\mathcal{V}}(t) = \{A_j(t) : j \in \mathcal{V}\}$ is a discrete random vector with each element $A_j(t)$ taking values on a finite set of ordered categories $\mathcal{A}_j = \{a_{j1}, ..., a_{js_j}\}$, $j \in \mathcal{V}$. The numbering is assumed to be consistent with the order of the categories. For every $\mathcal{S} \subset \mathcal{V}$, a marginal process of the chain is represented by $\mathbf{A}_{\mathcal{S}} = \{A_{\mathcal{S}}(t) : t \in \mathcal{Z}\}$ where $A_{\mathcal{S}}(t) = \{A_j(t) : j \in \mathcal{S}\}$. When $\mathcal{S} = \{j\}$ the univariate marginal process is indicated by $\mathbf{A}_j = \{A_j(t) : t \in \mathcal{Z}\}$, $j \in \mathcal{V}$. Moreover, we use the notation of conditional independence $X \perp\!\!\!\perp Y | W$ when the random variables X and Y are independent once the value of a third variable W is given.

3   Monotone and graphical multivariate Markov chains

We provide a graphical representation of the dynamic dependence among the component processes of an MMC by employing the multi edge graph. This is a graph that encodes Granger noncausal and contemporaneous independence statements. Here, we briefly recall some features of the ME graphs and refer to Colombi and Giordano (2009) for a deeper discussion of its properties.

In the ME graph $G = (\mathcal{V}, \mathcal{E})$, each node j belonging to the node set $\mathcal{V}$ corresponds to the univariate marginal process $\mathbf{A}_j$, $j \in \mathcal{V}$, of the q-variate MMC $\mathbf{A}_{\mathcal{V}}$, and the edges in the edge set $\mathcal{E}$ describe the interdependence among these processes. A pair of nodes $i, k \in \mathcal{V}$ of the ME graph may be joined by the directed edges $i \rightarrow k$, $i \leftarrow k$, and by the bi-directed edge $i \leftrightarrow k$, denoted also by $(i, k]$, $[i, k)$ and $[i, k]$, respectively. Each pair of distinct nodes $i, k \in \mathcal{V}$ can be connected by up to all the three types of edges. For each single node $i \in \mathcal{V}$, the bi-directed edge $[i, i]$ is implicitly introduced and the directed edge $(i, i]$ (or equivalently $[i, i)$) may or may not be present. If $(i, k] \in \mathcal{E}$ then i is a *parent* of k and k is a *child* of i. The set of parents of the node i is denoted by $Pa(i) = \{j \in \mathcal{V} : (j, i] \in \mathcal{E}\}$. Moreover, when $[i, k] \in \mathcal{E}$ the nodes i, k are *neighbors*. Thus, the set of neighbors of i is $Nb(i) = \{j \in \mathcal{V} : [i, j] \in \mathcal{E}\}$. Note that the generic node i is neighbor of itself ($i \in Nb(i)$) and may also be parent and child of itself. More generally, $Pa(\mathcal{S})$ and $Nb(\mathcal{S})$ are the collection of parents and neighbors of nodes in $\mathcal{S}$, for every non-empty subset $\mathcal{S}$ of $\mathcal{V}$ (see the wide ranging literature on graphical models for basic concepts).

ME graphs obey Markov properties which associate sets of G-noncausality and contemporaneous independence restrictions with missing directed and bi-directed edges, respectively. In particular, missing bi-directed arrows lead to independencies of marginal processes at the same point in time; missing directed edges, instead, refer to independencies which involve marginal processes at two consecutive instants.

Definition 1. (Graphical MMC). *A multivariate Markov chain is graphical with respect to an ME graph* $G = (\mathcal{V}, \mathcal{E})$ *if and only if its transition probabilities satisfy the following conditional independencies for all* $t \in \mathcal{Z} \setminus \{0\}$

$$A_{\mathcal{S}}(t) \perp\!\!\!\perp A_{\mathcal{V}\setminus Pa(\mathcal{S})}(t-1)|A_{Pa(\mathcal{S})}(t-1) \qquad \forall \mathcal{S} \in \mathcal{P}(\mathcal{V}) \tag{1}$$

$$A_{\mathcal{S}}(t) \perp\!\!\!\perp A_{\mathcal{V}\setminus Nb(\mathcal{S})}(t)|A_{\mathcal{V}}(t-1) \qquad \forall \mathcal{S} \in \mathcal{P}(\mathcal{V}). \tag{2}$$

In the context of first order MMC, condition (1) corresponds to the classical notion of Granger non-causality. Henceforth, we will refer to (1) with the term *Granger non-causality condition* saying that $\mathbf{A}_{\mathcal{S}}$ is not G-caused by $\mathbf{A}_{\mathcal{V}\setminus Pa(\mathcal{S})}$ with respect to $\mathbf{A}_{\mathcal{V}}$, and use the shorthand notation $\mathbf{A}_{\mathcal{V}\setminus Pa(\mathcal{S})} \nrightarrow \mathbf{A}_{\mathcal{S}}$.

Condition (2), on the other hand, is a restriction on marginal transition probabilities because it does not involve the marginal processes $\mathbf{A}_j : j \in Nb(\mathcal{S})\setminus\mathcal{S}$, at time t, and more precisely it states that the transition probabilities must satisfy the bi-directed Markov property (Richardson (2003)) with respect to the graph obtained by removing the directed edges from G. Here, we will refer to (2) with the term *contemporaneous independence condition* using a shorthand notation $\mathbf{A}_{\mathcal{S}} \nleftrightarrow \mathbf{A}_{\mathcal{V}\setminus Nb(\mathcal{S})}$, and say that $\mathbf{A}_{\mathcal{S}}$ and $\mathbf{A}_{\mathcal{V}\setminus Nb(\mathcal{S})}$ are contemporaneously independent.

For example, the graph in Figure 1 displays the contemporaneous independence relation $\mathbf{A}_{23} \nleftrightarrow \mathbf{A}_1$ and the G-noncausal restrictions: $\mathbf{A}_3 \nrightarrow \mathbf{A}_2$; $\mathbf{A}_1 \nrightarrow \mathbf{A}_3$; $\mathbf{A}_{23} \nrightarrow \mathbf{A}_1$; $\mathbf{A}_3 \nrightarrow \mathbf{A}_{12}$. Note that in this example the presence of the edges $(i, i]$ is assumed even if these edges are not drawn in Figure 1.

The above definition suggests that the lack of a directed edge from node i to k, $(i, k \in \mathcal{V})$, is equivalent to the independence of the present of the univariate marginal process $\mathbf{A}_k$ from the immediate past of $\mathbf{A}_i$ given the most recent past of the marginal process $\mathbf{A}_{\mathcal{V}\setminus\{i\}}$, that is, for all $t \in \mathcal{Z} \setminus \{0\}$

$$(i, k] \notin \mathcal{E} \iff A_k(t) \perp\!\!\!\perp A_i(t-1)|A_{\mathcal{V}\setminus\{i\}}(t-1). \tag{3}$$

Moreover, from Definition 1, we deduce that a missing bi-directed arrow between i and k is equivalent to stating that the corresponding marginal processes are contemporaneously independent given the recent past of the MMC, that is, for all $t \in \mathcal{Z} \setminus \{0\}$

$$[i, k] \notin \mathcal{E} \iff A_i(t) \perp\!\!\!\perp A_k(t)|A_{\mathcal{V}}(t-1). \tag{4}$$

The conditional independencies (3) and (4) are interpretable in terms of pairwise Granger non-causality and contemporaneous independence conditions, respectively. However, note that (1), (2) are not equivalent to the implied set of pairwise conditions.

Beside the Granger non-causality and independence conditions, the form of dependence of $\mathbf{A}_j$ on its parents $\mathbf{A}_{Pa(j)}$, $j \in \mathcal{V}$, is also relevant. We address the problem of assessing the aforementioned dependencies by using the concept of monotone dependence.

Fig. 1. *Example of a multi edge graph*

In the ME graph $G = (\mathcal{V}, \mathcal{E})$, the hypothesis of monotone dependence of $\mathbf{A}_j$ on its parents $\mathbf{A}_{Pa(j)}$, $j \in \mathcal{V}$, states that the distributions of $\mathbf{A}_j$ conditioned by $\mathbf{A}_{Pa(j)}$ can be ordered according to a stochastic dominance criterion in a coherent way with the partial order on $\times_{k \in Pa(j)} \mathcal{A}_k$ which is induced by the orderings on the sets $\mathcal{A}_k$, $k \in Pa(j)$.

The dominance criterion can be chosen from the *simple, uniform* and *likelihood ratio* stochastic orderings. Remember that the likelihood ratio is the strongest stochastic ordering and the simple ordering is the weakest.

A graphical MMC which allows a monotone dependence of at least one marginal component on its parents is defined below.

Definition 2. (Monotone Graphical MMC). *A multivariate Markov chain is monotone and graphical if and only if it is graphical with respect to an ME graph $G = (\mathcal{V}, \mathcal{E})$ and there exists a set $\mathcal{M} \subseteq \mathcal{V}$, $\mathcal{M} \neq \emptyset$, such that for every $j \in \mathcal{M}$ the dependence of $\mathbf{A}_j$ on its parents is monotone.*

It is worth noting that the dominance criterion concerns only the marginal processes in an MMC and does not refer to their joint behavior.

In the next Section, we will show how the conditions of Granger noncausality, contemporaneous independence and monotone dependence that specify a monotone graphical MMC can be tested.

4   A multivariate logistic model for transition probabilities

Here, we clarify that the requirements of Definition 2 are equivalent to equality and inequality constraints on suitable interactions of a multivariate logistic model which parameterize the transition probabilities. We remind the reader that $\mathcal{I} = \times_{j \in \mathcal{V}} \mathcal{A}_j$ is the q-dimensional discrete joint state space. The time-homogeneous joint transition probabilities are denoted by $p(i|i')$, for every pair of states $i \in \mathcal{I}$, $i' \in \mathcal{I}$. Given a vector $i = (i_1, i_2, ..., i_q)' \in \mathcal{I}$, if $\mathcal{H} \subset \mathcal{V}$ then $i_{\mathcal{H}}$ denotes the vector with components $i_j, j \in \mathcal{H}$. Any state which includes categories $a_{ji} \in \mathcal{A}_j$, for $j \notin S$, $S \subset \mathcal{V}$, at the baseline value (usually the first category) is denoted by $(i_S, i*_{V \setminus S})$. Given a state i', for the transition probabilities $p(i|i')$, we adopt the Glonek-McCullagh (1995) multivariate logistic model whose marginal interaction parameters are denoted by $\eta^P(i_P|i')$, for every non empty subset P of $\mathcal{V}$ and for every $i_P \in \times_{j \in P} \mathcal{A}_j$. The Glonek-McCullagh baseline interactions $\eta^P(i_P|i')$ are given by the following contrasts of logarithms of marginal transition probabilities $p(\boldsymbol{i}_P|\boldsymbol{i}')$ from the state $\boldsymbol{i}'$ to one of the states in $\times_{j\in P}\mathcal{A}_j$

$$\eta^P(\boldsymbol{i}_P|\boldsymbol{i}') = \sum_{\mathcal{K}\subseteq P} (-1)^{|P\setminus\mathcal{K}|} \log p((\boldsymbol{i}_\mathcal{K}, \boldsymbol{i}^*_{P\setminus\mathcal{K}})|\boldsymbol{i}'). \tag{5}$$

Hence the Glonek-McCullagh interactions are not log-linear parameters because they are not contrasts of logarithms of the joint transition probabilities $p(\boldsymbol{i}|\boldsymbol{i}')$.

The proof of the next proposition follows from classical results on the logistic regression and a result by Lupparelli et al. (2009).

Proposition 1. *For an MMC with positive time-homogeneous transition probabilities, it holds that: (i) the Granger non-causality condition (1) is true if and only if $\eta^P(\boldsymbol{i}_P|\boldsymbol{i}') = \eta^P(\boldsymbol{i}_P|\boldsymbol{i}'_{Pa(P)})$, $P \subseteq \mathcal{V}, P \neq \emptyset$, and (ii) the contemporaneous independence condition (2) is equivalent to $\eta^P(\boldsymbol{i}_P|\boldsymbol{i}') = 0$ for all P that are not connected sets in the bi-directed graph obtained by removing every directed edge from the ME graph G.*

The Proposition states that requirements (1) and (2) of a graphical MMC correspond to simple linear constraints on the $\eta^P(\boldsymbol{i}_P|\boldsymbol{i}')$ parameters. The testing such a hypothesis is a standard parametric problem when the alternative hypothesis is that at least one constraint is not satisfied.

Hypotheses of monotone dependence hold if and only if inequality constraints on certain interaction parameters are satisfied as shown by the next proposition.

Proposition 2. *For a graphical MMC with positive time-homogeneous transition probabilities, a positive (negative) monotone dependence hypothesis is true if and only if $\eta^j(\boldsymbol{i}_j|\boldsymbol{i}'_{Pa(j)\setminus k}, \boldsymbol{i}'_k) \leq (\geq)\eta^j(\boldsymbol{i}_j|\boldsymbol{i}'_{Pa(j)\setminus k}, \boldsymbol{i}'_k+1)$, $k \in Pa(j)$, $j \in \mathcal{M}, \mathcal{M} \subseteq \mathcal{V}, \mathcal{M} \neq \emptyset$.*

The *simple*, *uniform* and *likelihood ratio* orderings are obtained when the logits $\eta^j(\boldsymbol{i}_j|\boldsymbol{i}'_{Pa(j)})$ subjected to inequality constraints are of global, continuation and local types, respectively. For the correspondence between inequality constraints on different types of interactions and stochastic orderings see Shaked and Shantikumar (1994), among others.

Following Bartolucci et al. (2007), it can be proved that the set of zero restrictions imposed under the G-noncausality and contemporaneous independence hypotheses of Proposition 1 can be rewritten in the form $\boldsymbol{C}\ln(\boldsymbol{M}\boldsymbol{\pi}) = \boldsymbol{0}$, while the inequality constraints of Proposition 2 for monotone dependence have a compact expression given by $\boldsymbol{K}\ln(\boldsymbol{M}\boldsymbol{\pi}) \geq \boldsymbol{0}$, where $\boldsymbol{\pi}$ is the vector of all the transition probabilities and $\boldsymbol{C}, \boldsymbol{K}$ are matrices of contrasts and $\boldsymbol{M}$ is a zero-one matrix.

5   Likelihood ratio tests

Let H_G be the hypothesis: $\boldsymbol{C}\ln(\boldsymbol{M}\boldsymbol{\pi}) = \boldsymbol{0}$, stating that an MMC is graphical, and let $H_M : \boldsymbol{C}\ln(\boldsymbol{M}\boldsymbol{\pi}) = \boldsymbol{0}$, $\boldsymbol{K}\ln(\boldsymbol{M}\boldsymbol{\pi}) \geq \boldsymbol{0}$ be the hypothesis of a monotone graphical MMC. Let L_G, L_M and L_U denote the maximum of the log-likelihood functions under the previous constraints and the unrestricted model. Under the assumptions provided by Fahrmeir and Kaufmann (1987) for autoregressive categorical time series, the likelihood ratio test (LRT) statistic $2(L_U - L_G)$ for testing H_G has the classical chi-square asymptotic distribution. In contrast, the statistics $2(L_G - L_M)$ and $2(L_U - L_M)$, for H_M against H_G and H_M against the unrestricted alternative, are asymptotically chi-bar-square distributed (Silvapulle and Sen (2005)). The chi-bar-square distribution is a mixture of chi-square random variables. The asymptotic chi-bar-square distribution follows from the same assumptions of Fahrmeir and Kaufmann (1987) needed for the asymptotic distribution of $2(L_U - L_G)$, and from the fact that the parametric space under the null hypothesis is defined by linear inequality and equality constraints on the model parameters. See Silvapulle and Sen (2005) for the technical details of the maximum likelihood (ML) estimation under inequality constraints. It may be also interesting to test the null hypothesis $H_0 : C \ln(M\pi) = 0$, $K \ln(M\pi) = 0$ against H_M. In this case, the LRT statistic $2(L_M - L_0)$ has a chi-bar-square asymptotic distribution as well. According to Silvapulle and Sen's terminology, testing H_0 against H_M is a testing problem of type A and in this case the alternative hypothesis is specified by inequality constraints. Testing H_M against H_G or H_U is of type B and the inequalities are under the null hypotheses.

The ML estimation methods developed by Cazzaro and Colombi (2009) for multinomial data under equality and inequality constraints are easily adapted to the MMC context of this work. Moreover, Monte Carlo methods can be employed to compute the p-values of the LRT statistics $2(L_G - L_M)$, $2(L_U - L_M)$ and $2(L_M - L_0)$. All the procedures for computing ML estimates and p-values, used in the next example, are implemented in the R-package *hmmm*, Cazzaro and Colombi (2008).

6 Example

The introduced hypotheses are tested on a data set that includes a 3-dimensional binary time series of sales levels (low, high) of three well-known Italian brands (*Amato, Barilla, Divella*) of pasta (*spaghetti*) sold by a wholesale dealer operating in a region of Southern Italy. The data were collected on 365 days in the period between December, 2006 and January, 2009. The sale rate series are reasonably assumed to be modeled by a first order 3-variate Markov chain. One question that arises in managing the sales inventory of pasta is whether the quantity of *spaghetti* sold by one brand depends on the amount of sales of the two competitors on the same day, given the past sales of all brands. Moreover, it is also important to ascertain whether the current sales of one brand of *spaghetti* are influenced by the previous demand for every brand of *spaghetti*. Monotone dependence hypotheses can also be plausible. For example, we can hypothesize that the probability of selling a high amount of *spaghetti* of a certain brand is greater when a large quantity of spaghetti of all three companies has been sold in the past. The answer to these questions can be obtained by testing hypotheses of G-noncausality, contemporaneous independence and stochastic order. This boils down to testing equality and inequality constraints on the interactions which parameterize the transition probabilities of the *spaghetti* Markov chain and to identifying the ME graph which encodes the underlying independence conditions.

To this end, various hypotheses associated with edges of the ME graph $G = (\mathcal{V}, \mathcal{E})$, with one node for each brand of pasta $\mathcal{V} = \{1, 2, 3\}$, have been tested. In short $1, 2, 3$ stand for brands *Amato, Barilla,* and *Divella.* In this example, all the marginal processes have only two states $0, 1$ which correspond to low and high sales level, respectively; thus for every $P \subseteq \{1, 2, 3\}$ and every level $i' = (l, m, n)$, $l = 0, 1$, $m = 0, 1$, $n = 0, 1$, of the past sales, there is only one Gloneck-McCullagh multivariate logistic interaction $\eta^P(i_P|i')$ which will be denoted by $\eta^P(l, m, n)$. According to Proposition 1, the hypothesis of contemporaneous independence $\mathbf{A}_1 \not\leftrightarrow \mathbf{A}_2 \not\leftrightarrow \mathbf{A}_3$ requires that all the interactions $\eta^P(l, m, n)$ are null, except the 24 logits $\eta^j(l, m, n)$, $j \in \{1, 2, 3\}$ which, instead, are to be constrained to satisfy the Granger non-causality and the monotone dependence conditions. The hypothesis of contemporaneous independence can be accepted as $LRT = 34.212$, $df = 32$, $p-value = 0.362$. The graph corresponding to this accepted hypothesis has all the directed edges and no bi-directed edges.

An useful restriction that simplifies considerably the monotone dependence constraints of Proposition 2 is the hypothesis of additivity of the past sale effects on the current sale level. Under this assumption, the logits $\eta^j(l, m, n)$ have the factorial expansion $\eta^j(l, m, n) = \theta^j + \theta_l^{j1} + \theta_m^{j2} + \theta_n^{j3}$ in terms of a general effect and three main effects. The previous main effects are null if their index l, m or n is zero. Note that under this hypothesis, the 24 logits are parameterized by three general effects θ^j and nine main effects θ_1^{ji}, moreover the requirements of Proposition 2 are reduced to simple inequality constraints on the previous main effects. More precisely, assuming additivity, the main effect θ_1^{ji} corresponds bi-univocally to the edge $(i, j]$, and by Proposition 1 it must be null when this edge is missing in the ME graph and positive (negative) if the dependence of $\mathbf{A}_j$ on $\mathbf{A}_i$ is positive (negative) monotone (Proposition 2).

The hypothesis of contemporaneous independence together with additivity can be accepted as $LRT = 44.81$, $df = 44$, $p-value = 0.44$. Then, we add the order-restricted hypothesis that all causal relations are monotone. In particular, the hypothesis that the monotone dependence associated to all the edges is positive except for $(2, 3]$ and $(3, 2]$ which correspond to a negative relation, is not rejected ($LRT = 1.24$, $p-value = 0.86$). These properties impose that the main effects θ_1^{ji} are non-negative when associated with the edges $(1, 1]$, $(2, 2]$, $(3, 3]$, $(2, 1]$, $(1, 2]$, $(1, 3]$ and $(3, 1]$; while the main effects are non-positive when related to $(2, 3]$ and $(3, 2]$. Alternatively, we can proceed by considering that the graph which includes all directed and no bi-directed edges may be simplified since the hypothesis that the edges $(2, 1]$ and $(3, 1]$ can be removed is accepted ($LRT = 4.4$, $df = 2$, $p-value = 0.11$). Therefore, the order-restricted hypotheses may be tested on this reduced graph where $(2, 1]$ and $(3, 1]$ are missing. In this case the hypothesis of monotone dependence of positive type for the edges $(1, 1]$, $(2, 2]$, $(3, 3]$, $(1, 2]$, $(1, 3]$ and negative for $(2, 3]$ and $(3, 2]$ is clearly accepted, in fact $LRT = 0$, $p - value = 1$.

In conclusion, the *spaghetti* Markov chain can be described by a monotone graphical model with respect to the ME graph with edges $(1, 1]$, $(2, 2]$, $(3, 3]$, $(1, 2]$, $(1, 3]$, $(2, 3]$ and $(3, 2]$. This means that the current sales level of *Amato* does not depend on previous sales of either *Divella* or *Barilla*. Moreover, a high level of sales of *Barilla* and *Divella* on one day is more probable when the quantity which *Amato* previously sold was high. On the contrary, given previous high sales level of *Divella spaghetti*, a low level of *Barilla* sales is more probable, and vice versa. Moreover, there is no influence between the contemporaneous sales of all 3 brands, while sales of all brands depend positively on their own previous sales performance.

References

BARTOLUCCI, F. COLOMBI, R. and FORCINA, A. (2007): An extended class of marginal link functions for modelling contingency tables by equality and inequality constraints. *Statistica Sinica, 17, 691-711*.

CAZZARO, M. and COLOMBI, R. (2008): Hierarchical multinomial marginal models: the R package hmmm. *www.unibg.it/pers/?colombi*.

CAZZARO, M. and COLOMBI, R. (2009): Multinomial-Poisson models subject to inequality constraints. *Statistical Modelling, 9(3), 215-233*.

COLOMBI, R. and GIORDANO, S. (2009): Multi edges graphs for multivariate Markov chains. In: J. G. Booth (Eds.): *Proceedings of 24th International Workshop on Statistical Modelling*. Ithaca (NY), 102 – 109.

FAHRMEIR, L. and KAUFMANN, H. (1987): Regression models for nonstationary categorical time series. *Journal of Time Series Analysis, 8(2), 147-160*.

GLONEK, G. J. N. and McCULLAGH, P. (1995): Multivariate logistic models. *Journal of Royal Statistical Society, B, 57, 533-546*.

LUPPARELLI, M., MARCHETTI, G. M. and BERGSMA, W. P. (2009): Parameterization and fitting of discrete bi-directed graph models. *Scandinavian Journal of Statistics, 36, 559-576*.

RICHARSON, T. (2003): Markov properties for acyclic directed mixed graphs. *Scandinavian Journal of Statistics, 30, 145-157*.

SHAKED, M. and SHANTIKUMAR, J. G. (1994): *Stochastic Orders and Their Applications*. MA: Academic Press, Boston.

SILVAPULLE, M. J. and SEN, P. K. (2005): *Constrained Statistical Inference*. Wiley, New-Jersey.

Using Observed Functional Data to Simulate a Stochastic Process via a Random Multiplicative Cascade Model

G. Damiana Costanzo[1], S. De Bartolo[2], F. Dell'Accio[3], and G. Trombetta[3]

[1] Dip. Di Economia e Statistica, UNICAL, Via P. Bucci, 87036 Arcavacata di Rende (CS), Italy, *dm.costanzo@unical.it*
[2] Dip. di Difesa del Suolo *V. Marone*, UNICAL, Via P. Bucci, 87036 Arcavacata di Rende (CS), *samuele.debartolo@unical.it*
[3] Dip. di Matematica, UNICAL, Via P. Bucci, 87036 Arcavacata di Rende (CS), *fdellacc@unical.it, trombetta@unical.it*

Abstract. Considering functional data and an associated binary response, a method based on the definition of special Random Multiplicative Cascades to simulate the underlying stochastic process is proposed. It will be considered a class S of stochastic processes whose realizations are real continuous piecewise linear functions with a constrain on the increment and the family $\mathcal{R}$ of all binary responses Y associated to a process X in S. Considering data from a continuous phenomenon evolving in a time interval $[0, T]$ which can be simulated by a pair $(X, Y) \in S \times \mathcal{R}$, a prediction tool which would make it possible to predict Y at each point of $[0, T]$ is introduced. An application to data from an industrial kneading process is considered.

Keywords: functional data, stochastic process, multiplicative cascade

1 Introduction

When data represent functions or curves it is standard practice in the literature to consider them as paths of a stochastic process $X = \{X_t\}_{t \in [0,T]}$ taking values in a space of functions on some time interval $[0, T]$. *Functional data* has received in recent years considerable interest from researchers and the classical tools from finite multivariate analysis have been adapted to this kind of data. When dealing with functional data a major interest is to develop linear regression and classification methods (see Escabias et al., 2004, 2007, James, 2002, Ratcliffe et al. 2002a, 2002b, Saporta et al., 2007). In particular, when predictors are of functional type (generally, curves or real time functions) and response is a categorical variable Y defining K groups, $K \geq 2$, linear discriminant analysis (LDA) models for functional data are considered. Preda and Saporta (2005) proposed PLS regression in order to perform LDA on functional data. Following this approach, to address the problem of *anticipated prediction* of the outcome at time T of the process in $[0, T]$, in Costanzo *et al.* (2006) we measured the predictive capacity of a LDA for functional data

Y. Lechevallier, G. Saporta (eds.), *Proceedings of COMPSTAT'2010*,
DOI 10.1007/978-3-7908-2604-3_44, © Springer-Verlag Berlin Heidelberg 2010

model on the whole interval $[0, T]$. Then, depending on the quality of prediction, we determined a time $t^* < T$ such that the model considered in $[0, t^*]$ gives similar predictions to that considered in $[0, T]$. We consider here a new approach based on the definition of special Random Multiplicative Cascades (RMC for short) to model the underlying stochastic process. In particular, we consider a class $\mathcal{S}$ of stochastic processes whose realizations are real continuous piecewise linear functions with a constrain on the increment. Let $\mathcal{R}$ be the family of all binary responses Y associated to a process X in $\mathcal{S}$ and consider data from a continuous phenomenon which can be simulated by a pair $(X, Y) \in \mathcal{S} \times \mathcal{R}$, with the same objective of prediction of the binary outcome earlier than the end of the process, we introduce the *adjustement curve* for the binary response Y of the simulated stochastic process X. Such a tool is a decreasing function which would make it possible to predict Y at each point in time before time T. For real industrial processes this curve can be a useful tool for monitoring and predicting the quality of the outcome before completion. The paper is organized as follows. In Sec. 2 we describe our method based on the definition of special RMCs. In Sec. 3 we present the adjustment curve. Finally, in Sec. 4 we illustrate an application.

2   The Random Multiplicative Cascade Model

We start by considering a matrix of data of functional type $FD = \left[x^i\left(t_j\right) \right], i = 1, \ldots L$, $t_j = j \cdot \frac{T}{S}$ for $j = 0, \ldots, S$, where each row represents a continuous curve observed at discrete time $t_j, j = 0, \ldots, S$. Next, we consider the column vector $R = \left(r^i\right)$, $i = 1, \ldots, L$, where r^i is a binary outcome associated to the row $\left(x^i\left(0\right) \ldots x^i\left(t_j\right) \ldots x^i\left(T\right)\right)$ for $i = 1, \ldots, L$; for example $r^i \in \{bad, good\}$. As an example consider the situation depicted in Fig. 1 where dough resistance (density) has been recorded in a time interval $[0, T]$ during the kneading process for each type of flour. The achieved dough resistance in T affects the outcome of the process, that is the quality - good or bad - of the resulting cookies. The obtained curves could be used to predict the quality of cookies made with this dough before completion of the kneading. We assume that the data FD and R jointly arise from a continuous phenomenon which can be simulated by a pair (X, Y), where X is a stochastic process whose realizations are real continuous functions with $\{x(0) : x \in X\} = \left\{x_0^i : i = 1, \ldots, L\right\}$, linear on the intervals $[t_j, t_{j+1}]$, $t_j = j \cdot \frac{T}{S}$ for $j = 0, \ldots, S-1$, with a constraint on the increment, i.e. $|x(t_{j+1}) - x(t_j))| \leq M(x, j)$ for $j = 0, \ldots, S-1$. In the simplest case we can assume that the increment does not exceed a certain mean constant value obtainable from the real data, i.e. $M(x, j) = M$ for each $x \in X, j = 0, \ldots, S-1$. We will denote by $\mathcal{S}$ the class of such stochastic processes, $X = \{X(t)\}_{t \in [0, T]}$ a stochastic process in $\mathcal{S}$, $x = x(t)$ $(t \in [0, T])$ a realization of X. Moreover $\mathcal{R}$ will denote the class of all binary responses Y associated to X. Without loss of generality we can assume $Y \in \{bad, good\}$. We propose a method by means of which X and Y can be realized via RMCs which depend on a certain number of constants (obtained from the data FD and R) and real positive parameters.

A multiplicative cascade is a single process that fragments a set into smaller and smaller components according to a fixed rule and, at the same time, fragments the *measure* of components by another rule. The central role that the multiplicative cascades play in the theory of multifractal measures is well known. The notion of multiplicative cascades was introduced in the statistical theory of turbulence by Kolmogorov (1941) as a phenomenological framework intended to accommodate the intermittency and large fluctuations observed in flows. RMCs have been used as models to compress, infer future evolutions and characterize underlying forces driving the dynamics for a wide variety of other natural phenomena (cfr. Pont et al., 2009) such as rainfall (see Gupta and Waymire, 1993), internet packet traffic (see Resnick at al., 2003), market price (see Mandelbrot, 1998). Recently statistical estimation theory for random cascade models has been investigated by Ossiander and Waymire (2000, 2002). We defined a RMC generating recursively a multifractal measure μ on the family of all dyadic subintervals of the unit interval $[0, 1]$. This measure μ is recursively generated with the cascade that is schemetically depicted in Fig. 2 and fully detailed in (Costanzo et al., 2009). In this section we summarize the main steps of our RMC model and describe how to use it to model a real phenomenon using a pair $(X, Y) \in \mathcal{S} \times \mathcal{R}$. Let us consider the FD matrix of functional data and the vector R of the associated outcome and define sets $B = \{x^i(T) : i = 1, \ldots, L \text{ and } r^i = bad\}$ and $G = \{x^i(T) : i = 1, \ldots, L \text{ and } r^i = good\}$. We assume that $\min(G) > \max(B)$.

Step 1. We use the data FD and R in order to define, among others, the following constants ($|A|$ denotes the number of elements of the set A):

$$q^0 = |G| / (|G| + |B|) \text{ and } 1 - q^0 = |B| / (|G| + |B|),$$

$$p = \left(\max_{i=1,\ldots,L} \left(x^i(T) - x^i(0) \right) - \min_{i=1,\ldots,L} \left(x^i(T) - x^i(0) \right) \right) / \delta,$$

$$\delta = \left(\sum_{i=1}^{L} \sum_{j=1}^{S} |x^i(t_j) - x^i(t_{j-1})| \right) / (LS).$$

In particular q^0 is the ratio between the number of good realizations of the real process - that is the number of those curves whose outcome was good at time T - and the totality of such curves while p determines the number of stages (steps) of the multiplicative cascade.

Step 2. Let (α, β) be a pair of random generated numbers in the square $[10^{-1}, 10] \times [10^{-1}, 10]$. For given α, β and $q \in (0, 1)$ and for each $i \in \{1, \ldots, L\}$, if $r^i = good$ ($r^i = bad$) we start the cascade with $q = q^0$ ($q = 1 - q^0$) by truncating it at the stage p. To the resulting $(p + 1)$-uple of positive integers we associate a *proof of length* $p + 1$ that is a real piecewise linear function with a constrain on the increment which simulates a single row of the matrix FD. For each $i = 1, \ldots, L$ the set E_p of L proofs of lenght $p + 1$ is called an *experiment of size L and length $p + 1$*. Each simulated experiment E_p is rearranged in a matrix $SFD_{\alpha,\beta}$ of experiment data (*simulated functional data*).

Step 3. The closeness of the functional data FD with the simulated functional data $SFD = SFD_{\alpha,\beta}$ evaluated for the same subdivision in K classes $[0, \frac{1}{K}[, \ldots, [\frac{K-1}{K}, 1]$ of $[0, 1]$ in terms of the frequency distribution of the original data $\mathcal{I}_{FD}$ and the corresponding frequency distribution of the simulated data $\mathcal{I}_{SFD_{\alpha,\beta}}$, allows to define the set $\mathcal{E}_{\eta,\theta}$ of all admissible experiments E_p of size L and length $p+1$. The two fixed positive real numbers η and θ provide a measure of the closeness of the simulated experiment to the real data. Admissible experiments E_p can be obtained via the Monte-Carlo method based on the generated random pairs $(\alpha, \beta) \in [10^{-1}, 10] \times [10^{-1}, 10]$.

Step 4. Let $\mathcal{E}_{\eta,\theta}$ be the set of all admissible experiments E_p of size L and length $p + 1$, denote by $S(E_p)$ the set of L piecewise linear interpolant the data in each single row of SFD, we define the stochastic process X as the set $X = \bigcup\limits_{E_p \in \mathcal{E}_{\eta,\theta}} S(E_p)$. The associated binary response $Y : X \to \{bad, good\}$, $Y(s) = Y_{E_p}(s)$ is univocally determined since it does not depend on the particular experiment E_p.

3 The Adjustment Curve for Binary Response of a Simulated Stochastic Process

In Costanzo et al (2009) we introduced the notion of adjustement curve as a predictive tool of the binary outcome of a process. We first introduced the definition of the adjustment curve $\gamma_{a,D} : [0, T] \to [0, 1]$ for the binary outcome R of the functional data FD. We required that for real data the condition $x^i(T) < x^j(T)$ for each $i : r^i = bad$ and $j : r^j = good, i, j = 1, \ldots, L$ is satisfied. That is, we assumed there exist a value $X(T) \in \mathbb{R}$ such that $r^i = bad$ if, and only if, $x^i(T) < X(T)$ and $r^i = good$ if, and only if, $x^i(T) \geq X(T)$ for each $i = 1, \ldots, L$. Let $s_D^i : [0, T] \to \mathbb{R}$ $(i = 1, \ldots, L)$ be the piecewise linear functions whose node-sets are $N^i = \left\{ (j, x^i(t_j)) : t_j = j \cdot \frac{T}{S} \text{ for } j = 0, \ldots, S \right\}$ $(i = 1, \ldots, L)$. We defined:

$$b_D(j) = \max \left\{ x^i(t_j) : i = 1, \ldots, L \text{ and } r^i = bad \right\} \quad (j = 0, \ldots, S) \quad (1)$$

$$g_D(j) = \min \left\{ x^i(t_j) : i = 1, \ldots, L \text{ and } r^i = good \right\} \quad (j = 0, \ldots, S). \quad (2)$$

Let $i \in \{1, \ldots, L\}$ and $r^i = bad$ (or $r^i = good$). The piecewise linear interpolant s_D^i is called adjustable at the time $t \in [0, T]$ (for short $t-adjustable$) if there exists $t_j \geq t$ with $j \in \{0, 1, \ldots, S\}$ such that $s_D^i(t) \geq g_D(t_j)$ (or $s_D^i(t) \leq b_D(t_j)$). The adjustment curve $\gamma_{a,D} : [0, T] \to \mathbb{R}$ for the binary outcome R of the functional data FD is the function

$$\gamma_{a,D}(t) = \frac{\left| \left\{ s_D^i(t) : i = 1, \ldots, L \text{ and } s_D^i(t) \text{ is } t - adjustable \right\} \right|}{L} \quad (t \in [0, T]).$$

Given a set of curves coming from a real continuous process the *adjustment curve* is a decreasing step function which gives the relative frequency of curves adjustable (with respect to the final outcome in T) at each time $t \in [0, T]$. The complementary curve $1 - \gamma_{a,D}(t)$ gives then, at each time, the relative frequency of the curves that are definitively good or bad. Let us observe that by the two data sets (1) and (2) it was possible to deduce the binary response $r^i(t_j)$ associated to $s_D^i, i \in \{1, \ldots, L\}$ at each time $t_j, j = 0, \ldots, S - 1$, before time T; indeed: if $s_D^i(t_j) > b_D(j)$ then $r^i(t_j) = good$ or if $s_D^i(t_j) < g_D(j)$ then $r^i(t_j) = bad$ otherwise $r^i(t_j)$ is not yet definite.

By analogy with the case of real data we can introduce the adjustment curve $\gamma_{a,E_p} : [0, p] \to [0, 1]$ for the binary outcome Y_{E_p} of the admissible experiment $E_p \in \mathcal{E}_{\eta,\theta}$. We first consider the change of variable $\tau = \dfrac{p}{T} \cdot t$ ($t \in [0, T]$) and obtain, for every $E_p \in \mathcal{E}_{\eta,\theta}$, $\gamma_{a,E_p}(t) = \gamma_{a,E_p}(\dfrac{p}{T} \cdot t)(t \in [0, T])$. The set $\{\gamma_{a,E_p} : E_p \in \mathcal{E}_{\eta,\theta}\} = \{\gamma_1, \gamma_2, \ldots, \gamma_N\}$ is finite. We then consider the random experiment "*obtain an admissible experiment E_p*" whose sample space is the **infinite** set $\mathcal{E}_{\eta,\theta}$. We set $\mathcal{E}_{\eta,\theta}^i = \{E_p \in \mathcal{E}_{\eta,\theta} : \gamma_{a,E_p} = \gamma_i\}$ ($i = 1, \ldots, N$). Let ν_i be the frequencies of the curves γ_i ($i = 1, \ldots, N$). We define the *adjustment curve* $\gamma_a : [0, T] \to [0, 1]$ for the binary response Y of the process X as the function $\gamma_a(t) = \sum\limits_{i=1}^{N} \nu_i \gamma_i(t)(t \in [0, T])$. In practice, given a couple $(X, Y) \in \mathcal{S} \times \mathcal{R}$ we can choose a tolerance $\epsilon > 0$ such that, if $E_p^1 = (x_1^1, \ldots, x_L^1)$, $E_p^2 = (x_1^2, \ldots, x_L^2)$ are two admissible experiments such that $\max\limits_{i=1}^{L} \|x_i^1 - x_i^2\|_\infty \leq \epsilon$ (here $\|\cdot\|_\infty$ denotes the usual sup-norm) then E_p^1, E_p^2 can be considered indistinguishable. Therefore X becomes a process with a discrete number of realizations and thus we can assume that for $i = 1, \ldots, N$, $\nu_i = \lim\limits_{n \to \infty} \nu_i^n$, where ν_i^n is the relative frequency of γ_i observed on a sample $(\gamma_1, \ldots, \gamma_n)$ of size n. We set $\gamma_a^n = \sum\limits_{i=1}^{N} \nu_i^n \gamma_i$ ($n = 1, 2, \ldots$). The sequence $\{\gamma_a^n\}$ converges to γ_a on $[0, T]$ and the variance $Var(\gamma_a)$ of the random variable γ_a is less or equal 2. Consequently the classical Monte Carlo method can be used to produce approximations of γ_a with the needed precision.

4 Application

We present an application of our method to a real industrial process; namely we will show how our model can be used to monitor and predict the quality of a product resulting from a kneading industrial process. We will use a sample of data provided by Danone Vitapole Research Department (France). In kneading data from Danone, for a given flour, the resistance of dough is recorded during the first 480 seconds of the kneading process. There are 136 different flours and then 136 different curves or trajectories (functions of time). Each curve is observed in 240 equispaced time points (the same for all flours) of the interval time $[0, 480]$. Depending on its quality, after kneading, the dough is processed to obtain cookies. For each flour the quality of the dough can be *bad* or *good*. The sample we considered contains 44 *bad* and 62 *good* observations. In Fig. 1 grey curves (black curves) are those corresponding to the cookies that were considered of good quality (bad quality) after the end of the kneading process. In order to introduce the adjustment curve, we required that with respect to the end values of the process, we have a clear separation between bad and good curves, that is R must depend only on the values at the time T of the real process (see Sec.3). To meet such condition we introduced the concept of $\epsilon - (m, n)$ separability for two sets by means of which we find the minimum number of bad curves and/or good curves that can be discarded in such way that the ratio q^0 is kept in a prefixed error ϵ. For $\epsilon = 0.05$ we discarded from our analysis eight good curves and six bad curves; the remaining 54 good curves and 38 bad curves are separated in $T = 480$ at the dough resistance's value $c = X(T) = 505$. In Fig. 3 we show one admissible experiment E_p obtained by the method outlined in Sec.2. In order to obtain by application of Monte Carlo Method the adjustment curve γ_a with an error less than 10^{-1} and probability greater than 90% we need to perform $n = 4000$ admissible experiments. In Fig. 4 we depicted the adjustment curve γ_a for the binary response Y of the stochastic process X related to Danone's data. Such curve has been computed on the basis of $n = 1000$ admissible experiment E_p, obtained requesting a value of the χ^2 index less or equal to seven. For each $t \in [0, T]$, the standard deviation is not greather than $0.09 \approx 10^{-1}$. The intervals of one standard deviation from the mean curve value comprise a frequency of adjustment curves of the E_p's admissible experiments which range from a minimum of 65% about - in the time interval between $t = 150$ and $t = 320$ about - to a maximum of 87% about; while in the intervals of two standard deviation, such frequency range between 92% and 97%. These last intervals are illustrated in the figure 4 by the plus and minus signs and they comprise the adjustment curve $\gamma_{a,D}$ of real Danone's data. In such figure we can observe that the simulated process prediction curve gives the same results as the real data one at times near to $t = 186$, which was the same time $t^* < T$ we determined in Costanzo et al. (2006) on the whole interval $[0, 480]$; the average test error rate was of about 0.112 for an average $\overline{AUC}(T) = 0.746$. However, in our case we can observe that after such time and until time $t = 326$ the $\gamma_{a,D}$ gives an adjustment higher than γ_a, which denotes instability for such data since from 65% to 42% of the curves are not yet definitively bad or good. Let us remark that the mean absolute difference between the two curves is 0.06 on the whole time interval, while its value is 0.112 in the time interval $[186, 326]$. Starting from time $t = 330$ γ_a is over $\gamma_{a,D}$ so that such time seems for such data a good time to start to predict. An adjustment value of about $\gamma_a = 0.20$ implies in fact, that bad outcomes at such time has a low probability (0.20) of adjustment before the end of the process and they could be discarded or the process could be modified; while at the same time a good outcome has an high probability $1 - \gamma_a = 0.80$ to remain the same until the end of the process. Further details on the adjustment curve and its interpretation can be found in Costanzo et al. (2009).

5 Conclusion and perspectives

The RMC model proposed in this work is characterized by an intrinsic complexity of the recursive relation generating the cascade structure in terms of multifractal measures. This causes a non immediate (or direct) writing of the partition function and of so called sequence of mass exponents (Feder, 1988). The last is very important since it allows the definition, via Legendre transform, of the generalized fractal dimensions that controls the multi-scaling behaviours of the support of the measures. Works in progress comprise the formulation of such partition function to obtain, if it exists, the multiplicative processes limit and so way define a multifractal spectrum analitically; the validation of the multifractality of a kneading industrial process by means of the analysis of the relative scalings of the observed functional data. For such validation, in accordance to the standards requested by numerical convergence of the multifractal measures we need however of curves constituted by a very high number of data points (Fuchslin et al., 2001).

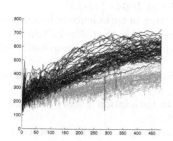

Fig. 1. Danone's data

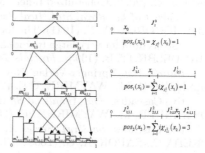

Fig. 2. The first four stages of the multiplicative cascade

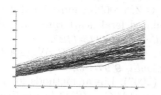

Fig. 3. An admissible experiment E_p

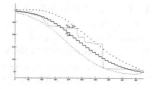

Fig. 4. The adjustment curves of the process and of Danone's data

Acknowledgements. Thanks are due for their support to Food Science & Engineering Interdepartmental Center of University of Calabria and to L.I.P.A.C., Calabrian Laboratory of Food Process Engineering (Regione Calabria APQ-Ricerca Scientifica e Innovazione Tecnologica I atto integrativo, Azione 2 laboratori pubblici di ricerca mission oriented interfiliera).

References

COSTANZO, G. D., PREDA, C., SAPORTA, G. (2006): Anticipated Prediction in Discriminant Analysis on Functional Data for binary response. In: Rizzi, A., Vichi, M. (eds.) *COMPSTAT'2006 Proceedings*, pp. 821-828. Springer, Heidelberg.

COSTANZO, G. D., DELL'ACCIO, F., TROMBETTA, G. (2009): Adjustment curves for binary responses associated to stochastic processes. *Dipartimento di Economia e Statistica, Working paper n. 17, Anno 2009*, submitted.

ESCABIAS, A.M., AGUILERA, A. M. and VALDERRAMA, M.J. (2004): Principal component estimation of functional logistic regression: discussion of two different approaches. *Journal of Nonparametric Statistics 16:365-384*.

ESCABIAS, A.M., AGUILERA, A. M. and VALDERRAMA, M.J. (2007): Functional PLS logit regression model. *Computational Statistics and Data Analysis 51:4891-4902*.

FEDER, J. (1988): *Fractals*. Plenum.

FUCHSLIN, R.M., SHEN, Y. and MEIER, P.F. (2001): An efficient algorithm to determine fractal dimensions of points sets. *Physics Letters A, 285, pp. 69-75*.

GUPTA, V.K., WAYMIRE, E. (1993): A statistical analysis of mesoscale rainfall as a random cascade. *J. Appl. Meteor. 32:251-267*.

JAMES, G. (2002) Generalized Linear Models with Functional Predictor Variables, *Journal of the Royal Statistical Society Series B 64: 411-432*.

KOLMOGOROV, A. N. (1941): The local structure of turbulence in incompressible viscous fluid for very large Reynolds number. *Dokl. Akad. Nauk SSSR 30 :9-13*.

MANDELBROT, B. (1998): *Fractals and scaling in finance: Discontinuity, concentration, risk*. Springer-Verlag, New York.

OSSIANDER, M., WAYMIRE, C.E. (2000): Statistical Estimation for Multiplicative Cascades. *The Annals od Statistics, 28(6):1533-1560*.

OSSIANDER, M., WAYMIRE, C.E. (2002): On Estimation Theory for Multiplicative Cascades. *Sankhyā, Series A, 64:323-343*.

PREDA C., SAPORTA, G. (2005): PLS regression on a stochastic process. *Computational Satistics and Data Analysis, 48:149-158*.

RATCLIFFE, S.J., LEADER, L.R., and HELLER G.Z. (2002a): Functional data analysis with application to periodically stimulated fetal heart rate data: I. Functional regression. *Statistics in Medicine 21:1103-1114*.

RATCLIFFE, S.J., LEADER, L.R., and HELLER G.Z. (2002b): Functional data analysis with application to periodically stimulated fetal heart rate data: II. Functional logistic regression. *Statistics in Medicine 21:1115-1127*.

RESNICK, S., SAMORODNITSKY, G., GILBERT, A., WILLINGER, W. (2003): Wavelet analysis of conservative cascades. *Bernoulli, 9:97-135*.

SAPORTA, G., COSTANZO, G. D., PREDA, C., (2007): Linear methods for regression and classification with functional data. In: *IASC-ARS'07 Proceedings, Special Conf., Seoul, 2007* (ref. CEDRIC 1234):

A Clusterwise Center and Range Regression Model for Interval-Valued Data

Francisco de A. T. de Carvalho[1], Gilbert Saporta[2], and Danilo N. Queiroz[1]

[1] Centro de Informática - CIn/UFPE
    Av. Prof. Luiz Freire, s/n - Cidade Universitária, CEP 50740-540, Recife-PE,
    Brazil {fatc,dnq}@cin.ufpe.br
[2] Chaire de statistique appliquée & CEDRIC, CNAM
    292 rue Saint Martin, Paris, France, gilbert.saporta@cnam.fr

Abstract. This paper aims to adapt clusterwise regression to interval-valued data. The proposed approach combines the dynamic clustering algorithm with the center and range regression method for interval-valued data in order to identify both the partition of the data and the relevant regression models, one for each cluster. Experiments with a car interval-valued data set show the usefulness of combining both approaches.

Keywords: clusterwise regression, interval-valued data, symbolic data analysis

1 Introduction

There is a large amount of publications on symbolic interval-valued data (see Billard and Diday (2007)). Symbolic interval-valued data occur in two contexts: either when one has uncertainty on individual values, or when one has variation like eg in medical data such as blood pressure, pulse rate observed on a daily time period. We will consider here only the second case.

Several methods have been proposed to deal with the case where the response y as well as the predictors are interval-valued variables. We will use the centre and range method proposed by Lima Neto and De Carvalho (2008). Assuming that data are homogeneous (ie there is only one regression model for the whole data set) can be misleading. Clusterwise regression has been proposed long ago, as a way to identify both the partition of the data and the relevant regression models, one for each class. Clusterwise regression may be viewed as a particular mixture or latent class model, or from a data analytic perspective as a combination of cluster and regression analysis.

In this paper we adapt clusterwise regression to interval-valued data. The paper is organized as follows. Section 2.1 presents approaches for interval data regression, section 2.2 is a short presentation of clusterwise regression. Section 3 presents how clusterwise regression is extended to interval data. Section 4 presents experiments with a car interval-valued data set in order to show the usefulness of combining both approaches. Finally, section 5 gives concluding remarks.

Y. Lechevallier, G. Saporta (eds.), *Proceedings of COMPSTAT'2010*,
DOI 10.1007/978-3-7908-2604-3_45, © Springer-Verlag Berlin Heidelberg 2010

2   A Brief Overview of Regression for Interval-Valued Data and Clusterwise Linear Regression

2.1   Regression for Interval Data

Billard and Diday (2000) considered the center method where one fits a regression model to the mid-points of the intervals. They predict the bounds of y by applying the model for the centers to the upper bounds of the predictors (resp. the lower bounds). The same model is thus applied to predict the centers and the (upper and lower) bounds. The MinMax method (Billard and Diday (2002)) consists in fitting two different regressions, one for all upper bounds, the other for all lower bounds.

Recently Lima Neto and de Carvalho (2008) presented the *"center and range method"*: in short, this method consists of fitting two linear models, one for the centers of the intervals, another one for the range. The prediction for a new example is given by the prediction of the center ± the half of the predicted range. In their paper, Lima Neto and de Carvalho (2008) proved with extensive simulations the superiority of the last method compared to the centre and the MinMax method, and it is why we will use it in the following.

2.2   Clusterwise Linear Regression

Clusterwise linear regression is a useful technique when heterogeneity is present in the data. It is a mix of cluster analysis and regression where clusters are obtained in a supervised way in order that for each cluster we have the "best" regression model.

This "local" regression model may also be viewed as a particular mixture model (Wayne et al 1988 and Hennig 2000) who used maximum likelihood estimation. Clusterwise linear regression has been also analyzed in a fuzzy framework (D'Urso and Santoro (2006)). We focus here on least squares techniques. In the basic model the number of clusters is supposed to be known.

Let y be a response variable and $\mathbf{x}$ a p-dimensional vector of regressors. From an algorithmic point of view the aim is to find simultaneously an optimal partition of the data in K clusters, $1 < K < n$ and K regression vectors $\beta_{(k)}$ $(1 < k < K)$ one for each cluster such that one maximizes the overall fit or minimize the sum of squared residuals:

$$\sum_{k=1}^{K} \sum_{i \in P_k} \left(\epsilon_{i(k)} \right)^2$$

where P_k is the kth cluster, $\hat{y}_{i(k)}$ is the prediction of y (assuming $i \in P_k$) and

$$y_i = (\mathbf{x}_i)^T \beta_{(k)} + \epsilon_{i(k)} = \sum_{j=1}^{p} \beta_{j(k)} x_i j + \epsilon_{i(k)} = \hat{y}_{i(k)} + \epsilon_{i(k)}$$

Numerous algorithms have been proposed to solve this problem: some use combinatorial optimisation techniques like Spaeth (1979) who proposes an exchange algorithm. We will use here the special case of k-means clustering which has been proposed by Diday and Simon (1976) and Bock (1989) and belongs to the family of alternated least squares techniques:

Step 1: Starting from an initial partition, one estimates separately a regression model for each cluster.

Step 2: Each observation is moved to the cluster (or model) giving the smallest square residual (i.e, the best prediction). Once all observations have been reclassified, we obtain a new partition.

Step 1 and 2 are then iterated until convergence (i.e, stability of the partition), or when the criterium does not decrease enough. It is necessary to have enough observations in each cluster (Charles (1977)) in order to estimate the regression coefficients by OLS. Like in k-means clustering, it is possible that some clusters become empty and that the final number of clusters may be less than the initial guess K. Choice of K remains difficult: some have advocated for AIC or BIC- like criteria (Plaia 2001)). From a empirical machine learning point of view, K should be chosen by some validation technique (cross-validation, bootstrap. etc.). The existence of many local minima have been stressed by Caporossi and Hansen (2007): this implies to choose wisely the starting partition.

3   Clusterwise regression on interval-valued data

This section presents a clusterwise regression model based on both the dynamic clustering algorithm (Diday and Simon (1976)) and the center and range regression model for interval-valued data (Lima Neto and De Carvalho (2008)).

Let $E = \{1, \ldots, n\}$ be a set of observations that are described by $p + 1$ interval-valued variables $z, w_1, \ldots, w_p$. Each observation $i \in E$ $(i = 1, \ldots, n)$ is represented by a vector of intervals $\mathbf{e}_i = (w_{i1}, \ldots, w_{ip}, z_i)$, where $w_{ij} = [w_{ij}^L, w_{ij}^U]$ $(j = 1, \ldots, p)$ and $z_i = [z_i^L, z_i^U]$.

Let $\mathbf{y}$ and $\mathbf{x}_j$ $(j = 1, \ldots, p)$ be, respectively, quantitative bi-variate variables that assume as their values the midpoints and half ranges of the interval assumed by the interval-valued variables z and w_j. Thus, each observation $i \in E$ $(i = 1, \ldots, n)$ is also represented as a vector of bi-variate quantitative vectors $\mathbf{t}_i = (\mathbf{x}_{i1}, \ldots, \mathbf{x}_{ip}, \mathbf{y}_i)$, with

$$\mathbf{x}_{ij} = \begin{pmatrix} x_{ij}^c \\ x_{ij}^r \end{pmatrix} (j = 1, \ldots, p) \text{ and } \mathbf{y}_i = \begin{pmatrix} y_i^c \\ y_i^r \end{pmatrix}$$

where $x_{ij}^c = (w_{ij}^L + w_{ij}^U)/2$, $x_{ij}^r = (w_{ij}^U - w_{ij}^L)/2$, $y_i^c = (z_i^L + z_i^U)/2$ and $y_i^r = (z_i^U - z_i^L)/2$.

This clusterwise regression model for interval-valued data looks for a partition of E in K clusters $P_1, \ldots, P_K$, each cluster being represented by a prototype, such that an adequacy criterion measuring the fit between the clusters and their prototypes are locally minimized. The particularity of this kind of method is that the prototype of each cluster is represented by the hyper-plane given by the linear regression relationship between the dependent variable and the independent predictor variables:

$$\mathbf{y}_{i(k)} = \boldsymbol{\beta}_{0(k)} + \sum_{j=1}^{p} \boldsymbol{\beta}_{j(k)} \mathbf{x}_{ij} + \boldsymbol{\epsilon}_{i(k)} \ (\forall i \in P_k) \qquad \text{where} \qquad (1)$$

$$\boldsymbol{\beta}_{0(k)} = \begin{pmatrix} \beta^c_{0(k)} \\ \beta^r_{0(k)} \end{pmatrix}, \quad \boldsymbol{\beta}_{j(k)} = \begin{pmatrix} \beta^c_{j(k)} & 0 \\ 0 & \beta^r_{j(k)} \end{pmatrix} \ (j = 1, \ldots, p) \qquad \text{and}$$

$$\boldsymbol{\epsilon}_{i(k)} = \begin{pmatrix} \epsilon^c_{i(k)} \\ \epsilon^r_{i(k)} \end{pmatrix} = \begin{pmatrix} y^c_i - \left(\beta^c_{0(k)} + \sum_{j=1}^{p} \beta^c_{j(k)} x^c_{ij} \right) \\ y^r_i - \left(\beta^r_{0(k)} + \sum_{j=1}^{p} \beta^r_{j(k)} x^r_{ij} \right) \end{pmatrix} \ (\forall i \in P_k)$$

The adequacy criterion is defined as:

$$J = \sum_{k=1}^{K} \sum_{i \in P_k} (\boldsymbol{\epsilon}_{i(k)})^T \boldsymbol{\epsilon}_{ik} = \sum_{k=1}^{K} \sum_{i \in P_k} \left[(\epsilon^c_{i(k)})^2 + (\epsilon^r_{i(k)})^2 \right] \qquad (2)$$

$$= \sum_{k=1}^{K} \sum_{i \in P_k} \left\{ \left[y^c_i - \left(\beta^c_{0(k)} + \sum_{j=1}^{p} \beta^c_{j(k)} x^c_{ij} \right) \right]^2 + \left[y^r_i - \left(\beta^r_{0(k)} + \sum_{j=1}^{p} \beta^r_{j(k)} x^r_{ij} \right) \right]^2 \right\}$$

This algorithm sets an initial partition and alternates two steps until convergence when the criterion J reaches a local minimum.

3.1   Step 1: definition of the best prototypes

In the first stage, the partition of E in K clusters is fixed.

Proposition 1. *The prototype*

$$\hat{\mathbf{y}}_{i(k)} = \begin{pmatrix} \hat{y}^c_{i(k)} \\ \hat{y}^r_{i(k)} \end{pmatrix} = \begin{pmatrix} \hat{\beta}^c_{0(k)} + \sum_{j=1}^{p} \hat{\beta}^c_{j(k)} x^c_{ij} \\ \hat{\beta}^r_{0(k)} + \sum_{j=1}^{p} \hat{\beta}^r_{j(k)} x^r_{ij} \end{pmatrix} \ (\forall i \in P_k)$$

of cluster P_k $(k = 1, \ldots, K)$ has the least square estimates of the parameters $\hat{\beta}^c_{j(k)}$ and $\hat{\beta}^r_{j(k)}$ $(j = 0, 1, \ldots, p)$, which minimizes the clustering criterion J, given by the solution of the system of $2(p+1)$ equations:

$$\hat{\boldsymbol{\beta}} = \left(\hat{\beta}^c_{0(k)}, \hat{\beta}^c_{1(k)}, \ldots, \hat{\beta}^c_{p(k)}, \hat{\beta}^r_{0(k)}, \hat{\beta}^r_{1(k)}, \ldots, \hat{\beta}^r_{p(k)} \right)^T = (\mathbf{A})^{-1} \mathbf{b} \qquad (3)$$

where $\mathbf{A}$ is a matrix $2(p+1) \times 2(p+1)$ and $\mathbf{b}$ is a vector $2(p+1) \times 1$, denoted as:

$$\mathbf{A} = \begin{pmatrix} |P_k| & \sum_{i \in P_k} x_{i1}^c & \cdots & \sum_{i \in P_k} x_{ip}^c & 0 & 0 & \cdots & 0 \\ \sum_{i \in P_k} x_{i1}^c & \sum_{i \in P_k} (x_{i1}^c)^2 & \cdots & \sum_{i \in P_k} x_{ip}^c x_{i1}^c & 0 & 0 & \cdots & 0 \\ \vdots & \vdots & \vdots & \vdots & \vdots & \vdots & \vdots & \vdots \\ \sum_{i \in P_k} x_{ip}^c & \sum_{i \in P_k} x_{i1}^c x_{ip}^c & \cdots & \sum_{i \in P_k} (x_{ip}^c)^2 & 0 & 0 & \cdots & 0 \\ 0 & 0 & \cdots & 0 & |P_k| & \sum_{i \in P_k} x_{i1}^r & \cdots & \sum_{i \in P_k} x_{ip}^r \\ 0 & 0 & \cdots & 0 & \sum_{i \in P_k} x_{i1}^r & \sum_{i \in P_k} (x_{i1}^r)^2 & \cdots & \sum_{i \in P_k} x_{ip}^r x_{i1}^r \\ \vdots & \vdots & \vdots & \vdots & \vdots & \vdots & \vdots & \vdots \\ 0 & 0 & \cdots & 0 & \sum_{i \in P_k} x_{ip}^r & \sum_{i \in P_k} x_{i1}^r x_{ip}^r & \cdots & \sum_{i \in P_k} (x_{ip}^r)^2 \end{pmatrix}$$

$$\mathbf{b} = \left(\sum_{i \in P_k} y_i^c, \sum_{i \in P_k} y_i^c x_{i1}^c, \ldots, \sum_{i \in P_k} y_i^c x_{ip}^c, \sum_{i \in P_k} y_i^r, \sum_{i \in P_k} y_i^r x_{i1}^r, \ldots, \sum_{i \in P_k} y_i^r x_{ip}^r \right)^T$$

3.2   Step 2: definition of the best partition

In this step, the prototypes $\hat{\mathbf{y}}_{i(k)}$ ($k = 1, \ldots, K$) are fixed.

Proposition 2. *The optimal clusters P_k ($k = 1, \ldots, K$), which minimize the criterion J, are obtained according to the following allocation rule:*

$$P_k = \{i \in E : (\boldsymbol{\epsilon}_{i(k)})^T \boldsymbol{\epsilon}_{i(k)} \leq (\boldsymbol{\epsilon}_{i(h)})^T \boldsymbol{\epsilon}_{i(h)}, \forall h \neq k \, (h = 1, \ldots, K)\} \quad (4)$$

Given a new observation $\mathbf{e} = (w_1, \ldots, w_p, z)$ described by the vector of bivariate quantitative vectors $\mathbf{t} = (\mathbf{x}_1, \ldots, \mathbf{x}_p, \mathbf{y})$, the interval $z = [z^L, z^U]$ is predicted from the estimated bivariate vector $\hat{\mathbf{y}}_{(k)} = (\hat{y}_{(k)}^c, \hat{y}_{(k)}^r)$ ($k = 1, \ldots, K$), as follows

$$\hat{z}_{(k)}^L = \hat{y}_{(k)}^c - \hat{y}_{(k)}^r \text{ and } \hat{z}_{(k)}^U = \hat{y}_{(k)}^c + \hat{y}_{(k)}^r$$

where $\hat{y}_{(k)}^c = \hat{\beta}_{0(k)}^c + \sum_{j=1}^p \hat{\beta}_{j(k)}^c x_j^c$ and $\hat{y}_{(k)}^r = \hat{\beta}_{0(k)}^r + \sum_{j=1}^p \hat{\beta}_{j(k)}^r x_j^r$.

"Goodness-of-fit measures" (determination coefficients) for these cluster-wise regression models are computed, for k=1,...,K, as:

$$R_{c(k)}^2 = \frac{\sum\limits_{i \in P_k} \left(\hat{y}_{i(k)}^c - \bar{y}_{c(k)} \right)^2}{\sum\limits_{i \in P_k} \left(y_i^c - \bar{y}_{c(k)} \right)^2} \; ; \; R_{r(k)}^2 = \frac{\sum\limits_{i \in P_k} \left(\hat{y}_{i(k)}^r - \bar{y}_{r(k)} \right)^2}{\sum\limits_{i \in P_k} \left(y_i^r - \bar{y}_{r(k)} \right)^2} \quad (5)$$

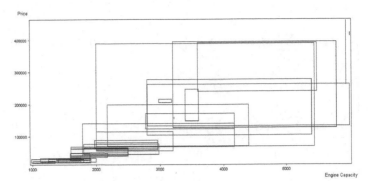

Fig. 1. The car interval-valued data set.

where $\bar{y}_{c(k)} = \sum_{i \in P_k} y_i^c/n$, $\bar{y}_{r(k)} = \sum_{i \in P_k} y_i^r/n$ and $R^2_{c(k)}$, $R^2_{r(k)}$ are, respectively, the determination coefficient of "center" and "range" models.

Other measures, in order to obtain the performance assessment of these linear regression models, are the lower ($RMSE_L$) and the upper ($RMSE_U$) boundaries root-mean-square error. They are computed as

$$RMSE_L = \sqrt{\frac{\sum_{i=1}^{n} \left(z_i^L - \hat{z}_i^L\right)^2}{n}} \; ; \; RMSE_U = \sqrt{\frac{\sum_{i=1}^{n} \left(z_i^U - \hat{z}_i^U\right)^2}{n}} \qquad (6)$$

4   Application: a car interval-valued data set

The car data set[1] (Figure 1) consists of a set of 33 car models described by 2 interval-valued variables: price y and engine capacity x_1. The aim is to predict the interval values of y (the dependent variable) from x_1 through linear regression models. In this application, the 2 interval-valued variables – Price and Engine Capacity –, have been considered for clustering purposes. The clusterwise regression algorithm has been performed on this data set in order to obtain a partition in $K = \{1, 2, 3\}$ clusters. For a fixed number of clusters K, the clustering algorithm is run 100 times and the best result according to the adequacy criterion is selected.

Table 1 presents the regression equations fitted over the car interval-valued data set. Table 2 gives the determination coefficients for the 1-cluster, 2-cluster and 3-cluster partitions.

In order to obtain a better preditive model, the estimates of the K regression models given by the K-cluster partition ($K = 1, 2, 3$), obtained with this algorithm, were combined according to the "stacked regressions" approach. According to Breiman (1996), this approach uses cross validation data and

[1] This   data   set   is   available   with   the   SODAS   software   at
http://www.info.fundp.ac.be/asso/index.html.

Table 1. Fitted regression equations over the whole car interval-valued data set

K − partition	cluster k	"Center Model"	"Range Model"
1	1	$\hat{y}^c_{(1)} = -98840.9 + 79.2\,x^c_1$	$\hat{y}^r_{(1)} = -341.4 + 60.9\,x^r_1$
2	1	$\hat{y}^c_{(1)} = -63462.2 + 59.6\,x^c_1$	$\hat{y}^r_{(1)} = -4560.1 + 47.1\,x^r_1$
	2	$\hat{y}^c_{(2)} = -22836.5 + 68.8\,x^c_1$	$\hat{y}^r_{(2)} = 34563.6 + 68.6\,x^r_1$
3	1	$\hat{y}^c_{(1)} = -77422.1 + 82.0\,x^c_1$	$\hat{y}^r_{(1)} = 2229.7 + 92.2\,x^r_1$
	2	$\hat{y}^c_{(2)} = -58484.1 + 71.1\,x^c_1$	$\hat{y}^r_{(2)} = 101952.9 - 546.7\,x^r_1$
	3	$\hat{y}^c_{(3)} = -73362.1 + 62.0\,x^c_1$	$\hat{y}^r_{(3)} = -9755.9 + 53.2\,x^r_1$

Table 2. Determination coefficients for the fitted regression equations over the whole car interval-valued data set

K-partition	1	2		3		
cluster k	1	1	2	1	2	3
$R^2_{c(k)}$	0.93	0.95	0.91	0.97	0.99	0.98
$R^2_{r(k)}$	0.53	0.79	0.66	0.98	0.98	0.83

least squares under non-negativity constraints for forming linear combinations of different predictors to give improved prediction accuracy.

The car interval-valued data set $\mathcal{L}$ was partitioned into 10 folds $\mathcal{L}_{(j)}$ ($j = 1, \ldots, 10$) of size as nearly equal as possible. For a fixed number of clusters K, the clustering algorithm is run 100 times on 9 folds $\mathcal{L}^{(j)} = \mathcal{L} - \mathcal{L}_{(j)}$ and the best result according to the adequacy criterion is selected. The K regression models are used to give preditions for the lower and upper boundary of the dependent variable on the $\mathcal{L}^{(j)}$ learning data set. These predictions were combined according to the "stacked regressions" approach to obtain the predictions for the observations belonging to the test data set $\mathcal{L}_{(j)}$. The $RMSE_L$ and $RMSE_U$ measures are computed from the predicted values on the test data sets $\mathcal{L}_{(j)}$ ($j = 1, \ldots, 10$).

This process is repeated 100 times and it is calculated the average and standard deviation of the $RMSE_L$ and $RMSE_U$ measures (Table 3). Even if the observed mean differences are not statistically significant, we can conclude that 2 regression models given by the 2-cluster partition give the best preditive model through the "stacked regressions" approach.

Table 3. Average Root-mean-square error for the combined estimates of the K regression models

K-partition	1	2	3
$RMSE_L$	96649.28 (13812.49)	90417.42 (13538.22)	94993.75 (11376.24)
$RMSE_U$	143416.6 (17294.02)	135471.4 (17027.49)	137825.9 (14243.29)

5 Concluding Remarks

This paper introduced a suitable clusterwise regression model for interval-valued data. The proposed model combines the dynamic clustering algorithm with the center and range regression model for interval-valued data in order to identify both the partition of the data and the relevant regression models (one for each cluster). Experiments with a car interval-valued data set showed the interest of this approach. Other experiments on medical data sets are in progress.

References

BILLARD, L. and DIDAY, E. (2000): Regression Analysis for Interval-Valued Data. In: H.A.L. Kiers, J.P. Rasson, P.J.F. Groenen and M. Schader (Eds.): *Data Analysis, Classification and Related Methods*. Springer, Berlin, 369–374.

BILLARD, L. and DIDAY, E. (2007): *Symbolic Data Analysis: Conceptual Statistics and Data Mining*. Wiley-Interscience, San Francisco.

BILLARD, L. and DIDAY, E. (2002): Symbolic Regression Analysis. In: K. Jajuga, A. Sokolowski and H.-H. Bock (Eds.): *Classification, Clustering, and Data Analysis. Recent Advances and Applications*. Springer, Berlin, 281–288.

BOCK, H.-H. (1989): The equivalence of two extremal problems and its application to the iterative classification of multivariate data. *Lecture* note. Mathematisches Forschungsinstitut Oberwolfach.

BREIMAN, L. (1996): Stacked Regressions. *Machine Learning 24, 49–64*.

CAPAROSSI, G. and HANSEN, P. (2007): Variable Neighborhood Search for Least Squares Clusterwise Regression. *Les Cahiers du GERAD, G 2005-61*. HEC Montréal

CHARLES, C. (1977): Régression typologique et reconnaissance des formes. *Thèse de doctorat* Université Paris IX.

DIDAY, E. and SIMON, J.C. (1976): Clustering analysis. In: K.S. Fu (Eds.): *Digital Pattern Classification*. Springer, Berlin, 47–94.

D'URSO, P. and SANTORO, A. (2006): Fuzzy clusterwise linear regression analysis with symmetrical fuzzy output variable. *Computational Statistics and Data Analysis, 51 (1): 287–313*.

GONZÁLEZ-RODRIGUES, G., BLANCO, A., CORRAL, N. and COLUBI, A. (2007): Least squares estimation of linear regression models for convex compact random sets. *Advances in Data Analysis and Classification 1, 67–81*.

HENNIG, C. (2000): Identifiability of models for clusterwise linear regression. *J. Classification 17 (2), 273–296*.

LIMA NETO, E. A. and DE CARVALHO, F.A.T. (2008): Centre and Range method for fitting a linear regression model to symbolic interval data. *Computational Statistics and Data Analysis, 52 (3): 1500–1515*.

PLAIA, A. (2001): On the number of clusters in clusterwise linear regression. In: *Xth International Symposium on Applied Stochastic Models and Data Analysis, Proceedings, vol. 2*. Compiegne, France, 847–852.

SPAETH, H. (1979): Clusterwise Linear Regression. *Computing 22 (4), 367–373*.

WAYNE, S., DESARBO, W.S. and CRON, W.L. (1988): A maximum likelihood methodology for clusterwise linear regression. *J. Classification 5 (2), 249–282*.

Contributions to Bayesian Structural Equation Modeling

Séverine Demeyer[1][2], Nicolas Fischer[1], and Gilbert Saporta[2]

[1] LNE, Laboratoire National de Métrologie et d'Essais
    29 avenue Roger Hennequin, 78197 Trappes, France, *severine.demeyer@lne.fr*
[2] Chaire de statistique appliquée & CEDRIC, CNAM
    292 rue Saint Martin, Paris, France

Abstract. Structural equation models (SEMs) are multivariate latent variable models used to model causality structures in data. A Bayesian estimation and validation of SEMs is proposed and identifiability of parameters is studied. The latter study shows that latent variables should be standardized in the analysis to ensure identifiability. This heuristics is in fact introduced to deal with complex identifiability constraints. To illustrate the point, identifiability constraints are calculated in a marketing application, in which posterior draws of the constraints are derived from the posterior conditional distributions of parameters.

Keywords: structural equation modeling, Bayesian statistics, Gibbs sampling, latent variables, identifiability

1 Structural equation models

1.1 Context

Structural equation models (SEMs) are multivariate latent variable models used to represent latent structures of causality in data. The observed (manifest) variables are associated with latent variables in the outer (measurement) model and causality links are assumed between latent variables in the inner (structural) model. This situation typically arises with satisfaction surveys as illustrated in section 3 where the observed variables are the questions and the latent variables are loyalty, satisfaction and image as in figure 2.

1.2 Model

Denoting Y_i the row vector of observed values for individual i on the p manifest variables and Z_i the row vector of scores of individual i on the q latent variables, the measurement model is expressed as

$$Y_i = Z_i\theta + E_i, \, 1 \leq i \leq n \tag{1}$$

where E_i is the measurement error term distributed $E_i \sim \mathcal{N}(0, \Sigma_\varepsilon)$ with Σ_ε diagonal and θ is the $q \times p$ matrix of regression coefficients.

Y. Lechevallier, G. Saporta (eds.), *Proceedings of COMPSTAT'2010*,
DOI 10.1007/978-3-7908-2604-3_46, © Springer-Verlag Berlin Heidelberg 2010

If Z_i were known, the measurement model (1) would reduce to a linear regression model.

Denoting H_i the endogenous latent variables and Ξ_i the exogeneous latent variables, the structural equations are equivalently given by the following expressions

$$H_i = H_i \Pi + \Xi_i \Gamma + \Delta_i$$
$$H_i = Z_i \Lambda + \Delta_i \qquad \Lambda^t = \left(\Pi^t \ \Gamma^t \right) \qquad (2)$$
$$\Pi_0^t H_i = \Gamma^t \Xi_i + \Delta_i \qquad \Pi_0 = Id - \Pi$$

where Π is the $q_1 \times q_1$ matrix of regression coefficients between endogeneous latent variables , Γ is the $q_2 \times q_1$ matrix of regression coefficients between endogeneous and exogeneous latent variables. Δ_i is the error term distributed $\Delta_i \sim \mathcal{N}(0, \Sigma_\delta)$, independent with Ξ_i and Ξ_i is distributed $\mathcal{N}(0, \Phi)$.

1.3   The role of latent variables and identifiability constraints

Basically LV are unidimensional concepts, measured on manifest variables (usually on different scales). They provide practitioners with useful unobserved information on individuals. Since latent variables are not observed they are unscaled. Unlike Palomo et al. (2007) who advocate a free mean and variance model for latent variables, this paper aims to prove that latent variables should be standardized in the run of the analysis, for identifiability concerns, see section 2.6 for a brief overview. This standardization step is showed to be an heuristics leading to the improved Gibbs sampling algorithm presented in section 2.4.

2   Bayesian estimation of SEM

2.1   Bayesian estimation

In the latent variable model defined by equations (1) and (2), well-known techniques of data augmentation and imputation, see Tanner and Wong (1987), are implemented in a Gibbs algorithm (see section 2.4) under normality and conjugacy assumptions. See Box and Tiao (1973) for calculations in multivariate Normal models and Gelman et al.(2004) for Gibbs sampling.

2.2   Conditional posterior distribution of latent variables

Let $\Theta = \{\theta, \Sigma_\varepsilon, \Pi_0, \Gamma, \Sigma_\delta, \Phi\}$. The conditional posterior distribution of the latent variables is expressed as

$$[Z_i | Y_i, \Theta] \propto [Y_i | Z_i, \Theta] [Z_i | \Theta]$$
$$\propto [Y_i | Z_i, \theta, \Sigma_\varepsilon] [Z_i | \Pi_0, \Gamma, \Sigma_\delta, \Phi] \qquad (3)$$
$$\propto [Y_i | Z_i, \theta, \Sigma_\varepsilon] [H_i | \Xi_i, \Pi_0, \Gamma, \Sigma_\delta] [\Xi_i | \Phi]$$

where $[Y_i|Z_i, \theta, \Sigma_\varepsilon]$ is the likelihood of individual i computed from the measurement model (1) and $[Z_i|\Pi_0, \Gamma, \Sigma_\delta]$ is the joint prior distribution of latent variables deduced from the structural equations (2)

$$Z_i|\Pi_0, \Gamma, \Sigma_\delta, \Phi \sim \mathcal{N}(0, \Sigma_Z) \tag{4}$$

$$\Sigma_Z = \begin{pmatrix} (\Pi_0^t)^{-1}(\Gamma^t\Phi\Gamma + \Sigma_\delta)\Pi_0^{-1} & (\Pi_0^t)^{-1}\Gamma^t\Phi \\ \Phi\Gamma\Pi_0^{-1} & \Phi \end{pmatrix} \tag{5}$$

Immediate computation gives

$$Z_i|Y_i, \theta, \Sigma_\varepsilon, \Lambda, \Sigma_\delta, \Phi \sim \mathcal{N}(D\theta\Sigma_\varepsilon^{-1}Y_i, D) \tag{6}$$

where $D^{-1} = \theta\Sigma_\varepsilon^{-1}\theta^t + \Sigma_Z^{-1}$.

2.3   Conditional posterior distributions of parameters

The conditional posterior distribution of parameters is expressed as

$$\begin{aligned}[\Theta|Y, Z] &\propto [Y, Z|\Theta][\Theta] \\ &\propto [Y|Z, \theta, \Sigma_\varepsilon][\theta, \Sigma_\varepsilon][H|\Xi, \Lambda, \Sigma_\delta][\Lambda, \Sigma_\delta][\Xi|\Phi][\Phi]\end{aligned} \tag{7}$$

where prior independance between inner and outer parameters is assumed.

The last expression implies that the posterior distributions of parameters can be computed separately from the following expressions

$$\begin{aligned} [\theta, \Sigma_\varepsilon|Y, Z] &= [Y|Z, \theta, \Sigma_\varepsilon][\theta, \Sigma_\varepsilon] \\ [\Lambda, \Sigma_\delta|Y, Z] &= [H|\Xi, \Lambda, \Sigma_\delta][\Lambda, \Sigma_\delta] \\ [\Phi|Z] &= [\Xi|\Phi][\Phi] \end{aligned} \tag{8}$$

Let $\theta_k = (\theta_{k1} \ldots \theta_{kn_k})$, the vector of regression coefficients of block k where n_k is the number of manifest variables in block k with $\theta_{k1} = 1$ for identifiability (see section 2.6), Λ_k the kth column of Λ and $\Sigma_{\varepsilon k}$ and $\Sigma_{\delta k}$ the associated error terms. Conjugate prior distributions are

$$\begin{aligned} \theta_{kj}|\Sigma_{\varepsilon kj} &\sim \mathcal{N}(\theta_{0k}, \Sigma_{\varepsilon kj}\Sigma_{\varepsilon 0k}), \quad \Sigma_{\varepsilon kj}^{-1} \sim Gamma(\alpha_{0\varepsilon k}, \beta_{0\varepsilon k}) \\ \Lambda_k|\Sigma_{\delta k} &\sim \mathcal{N}(\Lambda_{0k}, \Sigma_{\delta k}\Sigma_{\delta 0k}), \quad \Sigma_{\delta k}^{-1} \sim Gamma(\alpha_{0\delta k}, \beta_{0\delta k}) \\ &\qquad\qquad \Phi^{-1} \sim InvWishart(R_0, d_0) \end{aligned} \tag{9}$$

Let Y_{kj} the jth manifest variable of block k, and Z_k the associated latent variable. Combining (8) and (9) gives the posterior distributions

$$\theta_{kj}|Y, Z, \Sigma_{\varepsilon kj} \sim \mathcal{N}\left(D_{kj}A_{kj}, \Sigma_{\varepsilon kj}D_{kj}\right)$$

$$\Sigma_{\varepsilon k1}^{-1} \sim \mathcal{G}\left(\frac{n}{2} + \alpha_{0\varepsilon kj}, \beta_{0\varepsilon kj} + \frac{1}{2}\left(Y_{kj} - Z_k\right)^t\left(Y_{kj} - Z_k\right)\right)$$

$$\Sigma_{\varepsilon kj}^{-1} \sim \mathcal{G}\left(\frac{n}{2} + \alpha_{0\varepsilon kj}, \beta_{0\varepsilon kj} + \frac{1}{2}\left[Y_{kj}^t Y_{kj} - (D_{kj}A_{kj})^t D_{kj}^{-1} D_{kj} A_{kj} + \frac{\theta_{0k}^2}{\Sigma_{\varepsilon 0k}}\right]\right)$$

$$D_{kj} = \left(Z_k^t Z_k + \Sigma_{\varepsilon 0k}^{-1}\right)^{-1}, \quad A_{kj} = \Sigma_{\varepsilon 0k}^{-1}\theta_{0k} + Z_k^t Y_{kj}$$

$$\Lambda_k|Y, Z, \Sigma_{\delta k} \sim \mathcal{N}\left(\tilde{D}_k \tilde{A}_k, \Sigma_{\varepsilon k}\tilde{D}_k\right)$$

$$\Sigma_{\delta k}^{-1} \sim \mathcal{G}\left(\frac{n}{2} + \alpha_{0\delta k}, \beta_{0\delta k} + \frac{1}{2}\left[Y_k^t Y_k - \left(\tilde{D}_k \tilde{A}_k\right)^t \tilde{D}_k^{-1} \tilde{D}_k \tilde{A}_k + \Lambda_{0k}^t \Sigma_{\delta k}^{-1} \Lambda_{0k}\right]\right)$$

$$\tilde{D}_k = \left(Z_k^t Z_k + \Sigma_{\delta k}^{-1}\right)^{-1}, \quad \tilde{A}_k = \Sigma_{\delta k}^{-1} \Lambda_{0k} + Z^t H_k$$

$$\Phi|Z \sim InvWishart\left(\Xi^t \Xi + R_0^{-1}, n + d_0\right)$$

2.4   The Gibbs sampler

Gibbs algorithm (see figure 1) alternates sampling in the conditionnal posterior distribution of parameters given data and latent variables (step 1), and sampling in the conditional posterior distributions of latent variables given data and parameters (step 3 to 7). Step 2 is the heuristics whose role is to ensure identifiability of the model by scaling the latent variables.

Initialisation : $\theta^0, \Sigma_\varepsilon^0, \Lambda^0, \Sigma_\delta^0, \Phi^0$
At iteration t :

   a. sampling in the conditional posterior distribution of latent variables:
      $Z^t \sim Z|Y, \theta^{t-1}, \Sigma_\varepsilon^{t-1}, \Lambda^{t-1}, \Sigma_\delta^{t-1}, \Phi^{t-1}$
   b. **standardization of latent variables:** define Z^{*t} the standardized LV
   c. $\Sigma_\varepsilon^t \sim \Sigma_\varepsilon|Y, Z^{*t}, \theta^{t-1}, \Lambda^{t-1}, \Sigma_\delta^{t-1}, \Phi^{t-1}$
   d. $\theta^t \sim \theta|Y, Z^{*t}, \Sigma_\varepsilon^t, \Lambda^{t-1}, \Sigma_\delta^{t-1}, \Phi^{t-1}$
   e. $\Sigma_\delta^t \sim \Sigma_\delta|Y, Z^{*t}, \Lambda^{t-1}, \theta^t, \Sigma_\varepsilon^t, \Phi^{t-1}$
   f. $\Lambda^t \sim \Lambda|Y, Z^{*t}, \Sigma_\delta^t, \theta^t, \Sigma_\varepsilon^t, \Phi^{t-1}$
   g. $\Phi^t \sim \Phi|Y, Z^{*t}, \theta^t, \Sigma_\varepsilon^t, \Lambda^t, \Sigma_\delta^t$

Fig. 1. Steps of Gibbs algorithm

After enough runs of Gibbs algorithm, conditional posterior simulations are supposed to be drawn from the marginal distributions of parameters.

2.5   Validation

Validation is based on Posterior Predictive p-values as developed in Gelman and al. (1996). PP p-values are derived from posterior predictive distributions, integrated out both parameters and latent variables. Let y_{rep} be a simulated dataset under the same model that generated the observed dataset y, say H_0, and the same parameters Θ and latent variables Z. The posterior predictive distribution of y_{rep} is then defined as:

$$
\begin{aligned}
\mathbb{P}^{H_0}\left(y_{rep}|y\right) &= \int \mathbb{P}^{H_0}\left(y_{rep}, \Theta, Z|y\right) \, d\Theta dZ \\
&= \int \mathbb{P}^{H_0}\left(y_{rep}|\Theta, Z\right)\left[\Theta, Z|y\right] d\Theta dZ
\end{aligned}
\tag{10}
$$

The PP p-value is defined as the tail probability of a given discrepancy function D (analogous to the use of statistics to compute classical p-values) under the posterior predictive distribution :

$$
\begin{aligned}
PPp\left(y\right) &= \mathbb{P}^{H_0}\left(D\left(y_{rep}, \Theta, Z\right) \geq D\left(y, \Theta, Z\right)|y\right) \\
&= \int \mathbb{P}^{H_0}\left(D\left(y_{rep}, \Theta, Z\right) \geq D\left(y, \Theta, Z\right)\right)\left[\Theta, Z|y\right] d\Theta dZ
\end{aligned}
\tag{11}
$$

Lee (2007) selected the following discrepancy function to test SEMs:

$$
D\left(y_{rep}, \Theta, Z\right) = \sum_{i=1}^{n}\left(y_{rep_i} - Z^i\theta^i\right)^t \Sigma_\varepsilon^i \left(y_{rep_i} - Z^i\theta^i\right)
\tag{12}
$$

where θ^i and Σ_ε^i are the current values in the run of Gibbs algorithm.

The PP p-value is thus computed as the proportion of runs for which $D\left(y_{rep}, \Theta^i, Z^i\right)$ is higher than $D\left(y, \Theta^i, Z^i\right)$. H_0 is not rejected if the PP p-value is near 0.5.

2.6   Identifiability issues

Identifiability of structural equation models is the injectivity of the likelihood function integrated out the latent variables namely

$$
\forall Y_i, \; [Y_i|\Theta] = \left[Y_i|\tilde{\Theta}\right] \Longrightarrow \Theta = \tilde{\Theta}
\tag{13}
$$

where Y_i is marginally distributed as $\mathcal{N}\left(0, \Sigma_Y\right)$ and $\Sigma_Y = \theta^t \Sigma_Z \theta + \Sigma_\varepsilon$.

With the notations of section 2.3 and denoting $\Sigma_Z = \{\rho_{ij}, 1 \leq i, j \leq K\}$, Σ_Y is the block matrix

$$
\Sigma_Y = \begin{pmatrix} \rho_{11}\theta_1\theta_1^t + \Sigma_{\varepsilon 1} & \rho_{12}\theta_1\theta_2^t & \cdots & \rho_{1K}\theta_1\theta_K^t \\ \rho_{12}\theta_1\theta_2^t & \rho_{22}\theta_2\theta_2^t + \Sigma_{\varepsilon 2} \cdots & & \vdots \\ \vdots & & & \\ \rho_{1K}\theta_1\theta_K^t & \cdots & \cdots & \rho_{KK}\theta_K\theta_K^t + \Sigma_{\varepsilon K} \end{pmatrix}
\tag{14}
$$

Identifiability constraints are directly derived from definition (13) applied to the Normal likelihood, giving $\Sigma_Y = \tilde{\Sigma}_Y$.

The identifiability equations arising from this equality are

$$\rho_{kk}\theta_{ki}^2 + \sigma_{ki}^2 = \tilde{\rho}_{kk}\tilde{\theta}_{ki}^2\tilde{\sigma}_{ki}^2, \; i = 1 \ldots n_k, \; k = 1 \ldots K \tag{15}$$

$$\rho_{kk}\theta_{ki}\theta_{kj} = \tilde{\rho}_{kk}\tilde{\theta}_{ki}\tilde{\theta}_{kj}, \; 1 \le i < j \le n_k, \; k = 1 \ldots K \tag{16}$$

$$\rho_{kk'}\theta_{ki}\theta_{k'j} = \tilde{\rho}_{kk'}\tilde{\theta}_{ki}\tilde{\theta}_{k'j}, \; 1 \le i \le n_k, \; 1 \le j \le n_{k'}, \; k = 1 \ldots K \tag{17}$$

Equations (15) and (16) are derived from the block diagonal elements of Σ_Y and equation (17) is derived from the extra block diagonal elements of Σ_Y.

If $\theta_{k1} = \tilde{\theta}_{k1}$ and $\rho_{kk} = \rho_{kk'}$ for a fixed k then equation (16) gives $\theta_{kj} = \tilde{\theta}_{kj}$ for all j. Reporting in equation 15 gives $\sigma_{ki}^2 = \tilde{\sigma}_{ki}^2$ for all k, i. Reporting in equation (17) gives $\rho_{kk'} = \tilde{\rho}_{kk'}$ for all k, k'. Consequently, a sufficient set of conditions for identifiability is $\theta_{k1} = 1$ and $\rho_{kk} = 1$ for all k.

The latter constraint is actually expressed in terms of the inner parameters, see the application, obtained by equating to 1 the diagonal elements of Σ_Z given in expression 5. However, posterior sampling of parameters given these constraints is complicated. The heuristics, consisting in standardizing latent variable after they have been drawn in their posterior distribution, should overcome this difficulty, as shown in the application.

3   Application

Consider a part of ECSI model considering only relationships between loyalty, satisfaction and image (see figure 2), on a subset of $n = 202$ individuals with no missing data. The full dataset is the demonstration dataset of XLStat software (http://www.xlstat.com/) with ordinal variables treated as continuous variables. The algorithm is implemented with R software.

Let θ_0 and λ_0 denote the common prior values of parameters. Priors on parameters are chosen to reflect confidence in the causality links: $\theta_0 = 0.5$, $\Lambda_0 = 0.5$, $\Sigma_{\varepsilon 0} = 1$, $\Sigma_{\delta 0} = 1$ and $\Phi_0 = 1$. Early convergence of Gibbs algorithm for all the parameters and law autocorrelation in posterior samples is observed. Formula (5) applied to this model with $\Pi_0 = \begin{pmatrix} 1 & 0 \\ -\pi_{12} & 1 \end{pmatrix}$ and $\Gamma = (\lambda_1 \lambda_2)$ gives the following expression of Σ_Z

$$\begin{pmatrix} \lambda_1^2 + \Sigma_{\delta 1} + \pi_{12}\lambda_1\lambda_2 + \pi_{12}^2 \left(\lambda_2^2 + \Sigma_{\delta 2}\right) \; ; \; \lambda_1\lambda_2 + \pi_{12}^2 \left(\lambda_2^2 + \Sigma_{\delta 2}\right) \; ; \; \Phi\left(\lambda_1 + \lambda_1\lambda_2\right) \\ \lambda_1\lambda_2 + \pi_{12}^2 \left(\lambda_2^2 + \Sigma_{\delta 2}\right) \qquad \lambda_2^2 + \Sigma_{\delta 2} \qquad \Phi\lambda_2 \\ \Phi\left(\lambda_1 + \lambda_1\lambda_2\right) \qquad \Phi\lambda_2 \qquad \Phi \end{pmatrix}$$

Identifiability constraints are given by equating to 1 the diagonal elements (see section 2.6)

$$a)\Phi = 1, \; b)\lambda_2^2 + \Sigma_{\delta 2} = 1, \; c)\lambda_1^2 + \Sigma_{\delta 1} + \pi_{12}\lambda_1\lambda_2 + \pi_{12}^2 \left(\lambda_2^2 + \Sigma_{\delta 2}\right) = 1$$

Posterior samples of these constraints are computed from the posterior samples of parameters. These distributions are centred in 1 with low dispersion as showed in figure 2, which tends to support the heuristics.

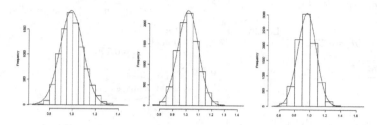

Fig. 2. Posterior distributions of the constraints a), b) and c) from left to right

Parameters of interest in SEMs are the correlations between manifest variables and latent variables and between latent variables. In table 1 θ_{12}, θ_{22}, θ_{23}, θ_{32}, θ_{33}, θ_{34}, θ_{35} and λ_2 are correlation coefficients whereas π_{12} and λ_1 are coefficients of a multiple regression. For identifiability $\theta_{11} = 1$, $\theta_{21} = 1$ and $\theta_{31} = 1$ (see section 2.6). From table 1, *satisfaction* and *Image* are highly correlated (0.796), meaning that *Image* has a great influence on *Satisfaction*. All the correlations are represented in the summary graph of figure 2.

	θ_{12}	θ_{22}	θ_{23}	θ_{32}	θ_{33}	θ_{34}	θ_{35}	π_{12}	λ_1	λ_2
mean	0.774	0.705	0.784	0.605	0.457	0.732	0.658	0.475	0.307	0.796
sd	0.060	0.051	0.053	0.063	0.067	0.059	0.059	0.127	0.130	0.047

Table 1. Regression coefficients: posterior mean and standard deviation (sd)

The PPp-value $0.37 < 0.5$ is due to the poor adjustment of data with the Normal distribution. This example however shows interesting features of Bayesian analysis, like hypothesis testing with PPp-values and the possibility to look at the variability of parameters and to the variability of functions of parameters.

4 Conclusion and perspectives

Posterior distributions of all the parameters of SEMs are derived under Normality and conjugacy assumptions. They are useful material to investigate aspects of the model like the variability of parameters and functions of parameters and hypothesis testing. The Gibbs algorithm augmented by the heuristics presented in this paper, converges rapidly, with low autocorrelations in posterior samples, thus reducing the number of iterations needed.

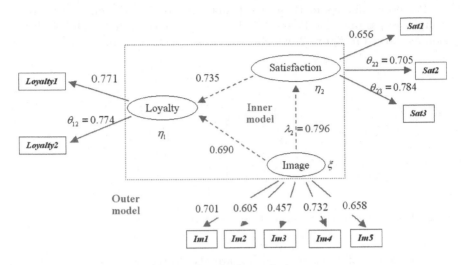

Fig. 3. Graph of correlations

More generally, this paper advocates systematic computation of identifiability constraints. Future work will concern structural equation modelling of mixed continuous and categorical data.

Acknowledgements

Jean-Baptiste Denis, Estelle Kuhn, Jean-Louis Foulley and René Ecochard are gratefully acknowledged. The authors particularly thank Eric Parent for his contribution to this work.

References

BOX, G. E. P. and TIAO G.C. (1973) : *Bayesian Inference in Statistical Analysis (Wiley Classics Library)*. Wiley.

GELMAN, A., MENG, X. L. and STERN, H. (1996) : Posterior Predictive Assessment of Model Fitness via Realized Discrepancies. *Statistica Sinica 6, 733-807.*

GELMAN, A., CARLIN, J.B., STERN, H.S., RUBIN, D.B. (2004) : *Bayesian Data Analysis (Texts in Statistical Science)*. Chapman & Hall/CRC.

LEE, S. Y. (2007) : *Structural Equation Modelling: A Bayesian Approach (Wiley Series in Probability and Statistics)*. Wiley.

PALOMO, J., DUNSON, D. B. and BOLLEN, K. (2007) : Bayesian Structural Equation Modeling. In: S. Y. Lee (Ed): *Handbook of latent variable and related models*. Elsevier, 163–188.

TANNER, M.A., WONG, W.H. (1987) : The Calculation of Posterior Distributions by Data Augmentation. *Journal of the American Statistical Association 82, 528-540.*

Some Examples of Statistical Computing in France During the 19th Century

Antoine de Falguerolles

Université de Toulouse, IMT, Laboratoire de Statistique et Probabilités
118 route de Narbonne, F-31068 Toulouse, France,
Antoine.Falguerolles@math.univ-toulouse.fr

Abstract. Statistical computing emerged as a recognised topic in the seventies. Remember the first COMPSTAT symposium held in Vienna (1974)! But the need for proper computations in statistics arose much earlier. Indeed, the contributions by Laplace (1749-1829) and Legendre (1752-1833) to statistical estimation in linear models are well known. But further works of computational interest originated in the structuring of the concept of regression during the 19th century. While some were fully innovative, some appear now unsuccessful but nevertheless informative. The paper discusses, from a French perspective, the computational aspects of selected examples.

Keywords: history of statistics, regression, statistical computing

1 Introduction

The contributions by Laplace (1749-1829) and Legendre (1752-1833) to the statistical estimation in linear models are well known: least absolute values ($\mathbf{L}_1$), least squares ($\mathbf{L}_2$), and minimax ($\mathbf{L}_\infty$) for the former and the derivation of least squares estimates for the latter (end of 18th century to early 19th century). These are detailed in comprehensive books by Farebrother (1998), Hald (2007) and Stigler (1990, 2002). The 19th century saw in France many further interesting developments. Some simply echo Peter Sint's invited talk presented at the COMPSTAT meeting held in Prague (1984). Examples include: Charles Dupin[1] reviewing favourably a letter which Charles Babbage had sent to the *Académie des Sciences* in support of the computing machine of the Swedish inventors named Scheutz (Falguerolles (2009)); Jacques Bertillon[2] and Émile Cheysson[3] (Peaucelle (2004)) advocating the use of

---

[1] COMPSTAT 2010 takes place in an institution founded in 1794, then called the *Conservatoire des Arts et Métiers*, where the first French statistical chair was created for baron Charles Dupin (1750-1873).

[2] Jacques Bertillon (1851-1922), statistician and demographer, not to be confused with his younger brother Adolphe, is President of the *Société de Statistique de Paris* in 1897.

[3] Émile Cheysson (1836-1910), a graduate from the *École Polytechnique*, is the famous advocate and theoretician of statistical cartography. Cheysson is also a President of the *Société de Statistique de Paris* (1883).

Y. Lechevallier, G. Saporta (eds.), *Proceedings of COMPSTAT'2010*,
DOI 10.1007/978-3-7908-2604-3_47, © Springer-Verlag Berlin Heidelberg 2010

the Hollerith machine for the French Census; Léon Lalanne[4] and Maurice
d'Ocagne[5], central characters of the *Nomographic School* (Hankins (1999)),
designing sophisticated *abaci*. But the spread of the general ideas of linear
fitting in France during the 19th century go beyond the mere development
of computing means. Specific situations led to interesting statistical developments. A well known example is given by Legendre[6] who considered autocorrelated errors (MA(1) in modern parlance) in his illustrative analysis (1805).
But there are other examples published later than Legendre's least squares
(from the Thirties to the Nineties). This paper presents a selection of these.

2   Covariance analysis

This section combines approaches in covariance analysis developed in two
different areas, namely the econometry of road building and the metrology
for cartographic triangulation. Let $E[Y] = \beta_{g0}^G + \beta_{g1}^G\, x$ be the full model
for a continuous random response variable given the explanatory variables, a
group factor G (with levels $1, \ldots, g, \ldots, \#G$) and a quantitative variable x.

2.1   Constant intercept and different slopes

Georges Müntz (1807-1887), a road engineer who graduated from *l'École
Polytechnique* and *l'École des Ponts et Chaussées*, considers a model[7] for the
costs of stone transportation where there is a common fixed part, $\beta_{g0}^G = \beta_0$,
and a part proportional to distance which varies across groups (the levels
of factor G), β_{g1}^G. In one of his examples, there are two unbalanced groups
of respective size $n_1^G > n_2^G > 0$. Müntz uses least squares on the data of
the largest group, $(y[G(i) == 1], x[G(i) == 1])$, to get estimates b_0 and
b_{11}^G of β_0 and β_{11}^G. Müntz then estimates β_{21}^G by computing the mean of the
$\frac{(y[G(i)==2]-b_0)}{x[G(i)==2]}$. Clearly, the estimators thus introduced are linear but do not

---

[4] Léon - Louis (Chrestien -) Lalanne (1811-1892), a graduate from the *École polytechnique*, is a recognised theoretician of computing, with definite skills in probability and statistics. His work on graphical computing was rapidly translated in
English (LALANNE, L.-L. (1846): *Explanation and use of the abacus or french
universal reckoner*. London: Joseph Thomas).

[5] The name of Maurice d'Ocagne (1862-1938), a nomographist in the line of
Lalanne, is often linked to the use of parallel coordinates. He graduated from
l'École polytechnique and *l'École des Ponts et Chaussées*, where he later taught.
D'OCAGNE, M. (1891): Nomographie: les calculs usuels effectués au moyen des
abaques: essai d'une théorie générale, ... Paris: Gauthiers-Villars et fils.

[6] LEGENDRE, A. M. (1805): *Nouvelles méthodes pour la détermination des orbites
des comètes* .... Paris: Courcier.

[7] MÜNTZ, G. (1834): Note sur l'évaluation du prix du transport des matériaux
de construction dans l'arrondissement du Nord, *Annales des Ponts et Chaussées*,
167, 86-100.

coincide with the least squares estimators that we would use now. Müntz had certainly the mathematical ability for solving a 3×3 linear system of normal equations, but the statistical concept of indicator variable had yet to be invented.

2.2   Different intercept and constant slopes

This problem arose in the calibration of some parts of an apparatus to be used in geographical triangulation by a Franco-Spanish team[8]. A leading French member was Aimé Laussedat (1819-1907), a Military Engineer who graduated from the *École Polytechnique*[9]. The number of levels for the group factor is large and the design is balanced. A constant slope over groups is assumed ($\beta_{g1}^G = \beta_1$). Least squares are used. The block pattern of the normal equations is recognised and closed form estimators are obtained.

3   Cauchy's heuristic for regression

In a 1835 paper[10] Augustin Cauchy (1789-1857) considers a situation in which the response is a non-linear function of an explanory variable which can be approximated by a linear combination of the leading terms of a series of simpler functions; special attention is given to the estimation of the order of the approximation to be carried out (see p. 195). With this situation in mind, Cauchy introduces a sequential procedure based on the repeated use of simple regressions. Although the least squares estimator can be used in these regressions, Cauchy proposes a heuristic linear estimator for the slope.

3.1   Cauchy's linear estimators for simple regression

Legendre's estimator (least squares) for the slope involves $2n$ multiplications which are potential sources of numerical errors. Hence, Cauchy proposes a formula which is less prone to errors:

$$\widehat{\beta_1} = \frac{\sum_{i=1}^n \text{sign}(x_i - \overline{x})(Y_i - \overline{Y})}{\sum_{i=1}^n |x_i - \overline{x}|}.$$

Note that this formula coincides with a weighted least squares estimator using weights $\frac{1}{|x_i - \overline{x}|}$ for $x_i \neq \overline{x}$ and 0 for $x_i = \overline{x}$. Nevertheless, Cauchy keeps the intuitive form of the least squares estimator for the intercept, $\widehat{\beta_0} = \overline{Y} - \widehat{\beta_1}\overline{x}$.

---

[8] LAUSSEDAT, A. (translator) (1860): *Expériences faites avec l'appareil à mesurer les bases appartenant à la commission de la carte d'Espagne*. Paris: Librairie militaire.

[9] Laussedat taught later at the *École Polytechnique*. He also taught at the *Conservatoire des Arts et Métiers* and became its director in 1884.

[10] CAUCHY, A. (1837): Mémoire sur l'interpolation, *Journal de mathématiques pures et appliquées*, Série 1, Tome 2, 193-205. In a note, the Editor (Joseph Liouville) acknowledges that the manuscript was sent to the *Académie des Sciences* in 1835.

3.2   Cauchy's multiple regression

Cauchy's approach to multiple regression combines the ideas of triangularization and step by step conditioning of the variables. First, all variables are centered to their means. Then iteratively at each step, a not-yet-considered currently revised explanatory variable is introduced; the currently revised response variable and all other not-yet-considered curently revised variables are regressed onto this variable according to Cauchy's formula; the slope coefficients thus obtained are stored; the residuals from all these regressions are computed and constitute the updated revised variables. The inspection of the values of the revised response variable may tell if the iterative process is to be stopped; that of the revised explanatory variables may help in finding the 'best' explanatory variable to introduce next. When the process is stopped, back calculation gives the estimated regression coefficients.

The main drawback of Cauchy's method is that the estimated values for the regression coefficients may depend on the order of introduction of the explanatory variables. However, if Legendre's formula for the slope is used in place of Cauchy's formula, the unique solution given by multiple regression based on least squares is obtained.

Cauchy's approach is a heuristic which received some attention in France but was criticized by the *aficionados* of least squares (see for instance Jules Bienaymé[11]). Still, the idea of having a large number of fast simple regressions computed and combined into a final result can be found in cutting-edge methods.

3.3   Spurious correlation and differencing

An example of the use of Cauchy's method is given in an article by Vilfredo Pareto presented at the *Société de Statistique de Paris*[12]. The general problem addresses the relationship between the number of marriages in England and economic prosperity, indices for the latter being Exports and Coal extraction. The data are indexed by time (year 1855 to 1895). Pareto recognizes the problem that arises in the analysis of time series, namely the opportunity of differencing the series to avoid spurious correlation (see his discussion pp. 376-378). Pareto chooses here not to differentiate the data and presents the estimates obtained by using Cauchy's heuristic.

---

[11] BIENAYMÉ, J. (1853): Remarques sur les différences qui distinguent l'interpolation de M. Cauchy de la méthode des moindres carrés, et qui assurent la supériorité de cette méthode. *Comptes rendus hebdomadaires des séances de l'Académie des Sciences*, 5-13.

[12]   PARETO, V. (1897): Quelques exemples d'application des méthodes d'interpolation à la Statistique, *Journal de la Société de Statistique de Paris*, 58 (novembre), 367-379.

4 Iteratively weighted least squares

Pareto's approach to non-linear least squares can be found again in his 1897 article (referenced in note 12). The motivating example consists in the estimation of the coefficients of an evolution curve over time for the population in England and Wales (Pareto, 1897, pp. 371-372). It turns out Pareto discusses the direct minimisation of $\sum_{i=1}^{n}(y_i - \mu_i)^2$ where $\mu_i = \exp \eta_i$ with $\eta_i = \beta_0 + \beta_1 x_i$ (a log link function for a normal distribution in modern notation). The gradient is:

$$\nabla_S(\beta_0, \beta_1) = - \begin{bmatrix} \sum_{i=1}^{n}(y_i - \mu_i)\mu_i \\ \sum_{i=1}^{n}(y_i - \mu_i)\mu_i x_i \end{bmatrix}$$

while the Hessian is:

$$H_S(\beta_0, \beta_1) = - \begin{bmatrix} \sum_{i=1}^{n}\left((y_i - \mu_i)\mu_i - \mu_i^2\right) & \sum_{i=1}^{n}\left((y_i - \mu_i)\mu_i x_i - \mu_i^2 x_i\right) \\ \sum_{i=1}^{n}\left((y_i - \mu_i)\mu_i x_i - \mu_i^2 x_i\right) & \sum_{i=1}^{n}\left((y_i - \mu_i)\mu_i x_i^2 - \mu_i^2 x_i^2\right) \end{bmatrix}.$$

At a stationary point $(\beta_0^\star, \beta_1^\star)'$, the Hessian simplifies to:

$$H_S(\beta_0^\star, \beta_1^\star) = \sum_{i=1}^{n} \mu_i^{\star 2} \begin{bmatrix} 1 & x_i \\ x_i & x_i^2 \end{bmatrix} - \sum_{i=1}^{n} \mu_i^\star x_i^2 \begin{bmatrix} 0 & 0 \\ 0 & y_i - \mu_i^\star \end{bmatrix}$$

Pareto proposes to search for a stationnary point by using a Newton-Raphson algorithm in which a simplified version of the Hessian is used:

$$\begin{bmatrix} \beta_0^{(k+1)} \\ \beta_1^{(k+1)} \end{bmatrix} = \begin{bmatrix} \beta_0^{(k)} \\ \beta_1^{(k)} \end{bmatrix} - \left(\sum_{i=1}^{n} \mu_i^{(k)2} \begin{bmatrix} 1 & x_i \\ x_i & x_i^2 \end{bmatrix} \right)^{-1} \nabla_S(\beta_0^{(k)}, \beta_1^{(k)}).$$

Has Pareto realized that $E[\mu_i x_i^2 (Y_i - \mu_i)] = 0$ and that he uses what is called now Fisher's scoring method?

However, Pareto finds such an iterative method too burdensome to use in practice and states that, by properly weighting the regression of the log-transformed response, a fair approximation to the coefficients can be easily calculated. Pareto's proposal is to consider the minimisation of

$$\sum_{i=1}^{n} y_i^2 (\log(y_i) - (\beta_0 + \beta_1 x_i))^2$$

How does this relate to the well known iteratively weighted least squares? Assuming independent observations with constant variance and log link ($g(\mu_i) = \log(\mu_i) = \eta_i = \beta_0 + \beta_1 x_i$), the loss function is $\sum_{i=1}^{n}(y_i - \exp\{\beta_0 + \beta_1 x_i\})^2$. At iteration k, the loss function is $\sum_{i=1}^{n}(\exp\{\eta_i^{(k-1)}\})^2(z_i^{(k)} - (\beta_0 + \beta_1 x_i))^2$ where the working response is $z_i^{(k)} = \frac{y_i - \exp\{\eta_i^{(k-1)}\}}{\exp\{\eta_i^{(k-1)}\}} + \eta_i^{(k-1)}$. Taking the convenient starting values $\eta_i^{(0)} = \log(y_i)$, the loss function at iteration 1 is exactly what Pareto has in mind.

5 Unsuccessful attempts

In this section, the two papers under consideration exemplify the case of modest treatment with genuine intuitions.

5.1   A weighted mean with data driven weights

In 1821, an anonymous subscriber[13] discusses at length the notion of mean. Among other considerations: expected mean or *moyenne absolue* versus estimated mean or *moyenne relative* (p. 188); trimmed means (p.189); weighted mean with data driven weights (p. 200):

$$m = \frac{\sum_{i=1}^{n} \frac{x_i}{(m-x_i)^2}}{\sum_{i=1}^{n} \frac{1}{(m-x_i)^2}}$$

But this choice is rather unfortunate since, as noted by the anonymous author, the definition can be rewritten as $\frac{1}{dm} \prod_{i=1}^{n} (m - x_i)^2 = 0$. Still, the idea of having data driven weights related to $|m - x_i|$ remains.

5.2   Fitting a Gamma density

In a talk at the *Société de Statistique de Paris*[14], Lucien March (1859-1933), a graduate from the *École Polytechnique* working at the *Office du Travail* (Armatte (2008)), introduces a theoretical model for the density of wages distribution of the form: $f(x) = \alpha x^{\beta} \exp\{-\gamma x\}$. March ascribes the theoretical curve to the German Otto Ammon. (However, Kleiber and Kotz (2003) claim that they did not trace any such thing in Ammon's publications!) March derives two indices of inequality for comparing curves, the mean to mode difference ($\delta = \frac{1}{\gamma} = \frac{\text{Var}(X)}{E[X]}$) and the difference between the two inflexion points ($\Delta = 2\frac{\sqrt{\beta}}{\gamma} = 2\sqrt{\text{Var}(X) - (\frac{\text{Var}(X)}{E[X]})^2}$) which he estimates using Pearson's newly available method of moments. Curiously, March also proceeds to the estimation of the unknown coefficients by using a regression. Noting the linear form of the log transformed density, $\log f(x) = \log \alpha + \beta \log x - \gamma x$, and using grouped data, March considers the regression of the log transformed empirical density onto the centers of classes and their logarithms. As expected in France, March uses the two strategies for regression, namely least squares and Cauchy's heuristic, and mentions the possible introduction of the weights suggested by Pareto in these. Nowadays March's approach is highly questionable. First, the fact that α is a function of β and γ is not recognised. Second, empty classes cannot easily be taken into account. The introduction of null weights for these, which bias the estimations, is a possibility but there is no justification for using the squared empirical density for non-empty classes. A constant model for the weighted mid-class values in the generalized linear model settings for the Gamma distribution would be a starting point nowadays.

---

[13]   ANONYMOUS (1821): Probabilités. Dissertation sur la recherche du milieu entre les résultats de plusieurs observations ou expériences. *Annales de Mathématiques pures et appliquées*, Vol. 12, 6, 1821, 181–204.

[14]   MARCH, L. (1898): Quelques exemples de distribution des salaires, contribution à l'étude comparative des méthodes d'ajustement, *Journal de la Société de Statistique de Paris*, 1898, 39 (June), 193-206

6   Concluding remarks

It would be a challenging task to identify all the statistical work introducing computational innovations between Legendre's estimation of the shape of the Earth by generalized least squares[15] in 1805 and the Cholesky[16] transform in topography in 1909 (Brezinski (2005)). Statistical computing is scattered in journals and books which were published under the auspices of a diversity of groups. Bygone Statistical Societies[17] had their journals with limited mathematical contents, the papers by Pareto (1897) and March (1898) being notable exceptions. Artillery publications offer a genuine blend of probability and statistics, e.g., Isidore Didion's curves of equal probability[18], published in 1858 and possibly considered as early as 1823 (Bru (1996)), and Paul Henry's *qnorm plot*[19] (Crépel (1993)). But the 'information superhighways' are the *Comptes rendus hebdomadaires des séances de l'Académie des sciences* and the *Journal de mathématiques pures et appliquées* (see note 21) with a great variety of contents. Some publications deal with theoretical matters. An example is the report[20] made by Gabriel Lamé, Michel Chasles and Joseph Liouville[21], members of the *Académie*, on a report by Jules Bienaymé[22] in appreciation of the work of Laplace on least squares. Technical pieces of research can also be found. An example of the latter is provided by Auguste(?) Pont[23] who describes how to reduce the computational burden of fitting a

---

[15] See reference in note 6.

[16] André-Louis Cholesky (1875-1918), a graduate from the *École Polytechnique*, served as an artillery officer and a military geographer. He never published 'his' method.

[17] During the 19th century several Societies having the word *statistique* in their name were founded all over France. The three main statistical Societies created in Paris (thus with a national dimension) are the *Société de Statistique* (1802) with its journal the *Annales de statistique*, the *Société française de Statistique universelle* (1829) with its journal the *Journal des travaux de la SfdSu*, and the *Société de Statistique de Paris* (1860) with its journal the *Journal de la SSP*. For this last, see Caussinus and Falguerolles (2006).

[18] DIDION, I. (1858): *Calcul des probabilités appliqué au tir des projectiles*, Paris: Dumaine, Mallet-Bachelier.

[19] HENRY, P. (1894): *Cours d'artillerie, Probabilité du Tir (1er Fascicule)*. Lithographie de l'École d'Application de l'Artillerie et du Génie.

[20] LAMÉ, G., CHASLES, M., and LIOUVILLE, J. (1852): Rapport sur un mémoire de M. Jules Bienaymé, Inspecteur général des finances, concernant la probabilité des erreurs d'après la méthode des moindres carrés. *Comptes rendus hebdomadaires des séances de l'Académie des Sciences*. Bachelier: Paris, 34, 90-92.

[21] Joseph Liouville is the founder in 1836 of the *Journal de mathématiques pures et appliquées* which is still published.

[22] Bienaymé also wrote two papers on least squares in the *Journal de mathématiques pures et appliquées*. See also note 11.

[23] PONT, A. (1887): Sur la résolution, dans un cas particulier, des équations normales auxquelles conduit la méthode des moindres carrés. *Comptes rendus hebdo-*

polynomial regression when the values of the explanatory variable are specified by an arithmetic progression.

It turns out that most papers mentioned in this article are authored by former graduates and/or professors from the *École Polytechnique*. This institution is certainly the common denominator for mathematical statistics and statistical computing in the 19th century in France. But the *Conservatoire National des Arts et Métiers* is not too far behind.

References

ALDRICH, J. (1998): Doing Least squares: Perpspectives from Gauss and Yule. *International Statistical Review, 66(1), 61–81.*

ARMATTE, M. (2008): Lucien March (1859-1933): une statistique sans probabilité? *Courrier des Statistiques, Vol. 123, 7-12.*

BREZINSKI, C. (2005): La méthode de Cholesky. *Revue d'histoire des mathématiques, 11, 205-238.*

BRU, B. (1996): Problème de l'efficacité du tir à l'École d'Artillerie de Metz. *Mathématiques Informatique et Sciences Humaines, 136, 29–42.*

CAUSSINUS, H. and FALGUEROLLES, A. de (2006): Journal de la Société Française de Statistique. In: *Encyclopedia of Statistical Sciences*, Second Edition, Vol. 6 (IN-L), 3765–3767, Wiley.

CRÉPEL, P. (1993): Henri et la droite de Henry. *MATAPLI, 36, 19-22.*

FALGUEROLLES, A. de (2009): Charles Dupin, statisticien. In: C. Christen and F. Vatin (Eds.):*Charles Dupin (1784-1873).* PUR, Rennes, 115-127.

FAREBROTHER, R. W. (1998): *Fitting linear relationships, a history of the calculus of observations (1750–1900).* Springer, New York.

HALD, A. (2007): *Sources and studies in the history of mathematics and physical sciences.* Springer, New York, 2007.

HANKINS, T.L. (1999): Blood, dirt and nomograms, a particular history of graphs. *Isis, 90, 50-80.*

KLEIBER, Chr. and KOTZ, S. (2003): *Statistical size distributions in economics and actuarial sciences.* Series in probability and statistics. Wiley.

PEAUCELLE, J.-L. (2004): À la fin du XIXe Siècle, l'adoption de la mécanographie est-elle rationnelle ? *Gérer et Comprendre, Annales des Mines, 77, 61-76.*

SINT, P. (1984): Roots of computational statistics. In: T. Havranek, Z. Šidák and M. Novák (Eds): *COMPSTAT 1984, proceedings in computational statistics.* Physica-Verlag, Wien, 9-20.

STIGLER, S. M. (1990): *The History of Statistics: The measurement of uncertainty before 1900.* Harvard University Press: Cambridge (Mass).

STIGLER, S. M. (2002): *Statistics on the Table: The History of statistical soncepts and methods.* Graphic Press: Cambridge (Mass).

---

madaires des séances de l'Académie des Sciences, Vol. 105, 491-494. In his note, Pont refers to the mathematical notation used by Esprit Jouffret in the *Revue d'Artillerie* in 1873. Jouffret is also referred to by Bru (1996). Jouffret is mostly remembered for his *Traité élémentaire de géométrie à quatre dimensions et introduction à la géométrie à n dimensions* (Paris, Gauthier-Villars (1903)) which is sometimes credited to have inspired the cubist painters, Jean Metzinger, Pablo Picasso . . .

Imputation by Gaussian Copula Model with an Application to Incomplete Customer Satisfaction Data

Meelis Käärik[1] and Ene Käärik[2]

[1] Senior researcher, Institute of Mathematical Statistics
University of Tartu, Estonia, *Meelis.Kaarik@ut.ee*
[2] Researcher, Institute of Mathematical Statistics
University of Tartu, Estonia, *Ene.Kaarik@ut.ee*

Abstract. We propose the idea of imputing missing value based on conditional distributions, which requires the knowledge of the joint distribution of all the data. The Gaussian copula is used to find a joint distribution and to implement the conditional distribution approach.

The focus remains on the examination of the appropriateness of an imputation algorithm based on the Gaussian copula.

In the present paper, we generalize and apply the copula model to incomplete correlated data using the imputation algorithm given by Käärik and Käärik (2009a).

The empirical context in the current paper is an imputation model using incomplete customer satisfaction data. The results indicate that the proposed algorithm performs well.

Keywords: Gaussian copula, incomplete data, imputation

1 Introduction

Traditionally correlated data analysis deals with repeated measurements over time or over space (Song (2007)). Here, we look at correlated data in a broader perspective (for example, battery of tests, etc.) and generalize the results we have obtained using incomplete repeated measurements.

We consider incomplete correlated data, which may cause complicated problems in many statistical analyses, especially in the case of small sample sizes when every value is substantial. So, we can say that we are interested in missing response values, i.e., in observations that potentially could be obtained and we try to find a reasonable estimation that can be substituted for a missing value. The basic idea of imputation is to fill in gaps in the incomplete data using existing observations following certain model with given assumptions. We focus on an imputation model based on conditional distributions. The main drawback there is that the joint distribution may not exist theoretically and finding conditional distributions may be therefore impossible.

Y. Lechevallier, G. Saporta (eds.), *Proceedings of COMPSTAT'2010*,
DOI 10.1007/978-3-7908-2604-3_48, © Springer-Verlag Berlin Heidelberg 2010

In this paper, we use copulas to overcome this problem. The term copula refers to the joining of distributions and copula is a good tool for modeling dependent data. We do not make assumptions on the functional form of the marginal distributions. We focus on the Gaussian copula and generalize the imputation strategy for dropouts which is examined in Käärik (2007), Käärik and Käärik (2009a).

For incomplete repeated measurements the natural assumption is the monotone missingness, which means there exists a permutation of the observations such that if a measurement for a given subject is observed, it is observed for all preceding measurements for that subject. In the presence of a monotone missingness pattern, the imputation can be reduced to a series of single variable imputations, starting with the variable which has the lowest proportion of missingness and impute variable by variable in a sequential fashion. For arbitrary missing data, we can order the data from most complete to most incomplete and call them ordered missing data (definition given in Käärik and Käärik (2009b)). We work iteratively through imputation for each variable starting from the variable with the least missing data and imputing the data by specifying an imputation model based on the conditional distribution.

2   Preliminaries

Consider random vector $\boldsymbol{Y}$ with correlated components Y_j, so $\boldsymbol{Y} = (Y_1, \ldots, Y_m)$. We have n observations from $\boldsymbol{Y}$ and data forms the $n \times m$ matrix $\boldsymbol{Y} = (Y_1, \ldots, Y_m)$, $Y_j = (y_{1j}, \ldots, y_{nj})^T$, $j = 1, \ldots, m$. Usually the data matrix is not complete, that means we have k completely observed variables and $m - k$ partially observed variables. For simplicity we suppress the subscript index for individual, writing simply y_j instead of y_{ij} (usually referring to an individual i having incomplete data). Assuming ordered missing data means, that we have the random vector $\boldsymbol{Y} = (Y_1, \ldots, Y_k, Y_{k+1}, \ldots, Y_m)$ where the data for first k $(k \geq 2)$ components are complete. We need to specify the joint distribution of components. We focus on imputing the first incomplete variable Y_{k+1} using the complete part $Y_1, \ldots, Y_k$, the same idea can be used later to work iteratively through all variables.

According to complete and incomplete parts of data, we can partition the correlation matrix of data $\mathbf{R}$ as follows

$$\mathbf{R} = \begin{pmatrix} \mathbf{R}_k & \mathbf{r} \\ \mathbf{r}^T & 1 \end{pmatrix}, \tag{1}$$

where $\mathbf{R}_k$ is the correlation matrix of the complete part and $\mathbf{r} = (r_{1,k+1}, \ldots, r_{k,k+1})^T$ is the vector of correlations between the complete part and the incomplete Y_{k+1}.

If the marginal distributions of $(Y_1, \ldots, Y_k)$ and Y_{k+1} are continuous and known and the correlation matrix is estimated directly from data, we can use a copula model for specifying the joint distribution. Of course, the marginal distribution functions are not typically known and we have to use some estimation strategy to find them and there may arise serious problems, but here we do not deal with these questions.

By definition, a $(k+1)$-variate copula is a joint distribution function with uniform marginals on the unit interval. If F_j is the marginal distribution function of a univariate random variable Y_j, then $C(F_1(y_1), \ldots, F_{k+1}(y_{k+1}))$ is a $(k+1)$-variate joint distribution for $\boldsymbol{Y} = (Y_1, \ldots, Y_{k+1})$ with marginal distributions F_j, $j = 1, \ldots, k+1$ (Nelsen (2006)). We focus on the most familiar Gaussian copula model because of easy implementation in practice and handling the dependence in a natural way as pairwise correlations among the variables (Clemen and Reilly (1999), Schölzel and Friederichs (2008), Song et al. (2009), etc). Using the Gaussian copula, we obtain the following expression for the joint multivariate distribution function $F_Y(y_1, \ldots, y_{k+1}; \mathbf{R}) = C[F_1(y_1), \ldots, F_{k+1}(y_{k+1}); \mathbf{R}] = \Phi_{(k+1)}[\Phi^{-1}(F_1(y_1)), \ldots, \Phi^{-1}(F_{k+1}(y_{k+1}))]$. After some transformations we obtain the conditional probability density function (see Käärik and Käärik (2009a))

$$f_{Z_{k+1}|Z_1,\ldots,Z_k}(z_{k+1}|z_1, \ldots, z_k; \mathbf{R}) = \frac{\exp\left\{-\frac{(z_{k+1} - \mathbf{r}^T \mathbf{R}_k^{-1} \mathbf{z}_k)^2}{2(1 - \mathbf{r}^T \mathbf{R}_k^{-1} \mathbf{r})}\right\}}{\sqrt{2\pi(1 - \mathbf{r}^T \mathbf{R}_k^{-1} \mathbf{r})}}, \qquad (2)$$

where $Z_j = \Phi^{-1}[F_j(Y_j)]$, $j = 1, \ldots, k+1$, are standard normal random variables and $\mathbf{z}_k = (z_1, \ldots, z_k)^T$.

As a result we have the (conditional) probability density function of a normal random variable with expectation $\mathbf{r}^T \mathbf{R}_k^{-1} \mathbf{z}_k$ and variance $1 - \mathbf{r}^T \mathbf{R}_k^{-1} \mathbf{r}$, i.e.,

$$E(Z_{k+1}|Z_1 = z_1, \ldots, Z_k = z_k) = \mathbf{r}^T \mathbf{R}_k^{-1} \mathbf{z}_k, \qquad (3)$$

$$Var(Z_{k+1}|Z_1 = z_1, \ldots, Z_k = z_k) = 1 - \mathbf{r}^T \mathbf{R}_k^{-1} \mathbf{r}. \qquad (4)$$

3 Imputation algorithms based on Gaussian copula

In this section, we present the strategy of the copula-based imputation method.

The formula (3) leads us to the general formula of replacing the missing value z_{k+1} by the estimate $\hat{z}_{k+1}$ using the conditional mean imputation

$$\hat{z}_{k+1} = \mathbf{r}^T \mathbf{R}_k^{-1} \mathbf{z}_k, \qquad (5)$$

where $\mathbf{r}$ is the vector of correlations between $(Z_1, \ldots, Z_k)$ and Z_{k+1}, $\mathbf{R}_k^{-1}$ is the inverse of the correlation matrix of $(Z_1, \ldots, Z_k)$ and $\mathbf{z}_k = (z_1, \ldots, z_k)^T$ is the vector of complete observations for the subject which has missing value z_{k+1}.

From expression (4) we obtain the (conditional) variance of imputed value as follows

$$(\hat{\sigma}_{k+1})^2 = 1 - \mathbf{r}^T \mathbf{R}_k^{-1} \mathbf{r}. \qquad (6)$$

These results for dropouts are proved by Käärik and Käärik (2009a) and are generalized in Käärik and Käärik (2009b) for correlated data.

To implement general formulas (5) and (6) we have to specify the structure of the correlation matrix. The natural start is from a simple correlation structure, depending on one parameter only.

(1) The *compound symmetry (CS)* or the constant correlation structure, when the correlations between all measurements are equal, $r_{ij} = \rho$, $i, j = 1, \ldots, m, i \neq j$.

(2) The *first order autoregressive* correlation structure (AR), when the observations on the same subject that are closer are more highly correlated than measurements that are further apart, $r_{ij} = \rho^{|j-i|}$, $i, j = 1, \ldots, m, i \neq j$.

Consider correlated data with ordered missingness, then the simplest CS structure may be ordinary, but the AR structure may be also suspected in some situations. Imputation strategy in the case of an existing CS correlation structure is studied in detail in Käärik and Käärik (2009b). For the ordered missing data with CS correlation structure, we had the following imputation formula

$$\hat{z}_{k+1}^{CS} = \frac{\rho}{1 + (k-1)\rho} \sum_{j=1}^{k} z_j, \tag{7}$$

where $z_1, \ldots, z_k$ are the observed values for the subject with missing value z_{k+1}.

We will now gather some properties of important characteristics of the AR structure case into a lemma and apply the results later to our imputation case.

Lemma 1. Let $\mathbf{Z} = (Z_1, \ldots, Z_{k+1})$ be a random vector with standard normal components and let the corresponding correlation matrix have AR correlation structure with correlation coefficient ρ. Then the following assertions hold:

$$E(Z_{k+1}|Z_1 = z_1, \ldots, Z_k = z_k) = E(Z_{k+1}|Z_k = z_k) = \rho z_k, \tag{8}$$

$$Var(Z_{k+1}|Z_1 = z_1, \ldots, Z_k = z_k) = 1 - \rho^2. \tag{9}$$

Formula (8) can be proved starting from (5) similarly to incomplete repeated measurements (Käärik (2007)); a detailed proof of (9) can be found in Appendix 1.

By Lemma 1, the conditional mean imputation formula for standardized measurements with an AR structure has the simple form

$$\hat{z}_{k+1}^{AR} = \rho z_k, \tag{10}$$

where z_k is the last observed value for the subject, and the corresponding variance is

$$(\hat{\sigma}_{k+1}^{AR})^2 = 1 - \rho^2. \tag{11}$$

In summary, the implementation of an imputation algorithm based on the Gaussian copula approach requires the following steps.

1. Sort the columns of the data matrix to get ordered missing data, and fix Y_{k+1} (column with the least number of missing values) as the starting point for imputation.

2. Estimate the marginal distribution functions of $Y_1, \ldots, Y_k, Y_{k+1}$. The copula method works with arbitrary marginal distributions; use a normalizing transformation, if needed.

3. Estimate the correlation structure between variables $Y_1, \ldots, Y_k, Y_{k+1}$. If we can accept the hypothesis of compound symmetry or autoregressive structure, estimate the Spearman's correlation coefficient ρ. If there is no simple correlation structure, estimate $\mathbf{R}$ by an empirical correlation matrix.

4. In the case of CS correlation structure, use imputation formula (7). In the case of AR correlation structure, use imputation formula (10) and estimate the variance of the imputed value using formula (11). If there is no simple correlation structure, then use general formulas (5) and (6).

5. Use the inverse transformation to impute the missing value into initial data, if needed.

6. Repeat steps 4-5 until all missing values in column Y_{k+1} are imputed. If $k < m - 1$, then take $k = k + 1$, take a new Y_{k+1}, estimate the marginal distribution of Y_{k+1} and go to step 3. In the following steps the imputed values are treated as if they were observed.

4   Imputing incomplete customer satisfaction data

Customer satisfaction index (CSI) is an economic indicator that measures the satisfaction of consumers. This is found by a customer satisfaction survey, which consists of two main parts: a questionnaire where the respondents (customers) are requested to give scores (in our example on a scale from 0 to 10, from least to most satisfied), and a structural equation model on the gathered data to obtain the CSI.

In our particular example each customer actually represents a certain company. While the overall satisfaction index is still the main focus, the scores given by individual customers are important for people involved with each particular customer (especially project managers), but each score also provides valuable information for division leaders, managers, and decision makers. Therefore finding reasonable substitutes for missing values in the survey is of high interest. The whole customer satisfaction survey has usually several blocks of similar questions. In the current paper we are focusing on a group of five questions (from 20 customers) directly related to customer satisfaction.

We have complete data and we will delete the values from one variable step by step and analyze the reliability of the proposed method. The imputation study has the following general steps.

1. *Estimation of marginal distributions.* We used the Kolmogorov-Smirnov and Anderson-Darling tests for normality; and, as usual, small samples passed the normality test, thus we did not reject the normality assumption.

2. *Estimation of the correlation structure.* It is difficult to specify the correct correlation structure in practical tasks. Many methods allow the specification of a 'working' correlation matrix that intends to approximate the true correlation matrix. In our correlation matrix, the correlations decreased monotonically over time, so the natural choice was an autoregressive correlation structure. Calculation of the 'working' correlation matrix gave us Spearman's $\hat{\rho} = 0.784$ as an estimate of the parameter of the AR-structure.

3. *Estimation of the missing values.* To validate the imputation algorithm we repeat the imputation procedure for every value in the data column Y_5. Here we have nonstandard normal variables and use the following modified formulas (instead of (10) and (11)):

$$\hat{z}_{k+1}^{AR} = \rho \frac{s_{k+1}}{s_k}(z_k - \bar{Z}_k) + \bar{Z}_{k+1}, \tag{12}$$

where $\bar{Z}_k$ and $\bar{Z}_{k+1}$ are the mean values of data columns Z_{k+1} and Z_k respectively, and s_{k+1} and s_k are the corresponding standard deviations, and

$$(\hat{\sigma}_{k+1}^{AR})^2 = s_{k+1}^2(1 - \rho^2). \tag{13}$$

To examine the quality of imputation, the average L_1 error (absolute distance between the observed and imputed value) and L_2 error (root mean square distance) were calculated; the corresponding values are 0.641 and 0.744. Analyzing the values of L_1 and L_2 errors allows us to conclude that the proposed imputation method is rather conservative.

4. *Estimation of the variance of imputed values.* Calculating the variance of an imputed value by (13) and repeating the imputation process for every value we obtain following results (see Table 1, where y_5 is the observed value, $\hat{z}_5^{AR}$ is the corresponding imputed value and 0.95 CI is its 0.95-level confidence interval based on the normal approximation and calculated in the standard way).

No	y_5	$\hat{z}_5^{AR}$	0.95 CI	No	y_5	$\hat{z}_5^{AR}$	0.95 CI
1	6	6.77	(5.12; 8.41)	11	8	7.57	(5.89; 9.24)
2	8	8.52	(6.84; 10.19)	12	4	5.43	(3.89; 6.97)
3	9	8.46	(6.79; 10.13)	13	7	6.68	(5.01; 8.35)
4	6	5.85	(4.21; 7.50)	14	5	6.89	(5.28; 8.49)
5	9	8.46	(6.79; 10.13)	15	10	9.30	(7.66; 10.95)
6	10	9.30	(7.66; 10.95)	16	8	8.52	(6.84; 10.19)
7	10	9.30	(7.66; 10.95)	17	7	6.68	(5.01; 8.35)
8	10	9.30	(7.66; 10.95)	18	8	8.52	(6.84; 10.19)
9	9	8.46	(6.79; 10.13)	19	7	7.62	(5.95; 9.29)
10	9	8.46	(6.79; 10.13)	20	9	9.40	(7.73; 11.07)

Table 1. Results of imputations

As illustrated by this example, our imputation strategy allows us to obtain applicable results for practical usage.

5   Concluding remarks

It is important to remember that the imputation methodology does not give us qualitatively new information but enables us to use all available information about the data with maximal efficiency. In general, most of the missing data handling methods deal with incomplete data primarily from the perspective of estimation of parameters and computation of test statistics rather than predicting the values for specific cases. We, on the other hand, are interested in small sample sizes where every value is essential and imputation results are of scientific interest itself.

The results of this study indicate that in the empirical context of the current study the algorithm performs well for modeling missing values in correlated data.

As importantly, the following advantages can be pointed out.

(1) The marginals of variables do not have to be normal, they can even be different.

(2) The simplicity of formulas (10)–(13).

The class of copulas is wide and growing, the copula approach used here can be extended to the case of other copulas. Choosing a copula to fit the given data is an important but difficult question. These relevant problems obviously merit further research and we will study them in our future work.

Appendix 1. Proof of Lemma 1

As the proof of formula (8) is discussed before, we only need to prove the validity of formula (9). Recall the general formula (4) for conditional variance

$$Var(Z_{k+1}|Z_1 = z_1, \ldots, Z_k = z_k) = 1 - \mathbf{r}^T \mathbf{R}_k^{-1} \mathbf{r}.$$

According to the partition of the correlation matrix $\mathbf{R}$ with autoregressive correlation structure the vector of correlations between the complete data and the $(k+1)$-th variable is of the form $\mathbf{r} = (\rho^k, \rho^{k-1} \ldots, \rho)^T$. The inverse of the correlation matrix $\mathbf{R}_k$ is a three-diagonal matrix. The main properties of this type of three-diagonal matrices are well-known (Kendall and Stuart (1976)).

The inverse matrix of the correlation matrix $\mathbf{R}_k$ has the following structure

$$\mathbf{R}_k^{-1} = \frac{1}{\rho^2 - 1} \begin{pmatrix} -1 & \rho & 0 \ldots & 0 & 0 \\ \rho & -(1+\rho^2) & \rho \ldots & 0 & 0 \\ \vdots & \vdots & \vdots \ddots & \vdots & \vdots \\ 0 & 0 & 0 \ldots & -(1+\rho^2) & \rho \\ 0 & 0 & 0 \ldots & \rho & -1 \end{pmatrix}.$$

Further, using the matrix $\mathbf{R}_k^{-1}$, we attain

$$\mathbf{r}^T \cdot \mathbf{R}_k^{-1} = \frac{1}{\rho^2 - 1} \cdot (0, 0, \ldots, 0, \rho(\rho^2 - 1)) = (0, 0, \ldots, 0, \rho).$$

Thus considering (4), we have

$$Var(Z_{k+1}|Z_1 = z_1, \ldots, Z_k = z_k) = 1 - (0, 0, \ldots, 0, \rho) \cdot (\rho^k, \rho^{k-1}, \ldots, \rho)^T = 1 - \rho^2.$$

Lemma is proved.

Acknowledgments

This work is supported by Estonian Science Foundation grants No 7313 and No 8294.

References

CLEMEN, R.T. and REILLY, T. (1999): Correlations and copulas for decision and risk analysis. *Management Science 45(2), 208-224.*

KENDALL, M. and STUART, A. (1976): *Design and analysis, and time-series. The advanced theory of statistics.* Nauka, Moscow (in Russian).

KÄÄRIK, E. (2007): *Handling dropouts in repeated measurements using copulas.* Diss. Math. Universitas Tartuensis, 51, UT Press, Tartu.

KÄÄRIK, E. and KÄÄRIK, M. (2009a): Modelling dropouts by conditional distribution, a copula-based approach. *Journal of Statistical Planning and Inference, 139(11), 3830 - 3835.*

KÄÄRIK, M. and KÄÄRIK, E. (2009b): Copula-based approach to modelling incomplete correlated data. In: ATINER Publications (Submitted).

NELSEN, R. B. (2006): *An introduction to copulas.* 2nd edition. Springer, New York.

SCHÖLZEL, C. and FRIEDERICS, P. (2007): Multivariate non-normally distributed random variables in climate research introduction to the copula approach. *Nonlinear Processes in Geophysics. 15, 761-772.*

SONG, P.X.K. (2007): *Correlated data analysis. Modeling, analytics, and applications.* Springer, New York.

SONG, P.X-K., LI, M., YUAN, Y. (2009): Joint regression analysis of correlated data using Gaussian copulas. *Biometrics 64 (2), 60-68.*

On Multiple-Case Diagnostics in Linear Subspace Method

Kuniyoshi Hayashi[1], Hiroyuki Minami[2] and Masahiro Mizuta[2]

[1] Graduate School of Information Sciences and Technology, Hokkaido University, N14W9, Kita-ku, Sapporo, JAPAN, *k-hayashi@iic.hokudai.ac.jp*
[2] Information Initiative Center, Hokkaido University, N11W5, Kita-ku, Sapporo, JAPAN, *min@iic.hokudai.ac.jp, mizuta@iic.hokudai.ac.jp*

Abstract. In this paper, we discuss sensitivity analysis in linear subspace method, especially on multiple-case diagnostics.

Linear subspace method by Watanabe (1973) is a useful discriminant method in the field of pattern recognition. We have proposed its sensitivity analyses, with single-case diagnostics and multiple-case diagnostics with PCA.

We propose a modified multiple-case diagnostics using clustering and discuss its effectiveness with numerical simulations.

Keywords: CLAFIC, sensitivity analysis, perturbation

1 Introduction

In the field of pattern recognition, Watanabe (1967, 1970, 1973) proposed linear subspace method which is one of discriminant methods. The performance is effective, even if the target dataset was sparse. It and its extensions have been used in recognition systems. In statistics, sensitivity analysis with influence functions have been studied in many multivariate methods (Campbell (1978); Radhakrishnan and Kshirsagar (1981); Critchley (1985); Tanaka (1988)). The main purpose is to evaluate the influence of observations to the result of analysis and find outliers. We have already proposed sensitivity analysis in linear subspace method for single-case diagnostics (Hayashi *et al.* (2008)). In multiple-case diagnostics, we used PCA to find influence directions but we do not always find them when the cumulative proportion is low. To overcome this problem, we propose a multiple-case diagnostics by clustering based on all dimensions and show its effectiveness through simulations.

2 Sensitivity analysis in linear subspace method

In this section, we briefly give an explanation of sensitivity analysis in linear subspace method. We especially focus on class-featuring information compression (CLAFIC) that is one of linear subspace methods (Watanabe (1973)).

Y. Lechevallier, G. Saporta (eds.), *Proceedings of COMPSTAT'2010*,
DOI 10.1007/978-3-7908-2604-3_49, © Springer-Verlag Berlin Heidelberg 2010

2.1   CLAFIC

We suppose that the number of classes is K and denote the number of variables as p and a training observation in k-th class as $\boldsymbol{x}_i^k$ $(i = 1, 2, \ldots, n_k,\ \ k = 1, \ldots, K)$, where n_k is the number of the samples in k-th class. Then, the autocorrelation matrix of the training data in k-th class is defined as follows:

$$\hat{G}_k = \frac{1}{n_k} \sum_{i=1}^{n_k} \boldsymbol{x}_i^k \boldsymbol{x}_i^{k\mathrm{T}}. \tag{1}$$

A covariance matrix is generally calculated from sample observed values with subtracting a mean, but $\hat{G}_k$ is calculated in the same way without subtractions. We solve the eigenvalue problem for $\hat{G}_k$ and denote the p eigenvalues as $\hat{\lambda}_1^k \geq \hat{\lambda}_2^k \geq \cdots \geq \hat{\lambda}_p^k \geq 0$. We denote the eigenvector corresponding to $\hat{\lambda}_s^k$ as $\hat{\boldsymbol{u}}_s^k$ $(s = 1, \ldots, p)$. A projection matrix in k-th class is defined as follows:

$$\hat{P}_k = \sum_{s=1}^{p_k} \hat{\boldsymbol{u}}_s^k \hat{\boldsymbol{u}}_s^{k\mathrm{T}}, \qquad (1 \leq p_k \leq p), \tag{2}$$

where p_k is the minimum value m, satisfied with the following inequation, $\tau \leq \sum_{s=1}^{m} / \sum_{s=1}^{p} \hat{\lambda}_s^k$, $(1 \leq m \leq p)$, for given τ, which is a threshold like cumulative proportion in PCA. We project a test observation $\boldsymbol{x}^*$ into all subspaces and calculate the squares of the projection norms $(\boldsymbol{x}^{*\mathrm{T}} \hat{P}_k \boldsymbol{x}^*,\ \ k = 1, \ldots, K)$. We classify the test observation into the most appropriate class that gives the maximum value $(\max_k \{\boldsymbol{x}^{*\mathrm{T}} \hat{P}_k \boldsymbol{x}^*\})$.

2.2   Discriminant score

We define a discriminant score for $\boldsymbol{x}_i^k$ as follows:

$$\hat{z}_i^k = \boldsymbol{x}_i^{k\mathrm{T}} \hat{Q}_k \boldsymbol{x}_i^k \qquad (1 \leq i \leq n_k), \tag{3}$$

where

$$\hat{Q}_k = \frac{1}{K-1} \left(K\hat{P}_k - \sum_{\ell=1}^{K} \hat{P}_\ell \right). \tag{4}$$

We calculate the average of the discriminant scores in each class,

$$\hat{Z}^k = \frac{1}{n_k} \sum_{i=1}^{n_k} \hat{z}_i^k. \tag{5}$$

We evaluate the change for the influence of observation with $\hat{Z}^k$ because an average can be greatly affected by outlier.

2.3   EIF and SIF

We regard $\mathrm{vech}(\hat{Q}_k)$ $(k = 1, \ldots, K)$ as differentiable functionals of the empirical cumulative distribution functions $\hat{F}^g$ $(g = 1, \ldots, K)$. From the definition of influence functions (Hampel (1974, 1986)), the empirical influence function is given by

$$\mathrm{EIF}(\boldsymbol{x}_j^g; \mathrm{vech}(\hat{Q}_k)) =$$

$$
\begin{cases}
\mathrm{vech}\left(\sum_{s=1}^{p_g} \sum_{t=p_g+1}^{p} (\hat{\lambda}_s^g - \hat{\lambda}_t^g)^{-1} \hat{\boldsymbol{u}}_s^{g\mathrm{T}} \hat{G}_g^{gj} \hat{\boldsymbol{u}}_t^g (\hat{\boldsymbol{u}}_s^g \hat{\boldsymbol{u}}_t^{g\mathrm{T}} + \hat{\boldsymbol{u}}_t^g \hat{\boldsymbol{u}}_s^{g\mathrm{T}}) \right) & (g = k), \\[2ex]
\mathrm{vech}\left(-\frac{1}{K-1} \sum_{s=1}^{p_g} \sum_{t=p_g+1}^{p} (\hat{\lambda}_s^g - \hat{\lambda}_t^g)^{-1} \hat{\boldsymbol{u}}_s^{g\mathrm{T}} \hat{G}_g^{gj} \hat{\boldsymbol{u}}_t^g (\hat{\boldsymbol{u}}_s^g \hat{\boldsymbol{u}}_t^{g\mathrm{T}} + \hat{\boldsymbol{u}}_t^g \hat{\boldsymbol{u}}_s^{g\mathrm{T}}) \right) & (g \neq k),
\end{cases}
\tag{6}
$$

where p_g is the number of the basis vectors for the projection matrix in g-th class. $\hat{G}_g^{gj}$ is $\hat{\boldsymbol{x}}_j^g \hat{\boldsymbol{x}}_j^{g\mathrm{T}} - \hat{G}_g$ $(j = 1, \ldots, n_g)$. In the derivation of (6), we can refer to Tanaka (1988, 1994). The sample influence function is calculated as

$$\mathrm{SIF}(\boldsymbol{x}_j^g; \mathrm{vech}(\hat{Q}_k)) = -(n_g - 1) \cdot \left\{ \mathrm{vech}(\hat{Q}_{kg(j)}) - \mathrm{vech}(\hat{Q}_k) \right\}, \tag{7}$$

where $\mathrm{vech}(\hat{Q}_{kg(j)})$ is $\mathrm{vech}(\hat{Q}_k)$ by deleting j-th observation in g-th class.

To evaluate the influence of a perturbed observation for $\hat{Z}^k$, we summarize $\mathrm{EIF}(\boldsymbol{x}_j^g; \mathrm{vech}(\hat{Q}_k))$ and $\mathrm{SIF}(\boldsymbol{x}_j^g; \mathrm{vech}(\hat{Q}_k))$ into scalars according to Tanaka (1994). We summarize them as $\hat{Z}_k^{gj}$ and $\hat{Z}_k^{g(j)}$,

$$\hat{Z}_k^{gj} = \frac{1}{n_k} \sum_{i=1}^{n_k} \boldsymbol{x}_i^{k\mathrm{T}} \hat{Q}_k^{gj} \boldsymbol{x}_i^k \quad (g \neq k) \tag{8}$$

$$\hat{Z}_k^{g(j)} = \frac{1}{n_k} \sum_{i=1}^{n_k} \boldsymbol{x}_i^{k\mathrm{T}} \hat{Q}_k^{g(j)} \boldsymbol{x}_i^k, \tag{9}$$

where $\hat{Q}_k^{gj} = -\frac{1}{K-1} \sum_{s=1}^{p_g} \sum_{t=p_g+1}^{p} (\hat{\lambda}_s^g - \hat{\lambda}_t^g)^{-1} \hat{\boldsymbol{u}}_s^{g\mathrm{T}} \hat{G}_g^{gj} \hat{\boldsymbol{u}}_t^g (\hat{\boldsymbol{u}}_s^g \hat{\boldsymbol{u}}_t^{g\mathrm{T}} + \hat{\boldsymbol{u}}_t^g \hat{\boldsymbol{u}}_s^{g\mathrm{T}})$ and $\hat{Q}_k^{g(j)} = -(n_g - 1) \cdot (\hat{Q}_{kg(j)} - \hat{Q}_k)$.

2.4   Diagnostics

On single-case diagnostics in linear subspace method, we use $\hat{Z}_k^{g(j)}$ or $\hat{Z}_k^{gj}$ to evaluate the influence of each observation. To deal with the influence of multiple individuals in theoretical influence function (TIF), we consider a perturbation from F^g to $\tilde{F}^g = (1 - \varepsilon)F^g + \varepsilon G^g$, where $G^g = \alpha^{-1} \sum_{\boldsymbol{x}_i^g \in A} \delta_{\boldsymbol{x}_i^g}$ (Tanaka (1994)). A and α represent a set of observations and the number of observations belonging to the set, respectively. We can define a generalized influence function for A as $\mathrm{TIF}(A; \mathrm{vech}(Q_k)) = \lim_{\varepsilon \to 0}[\mathrm{vech}(Q_k)(\tilde{F}^g) - \mathrm{vech}(Q_k)(F^g)]/\varepsilon$. This can be rewritten as follows:

$$\mathrm{TIF}(A; \mathrm{vech}(Q_k)) = \frac{1}{\alpha} \cdot \sum_{\boldsymbol{x}_i^g \in A} \mathrm{TIF}(\boldsymbol{x}_i^g; \mathrm{vech}(Q_k)). \tag{10}$$

Equation (10) indicates that the generalized influence function for a subset A is obtained as the average of the influence functions calculated from observations in the subset A.

We denote $\hat{F}^g_{(A)}$ as the empirical cumulative distribution function based on the observations not in the subset A. $\hat{F}^g_{(A)} = (n_g - \alpha)^{-1} \cdot \{\sum_{i=1}^{n_g} \delta_{\boldsymbol{x}_i^g} - \sum_{\boldsymbol{x}_i^g \in A} \delta_{\boldsymbol{x}_i^g}\}$. $\hat{F}_{(A)}$ can be rewritten as

$$\hat{F}^g_{(A)} = \frac{1}{n_g - \alpha} \sum_{i=1}^{n_g} \delta_{\boldsymbol{x}_i^g} - \frac{\alpha}{n_g - \alpha} \cdot \frac{1}{\alpha} \sum_{\boldsymbol{x}_i^g \in A} \delta_{\boldsymbol{x}_i^g}. \tag{11}$$

When we put $-\alpha/(n_g-\alpha)$ as ε, $\hat{F}^g_{(A)}$ is equal to $(1-\varepsilon)\sum_{i=1}^{n_g} + \varepsilon\alpha^{-1}\sum_{\boldsymbol{x}_i^g \in A} \delta_{\boldsymbol{x}_i^g}$. Therefore, we can understand that the additive property in TIF is also satisfied in EIF (Critchley (1985); Tanaka (1984)). Based on the additive property, Tanaka (1994) proposed the procedure of multiple-case diagnostics using PCA. When we use SIF in multiple-case diagnostics, the number of all possible combinations of deleting observations rapidly increases in proportion to the number of classes and observations. Therefore, in the analysis of tons of data, we can not generally use SIF in multiple-case diagnostics.

3   A multiple-case diagnostics with clustering

We have developed sensitivity analysis in linear subspace method including single-case and multiple-case diagnostics. In multiple-case diagnostics, we use PCA and PCA with metric $[\widehat{\mathrm{acov}}(\hat{Q}_k)]^{-1}$ to search the influential directions of observations and deleted the observations which have a similar influence direction, so that we evaluate the change of the result of analysis.

However, if the influence directions of observations can not be represented with a few dimensions, we have to pick up many dimensions. In addition, there is not an criterion to measure the similarity of observations. To overcome these problems, we can apply clustering to influence directions of observations and can confirm the relationship of them. A multiple-case diagnostics with PCA is appropriate for searching a few of large influential directions of observations, but not for searching grouping them. Considering the stability of statistical model by deleting multiple observations, the main purpose is to evaluate the changes of the result of analyses by deleting observations based on all possible combinations of observations. Therefore, in multiple-case diagnostics, the technique of clustering is as important as PCA.

Here, we modify the procedure of multiple-case diagnostics with PCA from a point of view of clustering. In this regard, we particularly focus on hierarchical clustering. We denote the eigenvalues calculated in eigenvalue problem to obtain influence directions of observations as $\xi_1 \geq \xi_2 \geq \cdots \geq \xi_{n_g} \geq 0$ and also denote a component of the eigenvectors as $\boldsymbol{a}_{ji}$ $(j, i = 1, \ldots, n_g)$. We determine a threshold ρ and pick up $\xi_1, \xi_2, \ldots, \xi_{n'_g}$ $(1 \leq n'_g < n_g)$ satisfied with $\sum_{i=1}^{n'_g} \xi_i / \sum_{i=1}^{n_g} \xi_i < \rho \leq \sum_{i=1}^{n'_g+1} \xi_i / \sum_{i=1}^{n_g} \xi_i$. Using the eigenvectors associated with these eigenvalues, we make up $A = (\boldsymbol{a}_{ji})$ $(j = 1, \ldots, n_g, \ i = 1, \ldots, n'_g)$.

Before clustering, to get the similarity matrix for A, we calculate the Euclidean norm, $d_{jj'} = \sqrt{\sum_{i=1}^{n'_g} (\boldsymbol{a}_{ji} - \boldsymbol{a}_{j'i})^{\mathrm{T}} (\boldsymbol{a}_{ji} - \boldsymbol{a}_{j'i})}$ $(j, j' = 1, \ldots, n_g)$. We apply Ward's method to the matrix $D = (d_{jj'})$ and search the similar influence patterns of observations. If we can know the number of clusters from the power of computer and calculation time, we can also adapt a nonhierarchical clustering like k-means.

Finally, we group the influence patterns of observations and delete the subsets which have the same influence pattern and evaluate the change of the result of analysis. This approach in multiple-case diagnostics is superior to one by deleting observations in all possible combinations. The first reason is that we can visually find the influence patterns of observations. The second reason is that we can perform the diagnostics within a reasonable time. In the following, we summarize the procedure of multiple-case diagnostics with clustering again.

(Step1) Calculate the eigenvectors $\boldsymbol{a}_{\cdot i}$s with EIF and $\widehat{\mathrm{acov}}(\hat{Q}_k)$.

(Step2) Determine a threshold ρ from a screeplot and build $D = (d_{jj'})$ with $A = (\boldsymbol{a}_{ji})$.

(Step3) Group the similar influence patterns of observations applying Ward's method to $D = (d_{jj'})$.

(Step4) Delete the subsets that have the similar influence pattern and evaluete the variant of the result of analysis.

In the next section, we show the effectiveness of the multiple-case diagnostics with simulations, comparing one by deletion in all possible combinations.

4 Numerical examples

To show the effectiveness of the modified diagnostics in linear subspace method, we perform simple examples. We set up two datasets generated in multivariate normal distributions and we add noises to them, respectively. We call them as Group 1 and Group 2 and denote the index of them as 1 and 2, respectively. Each dataset consists of $n = 10$ observations and 8 variables. We set the value of τ up as 0.999 and develop the classifier using the data.

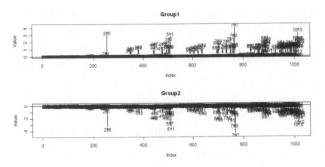

Fig. 1. $\hat{Z}_k^{1(J)}$ in Group1

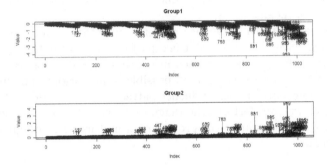

Fig. 2. $\hat{Z}_k^{2(J)}$ in Group2

We firstly perform the multiple-case diagnostics by omitting observations in all possible combinations. In this case, the number of combinations deleting observations in each class is 1023 ($2^{10} - 1$). We study the change of $\hat{Z}_k^{g(J)}$ ($k, g = 1, 2$, $J \in \{x_1^g, \ldots, x_{n_g}^g\}$). $\hat{Z}_k^{g(J)}$s are shown in Fig. 1 and Fig. 2, respectively.

In Group 1, the four combinations which are No. 255, No. 511, No. 767 and No. 1015 show the large value in $\hat{Z}_k^{1(J)}$. In Group 2, No. 703, No. 831, No. 895 and No. 959 have the large $\hat{Z}_k^{1(J)}$. These numbers correspond to the subsets of observations (Table 1).

Table 1. Large influential subsets

Group 1	Subset	Group 2	Subset
No. 255	{ 3, 4, 5, 6, 7, 8, 9, 10 }	No. 703	{ 1, 3, 5, 6, 7, 8, 9, 10 }
No. 511	{ 2, 3, 4, 5, 6, 7, 8, 9, 10 }	No. 831	{ 1, 2, 5, 6, 7, 8, 9, 10 }
No. 767	{ 1, 3, 4, 5, 6, 7, 8, 9, 10 }	No. 895	{ 1, 2, 4, 5, 6, 7, 8, 9, 10 }
No. 1015	{ 1, 2, 3, 4, 5, 6, 8, 9, 10 }	No. 959	{ 1, 2, 3, 5, 6, 7, 8, 9, 10 }

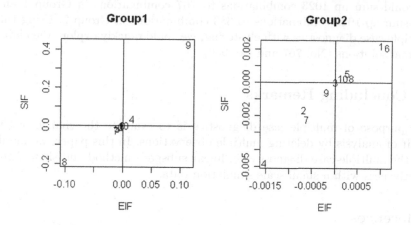

Fig. 3. EIF vs SIF

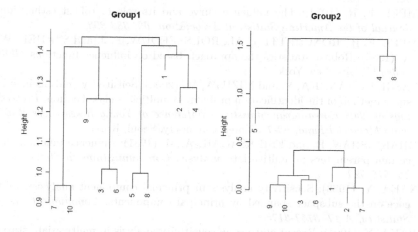

Fig. 4. Clusters of influence directions in each class

Secondly, we carry out the multiple-case diagnostics. The approximations of EIF and SIF in each class are shown in Fig. 3. From Fig. 3, we can understand that the approximations are good. According to the procedure of Section 4, we calculate the influence directions of observations with EIF and $\widehat{acov}(\hat{Q}_k)$ and determine a threshold $\rho(= 0.90)$. We constitute $D = (d_{jj'})$ $(j, j' = 1, \ldots, 10)$ and apply Ward's method to $D = (d_{jj'})$. This result is represented in Fig. 4. Finally, we could reduce 10 observations to 5 clusters ({ 7, 10 } , { 3, 6, 9 } , { 5, 8 } , { 1 } , { 2, 4 }) in Group 1 and can also summarize 10 observations to 4 clusters ({ 5 } , { 9, 10, 3, 6 } , { 1, 2, 7 } , { 4, 8 }) in Group 2. Using the modified multiple-case diagnostics, we could sum up 1023 combinations to 767 combinations in Group 1 and also sum up 1023 combinations to 383 combinations in Group 2. Using this multiple-case diagnostics with clustering, we could quickly explore the global optimal solutions (No. 767 and No. 959).

5   Concluding Remarks

The purpose of multiple-case diagnostics is to evaluate the change of the result of analysis by deleting multiple observations. In this paper, we modified the multiple-case diagnostics in linear subspace method and showed the effectiveness with a small scale simulation data.

References

CRITCHLEY, F. (1985): Influence in principal component analysis. *Biometrika, 72, 627-636.*

HAMPEL, F. R. (1974): The influence curve and its role in robust estimation. *Journal of the American Statistical Association, 69, 383-393.*

HAMPEL, F. R., RONCHETTI, E. M., ROUSSEEOUW, P. J. and STAHEL, W. A. (1986): Robust statistics the approach based on influence functions. *Jhon Wiley & Sons, New York.*

HAYASHI, K., TANAKA, Y. and MIZUTA, M. (2008): Sensitivity analysis in subspace method of the identification problem in multiclass classification. *Proceedings of 2008 Korea-Japan Statistics Conference of Young Researchers Wakimoto Memorial Fund, 63-75,* Korea University, Seoul, Korea.

RADHAKRISHAN, R. and KSHIRSAGAR, A. M. (1981): Influence functions for certain parameters in multivariate analysis. *Communications in Statistics, A 10, 515-529.*

TANAKA, Y. (1988): Sensitivity analysis in principal component analysis: Influence on the subspace spanned by principal components. *Communications in Statistics, A 17, 3157-3175.*

TANAKA, Y. (1994): Recent advance in sensitivity analysis in multivariate statistical methods. *Journal of the Japanese Society of Computational Statistics, 7, 1-25.*

WATANABE, S. (1970): Featuring compression. *Advances in Information Systems Science Volume 3 (Edited by Tou, J. T.),* Plenum Press, New York.

WATANABE, S., LAMPERT, P. F., KULIKOWSKI, C. A., BUXTON, J. L. and Walker, R. (1967): Evaluation and selection of variables in pattern recognition. *Computer and Information Sciences II,* Academic Press, New York.

WATANABE, S. and PAKVASA, N. (1973): Subspace method of pattern recognition, *Proceedings of 1st International Joint Conference of Pattern Recognition, 25-32.*

Fourier Methods for Sequential Change Point Analysis in Autoregressive Models

Marie Hušková[1], Claudia Kirch[2], and Simos G. Meintanis[3]

[1] Charles University of Prague, Department of Statistics
Sokolovská 83, CZ – 186 75, Praha 8, Czech Republic,
marie.huskova@karlin.mff.cuni.cz
[2] Karlsruhe Institute of Technology, Institute for Stochastics
Kaiserstr. 89, 76133 Karlsruhe, Germany, *claudia.kirch@kit.edu*
[3] National and Kapodistrian University of Athens, Department of Economics,
8 Pesmazoglou Street, 105 59 Athens, Greece, *simosmei@econ.uoa.gr*

Abstract. We develop a procedure for monitoring changes in the error distribution of autoregressive time series. The proposed procedure, unlike standard procedures which are also referred to, utilizes the empirical characteristic function of properly estimated residuals. The limit behavior of the test statistic is investigated under the null hypothesis, while computational and other relevant issues are addressed.

Keywords: empirical characteristic function, change point analysis

1 Introduction

Change–point analysis for distributional change with i.i.d. observations and the study of structural breaks in the parameters of time series has received wide attention; see for instance Yao (1990), Einmahl and McKeague (2003), Hušková and Meintanis (2006a), Hušková et al. (2007), Hušková et al. (2008), Gombay and Serban (2009), to name a few. (For a full–book treatment on theoretical and methodological issues of change–point analysis the reader is referred to Csörgő and Horváth (1997)). On the other hand works on structural breaks due to change in the distribution of a time series are relatively few. The purpose of this paper is to develop novel sequential procedures for change in the error distribution of autoregressive models and to compare these procedures to alternative monitoring schemes.

Testing hypotheses in the context of monitoring schemes assumes that data arrive sequentially and that an initial subset of these data, termed 'training data', involve no change. Then after each new observation we should decide whether there is evidence of change, and terminate testing in favor of the alternative hypothesis, or that there is no evidence of change, in which case we continue the testing procedure.

Let X_t be an AR(p) process defined by the equation

$$X_t - \mathbf{X}'_{t-1}\boldsymbol{\beta} = \varepsilon_t, \tag{1}$$

Y. Lechevallier, G. Saporta (eds.), *Proceedings of COMPSTAT'2010*,
DOI 10.1007/978-3-7908-2604-3_50, © Springer-Verlag Berlin Heidelberg 2010

where $\mathbf{X}_t = (X_t, ..., X_{t-p+1})'$, and $\boldsymbol{\beta} = (\beta_1, ..., \beta_p)'$. In (1) the errors ε_t are i.i.d. with distribution function F_t having mean zero and finite variance. Also the AR process is assumed to be stationary i.e., the characteristic polynomial $P(z) = 1 - \beta_1 z - ... - \beta_p z^p$, is assumed to satisfy $P(z) \neq 0, \forall |z| \leq 1$. For some $T < \infty$, and given the training data $X_1, ..., X_T$, we are interested in testing the hypothesis

$$\mathbb{H}_0 : F_t = F_0, \forall t > T \ vs. \ \mathbb{H}_1 : F_t \neq F_0 \text{ for some } t > T,$$

where F_0 is assumed unknown. In view of the fact that the errors are unobserved, typically one computes the residuals

$$\widehat{\varepsilon}_t = X_t - \mathbf{X}'_{t-1} \widehat{\boldsymbol{\beta}}_T, \tag{2}$$

from (1) by using some standard (possibly $\sqrt{T}$ consistent) estimator $\widehat{\boldsymbol{\beta}}_T$ of $\boldsymbol{\beta}$, such as the least squares (LS) estimator. This estimator is computed on the basis of the training data $X_1, ..., X_T$. Then standard goodness–of–fit statistics are employed which make use of the empirical distribution function (EDF) of these residuals. In this paper we deviate from these standard approaches by proposing a unified method for estimation, and for testing $\mathbb{H}_0$ that utilizes the empirical characteristic function (ECF) of the residuals. The rationale for following this approach is that test statistics analogous to these proposed herein have been used to test structural change in the context of i.i.d. observations with satisfactory performance; see Hušková and Meintanis (2006a, 2006b). Also the estimation method employed here in computing the residuals in (2) is more general and robust to outliers than least squares and contains the LS method as a special case.

2   Test statistics

We assume that the chosen estimator $\widehat{\boldsymbol{\beta}}_T$ of $\boldsymbol{\beta}$, which is computed on the basis of the training data $\{X_t\}_{t=1}^T$, satisfies the property

$$\sqrt{T}(\widehat{\boldsymbol{\beta}}_T - \boldsymbol{\beta}) = O_P(1), \ T \to \infty.$$

On the basis of the residuals $\widehat{\varepsilon}_t$ defined in (2), classical procedures for testing the null hypothesis $\mathbb{H}_0$ utilize the EDF,

$$\widehat{F}_k(z) = \frac{1}{k-p} \sum_{t=p+1}^k \mathbb{I}(\widehat{\varepsilon}_t \leq z),$$

where $\mathbb{I}(\cdot)$ denotes the indicator function. In particular the Kolmogorov–Smirnov (KS) statistic is defined by the critical region

$$KS := \sup_{k \geq T} T_{KS}(k) \geq C_{KS,\alpha}, \tag{3}$$

where α denotes the nominal level of significance and

$$T_{KS}(k) = c_{k,T}(\gamma) \sup_{-\infty < z < \infty} |\widehat{F}_k(z) - \widehat{F}_T(z)|,$$

with $c_{k,T}(\gamma)$ being a normalizing function depending on a parameter $\gamma \geq 0$. The Crámer–von Mises (CM) statistic is defined likewise by replacing in (3) $T_{KS}(k)$ by

$$T_{CM}(k) = c_{k,T}(\gamma) \int_{-\infty}^{\infty} |\widehat{F}_k(z) - \widehat{F}_T(z)|^2 d\widehat{F}_T(z).$$

In the asymptotic behavior for classical statistics one uses functionals of the processes

$$c_{k,T}(\gamma) \left[\widehat{F}_k(z) - \widehat{F}_T(z) \right].$$

For these processes the limit behavior has been studied by Bai (1994). Follow–up articles on the KS and CM statistics are by Inoue (2001), and by Lee et al. (2009), while Ling (2007) studies the behavior of a Wald–type statistic for the same problem.

It should be pointed out, that in the KS and CM statistics the underlying distribution function F_t is usually assumed to be absolutely continuous. On the other hand, the Fourier approach which we advocate does not require smoothness of F_t since it utilizes the ECF of the residuals

$$\widehat{\phi}_{k_1,k_2}(u) = \frac{1}{k_2 - k_1} \sum_{t=k_1+1}^{k_2} e^{iu\widehat{\varepsilon}_t},$$

which is continuous regardless of the type of F_t. In the proposed test statistic, we reject the null hypothesis $\mathbb{H}_0$ whenever

$$CF := \sup_{1 \leq k \leq L_T} T_{CF}(k) \geq C_{CF,\alpha} \tag{4}$$

with $L_T \to \infty$ as $T \to \infty$, where

$$T_{CF}(k) = \rho_{k,T}(\gamma) \int_{-\infty}^{\infty} |\widehat{\phi}_{T,T+k}(u) - \widehat{\phi}_{p,T}(u)|^2 w(u) du.$$

In the CF–test, and in addition to the normalization $\rho_{k,T}(\gamma)$, $w(u)$ is an extra weight function introduced to smooth out the periodic components of the ECF.

3   Sketch of asymptotics

It can be shown that the limit null distribution of the CF–statistic does not depend on the estimator of $\widehat{\beta}_T$. Moreover the aforementioned limit distribution is the same as if we replace the residuals $\widehat{\varepsilon}_t$ by ε_t. To get the limit distribution of the test statistics with ε_t we follow the proof of Hušková and Meintanis (2006a). It can be shown that for $k = \lfloor Ts \rfloor$, $s > 0$ fixed, $T \to \infty$, the limit behavior of

$$\frac{kT}{k+T} \int_{-\infty}^{\infty} |\widehat{\phi}_{T,T+k}(u) - \widehat{\phi}_{p,T}(u)|^2 w(u)du$$

is the same as

$$\int w(t)dt - \mathbb{E}\left[h_w(\varepsilon_1, \varepsilon_2)\right] + \sum_{j=1}^{\infty} \lambda_j \left\{ \frac{(W_{j,1}(s) - sW_{j,2}(1))^2}{s(1+s)} - 1 \right\},$$

where $h_w(x,y) := h_w(x-y) = \int \cos(u(x-y))w(u)du$, $W_{j,1}(\cdot)$, $j \geq 1$ and $W_{j,2}(\cdot)$, $j \geq 1$, are independent Wiener processes, and λ_j, $j \geq 1$, are eigenvalues which depend on the underlying distribution function F_0 which is unknown. Hence the limit distribution depends on unknown quantities and does not provide an approximation for critical values of the CF–statistic. One can use a special bootstrap for this sequential setup. Possible versions can be obtained by adapting the procedures suggested by Kirch (2008) and Hušková and Kirch (2009) to the present situation.

Concerning more general standardized constants $\rho_{k,T}(\gamma)$ we suggest:

$$\rho_{k,T}(\gamma) = \frac{kT}{k+T}\left(k/(T+k)\right)^\gamma, \quad 0 \leq \gamma < 1.$$

The proposed procedure based on CF defined in (4) can be used also for situation when $\{X_t\}_t$ follow either linear regression model or ARMA sequence.

In the following section we examine some aspects of the estimation method and the new statistics.

4   FLS estimation and ECF statistics

(i) FLS estimation: The proposed estimator is the functional least squares (FLS) estimator proposed by Heathcote and Welsh (1983). For fixed $u \in \mathbb{R}$, the FLS estimator is obtained by minimizing the loss function

$$H_T(\boldsymbol{\beta}, u) = -\frac{1}{u^2} \log \left|\widehat{\phi}_{p,T}(u)\right|^2, \tag{5}$$

where $\widehat{\phi}_{p,T}(u)$ is the ECF computed from the residuals $\widehat{\varepsilon}_t$, $t = p+1, ..., T$. Under standard assumptions the FLS method produces consistent and asymptotically normal estimators, which are robust to 'innovation' outliers, i.e. to outliers with respect to the error distribution; see Dhar (1993) and Meintanis and Donatos (1999) . Note also that an efficient FLS estimator can be adaptively defined by choosing the argument $u := \widehat{u}_T$ so that the estimated asymptotic variance is minimized; refer to Csörgő (1983).

The first thing to notice in FLS estimation is that

$$\left|\widehat{\phi}_{p,T}(u)\right|^2 = \frac{1}{(T-p)^2} \sum_{t,s=p+1}^{T} \cos\left[u(\widehat{\varepsilon}_t - \widehat{\varepsilon}_s)\right],$$

is location invariant and hence the constant term can not be estimated by FLS. Despite the fact that Welsh (1985), motivated by circular statistics, proposed an estimator of the intercept based on the FLS–slope estimate, in what follows we will consider the case of no intercept. It is illuminating to further investigate which factors play part in the FLS loss function $H_T(\beta, u)$ in (5). To this end, by the previous equation and by simple Taylor expansions of $\cos(u)$ and $\log(1 + u)$ one has after some algebra that

$$\log\left|\widehat{\phi}_{p,T}(u)\right|^2 = -\tfrac{u^2}{2}M_2 + \tfrac{u^4}{24}\left(M_4 - 3M_2^2\right) + \tfrac{u^6}{720}\left(15M_2M_4 - M_6 - 30M_2^3\right) + \ldots,$$

(6)

where $M_k = (T - p)^{-2} \sum_{t,s=p+1}^{T} (\widehat{\varepsilon}_t - \widehat{\varepsilon}_s)^k$, $k = 2, 3, \ldots$. Equation (6) contains powers of u and associated contrasts incorporating empirical moments (in forms reminiscent of V–statistics) computed from the FLS residuals. Notice however that as $T \to \infty$, the coefficients of u^k in (6) vanish identically for $k > 2$, if the corresponding errors follow the normal distribution, since the aforementioned contrasts hold true for this distribution; for instance the coefficient of u^4 expresses, the moment relation $\mathbb{E}(X^4) = 3(\mathbb{E}(X^2))^2$, while the coefficient of u^6, the moment relation $\mathbb{E}(X^6) = 15\mathbb{E}(X^4)\mathbb{E}(X^2) - 30(\mathbb{E}(X^2))^2$. Hence from this Taylor approximation, it becomes transparent that when estimating β on the basis of the loss function $H_T(\beta, u)$, it is unnecessary, at least asymptotically, to go beyond u^2 in that Taylor expansion when the errors are normal. In fact by replacing (6) in (5) one has $\lim_{u \to 0} H_T(\beta, u) = M_2$, which is the loss function of the LS–slope coefficients in deviation form, and shows that LS is a special case of the FLS estimator, and recovers the fact that under normal errors LS estimation is optimal.

(ii) ECF statistics: By similar expansions as in (i) above one has

$$|\ddot{\phi}_{T,T+k}(u) - \widehat{\phi}_{p,T}(u)|^2 = u^2(m_{T,T+k}^{(1)} - m_{p,T}^{(1)})^2$$

$$+\frac{u^4}{12}\left[3(m_{T,T+k}^{(2)} - m_{p,T}^{(2)})^2 - 4(m_{T,T+k}^{(1)} - m_{p,T}^{(1)})(m_{T,T+k}^{(3)} - m_{p,T}^{(3)})\right]$$

$$+\frac{u^6}{360}\left[6(m_{T,T+k}^{(1)} - m_{p,T}^{(1)})(m_{T,T+k}^{(5)} - m_{p,T}^{(5)}) + 10(m_{T,T+k}^{(3)} - m_{p,T}^{(3)})^2\right.$$

$$\left. -15(m_{T,T+k}^{(2)} - m_{p,T}^{(2)})(m_{T,T+k}^{(4)} - m_{p,T}^{(4)})\right] + o(u^6), \quad u \to 0,$$

where $m_{k_1,k_2}^{(\rho)} = (k_2 - k_1)^{-1} \sum_{t=k_1+1}^{k_2} \widehat{\varepsilon}_t^\rho$, $\rho = 1, 2, \ldots$. It is transparent from this equation that moment matching takes place in the test statistic in (4) between the sample moments computed from $\{\widehat{\varepsilon}_t\}_{t=T+1}^{T+k}$ and the corresponding sample moments computed from $\{\widehat{\varepsilon}_t\}_{t=p+1}^{T}$. The role then of the weight function $w(u)$ is to assign specific weights with which each of these moment–matching equations enters the test statistic. In this connection, a weight function with rapid rate of decay assigns little weight to higher sample moments, and the value of the test statistic is dominated by matching the low–order moments of $\{\widehat{\varepsilon}_t\}_{t=T+1}^{T+k}$ and $\{\widehat{\varepsilon}_t\}_{t=p+1}^{T}$. In contrast a slower rate of decay of $w(u)$ allows moments of higher order to also have an significant impact on the test statistic. Standard choices such as $w(u) = \exp(-a|u|^b), a, b > 0$ in (4), yield for $b = 1$ the limit statistic

$$CF_\infty^{(1)} := \lim_{a \to \infty} a^3 CF_a^{(1)} = 4\rho_{k,T}(\gamma) \sup_{1 \le k \le L_T} (m_{T,T+k}^{(1)} - m_{p,T}^{(1)})^2,$$

and for $b = 2$ the limit statistic

$$CF_\infty^{(2)} := \lim_{a \to \infty} a^{3/2} CF_a^{(2)} = \frac{\sqrt{\pi}}{2} \rho_{k,T}(\gamma) \sup_{1 \le k \le L_T} (m_{T,T+k}^{(1)} - m_{p,T}^{(1)})^2,$$

where $CF_a^{(m)}$, $m = 1, 2$, denotes the test statistic in (4) with weight function $e^{-a|u|^m}$. These limit statistics show that extreme smoothing of the periodic component of the ECF leads to rejection of the null hypothesis for large values in the sequential matching of the sample means of the residuals before and after a hypothetical change.

5   Computational issues

The FLS estimating equations are given by $h_T(\beta, u) = 0$ where $h_T := \partial H_T / \partial \beta$ is a vector of dimension p with m^{th} element

$$h_{T,m}(\beta, u) = \frac{1}{(T-p)^2} \frac{1}{u} \sum_{t,s=p+1}^{T} X_{t-m} \sin \left[u(X_t - X_s) - u(\mathbf{X}_{t-1}' - \mathbf{X}_{s-1}')\beta \right],$$

$m = 1, ..., p$. The numerical procedure for obtaining the adaptive and efficient FLS estimate is described in Meintanis and Donatos (1997, 1999). This procedure is iterative whereby at step j and given the current value of the estimate $\widehat{\beta}_T^{(j)}$, the empirical variance is calculated as $Var_T^{(j)}(u) := Var(\widehat{\phi}_{p,T}^{(j)}(u), u)$ where $\widehat{\phi}_{p,T}^{(j)}(u)$ denotes the ECF calculated from the current residuals $\widehat{\varepsilon}_t := \widehat{\varepsilon}_t(\widehat{\beta}_T^{(j)})$ and $Var(u) := Var(\phi(u), u)$ denotes the asymptotic variance of the FLS estimator under a hypothesized error distribution with characteristic function denoted by $\phi(u)$. Then the adaptive and efficient FLS estimator at this step corresponds to the argument $u := \widehat{u}_T^{(j)}$ which minimizes $Var_T^{(j)}(u)$ over an interval around zero.

Computationally convenient expressions for the ECF test statistic may be obtained from (4) by straightforward algebra as (see also Hušková and

Meintanis (2006a)), $T_{CF}(k) = \rho_{k,T}(\gamma)\Sigma_k$ where

$$\Sigma_k = \frac{1}{k^2}S_{1,k} + \frac{1}{(T-p)^2}S_{2,T} - 2\frac{1}{k(T-p)}S_{3,k},$$

with

$$S_{1,k} = \sum_{t,s=T+1}^{T+k} h_w(\widehat{\varepsilon}_t - \widehat{\varepsilon}_s), \quad S_{2,k} = \sum_{t,s=p+1}^{k} h_w(\widehat{\varepsilon}_t - \widehat{\varepsilon}_s),$$

and

$$S_{3,k} = \sum_{t=T+1}^{T+k}\sum_{s=p+1}^{T} h_w(\widehat{\varepsilon}_t - \widehat{\varepsilon}_s).$$

In fact, some further algebra shows that the computation of the test statistic is facilitated by the recursive relations

$$S_{1,k+1} = S_{1,k} + 2\sum_{t=T+1}^{T+k} h_w(\widehat{\varepsilon}_t - \widehat{\varepsilon}_{T+k+1}) + h_w(0),$$

$$S_{3,k+1} = S_{3,k} + \sum_{t=p+1}^{T} h_w(\widehat{\varepsilon}_t - \widehat{\varepsilon}_{T+k+1}).$$

(For $S_{2,k}$ the recursive relation is obtained from that of $S_{1,k}$ by simply setting $T = 0$).

Preliminary simulations indicate that the proposed test procedure is sensitive w.r.t. a large spectrum of changes, either local or fixed. Results of a more extensive simulation study will be presented during the talk, along with a comparison with the procedure suggested by Lee et al. (2009).

Acknowlegements: The work of M. Hušková was partially supported by the grants GACR 201/09/j006, 201/09/0755 and MSM 0021620839, and the work of S. Meintanis by grant number KA: 70/4/7658 of the program 'Kapodistrias' of the special account for reasearch of the National and Kapodistrian University of Athens. The position of C. Kirch was financed by the Stifterverband für die Deutsche Wissenschaft by funds of the Claussen-Simon-trust.

References

BAI, J. (1994): Weak convergence of the sequential empirical processes of residuals in ARMA models. *Ann. Statist. 22, 2051–2061.*

CSÖRGŐ, S. (1983): The theory of functional least squares. *J. Austral. Math. Soc. Ser. A 34, 336–355.*

CSÖRGŐ, M. and HORVÁTH, L. (1997): *Limit Theorems in Change-point Analysis.* J. Wiley, New York.

DHAR, S.K. (1993): Computation of certain minimum distance estimators in AR[k] models. *J.Amer.Statist.Assoc. 88, 278–283.*

EINMAHL, J.H.J. and MCKEAGUE, I.W. (2003): Empirical likelihood based hypothesis testing. *Bernoulli 9, 267–290.*

GOMBAY, E. and SERBAN, D. (2009): Monitoring parameter change in AR(p) time series models. *J.Multivar.Anal. 100, 715–725.*

HEATHCOTE, C.R. and WELSH, A.H. (1983): The robust estimation of autoregressive processes by functional least squares. *J.Appl.Probab. 20, 737–753.*

HUŠKOVÁ, M., KIRCH, C., PRAŠKOVÁ, Z. and STEINEBACH, J. (2008): On the detection of changes in autoregressive time series: II. Resample procedures. *J.Statist.Plann.Infer. 138, 1697–1721.*

HUŠKOVÁ, M. and KIRCH, C. (2009): Bootstrapping sequential change-point tests for linear regression, *submitted.*

HUŠKOVÁ, M. and MEINTANIS, S.G. (2006a): Change point analysis based on empirical characteristic functions. *Metrika 63, 145–168.*

HUŠKOVÁ, M. and MEINTANIS, S.G. (2006b): Change Point Analysis Based on the Empirical Characteristic Functions of Ranks. *Sequential Analysis 25, 421–436.*

HUŠKOVÁ, M., PRAŠKOVÁ, Z. and STEINEBACH, J. (2007): On the detection of changes in autoregressive time series: I. Asymptotics. *J.Statist.Plann.Infer. 137, 1243–1259.*

INOUE, A. (2001): Testing for distributional change in time series. *Econometr. Theor. 17, 156–187.*

KIRCH, C. (2008): Bootstrapping sequential change-point tests. *Sequential Anal. 27, 330–349.*

LEE, S., LEE, Y. and NA, O. (2009): Monitoring distributional changes in autoregressive models. *Commun.Statist.Theor.Meth. 38, 2969–2982.*

LING, S. (2007): Tests for change points in time series models and limiting theorems for NED sequences. *Ann. Statist. 35, 1213–1237.*

MEINTANIS, S.G. and DONATOS, G. (1997): A comparative study of some robust methods for coefficient–estimation in linear regression. *Comput.Statist.Dat. Anal. 23, 525–540.*

MEINTANIS, S.G. and DONATOS, G. (1999): Finite–sample performance of alternative estimators for autoregressive models in the presence of outliers. *Comput.Statist.Dat. Anal. 31, 323–340.*

WELSH, A.H. (1985): An angular approach for linear data. *Biometrika 72, 441–450.*

YAO, Y.C. (1990): On the asymptotic behavior of a class of nonparametric tests for a change–point problem. *Statist.Probab.Lett. 9, 173–177.*

Computational Treatment of the Error Distribution in Nonparametric Regression with Right-Censored and Selection-Biased Data

Géraldine Laurent[1] and Cédric Heuchenne[2]

[1] QuantOM, HEC-Management School of University of Liège
boulevard du Rectorat, 7 Bât.31, B-4000 Liège, Belgium,
G.Laurent@student.ulg.ac.be
[2] QuantOM, HEC-Management School of University of Liège
boulevard du Rectorat, 7 Bât.31, B-4000 Liège, Belgium,
C.Heuchenne@ulg.ac.be

Abstract. Consider the regression model $Y = m(X) + \sigma(X)\varepsilon$, where $m(X) = E[Y|X]$ and $\sigma^2(X) = Var[Y|X]$ are unknown smooth functions and the error ε (with unknown distribution) is independent of X. The pair (X, Y) is subject to parametric selection bias and the response to right censoring. We construct a new estimator for the cumulative distribution function of the error ε, and develop a bootstrap technique to select the smoothing parameter involved in the procedure. The estimator is studied via extended simulations and applied to real unemployment data.

Keywords: nonparametric regression, selection bias, right censoring, bootstrap, bandwidth selection

1 Introduction and model

Let (X, Y) be a bivariate random vector, where Y is the unemployment duration of an individual and X is, for example, his age when he lost his job. The objective is to study the relation between Y and X. In Figure 1, an example of a scatter plot with these two variables is displayed. It comes from the Spanish Institute for Statistics and is completely described in Section 4. Unfortunately, this kind of data set suffers from some 'incompleteness' (due to sampling), as explained hereunder.

Indeed, (X, Y) is supposed to be obtained from cross-sectional sampling meaning that only individuals whose unemployment duration is in progress at a fixed sampling time are observed and followed. As a result, a bias appears due to the length of Y: conditionally on X, longer durations have a larger probability to be observed. Moreover, we assume that durations of the followed individuals are possibly right-censored; for example, this may happen if an individual stops the follow-up or if the follow-up itself comes to an end.

Y. Lechevallier, G. Saporta (eds.), *Proceedings of COMPSTAT'2010*,
DOI 10.1007/978-3-7908-2604-3_51, © Springer-Verlag Berlin Heidelberg 2010

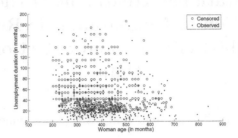

Fig. 1. Scatter plot of unemployment data

In this context, the following general nonparametric regression model can be assumed in most applications:

$$Y = m(X) + \sigma(X)\varepsilon, \tag{1}$$

where $m(X) = E[Y|X]$ and $\sigma^2(X) = Var[Y|X]$ are unknown smooth functions and ε (with zero mean, unit variance and distribution F_ε) is independent of X. This enables to define the error ε and estimate its distribution $F_\varepsilon(\cdot)$. Indeed, such an estimator can be very useful in the sense that it is naturally related to the commonly used graphical procedures based on visual examination of the residuals (see Atkinson (1985)). Furthermore, a complete set of testing procedures can be based on this estimated distribution (e.g. tests for the model (1), goodness-of-fit tests for $F_\varepsilon(\cdot)$, $m(\cdot)$ and $\sigma(\cdot)$...).

As explained above, the incompleteness of the data is characterized by two phenomena: cross-sectional sampling and right censoring. We can therefore model them by using the following variables.

a. T, the truncation variable (duration between the time point when the individual loses his job and the sampling time) assumed to be here independent of Y conditionally on X (usual assumption when truncated data are present): T is observed if $Y \geq T$.

b. C, the censoring variable making Y (larger or equal to T) observable only if $Y \leq C$. (Y, T) is assumed to be independent of $C - T$, conditionally on $T \leq Y$ and X (assumption needed to construct conditional distribution estimators with censored data).

Here, $F_{T|X}(y|x) = \mathbb{P}(T \leq y|x)$ is assumed to be a parametric function. This assumption is satisfied by classical length-biased data but also by other types of selection biases where the process that counts individuals who lose their job can be considered as parametric. By construction, we also impose that the support of $F_{Y|X}(y|x) = \mathbb{P}(Y \leq y|x)$ is included into the support of $F_{T|X}(y|x)$ and that the lower bound of the support of $F_{T|X}(y|x)$ is zero. Defining $Z = \min(C - T, Y - T)$ and $\Delta = I(Y \leq C)$, we therefore obtain a sample $\{(X_1, T_1, Z_1, \Delta_1), \ldots, (X_n, T_n, Z_n, \Delta_n)\}$ of independent copies of (X, T, Z, Δ) with the same distribution as (X, T, Z, Δ) conditionally on $Y \geq T$. Special cases of these data have been widely studied in the literature (see, e.g., de Uña-Alvarez and Iglesias-Pérez (2008) for a literature overview).

The paper is organized as follows. In the next section, we describe the estimation procedure in detail. Section 3 presents the results of a simulation study while Section 4 is devoted the analysis of the unemployment data introduced hereabove.

2   Description of the method

To address the problem introduced in Section 1, we first propose to write

$$H_{X,Y}(x, y) = \mathbb{P}(X \leq x, Y \leq y | T \leq Y \leq C) = \frac{\mathbb{P}(X \leq x, Y \leq y, T \leq Y \leq C)}{\mathbb{P}(T \leq Y \leq C)}.$$

We can show that

$$\mathbb{P}(X \leq x, Y \leq y, T \leq Y \leq C) =$$
$$\int_{r \leq x} \int_{s \leq y} \int_{u \leq s} (1 - \mathcal{G}(s - u|r)) \, dF_{T|X}(u|r) dF_{Y|X}(s|r) dF_X(r),$$

where $F_X(x) = \mathbb{P}(X \leq x)$ and $\mathcal{G}(z|x) = \mathbb{P}(C - T \leq z | X = x, T \leq Y)$. That leads to

$$H_{X,Y}(x, y) = (E[w(X, Y)])^{-1} \int_{r \leq x} \int_{s \leq y} w(r, s) dF_{X,Y}(r, s), \qquad (2)$$

where $F_{X,Y}(x, y) = \mathbb{P}(X \leq x, Y \leq y)$ and the weight function is defined by

$$w(x, y) = \int_{t \leq y} (1 - \mathcal{G}(y - t|x)) \, dF_{T|X}(t|x). \qquad (3)$$

In particular, a similar expression can be obtained for a constant follow-up τ, i.e. $C = T + \tau$ where τ is a positive constant. By applying the same reasoning, it's easy to check that the weight $w(x, y)$ can be written as

$$w(x, y) = \int_{0 \vee y - \tau}^{y} dF_{T|X}(t|x). \qquad (4)$$

Thanks to (2), we have

$$dF_{X,Y}(x, y) = \frac{E[w(X, Y)]}{w(x, y)} dH_{X,Y}(x, y),$$

leading to

$$F_\varepsilon(e) = \iint_{\{(x,y): \frac{y - m(x)}{\sigma(x)} \leq e\}} \frac{E[w(X, Y)]}{w(x, y)} dH_{X,Y}(x, y). \qquad (5)$$

Next, we estimate the unknown quantities in (5). For $\mathcal{G}(y - t|x)$, we use the Beran (1981) estimator, defined by (in the case of no ties):

$$\hat{\mathcal{G}}(y - t|x) = 1 - \prod_{\substack{Z_i \leq y-t \\ \Delta_i = 0}} \left(1 - \frac{W_i(x, h_n)}{\sum_{j=1}^n I\{Z_j \geq Z_i\} W_j(x, h_n)} \right),$$

where $W_i(x, h_n) = K\left(\dfrac{x - X_i}{h_n}\right) \Big/ \sum_{i=1}^n K\left(\dfrac{x - X_i}{h_n}\right)$, K is a kernel function and h_n is a bandwidth sequence tending to 0 when $n \to \infty$. We thus obtain for $w(x, y)$

$$\hat{w}(x, y) = \int_{t \leq y} \left(1 - \hat{\mathcal{G}}(y - t|x) \right) dF_{T|X}(t|x).$$

For $m(\cdot)$ and $\sigma(\cdot)$, we use

$$\hat{m}(x) = \frac{\sum_{i=1}^n \frac{W_i(x, h_n) Y_i \Delta_i}{\hat{w}(x, Y_i)}}{\sum_{i=1}^n \frac{W_i(x, h_n) \Delta_i}{\hat{w}(x, Y_i)}}, \qquad \hat{\sigma}^2(x) = \frac{\sum_{i=1}^n \frac{W_i(x, h_n) \Delta_i (Y_i - \hat{m}(x))^2}{\hat{w}(x, Y_i)}}{\sum_{i=1}^n \frac{W_i(x, h_n) \Delta_i}{\hat{w}(x, Y_i)}},$$

obtained by extending the conditional estimation methods introduced in de Uña-Alvarez and Iglesias-Pérez (2008). Consequently, the estimator of the error distribution is

$$\hat{F}_\varepsilon(e) = \frac{1}{M} \sum_{i=1}^n \frac{\hat{E}[w(X, Y)]}{\hat{w}(X_i, Y_i)} I\{\hat{\varepsilon}_i \leq e, \Delta_i = 1\}, \tag{6}$$

where

$$\hat{\varepsilon}_i = \frac{Y_i - \hat{m}(X_i)}{\hat{\sigma}(X_i)}, \qquad M = \sum_{i=1}^n \Delta_i, \qquad \hat{E}[w(X, Y)] = \left(\frac{1}{M} \sum_{i=1}^n \frac{\Delta_i}{\hat{w}(X_i, Y_i)} \right)^{-1}$$

and $\hat{H}_{X,Y}(x, y)$ is the bivariate empirical distribution based on pairs (X_i, Y_i) verifying $T_i \leq Y_i \leq C_i$, $i = 1, \ldots, n$.

Remark 2.1 Under some assumptions, weak convergence of $\hat{F}_\varepsilon$ can be obtained by extensions of the proofs of de Uña-Alvarez and Iglesias-Pérez (2008), Ojeda-Cabrera and Van Keilegom (2008) and Van Keilegom and Akritas (1999). For more information about that, details can be given on request to the authors.

3   Practical implementation and simulations

3.1   Bandwidth selection procedure

We want to determine the smoothing parameter h_n which minimizes

$$MISE = E[\int \{\hat{F}_{\varepsilon, h_n}(e) - F_\varepsilon(e)\}^2 de], \tag{7}$$

where $\hat{F}_{\varepsilon,h_n}(e)$ denotes $\hat{F}_\varepsilon(e)$ used with bandwidth h_n. Considering asymptotic expansions for (7) will lead to complicated expressions with too many unknown quantities. As a consequence, we propose a bootstrap procedure. This is an extension of the method of Li and Datta (2001) to the truncation case.

The bootstrap procedure is as follows.
For $b = 1, \ldots, B$,

a. for $i = 1, \ldots, n$,
   Step 1. Generate $X_{i,b}^*$ from the distribution

$$\hat{F}_X(\cdot) = \sum_{j=1}^n \frac{\hat{E}[w(X,Y)]}{\hat{E}[w(X,Y)|X = \cdot]} I\{X_j \leq \cdot, \Delta_j = 1\},$$

where $\hat{E}[w(X,Y)|X = \cdot] = \sum_{j=1}^n W_j(\cdot, g_n)\Delta_j / \sum_{j=1}^n \frac{W_j(\cdot, g_n)\Delta_j}{\hat{w}(\cdot, Y_j)}$, g_n is a

pilot bandwidth asymptotically larger than the original h_n and $\hat{F}_X(\cdot)$ is an extension to the censored case of the estimator of $F_X(\cdot)$ found, for example, in Ojeda-Cabrera and Van Keilegom (2008).
   Step 2. Select at random $Y_{i,b}^*$ from the distribution

$$\hat{F}_{Y|X}(\cdot|X_{i,b}^*) = \sum_{j=1}^n \frac{\hat{E}[w(X,Y)|X = X_{i,b}^*]W_j(X_{i,b}^*, g_n)}{\hat{w}(X_{i,b}^*, Y_j)(\sum_{k=1}^n W_k(X_{i,b}^*, g_n)\Delta_k)} I\{Y_j \leq \cdot, \Delta_j = 1\},$$

where $\hat{F}_{Y|X}(y|x)$ is a straightforward extension of the conditional distribution estimator of de Uña-Alvarez and Iglesias-Pérez (2008).
   Step 3. Draw $T_{i,b}^*$ from the distribution $F_{T|X}(\cdot|X_{i,b}^*)$. If $T_{i,b}^* > Y_{i,b}^*$, then reject $(X_{i,b}^*, Y_{i,b}^*, T_{i,b}^*)$ and go to Step 1. Otherwise, go to Step 4.
   Step 4. Select at random $V_{i,b}^*$ from $\hat{\mathcal{G}}(\cdot|X_{i,b}^*)$ calculated with g_n and define $Z_{i,b}^* = \min(Y_{i,b}^* - T_{i,b}^*, V_{i,b}^*)$ and $\Delta_{i,b}^* = I(Y_{i,b}^* - T_{i,b}^* \leq V_{i,b}^*)$.
b. Compute $\hat{F}_{\varepsilon,h_n,b}^*$, the error distribution (6) based on the bandwidth h_n and the obtained resample $\{(X_{i,b}^*, T_{i,b}^*, Z_{i,b}^*, \Delta_{i,b}^*) : i = 1, \ldots, n\}$.

From this, (7) can be approximated by $B^{-1} \sum_{b=1}^B \int \{\hat{F}_{\varepsilon,h_n,b}^*(e) - \hat{F}_{\varepsilon,g_n}(e)\}^2 de$.

3.2 Simulations

We study the $\widehat{MISE}$ (obtained from (7) where $E[\cdot]$ is estimated by the average over all the samples and h_n is defined by the above bootstrap procedure) of the error distribution for two homoscedastic and two heteroscedastic models for random $C - T$ (many other simulations, not reported here, have been carried out for a constant $C - T$). In the homoscedastic cases, we compute

Dist. of T	Dist. of $C - T$	% Censor.	$\widehat{MISE}$ $(*10^{-3})$
$T \sim \mathrm{Unif}([0; 4])$	$C - T \sim \mathrm{Exp}(2/5)$	0.37	5.5
$T \sim \mathrm{Unif}([0; 4])$	$C - T \sim \mathrm{Exp}(2/7)$	0.28	4.9
$T \sim \mathrm{Unif}([0; X + 2])$	$C - T \sim \mathrm{Exp}(2/7)$	0.29	5.0
$T \sim \mathrm{Unif}([0; X + 2])$	$C - T \sim \mathrm{Exp}(2/5)$	0.36	5.2
$T \sim 4 * \mathrm{Beta}(0.5; 1)$	$C - T \sim \mathrm{Exp}(2/7)$	0.34	4.2
$T \sim 4 * \mathrm{Beta}(0.5; 1)$	$C - T \sim \mathrm{Exp}(2/9)$	0.29	4.0
$T \sim \mathrm{Unif}([0; 4])$	$C - T \sim \mathrm{Exp}(1/(X + 1.5))$	0.28	4.6
$T \sim 4 * \mathrm{Beta}(0.5; 1)$	$C - T \sim \mathrm{Exp}(1/(X^2 - 1))$	0.34	4.5

Table 1. Results for the $\widehat{MISE}$ for regression model (8)

error distributions based on $Y_i - \hat{m}(X_i)$, avoiding the estimation of $\sigma(X_i)$, $i = 1, \ldots, n$. For each model, we consider both finite and infinite supports for the error distribution. We choose to work with the Epanechnikov kernel. The simulations are carried out for $n = 100$, $B = 250$ and the results are obtained for 250 simulations.

In the first setting, we generate i.i.d. observations from the homoscedastic regression model

$$Y = X + \varepsilon, \tag{8}$$

where X and ε have uniform distributions on $[1, 7321; 2]$ and $[-\sqrt{3}; \sqrt{3}]$ respectively. Table 1 summarizes the simulation results for different $F_{T|X}$ and $\mathcal{G}$ (first and second column respectively). Clearly, the $\widehat{MISE}$ decreases when the censoring percentage, proportion of censored data in the 250 simulations, (third column) decreases whatever the distributions of T and $C - T$. Notice that, for the same censoring percentage, the $\widehat{MISE}$ is weaker when T has a beta distribution instead of a uniform distribution. It's explained by the shape of the beta distribution.

In the second setting, we consider a heteroscedastic regression model

$$Y = X^2 + X * \varepsilon, \tag{9}$$

where X and ε have uniform distributions on $[2; 2\sqrt{3}]$ and $[-\sqrt{3}; \sqrt{3}]$ respectively. In Table 2, when looking at a heteroscedastic instead of a homoscedastic model, introduced variability seems to increase the $\widehat{MISE}$ in a reasonable way. The $\widehat{MISE}$ increasing is not surprising because we don't estimate $\sigma(x)$ in the homoscedastic model. If the distributions of T or $C - T$ depend on X, the $\widehat{MISE}$ doesn't seem to vary significantly whatever the model.

In the third setting, we study both the homoscedastic and heteroscedastic models

$$\log(Y) = X + \varepsilon \qquad \text{and} \qquad \log(Y) = X^2 + X * \varepsilon, \tag{10}$$

where X has a uniform distribution on $[0; 1]$ and ε has a standard normal distribution. In this case, Y is submitted to selection bias and right censoring

Dist. of T	Dist. of $C - T$	% Censor.	$\widehat{MISE}$ ($*10^{-3}$)
$T \sim \text{Unif}([0; 18])$	$C - T \sim \text{Exp}(0.1)$	0.34	6.9
$T \sim \text{Unif}([0; 18])$	$C - T \sim \text{Exp}(0.05)$	0.19	6.2
$T \sim 18 * \text{Beta}(0.5; 1)$	$C - T \sim \text{Exp}(1/12)$	0.35	6.3
$T \sim 18 * \text{Beta}(0.5; 1)$	$C - T \sim \text{Exp}(1/15)$	0.3	6.2
$T \sim \text{Unif}([0; X + 16])$	$C - T \sim \text{Exp}(1/12)$	0.3	6.2
$T \sim 18 * \text{Beta}(0.5; 1)$	$C - T \sim \text{Exp}(1/(2X^2 - 1))$	0.3	6.6

Table 2. Results for the $\widehat{MISE}$ for regression model (9)

Dist. of T	Dist. of $C - T$	% Censor.	$\widehat{MISE}$ ($*10^{-3}$)
$T \sim \text{Exp}(2)$	$C - T \sim \text{Exp}(0.25)$	0.27	6.6
$T \sim \text{Exp}(2)$	$C - T \sim \text{Exp}(2/9)$	0.25	6.5
$T \sim \text{Exp}(2)$	$C - T \sim \text{Exp}(0.2)$	0.23	6.3

Table 3. Results for the $\widehat{MISE}$ for the heteroscedastic regression model (10)

while the error distribution to estimate is here $\mathbb{P}\left(\frac{\log(Y) - m(X)}{\sigma(X)} \leq e\right)$. This is achieved by a straightforward transformation of expression (5). Results are similar to finite supports but generally less good. To illustrate this, Table 3 displays some results for the heteroscedastic model.

When looking at the shape of the estimations of the error distributions, we observe that the estimations are quite good for ε-values included between minus 1 and 1 for the homoscedastic models, whatever the support of F_ε. The loss of ε-values in the tails of the distribution is caused by the combined selection bias and right censoring processes (this loss is slightly harder for infinite supports). Concerning the heteroscedastic models, this phenomenon is increased due to local variance estimation.

4   Data analysis

The proposed method is illustrated on the unemployment data set introduced in Section 1. These data result from the survey, Encuesta de Población Activa (Labour Force Survey), of the Spanish Institute for Statistics between 1987 and 1997. The available information consists of 1009 unemployment spells of married women being unemployed at the time of inquiry. Sampled women were asked to provide the date they started searching a job and their age (in years) at this date. After, they were followed for 18 months. If they did not find any job at the end of this period, their unemployment durations were considered as censored. This results in a constant $C - T = \tau$ leading to weights (4). We consider a uniform distribution for the truncation variable. This assumption was informally checked through a graphical comparison between the empirical truncation distribution function and the uniform model (Wang

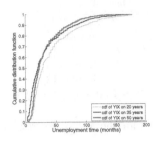

Fig. 2. Representation of $\hat{F}_{Y|X}$ for different values of x

(1991)), showing a good fit. The bootstrap approximation gives an optimal smoothing parameter of seventy months.

The estimator $\hat{F}_{Y|X}(\cdot|x) = \hat{F}_{\varepsilon}\left(\frac{\cdot - \hat{m}(x)}{\hat{\sigma}(x)}\right)$ is displayed in Figure 2 for $x = 20, 35$ and 50. The 35 years old unemployed women seem to find a job earlier in the short run and later in the long run than the 50 years old unemployed women.

Acknowledgements. Thanks to G. Alvarez-Llorente, M. S. Otero-Giráldez, and J. de Uña-Alvarez (University of Vigo, Spain) for providing the Galician unemployment data.

References

ASGHARIAN, M., M′LAN, C. E., WOLFSON, D. B. (2002): Length-biased sampling with right-censoring: an unconditional approach. *Journal of the American Statististical Association 97, 201-209.*

ATKINSON, A. C. (1985): *Plots, transformations and regression: an introduction to graphical methods of diagnostic.* Clarendon Press, Oxford.

BERAN, R. (1981): *Nonparametric regression with randomly censored survival data.* Technical Report, University of California, Berkeley.

de UNA-ALVAREZ, J., IGLESIAS-PEREZ, M.C. (2008): Nonparametric estimation of a conditional distribution from length-biased data. *Annals of the Institute of Statistical Mathematics, in press. doi: 10.1007/s10463-008-0178-0.*

LI, G., DATTA, S. (2001): A bootstrap approach to non-parametric regression for right censored data. *Annals of the Institute of Statistical Mathematics 53, 708-729.*

OJEDA-CABRERA, J.L., VAN KEILEGOM, I. (2008): Goodness-of-fit tests for parametric regression with selection biased data. *Journal of Statistical Planning and Inference 139 (8), 2836-2850.*

VAN KEILEGOM, I., AKRITAS, M.G. (1999): Transfer of tail information in censored regression models. *The annals of Statistics 27 (5), 1745-1784.*

WANG, M.-C. (1991): Nonparametric estimation from cross-sectional survival data. *Journal of the American Statistical Association 86, 130-143.*

Mixtures of Weighted Distance-Based Models for Ranking Data

Paul H. Lee[1] and Philip L. H. Yu[2]

[1] Department of Statistics and Actuarial Science,
   The University of Hong Kong, Hong Kong, *honglee@hku.hk*
[2] Department of Statistics and Actuarial Science,
   The University of Hong Kong, Hong Kong, *plhyu@hku.hk*

Abstract. Ranking data has applications in different fields of studies, like marketing, psychology and politics. Over the years, many models for ranking data have been developed. Among them, distance-based ranking models, which originate from the classical rank correlations, postulate that the probability of observing a ranking of items depends on the distance between the observed ranking and a modal ranking. The closer to the modal ranking, the higher the ranking probability is. However, such a model basically assumes a homogeneous population, and the single dispersion parameter may not be able to describe the data very well.

To overcome the limitations, we consider new weighted distance measures which allow different weights for different ranks in formulating more flexible distance-based models. The mixtures of weighted distance-based models are also studied for analyzing heterogeneous data. Simulations results will be included, and we will apply the proposed methodology to analyze a real world ranking dataset.

Keywords: ranking data, distance-based model, mixture model

1 Introduction

Ranking data frequently occurs where judges (individuals) are asked to rank a set of items, which may be types of soft drinks, political goals, candidates in an election, etc. By studying ranking data, we can understand judges' perception and preferences on the ranked alternatives. Modeling ranking data have been a popular topic recently in the data mining field, for example decision tree models (Yu et al. (2008)).

Over the years, various statistical models for ranking data have been developed, such as order statistics models, rankings induced by paired comparisons (for instance, Bradley-Terry Model), distance-based models and multistage models. See Critchlow et al. (1991) and Marden (1995) for more details of these models. Among many models for ranking data, distance-based models have the advantages of being simple and elegant.

Distance-based models (Fligner and Verducci (1986)) assume a modal ranking π_0 and the probability of observing a ranking π is inversely proportional to its distance from the modal ranking. The closer to the modal

Y. Lechevallier, G. Saporta (eds.), *Proceedings of COMPSTAT'2010*,
DOI 10.1007/978-3-7908-2604-3_52, © Springer-Verlag Berlin Heidelberg 2010

ranking π_0, the more frequent the ranking π is observed. Many distance measures have been proposed in the literature. Typical examples of distances are Kendall, Spearman and Cayley distances (see Mallows (1957), Critchlow (1985) and Diaconis (1988)).

Distance-based models have received much less attention than what they should deserve, probably because the models are not flexible. With the aim of increasing model flexibility, Fligner and Verducci (1986) generalized the one-parameter distance-based models to $k - 1$-parameter models, based on the decomposition of a distance measure. However, certain distance property is lost in the extended models. In this paper, we propose an extension of distance-based models using new weighted distance measures, which can retain the properties of distance and at the same time increase model flexibility.

In the case of heterogenous data, one can adopt a mixture modeling framework to produce more sophisticated models. EM algorithm (Demster et al. (1977)) can fit the mixture models in a simple and fast way. Recently, Murphy and Martin (2003) extended the use of mixtures to distance-based models to describe the presence of heterogeneity among the judges. In this way, the limitation of assumption of homogenous population can be relaxed. We will develop a mixture of weighted distance-based models for ranking data. It generalized Murphy and Martin's model by using a weighted distance.

The remainder of this paper is organized as follows. Section 2 reviews the distance-based models for ranking data and Section 3 proposes the new weighted distance-based models. To illustrate the feasibility of the proposed model, a simulation study and a case study of real data are presented in Sections 4 and 5 respectively. Finally, some concluding remarks are given in Section 6.

2   Distance-based models for ranking data

2.1   Distance-based models

Some notations are defined here for better description of ranking data. When ranking k items, labeled $1, ..., k$, a ranking π is a mapping function from $1, ..., k$ to $1, ...k$, where $\pi(i)$ is the rank given to item i. For example, $\pi(2) = 3$ means that item 2 is ranked third.

Distance function is useful in measuring the discrepancy in two rankings. The usual properties of a distance function are: (1): $d(\pi, \pi) = 0$, (2): $d(\pi, \sigma) > 0$ if $\pi \neq \sigma$, and (3): $d(\pi, \sigma) = d(\sigma, \pi)$. For ranking data, we require the distance, apart from the usual properties, to be right invariant, i.e. $d(\pi, \sigma) = d(\pi \circ \tau, \sigma \circ \tau)$, where $\pi \circ \tau(i) = \pi(\tau(i))$. This requirement makes sure relabeling of items has no effect on the distance.

Some popular distances are given in Table 1, where $I\{\}$ is an indicator function. Apart from these distances, there are other distances for ranking data, and readers can refer to Critchlow et al. (1991) for details.

Table 1. Some distances for ranking data

Name	Short form	Formula
Spearman's rho	$R(\boldsymbol{\pi}, \boldsymbol{\sigma})$	$\left(\sum_{i=1}^{k}[\pi(i) - \sigma(i)]^2\right)^{0.5}$
Spearman's rho square	$R^2(\boldsymbol{\pi}, \boldsymbol{\sigma})$	$\sum_{i=1}^{k}[\pi(i) - \sigma(i)]^2$
Spearman's footrule	$F(\boldsymbol{\pi}, \boldsymbol{\sigma})$	$\sum_{i=1}^{k}|\pi(i) - \sigma(i)|$
Kendall's tau	$T(\boldsymbol{\pi}, \boldsymbol{\sigma})$	$\sum_{i<j} I\{[\pi(i) - \pi(j)][\sigma(i) - \sigma(j)] < 0\}$

Diaconis (1988) developed a class of distance-based models,

$$P(\boldsymbol{\pi}|\lambda, \boldsymbol{\pi}_0) = \frac{e^{-\lambda d(\boldsymbol{\pi}, \boldsymbol{\pi}_0)}}{C(\lambda)},$$

where $\lambda \geq 0$ is the dispersion parameter, and $d(\boldsymbol{\pi}, \boldsymbol{\pi}_0)$ is an arbitrary right invariant distance. In particular, when d is Kendall's tau, the model is named Mallows' ϕ-model (Mallows (1957)). The parameter λ measures how individuals' preferences differ from the modal ranking $\boldsymbol{\pi}_0$. The closer to $\boldsymbol{\pi}_0$, the higher probability of observing the ranking $d(\boldsymbol{\pi})$. When λ approaches zero, the distribution of a ranking will become uniform.

3 Mixtures of weighted distance-based models

3.1 Weighted distance-based models

We propose an extension of distance-based model by replacing the (un-weighted) distance with a new weighted distance measure, so that different weights can be assigned to different ranks.

Motivated from the weighted Kendall's tau correlation coefficient proposed by Shieh (1998), we define weighted Kendall's tau distance by

$$T_{\mathbf{w}}(\boldsymbol{\pi}, \boldsymbol{\sigma}) = \sum_{i<j} w_{\pi_0(i)} w_{\pi_0(j)} I\{[\pi(i) - \pi(j)][\sigma(i) - \sigma(j)] < 0\}.$$

Note that this weighted distance satisfies all the usual distance properties, in particular, the symmetric property: $T_{\mathbf{w}}(\boldsymbol{\pi}, \boldsymbol{\sigma}) = T_{\mathbf{w}}(\boldsymbol{\sigma}, \boldsymbol{\pi})$.

Other distance measures can be generalized to weighted distance in a similar manner as what we have done in generalizing Kendall's tau distance. Some examples are given in Table 2.

Apart from the weighted Kendall's tau (Shieh (1998)) and weighted Spearman rho square (Shieh et al. (2000)), there are many other weighted rank correlations proposed, see, for example, Tarsitano (2009).

Applying a weighted distance measure $d_{\mathbf{w}}$ to distance-based model, the probability of observing a ranking $\boldsymbol{\pi}$ under the weighted distance-based ranking model is

$$P(\boldsymbol{\pi}|\mathbf{w}, \boldsymbol{\pi}_0) = \frac{e^{-d_{\mathbf{w}}(\boldsymbol{\pi}, \boldsymbol{\pi}_0)}}{C(\mathbf{w})}.$$

Table 2. Some weighted distances for ranking data

Name	Short form	Formula
Weighted Spearman's rho	$R_\mathbf{w}(\boldsymbol{\pi}, \boldsymbol{\sigma})$	$\left(\sum_{i=1}^{k} w_{\pi_0(i)}[\pi(i) - \sigma(i)]^2\right)^{0.5}$
Weighted Spearman's rho square	$R_\mathbf{w}^2(\boldsymbol{\pi}, \boldsymbol{\sigma})$	$\sum_{i=1}^{k} w_{\pi_0(i)}[\pi(i) - \sigma(i)]^2$
Weighted Spearman's footrule	$F_\mathbf{w}(\boldsymbol{\pi}, \boldsymbol{\sigma})$	$\sum_{i=1}^{k} w_{\pi_0(i)}|\pi(i) - \sigma(i)|$

Generally speaking, if w_i is large, few people will disagree the item which ranked i in $\boldsymbol{\pi}_0$, because this disagreement will greatly increase the distance and hence probability of observing it will be very small. If w_i is close to zero, people have no preference about how the item which ranked i in $\boldsymbol{\pi}_0$ is ranked, because the change of its rank will not affect the distance at all.

Based on a set of a ranking $\boldsymbol{\pi}$ of k items, the MLE $\hat{\mathbf{w}}$ of the weighted distance-based ranking model satisfies the following equation

$$\sum_{i=1}^{n} d_\mathbf{w}(\boldsymbol{\pi}_i, \boldsymbol{\pi}_0) = n \sum_{j=1}^{k!} P(\boldsymbol{\pi}_j|\mathbf{w}, \boldsymbol{\pi}_0) d_\mathbf{w}(\boldsymbol{\pi}_j, \boldsymbol{\pi}_0).$$

3.2 Mixture models

If a population contains G sub-populations with probability mass function (pmf) $P_g(x)$, and the proportion of sub-population g equals p_g, the pmf of the mixture model is $P(x) = \sum_{g=1}^{G} p_g P_g(x)$. Hence, the probability of observing a ranking $\boldsymbol{\pi}$ under a mixture of G weighted distance-based ranking models is :

$$P(\boldsymbol{\pi}) = \sum_{g=1}^{G} p_g P(\boldsymbol{\pi}|\mathbf{w}_g, \boldsymbol{\pi}_g) = \sum_{g=1}^{G} p_g \frac{e^{-d_{\mathbf{w}_g}(\boldsymbol{\pi}, \boldsymbol{\pi}_g)}}{C(\mathbf{w}_g)}$$

And the loglikelihood for n observations is:

$$L = \sum_{i=1}^{n} \log \left(\sum_{g=1}^{G} p_g \frac{e^{-d_{\mathbf{w}_g}(\boldsymbol{\pi}_i, \boldsymbol{\pi}_g)}}{C(\mathbf{w}_g)} \right)$$

Estimating the model parameters by direct maximizing of the loglikelihood function may lead to a high-dimensional numerical optimization problem. Instead, this can be done by applying the EM algorithm (Demsters et al. (1977)). In the E-step of an EM algorithm computes, for all observations, the probabilities of belonging to every sub-population. The M-step maximizes the conditional expected complete-data loglikelihood given the estimates generated in E-step.

To derive the EM algorithm, we define a latent variable $z_i = (z_{1i}, ..., z_{Gi})$ as: $z_{gi} = 1$ if observation i belongs to sub-population g, otherwise $z_{gi} = 0$.

The complete-data loglikelihood is:

$$L_{com} = \sum_{i=1}^{n} \sum_{g=1}^{G} z_{gi}[\log(p_g) - d_{\mathbf{w}_g}(\boldsymbol{\pi}_i, \boldsymbol{\pi}_g) - log(C(\mathbf{w}_g))]$$

In the E-step, $\hat{z}_{gi}$, $g = (1, 2, ..., G)$ are updated for observations $i = 1, 2..., n$, by $\hat{z}_{gi} = \frac{\hat{p}_g P(\hat{\boldsymbol{\pi}}_i | \hat{\mathbf{w}}_g, \hat{\boldsymbol{\pi}}_g)}{\sum_{h=1}^{G} \hat{p}_h P(\hat{\boldsymbol{\pi}}_i | \hat{\mathbf{w}}_h, \hat{\boldsymbol{\pi}}_h)}$.

In the M-step, model parameters are updated by maximizing complete-data loglikelihood, z_{gi} replaced by $\hat{z}_{gi}$. Such maximization can be done similar to the estimation method described in Section 3.1.

To determine the number of mixtures, we use the Bayesian information criterion (BIC). BIC equals $-2L + v \log(n)$ where L is the loglikelihood, n is the sample size and v is the number of model parameters. The model with the smallest BIC is chosen to be the best model. Murphy and Martin (2003) showed that BIC worked quite well if there is no noise component in the mixed population.

4   Simulation Studies

In this section, two simulations results are reported. The first simulation studies the performance of the estimation algorithm of our weighted distance-based models, while the second simulation investigates the effectiveness of using BIC in selecting the number of mixtures.

In the first simulation, ranking data sets of 4 items and sample size 2000 were simulated to test the accuracy of model fitting, using weighted Kendall's tau. We use 4 models in simulation, and the parameters of the models are listed in Table 3. The initial values for $\hat{\mathbf{w}}$ are drawn from uniform $(0, 1)$. Furthermore, we assume the number of mixtures is known. The simulation results, based on 30 replications, are summarized in Table 4.

Table 3. Simulation settings

Model	π_0	w_1	w_2	w_3	w_4
1	(1,2,3,4)	2	1.5	1	0.5
2	(1,2,3,4)	1	0.75	0.5	0.25

Model	p	π_0	w_1	w_2	w_3	w_4
3	0.5	(1,2,3,4)	2	1.5	1	0.5
	0.5	(4,3,2,1)	2	1.5	1	0.5
4	0.5	(1,2,3,4)	2	1.5	1	0.5
	0.5	(4,3,2,1)	1	0.75	0.5	0.25

There are two implications from these simulation results. First, The model estimates are very close to their actual values, therefore we can conclude that our proposed algorithm works fine for 1 and 2 mixtures cases. Second, by comparing cases 1 and 2, models with larger weights have smaller standard deviation. The same conclusion can be drawn by comparing cases 3 and 4.

Table 4. Simulation results (standard deviation)

Model	1	2	3		4	
$\hat{\pi}_0$	(1,2,3,4)	(1,2,3,4)	(1,2,3,4)	(4,3,2,1)	(1,2,3,4)	(4,3,2,1)
$\hat{p}(s.d.)$	-	-	0.503(0.011)	0.497	0.502(0.026)	0.498
$\hat{w}_1(s.d.)$	1.985(0.082)	0.985(0.085)	2.004(0.105)	2.005(0.075)	2.070(0.214)	1.041(0.163)
$\hat{w}_2(s.d.)$	1.523(0.057)	0.782(0.093)	1.525(0.102)	1.534(0.100)	1.441(0.161)	0.752(0.172)
$\hat{w}_3(s.d.)$	0.997(0.040)	0.491(0.032)	0.969(0.055)	0.983(0.062)	1.037(0.174)	0.499(0.062)
$\hat{w}_4(s.d.)$	0.495(0.010)	0.247(0.031)	0.497(0.045)	0.509(0.029)	0.493(0.044)	0.255(0.065)

It is because models with larger weights in average have larger distances, therefore the probability of an observation being modal ranking is higher. In other words, models with larger weights are more certain at the model ranking.

In the second simulation, we will use the four models described in the first simulation. Mixtures of weighted distance-based models were fitted for mixture number 1 to 3. We repeated this process 50 times and recorded the frequencies that each type of mixture model was selected (Table 5). The $+N$ notation indicates an additional noise component (uniform model).The simulation results show that BIC provides a good estimate of the number of mixtures, and the performance improves when the weights are larger. However, occasionally BIC will include a noise component in addition to the true mixture model, probably because there is only 1 parameter in the noise component and hence the improvement in loglikelihood is less penalized.

Table 5. Simulations results

Model	N	1	$1+N$	2	$2+N$	3
1	0	45	5	0	0	0
2	0	37	13	0	0	0
3	0	0	0	49	1	0
4	0	0	0	47	3	0

5   Application to real data: social science research on political goals

To illustrate the applicability of the weighted distance-based models described in Section 3, we have made use of the ranking dataset obtained from Croon (1989). It is a survey covering topics important for social science research conducted in 5 western countries, however Croon only analyzed 2262 observations from Germany. Respondents were asked to rank the political goals for their Government from the following four alternatives: (A): maintain order in nation, (B): give people more say in Government decisions,(C): fight rising prices and (D): protect freedom of speech.

Weighted distance-based models were fitted for four types of weighted distance($T_{\mathbf{w}}$, $R_{\mathbf{w}}$, $R_{\mathbf{w}}^2$ and $F_{\mathbf{w}}$), with number of mixtures 1 to 4, and the models' BIC are listed in Table 6. Among models with same distance measure, the mixtures models with smallest BIC values are underlined. Our best model is weighted footrule with 3 classes. The BIC is 12670.82 which is better than the strict utility (SU) model (12670.87) and Pendergrass-Bradley (PB) model (12673.07) discussed in Croon (1989), as well as distance-based model (12733.08). For all types of distances, the mixtures number selected are either 3 or 3+N. However, we can't draw conclusion about which distance measure best fit the data.

Table 6. BIC of the models

# Mixture	Weighted Distance				Distance			
	$T_{\mathbf{w}}$	$R_{\mathbf{w}}$	$R_{\mathbf{w}}^2$	$F_{\mathbf{w}}$	T	R	R^2	F
N	14377.52	14377.52	14377.52	14377.52	14377.52	14377.52	14377.52	14377.52
1	12974.28	13011.22	12951.34	13174.30	13052.58	13001.36	12988.06	13163.26
1 + N	12943.44	13018.94	12863.46	13172.96	13014.91	13009.09	12889.45	13162.11
2	12797.52	12774.10	12864.90	12806.18	12908.05	12848.57	12851.75	12980.63
2 + N	12688.72	12713.96	12691.64	12697.92	12860.70	12856.28	12758.02	12944.18
3	12692.20	<u>12678.88</u>	<u>12671.24</u>	**12670.82**	12846.88	12832.44	<u>12754.64</u>	<u>12902.74</u>
3 + N	<u>12678.06</u>	12688.20	12673.36	12843.80	<u>12839.56</u>	**12733.08**	12770.09	12932.52
4	12730.74	12716.28	12709.86	12701.08	12851.53	12847.89	12770.09	12918.19

The model estimates of thae best model, mixtures of 3 weighted footrule models, are shown in Table 7. The first 2 groups, which comprises 79% of respondents, ranked (A) and (C) more important than the other 2 goals, and the third group ranked (B) and (D) more important. For groups 1 and 2, weights w_3 and w_3 are very close to zero and w_1 and w_2 are much larger, indicating that observations from groups 1 and 2 are mainly (C,A,?,?) and (A,C,?,?) respectively. As compared with that in groups 1 and 2, the weights in group 3 are relatively closer to zero, this implies that people belonging to this group are less certain about their preferences than people in the other groups.

Table 7. Parameters of weighted footrule mixtures model

Group	Ordering of goals in π_0	p	w_1	w_2	w_3	w_4
1	$C \succ A \succ B \succ D$	0.352	2.030	1.234	~ 0	0.191
2	$A \succ C \succ B \succ D$	0.441	1.348	0.917	0.107	0.104
3	$B \succ D \succ C \succ A$	0.208	0.314	~ 0	0.151	0.552

6   Conclusion

We propose a new class of distance-based models using weighted distance. Our weighted distance-based ranking models can keep the nature of distance and maintain a great flexibility. Our simulations show that the algorithm can accurately estimate the model parameters. Our real data application shows that our models can fit the data better than some existing models. Furthermore, the interpretation of the model is kept simple and straightforward too.

Acknowledgement

The research of Philip L. H. Yu was supported by a grant from the Research Grants Council of the Hong Kong Special Administrative Region, China (Project No. HKU 7473/05H).

References

CRITCHLOW, D. E. (1985): *Metric methods for analyzing partially ranked data.* Lecture Notes in Statistics, 34, Springer, Berlin.

CRITCHLOW, D. E., FLIGNER, M. A. and VERDUCCI, J. S. (1991): Probability models on rankings. *Journal of Mathematical Psychology 35, 294-318.*

CROON, M. A. (1989): Latent class models for the analysis of rankings. In: G. De Soete, H. Feger, K. C. Klauer (Eds.), *New developments in psychological choice modeling,* Elsevier Science, North-Holland, 99-121,.

DEMPSTER, A. P., LAIRD, N. M. and RUBIN, D. B. (1977): Maximum likelihood from incomplete data via the EM algorithm. *Journal of Royal Statistical Society Series B, 39(1):1-38.*

DIACONIS, P. (1988): *Group representations in probability and statistics.* Institute of Mathematical Statistics, Hayward.

FLIGNER, M. A. and VERDUCCI, J. S. (1986): Distance based ranking models. *Journal of Royal Statistical Society Series B 48(3), 359-369*

MALLOWS, C. L. (1957): Non-null ranking models. I. *Biometrika, 44, 114-130.*

MARDEN, J. I. (1995): *Analyzing and modeling rank data.* Chapman and Hall.

MURPHY, T. B. and MARTIN, D. (2003): Mixtures of distance-based models for ranking data. *Computational Statistics and Data Andlysis, 41, 645-655.*

SHIEH, G. S. (1998): A weighted Kendall's tau statistic. *Statistics and Probability Letters, 39, 17-24.*

SHIEH, G. S., BAI, Z. and TSAI, W.-Y. (2000): Rank tests for independence - with a weighted contamination alternative. *Statistica Sinica, 10, 577-593.*

TARSITANO, A. (2009): Comparing the effectiveness of rank correlation statistics. *Working Papers, Università della Calabria, Dipartimento di Economia e Statistica, 200906.*

YU, P. L. H., WAN, W. M., LEE. P. H. (2008): Analyzing Ranking Data Using Decision Tree. *European Conference on Machine Learning and Principles and Practice of Knowledge Discovery in Databases.*

Fourier Analysis and Swarm Intelligence for Stochastic Optimization of Discrete Functions

Jin Rou New and Eldin Wee Chuan Lim

Department of Chemical & Biomolecular Engineering
National University of Singapore
4 Engineering Drive 4, Singapore 117576, *chelwce@nus.edu.sg*

Abstract. A new methodology for solving discrete optimization problems by the continuous approach has been developed in this study. A discrete Fourier series method was derived and used for re-formulation of discrete objective functions as continuous functions. Particle Swarm Optimization (PSO) was then applied to locate the global optimal solutions of the continuous functions derived. The continuous functions generated by the proposed discrete Fourier series method correlated almost exactly with their original model functions. The PSO algorithm was observed to be highly successful in achieving global optimization of all such objective functions considered in this study. The results obtained indicated that the discrete Fourier series method coupled to the PSO algorithm is indeed a promising methodology for solving discrete optimization problems via the continuous approach.

Keywords: discrete optimization, Fourier series, particle swarm optimization, simulation, global optimization

1 Introduction

Discrete optimization refers to the maximization or minimization of an objective function over a set of feasible parameter values where the objective function cannot be evaluated analytically. In such problems, values of the objective function may have to be measured, estimated or evaluated from simulations and the domain(s) of the objective function and/or feasible region is discrete in nature. Such optimization problems are ubiquitous in engineering, operations research and computer science.

The solution methods for discrete optimization problems can generally be classified into combinatorial and continuous approaches. In the former, a sequence of states is generated from a discrete finite set to represent a partial solution while in continuous approaches, the discrete optimization problem is characterized using equivalent continuous formulations or continuous relaxations (Pardalos et al. (2000)). There are many methods to formulate discrete optimization problems as equivalent continuous ones. For example, Goyal and Ierapetritou (2007) recently proposed combining a simplicial-based approach and the Sample Average Approximation approach for solving convex stochastic MINLP problems. This was based on the idea of closely describing the

Y. Lechevallier, G. Saporta (eds.), *Proceedings of COMPSTAT'2010*,
DOI 10.1007/978-3-7908-2604-3_53, © Springer-Verlag Berlin Heidelberg 2010

feasible region by a set of linear constraints representing an approximation of its convex hull. The objective function was linearized at the simplicial boundary points and the global optimal solution was obtained using the linear representation of the feasible space and the linear approximation of the objective function. Aytug and Sayin (2009) used support vector machines (SVM) to learn the efficient set of a multiple objective discrete optimization problem. They conjectured that a surface generated by SVM could provide a good approximation to the efficient set. To evaluate their idea, the authors incorporated the SVM-learned efficient set into a multi-objective genetic algorithm through the fitness function to generate feasible solutions that were representative of the true efficient set.

In this paper, a new continuous approach to the solution of discrete optimization problems is presented. The goal of the optimization process is to obtain the value(s) of the independent variable(s) which will maximize (or minimize) the objective function, keeping in mind that the optimal solution may not correspond to any of the available discrete points representing the objective function. Currently available methods that make use of linearization, smoothing or averaging techniques to derive an equivalent continuous formulation of the discrete objective function tend to distort the objective function and are approximations to the true analytical model at best. On the other hand, it is also well-established that a function (continuous or discontinuous) may be represented as a Fourier series consisting of a large number of trigonometric terms. In the limit that the number of such terms approaches infinity, the Fourier series will converge exactly to the original function it represents, thus making it effectively a universal mathematical regression technique. Based on this premise, it was conjectured that a Fourier series representation of a discrete objective function may be derived that will correspond exactly or almost exactly to the true analytical model and which also effectively converts the discrete optimization problem into a continuous problem. A stochastic global optimization method may then be applied to solve the continuous optimization problem. Such an approach that exploits the superior regression capabilities of the Fourier series method towards solving discrete optimization problems has not been attempted in the research literature to date. In the next section, the formulation of the Fourier series method as applied to discrete functions will be derived and the basic principles of a stochastic method, Particle Swarm Optimization, which will be applied towards solving the resulting continuous optimization problem will be introduced.

2   Computational method

2.1   Discrete fourier analysis

The sampling theorem states that if the Fourier transform of a function f(x) is zero for all frequencies greater than a certain frequency f_c, then the continuous function f(x) can be uniquely determined from a knowledge of its sampled values. Consider a discrete function containing N data points for which the corresponding continuous function is to be determined. Without loss of generality, the smallest interval between any two adjacent data points may be used to define the highest frequency component of the Fourier transform of the corresponding continuous function. Further, the domain of the discrete function may be assumed to be one period of a periodic waveform of the corresponding continuous function. This allows the discrete Fourier transform of the discrete function to be calculated and by the convolution theorem, these will be equal to the coefficients of the Fourier series expansion of the corresponding continuous function. By this argument, the following expression for the double Fourier sine series of a continuous two-dimensional function may be derived from its discrete counterpart:

$$f(x,y) = \sum_{m=1}^{M}\sum_{n=1}^{N} a_{mn} sin\frac{m\pi x}{L_x} sin\frac{n\pi y}{L_y} \tag{1}$$

$$a_{mn} = \frac{4}{MN}\sum_{h=1}^{M}\sum_{k=1}^{N} f(\frac{h}{M},\frac{k}{N}) sin\frac{m\pi h}{M} sin\frac{n\pi k}{N} \tag{2}$$

2.2 Particle Swarm Optimization

The Particle Swarm Optimization (PSO) algorithm is a population based search algorithm based on the simulation of the social behavior of birds within a flock (Engelbrecht 2002)). The initial intent of the particle swarm concept was to graphically simulate the graceful and unpredictable choreography of a bird flock (Kennedy and Eberhart (1995)), with the aim of discovering patterns that govern the ability of birds to fly synchronously and to suddenly change direction with a regrouping in an optimal formation. In PSO, a swarm of individuals are referred to as particles, with each representing a potential solution. Each particle is flown through a hyperdimensional search space in such a manner that the behavior of each particle is influenced by its own experience as well as those of its neighbors. The concept behind PSO is based on the social-psychological tendency of individuals to emulate the success of other individuals and therefore represents a kind of symbiotic cooperative algorithm. The position of each particle, P_i, in the swarm is updated at each time step according to the following equation:

$$x_i(t) = x_i(t-1) + v_i(t) \tag{3}$$

where $x_i(t)$ and $v_i(t)$ are the position and velocity of particle P_i at time step t respectively.

The velocity of each particle is updated at each time step according to the following equation:

$$v_i(t) = \phi v_i(t) + \rho_1\{x_{pbest,i} - x_i(t)\} + \rho_2\{x_{gbest} - x_i(t)\} \tag{4}$$

where ϕ is an inertia weight, ρ_1 and ρ_2 are random variables, $x_{pbest,i}$ is the position giving the best performance of P_i up to time step t and x_{gbest} is the position giving the globally best performance of the entire swarm up to the current time step.

3   Results and discussion

Fig. 1 shows an arbitrary two-dimensional function with the gray scale contours representing values of the dependent variable. Here, this function is used to represent a system or model whose combination of its independent variables which will result in the global maximum of its dependent variable is to be located. In principle, the entire contour surface can be constructed by performing a large number of experiments or simulations at various combinations of values of the independent variables but this is almost never practically possible in actual practice. Instead, it was assumed that experiments or simulations were performed at values of independent variables indicated by white dots on the figure so that only a small, finite number of discrete values of the entire function was known. Treating this set of discrete values as a discrete function whose continuous equivalent was to be derived via the discrete Fourier series method presented in the previous section, equation (1) was applied to this discrete function. Fig. 2 shows the resulting continuous function that was re-constructed from this set of discrete values. On comparison between the two figures, it may be seen that the major features of the original two-dimensional function had been re-constructed although quantitative differences may also be discerned. The re-constructed two-dimensional function may be adequate for the current purpose if it allows a good approximate of the global maximal point of the original function to be located. Otherwise, a larger number of discrete values of the original function may be required for a more accurate re-construction.

Fig. 3 shows another arbitrarily generated two-dimensional function which contains more complex features than the previous one. Correspondingly, as depicted by the white dots shown on the figure, it was assumed that a larger number of experiments or simulations was performed to sample this function. On performing the re-construction process by applying the discrete Fourier series method to this set of discrete values, Fig. 4 shows that a much more accurate representation of the original function was obtained. In fact, the original and re-constructed continuous functions were almost indistinguishable from each other. It may then be expected that an accurate approximate of the global maximum of the original function can be obtained by applying the PSO algorithm to the re-constructed function and this will be presented next.

Fig. 5 shows positions of 100 particles randomly distributed over the domain of the re-constructed two-dimensional function at the start of the optimization process. The positions of these particles were updated via equations

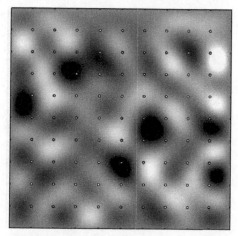

Fig. 1. Gray scale contours of a two-dimensional continuous function. White dots represent positions where sampling are performed via experiments or simulations.

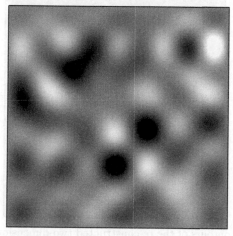

Fig. 2. Gray scale contours of the re-constructed two-dimensional continuous function.

(3) and (4) presented previously and after 1000 iterations, Fig. 6 shows that almost all particles converged to a common location on the contour map. It was verified manually that this final position of all particles was the global maximal point of both the original and re-constructed two-dimensional functions. This indicates that the PSO algorithm had been successful in achieving global optimization of these functions. The proposed methodology of deriving a continuous equivalent of a discrete function via a discrete Fourier series method and then applying a stochastic global optimization algorithm to locate the global optimum of this continuous function is thus a promising, novel

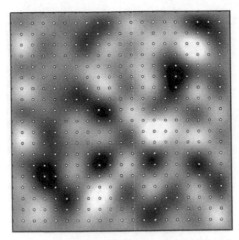

Fig. 3. Gray scale contours of a more complex two-dimensional continuous function. A larger number of discrete samples was obtained as indicated by the white dots.

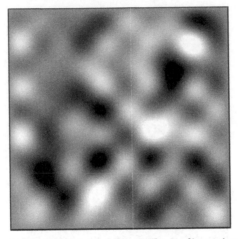

Fig. 4. Gray scale contours of the re-constructed two-dimensional continuous function. A more accurate re-construction has been obtained with the larger number of sampling points.

methodology for solving discrete optimization problems via the continuous approach.

4   Conclusions

A new methodology for solving discrete optimization problems by the continuous approach has been developed in this study. A discrete Fourier series method was derived from the conventional Fourier series formulation and

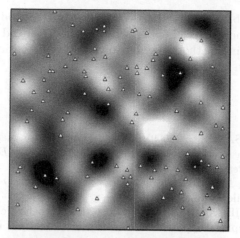

Fig. 5. Initial positions of PSO particles at the start of the optimization process.

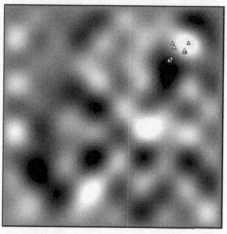

Fig. 6. Final positions of PSO particles after 1000 iterations of the optimization process. The global maximum of the original two-dimensional function has been successfully located.

principles associated with the discrete Fourier transform and used for reformulation of discrete objective functions as continuous functions. A stochastic global optimization technique known as Particle Swarm Optimization (PSO) was then applied to locate the global optimal solutions of the continuous functions derived. In contrast with conventional linearization, smoothing or averaging approaches, it was found that the continuous functions generated by the proposed discrete Fourier series method correlated almost exactly with their original model functions. The structure of each continuous function was unknown a priori and always non-convex in nature and the stochastic PSO algorithm was observed to be highly successful in achieving global optimization of all such objective functions considered in this study. It may thus be concluded that the discrete Fourier series method coupled to the PSO algorithm is a promising methodology for solving discrete optimization problems via the continuous approach.

References

AYTUG, H. and SAYIN, S. (2009): Using support vector machines to learn the efficient set in multiple objective discrete optimization. *European Journal of Operational Research 193, 510-519.*

ENGELBRECHT, A.P. (2002): *Computational Intelligence An Introduction.* England: John Wiley & Sons Ltd.

GOYAL, V. and IERAPETRITOU, M.G. (2007): Stochastic MINLP optimization using simplicial approximation. *Computers and Chemical Engineering 31, 1081-1087.*

KENNEDY, J. and EBERHART, R.C. (1995): Particle Swarm Optimization. In: *Proceedings of the IEEE International Conference on Neural Networks.* 4, 1942.

PARDALOS, P.M., ROMEIJIN, H.E. and TUY, H. (2000): Recent developments and trends in global optimization. *Journal of Computational and Applied Mathematics 124, 209-228.*

Global Hypothesis Test to Simultaneously Compare the Predictive Values of Two Binary Diagnostic Tests in Paired Designs: a Simulation Study

J. A. Roldán Nofuentes,[1] J. D. Luna del Castillo[2] and
M. A. Montero Alonso[3]

[1] Biostatistics, School of Medicine, University of Granada,
18071, Spain, *jaroldan@ugr.es*
[2] Biostatistics, School of Medicine, University of Granada,
18071, Spain, *jdluna@ugr.es*
[3] School of Social Sciences, Campus of Melilla, University of Granada,
52071, Spain, *mmontero@ugr.es*

Abstract. The positive and negative predictive values of a binary diagnostic test are measures of the clinical accuracy of the diagnostic that depend on the sensitivity and the specificity of the binary test and on the disease prevalence. Moreover, the positive predictive value and the negative predictive value are not parameters which are independent of each other. In this article, a global hypothesis test is studied to simultaneously compare the positive and negative predictive values of two binary diagnostic tests in paired designs.

Keywords: binary diagnostic test, predictive values, simultaneously comparison

1 Introduction

The classic parameters to assess the accuracy of a binary diagnostic test with regard to a gold standard are sensitivity and specificity. The sensitivity (Se) is the probability of a diagnostic test being positive when the individual is diseased and the specificity (Sp) is the probability of the diagnostic test being negative when the individual is not diseased. Other parameters to assess the accuracy of a binary diagnostic test are the positive predictive value and the negative predictive value. The positive predictive value (PPV) is the probability of a patient being diseased given that the test is positive, and the negative predictive value (NPV) is the probability of a patient being non-diseased given that the test is negative. The predictive values (PVs) represent the accuracy of the diagnostic test when it is applied to a cohort of individuals, depend on the sensitivity and specificity of the diagnostic test and on the disease prevalence, and are easily calculated applying Bayes'

Y. Lechevallier, G. Saporta (eds.), *Proceedings of COMPSTAT'2010*,
DOI 10.1007/978-3-7908-2604-3_54, © Springer-Verlag Berlin Heidelberg 2010

Theorem, i.e.

$$PPV = \frac{p \times Se}{p \times Se + q \times (1 - Sp)} \text{ and } NPV = \frac{q \times Sp}{p \times (1 - Se) + q \times Sp} \quad (1)$$

where p is the disease prevalence and $q = 1 - p$.

Furthermore, the comparison of the positive predictive values and the negative predictive values of two binary diagnostic tests in paired designs has been the subject of several studies (Bennett (1972); Leisenring et al. (2000); Wang et al. (2006)). Nevertheless, in all of these studies the positive and negative predictive values are compared independently. A global hypothesis test is studied to simultaneously compare the positive and negative predictive values of two binary diagnostic tests when both diagnostic tests and the gold standard are applied to all of the individuals in a random sample.

2   Global hypothesis test

Let there be two binary diagnostic tests (modeled through the binary variables T_1 and T_2, $T_i = 1$ when the diagnostic test is positive and $T_i = 0$ when the diagnostic test is negative) and a gold standard (modeled through the binary variable D, $D = 1$ when the gold standard is positive and $D = 0$ when the gold standard is negative) which are applied to all of the individuals in a random sample sized n, producing Table 1.

Table 1. Frequencies observed applying the two diagnostic tests and the gold standard to a random sample of n individuals.

	$T_1 = 1$		$T_1 = 0$		
	$T_2 = 1$	$T_2 = 0$	$T_2 = 1$	$T_2 = 0$	Total
$D = 1$	s_{11}	s_{10}	s_{01}	s_{00}	s
$D = 0$	r_{11}	r_{10}	r_{01}	r_{00}	r
Total	n_{11}	n_{10}	n_{01}	n_{00}	n

The data from Table 1 are the product of a multinomial distribution with probabilities p_{ij} for $D = 1$ and q_{ij} for $D = 0$, with $i, j = 0, 1$, so that $\sum_{i,j=0}^{1} p_{ij} + \sum_{i,j=0}^{1} q_{ij} = 1$. Let $\pi = (p_{00}, p_{10}, p_{01}, p_{11}, q_{00}, q_{10}, q_{01}, q_{11})^T$ be a vector sized 8. As π is the probability vector of a multinomial distribution, the variance-covariance matrix of $\hat{\pi}$ is

$$\Sigma_{\hat{\pi}} = \frac{diag(\pi) - \pi \pi^T}{n}, \quad (2)$$

where $diag(\pi)$ is an 8×8 diagonal matrix. In terms of the components of vector π, the predictive values of diagnostic test 1 are

$$PPV_1 = \frac{p_{10} + p_{11}}{p_{10} + p_{11} + q_{10} + q_{11}} \text{ and } NPV_1 = \frac{q_{00} + q_{01}}{p_{00} + p_{01} + q_{00} + q_{01}}, \quad (3)$$

and those of test 2 are

$$PPV_2 = \frac{p_{01} + p_{11}}{p_{01} + p_{11} + q_{01} + q_{11}} \text{ and } NPV_2 = \frac{q_{00} + q_{10}}{p_{00} + p_{10} + q_{00} + q_{10}}. \quad (4)$$

As p_{ij} and q_{ij} are probabilities of a multinomial distribution, their maximum likelihood estimators are $\hat{p}_{ij} = s_{ij}/n$ and $\hat{q}_{ij} = r_{ij}/n$, and therefore the maximum likelihood estimators of the predictive values are

$$\widehat{PPV_1} = \frac{s_{10} + s_{11}}{s_{10} + s_{11} + r_{10} + r_{11}} \text{ and } \widehat{NPV_1} = \frac{r_{00} + r_{01}}{s_{00} + s_{01} + r_{00} + r_{01}} \quad (5)$$

for test 1, and

$$\widehat{PPV_2} = \frac{s_{01} + s_{11}}{s_{01} + s_{11} + r_{01} + r_{11}} \text{ and } \widehat{NPV_2} = \frac{r_{00} + r_{10}}{s_{00} + s_{10} + r_{00} + r_{10}} \quad (6)$$

for test 2. The global hypothesis test to simultaneously compare the predictive values of the two binary tests is

$$H_0 : PPV_1 = PPV_2 \text{ and } NPV_1 = NPV_2$$

$$H_1 : PPV_1 \neq PPV_2 \text{ and/or } NPV_1 \neq NPV_2.$$

Let vector $\eta = (PPV, NPV)^T$, with $PPV = PPV_1 - PPV_2$ and $NPV = NPV_1 - NPV_2$. As this vector is the probability function of vector π, applying the delta method (Agresti (2002)), the variance-covariance matrix of $\hat{\eta}$ is

$$\Sigma_{\hat{\eta}} = \left(\frac{\partial \eta}{\partial \pi} \right) \Sigma_{\hat{\pi}} \left(\frac{\partial \eta}{\partial \pi} \right)^T, \quad (7)$$

and the statistic for the global hypothesis test is

$$Q^2 = \hat{\eta}^T \hat{\Sigma}_{\hat{\eta}}^{-1} \hat{\eta}, \quad (8)$$

which is distributed asymptotically according to a central chi-square distribution with 2 degrees of freedom.

In the studies carried out by Leisenring et al (2000) and Wang et al (2006) the comparison of the predictive values is carried out independently i.e. solving the marginal hypothesis tests

$$H_0 : PPV_1 = PPV_2 \text{ vs } H_1 : PPV_1 \neq PPV_2$$

and

$$H_0 : NPV_1 = NPV_2 \text{ vs } H_1 : NPV_1 \neq NPV_2,$$

each of these to an error α, and therefore the comparisons are made assuming that the positive and negative predictive values are independent parameters. In our opinion, if the marginal hypothesis tests are carried out, some penalization should be made in terms of the error α. Thus, each marginal hypothesis test could be carried out to an error of $\alpha/2$ so that the global error would be α. Therefore, the global hypothesis test could also be solved by applying marginal hypothesis tests with Bonferroni correction. Consequently, the simultaneous comparison of the two positive predictive values and of the two negative predictive values could also be solved by comparing the two positive (negative) predictive values applying the method proposed by Leisenring et al (2000) (Wang et al.(2006)) using Bonferroni correction (carrying out each marginal test to an error rate $\alpha/2$, i.e. comparing the positive predictive values to an error rate $\alpha/2$ and comparing the negative predictive values to an error rate $\alpha/2$).

3   Simulation experiments

Monte Carlo simulation experiments were carried out to study the type I error and the power of the global hypothesis test and a comparison was made with the type I errors and the powers of the methods proposed by Leisenring et al (2000) and Wang et al (2006), both if the marginal hypothesis tests are carried to an error of α and if they are carried out to an error of $\alpha/2$ (applying Bonferroni's method). These experiments consisted in the generation of 5000 random samples with multinomial distributions of different sizes, whose probabilities were calculated through the method proposed by Vacek (1985) i.e.

$$P(T_1 = i, T_2 = j | D = 1) = P(T_1 = i | D = 1) \times P(T_2 = j | D = 1) + \delta_{ij}\varepsilon_1$$
$$P(T_1 = i, T_2 = j | D = 0) = P(T_1 = i | D = 0) \times P(T_2 = j | D = 0) + \delta_{ij}\varepsilon_0,$$
$$(9)$$

where $\delta_{ij} = 1$ when $i = j$ and $\delta_{ij} = -1$ when $i \neq j$, and ε_k is the dependence factor between the two diagnostic tests $(\varepsilon_k \geq 0) : \varepsilon_1$ is the dependence factor between the diagnostic test and the gold standard when $D = 1$ and ε_0 when $D = 0$; and it is verified that $\varepsilon_k \leq \theta_1(1-\theta_2)$ when $\theta_2 > \theta_1$ and $\varepsilon_k \leq \theta_2(1-\theta_1)$ when $\theta_1 > \theta_2$, where θ is the sensitivity or the specificity. For the type I error we have taken as predictive values

$$PPV_1 = PPV_2 = 0.80, NPV_1 = NPV_2 = 0.70$$

and

$$PPV_1 = PPV_2 = 0.90, NPV_1 = NPV_2 = 0.80,$$

and for the power we have taken the values

$$PPV_1 = 0.85, PPV_2 = 0.75, NPV_1 = 0.80, NPV_2 = 0.70$$

and

$$PPV_1 = 0.90, PPV_2 = 0.80, NPV_1 = 0.85, NPV_2 = 0.70,$$

which are common values in clinical practice. For all of the study the nominal error α was set at 5%. For the type I error, in Table 2 we show some of the results obtained for $PPV_1 = PPV_2 = 0.8, NPV_1 = NPV_2 = 0.7$ for intermediate values of the dependence factors between the two binary tests indicating the values of sensitivity, specificity and prevalence which produce the aforementioned predictive values. From the results obtained in the simulation experiments the following conclusions are reached:

a. If the global hypothesis test is solved by applying the marginal hypothesis tests ($H_0 : PPV_1 = PPV_2$ and $H_0 : NPV_1 = NPV_2$) applying the method proposed by Leisenring et al (2000) or the method proposed by Wang et al (2006) to an error rate $\alpha = 5\%$, the type I error is higher than the nominal error of 5%, so that the method can give rise to erroneous results.

b. If the global hypothesis test is solved by applying the marginal hypothesis tests ($H_0 : PPV_1 = PPV_2$ and $H_0 : NPV_1 = NPV_2$) applying the method proposed by Leisenring et al (2000) or the method proposed by Wang et al (2006) to an error rate $\alpha/2 = 2.5\%$, i.e. applying Bonferroni correction, the type I error is always lower than the nominal error $\alpha = 5\%$, so that it is a conservative method whose type I error has a similar performance to that of an exact hypothesis test. Therefore, this method for solving the global hypothesis test has a type I error that does not usually reach the fixed nominal error.

c. The global hypothesis test to simultaneously compare the two positive predictive values and the two negative predictive values has a type I error that fluctuates around the nominal error of 5%, especially for sample sizes starting from $200 - 400$ individuals, depending on the disease prevalence and the dependence factors. Therefore, the global hypothesis test shows the classic performance of an asymptotic hypothesis test for medium-sized samples.

Regarding the power of the different methods, in Table 3 we show some of the results obtained for $PPV_1 = 0.85, PPV_2 = 0.75, NPV_1 = 0.80, NPV_2 = 0.70$, and in general it is observed that it is necessary to have samples of between 200 and 300 individuals (depending on the factors of dependence between the two binary tests) so that the power is reasonable (higher than 80%).

Table 2. Type I error of the hypothesis tests of comparison of predictive values of two diagnostic tests.

	$Se_1 = Se_2 = 0.2286$, $Sp_1 = Sp_2 = 0.9692$, $p = 0.35$				
	$\varepsilon_1 = 0.080$, $\varepsilon_0 = 0.013$				
	Leisenring et al		Wang et al		Global test
n	$\alpha = 5\%$	$\alpha = 2.5\%$	$\alpha = 5\%$	$\alpha = 2.5\%$	$\alpha = 5\%$
100	0.021	0.005	0.022	0.006	0.003
200	0.056	0.026	0.058	0.027	0.023
300	0.060	0.025	0.062	0.026	0.029
400	0.076	0.037	0.079	0.039	0.043
500	0.086	0.042	0.089	0.043	0.046
1000	0.090	0.045	0.091	0.047	0.053
2000	0.092	0.045	0.092	0.045	0.050
	$Se_1 = Se_2 = 0.7273$, $Sp_1 = Sp_2 = 0.7778$, $p = 0.55$				
	$\varepsilon_1 = 0.090$, $\varepsilon_0 = 0.080$				
	Leisenring et al		Wang et al		Global test
n	$\alpha = 5\%$	$\alpha = 2.5\%$	$\alpha = 5\%$	$\alpha = 2.5\%$	$\alpha = 5\%$
100	0.076	0.034	0.077	0.035	0.039
200	0.083	0.041	0.084	0.041	0.046
300	0.096	0.047	0.097	0.047	0.053
400	0.084	0.042	0.085	0.043	0.045
500	0.090	0.047	0.090	0.047	0.051
1000	0.085	0.044	0.085	0.044	0.049
2000	0.085	0.042	0.085	0.042	0.047

Table 3. Powers of the hypothesis tests of comparison of predictive values of two diagnostic tests.

	$Se_1 = 0.4048$, $Sp_1 = 0.9615$, $Se_2 = 0.2286$, $Sp_2 = 0.9692$, $p = 0.35$				
	$\varepsilon_1 = 0.060$, $\varepsilon_0 = 0.013$				
	Leisenring et al		Wang et al		Global test
n	$\alpha = 5\%$	$\alpha = 2.5\%$	$\alpha = 5\%$	$\alpha = 2.5\%$	$\alpha = 5\%$
100	0.375	0.253	0.375	0.254	0.208
200	0.726	0.619	0.726	0.619	0.635
300	0.881	0.808	0.880	0.809	0.844
400	0.948	0.912	0.948	0.912	0.938
500	0.982	0.963	0.982	0.962	0.978
	$\varepsilon_1 = 0.120$, $\varepsilon_0 = 0.026$				
	Leisenring et al		Wang et al		Global test
n	$\alpha = 5\%$	$\alpha = 2.5\%$	$\alpha = 5\%$	$\alpha = 2.5\%$	$\alpha = 5\%$
100	0.398	0.245	0.399	0.245	0.170
200	0.920	0.853	0.920	0.854	0.832
300	0.987	0.975	0.987	0.975	0.976
400	0.999	0.997	0.999	0.997	0.997
500	1	1	1	1	1

4 Conclusions

The positive predictive value and the negative predictive value of a binary test, along with the sensitivity and the specificity, are fundamental values to assess and compare the classificatory accuracy of binary diagnostic tests. For the same binary test, both parameters depend on the sensitivity and the specificity of the test and on the disease prevalence, so that this dependence should be considered when comparing the predictive values of two binary tests in paired designs. In this study, we have proposed a global hypothesis test to simultaneously compare the positive predictive values and the negative predictive values of two binary diagnostic tests in paired designs. The hypothesis test proposed is based on the chi-square distribution and on the estimation of the variance-covariance matrix of the difference between the predictive values through the delta method. Simulation experiments were carried out to study the type I error and the power of various methods to simultaneously compare the predictive values. The type I error of the global hypothesis test fluctuates around the nominal error starting from sample sizes of between 200 and 400 individuals (depending on the disease prevalence and the dependence factors between the two binary tests), and is a conservative method (like the other methods) for small sample sizes. Regarding the power of the global hypothesis test, we need samples of between 200 and 400 individuals (depending on the prevalence and the dependence factors between the two binary tests) so that the power is higher than 80%. Based on the results of the simulation experiments, we propose the following method to compare the positive predictive values and the negative predictive values of two binary diagnostic tests in paired designs: 1) carry out the global hypothesis test to an error of α; 2) if the test is not significant, the homogeneity of the predictive values is not rejected, but if the test is significant to an error of α, the study of the causes of the significance should be carried out applying marginal hypothesis tests through the method by Leisenring et al (2000) or the method of Wang et al (2006) to an error of $\alpha/2$ (so that the global error is α). The reason why the marginal hypothesis tests should be carried out to an error of $\alpha/2$ and not α is because the method proposed by Leisenring et al (Wang et al) to an error of α has a type I error that is clearly higher than the nominal error α. We employed the Bonferroni method because it so commonly used. Other, less conservative methods could also have been applied, for example, Holm's method (1979) or Hochberg's method (1988).

The method that we propose allows us to simultaneously compare the positive and negative predictive values of two binary tests in paired designs, and when the global test is significant to an error rate α the causes of the significance are investigated applying multiple comparison procedures (such as the Bonferroni method or another sequential method). If the researcher is only interested in comparing the two positive (or negative) predictive values, the problem is solved by applying the method proposed by Leisenring et al (2000) or the method proposed by Wang et al (2006) to an error rate α.

References

AGRESTI, A. (2002): *Categorical data analysis*. John Wiley & Sons, New York.

BENNETT, B.M. (1972): On comparison of sensitivity, specificity and predictive value of a number of diagnostic procedures. *Biometrics 28, 793-800*.

HOLM, S. (1979): A simple sequentially rejective multiple test procedure. *Scandinavian Journal of Statistic 6, 65-70*.

HOCHBERG, Y. (1988): A sharper Bonferroni procedure for multiple tests of significance. *Biometrika 75, 800-802*.

LEISENRING, W., Alonzo, T., PEPE, M.S. (2000): Comparisons of predictive values of binary medical diagnostic tests for paired designs. *Biometrics 56, 345-351*.

VACEK, P.M. (1985): The effect of conditional dependence on the evaluation of diagnostic tests. *Biometrics 41, 959-968*.

WANG, W., DAVIS, C.S., SOONG, S.J. (2006): Comparison of predictive valus of two diagnostic tests from the same sample of subjects using weighted least squares. *Statistics in Medicine 25, 2215-2229*.

Modeling Operational Risk: Estimation and Effects of Dependencies

Stefan Mittnik, Sandra Paterlini, and Tina Yener

Center for Quantitative Risk Analysis (CEQURA), Department of Statistics, LMU Munich, Germany

Abstract. Being still in its early stages, operational risk modeling has, so far, mainly been concentrated on the marginal distributions of frequencies and severities within the context of the Loss Distribution Approach (LDA). In this study, drawing on a fairly large real–world data set, we analyze the effects of competing strategies for dependence modeling. In particular, we estimate tail dependence both via copulas as well as nonparametrically, and analyze its effect on aggregate risk–capital estimates.

Keywords: operational risk, risk capital, value–at–risk, correlation, tail dependence

1 Introduction

The Basel Committee defines operational risk as "the risk of loss resulting from inadequate or failed internal processes, people and systems or from external events". Based on aggregate losses, L, banks are required to calculate the minimum capital requirement (MCR) as the 99.9 % Value–at–Risk (VaR) of the loss distribution, that is,

$$MCR = \text{VaR}_{.999}(L) = \text{VaR}_{.999} \left(\sum_{i=1}^{56} L_i \right), \qquad (1)$$

where L_i refers to the aggregate loss of one of 56 event–type/business–line combinations. In the Loss Distribution Approach (LDA) (see, e.g., Panjer (2006)), L_i is generated by $L_i = \sum_{n=1}^{N_i} X_{i,n}$ that is, a random number of events, N, each associated with loss amounts $X_1, \ldots, X_N$.

The standard LDA approach avoids the complexities of modeling dependencies among aggregate losses. To obtain a conservative risk–capital estimate, the calculation prescribed by the Basel Committee,

$$MCR^* = \sum_{i=1}^{56} \text{VaR}_{.999}(L_i), \qquad (2)$$

Y. Lechevallier, G. Saporta (eds.), *Proceedings of COMPSTAT'2010*,
DOI 10.1007/978-3-7908-2604-3_55, © Springer-Verlag Berlin Heidelberg 2010

implicitly assumes comonotonicity (and, thus, a perfect positive linear correlation) between all aggregate loss pairs L_i and L_j. Nevertheless, under certain conditions, banks may explicitly model correlations (Basel Committee on Banking Supervision (2006), p. 148). In this way, the regulators aim at providing an incentive for a bottom–up development of more sophisticated modeling approaches.

Based on operational losses from the *"Database Italiano delle Perdite Operative"*[1] (DIPO) collected between January 2003 and December 2007, we analyze the effects of different dependency assumptions on risk–capital estimates. We find that the departure from the comonotonicity assumption and an explicit modeling of tail dependence, based on the parameter estimates obtained from our data base, do not always lead, as inuitively expected, to a decrease in risk–capital estimates.

2   Correlation

Table 5 reports estimates of linear (Pearson) correlations among event types. The estimates in the upper–right triangle are based on the entire sample (January 2003 – December 2007); the lower triangular part shows estimates based only on the first two–thirds of the sample (January 2003 – April 2006). As is well–known, linear correlation is mainly driven by extreme observations.

	ET 1	ET 2	ET 3	ET 4	ET 5	ET 6	ET 7
ET 1	1	0.0454	0.2208	0.0462	0.0098	0.0854	0.2231
ET 2	0.0622	1	0.1624	0.1606	0.0258	-0.0658	0.0523
ET 3	0.1260	0.2830	1	0.5284	0.2954	0.1815	0.4430
ET 4	-0.0281	0.2420	0.5882	1	0.1431	0.0633	0.2012
ET 5	-0.0117	-0.1144	0.2899	0.1765	1	-0.0459	-0.0498
ET 6	0.0302	-0.0388	0.1507	0.0121	-0.0530	1	0.0648
ET 7	0.1550	0.0625	0.3653	0.2017	-0.1036	0.0450	1

Table 1. Linear correlation coefficients for aggregate losses of different event types; upper part: period 01/03–12/07, lower part: period 01/03–04/06

For example, reducing the sample leads to a change of sign for event types 2 and 5; this is caused by the two most extreme observations dropping out of the sample. Likewise, the correlation between event types 3 and 4 does not change substantially when shortening the period, because the common extremes are present in both samples.

As alternatives to the popular linear correlation, we also consider the two most commonly used rank correlation measures, namely Kendall's τ and

---

[1] www.dipo-operationalrisk.it

Spearman's ρ. In contrast to Pearson's linear correlation coefficient, they are not based on the *value* of two observations i and j, but rather on their *ranks* within the sample. They are thus by their very nature more robust towards effects of extreme observations.

However, looking at Table 2, which is organized as Table 1, confirms the high correlations, for example, between event types 3 and 4. Furthermore, the rank correlation estimates can also change considerably as the sample varies.[2]

	ET 1	ET 2	ET 3	ET 4	ET 5	ET 6	ET 7
ET 1	1	0.1345	0.2475	0.2136	0.1424	0.1051	0.1898
ET 2	0.0974	1	0.1480	0.2113	0.0045	-0.0237	0.1107
ET 3	0.0641	0.1923	1	0.5096	0.2599	0.2068	0.1831
ET 4	0.0487	0.2179	0.4513	1	0.3073	0.3130	0.0723
ET 5	0.0462	-0.0051	0.1615	0.3564	1	0.0520	-0.0328
ET 6	0.041	0.0974	0.1513	0.2795	0.0513	1	0.1718
ET 7	0.1333	0.0821	0.0897	-0.0436	-0.1385	0.1385	1

Table 2. Kendall's τ among aggregate losses; upper part: period 01/03–12/07, lower part: period 01/03–04/06

3 Tail dependence

To account for possibly nonlinear dependencies in extreme observations, we leave the correlation framework and focus explicitly on modeling joint behavior. Intuitively, the intention in our context is to capture the joint probability that, if a loss in one category exceeds a (high) threshold, this also happens in another category. The concept of tail dependence can be traced back to Sibuya (1960). Note that we analyze loss distributions, so that only upper tail dependence needs to be considered. The upper-tail dependence coefficient, λ_U, is defined by

$$\lambda_U = \lim_{t \to 1^-} \Pr[F(X) > t | G(Y) > t] = \lim_{t \to 1^-} 2 - \frac{1 - C(t,t)}{1 - t}, \qquad (3)$$

where $C(t,t)$ refers to the copula of X and Y.

3.1 Estimation via copulas

We estimate several popular parametric copulas via Maximum Likelihood, using the empirical distribution functions of the margins (the so-called *Canonical Maximum Likelihood* or CML method). In this way, we avoid any influence

---

[2] The results for Spearman's ρ are similar and therefore not reported here.

from misspecifications of the margins on dependency estimation. The copulas we consider have different properties with respect to tail dependence. The Gaussian copula does not imply any tail dependence; the Student–t is able to model symmetric, i.e., upper and lower tail dependence; and the Archimedean copulas considered here can capture asymmetric tail dependence structures.

Interestingly, only one of the three parametric copulas, which are able to capture tail dependence, suggests that the data are characterized by tail dependence. Whereas the Gumbel and Student–t copula parameter estimates amount to zero tail dependence, the Clayton survival copula implies positive values of λ_U . Table 3 reports strong dependencies between event types 3 and 4 and between event types 4 and 5 which is in line with the results from linear and rank correlation estimation. However, for many event types, the estimated parameter values of the Clayton survival copula suggest zero tail dependence.

	ET 1	ET 2	ET 3	ET 4	ET 5	ET 6	ET 7
ET 1	1	0.1017	0.0002	0.0001	0	0.0892	0.0908
ET 2	0.0567	1	0.2295	0.2733	0	0.2212	0.184
ET 3	0.1399	0.1142	1	0.5308	0.0928	0.0534	0.1334
ET 4	0.1687	0.1334	0.5869	1	0.4309	0.2349	0
ET 5	0.0521	0	0.2438	0.4264	1	0	0
ET 6	0.1452	0.0001	0.1222	0.3157	0	1	0.3131
ET 7	0.2281	0.052	0.2781	0	0	0.2564	1

Table 3. Upper tail dependence coefficient implied by the Clayton survival copula; upper part: period 01/03–12/07, lower part: period 01/03–04/06

3.2 Nonparametric estimation

As seen in the previous subsection, the results from copula fitting do not yield a clear picture with respect to the presence of upper tail dependence. We therefore further assess this question without imposing a parametric structure in the form of a copula. That is, we estimate tail dependence nonparametrically. Several nonparametric estimators of tail dependence inspired by Equation (3) have been developed. A review of these can be found, for example, in Frahm et al. (2005).

The first nonparametric estimator is based on Coles et al. (1999) and defined by

$$\widehat{\lambda}_U^{\text{LOG}} = 2 - \frac{\ln \widehat{C}_n \left(\frac{n-k}{n}, \frac{n-k}{n} \right)}{\ln \left(\frac{n-k}{n} \right)} , \quad 0 < k < n ,$$

where $\widehat{C}_n$ is the empirical copula. From (3), it follows that

$$\lambda_U = \lim_{t \to 1^-} \widehat{\lambda}_U^{LOG}(t);$$

but $\widehat{\lambda}_U^{LOG}$ can also be used as a measure of dependence for thresholds $t < 1$, whose sign depends on whether the random variables under consideration are positively or negatively associated at the level t. A similar estimator,

$$\widehat{\lambda}_U^{SEC} = 2 - \frac{1 - \widehat{C}_n\left(\frac{n-k}{n}, \frac{n-k}{n}\right)}{1 - \frac{n-k}{n}}, \quad 0 < k < n$$

goes back to Joe et al (1992).
A third nonparametric estimator is developed by Frahm et al. (2005). Assuming that the empirical copula approximates an extreme value copula, they propose the estimator

$$\widehat{\lambda}_U^{CFG} = 2 - 2 \exp\left(\frac{1}{n} \sum_{i=1}^{n} \ln\left(\sqrt{\ln(U_i^{-1}) \ln(V_i^{-1})}/\ln(\max(U_i, V_i)^{-2})\right)\right),$$

which is based on n random samples U_i and V_i from the copula. Here, no threshold needs to be chosen; but this advantage comes at the cost of the extreme–value copula assumption, which induces a bias that increases with the number of block maxima used.[3] In their simulation study, Frahm et al. (2005) find $\widehat{\lambda}_U^{CFG}$ to be superior to the other nonparametric estimators in terms of sample variances and root mean square errors. In contrast, $\widehat{\lambda}_U^{SEC}$ is found to react sensitively to the distribution of extremal data.

Figure 1 shows the empirical results for $j = 3$ vs. $j = 4$ and $j = 2$ vs. $j = 5$. We observe that $\widehat{\lambda}_U^{SEC}$ approaches 1 with increasing thresholds. This effect can be reproduced in a simulation setup which leads us to conclude that this latter behavior is not due to tail dependence. The estimators $\widehat{\lambda}_U^{LOG}$ and $\widehat{\lambda}_U^{SEC}$ suggest absence of tail dependence for event types 2 and 5, but suggest a presence in case of types 3 and 4. We, therefore, consider an additional estimator. As pointed out by Coles et al. (1999), asymptotic dependence implies not only that $\widehat{\lambda}_U > 0$, but also that

$$\bar{\chi} = \lim_{t \to 1^-} \frac{2 \ln(1 - t)}{\widetilde{C}(t,t) - 1} = \lim_{t \to 1^-} \bar{\chi}(t) = 1, \tag{4}$$

where $\widetilde{C}(t,t)$ denotes the survival copula of $C(t,t)$. We thus include the estimator $\widehat{\bar{\chi}}(t)$ based on (4), using the empirical survival copula. The results for event types 3 and 4 suggest that also for this event type combination, no clear evidence of tail dependence can be found.

---

[3] For our application, due to the small sample, we do not select block maxima. In other words, we use 60 blocks each containing one observation.

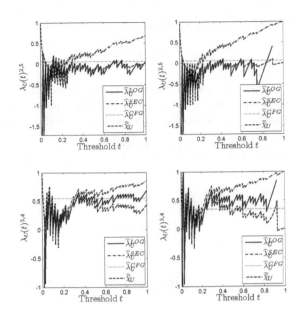

Fig. 1. Nonparametric estimators of tail dependence for the entire sample (left) and using 2/3 of the data (right) for event type combinations 2/5 (top) and 3/4 (bottom).

4   Effects on risk–capital estimation

In order to assess the sensitivity of results and the possible range of outcomes, we estimate 250 VaR$_{.999}$ figures per model and event type combination, using different numbers of replications for the estimation, and subtract the resulting risk–capital estimate from the sum of the single VaRs. For each model and event type combination, we use the copula parameter values obtained from Maximum Likelihood estimation. The results are depicted in Figure 2 for the Clayton Survival copula—which is the only one implying positive upper tail dependence—and lognormal margins. We see that using $B_{rc} = 10,000$ replications in the Monte Carlo setup can lead to increases in risk capital compared to those resulting from the comonotonicity assumption: For event types 1 and 2, the upper boxplots shows that risk capital may increase by more than 20%.

The fact that the sum of the single VaRs does, in fact, not represent the most conservative risk–capital estimate has been pointed out, for example, by Embrechts et al. (2002). The reason for this is the lack of subadditivity of the VaR measure (see Artzner et al. (1999)). However, and this can be seen for all models, this effect diminishes as the number of replications in the VaR simulation is increased. For example, in the lower boxplot of Figure 2,

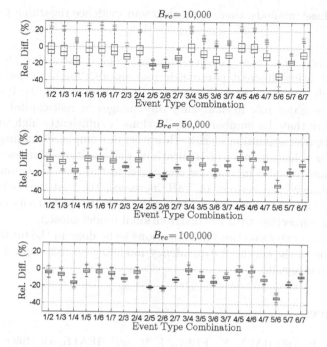

Fig. 2. Boxplots of 250 VaR$_{.999}$ estimates for the Clayton survival copula and lognormal margins.

which uses 100,000 losses per risk–capital estimate, the maximum increase observed for event types 1 and 2 is below 5%. Hence, the simulation setup is of paramount importance to avoid a substantial overestimation of risk.

5 Conclusion

We confirm the well-known finding that linear correlations are unstable and mainly driven by extreme observations. Rank correlations offer an alternative, but they do not necessarily provide more stability in case of common movements of monthly losses. Therefore, we consider copula approaches—a concept going beyond correlation and being more appropriate for modeling extremes—as an alternative.

We do, however, not find clear evidence of upper–tail dependence. While two parametric copulas, which are able to model upper–tail dependence, indicate absence of such dependence, the Clayton survival copula estimates imply nonzero upper–tail dependence for some event type combinations. As these combinations coincide with those displaying high correlations, we investigate tail dependence further and examine several nonparametric estimators. But also with these methods, there is no clear–cut evidence regarding tail dependence.

We analyze the ranges of possible risk–capital estimates in a simplified context using different parametric assumptions for the copula and the marginals. It turns out that the number of replications in the loss simulation plays a major role in analyzing the changes in risk capital. It has to be made sure that the number of replications is sufficiently high in order to avoid severe overestimation of risk. However, our empirical findings suggest also that for a high number of replications risk–capital estimates could not only decrease but also increase as compared to the case of comonotonicity. We thus observe two sources of VaR increases, the first one being purely computational and the second one being the lack of subadditivity of this risk measure in connection with the distributional model chosen.

Besides several extensions and modifications to be done in the future, further investigation of the effects of dependency modeling on risk–capital estimates is high on our agenda.

References

ARTZNER, P., DELBAEN, F., EBER, J. M. and HEATH, D. (1999): Coherent Measures of Risk. *Mathematical Finance, 9, 203–228.*

BASEL COMMITTEE ON BANKING SUPERVISION (2006): International Convergence of Capital Measurement and Capital Standards: A Revised Framework. *Technical Report, Bank for International Settlements.*

COLES, S. G., HEFFERNAN, J. E. and TAWN, J. A. (1999): Dependence measures for extreme value analyses. *Extremes, 2, 339–365.*

DEHEUVELS, P. (1981): A nonparametric test for independence. *Publications de l'Institut de Statistique de l'Université de Paris, 26, 29-50.*

EMBRECHTS, P., MCNEIL, A. and STRAUMANN, D. (2002): Correlation and dependence in risk management: properties and pitfalls. In Dempster, M.A.H. (Ed.): *Risk Management: Value at Risk and Beyond,* Cambridge University Press, Cambridge, 176–223.

FRAHM, G., JUNKER, M., SCHMIDT, R. (2005): Estimating the tail-dependence coefficient: Properties and pitfalls. *Insurance: Mathematics and Economics, 37, 80-100.*

JOE, H., SMITH, R. L. and WEISSMAN, I. (1992): Bivariate threshold models for extremes. *Journal of the Royal Statistical Society, Series B, 54, 171-183.*

PANJER, H. (2006): *Operational Risk: Modeling Analytics.* Wiley, New York.

SIBUYA, M. (1960): Bivariate extreme statistics. *Annals of the Institute of Statistical Mathematics, 11, 195-210.*

Learning Hierarchical Bayesian Networks for Genome-Wide Association Studies

Raphaël Mourad[1], Christine Sinoquet[2], and Philippe Leray[1]

[1] LINA, UMR CNRS 6241, Ecole Polytechnique de l'Université de Nantes,
rue Christian Pauc, BP 50609, 44306 Nantes Cedex 3, France,
{*raphael.mourad,philippe.leray*}*@univ-nantes.fr*
[2] LINA, UMR CNRS 6241, Université de Nantes,
2 rue de la Houssinière, BP 92208, 44322 Nantes Cedex 3, France,
christine.sinoquet@univ-nantes.fr

Abstract. We describe a novel probabilistic graphical model customized to represent the statistical dependencies between genetic markers, in the Human genome. Our proposal relies on a forest of hierarchical latent class models. The motivation is to reduce the dimension of the data to be further submitted to statistical association tests with respect to diseased/non diseased status. A generic algorithm, CFHLC, has been designed to tackle the learning of both forest structure and probability distributions. A first implementation has been shown to be tractable on benchmarks describing 10^5 variables for 2000 individuals.

Keywords: Bayesian networks, hierarchical latent class model, data dimensionality reduction, genetic marker dependency modelling

1 Introduction

Genetic association studies are designed to identify genes underlying human complex diseases. Decreasing genotyping costs now enable the generation of hundreds of thousands of genetic variants, or SNPs, spanning whole Human genome, accross cohorts of cases and controls. The purpose is to find patterns of SNPs highly correlated with the diseased status. This scaling up to genome-wide association studies (GWAS) makes the analysis of high-dimensional data a hot topic. Yet, the search for associations between single SNPs and the variable describing case/control status requires carrying out a large number of statistical tests. Still more worrying, SNP patterns, rather than single SNPs, are likely to be causal with regard to complex diseases. Therefore, a high rate of false positives as well as a perceptible statistical power decrease, not to speak of untractability, are severe issues to be overcome.

To reduce data dimensionality, a promising lead consists in exploiting the existence of statistical dependencies between SNPs, also called linkage disequilibrium (LD). In eukaryotic genomes, LD is highly structured into the so-called "haplotype block structure": regions where correlation between markers is high alternate with shorter regions characterized by low correlation.

Y. Lechevallier, G. Saporta (eds.), *Proceedings of COMPSTAT'2010*,
DOI 10.1007/978-3-7908-2604-3_56, © Springer-Verlag Berlin Heidelberg 2010

Relying on this feature, various approaches were proposed to achieve data dimensionality reduction: testing association with haplotypes (*i.e.* inferred data underlying genotypic data) (Schaid (2004)); partitioning the genome according to spatial correlation (Pattaro *et al.* (2008)); selecting SNPs informative about their context, or SNP tags, to name but a few. Unfortunately, these methods do not take into account all existing dependencies, in particular dependencies between haplotype blocks.

Probabilistic graphical models offer an adapted framework for a fine modelling of dependencies between SNPs. Various models have been used for this peculiar purpose, mainly Markov fields (Verzilli *et al.* (2006)) and Bayesian networks (BNs), with the use of hierarchical latent BNs (embedded BNs (Nefian (2006)); two-layer BNs with multiple latent (hidden) variables (Zhang and Ji (2009))). Although modelling SNP dependencies through hierarchical BNs is undoubtedly an attractive lead, there is still room for improvement. Notably, scalability remains a crucial issue.

In this paper, we propose to use a forest of Hierarchical Latent Class models (HLCMs) to reduce the dimension of the data to be further submitted to association tests. Basically, latent variables (LVs) capture the information born by underlying markers. To their turn, LVs are clustered into groups and, if relevant, such groups are subsequently subsumed by additional LVs. Iterating this process yields a hierarchical structure. First, the great advantage to GWASs is that further association tests will be chiefly performed on LVs. Thus, a reduced number of variables will be examined. Second, the hierarchical structure is meant to efficiently conduct refined association testing: zooming in through narrower and narrower regions in search for stronger association with the disease ends pointing out the potential markers of interest.

However, most algorithms dedicated to HLCM learning fail the scalability criterion when data describe thousands of variables and a few hundreds of individuals. The contribution of this paper is twofold: (i) the modelling of dependencies between clusters of SNPs, (ii) the design of a scalable algorithm, CFHLC, fitted to learn a forest of HLCMs from spacially-dependent variables. In the line of a hierarchy-based proposal of Hwang and collaborators (Hwang *et al.* (2006)), our method yet implements data subsumption, meeting two additional requirements: (i) more flexible thus more faithful modelling of underlying reality, (ii) control of information decay due to subsumption. Section 2 recalls some definitions about HLCMs and points out the few anterior works devoted to HLCM learning. Section 3 focuses on the general description of our method. In Section 4, we give the sketch of algorithm CFHLC. Section 5 presents experimental results and briefly discusses them.

2   Background for HLC model learning

In the sequel, we will restrain to discrete variables (either observed or latent). A Latent Class Model (LCM) is defined as containing a unique LV connected to each of the observed variables (OVs). Each value of the LV defines a class. In LCMs, the so-called local independence (LI) assumption states that the OVs are mutually independent conditional on latent class membership. Mainly used for data clustering, LCMs are generalized by HLCMs. The latter are tree-shaped BNs where leaf nodes are observed while internal nodes are not. HLCMs allow the relaxation of the LI constraint.

As for general BNs, besides learning of parameters (θ), *i.e.* unconditional and conditional probabilities, one of the tasks in HLCM learning is structure ($\mathcal{S}$) inference. The HLCM learning methods fall into one of two categories. The first category, structural Expectation Maximization (SEM), successively optimizes $\theta \mid \mathcal{S}$ and $\mathcal{S} \mid \theta$. Amongst few proposals, hill-climbing guided by a scoring function was designed (Zhang (2003)): the HLCM space is visited through addition or removal of latent nodes and states for existing nodes. Other authors adapted a SEM algorithm combined with simulated annealing to learn a two-layer BN with multiple LVs (Zhang and Ji (2009)). Alternative approaches implement agglomerative hierarchical clustering (AHC). Relying on pairwise correlation strength, Wang and co-workers first build a binary tree; then they apply regularization and simplification transformations which may result in subsuming more than two nodes through an LV (Wang *et al.* (2008)). Hwang and co-workers' approach confines the HLCM search space to binary trees augmented with possible connections between siblings (nodes sharing the same parent into immediate upper layer) (Hwang *et al.* (2006)). Moreover, they constrain LVs' arity to binarity. However, the latter approach is the only one we are aware of that succeeds in processing high-dimensional data: in an application dealing with a microarray dataset, more than 6000 genes have been processed for around 60 samples. To our knowledge, no running time was reported for this study.

Nevertheless, the twofold binarity restriction and the lack of control for information decay as the level increases are severe drawbacks to achieve realistic SNP dependency modelling and subsequent association study with sufficient power. Indeed, SNP dependencies would rather be more wisely modelled through a forest of HLCMs of various heights, best accounting for relevant higher-order dependencies on the genome. Moreover, not the least advantage of the FHLC model over the HLC model lies in that variables are not constrained to be dependent upon one another, either directly or indirectly.

3   Constructing the FHLC model

3.1   Principle

Our method takes as an input a matrix D_X defined on a finite discrete domain, say $\{0, 1, 2\}$ for SNPs, describing n individuals through p variables ($X = X_1, ..., X_p$). Algorithm CFHLC yields a forest of LHCMs (abbreviated as an FHLCM). An FHLCM consists of a Directed Acyclic Graph (DAG), also called the structure, whose non-connected components are trees, and of

θ, the parameters of a set of *a priori* distributions and local conditional distributions allowing the definition of the joint probability distribution. Two search spaces are explored: the space of directed forests and the probability space. In addition, H, the whole LV set of the FHLCM is output, together with the associated data matrix.

To handle high-dimensional data, our proposal combines two strategies. The first strategy splits up the genome-scale data into contiguous regions. In our case, splitting into (large) windows is not a mere implementational trick; it meets biological grounds: the overwhelming majority of dependencies between genetic markers (including higher-order dependencies) is observed for close SNPs. Then, an FHLCM is learnt for each window in turn. Within a window, subsumption is performed through an adapted AHC procedure: (i) at each agglomerative step, a partitioning method is used to identify clusters of variables; (ii) each such cluster is intended to be subsumed into an LV, through an LCM. For each LCM, parameter learning and missing data imputation (for the LV) are performed.

3.2   Node partitioning

Following Martin and VanLehn (1995), ideally, in the undirected graph of dependency relations between variables, we would propose to associate an LV with any clique exhibiting pairwise dependencies whose strengths are above a given threshold. However, searching for such cliques is an NP-hard task. Moreover, in contrast with the previous authors' objective, FHLCMs do not allow clusters to have more than one parent each: non-overlapping clusters are required for our purpose. Thus, an approximate method solving a *partitioning* problem when provided pairwise dependency measures is required.

3.3   Parameter learning and missing data imputation

A steep task is choosing - ideally optimizing - the cardinality of each LCM's LV. Instead of using an arbitrary constant value common to all LVs, we propose that the cardinality be estimated for each LV through a function of the underlying cluster's size.

At each step of the AHC process, parameter learning has to be performed for as many LCMs as there are clusters of at least two nodes identified. For each LCM, parameter learning may be performed through a standard EM procedure. This procedure takes as an input the cardinality of the LV and yields the probability distributions: *prior* distribution for the LV and conditional distributions for the remaining nodes. Once the distributions have been estimated, a way to impute the missing data corresponding to LVs may consist in directly inferring them through probabilistic inference in BNs. Finally, new data are available to seed next step of the FHLCM construction: LVs identified through step i will be considered as OVs during step $i + 1$.

3.4   Controlling information decay

In contrast with Hwang and co-workers' approach, whose main aim is data compression, information decay control is required: any LV candidate H in step i which does not bear sufficient information about its child nodes must be unvalidated. As a consequence, such child nodes will be seen as isolated nodes in step $i + 1$. The information criterion, $\mathcal{C}$, relies on average mutual information. It is scaled through entropy $\mathcal{H}$: $\mathcal{C} = \frac{1}{s_H} \sum_{i \in cluster(H)} \frac{\mathcal{I}(X_i, H)}{\min (\mathcal{H}(X_i), \mathcal{H}(H))}$, with s_H the size of $cluster(H)$.

4   Sketch of algorithm CFHLC

Due to space limitation, in this paper we will only present the sketch of algorithm CFHLC. The node partitioning algorithm chosen is longer discussed in Mourad *et al.* (2010), together with the justification for the estimation of LV cardinalities and the imputation method used by LCM parameter learning. To run CFHLC, the user has to tune various parameters: s, the window size, specifies the number of contiguous SNPs (*i.e.* variables) spanned per window; t is meant to constrain information dilution to a minimal threshold. Parameters a, b and $card_{max}$ participate in the estimation of the cardinality of each LV. Finally, parameter *PartitioningAlg* enables flexibility in the choice of the method devoted to cluster highly-correlated variables into non-overlapping groups.

Within each successive window, the AHC process is initiated from a first layer of univariate models. Each such univariate model is built for any OV in the set W_i (lines 4 to 6). The AHC process stops if all clusters identified each reduce to a single node (line 10) or if no cluster of size strictly greater than 1 could be validated (line 23). Each cluster of at least two nodes is subject to LCM learning followed by validation (line 13 to 22). In order to simplify the FHLCM learning, the cardinality of the LV is estimated as an affine function of the number of variables in the corresponding cluster (line 14). Algorithm *LCMLearning* is plugged into this generic framework (line 15). After validation through threshold t (lines 16 and 17), the LCM is used to enrich the FHLCM associated with current window (line 18): (i) a specific merging process links the additional node corresponding to the LV to its child nodes; (ii) the *prior* distributions of the child nodes are replaced with distributions conditional to the LV. In W_i, clusters of variables are replaced with the corresponding LVs; data matrix $D[W_i]$ is updated accordingly (lines 19 and 20). In contrast, the nodes in unvalidated clusters are kept isolated for the next step. At last, the collection of forests, DAG, is successively augmented with each forest built within a window (line 26). In parallel, due to assumed independency between windows, the joint distribution of the final FHLCM is merely computed as the product of the distributions associated with windows (line 26).

Algorithm $CFHLC(X, D_X, s, t, PartitioningAlg, a, b, c_{max})$

INPUT:
$\mathbf{X}, \mathbf{D_X}$: a set of p variables $X = X_1, ..., X_p$ and the corresponding data observed for n individuals,
$\mathbf{s}$: a window size,
$\mathbf{t}$: a threshold used to limit information decay while building the FHLC,
$\mathbf{a}, \mathbf{b}, \mathbf{c_{max}}$: parameters used to calculate the cardinality of latent variables.

OUTPUT:
DAG, θ: the DAG structure and the parameters of the FHLC model constructed,
H, D_H: the whole set of latent variables identified through the construction ($H = \{H_1, ..., H_m\}$) and the
      corresponding data imputed for the n individuals.

```
1:  numWin ← p/s;
2:  DAG ← ∅; θ ← ∅; H ← ∅; D_H ← ∅
3:  for i = 1 to numWin
4:      W_i ← {X_{(i-1)×s+1}, ..., X_{i×s}}; D[W_i] ← D[(i-1) × s + 1 : i × s)]
5:      {∪_{j∈W_i} DAG_{univ_j}, ∪_{j∈W_i} θ_{univ_j}} ← LearnUnivariateModels(W_i)
6:      DAG_i ← ∪_{j∈W_i} DAG_{univ_j}; θ_i ← ∪_{j∈W_i} θ_{univ_j}

7:      step ← 1
8:      while true
9:          {C_1, ..., C_{nc}} ← Partitioning(W_i, D[W_i], PartitioningAlg)
10:         if all clusters have size 1 then break end if

11:         C_{j_1}, ..., C_{j_{nc_2}} ← ClustersContainingAtLeast2Nodes(C_1, ..., C_{nc})
12:         nc_{2_valid} ← 0
13:         for k = 1 to nc_2
14:             card_H ← min(RoundInteger(a × NumberOfVariables(C_{j_k}) + b, c_{max})
15:             {DAG_{j_k}, θ_{j_k}, H_{j_k}, DH_{j_k}} ← LCMLearning(C_{j_k}, D[C_{j_k}], card_H)
16:             if (C(DAG_{j_k}, D[C_{j_k}] ∪ DH_{j_k}) ≥ t)    /* validation of current cluster - see Section 3.4 */
17:                 incr(nc_{2_valid})
18:                 DAG_i ← MergeDags(DAG_i, DAG_{j_k}); θ_i ← MergeParams(θ_i, θ_{j_k})
19:                 H ← H ∪ H_{j_k}; D_H ← D_H ∪ DH_{j_k}
20:                 D[W_i] ← (D[W_i] \ D[C_{j_k}]) ∪ DH_{j_k}; W_i ← (W_i \ C_{j_k}) ∪ H_{j_k}
21:             end if
22:         end for
23:         if (nc_{2_valid} = 0) then break end if
24:         incr(step)
25:     end while
26:     DAG ← DAG ∪ DAG_i; θ ← θ × θ_i
27: end for
```

Algorithm $LCMLearning(C_r, D[C_r], card_H)$

```
1:  H_r ← CreateNewLatentVariable()
2:  DAG_r ← BuildNaiveStructure(H_r, C_r)
3:  θ_r ← standardEM(DAG_r, D[C_r], card_H)
4:  DH_r ← Imputation(θ_r, D[C_r])
```

Table 1. Sketch of algorithm CFHLC.

5   Experimental results and discussion

Algorithm CFHLC has been implemented in C++, relying on the ProBT library dedicated to BNs (http://bayesian-programming.org). We have plugged into CFHLC a partitioning method designed by Ben-Dor and co-authors (1999). CFHLC was run on a standard PC (3.8 GHz, RAM 3.3 Go). We have generated simulated genotypic data using software HAPSIMU (http://l.web .umkc.edu/liujian/). Parameter n was set to 2000. Three sample sizes were considered: $1k$, $10k$ and $100k$ (OVs). Here, we show results obtained with a rough parameter adjustment : $a = 0.2$, $b = 2$, $c_{max} = 20$, $t = 0.5$ (see

Mourad *et al.* (2010) for investigations about the influence of CFHLC parameters). Figure 1(a) shows that only 15 hours are required for 10^5 SNPs, with the window size s set to 100. For the same dataset processed in the cases "$s = 200$" and "$s = 600$", running times are 20.5 h and 62.5 h, respectively. For the same number of OVs ($100k$), Wang *et al.* report running times in the order of two months. Figure 1(b) more thoroughly describes the influence of window size increase on running time. Interestingly, Figure 1(c) highlights the decrease in the number of variables to be tested for association with the disease (from 1000 observed variables to less than 200 forest roots in the case "$s = 100$"). In previous case, CFHLC allows a reduction in the number of variables to be tested of more than 80%. For this same case, Figure 1(d) exhibits the dramatical decrease of the number of LVs per layer (over the whole FHLCM) with the layer. As most of LVs are present in the first layer (64%), the information dilution of observed variables is shown to be limited. Finally, Figure 1(e) displays how information fades while the layer number increases. In the highest layers, average scaled mutual information is at least equal to 0.52 and 0.56 for the cases "$s = 100$" and "$s = 600$" respectively. Therefore, not only is a major point reached regarding tractability, information dilution is also controlled in an efficient way. Many more results are presented in Mourad *et al.* (2010), together with additional comments.

To our knowledge, our hierarchical model is the first one shown to achieve fast model learning for genome-scaled data sets. Whereas Hwang and collaborators' purpose is data compression, we are faced with a more demanding challenge: allow a sufficiently powerful down-stream association analysis. Relaxing the twofold binarity restriction of Hwang and collaborators' model

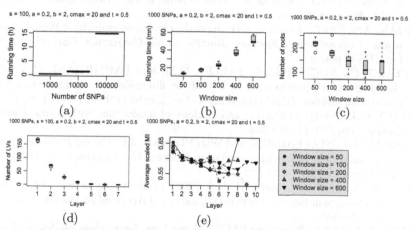

Figure 1: (a) Running time *versus* number of variables. (b) Running time *versus* window size. (c) Number of roots *versus* window size. (d) Number of latent variables per layer over the whole FHLC model. (e) Impact of window size on average scaled mutual information per layer over the whole FHLC model. N.B.: Boxplots have been produced from 20 benchmarks (exceptionally 5 in the $100k$ case of (a)).

(binary trees, binary LVs), the FHLC model is an appealing framework for GWASs: in particular, flexibility in the cluster size reduces the number of LVs.

6   Concluding remarks

Our contribution in this paper is twofold: (i) a variant of the HLC model, the FHLC model, has been described; (ii) CFHLC, a generic algorithm dedicated to learn such models, has been shown to be efficient when run on genome-scaled benchmarks. Regarding node partitioning and imputation for LVs, one of our current tasks is examining which plug-in methods are most relevant, especially for the purpose of GWASs. Finally, we will evaluate CFHLC as a promising algorithm enhancing genome wide genetic analyses, including study and visualization of linkage disequilibrium, mapping of causal SNPs and study of population structure.

References

BEN-DOR, A., SHAMIR, R. and YAKHINI, Z. (1999): Clustering gene expression patterns. *Journal of Computational Biology 6(3-4), 281-97.*

HWANG, K.B., KIM, B.-H. and ZHANG, B.-T. (2006): Learning hierarchical Bayesian networks for large-scale data analysis. *ICONIP (1), 670-679.*

MARTIN, J. and VANLEHN, K. (1995). Discrete factor analysis: learning hidden variables in Bayesian networks. *Technical report, Department of Computer Science, University of Pittsburgh.*

MOURAD, R., SINOQUET, C. and LERAY, P. (2010): Learning a forest of Hierarchical Bayesian Networks to model dependencies between genetic markers. *LINA, Research Report, hal-00444087.*

NEFIAN, A.V. (2006): Learning SNP dependencies using embedded Bayesian networks. *Computational Systems Bioinformatics Conference CSB'2006,* Stanford, USA, poster.

PATTARO, C., RUCZINSKI, I., FALLIN, D.M. and PARMIGIANI, G. (2008): Haplotype block partitioning as a tool for dimensionality reduction in SNP association studies. *BMC Genomics 9, 405, doi:10.1186/1471-2164-9-405.*

SCHAID, D.J. (2004): Evaluating associations of haplotypes with traits. *Genetic Epidemiology 27(4), 348-364.*

VERZILLI, C.J., STALLARD, N. and WHITTAKER, J.C. (2006): Bayesian graphical models for genomewide association studies. *The American Journal of Human Genetics 79(1), 100-112.*

WANG, Y., ZHANG, N.L. and CHEN, T. (2008): Latent tree models and approximate inference in Bayesian networks. *Journal of Artificial Intelligence Research 32(1), 879-900.*

ZHANG, N.L. (2003). Structural EM for hierarchical latent class model. *Technical report, HKUST-CS03-06.*

ZHANG, Y. and JI, L. (2009): Clustering of SNPs by a Structural EM Algorithm. *International Joint Conference on Bioinformatics, Systems Biology and Intelligent Computing, 147-150.*

Exact Posterior Distributions over the Segmentation Space and Model Selection for Multiple Change-Point Detection Problems

G. Rigaill[123], E. Lebarbier[12], S. Robin[12]

[1] AgroParisTech, UMR 518, F-75005, Paris, FRANCE
[2] INRA, UMR 518, F-75005, Paris, FRANCE
[3] Institut Curie, Département de Transfert, F-75005 Paris, France

Abstract. In segmentation problems, inference on change-point position and model selection are two difficult issues due to the discrete nature of change-points. In a Bayesian context, we derive exact, non-asymptotic, explicit and tractable formulae for the posterior distribution of variables such as the number of change-points or their positions. We also derive a new selection criterion that accounts for the reliability of the results. All these results are based on an efficient strategy to explore the whole segmentation space, which can be very large. We illustrate our methodology on both simulated data and a comparative genomic hybridisation profile.

Keywords: change-point detection, posterior distribution of change-points

1 Introduction

Segmentation and change-point detection problems arise in many scientific domains. In this problem, it is assumed that the observed data $\{y_t\}_{t=1,\ldots,n}$ is a realization of an independent random process $Y = \{Y_t\}_{t=1,\ldots,n}$. This process is drawn from a probability distribution G, which depends on a set of parameters denoted by θ. These parameters are assumed to be affected by $K-1$ abrupt changes, called change-points, at some unknown positions $\tau_2, \ldots, \tau_K$ (with the convention $\tau_1 = 1$ and $\tau_{K+1} = n+1$). Thus, the change-points delimit a partition m of $\{1, \ldots, n\}$, called here a segmentation, into K segments $r^{(k)}$ such that $r^{(k)} = [\tau_k, \tau_{k+1}[= \{\tau_k, \tau_k + 1, \ldots, \tau_{k+1} - 1\}$ and $m = \{r^{(k)}\}_{k=1,\ldots,K}$. The segmentation model has the following general form for a given m: if $t \in r$ and $r \in m$, $Y_t \sim G(\theta_r)$, where θ_r stands for the parameters of segment r. In this study, all the change-points are detected simultaneously. The question of finding the best segmentation in a given number of segments has already been largely studied (see for example Lavielle (2005), Braun et al. (2000), Bai and Perron (2003)). Two important issues remain: assessing the quality of the proposed segmentation and selecting the number of segments (also called dimension). In both cases, the main problem is the discrete nature of the change-points, which prevents the use of routine statistical inference.

Y. Lechevallier, G. Saporta (eds.), *Proceedings of COMPSTAT'2010*,
DOI 10.1007/978-3-7908-2604-3_57, © Springer-Verlag Berlin Heidelberg 2010

On the one hand, the quality of a segmentation can be assessed by study-ing the uncertainty of the change-point positions. From a non-asymptotic and non-parametric point of view, the likelihood-based inference is intricate, as the required regularity conditions for the change-point parameters are not satisfied (Feder (1975)). Different methods to obtain change-point confidence intervals have been proposed. Most of them are based on the limit distribu-tion of the change-point estimators (Feder (1975), Bai and Perron (2003)) or the asymptotic use of a likelihood-ratio statistic (Muggeo (2003)), others are based on bootstrap techniques (Hušková and Kirch (2008)). A practical comparison of these methods can be found in Toms and Lesperance (2003).

On the other hand, choosing the number of segments is also a critical issue. This is usually done by minimising a penalised contrast function. Gen-eral penalized criteria have been developed, such as AIC and BIC but they are not adapted in the segmentation framework since an exponential model collection is considered (Birgé and Massart (2007), Baraud et al. (2009)) and these criteria tend to overestimate the number of segments (Lavielle (2005)). Some criteria have been proposed specially for the segmentation framework. Some depend on constants to be calibrated (Lavielle (2005) and Lebarbier (2005)), but others do not (Zhang and Siegmund (2007)). More precisely, Zhang and Siegmund (2007) discussed the fact that the classical BIC was not theoretically justified in the segmentation context.

The purpose of our work is to provide exact, non-asymptotic, explicit and tractable formulae for both the posterior probability of a segmentation and that of a change-point occurring at a given position. More specifically, we consider the segmentation problem in a Bayesian framework so that the posterior probability of a segmentation is well defined. To tackle the discrete nature of change-points, we work at the segment level, where statistical in-ference is straightforward. From these segments, the issue is to get back to the segmentation or dimension level. If the segments are independent, it will be necessary to calculate quantities such as:

$$\sum_{m \in \mathcal{M}^*} P(Y|m)P(m) = \sum_{m \in \mathcal{M}^*} P(m) \prod_{r \in m} P(Y^r|r) \tag{1}$$

where Y^r stands for all observations in segment r and $\mathcal{M}^*$ is usually a very large set of segmentations. We propose a close-form (in terms of matrix prod-ucts) and tractable formulation of (1). Some similar quantities were computed by Guédon (2008) in a non-Bayesian context, using a forward-backward-like algorithm, but for fixed parameters. From our formula, we derive key quanti-ties to assess the quality of a segmentation and select the number of segments.

On the one hand, we obtain exact formulae for both the posterior prob-ability of a segmentation and that of a change-point occurring at a given position. This enables the construction of credibility intervals for change-points. Moreover, we retrieve the exact posterior probability of a segment within a given dimension and the exact entropy of the posterior distribution of the segmentations within a given dimension.

On the other hand, we derive a so-called 'exact' BIC criterion for choosing the number of segments K, taking $\mathcal{M}^* = \mathcal{M}_K$ which is the set of $\binom{n-1}{K-1}$ possible segmentations with K segments. In the same way, we derive the ICL criterion of Biernacki *et al.* (2000) in the segmentation framework. This last criterion takes into account the reliability of the results.

2   Exploring the segmentation space

In this section we propose a tractable and close-form formula of (1). We denote by $\mathcal{M}_K([i,j[)$ the set of all possible segmentations of $([i,j[)$ into K segments. The simplified notation $\mathcal{M}_K$ refers to $\mathcal{M}_K([1, n+1[)$.

Factorability assumption: A model satisfies the factorability assumption $\mathbf{H}$ if

$$\mathbf{H} : P(Y, m) = C \prod_{r \in m} a_r P(Y^r) \tag{2}$$

where $P(Y^r) = \int P(Y^r | \theta_r) P(\theta_r) d\theta_r$. This is false for the normal homoscedastic model $G(\theta_r) = \mathcal{N}(\mu_r, 1/\tau)$. When $\mathbf{H}$ holds, we derive an exact matrix product formulation of (1) enabling its computation in $O(Kn^2)$.

Theorem 1. *Consider a function F such that, for all $k \in [1, K]$ and for all segmentation $m \in \mathcal{M}_k([1, j[)$, there exists a function f such that: $F(m) = \prod_{r \in m} f(r)$. Let $\mathbf{A}$ be a square matrix with $n + 1$ columns such that $\mathbf{A}_{ij} = f([i, j[)$ if $1 \leq i < j \leq n+1$ and 0 otherwise. Then all elements of*

$$\left\{ \sum_{m \in \mathcal{M}_k([1,j[)} F(m) \right\}_{k \in [1,K] \cap j \in [1,n+1]}$$

can be computed in $O(Kn^2)$ using $\sum_{m \in \mathcal{M}_k([1,j[)} F(m) = (\mathbf{A}^k)_{1,j}$.

Theorem 1 will be used many times in the following sections, using a specific function $f(r)$ for each quantity of interest. Its proof is based on the following lemma, the proof of which is left to the reader.

Lemma 1. *Let $\mathbf{A}$ be a $n \times n$ square matrix. For all $k \in \mathbb{N}$, we define the function $f_{\mathbf{A},k}$ as: $\forall (i,j) \in [1,n]^2$, $f_{\mathbf{A},k}(i,j) = \sum_{(t_2 \cdots t_k) \in [1,n]^{k-1}}^{t_1 = i, \ t_{k+1} = j} \prod_{i=1}^{k} \mathbf{A}_{t_i, t_{i+1}}$. The Kn elements of $\{f_{\mathbf{A},k}(i,j)\}_{\{i \in [1,n], k \in [1,K]\}}$ can be computed in $O(Kn^2)$ as $f_{\mathbf{A},k}(i,j) = (\mathbf{A}^k)_{i,j}$.*

2.1   Calculation of $P(Y, m)$ and $P(Y, K)$

To calculate $P(Y, m)$ and $P(Y, K) = \sum_{m \in \mathcal{M}_K} P(Y, m)$, we need to define priors for the segmentation m. We now consider two typical priors.

Uniform conditional on the dimension: For any prior on the dimension $P(K)$, we define a uniform distribution for m given its dimension K:

$$P(m|K) = \binom{n-1}{K-1}^{-1} \quad \Rightarrow \quad P(m) = P(K(m)) \Big/ \binom{n-1}{K(m)-1} \tag{3}$$

that is $a_r = 1$ in (2), denoting $K(m)$ the number of segments of m.
Homogeneous segment lengths: Segmentation with balanced segment lengths
are sometimes desirable. They are favoured by the following prior:

$$P(m) = C \prod_{r \in m} n_r^{-1}, \qquad \text{where } C \text{ ensures that } \sum_{m \in \mathcal{M}} P(m) = 1. \qquad (4)$$

that is $a_r = n_r^{-1}$ in (2), where n_r is the length of segment r and $\mathcal{M}$ the set
of considered segmentations.

Proposition 3. *When* **H** *holds, for prior distributions* (3) *and* (4), $P(Y, K)$
can be computed in $O(Kn^2)$ *as* $P(Y, K) = C(\mathbf{A}^k)_{1,n+1}$ *with* $\mathbf{A}_{i,j} = 0$ *for* $j \leq i$
and, for $j > i$, *for prior* (3): $\mathbf{A}_{i,j} = P(Y^{[i,j[})$ *and* $C^{-1} = \binom{n-1}{K-1}$; *for prior*
(4): $\mathbf{A}_{i,j} = n_{[i,j[}^{-1} P(Y^{[i,j[})$ *and* $C^{-1} = \sum_{m \in \mathcal{M}_K} \prod_{r \in m} n_r^{-1}$.

Proof. For prior distribution (3), we use Theorem 1 with function $f(r) = P(Y^r)$, implying $\mathbf{A}_{i,j} = f([i, j[) = P(Y^{[i,j[})$. For prior distribution (4), we
first retrieve C using Theorem 1 with function $f(r) = n_r$. The result follows,
using Theorem 1 again, with function $f(r) = n_r^{-1} P(Y^r)$.$\square$

Poisson and Gaussian models. We recall two models that will be used later.
First is the segmentation problem of a piecewise constant Poisson rate model:

$$Y_t \sim \mathcal{P}(\mu_r) \text{ if } t \in r, \{\mu_r\} \text{ i.i.d., } \mu_r \sim \mathcal{G}\text{am}(\alpha_r, \beta_r); \qquad (5)$$

Second is the segmentation of a piecewise constant mean and variance Gaussian signal:

$$Y_t \sim \mathcal{N}(\mu_r, 1/\tau_r) \text{ if } t \in r, \begin{cases} \{\tau_r\} \text{ i.i.d., } & \tau_r \sim \mathcal{G}\text{am}(\nu_0/2, 2/s_0); \\ \{\mu_r\} \text{ indep., } & \mu_r | \tau_r \sim \mathcal{N}(\mu_0, (n_0\tau_r)^{-1}). \end{cases} \qquad (6)$$

2.2   Posterior distribution of the change-points and segments

We first define the corresponding segmentation sets:
$\mathcal{B}_{K,k}(t)$ is the set of segmentations from $\mathcal{M}_K$ such that the k-th segment
starts at position t;
$\mathcal{B}_K(t)$ is the subset of segmentations having a change-point at position t;
$\mathcal{S}_{K,k}([t_1, t_2[)$ is the subset of segmentations having segment $r = [t_1; t_2[$ as
their k-th segment;
$\mathcal{S}_K([t_1, t_2[)$ is the subset of segmentations including segment $[t_1, t_2[$.

We denote the conditional probability given the data Y and the dimension
K of each of these subsets by the corresponding capital letters with same
indices, e.g. $B_{K,k}(t) = \Pr\{m \in \mathcal{B}_{K,k}(t) | Y, K\}$. $B_K(t)$, $S_{K,k}(t)$ and $S_K(t)$ are
defined similarly. The following proposition gives explicit formulae for these
probabilities.

Proposition 4. *For all* $[t_1, t_2[$ *such that* $t_1 < t_2$, *we define, for* $K \geq 1$, $F_{t_1,t_2}(K) = \sum_{m \in \mathcal{M}_K([t_1,t_2[)} P(Y^{[t_1,t_2[}|m)P(m|K)$, *with* $F_{t_1,t_2}(K) = 0$ *if* $t_1 \geq t_2$. *Under assumption* **H**, *we have* $B_{K,k}(t) = P(Y|K)^{-1}F_{1,t}(k-1)F_{t,n+1}(K - k + 1)$ *and* $S_{K,k}(t_1, t_2) = P(Y|K)^{-1}F_{1,t_1}(k - 1)F_{t_1,t_2}(1)F_{t_2,n+1}(K - k)$, $B_K(t) = \sum_{k=1}^K B_{K,k}(t)$ *and* $S_K(t_1, t_2) = \sum_k S_{K,k}(t_1, t_2)$.

The proof is mainly based on set decompositions, such as $\mathcal{B}_{K,k}(t) = \mathcal{M}_{k-1}([1, t[) \times \mathcal{M}_{K-k+1}([t, n+1[)$ and all sums over $\mathcal{M}_{k-1}([1, t[)$ and $\mathcal{M}_{K-k+1}([t, n+1[)$ can be obtained with Theorem 1. The credibility of interval $[t_1, t_2]$ for change-point τ_k is $C_{K,k}([t_1, t_2]) = \Pr\{\tau_k \in [t_1, t_2]|Y, K\} = \sum_{t=t_1}^{t_2} B_{K,k}(t)$.

2.3   Posterior entropy

Segmentation problems are often reduced to choosing the best segmentation (i.e. the one with maximal posterior probability). Other segmentations with dimension K are rarely considered. The entropy of the distribution $P(m|Y, K)$ is $\mathcal{H}(K) = -\sum_{m \in \mathcal{M}_K} P(m|Y, K) \log P(m|Y, K)$ measures how the posterior distribution is concentrated around the best segmentation. Intuitively, a small entropy $\mathcal{H}(K)$ means that the best segmentation is a much better fit to the data than any other segmentation.

Proposition 5. *If* **H** *holds,* $\mathcal{H}(K) = \log A_K - \sum_r S_K(r) \log f(r)$. $A_K = \sum_{m \in \mathcal{M}_K} \prod_{r \in m} f(r)$ *is computed with Proposition 3 and* $f(r) = a_r P(Y^r)$.

3   Model selection

In a Bayesian framework, the BIC criterion aims to choose the model which maximises $P(M|Y)$, where M is the model. To calculate the BIC criterion, one needs to know $P(Y|M)$. In our case, the word 'model' is too broad and we have to distinguish between the selection of the dimension K and the selection of the segmentation m. However, we can bypass the problem by working at the segmentation level and going back at the dimension level using Proposition 3. Thus, the derivation of BIC criteria only requires the calculation of $P(Y^r) = \int P(Y^r|\theta_r)P(\theta_r)d\theta_r$, which can be obtained in a close form for simple models. Moreover, we derive an adaptation of the ICL criterion, first proposed for mixture models, to the segmentation context.

3.1   Exact BIC criterion

In segmentation problems, the selection of the 'best' number of segments K can be addressed per se, or as a first step to select the 'best' segmentation. The Bayesian framework suggests to choose $\widehat{K} = \arg\min_K \text{BIC}(K)$ where $\text{BIC}(K) = -\log P(Y, K)$. The best segmentation can be chosen in two ways. *Two-step strategy:* The 'best' segmentation can be chosen, conditionally to the pre-selected dimension $\widehat{K}$ as $\widehat{m}(\widehat{K}) = \arg\min_{m \in \mathcal{M}_{\widehat{K}}} \mathrm{BIC}(m|\widehat{K})$, where $\mathrm{BIC}(m|\widehat{K}) = -\log P(Y, m|\widehat{K})$.

One-step strategy: The 'best' segmentation can be chosen in $\mathcal{M} = \bigcup_{k=1}^{K} \mathcal{M}_k$ as $\widehat{m} = \arg\min_{m \in \mathcal{M}} \mathrm{BIC}(m)$, where $\mathrm{BIC}(m) = -\log P(Y, m)$.

$\mathrm{BIC}(K)$, $\mathrm{BIC}(m|K)$ and $\mathrm{BIC}(m)$ can all be computed with Proposition 3.

3.2   ICL criterion for dimension selection

In the framework of incomplete data models (e.g. mixture models), Biernacki *et al.* (2000) suggest the $\mathrm{ICL}(M)$ criterion, which is an estimate of $\mathbb{E}[\log P(Y, Z, M)|Y]$ where Z stands for the unobserved variables. The ICL criterion tend to select models that provide a reliable prediction of Z, i.e. with a small entropy. A segmentation m can be considered as an unobserved data and the dimension K can be chosen as $\widehat{K} = \arg\min_K \mathrm{ICL}(K)$ where $\mathrm{ICL}(K) = -\log P(Y, K) + H(m|Y, K)$. ICL favours dimensions where the best segmentation $\widehat{m}(K)$ outperforms other segmentations, so that $\widehat{m}(K)$ is more reliable.

4   Applications

4.1   Simulation study

Simulation design. We performed the simulation study in the Poisson model (5). We simulated a sequence of 150 observations affected by six changepoints. The segments have alternated mean 1 and $1 + \lambda$, where λ varies between 0 and 10. We set $\alpha = \beta = 1$ and simulated 300 sequences.

Model selection. The BIC criterion for dimension selection, $\mathrm{BIC}(K)$, almost never returned the true dimension, even for high values of λ (Figure 1). On the other hand, both the BIC criterion for model selection, $\mathrm{BIC}(m)$, and the ICL criterion, $\mathrm{ICL}(K)$, tend to recover the true dimension more often when λ became larger. $\mathrm{ICL}(K)$ even increased to a maximum of 99% true recoveries compared to a maximum of 91% for the $\mathrm{BIC}(m)$ criterion for model selection.

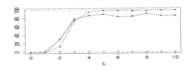

Fig. 1.   Percentage of true dimension recoveries as a function of λ for the three criteria. $\mathrm{BIC}(\widehat{m}_K)$: solid, $\mathrm{BIC}(K)$: dashed and $\mathrm{ICL}(K)$: dotted.

4.2 Analysis of a CGH profile

CGH enables the study of DNA copy number along the genome (Pinkel *et al.* (1998)). We used the Gaussian model defined in (6) that is often used for this type of data (Picard *et al.* (2005)). The profile shown in Figure 2 represents the copy number logratio of cell line BT474 to a normal reference sample, along chromosome 10.

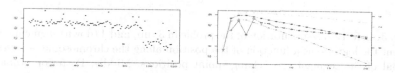

Fig. 2. Left: Chromosome 10 profile of cell line BT474. The DNA copy number logratio is represented as a function of its position along the chromosome. Right: (Left axis) BIC(m): triangle, BIC(K): bullet and ICL(K): black square as a function of the dimension K. (Right axis) $\mathcal{H}(K) - \mathcal{H}(K-1)$: circle as a function of K.

Model selection. The ICL(K) criterion selected 4 segments whereas BIC(m) selected 3 segments (see Figure 2 and 3 (left)). The additional penalty term of the ICL does not necessarily penalise larger dimensions. Here, ICL selected a segmentation with a larger dimension because it was more reliable. The choice of ICL was motivated by the small gain of entropy between $K = 3$ and 4 and was supported by the posterior distributions of the change-points and of the segments shown in Figure 3.

Posterior probability of the change-point positions. The distribution of the change-points for $K = 3$ and 4 are shown in Figure 3 (middle). For $K = 4$, the intervals were $[66, 78]$, $[78, 97]$ and $[91, 112]$ for τ_2, τ_3 and τ_4, respectively.

Posterior probability of a segment. In Figure 3 (Right) each point corresponds to a segment. The $K = 4$ model exhibits sharper peaks, which indicates a more reliable segmentation.

Acknowledgements. We thank M.P. Etienne for her helpful advice. We thank T. Dubois and E. Barillot for their support. G. Rigaill was supported by a grant of the INCA (Institut national du cancer).

References

BAI, J. and PERRON, P. (2003): Computation and analysis of multiple structural change models. *J. Appl. Econ.* **18** 1–22.

BARAUD, Y., GIRAUD, C. and HUET, S. (2009): Gaussian model selection with unknown variance. *AS.* **37 (2)** 630–672.

BIERNACKI, C., CELEUX, G. and GOVAERT, G. (2000): Assessing a mixture model for clustering with the integrated completed likelihood. *IEEE Trans. Pattern Anal. Machine Intel.* **22 (7)** 719–725.

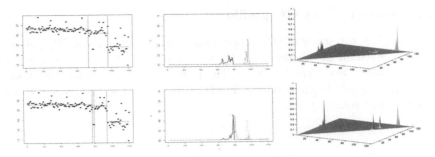

Fig. 3. Left: Best segmentation of the profile in 3 (up) and 4 (down) segments. • represent the logratio as a function of the position along the chromosome. $-$: averaged signal of the segment. $\cdots$: change-point positions. Middle: Posterior probability that the k-th change-point is at position t knowing that there is either 3 (up) or 4 (down) segments. Probability of the first change-point: $-$, probability of the second change-point: $--$ and probability of the third change-point: $\cdots$. Right: 3D plot of the probability of all segments. Up panel: $K = 3$ segments; down panel: $K = 4$ segments. x-axis: t_1, y-axis: t_2, z-axis: $S([t_1, t_2[)$.

BIRGÉ, L. and MASSART, P. (2007): Minimal penalties for gaussian model selection. *Probability Th. and Related Fields.* **138** 33–73.

BRAUN, R.-K., BRAUN, J.-V. and MÜLLER, H.-G. (2000): Multiple change-point fitting via quasilikelihood, with application to dna sequence segmentation. *Biometrika.* **87** 301–314.

FEDER, P. I. (1975): The loglikelihood ratio in segmented regression. *"AS".* **3 (1)** 84–97.

GUÉDON, Y. (2008), Explorating the segmentation space for the assessment of multiple change-points models. Technical report, Preprint INRIA n6619.

HUŠKOVÁ, M. and KIRCH, C. (2008): Bootstrapping confidence intervals for the change-point of time series. *Journal of Time Series Analysis.* **29 (6)** 947–972.

LAVIELLE, M. (2005): Using penalized contrasts for the change-point problem. *Signal Processing.* **85 (8)** 1501–1510.

LEBARBIER, E. (2005): Detecting multiple change-points in the mean of gaussian process by model selection. *Signal Processing.* **85** 717–736.

MUGGEO, V. M. (2003): Estimating regression models with unknown break-points. *Stat. Med.* **22 (19)** 3055–3071.

PICARD, F., ROBIN, S., LAVIELLE, M., VAISSE, C. and DAUDIN, J.-J. (2005): A statistical approach for array CGH data analysis. *BMC Bioinformatics.* **6 (27)** 1. www.biomedcentral.com/1471-2105/6/27.

PINKEL, D. *et al.* (1998): High resolution analysis of DNA copy number variation using comparative genomic hybridization to microarrays. *Nature Genetics.* **(20)** 207–211.

TOMS, J. D. and LESPERANCE, M. L. (2003): Piecewise regression: A tool for identifying ecological thresholds. *Ecology.* **84 (8)** 2034–2041.

ZHANG, N. R. and SIEGMUND, D. O. (2007): A modified Bayes information criterion with applications to the analysis of comparative genomic hybridization data. *Biometrics.* **63 (1)** 22–32.

Parcellation Schemes and Statistical Tests to Detect Active Regions on the Cortical Surface

Bertrand Thirion[1,2], Alan Tucholka[1,2], and Jean-Baptiste Poline[1,2]

[1] Parietal team, INRIA Saclay-Île-de-France, Saclay, France
CEA Saclay, Bâtiment 145, 91191, Gif-sur-Yvette, France
bertrand.thirion@inria.fr,
[2] CEA, DSV, I^2BM, Neurospin,
CEA Saclay, Bâtiment 145, 91191, Gif-sur-Yvette, France

Abstract. Activation detection in functional Magnetic Resonance Imaging (fMRI) datasets is usually performed by thresholding activation maps in the brain volume or, better, on the cortical surface. However, basing the analysis on a site-by-site statistical decision may be detrimental both to the interpretation of the results and to the sensitivity of the analysis, because a perfect point-to-point correspondence of brain surfaces from multiple subjects cannot be guaranteed in practice. In this paper, we propose a new approach that first defines anatomical regions such as cortical gyri outlined on the cortical surface, and then segments these regions into functionally homogeneous structures using a parcellation procedure that includes an explicit between-subject variability model, i.e. random effects. We show that random effects inference can be performed in this framework. Our procedure allows an exact control of the specificity using permutation techniques, and we show that the sensitivity of this approach is higher than the sensitivity of voxel- or cluster-level random effects tests performed on the cortical surface.

Keywords: statistical testing, EM algorithm, spatial models, neuroimaging

1 Introduction

In neuroimaging, brain activation detection is traditionally performed through the thresholding of statistical maps. In contrast with standard volume-based analyses, cortical surface mapping (CSM) consists in detecting brain activations on the cortical surface, after projection of the fMRI volume-based data onto the surface (Fischl et al. (1999), Andrade et al. (2001)). This offers the advantage of positioning functional activations in the two-dimensional space where they are indeed generated, as well as a better sensitivity/specificity compromise due to the limitation of the statistical tests to grey matter only. Although it has been suggested that CSM could be more sensitive in group studies than traditional volume-based studies (see e.g. Fischl et al. (1999)), inter-subject analyses have been limited by the problem of defining properly brain location on the surface in the absence of a standard coordinate system. A meaningful solution to this problem consists in defining intermediate representations, such as gyri, that represent a delineation of the main regions on

Y. Lechevallier, G. Saporta (eds.), *Proceedings of COMPSTAT'2010*,
DOI 10.1007/978-3-7908-2604-3_58, © Springer-Verlag Berlin Heidelberg 2010

the cortical surface, as obtained from an atlas, see Fischl et al. 2004. Then, one still has to decide how to take into account such gyral parcellations when making statistical tests, or how to test region-specific hypotheses based on the available data. Because gyri represent the cortex at a very coarse resolution, functional information should be used to test more precise regions.

A second aspect of the problem is that it is not possible to require a perfect match between brain meshes since they have different shapes, as seen with various sulci or gyrification indexes. But, even assuming that a perfect anatomical match can be obtained between the brains of several individuals, it is not clear that functional regions would be matched perfectly. A promising solution consists in introducing an intermediate representation between mesh vertices and gyri, for instance through the concept of brain parcellation (Tucholka et al. (2008)). Conceptually, such parcellations are defined through the use of both anatomical and functional information. Although this may provide meaningful entities, it is not clear how these structures can be used to infer active regions across subjects, i.e. how to make random effects analyses. In this work, we address this particular question by introducing a new probabilistic parcellation framework that includes random effects, and finally allows the test of some contrasts of interest. An unbiased assessment of these tests using permutations is possible thanks to the relatively mild computation cost of the proposed method.

In Section 2, we develop the random-effects anatomo-functional permutation model, then we described the validation procedure and give some results on a real dataset in Section 3.

2   Model

2.1   Inputs and notations

Let $X^s = \{x_i^s\}_{i=1..I^s}$ be a set of pre-defined coordinates that represent the position of cortical sites in a subject $s \in \{1,..,S\}$ in a certain gyrus $g \in \{1,..,G\}$ (in Sections 2.1-2.4, we omit the dependence on the gyrus to keep notations simple). These coordinates are assumed to yield an approximate correspondence across individuals. Let $Y^s = \{y_i^s\}_{i=1..I^s}$ be n_f-dimensional vectors that represent the functional activity related to these sites in subjects $s \in \{1,..,S\}$. In this work, we use $n_f = 1$. Let $K > 0$ be the number of components of the probabilistic parcellation.

Let $(w_{ik}^s)_{i=1..I^s,k=1..K}$ denote the probability that the site i belongs to component $k \in \{1,..,K\}$,i.e. $p(z_i^s = k)$, given its position. w_{ik}^s are function of the positions x_i^s and a set of two-dimensional coordinates $\mathcal{T} = (\tau_k)_{k=1..K}$ that describe the position of the clusters on the cortex, and a spatial variance parameter γ:

$$w_{ik}^s(\mathcal{T}) = \frac{\exp(-\frac{\|x_i^s - \tau_k\|^2}{2\gamma^2})}{\sum_{l=1}^{K} \exp(-\frac{\|x_i^s - \tau_l\|^2}{2\gamma^2})} \tag{1}$$

Note that the position variables $\mathcal{T}$ are shared across subjects.

2.2 Hierarchical parcellations

The parameters $\Theta = (\theta_k)_{k=1..K}$ used to model the functional information $(Y^s)_{s=1..S}$ are part of a hierarchical model that includes group-level and subject-specific activation maps in the chosen gyrus. The activation is assumed to be normally distributed in the population, and then normally distributed in each subject given the parameters of this subject: $\forall k \in \{1..K\}$, let (μ_k, Σ_k) be the population parameters, and $((\mu_k^s, \Sigma_k^s)_{s=1..S})$ be the individual parameters.

$$p(\mu_k^s | \mu_k, \Sigma_k) = \mathcal{N}(\mu_k^s; \mu_k, \Sigma_k) \tag{2}$$
$$p(y_i^s | z_i^s = k, \mu_k^s, \Sigma_k^s) = \mathcal{N}(y_i^s; \mu_k^s, \Sigma_k^s) \tag{3}$$

The parameters of the model are thus $\Theta = (\mu_k, \Sigma_k, (\Sigma_k^s)_{s=1..S})_{k=1..K}$, and the log-likelihood of the data can be written:

$$\mathcal{L}(Y | \Theta, \mathcal{T}) = \sum_{s=1}^{S} \sum_{i=1}^{I_s} \log \left(\sum_{k=1}^{K} w_{ik}^s(\mathcal{T}) \mathcal{N}(y_i^s; \mu_k, \Sigma_k + \Sigma_k^s) \right) \tag{4}$$

This assumes conditional independence of the functional information given the parcel parameters, as is classically done for mixture models. The model is summarized in Fig. 1. The important aspect with the random effects model is that it allows second level inference: let c be a certain contrast of experimental conditions; if we define second level statistics as

$$t_{RFX}(k) = \frac{c^T \mu_k}{\sqrt{c^T \Sigma_k c}} \sqrt{S - 1} \tag{5}$$

This statistic is readily computed for each parcel in each gyrus. Note the distribution of this quantity cannot be assumed as known under the null hypothesis, but a corrected threshold can be derived through statistical resampling procedures (see Sec. 2.5).

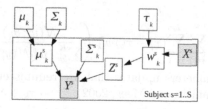

Fig. 1. Generative model of the data used in this work: in each subject $s \in 1..S$, the observed data Y_s, results from a spatial model, shared across subjects, that provides the probability w that each surface point belongs to a parcel, and a hierarchical model of the functional parameters, with both subject-specific (μ_k^s, Σ_k^s) and group-level (μ_k, Σ_k) mean and covariance parameters. The observed variables are shaded.

2.3   Estimation of the model

We use an alternate optimization scheme, in which Θ and $\mathcal{T}$ are optimized in turn in order to maximize the log-likelihood of the data in Eq. (4). $\max_\Theta p(Y|\Theta, \mathcal{T})$ is obtained through the standard EM algorithm while $\max_\mathcal{T} p(Y|\Theta, \mathcal{T})$ is obtained through gradient descent performed simultaneously.

- E-step: let $Z^s = (z_i^s)_{i=1..I}$ be the allocation variables of the mixture model.

$$p(z_i^s = k) = \frac{w_{ik}^s \mathcal{N}(y_i^s; \theta_k)}{\sum_{l=1}^K w_{il}^s \mathcal{N}(y_i^s; \theta_l)} \tag{6}$$

- M-step: $(\mu_k, \Sigma_k, \Sigma_k^s) = argmax_\Theta \mathbb{E}_z \log p(Y, Z|\theta, \mathcal{T})$, which yields an internal EM algorithm, where μ_k^s are the hidden variables, while the maximization is carried out over the other variables $(\mu_k, \Sigma_k, \Sigma_k^s)$:

$$p(\mu_k^s|\mu_k, \Sigma_k, \Sigma_k^s, Y^s, Z^s) = \mathcal{N}(\mu_k^s; \Lambda_k^s \left[(\Sigma_k)^{-1}\mu_k + m_k^s(\Sigma_k^s)^{-1}n_k^s \right], \Lambda_k^s) \tag{7}$$

where $m_k^s = \frac{\sum_{i=1}^{I_s} p(z_i^s=k)y_i}{\sum_{i=1}^{I_s} p(z_i^s=k)}$, $n_k^s = \sum_{i=1}^{I_s} p(z_i^s = k)$ and $\Lambda_k^s = \left[(\Sigma_k)^{-1} + n_k^s(\Sigma_k^s)^{-1} \right]^{-1}$. Then the internal M-step is performed:

$$\mu_k = \frac{1}{S} \sum_{s=1}^S \mu_k^s, \tag{8}$$

$$\Sigma_k = \frac{1}{S} \sum_{s=1}^S (\mu_k^s - \mu_k)^T (\mu_k^s - \mu_k), \tag{9}$$

$$\Sigma_k^s = \frac{\sum_{i=1}^{I_s} p(z_i^s = k)(y_i^s - \mu_k^s)^T (y_i^s - \mu_k^s)}{\sum_{i=1}^{I_s} p(z_i^s = k)} \tag{10}$$

Eqs. (7) and (8-10) are iterated until convergence. Furthermore, we use in this algorithm a regularization procedure (Fraley and Raftery (2007)) in order to ensure that the different terms do not converge toward a degenerated solution (e.g. null variance).

- C-step:

$$\frac{\nabla \mathcal{L}}{\nabla \tau_k} = \frac{1}{\gamma^2} \sum_{s=1}^S \sum_{i=1}^{I_s} (x_i^s - \tau_k)w_{ik}^s \left(\frac{\mathcal{N}(y_i^s; \theta_k)}{\sum_{l=1}^K w_{il}^s \mathcal{N}(y_i^s; \theta_l)} - 1 \right) \tag{11}$$

We perform parameters updates that are reminiscent of the mean-shift procedure (Comaniciu and Meer, 2002): $\tau_k \to \tau_k + \delta\tau_k$, where

$$\delta\tau_k = \sum_{s=1}^S \frac{1}{I_s} \sum_{i=1}^{I_s} (x_i^s - \tau_k)\omega_i^s, \text{ and } \omega_i^s = w_{ik}^s \left(\frac{\mathcal{N}(y_i^s; \theta_k)}{\sum_{l=1}^K w_{il}^s \mathcal{N}(y_i^s; \theta_l)} - 1 \right) \tag{12}$$

Alternating these three steps (6,7-10,12) is very effective in practice: the log likelihood often converges in 5 to 10 iterations.

2.4   Optimizing the parameters of the model

The two free parameters of the model are the number of parcels K and the spatial shrinkage parameter γ in each gyrus g. We optimize conjointly these parameters during a first analysis session using the cross-validated likelihood as criterion and a grid search approach. To compute the log-likelihood on a new dataset (X^σ, Y^σ), we need to estimate the covariance matrices Σ_k^σ within the new subject; we take the maximum likelihood estimator:

$$\mathcal{L}(Y^\sigma|X^\sigma, \Theta, \mathcal{T}) = \max_{(\Sigma_k^\sigma)_{k \in \{1..K\}}} \sum_{i=1}^{I_\sigma} \log \left(\sum_{k=1}^{K} w_{ik}^s(x_i^\sigma, \mathcal{T}) \mathcal{N}(y_i^\sigma; \mu_k, \Sigma_k + \Sigma_k^\sigma) \right)$$

$$(13)$$

The optimal values $(K^\star(g), \gamma^\star(g))$ are then retained for the RFX procedure.

2.5   Random-effects (RFX) inference procedure

In order to control the specificity of the parcel-based statistical procedure, we need to know the distribution of the statistic (5) under the null hypothesis, i.e. when no activation is present. This cannot be done analytically, because the value of the statistic depends on the whole parcellation procedure. We tabulate the distribution of the null hypothesis by randomly swapping the sign of the data related to the tested contrast across subjects, and then recomputing the parcels and the associated statistic $\tilde{t}$. Next, this procedure has to be carried out on the whole volume. After $R = 10^3$ randomizations, the maximal parcel-level statistic across gyri is tabulated:

$$\bar{t}_r = \max_{g \in 1..G} \max_{k \in \{1,..,K^\star(g)\}} \tilde{t}_k, \forall r \in \{1,..,R\} \tag{14}$$

and the threshold t_α for a specificity α ($\alpha = 0.05$ typically), corrected for multiple comparisons across parcels and gyri, is chosen as the $(1-\alpha)$ quantile of the distribution of $(\bar{t}_r)$. The probability of a parcel-based t-value being greater than t_α in any parcel of any gyrus by chance is thus lower than α.

3   Results on a real dataset

Dataset. A localizer protocol was acquired on a 1.5T GE MRI scanner. The Freesurfer package was used to segment different anatomical compartments from the anatomical image of the brain of each subject, providing white and grey matter mesh, and segmenting the sulci (Fischl et al. 1999). This sequence of processing was applied systematically to all available brains and the quality of resulting segmentation was visually checked. A surface-based coordinate system that represents sulco-gyral anatomy is finally obtained, and the cortical surface is subdivided into gyri. All cortical meshes are then resampled so that the nodes of the mesh are in one-to-one correspondence across subjects. For all subjects a standard preprocessing of fMRI data was performed using the SPM5 software. Functional images were then projected onto the grey/white interface using the method described in (Operto et al. (2008)). Subsequently, on each functional dataset a Linear Model-based analysis was carried out to obtain task-related activity maps Y for different contrasts of experimental conditions. We have tested 4 different contrasts related to motor, auditory, computation and reading functions respectively, but in separate analyses, so that we always have $n_f = 1$: taking $n_f > 1$ is possible, but would complicate the permutation framework described in Section 2.5.

Assessment of the PRFX statistic. Average left and right brain hemisphere meshes have been derived and are used for display. These average meshes are then parcelled using the maximum a posteriori label of each node given its position and the $\mathcal{T}$ parameters learnt by the algorithm. Our parcel-based inference (PRFX) is compared to more classical statistical procedures (Hayasaka etal. 2003, Rocheet al. 2007) used on the cortical surface: *i)* a vertex- or node-level control procedure yields the threshold t_α so that the probability of the random effects statistic at a single node being greater than t_α is less than α (0.05 typically); it is obtained by tabulating the maximal t-value of any node under the null hypothesis by a permutation procedure (VRFX); *ii)* a cluster-level procedure(CRFX) that considers all the clusters (connected components) of nodes with a t values higher than a certain threshold (we take the threshold corresponding to $p < 0.01$, uncorrected) and tabulates the distribution of the largest cluster size under the null hypothesis using the same permutation approach, so that the risk of detecting one cluster larger than the size threshold is less than α.

Outcome of the procedure. We concentrate on the contrast *sentence reading minus checkerboard viewing* that yields regions specifically involved in the reading task. Altogether, the parcellation outlines about 500 regions in each hemisphere. Activation detection images are given in Fig. 2. In the left hemisphere, activation specific to the reading task is found along the Superior Temporal Sulcus (superior and middle temporal gyrus), in Broca's area, in the middle part of the pre-central gyrus, and in the Superior Frontal Gyrus (Supplementary Motor Areas, SMA) by both PRFX and CRFX. Moreover, PRFX also detects significant activity in the temporal pole and the inferior temporal gyrus. VRFX detects tiny spots, barely visible in Fig. 2 in all these regions, except the superior Frontal region. In the right hemisphere, all three methods detect some activity in the Superior Temporal Sulcus (middle temporal gyrus), but only PRFX detects activity in the right SMA. Overall, the PRFX procedure is more sensitive than the other techniques. We also tested other contrasts and found that the PRFX procedure is at least as sensitive as the others. The VRFX procedure detects very few active nodes, but with a stronger control, in the sense that the null hypothesis is indeed rejected in

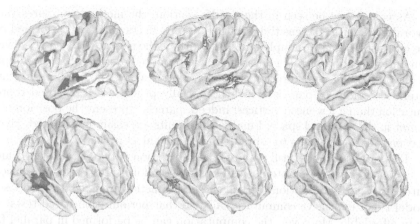

Fig. 2. Outcome of the parcel-based (left), cluster-based (middle) and node-based (right) random effects analyses in the left(top) and right (bottom) hemisphere. All the maps are corrected at the $p < 0.05$ parcel-, cluster- and voxel-level, respectively.

each detected node. Nevertheless, it detects at least one active node in almost all the regions found with the other approaches.

The CRFX procedure detects more extended regions than VRFX, but rejects only the global null hypothesis in these clusters, i.e. it does not reject the null hypothesis in any particular node. The same applies for the Parcel-based random effect procedure: it allows the rejection of the null hypothesis in a certain portion of a pre-defined gyrus, not on all the nodes of the finally outlined region.

4   Discussion

This work presents a new procedure to segment brain regions at a spatial scale that is intermediate between the mesh vertices and the anatomical gyri, which are too coarse (34 in each hemisphere with Freesurfer in (Fischl et al. (2004)) for an accurate functional description of the cortical surface. The main novelty of the presented work is to introduce a probabilistic model with random effects, which introduces the distinction between two sources of variance: *i)* the variance related to the spatial spread of the parcels, and thus simply represents the resolution which is chosen to analyse the data and *ii)* the between-subject variance, that represents the intrinsic functional variability between individuals, as well as potential spatial misfits. Besides, the introduction of the different variance components allows group-level inference, i.e. the computation of statistics that represent the magnitude of the average effect in the population, when compared to between-subjects fMRI signal variability.

As can clearly be seen in the results section, the method compares very favorably in terms of sensitivity with random effects analyses performed on the coregistered and resampled meshes, both at the cluster- and vertex- level. Our interpretation of this gain is that the proposed approach better adapts to the individual configurations.features. Importantly, the method outlines extended regions or parcels, which potentially provides a less biased representation than a few mesh vertices: indeed, parcels represent the position of a *region* in the standard space. Finally, the results are easily interpreted, given that each region belongs to a pre-defined anatomical gyrus.

The proposed model still requires the calibration of two parameters γ and K, which can be made automatically using standard model selection procedures (BIC, cross-validation). When these parameters are fixed, the proposed model is not expensive computationally, so that permutation-based tests remain affordable. Moreover, the computation can be performed in parallel for the different gyri. Using a python implementation, we could run the whole framework in less than 24 hours.

A relatively straightforward extension of the present framework includes the adaptation to more complex populations, where behavioural or clinical score are available to characterize the between subject variability of subgroup structure in the observed population. This might be particularly useful to derive interpretable, i.e. few discriminative features to separate the populations.

References

ANDRADE, A., KHERIF, F. et al. (2001): Detection of fMRI activation using cortical surface mapping. *Hum. Brain Mapp. 12, 79–93*

COMANICIU, D. and MEER, P. (2002): Mean shift: a robust approach toward feature space analysis. *IEEE PAMI 24(5), 603–619*

FISCHL, B., SERENO, M.I., TOOTELL, R.B. and DALE, A.M. (1999): High-resolution intersubject averaging and a coordinate system for the cortical surface. *Hum. Brain Mapp. 8(4), 272–284*

FISCHL, B., VAN DER KOUWE, A., et al. (2004): Automatically parcellating the human cerebral cortex. *Cereb. Cortex 14(1), 11–22*

FRALEY, C. and RAFTERY, A. (2007): Bayesian regularization for normal mixture estimation and model-based clustering. *Journal of Classif. 24, 155–181*

HAYASAKA, S. and NICHOLS, T.E.(2003): Validating Cluster Size Inference: Random Field and Permutation Methods *NeuroImage 20(4):2343–2356*

OPERTO, G., BULOT, R., ANTON, J.L. and COULON, O. (2008): Projection of fMRI data onto the cortical surface using anatomically-informed convolution kernels. *NeuroImage 39(1), 127–135*

ROCHE, A., MÉRIAUX, S., KELLER, M. and THIRION, B. (2007): Mixed-effects statistics for group analysis in fMRI: A nonparametric maximum likelihood approach. *NeuroImage, 38:501–510*

TUCHOLKA, A., THIRION, B., PERROT, M., PINEL, P., MANGIN, J.F. and POLINE, J.B. (2008): Probabilistic anatomo-functional parcellation of the cortex: how many regions? In: Metaxas, D.; Axel, L.; Fichtinger, G.; Szekely, G. (Eds.) *11th Proc. MICCAI* LNCS Vol. 5242, Springer Verlag, Berlin.

Robust Principal Component Analysis Based on Pairwise Correlation Estimators

Stefan Van Aelst[1], Ellen Vandervieren[2], and Gert Willems[1]

[1] Dept. of Applied Mathematics and Computer Science, Ghent University, Krijgslaan 281 S9, B-9000 Ghent, Belgium. *stefan.vanaelst@ugent.be ; gertllwillems@gmail.com*
[2] Dept. of Mathematics and Computer Science, University of Antwerp, Middelheimlaan 1, B-2020 Antwerp, Belgium. *ellen.vandervieren@ua.ac.be*

Abstract. Principal component analysis tries to explain and simplify the structure of multivariate data. For standardized variables, these principal components correspond to the eigenvectors of their correlation matrix. To obtain a robust principal components analysis, we estimate this correlation matrix componentwise by using robust pairwise correlation estimates. We show that the approach based on pairwise correlation estimators does not need a majority of outlier-free observations which becomes very useful for high dimensional problems. We further demonstrate that the "bivariate trimming" method especially works well in this setting.

Keywords: principal component analysis, robustness, high dimensional data, trimming.

1 Introduction

Principal component analysis (PCA) is a data-analytic technique that tries to explain the structure of multivariate data by means of a small number of principal components. These principal components are uncorrelated linear combinations of the original variables. As PCA is often used for data reduction, it is important to find those principal components that contain most of the information.

In the classical approach, the first principal component corresponds to the direction in which the variance of the projected data is maximal. Next, the second principal component is orthogonal to the first one and again maximizes the variance of the data projected on it and so on. We assume that the variables have been standardized. Then, the principal component estimates correspond to the eigenvectors of the sample correlation matrix.

Unfortunately, the classical correlations are very sensitive to aberrant observations. Consequently, when outliers are present in the data, the principal components may be affected by these outlying observations and thus become unreliable. Therefore, robust methods for PCA have been developed based on a robust covariance matrix (see e.g. Croux and Haesbroeck (2000), Salibian-Barrera et al. (2006)) or projection pursuit (see e.g. Croux and Ruiz-Gazen

Y. Lechevallier, G. Saporta (eds.), *Proceedings of COMPSTAT'2010*,
DOI 10.1007/978-3-7908-2604-3_59, © Springer-Verlag Berlin Heidelberg 2010

(2000)). Hubert et al. (2005) proposed the robpca approach which combines the advantages of projection pursuit with robust scatter matrix estimation. Atkinson et al. (2004) developed a method based on the forward search.

To study the performance of robust methods, contamination models are most often used. The standard contamination model assumes that the majority of the observations comes from a nominal distribution such as a multivariate normal distribution, while the remainder comes from another distribution that generates outliers (see e.g. Maronna et al. (2006)). This means that each data set is assumed to consist of at least 50% of uncontaminated observations. However, such models are not always realistic. In high dimensions, it can easily happen that an amount of outlying measurements is present in such a way that the majority of the observations is contaminated in at least one of their components.

To study robustness properties at high dimensional data, Alqallaf et al. (2009) proposed a flexible contamination model and discussed in more detail the independent contamination model which is very useful in this context. This model assumes that each variable is contaminated independently, which leads to componentwise outliers. Hence, each variable is assumed to have a majority of outlier-free values, but there is not necessarily a majority of outlier-free observations anymore.

In this paper, we standardize the data robustly, using the median and the median absolute deviation. We then consider several robust pairwise correlation estimators and investigate the robustness of the resulting robust PCA methods under different types of contamination. By estimating the correlation matrix componentwise, the resulting PCA methods should be able to resist better independent componentwise contamination.

2   Pairwise correlation estimators

Suppose $X = \{x_1, \ldots, x_n\} \subset \mathbb{R}^p$ is a set of n observations. Then, the off-diagonal elements of the corresponding correlation matrix $R \in \mathbb{R}^{p \times p}$ are obtained by pairwise robust correlation estimates $R_{jk} = \rho_T(X_j, X_k)$ $(j \neq k)$, with $X_l = \{x_{1l}, \ldots, x_{nl}\}$ $(l = 1, \ldots, p)$. We consider the following four choices for the robust pairwise correlation estimator ρ_T.

2.1   Univariate trimming.

An easy way to obtain a robust measure of correlation ρ_T is to trim the data componentwise as follows. For each (standardized) observation x_i; $i = 1, \ldots, n$ we define a vector of componentwise weights $(w_{i1}, \ldots, w_{ip})$ with $w_{ij} = I(|x_{ij}| \leq 2)$. Then, $\rho_{\text{Uni-Tr}}(X_j, X_k)$ is defined as the classical correlation coefficient of the weighted measurements of the corresponding variables.

2.2 Bivariate trimming.

Since the univariate trimming approach does not take into account the orientation of the bivariate data, Khan et al. (2007) developed a bivariate approach. For each set of variables (X_j, X_k) an initial correlation matrix $R^0 \in \mathbb{R}^{2 \times 2}$ is computed by using two different tuning constants to perform univariate trimming of the data. The size of the tuning constant is large (e.g. 2) for the quadrants of the bivariate space containing the majority of observations and small for the remaining two quadrants (see Khan et al. (2007) for details). Next, bivariate Mahalanobis distances are computed based on R^0 and a 95% tolerance ellipse is used to trim possible outliers. The final correlation estimate is the classical correlation of the trimmed bivariate data. We will refer to this method as $\rho_{\text{Bi-Tr}}$.

2.3 Gnanadesikan-Kettenring estimator.

Another alternative to define ρ_T is to use the Gnanadesikan-Kettenring estimator (Gnanadesikan and Kettenring (1972)) as used in e.g. Maronna and Zamar (2002). It is based on the identity

$$\text{Cor}(X, Y) = \frac{1}{4}(\sigma(X + Y)^2 - \sigma(X - Y)^2)$$

where σ is the standard deviation and X, Y is a pair of standardized random variables. By using a robust scale estimator to estimate σ, a robust correlation estimate is obtained. Here, we consider two choices for σ: the τ scale of Yohai and Zamar (1988) and the Q_n estimator of Rousseeuw and Croux (1992). The corresponding correlation estimates are denoted by $\rho_{\text{GK-tau}}$ and $\rho_{\text{GK-Qn}}$ respectively.

2.4 Quadrant correlation.

Finally, the quadrant correlation (see e.g. Alqallaf et al. (2002)) is defined as $\rho_{\text{QC}}(X_j, X_k) = \sin(\frac{\pi}{2} r_{jk})$ with

$$r_{jk} = \frac{\sum_{i=1}^{n} \text{sgn}(x_{ij})\, \text{sgn}(x_{ik})}{\sum_{i=1}^{n} |\text{sgn}(x_{ij})|\, |\text{sgn}(x_{ik})|}.$$

Note that the correlation matrix R, obtained by using one of these pairwise correlation estimators, is not necessarily positive (semi-)definite. Usually, this is not a problem because in PCA the focus is on the eigenvectors corresponding to the largest (positive) eigenvalues. However, if positive definiteness is needed, the techniques mentioned in Alqallaf et al. (2002) can be used.

3   Simulation Study

Through simulation we now investigate the effect of different types of outliers on the estimation of the principal components by classical and robust PCA. In particular, we present root mean squared errors and mean angles of the eigenvectors of the correlation matrices.

The study involved samples $X = \{x_1, \ldots, x_n\}$ of size $n = 100$ in $p = 5$ dimensions. The samples were randomly drawn from the multivariate normal distribution $N_p(\mathbf{0}, R_1)$ or $N_p(\mathbf{0}, R_2)$ where

$$R_1 = \begin{pmatrix} 1 & .8 & .6 & .4 & .2 \\ .8 & 1 & .8 & .6 & .4 \\ .6 & .8 & 1 & .8 & .6 \\ .4 & .6 & .8 & 1 & .8 \\ .2 & .4 & .6 & .8 & 1 \end{pmatrix} \quad \text{and} \quad R_2 = \begin{pmatrix} 1 & .9 & .9 & .9 & .9 \\ .9 & 1 & .9 & .9 & .9 \\ .9 & .9 & 1 & .9 & .9 \\ .9 & .9 & .9 & 1 & .9 \\ .9 & .9 & .9 & .9 & 1 \end{pmatrix}$$

Next, different types of contamination were added in such a way that they severely affect classical PCA:

- **Bivariate correlation outliers**: Since X_1 and X_2 are strongly positively correlated, for $\epsilon\%$ of the data these components were shifted over a distance of 2.5 in direction $(1, -1)$. Moreover, the variance of these components was multiplied by 0.1.
- **Multivariate correlation outliers**: We introduced $\epsilon\%$ of contamination in the direction of the eigenvector with the smallest eigenvalue. For R_1, the data were shifted over a distance of 15 in this direction and for R_2, we shifted the data over a distance of 20. The variance of the outliers was again multiplied by 0.1.
- **Componentwise outliers**: For each variable independently, a fraction ϵ of univariate outliers was introduced. The outlying values were obtained by shifting these values to center 10.

We present results for the cases of 0% and 20% outliers. For each setting, we generated $N = 500$ samples. For each of these samples $X^{(l)}; l = 1, \ldots, N$ we computed the correlation matrix estimates $R_T^{(l)}$, and its corresponding eigenvectors $v_{T,1}^{(l)}, v_{T,2}^{(l)}, v_{T,3}^{(l)}, v_{T,4}^{(l)}, v_{T,5}^{(l)}$. Next, for each of the eigenvectors $v_1, \ldots, v_5$ corresponding to R_1 or R_2 above, the root mean squared error (RMSE) and the mean angle of the various methods were calculated as

$$\text{RMSE}(v_{T,k}) = \sqrt{\underset{j=1,\ldots,p}{\text{ave}} \left(\underset{l=1,\ldots,N}{\text{ave}} (v_{T,kj}^{(l)} - v_{kj})^2 \right)}$$

and

$$\text{Mean Angle}(v_{T,k}) = \underset{l=1,\ldots,N}{\text{ave}} (\text{acos}(|v_k^t v_{T,k}^{(l)}|))$$

where $\text{acos}(|v_k^t v_{T,k}^{(l)}|) \in [0; \frac{\pi}{2}]$ is the angle between the normalized eigenvector v_k and its estimated counterpart $v_{T,k}^{(l)}$.

We first consider the uncontaminated case. The upper row of Figure 1 shows the RMSE of the eigenvectors for the robust pairwise correlation matrices, robpca and the classical PCA method (cpca). The bottom row shows the mean angle of these eigenvectors. On the left hand side, the result for R_1 is shown whereas the right side shows the result for R_2.

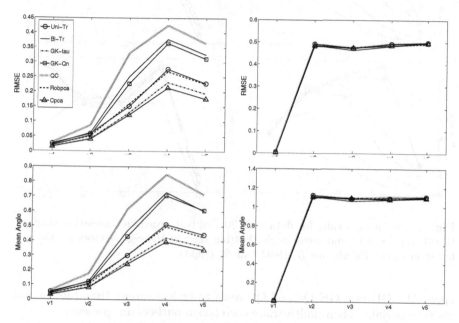

Fig. 1. Simulation results for uncontaminated data with correlation matrix R_1 (left) and R_2 (right): RMSE (upper row) and mean angle (bottom row) of the eigenvectors for the different methods.

Note that as PCA is a data reduction technique, we focus on the first K eigenvectors. To find a good value for K, one can make a screeplot of the eigenvalues or look at the percentage of variance explained by the first K eigenvectors. For R_1, the first three eigenvectors explain already 94.75% of the total variance so we focus on $K = 3$. For R_2, we use $K = 1$ as the first eigenvector explains 92% of the total variance.

When there are no outliers, the classical PCA method clearly performs best. However, the difference between cpca and the other methods is relatively small, especially for data with correlation matrix R_2.

Figure 2 shows the results for data with 20% of bad bivariate correlation outliers. We see that the RMSE and the mean angle become large for cpca, but robpca and Bi-Tr yield a considerable improvement.

The same holds for data with 20% of bad multivariate correlation outliers as can be seen from Figure 3. This clearly indicates the non-robustness of

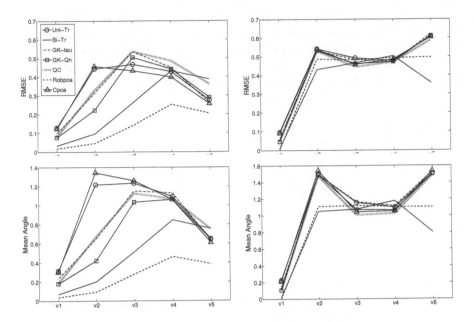

Fig. 2. Simulation results for data with 20% of bad bivariate correlation outliers: RMSE (upper row) and mean angle (bottom row) of the eigenvectors for the different methods. Results for R_1 (left) and R_2 (right).

cpca. Also GK-tau, GK-Qn and QC seem to be less robust than robpca and Bi-Tr, especially when multivariate correlation outliers are present.

Figure 4 shows the results for 20% of componentwise outliers. Now, robpca clearly performs much worse than the pairwise correlation approach, because there is no majority of uncontaminated observations anymore. Indeed, with 20% of contamination in each variable independently, there is only a slight minority of completely clean observations left. As robpca is based on at least 50% of the observations, it is forced to use contaminated observations, which results in an unreliable estimate. The pairwise correlation approach on the other hand, does not need a majority of outlier-free observations and thus better withstands this type of outliers. Of all pairwise correlation estimators, Bi-Tr performs best. It yields a small RMSE and mean angle, which indicates that the principal components are estimated accurately.

4   Conclusion

We considered robust PCA based on robust pairwise correlation estimates. The resulting robust PCA clearly estimates the principal components better in settings with independent contamination. It was shown empirically that the pairwise correlation estimates do not need a majority of outlier-free

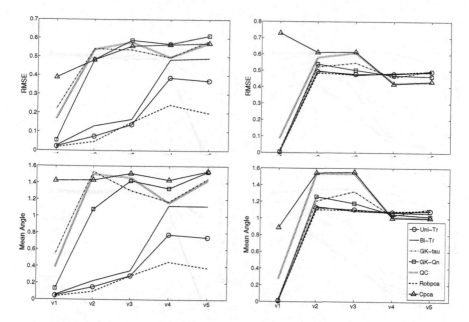

Fig. 3. Simulation results for data with 20% of bad multivariate correlation outliers: RMSE (upper row) and mean angle (bottom row) of the eigenvectors for the different methods. Results for R_1 (left) and R_2 (right).

observations and hence, can better withstand this type of outliers. The simulation study indicated that PCA based on correlation estimates obtained by bivariate trimming (Bi-Tr) works well, compared to robpca, when the data are contaminated and outperforms robpca with componentwise outliers.

References

ALQALLAF, F.A., KONIS, K.P., MARTIN, R.D. and ZAMAR, R.H. (2002): Scalable Robust Covariance and Correlation Estimates for Data Mining. In: *Proceedings of the Eighth ACM SIGKDD International Conference on Knowledge Discovery and Data Mining.* Edmonton, Alberta, Canada, 14-23.

ALQALLAF, F., VAN AELST, S., YOHAI, V.J. and ZAMAR, R.H. (2009): Propagation of Outliers in Multivariate Data. *Annals of Statistics 37, 311-331.*

ATKINSON, A.C., RIANI, M. and CERIOLI, A. (2004): *Exploring Multivariate Data With the Forward Search.* Springer Verlag, New York.

CROUX, C. and HAESBROECK, G. (2000): Principal Components Analysis based on Robust Estimators of the Covariance or Correlation Matrix: Influence Functions and Efficiencies. *Biometrika 87, 603-618.*

CROUX, C. and RUIZ-GAZEN, A. (2000): High Breakdown Estimators for Principal Components: the Projection-Pursuit Approach Revisited. *Journal of Multivariate Analysis 95, 206-226.*

580   Van Aelst, S. et al.

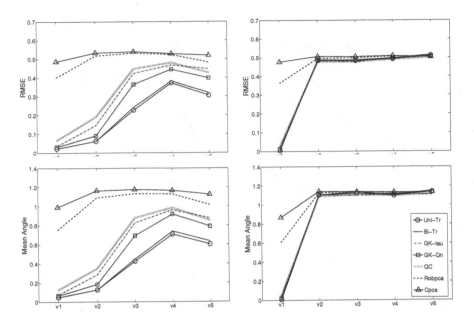

Fig. 4. Simulation results for data with 20% of bad componentwise outliers: RMSE (upper row) and mean angle (bottom row) of the eigenvectors for the different methods. Results for R_1 (left) and R_2 (right).

GNANADESIKAN, R. and KETTENRING, J.R. (1972): Robust Estimates, Residuals and Outlier Detection With Multiresponse Data. *Biometrics 28, 81-124.*

HUBERT, M., ROUSSEEUW, P.J. and VANDEN BRANDEN, K. (2005): ROBPCA: a New Approach to Robust Principal Component Analysis. *Technometrics 47, 64-79.*

KHAN, J.A., VAN AELST, S. and ZAMAR, R.H. (2007): Robust Linear Model Selection Based on Least Angle Regression. *Journal of the American Statistical Association 102 (12), 1289-1299.*

MARONNA, R.A., MARTIN, D.R. and YOHAI, V.J. (2006): *Robust Statistics: Theory and Methods.* John Wiley and Sons, New York.

MARONNA, R.A. and ZAMAR, R.H. (2002): Robust Estimates of Location and Dispersion for High-Dimensional Datasets. *Technometrics 44 (4), 307-317.*

ROUSSEEUW, P.J. and CROUX, C. (1992): Explicit Scale Estimators with High Breakdown Point. In: Y. Dodge (Ed.): L_1-*Statistical Analysis and Related Methods.* Amsterdam: North-Holland, 77-92.

SALIBIAN-BARRERA, M., VAN AELST, S. and WILLEMS, G. (2006): PCA Based on Multivariate MM-estimators with Fast and Robust Bootstrap. *Journal of the American Statistical Association 101, 1198-1211.*

YOHAI, V.J. and ZAMAR, R. (1988): High Breakdown Point Estimates of Regression by Means of the Minimization of an Efficient Scale. *Journal of the American Statistical Association 86, 403-413.*

Ordinary Least Squares for Histogram Data Based on Wasserstein Distance

Rosanna Verde and Antonio Irpino[1]

Dipartimento di Studi Europei e Mediterranei,
Seconda Universitá degli Studi di Napoli
Via del Setificio, Caserta, Italy, {*rosanna.verde, antonio.irpino*}*@unina2.it*

Abstract. Histogram data is a kind of symbolic representation which allows to describe an individual by an empirical frequency distribution. In this paper we introduce a linear regression model for histogram variables. We present a new Ordinary Least Squares approach for a linear model estimation, using the Wasserstein metric between histograms. In this paper we suppose that the regression coefficient are scalar values. After having illustrated the concurrent approaches, we corroborate the proposed estimation method by an application on a real dataset.

Keywords: probability distribution function, histogram data, ordinary least squares, Wasserstein distance

1 Introduction

Suppose the population is partitioned into K clusters, sub-populations or macro-unit observations, each of them consisting of n_k $(k = 1, \ldots, K)$ individuals: for example, studying the income of a region, we may observe the incomes of those citizens living in the municipalities. The population is observed with respect to two variables Y and X for which we want to investigate the causal relationship $Y = f(X) + e$. For each macro-unit we assume to know only the marginal distributions of X and Y, that we denote by $f_k(X)$ and $f_k(Y)$ and in some occasions we may not know the n_k too. Further, we do not know the joint distribution $f_k(X, Y)$. This situation is quite common in practise. For example, if we browse the SIMBAD (http://simbad.u-strasbg.fr/simbad/) astronomical database, for the stellar object *SIRIUS A* we obtain a Redshift in terms of V(km/s) equal to -7.6 ± 0.9 and a Parallaxes of 379.21 ± 1.58, or in other words, assuming a Gaussian distribution, we may say that variable $Redshift_{SIRIUS\,A} \sim N(-7.6, 0.9)$ and $Parallaxes_{SIRIUS\,A} \sim N(379.21, 1.58)$, but the database does not report how many observations have been done (n_k) and what is the joint density function $f(Redshift, Parallaxes)$. Other similar cases occur, when, for confidentiality matters, we obtain descriptions of groups of individuals at an aggregate level from the Official statistics databases. In particular, the description of the groups hold the following characteristics:

Y. Lechevallier, G. Saporta (eds.), *Proceedings of COMPSTAT'2010*,
DOI 10.1007/978-3-7908-2604-3_60, © Springer-Verlag Berlin Heidelberg 2010

Assumption of error-free representation of macro-units For a macro-unit, we assume that $X_1, X_2, \ldots$ are i.i.d random variables in $\mathbb{R}$ with cumulative distribution function $F(x)$. The empirical distribution function for $X_1, \ldots, X_n$ is defined by $F_n(x) = \frac{1}{n} \sum_{i=1}^{n} I_{(-\infty, x]}(X_i)$ where $I_{(-\infty, x]}$ is the indicator function. Assuming that n is large enough for each macro-unit, or the sample size in each macro-unit is chosen according to the Dvoretzky-Kiefer-Wolfowitz inequality (Dvoretzky et al. (1956)) derived from the Glivenko-Cantelli theorem, we assume that the description of a macro-unit by means of the empirical distribution function is error-free, i.e., we assume that the observed distribution function (or a model of it) corresponds to the theoretic distribution of X in the macro-unit.

First two moments are finite for each macro-unit, X and Y have finite the first two moments.

Internal independence Another assumption is the internal independence of X and Y,i.e., $f_k(x, y) = f_k(x) f_k(y)$. This is a common assumption in Symbolic Data Analysis.

The above conditions are in accordance with the definition of symbolic modal variable (Bock and Diday (2000)) equipped with a numerical (continuous) support. Bock and Diday (2000) give three kinds of possible description:

Histogram variable In this case the description is a classic histogram where the support is partitioned into intervals, where, each of them is weighted by the observed density (or by the observed frequency if the intervals are of equal width);

Empirical distribution function variable The description of a macro-unit is done according to the empirical distribution function $F_{n_k}(x)$;

Model of distribution variable The macro-unit description is done according to a predefined model of random variable. For example, the macro unit is described by a normal distribution $X \sim N(\mu_k, \sigma_k)$.

After presenting a formalization about histogram data, we introduce the Wasserstein distance in order to define an OLS criterion for a linear bivariate model.Considering two histogram variable Y and X observed on N macro-units, the aim is to find the best linear transformation of X that best (in a OLS way) fits the Y variable.

2   Histogram Data and Wasserstein Distance

Given a set $E = s_1, \ldots, s_n$ of n macro-units, we assume that each macro-unit is described by a histogram for the variable X, according to the definition of histogram variable of Bock and Diday (2000).A histogram can be described as a density function $f_i(x)$ where the support is a partition of a closed subset of $\Re$ consisting of intervals of $\Re$. With each density $f_i(x)$ is associated a cumulative distribution function $F_i(x) = \int\limits_{-\infty}^{x} f_i(x) dx$ corresponding to the quantile function (qf) is $F_{iX}^{-1}(t) = (x|F_i(x) = t)$. Quantile functions are non decreasing functions because they are the inverses of non decreasing functions (the cdf's). We must remember that, in general the sum of two qf's is again a quantile function. The same it is not true for the difference between two qf's. Indeed, the sum of two not decreasing is a not decreasing function too, while the difference is not monotonic in general. Further, the algebraic sum of a scalar with a qf is a qf, like the product of a positive real number and a qf. In order to simplify the notation, we denote the following quantities:

$$x_i(t) = F_{iX}^{-1}(t)$$
$$\bar{x}_i = \int_0^1 x_i(t)dt \text{ and } \sigma_{x_i}^2 = \int_0^1 [x_i(t)]^2 dt - [\bar{x}_i]^2 \Rightarrow \int_0^1 [x_i(t)]^2 dt = \sigma_{x_i}^2 + [\bar{x}_i]^2$$

According to Verde and Irpino (2008), we can write:

$$\bar{x}(t) = \frac{1}{n} \sum_{i=1}^n x_i(t) \; \forall t \in [0,1]; \quad \bar{x} = \frac{1}{n} \sum_{i=1}^n \int_0^1 x_i(t)dt = \frac{1}{n} \sum_{i=1}^n \bar{x}_i = \int_0^1 \bar{x}(t)dt$$
$$\rho(x_i, x_j) = \frac{\int_0^1 x_i(t)x_j(t)dt - \bar{x}_i\bar{x}_j}{\sigma_{x_i}\sigma_{x_j}} \Rightarrow \int_0^1 x_i(t)x_j(t)dt = \rho(x_i, x_j)\sigma_{x_i}\sigma_{x_j} + \bar{x}_i\bar{x}_j$$

In order to compare two histograms, the authors propose to use the L_2–Wasserstein-Kantorovich metric:

$$d_W(x_i, x_j) := \sqrt{\int_0^1 (x_i(t) - x_j(t))^2 dt}. \tag{1}$$

The squared L_2 Wasserstein metric can be decomposed (Irpino and Verde (2008)) as a sum of squared Euclidean distances between the means, the standard deviations and a residual part that can be assumed as a shape distance between two distributions:

$$d_W^2 = \underbrace{(\bar{x}_i - \bar{x}_j)^2}_{Location} + \underbrace{(\sigma_{x_i} - \sigma_{x_j})^2}_{Size} + \underbrace{2\sigma_{x_i}\sigma_{x_j}(1 - \rho(x_i, x_j))}_{Shape} \tag{2}$$

where $\rho(x_i, x_j)$ is the correlation of the quantiles of the two distributions as represented in a classical QQ plot.
We denote $x_i^c(t) = x_i(t) - \bar{x}_i$ as the centered qf of x_i. Under this notation Cuesta-Albertos et al. (1987) prove that:

$$d_W^2(x_i, x_j) = (\bar{x}_i - \bar{x}_j)^2 + d_W^2(x_i^c, x_j^c) \tag{3}$$

or, in other words, the (squared) Wasserstein distance between two distribution or random variables, is equal to the sum of the squared Euclidean distance between their means (the first moments) and the squared Wasserstein distance between the two centered random variables.

3   The Model

Given a vector of n histograms $(f_1(x), \ldots, f_n(x))$ for the X variable and a vector of n histograms for the Y variable $(f_1(y), \ldots, f_n(y))$, we propose a method for the investigation of a casual relationship between their quantile functions, or in other words, how to predict the quantile function of $y_i(t)$, once we observe the quantile function $x_i(t)$:

$$y_i(t) = \varphi\left(x_i(t)\right) + \varepsilon_i(t) \quad i = 1, \ldots, n \text{ and } t \in [0, 1] \tag{4}$$

such that the error term is the following function:

$$\varepsilon_i(t) = y_i(t) - \varphi\left(x_i(t)\right) \quad i = 1, \ldots, n \text{ and } t \in [0, 1]. \tag{5}$$

We assume a linear model for $\varphi\left(x_i(t)\right)$ of such kind:

$$\varphi\left(x_i(t)\right) = \alpha + \beta_1 \bar{x}_i + \beta_2 x_i^c(t) \ (\alpha, \beta_1, \beta_2) \in \Re^3. \tag{6}$$

The choice of considering two terms for the β's is founded on the fact a linear transformation of a quantile function into another can be done in two steps: we can translate the quantile function by multiplying the mean by a positive or a negative number and we can shrink or enlarge the quantile function by multiplying only by a positive number. Considering the linear transformation of quantile functions, we assume that the distribution functions that are related to the qf's should have a similar shape in terms of third (skew) and fourth (kurtosis) standardized moments (i.e., $\rho(x_i, x_j)$, $\rho(x_i, y_i)$ and $\rho(y_i, y_j)$ should be close to 1). For example, there is no linear transformation that can transform a Gaussian variable into a χ^2 one. Under this consideration we express the model as follows:

$$y_i(t) = \alpha + \beta_1 \bar{x}_i + \beta_2 x_i^c(t) + \varepsilon_i(t). \tag{7}$$

We propose to estimate the model parameters using the Ordinary Least Squares minimization problem based on the Wasserstein distance between $y_i(t)$ and $\varphi\left(x_i(t)\right)$, as follows:

$$\underset{(\alpha, \beta_1, \beta_2) \in \Re^3}{\arg \min} \ f(\alpha, \beta_1, \beta_2) = \sum_{i=1}^{n} d_W^2\left(y_i(t), \varphi\left(x_i(t)\right)\right) \tag{8}$$

where

$$f(\alpha, \beta_1, \beta_2) = \sum_{i=1}^{n} \int_0^1 \left[y_i(t) - \alpha - \beta_1 \bar{x}_i - \beta_2 x_i^c(t)\right]^2 dt. \tag{9}$$

The parameters are obtained according the usual first order conditions:

$$\begin{cases} \frac{\delta f}{\delta \alpha} = -2 \sum\limits_{i=1}^{n} \int\limits_{0}^{1} \left(\bar{y}_i + y_i^c(t) - \alpha - \beta_1 \bar{x}_i - \beta_2 x_i^c(t)\right) dt = 0 & (I) \\ \frac{\delta f}{\delta \beta_1} = -2 \sum\limits_{i=1}^{n} \int\limits_{0}^{1} \bar{x}_i \left(\bar{y}_i + y_i^c(t) - \alpha - \beta_1 \bar{x}_i - \beta_2 x_i^c(t)\right) dt = 0 & (II) \\ \frac{\delta f}{\delta \beta_2} = -2 \sum\limits_{i=1}^{n} \int\limits_{0}^{1} x_i^c(t) \left(\bar{y}_i + y_i^c(t) - \alpha - \beta_1 \bar{x}_i - \beta_2 x_i^c(t)\right) dt = 0 & (III) \end{cases} \quad (10)$$

The solution for α, β_1 and β_2 are the following:

$$\alpha = \bar{y} - \beta_1 \bar{x}; \quad \beta_1 = \frac{\sum\limits_{i=1}^{n} \bar{x}_i \bar{y}_i - n \bar{y}\,\bar{x}}{\sum\limits_{i=1}^{n} \bar{x}_i^2 - n\bar{x}^2}; \quad \beta_2 = \frac{\sum\limits_{i=1}^{n} \rho_i(X,Y)\sigma_{x_i}\sigma_{y_i}}{\sum\limits_{i=1}^{n} \sigma_{x_i}^2}.$$

The terms α and β_1 are the same of a regression between the means of the $y_i(t)$'s and the means of the $x_i(t)$'s. The interesting term is the β_2: it is always positive as is the ratio of two positive numbers. This solves naturally a problem that is presented, for example, in the regression method proposed by Lima Neto and De Carvalho (2010) for interval data. They propose a regression on midpoints and ranges of intervals using a constrained regression, where the constraint is the positivity of the coefficient related to the variability of ranges of the intervals of the explicative variable and that of the explained one.

3.1 Tools for the evaluation of the Goodness of Fit of the model

Verde and Irpino (2008) proved that the Wasserstein distance can be used for the definition of an inertia measure, that, for grouped data satisfies the Huygens theorem of decomposition.

$$SS(Y) = \sum\limits_{i=1}^{n} d_W^2\left(y_i(t), \bar{y}(t)\right) = \sum\limits_{i=1}^{n} \int\limits_{0}^{1} \left[y_i(t) - \bar{y}(t)\right]^2 dt.$$

A common tool for the evaluation of a fitting procedure is the well known R^2 statistics deriving from the following decomposition of $SS(Y)$:

$$SS(Y) = SS_{Error} + SS_{Regression}$$

where $\hat{y}_i$ are the predicted values. In our case, this equality holds only when the conditions of equality shape and of proportionality hold. In our case we may prove that:

$$SS(Y) = \sum_{i=1}^{n} d_W^2 \left(y_i(t), \bar{y}(t) \right) = \underbrace{\sum_{i=1}^{n} \int_0^1 \left[\hat{y}_i(t) - y_i(t) \right]^2 dt}_{SS_{Error}} +$$

$$+ \underbrace{\sum_{i=1}^{n} \int_0^1 \left[\bar{y}(t) - \hat{y}_i(t) \right]^2 dt}_{SS_{Regression}} \underbrace{- 2n \int_0^1 \bar{y}(t)\bar{e}(t)dt}_{Bias} \tag{11}$$

where $\hat{y}_i(t) = \alpha + \beta_1 \bar{x}_i + \beta_2 x_i^c(t)$,

$$bias = \int_0^1 \bar{y}(t)\bar{e}(t)dt = \left\{ \sigma_{\bar{y}}^2 - \beta_2 \rho(\bar{X}, \bar{Y}) \sigma_{\bar{x}} \sigma_{\bar{y}} \right\} \tag{12}$$

and $\bar{e}(t)$ is the mean (or barycenter) distribution of the distributions of the errors for each observation. The term in eq. 12 reflects the impossibility of the linear transformation of $\bar{x}(t)$ of reflecting the variability structure of $\bar{y}(t)$. In general, this term goes to zero when histograms have the same shape (i.e., from the third ones forward, the standardized moments of the histograms are equal) and the standard deviations of x_i's are proportional to the standard deviations y_i's. We assume that this term is related to the capacity of the model of predict the mean distribution $\bar{y}(t)$ from the mean distribution $\bar{x}(t)$, and can be considered as a bias of prediction of the variability of $\bar{y}(t)$ related to the linear form of the model. If we rewrite the $SS_{Regression}$ as

$$SS_{Regression} = \sum_{i=1}^{n} \left(\bar{y}_i - \bar{\hat{y}}_i \right)^2 + \sum_{i=1}^{n} \int_0^1 \left[\bar{y}^c(t) - \hat{y}_i^c(t) \right]^2 dt - \int_0^1 \bar{y}(t)\bar{e}(t)dt \tag{13}$$

In this case, the classical $R^2 = 1 - \frac{SS_{Error}}{SS(Y)}$ statistic can be lesser of zero or greater than 1. This occurs when the shapes (i.e, the internal variability structures) of the histograms are very different within the X or between the $x_i(t)$'s and the $y_i(t)$'s. In order to obtain a statistics that does not suffer of the described drawback, we propose to adopt the following general index that varies between 0 and 1:

$$PseudoR^2 = \min \left[\max \left[0; 1 - \frac{SS_{Error}}{SS(Y)} \right]; 1 \right]. \tag{14}$$

$PreudoR^2$ index should be presented also with the quantity $\frac{bias}{SS(Y)}$. Indeed, the $PseudoR^2$ show the goodness of fit when all the data have the same shape and a proportional standard deviation, while $\frac{bias}{SS(Y)}$ shows the effect of different variability structure in the data on the prediction model. In this formulation, this effect cannot be deleted from the model except if we formulate a different functional model for the regression problem.

4   Application

In this section, we show some results of clustering of data describing the mean monthly temperature, pressure, relative humidity, wind speed and total monthly precipitations of 60 meteorological stations of the People's Republic of China[1], recorded from 1840 to 1988. For the aims of this paper, we have considered the distributions of the variables for January (the coldest month) and July (the hottest month) as presented in Verde and Irpino (2008). For a simple comparison, we propose to evaluate if it is possible to predict temperature, pressure, relative humidity, wind speed and precipitation in January on the basis of the same histogram variable observed in July. For each bivariate model we collect the estimated parameters, the correlation among histogram variables (as proposed in Verde and Irpino, (2008)) and the components of the sum of squares of the dependent variable. In table 1, we present some

Variable	Y	X	α	β_1	β_2	$PseudoR^2$	$\frac{Bias}{SS(Y)}$
Relative Umidity (%)	July	January	472.52	0.393	0.593	0.1564	-0.0296
Station Pressure (mb)	July	January	515.31	0.929	0.993	0.9981	0.0007
Temperature (Cel)	July	January	254.68	0.196	0.521	0.3813	-0.0185
Wind Speed (m/s)	July	January	7.98	0.638	0.848	0.6563	-0.0564
Precipitation (mm)	July	January	1337.22	0.617	3.578	0.0000	-0.9275

Table 1. Five bivariate OLS regressions on China dataset. Main Results.

results about five bivariate regressions. In general, α's and β_1's can be read as a classic regression result. The β_2's indicates if the predicted histogram variable have a greater (when $\beta_2 > 1$) or a lower (when $0 < \beta_2 < 1$) variability with respect the explicative one. For example, the *Wind speed in July* have a lower variability than the Wind speed in January, while the *Station pressure* has the same variability in the two months. Particular attention shold be paid to the bias factor. For example, considering the variable *Precipitation*, the last column indicates that there is a 92.75% of bias due to the different variability structure of the Y and of the X. In this case, the linear model it is not useful, i.e., a linear transformation of the histogram variable *Precipitation in January* cannot give a good forecast of the *Precipitation in July*.

5   Conclusions

In the present paper, we have presented a novel method for the estimation of a linear regression using Ordinary Least Squares method and the Wasserstein distance for histogram data. The proposed model is evaluated on the basis of a variability measure based on Wasserstein distance as proposed in Verde

---

[1] Dataset URL: http://dss.ucar.edu/datasets/ds578.5/

and Irpino (2008). The model has good performance when the bias factor is low. It occurs when the histograms have a similar shape and the standard deviation of the $x_i(t)$'s are nearly proportional to the standard deviation of the $y_i(t)$'s. Considering the nature of data and the state of the art on histogram data it is not possible to explain the inferential aspect of the model as in the classic case. Indeed, it is not easy establish the characteristics of the error term (where errors are functions). The OLS guarantees only that the mean of the mean values of the error functions are equal to zero. A resampling technique like bootstrap estimation can allow an estimation of the variability of estimates. Further, starting from the definition of a scalar product of functions will be interesting to study the multivariate regression case.

References

BILLARD, L. (2007): Dependencies and Variation Components of Symbolic Interval–Valued Data. In: P. Brito, P. Bertrand, G. Cucumel, F. de Carvalho (Eds.): *Selected Contributions in Data Analysis and Classification*. Springer, Berlin, 3–12.

BILLARD, L. and DIDAY, E. (2007): *Symbolic Data Analysis: Conceptual Statistics and Data Mining*. Wiley Series in Computational Statistics. John Wiley & Sons.

BOCK, H.H. and DIDAY, E. (2000): *Analysis of Symbolic Data, Exploratory methods for extracting statistical information from complex data*. Studies in Classification, Data Analysis and Knowledge Organisation, Springer-Verlag.

CUESTA-ALBERTOS, J.A., MATRÁN, C., TUERO-DIAZ, A. (1997): Optimal transportation plans and convergence in distribution. *Journ. of Multiv. An., 60, 72–83*.

DVORETZKY, A., KIEFER, J. and WOLFOWITZ, J. (1956): Asymptotic minimax character of the sample distribution function and of the classical multinomial estimator. *Annals of Mathematical Statistics 27 (3), 642–669*.

GIBBS, A.L. and SU, F.E. (2002): On choosing and bounding probability metrics. *Intl. Stat. Rev. 7 (3), 419–435*.

IRPINO, A., LECHEVALLIER, Y. and VERDE, R. (2006): Dynamic clustering of histograms using Wasserstein metric. In: Rizzi, A., Vichi, M. (eds.) *COMPSTAT 2006*. Physica-Verlag, Berlin, 869–876.

IRPINO, A. and VERDE, R. (2006): A new Wasserstein based distance for the hierarchical clustering of histogram symbolic data. In: Batanjeli, V., Bock, H.H., Ferligoj, A., Ziberna, A. (eds.) *Data Science and Classification, IFCS 2006*. Springer, Berlin, 185–192.

VERDE, R. and IRPINO, A.(2008): Comparing Histogram data using a Mahalanobis–Wasserstein distance. In: Brito, P. (eds.) *COMPSTAT 2008*. Physica–Verlag, Springer, Berlin, 77–89.

LIMA NETO, E.d.A. and DE CARVALHO, F.d.A.T. (2010): Constrained linear regression models for symbolic interval-valued variables. *Computational Statistics and Data Analysis, 54, 2, 333–347*.

DetMCD in a Calibration Framework

Tim Verdonck[1], Mia Hubert[2], and Peter J. Rousseeuw[3]

[1] Department of Mathematics and Computer Science, University of Antwerp
  Middelheimlaan 1, Antwerp, Belgium, *Tim.Verdonck@ua.ac.be*
[2] Department of Mathematics, Katholieke Universiteit Leuven
  Celestijnenlaan 200b, Leuven, Belgium, *Mia.Hubert@wis.kuleuven.be*
[3] Department of Mathematics, Katholieke Universiteit Leuven
  Celestijnenlaan 200b, Leuven, Belgium, *peter@rousseeuw.net*

Abstract. The minimum covariance determinant (MCD) method is a robust estimator of multivariate location and scatter (Rousseeuw (1984)). Computing the exact MCD is very hard, so in practice one resorts to approximate algorithms. Most often the FASTMCD algorithm of Rousseeuw and Van Driessen (1999) is used. The FASTMCD algorithm is affine equivariant but not permutation invariant. Recently a deterministic algorithm, denoted as DetMCD, is developed which does not use random subsets and which is much faster (Hubert et al. (2010)). In this paper DetMCD is illustrated in a calibration framework. We focus on robust principal component regression and partial least squares regression, two very popular regression techniques for collinear data. We also apply DetMCD on data with missing elements after plugging it into the M-RPCR technique of Serneels and Verdonck (2009).

Keywords: deterministic algorithm, outliers, robustness, RPCR, RSIMPLS

1 Introduction

The Minimum Covariance Determinant (MCD) method of Rousseeuw (1984) is a highly robust estimator of multivariate location and scatter. Given an $n \times p$ data matrix $\boldsymbol{X} = (\boldsymbol{x}_1, \ldots, \boldsymbol{x}_n)^T$ with $\boldsymbol{x}_i = (x_{i1}, \ldots, x_{ip})^T$, its objective is to find h observations (with $n/2 \leq h \leq n$) whose covariance matrix has the lowest determinant. The MCD estimate of location is then the average of these h points, and the scatter estimate is a multiple of their covariance matrix. The MCD has a bounded influence function and can attain the highest possible breakdown value (i.e. 50%) when $h = \lfloor (n + p + 1)/2 \rfloor$. In addition to being highly resistant to outliers, the MCD is affine equivariant, i.e. the estimates behave properly under affine transformations of the data.

Although the MCD was already introduced in 1984, its practical use only became feasible since the introduction of the computationally efficient FASTMCD algorithm of Rousseeuw and Van Driessen (1999). The FASTMCD algorithm starts by drawing random subsets of size $p + 1$. It needs to draw many in order to obtain at least one that is outlier-free.

Y. Lechevallier, G. Saporta (eds.), *Proceedings of COMPSTAT'2010*,
DOI 10.1007/978-3-7908-2604-3_61, © Springer-Verlag Berlin Heidelberg 2010

Recently, Hubert et al. (2010) have developed a deterministic algorithm for the MCD, denoted as DetMCD, which does not use random subsets and runs even faster than FASTMCD. Unlike the latter it is permutation invariant, i.e. the result does not depend on the order of the observations in the data set. It starts from only a few well-chosen initial estimates. By an extensive simulation study Hubert et al. (2010) have shown that DetMCD is as robust as FASTMCD and that the lack of affine equivariance is small. In Hubert et al. (2010) the performance of the DetMCD algorithm is illustrated in the context of principal component analysis, discriminant analysis, and MCD regression (Rousseeuw et al. (2004)). The latter method is a robust multivariate regression technique for low-dimensional predictors x_i and vector-valued response variables y_i. The MCD regression estimates are obtained by matrix operations on the MCD location and scatter estimates of the joint (x_i, y_i) data. In this paper we investigate the use of the DetMCD algorithm in robust principal component regression (RPCR) and robust partial least squares regression (RSIMPLS). These two regression techniques fit a linear relationship between two sets of variables and are mostly used when the number of independent variables x_i is very large or when the regressors are highly correlated (also known as multicollinearity).

In Section 2 we describe the DetMCD algorithm in detail, whereas in Section 3 we briefly summarize RPCR and RSIMPLS. Section 4 presents the results of a simulation study in which we investigate the effect of replacing the FASTMCD algorithm with the DetMCD algorithm. We compare the robustness of the algorithms by adding different percentages of contamination in the simulated data sets, and we also compare their computation times. Moreover, both algorithms for MCD are compared on data with missing elements after plugging them into the M-RPCR method of Serneels and Verdonck (2009).

2 The DetMCD algorithm

In this section we describe the deterministic algorithm to compute the MCD, developed in Hubert et al. (2010). Given the data matrix X with rows x_i^T, we denote the columns as X_j $(j = 1, \ldots, p)$. For a data set X with estimated center $\hat{\mu}$ and scatter matrix $\hat{\Sigma}$, the statistical distance of the i-th observation x_i is written as

$$D(x_i, \hat{\mu}, \hat{\Sigma}) = \sqrt{(x_i - \hat{\mu})^T \hat{\Sigma}^{-1} (x_i - \hat{\mu})}.$$

2.1 General procedure

First, each variable X_j is standardized by subtracting its median and dividing by the Q_n scale estimator of Rousseeuw and Croux (1993). This standardization makes the algorithm location and scale equivariant. The standardized data set is denoted by Z with rows z_i^T $(i = 1, \ldots, n)$ and columns Z_j $(j = 1, \ldots, p)$.

Next, seven initial estimates $\hat{\boldsymbol{\mu}}_l(\boldsymbol{Z})$ and $\hat{\boldsymbol{\Sigma}}_l(\boldsymbol{Z})$ ($l = 1, \ldots, 7$) are constructed for the center and scatter of $\boldsymbol{Z}$. Apart from the last one, each computes a preliminary estimate $\boldsymbol{S}_l$ of the covariance or correlation matrix of $\boldsymbol{Z}$. They will be described in Section 2.2. As these $\boldsymbol{S}_l$ may have very inaccurate eigenvalues, the following steps are applied to each. The first two steps are performed to make the robust scatter matrix positive definite and more affine equivariant. They are similar to steps in the orthogonalized Gnanadesikan-Kettenring (OGK) algorithm (Maronna and Zamar (2002)).

a. Compute the matrix $\boldsymbol{E}$ of eigenvectors of $\boldsymbol{S}_l$ and put $\boldsymbol{B} = \boldsymbol{ZE}$.
b. Estimate the covariance of $\boldsymbol{Z}$ by $\hat{\boldsymbol{\Sigma}}_l(\boldsymbol{Z}) = \boldsymbol{ELE}^T$ where
$\boldsymbol{L} = \text{diag}\left(Q_n^2(\boldsymbol{B}_1), \ldots, Q_n^2(\boldsymbol{B}_p)\right)$.
Here $Q_n(\boldsymbol{B}_1)$ is the Q_n scale estimator applied to the first column of $\boldsymbol{B}$.
c. To estimate the center of $\boldsymbol{Z}$ sphere the data, apply the coordinatewise median, and transform it back, i.e. $\hat{\boldsymbol{\mu}}_l(\boldsymbol{Z}) = \hat{\boldsymbol{\Sigma}}_l^{1/2}(\text{med}(\boldsymbol{Z}\hat{\boldsymbol{\Sigma}}_l^{-1/2}))$.

For all estimates $(\hat{\boldsymbol{\mu}}_l(\boldsymbol{Z}), \hat{\boldsymbol{\Sigma}}_l(\boldsymbol{Z}))$ we compute the statistical distances

$$d_{i,l} = D(\boldsymbol{z}_i, \hat{\boldsymbol{\mu}}_l(\boldsymbol{Z}), \hat{\boldsymbol{\Sigma}}_l(\boldsymbol{Z})).$$

For each initial estimate l the h observations with smallest $d_{i,l}$ are taken and *concentration steps* (C-steps) are applied until convergence. (A C-step reduces the MCD objective function and is a major component of the FASTMCD algorithm.) The solution with smallest determinant is called the raw DetMCD. As in the FASTMCD algorithm, we then compute reweighted estimates to increase statistical efficiency while retaining high robustness.

2.2   Initial estimates

1) The first initial scatter estimate is obtained by computing the hyperbolic tangent (sigmoid) of each column of $\boldsymbol{Z}$, i.e. $Y_j = \tanh(Z_j)$ for $j = 1, \ldots, p$. Computing the classical correlation matrix of $\boldsymbol{Y}$ yields $\boldsymbol{S}_1 = \text{corr}(\boldsymbol{Y})$.
2) Let R_j be the ranks of the column Z_j, and put $\boldsymbol{S}_2 = \text{corr}(\boldsymbol{R})$. This is the Spearman correlation matrix of $\boldsymbol{Z}$.
3) For $\boldsymbol{S}_3$ normal scores are computed from these ranks, namely $T_j = \Phi^{-1}((R_j - 1/3)/(n + 1/3))$ where $\Phi(.)$ is the normal cumulative distribution function, and then we set $\boldsymbol{S}_3 = \text{corr}(\boldsymbol{T})$.
4) The fourth scatter estimate is based on the spatial sign covariance matrix of Visuri et al. (2000): define $\boldsymbol{a}_i = \boldsymbol{z}_i/\|\boldsymbol{z}_i\|$ for all i and let $\boldsymbol{S}_4 = \text{cov}(\boldsymbol{A})$.
5) For $\boldsymbol{S}_5$ we take the covariance matrix of the $\lceil n/2 \rceil$ standardized observations $\boldsymbol{z}_i$ with smallest norm.
6) The sixth scatter estimate is the raw OGK estimator.
7) Finally the classical mean $\hat{\boldsymbol{\mu}}_7(\boldsymbol{Z})$ and covariance matrix $\hat{\boldsymbol{\Sigma}}_7(\boldsymbol{Z})$ of the full data set are used.

3   Robust calibration methods

In practice one often needs to estimate a linear relation between an $n \times p$ predictor data matrix X and an $n \times q$ predictand matrix Y. When the errors are normally distributed, the optimal solution to this problem is to use the least squares estimator. However, when the number of predictors exceeds the number of cases the least squares regression estimator cannot be computed, and when the predictor data matrix X contains highly correlated columns the method is numerically unstable. Two popular regression techniques that tackle these problems are principal component regression (PCR) and partial least squares regression (PLSR).

The idea behind PCR is to replace the original regressors by their principal component scores (T). Hubert and Verboven (2003) have proposed a robust PCR method (RPCR) by robustifying both steps of PCR. First a robust principal component analysis (PCA) method is applied to the regressors. For low-dimensional data the MCD estimator is used for this, whereas for high-dimensional data ROBPCA (Hubert et al. (2005)) is applied. The latter is a hybrid method that combines projection pursuit with the MCD. Next, a robust regression is performed with the robust scores as predictor variables. For a univariate response variable ($q = 1$) this is done by means of LTS regression (Rousseeuw (1984)), and for $q > 1$ by means of MCD regression.

In PLSR the scores are computed by maximizing a covariance criterion between the x- and y-variables. Unlike PCR, this technique uses the responses already from the start. A well-known PLSR method is the SIMPLS algorithm (de Jong (1993)). A robust SIMPLS method, RSIMPLS (Hubert and Vanden Branden (2003)), starts by applying ROBPCA to the x- and y-variables and then proceeds analogously to the SIMPLS algorithm. In the second stage of the algorithm again a robust regression is applied.

Both RPCR and RSIMPLS thus apply the MCD estimator. For RPCR with $q > 1$ this is done in the PCA and in the regression step. RSIMPLS uses MCD in the first stage only, as part of ROBPCA.

When missing values occur in the data, RPCR and RSIMPLS cannot be applied anymore. However, in Serneels and Verdonck (2009) a method (M-RPCR) is presented to perform RPCR on data with missing elements according to the missing at random mechanism (MAR). As the algorithm is based on the expectation-maximization approach, it is iterative and consequently it applies MCD many times. Note that for RSIMPLS the same methodology could be applied, but this has not been worked out yet.

4   Simulation study

In this section we first compare RPCR and RSIMPLS using the FASTMCD and the DetMCD algorithms on several simulated data sets without missing values. Different types of outliers are added to the data. This allows to study the efficiency at uncontaminated data, as well as the robustness at contaminated data. Next, we study the M-RPCR method on data with missing elements.

4.1   Simulation design

A straightforward way to set up a simulation for PCR and SIMPLS is to generate data according to the bilinear latent variable model (Burnham et al. (1999)) with given complexity k. We will consider

$$\begin{cases} X = T_k P_k^T + N_p\left(0_p, 0.1 I_p\right) \\ Y = T_k Q_k^T + N_q\left(0_q, 0.1 I_q\right) \end{cases} \tag{1}$$

where $q = 3$, $k = 2$, $T_k \sim N_k\left(0_k, \Sigma\right)$, and $\Sigma = \mathrm{diag}(6, 2)$. We will specify p later. For the matrix Q_k we took

$$Q_k = \begin{pmatrix} -2 & 1 & 2 \\ 1 & -1 & -2 \end{pmatrix}.$$

The loadings P_k are defined as the eigenvectors of the covariance matrix of k independent uniform variables on $[0,1]$. The vector 0_p denotes the vector of length p with all entries equal to zero, and I_p is the identity matrix of size p.

The contaminated parts of the data T_ε, X_ε, and Y_ε were constructed as follows. Bad leverage points were generated as $X_\varepsilon = T_\varepsilon P_k^T + N_p(0_p, 0.1 I_p)$ with $T_\varepsilon \sim N_k\left(30\, 1_k, 0.1\Sigma\right)$. Vertical outliers are obtained as $Y_\varepsilon = T_k Q_k^T + N_p\left(30\, 1_p, 0.1 I_p\right)$.

Note that X and Y in the latent variable model (1) satisfy the regression relation

$$Y = X\mathfrak{B} + E$$

with $\mathfrak{B} = P_k Q_k^T$ and E normally distributed errors. In order to evaluate the different methods, the following criteria are used:

- The bias in the regression coefficients:

$$e_B = \frac{1}{pq} \left\| \mathfrak{B} - \hat{\mathfrak{B}} \right\|_F,$$

where $\| \cdot \|_F$ denotes the Frobenius norm of the matrix.
- The predictive ability for a test set (X_t, Y_t) of the same size as (X, Y):

$$e_P = \frac{1}{nq} \left\| Y_t - \hat{Y}_t \right\|_F.$$

- The computation time t (in seconds).

Each of these performance measures should be as close to zero as possible. We considered both low-dimensional ($n = 100$ and $p = 6$) and high-dimensional ($n = 40$ and $p = 200$) data, and 100 data sets were generated for each situation. The number of selected components in RPCR and RSIMPLS were fixed to the actual complexity $k = 2$.

For the contamination percentage ϵ we chose the values 0%, 10% and 25%. The parameter $\alpha = (n - h)/n$, denoting the fraction of outliers the method should be able to resist, was set to 25%, 25% and 50% respectively. To study M-RPCR with FASTMCD and DetMCD we randomly replaced 10% of the elements of X by missing values.

All simulations were carried out in MATLAB 7.4 (The MathWorks, Natick, MA). Many functions were taken from LIBRA, the Matlab library for Robust Analysis (Verboven and Hubert (2005)).

4.2 Results

In the following tables we report for each performance criterion the average over 100 runs. Tables 1 and 2 show the results for the low-dimensional and the high-dimensional data without missing elements. We can conclude that the algorithms perform similarly well for the first two performance criteria, irrespective of the data dimension. However, we see that the algorithms differ in computation time. As DetMCD is much faster than FASTMCD, its computational advantage carries over to RPCR and RSIMPLS. The speedup is most prominent for RPCR in low dimensions, because MCD is applied more often there than in RSIMPLS. In high dimensions this effect is reduced as RPCR then applies ROBPCA to the regressors, and ROBPCA includes MCD but also a time-consuming projection pursuit part that is not changed.

		Clean	Bad leverage		Vertical outliers	
	ϵ	0	0.10	0.30	0.10	0.30
RPCR (FASTMCD)	e_B	0.0147	0.0144	0.0153	0.0150	0.0175
	e_P	0.0446	0.0447	0.0450	0.0447	0.0450
	t	3.15	3.14	3.13	3.15	3.14
RPCR (DetMCD)	e_B	0.0143	0.0143	0.0152	0.0147	0.0159
	e_P	0.0446	0.0447	0.0449	0.0447	0.0449
	t	0.51	0.51	0.53	0.51	0.52
RSIMPLS (FASTMCD)	e_B	0.0147	0.0146	0.0154	0.0149	0.0163
	e_P	0.0446	0.0447	0.0450	0.0447	0.0449
	t	2.42	2.41	2.40	2.41	2.40
RSIMPLS (DetMCD)	e_B	0.0145	0.0145	0.0153	0.0148	0.0162
	e_P	0.0446	0.0447	0.0450	0.0447	0.0449
	t	1.76	1.75	1.76	1.76	1.76

Table 1. Simulation results for low-dimensional data.

		Clean	Bad leverage		Vertical outliers	
	ϵ	0	0.10	0.30	0.10	0.30
RPCR (FASTMCD)	e_B	0.0025	0.0026	0.0029	0.0025	0.0025
	e_P	0.0948	0.0974	0.1072	0.0946	0.0969
	t	3.79	3.78	3.78	3.79	3.78
RPCR (DetMCD)	e_B	0.0025	0.0026	0.0028	0.0025	0.0025
	e_P	0.0943	0.0976	0.1074	0.0946	0.0959
	t	1.90	1.89	1.89	1.90	1.90
RSIMPLS (FASTMCD)	e_B	0.0027	0.0027	0.0030	0.0027	0.0030
	e_P	0.0967	0.0979	0.1129	0.0992	0.1125
	t	2.38	2.37	2.36	2.38	2.37
RSIMPLS (DetMCD)	e_B	0.0026	0.0027	0.0030	0.0027	0.0030
	e_P	0.0962	0.0973	0.1118	0.0983	0.1100
	t	1.74	1.73	1.72	1.74	1.73

Table 2. Simulation results for high-dimensional data.

The same conclusions can be drawn when missing values are added to the data, as seen in Tables 3 and 4. Because the M-RPCR method iterates RPCR several times, the RPCR speedup is very useful.

		Clean	Bad leverage		Vertical outliers	
	ϵ	0	0.10	0.30	0.10	0.30
M-RPCR (FASTMCD)	e_B	0.0170	0.0170	0.0179	0.0172	0.0199
	e_P	0.0450	0.0455	0.0457	0.0455	0.0459
	t	45.89	44.09	64.11	45.65	69.22
M-RPCR (DetMCD)	e_B	0.0169	0.0169	0.0180	0.0170	0.0189
	e_P	0.0450	0.0455	0.0456	0.0455	0.0460
	t	5.03	4.91	7.05	4.91	5.59

Table 3. Simulation results for low-dimensional data with missing values.

		Clean	Bad leverage		Vertical outliers	
	ϵ	0	0.10	0.30	0.10	0.30
M-RPCR (FASTMCD)	e_B	0.0027	0.0027	0.0030	0.0027	0.0027
	e_P	0.1001	0.1022	0.1149	0.0995	0.1005
	t	14.81	14.83	18.25	15.19	15.51
M-RPCR (DetMCD)	e_B	0.0027	0.0027	0.0030	0.0027	0.0027
	e_P	0.0995	0.1024	0.1147	0.0993	0.1000
	t	4.83	4.74	5.83	4.87	4.67

Table 4. Simulation results for high-dimensional data with missing values.

5   Summary and conclusion

In this paper we have illustrated our recently proposed deterministic algorithm for MCD in a calibration framework. Replacing FASTMCD by DetMCD in the robust regression techniques RPCR and RSIMPLS gives similar results concerning robustness and predictive ability, but with improved computation speed. This becomes even more important when the data also contain missing elements and the DetMCD algorithm is applied many times in an iterative way. We conclude that DetMCD is a fast and robust alternative to FASTMCD in this calibration framework.

References

BURNHAM, A.J., MACGREGOR, J.F. and VIVEROS, R. (1999): Latent variable multivariate regression modeling. *Chemometrics and Intelligent Laboratory Systems 48(2), 167-180.*

DE JONG, S. (1993): SIMPLS: an alternative approach to partial least squares regression. *Chemometrics and Intelligent Laboratory Systems 18, 251-263.*

HUBERT, M., ROUSSEEUW, P.J. and VANDEN BRANDEN, K. (2005): ROBPCA: a new approach to robust principal component analysis. *Technometrics 47, 64-79.*

HUBERT, M., ROUSSEEUW, P.J. and VERDONCK, T. (2010): A deterministic algorithm for the MCD. *Submitted.*

HUBERT, M. and VANDEN BRANDEN, K. (2003): Robust methods for partial least squares regression. *Journal of Chemometrics 17, 537-549.*

HUBERT, M. and VERBOVEN, S. (2003): A robust PCR method for high-dimensional regressors. *Journal of Chemometrics 17, 438-452.*

MARONNA, R.A. and ZAMAR, R.H. (2002): Robust estimates of location and dispersion for high-dimensional data sets. *Technometrics 44, 307-317.*

ROUSSEEUW, P.J. (1984): Least median of squares regression. *Journal of the American Statistical Association 79, 871-880.*

ROUSSEEUW, P.J. and CROUX, C. (1993): Alternatives to the median absolute deviation. *Journal of the American Statistical Association 88, 1273-1283.*

ROUSSEEUW, P.J., VAN AELST, S., VAN DRIESSEN, K. and AGULLO, J. (2004) Robust multivariate regression. *Technometrics 46, 293-305.*

ROUSSEEUW, P.J. and VAN DRIESSEN, K. (1999): A fast algorithm for the minimum covariance determinant estimator. *Technometrics 41, 212-223.*

SERNEELS, S. and VERDONCK, T. (2009): Principal component regression for data containing outliers and missing elements. *Computational Statistics and Data Analysis 53(11), 3855-3863.*

VERBOVEN, S. and HUBERT, M. (2005): LIBRA: a Matlab library for robust analysis. *Chemometrics and Intelligent Laboratory Systems 75, 127-136.*

VISURI, S., KOIVUNEN, V. and OJA, H. (2000): Sign and rank covariance matrices. *Journal of Statistical Planning and Inference 91, 557-575.*

Separable Two-Dimensional Linear Discriminant Analysis

Jianhua Zhao[1], Philip L.H. Yu[2], and Shulan Li[3]

[1] School of Statistics and Mathematics, Yunnan University of Finance
   and Economics, Kunming, 650221, China. *jhzhao.ynu@gmail.com*
[2] Department of Statistics and Actuarial Science,
   The University of Hong Kong, Hong Kong. *plhyu@hku.hk*
[3] Department of Mathematics and Statistics,
   Yunnan University, Kunming, 650091, China. *lishulan0526@gmail.com*

Abstract. Several two-dimensional linear discriminant analysis LDA (2DLDA) methods have received much attention in recent years. Among them, the 2DLDA, introduced by Ye, Janardan and Li (2005), is an important development. However, it is found that their proposed iterative algorithm does not guarantee convergence. In this paper, we assume a separable covariance matrix of 2D data and propose separable 2DLDA which can provide a neatly analytical solution similar to that for classical LDA. Empirical results on face recognition demonstrate the superiority of our proposed separable 2DLDA over 2DLDA in terms of classification accuracy and computational efficiency.

Keywords: LDA, 2DLDA, two-dimensional data, face recognition

1 Introduction

Fisher linear discriminant analysis (LDA) is a popular supervised subspace learning technique and has been widely used in computer vision, patter recognition and machine learning. It looks for a linear transformation such that in the transformed subspace the between-class covariance is maximized relative to the within-class covariance.

Since LDA is simply formulated for 1D data (in which observations are in vector form), when applying LDA for 2D data such as images (in which observations are in matrix form), the 2D matrix data have to be converted into 1D vector ones. Unfortunately, the resulting 1D data are easily trapped into the so-called *curse of dimensionality*. Although several extensions of LDA have been proposed to deal with this problem such as high-dimensional LDA (Bouveyron et al. (2007)), regularized LDA, performing principal component analysis before LDA (Belhumeur et al. (1997)), pseudo-LDA and so on, such extensions have to rely on the vectorization of 2D data and the resulting very high dimension not only degrades the performance of LDA but also incurs expensive computation cost.

Y. Lechevallier, G. Saporta (eds.), *Proceedings of COMPSTAT'2010*,
DOI 10.1007/978-3-7908-2604-3_62, © Springer-Verlag Berlin Heidelberg 2010

In recent years, rather than resorting to the vectorization, another group of researchers have suggested performing LDA using 2D data directly. For instance, two-dimensional LDA (2DLDA) (Li and Yuan (2005), Liu et al. (1993), Xiong et al. (2005)) maximizes a generalized Fisher discriminant criterion that restricts the linear transformation to be row or column linear transformation. A drawback of this method is that it typically requires extracting much more features than LDA for recognition and representation. To overcome this disadvantage, Yang et al. (2005) presented a two-stage solution: finding column and row transformation sequentially, which, however, is an order-dependent algorithm (Inoue and Urahama (2006)). To find column and row transformation simultaneously, Ye et al. (2005) proposed a formulation that restricts the linear transformation to be a bilinear one, i.e., a Kronecker product of column and row linear transformations. Unfortunately, convergence of the proposed algorithm is not guaranteed (Inoue and Urahama (2006); Luo et al. (2009)). To overcome this problem, a new objective function is defined in Luo et al. (2009) but maximizing the objective function has to resort to numerical methods and the computation is much more complicated than that in Ye et al. (2005).

Compared with LDA, an appealing advantage of these 2DLDA methods is that the *curse of dimensionality* is overcome and the computation cost could be greatly alleviated. Importantly, their empirical results show that these 2DLDA methods can achieve competitive or better recognition than LDA, especially in small sample size cases. This advantage should be owed to the utilization of underlying 2D data structure.

In this paper, we propose utilizing the underlying 2D data structure not only to restrict the linear transformation but also to model the covariance matrix of 2D data as separable covariance. Based on this, we propose separable 2DLDA. Unlike existing iterative solutions (Luo et al. (2009); Ye et al. (2005)), a neatly analytical solution to a generalized Fisher discriminant criterion can be obtained as that in classical LDA. Separable covariance models have been used in many other applications where the structure of the problem suggests such assumption. Examples include spatial-temporal modeling for environmental data (Mardia and Goodall (1993)), channel modeling for multiple-input multiple-out communications (Werner and Jansson (2009)), signal modeling of MEG/EEG data (de Munck et al. (2002)), etc. In this paper, we argue that the underlying structure of 2D data suggests such assumption.

The remainder of the paper is organized as follows. Sec. 2 gives a brief review of LDA and the 2DLDA in Ye et al. (2005). Sec. 3 proposes our separable 2DLDA (S2DLDA). Sec. 4 constructs an empirical study to compare S2DLDA and 2DLDA. We end the paper with a conclusion in Sec. 5.

2   Review of LDA and 2DLDA

2.1   Review of LDA

Let $\mathbf{x} \in \mathbb{R}^d$ be a random vector and π_k and $\boldsymbol{\mu}_k$ be the prior probability and population mean of class $\mathcal{L}_k, k = 1, \ldots, K$, then the global population mean $\boldsymbol{\mu} = \sum_k \pi_k \boldsymbol{\mu}_k$ and between-class and within-class covariance matrices are

$$\boldsymbol{\Sigma}^b = \sum_{k=1}^K \pi_k (\boldsymbol{\mu}_k - \boldsymbol{\mu})(\boldsymbol{\mu}_k - \boldsymbol{\mu})', \quad \boldsymbol{\Sigma}^w = \sum_{k=1}^K \pi_k \mathbb{E}(\mathbf{x} - \boldsymbol{\mu}_k)(\mathbf{x} - \boldsymbol{\mu}_k)' | \mathbf{x} \in \mathcal{L}_k).$$

Consider the linear transformation $\mathbf{y} = \mathbf{V}' mathbf x$, where $\mathbf{V}$ is a $d \times q (q < d)$ matrix. The within-class and between-class covariance matrices in $\mathbf{y}$-space become $\mathbf{V}' \boldsymbol{\Sigma}^w \mathbf{V}$ and $\mathbf{V}' \boldsymbol{\Sigma}^b \mathbf{V}$. LDA aims to find $\mathbf{V}$ such that between-class covariance is large while within-class covariance is small. A commonly used *trace ratio* criterion (Fukunaga (1990)) is

$$\arg\max_{\mathbf{V}} \operatorname{tr} \left\{ (\mathbf{V}' \boldsymbol{\Sigma}^w \mathbf{V})^{-1} (\mathbf{V}' \boldsymbol{\Sigma}^b \mathbf{V}) \right\} \tag{1}$$

The closed form solution to (1) is given by the eigenvectors of $\boldsymbol{\Sigma}^{w-1} \boldsymbol{\Sigma}^b$ corresponding to the largest q eigenvalues. More details can be found in (Fukunaga (1990)).

Estimation of $\boldsymbol{\Sigma}^w$ and $\boldsymbol{\Sigma}^b$ can be obtained via maximum likelihood method under the assumption that all classes follow normal distributions with different means but common within-class covariance matrix (Hastie et al. (2009)). More specifically, given data $\{\mathbf{x}_1, \mathbf{x}_2, \ldots, \mathbf{x}_N\}$ from K classes and the n_k observations in class k following $\mathcal{N}(\boldsymbol{\mu}_k, \boldsymbol{\Sigma}^w), k = 1, \ldots, K$. Here, the total number of observations $N = \sum_k n_k$. The MLE of $\boldsymbol{\mu}_k$ is $\hat{\boldsymbol{\mu}}_k = \frac{1}{n_k} \sum_{n \in \mathcal{L}_k} \mathbf{x}_n$ and the MLE of $\boldsymbol{\mu}$ is $\hat{\boldsymbol{\mu}} = \frac{1}{N} \sum_n \mathbf{x}_n$. The MLE of between-class covariance matrix $\boldsymbol{\Sigma}^w$ is $\hat{\boldsymbol{\Sigma}}^w = \frac{1}{N} \sum_{k=1}^K \sum_{n \in \mathcal{L}_k} (\mathbf{x}_n - \hat{\boldsymbol{\mu}}_k)(\mathbf{x}_n - \hat{\boldsymbol{\mu}}_k)'$. On the centroids $\boldsymbol{\mu}_k$'s level, it can be regarded that class k has n_k copies of $\boldsymbol{\mu}_k$ and $\boldsymbol{\mu}_k \sim \mathcal{N}(\boldsymbol{\mu}, \boldsymbol{\Sigma}^b)$. Then the MLE of $\boldsymbol{\Sigma}^b$ is $\hat{\boldsymbol{\Sigma}}^b = \frac{1}{N} \sum_{k=1}^K n_k (\hat{\boldsymbol{\mu}}_k - \hat{\boldsymbol{\mu}})(\hat{\boldsymbol{\mu}}_k - \hat{\boldsymbol{\mu}})$.

2.2   Review of 2DLDA

In this section, we briefly review the 2DLDA proposed in Ye et al. (2005). For a 2D random matrix $\mathbf{X} \in \mathbb{R}^{d_c \times d_r}$, 2DLDA seeks a bilinear transformation $\mathbf{Y} = \mathbf{U}_c' \mathbf{X} \mathbf{U}_r$ that would maximize the between-class covariance while minimize the within-class covariance in $\mathrm{vec}(\mathbf{Y})$-space, where $\mathbf{U}_c$ and $\mathbf{U}_r$ are $d_c \times q_c (q_c < d_c)$ and $d_r \times q_r (q_r < d_r)$ matrices. Denote vectorization operator as $\mathrm{vec}(\cdot)$. Since $\mathrm{vec}(\mathbf{Y}) = (\mathbf{U}_r \otimes \mathbf{U}_c)' \mathrm{vec}(\mathbf{X})$, this amounts to substituting $\mathbf{x} = \mathrm{vec}(\mathbf{X})$ and $\mathbf{V} = \mathbf{U}_r \otimes \mathbf{U}_c$ into (1). Due to the difficulty in solving the resulting objective function with respect to $\mathbf{U}_c$ and $\mathbf{U}_r$ simultaneously, Ye et al. (2005) proposed an iterative algorithm. However, the algorithm does not guarantee to converge as detailed in Inoue and Urahama (2006); Luo et al. (2009). Due to this reason, Ye et al. (2005) suggest performing only one number of iteration with the iterative algorithm.

Like LDA, 2DLDA tries to maximize the class separability in the low-dimensional space. Unlike LDA that seeks linear transformation $\mathbf{V}$, 2DLDA seeks bilinear transformation $\mathbf{V} = \mathbf{U}_r \otimes \mathbf{U}_c$ that utilizes the underlying 2D data structure. However, the resulting optimization problem is difficult to solve. We attribute this problem to the fact that Ye et al. (2005) fail to define a suitable between-class and within-class covariance matrices that will utilize the underlying 2D data structure. In this paper we propose using separable covariance matrix to model 2D data, which is justified in Sec. 3.1. Based on this proposal, a neatly analytical solution similar to that in LDA can be obtained as detailed in Sec. 3.

3   Separable 2DLDA

3.1   Motivation: Using separable covariance matrix for 2D data

Let $\mathbf{C} = (\mathbf{c}_1, \mathbf{c}_2, \ldots, \mathbf{c}_{d_c})$ be a basis in $\mathbb{R}^{d_c}$ and $\mathbf{R} = (\mathbf{r}_1, \mathbf{r}_2, \ldots, \mathbf{r}_{d_r})$ be one in $\mathbb{R}^{d_r}$. For any matrix $\mathbf{X} \in \mathbb{R}^{d_c \times d_r}$, one can always find a matrix $\mathbf{Z} = \mathbf{C}^{-1}\mathbf{X}\mathbf{R}^{-1'} \in \mathbb{R}^{d_c \times d_r}$ such that

$$\mathbf{X} = \mathbf{CZR}'. \tag{2}$$

By vectorization operator, (2) can be written as $\mathrm{vec}(\mathbf{X}) = (\mathbf{R} \otimes \mathbf{C})\mathrm{vec}(\mathbf{Z})$. From a view of generative models, if the covariance matrix of $\mathrm{vec}(\mathbf{Z})$ is assumed to be the identity matrix $\mathbf{I}$, i.e., $\mathrm{cov}(\mathrm{vec}(\mathbf{Z}))=\mathbf{I}$, then

$$\mathrm{cov}(\mathrm{vec}(\mathbf{X})) = \mathbf{\Sigma}_r \otimes \mathbf{\Sigma}_c,$$

where $\mathbf{\Sigma}_r = \mathbf{RR}'$ and $\mathbf{\Sigma}_c = \mathbf{CC}'$ are row and column covariance matrices respectively. This result reveals that the underlying structure of 2D data suggests using separable covariance matrix for 2D data $\mathbf{X}$.

3.2   Separable 2DLDA

Under separable covariance assumption, the between-class and within-class covariance matrices in $\mathrm{vec}(\mathbf{X})$-space are $\mathbf{\Sigma}^b = \mathbf{\Sigma}_r^b \otimes \mathbf{\Sigma}_c^b$ and $\mathbf{\Sigma}^w = \mathbf{\Sigma}_r^w \otimes \mathbf{\Sigma}_c^w$. For the bilinear transformation $\mathbf{Y} = \mathbf{U}_c'\mathbf{X}\mathbf{U}_r$, the between-class covariance matrices in $\mathrm{vec}(\mathbf{Y})$-space is $(\mathbf{U}_r \otimes \mathbf{U}_c)'(\mathbf{\Sigma}_r^b \otimes \mathbf{\Sigma}_c^b)(\mathbf{U}_r \otimes \mathbf{U}_c) = (\mathbf{U}_r'\mathbf{\Sigma}_r^b\mathbf{U}_r) \otimes (\mathbf{U}_c'\mathbf{\Sigma}_c^b\mathbf{U}_c)$, where we have used the property of Kronecker product that $(\mathbf{A}\otimes\mathbf{B})(\mathbf{C}\otimes\mathbf{D}) = (\mathbf{AB}\otimes\mathbf{CD})$. Similarly, the within-class covariance matrices in $\mathrm{vec}(\mathbf{Y})$-space is $(\mathbf{U}_r'\mathbf{\Sigma}_r^w\mathbf{U}_r) \otimes (\mathbf{U}_c'\mathbf{\Sigma}_c^w\mathbf{U}_c)$. Using the property $\mathrm{tr}(\mathbf{A} \otimes \mathbf{B}) =$

$\text{tr}(\mathbf{A})\text{tr}(\mathbf{B})$, the objective function (1) can be written as two separable sub-functions:

$$\max_{\mathbf{U}_r}\left\{\text{tr}(\mathbf{U}_r'\boldsymbol{\Sigma}_r^w\mathbf{U}_r)^{-1}(\mathbf{U}_r'\boldsymbol{\Sigma}_r^b\mathbf{U}_r)\right\} \text{ and } \max_{\mathbf{U}_c}\left\{\text{tr}(\mathbf{U}_c'\boldsymbol{\Sigma}_c^w\mathbf{U}_c)^{-1}(\mathbf{U}_c'\boldsymbol{\Sigma}_c^b\mathbf{U}_c)\right\},$$

(3)

each of which solves a similar optimization problem to that in LDA. That is, $\mathbf{U}_c$ and $\mathbf{U}_r$ are given by the eigenvectors of $\boldsymbol{\Sigma}_c^{w-1}\boldsymbol{\Sigma}_c^b$ and $\boldsymbol{\Sigma}_r^{w-1}\boldsymbol{\Sigma}_r^b$ corresponding to the largest q_c and q_r eigenvalues, respectively. To sum up, separable 2DLDA consists of two steps: step 1 estimates separable between-class and within-class covariance matrices $\boldsymbol{\Sigma}_r^b \otimes \boldsymbol{\Sigma}_c^b$ and $\boldsymbol{\Sigma}_r^w \otimes \boldsymbol{\Sigma}_c^w$; step 2 obtains $\mathbf{U}_r$ and $\mathbf{U}_c$ using (3). Step 1 is treated in section Sec. 3.3 by using maximum likelihood estimation method.

3.3 Maximum likelihood estimation of separable covariance matrix

A natural estimation for separable covariance matrix is maximum likelihood estimation (MLE). For simplicity, in this paper we focus on matrix-variate normal distribution, which is a generalization from multivariate normal in 1D space to the one in 2D space. A random matrix $\mathbf{X} \in \mathbb{R}^{d_c \times d_r}$ is said to follow a matrix-variate normal with mean matrix $\mathbf{W}$, column and row covariance matrices $\boldsymbol{\Sigma}_c$ and $\boldsymbol{\Sigma}_r$, denoted as $\mathcal{N}_{d_c,d_r}(\mathbf{W}, \boldsymbol{\Sigma}_c, \boldsymbol{\Sigma}_r)$, then apart from a constant term, the log p.d.f is given by Gupta and Nagar (1999)

$$\ln p(\mathbf{X}) = -\frac{1}{2}\left\{d_r \ln|\boldsymbol{\Sigma}_c| + d_c \ln|\boldsymbol{\Sigma}_r| + \text{tr}\left[\boldsymbol{\Sigma}_c^{-1}(\mathbf{X} - \mathbf{W})\boldsymbol{\Sigma}_r^{-1}(\mathbf{X} - \mathbf{W})'\right]\right\}.$$

Like the link between multivariate normals and LDA, we assume that different classes have different means but the same column and row covariance matrices. In other words, given a set of i.i.d. 2D data $\{\mathbf{X}_1, \mathbf{X}_2, \ldots, \mathbf{X}_N\}$, the n_k observations in class k follow $\mathcal{N}(\mathbf{W}_k, \boldsymbol{\Sigma}_c^w, \boldsymbol{\Sigma}_r^w), k = 1, \ldots, K$. The total number of observations is $\sum_k n_k = N$. The MLE of $\mathbf{W}_k$ is given by the sample mean of class k: $\hat{\mathbf{W}}_k = \frac{1}{n_k}\sum_{n \in \mathcal{L}_k} \mathbf{X}_n$ and the MLE of $\mathbf{W}$ is given by the global population mean: $\hat{\mathbf{W}} = \frac{1}{n}\sum_n \mathbf{X}_n$. Given an initial value of $\boldsymbol{\Sigma}_r^w$, the separable within-class covariance matrix can be estimated by iterations of the following two steps until convergence is met (e.g. data log-likelihood):

Step 1. $\hat{\boldsymbol{\Sigma}}_c^w = \frac{1}{Nd_r}\sum_{k=1}^K \sum_{n \in \mathcal{L}_k}(\mathbf{X}_n - \hat{\mathbf{W}}_k)[\hat{\boldsymbol{\Sigma}}_r^w]^{-1}(\mathbf{X}_n - \hat{\mathbf{W}}_k)'$.

Step 2. $\hat{\boldsymbol{\Sigma}}_r^w = \frac{1}{Nd_c}\sum_{k=1}^K \sum_{n \in \mathcal{L}_k}(\mathbf{X}_n - \hat{\mathbf{W}}_k)'[\hat{\boldsymbol{\Sigma}}_c^w]^{-1}(\mathbf{X}_n - \hat{\mathbf{W}}_k)$.

Similarly, to estimate the separable between-class covariance matrix on the class centroids $\mathbf{W}_k$'s level, we view that class k has n_k copies of $\mathbf{W}_k$ and $\mathbf{W}_k \sim \mathcal{N}(\mathbf{W}, \boldsymbol{\Sigma}_c^b, \boldsymbol{\Sigma}_r^b), k = 1, \ldots, K$. Then the separable between-class covariance matrix can be estimated by iterations of the following two steps until convergence:

Step 1. $\hat{\boldsymbol{\Sigma}}_c^b = \frac{1}{Nd_r}\sum_{k=1}^K n_k(\hat{\mathbf{W}}_k - \hat{\mathbf{W}})[\hat{\boldsymbol{\Sigma}}_r^b]^{-1}(\hat{\mathbf{W}}_k - \hat{\mathbf{W}})'$.

Step 2. $\hat{\boldsymbol{\Sigma}}_r^b = \frac{1}{Nd_c}\sum_{k=1}^K n_k(\hat{\mathbf{W}}_k - \hat{\mathbf{W}})'[\hat{\boldsymbol{\Sigma}}_c^b]^{-1}(\hat{\mathbf{W}}_k - \hat{\mathbf{W}})$.

4   Experiments

In this section, we use real data to compare separable 2DLDA (S2DLDA) and 2DLDA. The performance of Fisherfaces (Belhumeur et al., 1997) is also included. For Fisherfaces, the dimension in the PCA stage is $N - K$. Due to the non-convergence problem suffered by 2DLDA, we use 1 iteration (2DLDA(1)) as suggested in Ye et al. (2005). To see whether more iterations are useful, we add the result of 2DLDA using 4 iterations (2DLDA(4)). For S2DLDA, we stop the iterations for MLE if the change of relative log-likelihood less than tol=10^{-5} or the number of iterations larger than 10. In our experiments, we use the following publicly available face image datasets:

- FRAV2D(http://www.frav.es/databases/FRAV2D/) (Ángel Serrano et al. (2007)) contains 109 individuals, each of which has 32 images with size 320×240. The 32 images were classified into six groups according to the pose and lighting conditions, of which 16 images are used in our experiment: the first 8 frontal images without gestures but with diffuse light, the 4 images with gestures and the 4 images with occluded face features. We subsample the images to the size 96×72.
- ORL(http://www.face-rec.org/databases/) contains 400 images of 40 individuals taken at different times, lighting, facial expressions and facial details. The image size is 92×112.
- PIX(http://peipa.essex.ac.uk/ipa/pix/faces/manchester/) consists of the images in the folder 'test-easy', containing 30 individuals. Each person has 10 images with the size 512×512. We subsample the images to the size 100×100.

The reduced feature of image $\mathbf{X}$ for two methods is computed by $\mathbf{Z} = \mathbf{U}'_c \mathbf{X} \mathbf{U}_r$ and the Nearest-Neighbors (NN) classifier based on Frobenius norm is naturally used for classification. To measure the misclassification error rate, we randomly split each data set into two parts: one part for training and the other for test. The training part consists of randomly chosen $r = 4, 6, 8$ or 11 images per individual with labels. We report the results from 50 replications. Since 2DLDA is an iterative algorithm, to save time we restrict $q_c = q_r = q$ and set q to a wide range from 1 to a large value q_{max} (65 for FRAV2D and 90 for PIX and ORL data.). The optimal averaged misclassification error rates and their corresponding latent dimensions are collected in Table 1. The main observations are summarized as follows:

a. S2DLDA and 2DLDA(1). From Table 1, S2DLDA outperforms 2DLDA(1) in terms of misclassification error and the corresponding optimal latent dimension q_{opt} by S2DLDA is generally comparable with or smaller than that by 2DLDA(1).

b. 2DLDA(1) vs. 2DLDA(4). From Table 1, 2DLDA(1) is better than 2DLDA(4), which indicates that more iterations do not improve the performance of 2DLDA.

Table 1. The averaged lowest error rates and their corresponding dimensions q_{opt} shown as mean±std.(q_{opt}) by different methods. Bold face indicates the best one.

Data	train	S2DLDA	2DLDA(1)	2DLDA(4)	Fisherfaces
FRAV2D	8	**21.1±9.0(21)**	23.5±8.2(38)	24.3±8.8(15)	44.3±6.0(108)
	11	**16.0±8.0(14)**	17.4±8.2(39)	18.7±8.4(31)	42.6±6.6(108)
PIX	4	**22.4±5.2(24)**	28.4±5.6(66)	40.3±7.2(76)	28.9±5.3(29)
	6	**15.3±4.3(36)**	20.2±3.8(59)	30.2±5.2(61)	21.7±4.1(29)
ORL	4	**5.4±1.8(53)**	5.9±1.7(45)	7.1±1.9(38)	9.5±2.3(39)
	6	**2.9±1.2(66)**	3.3±1.4(57)	3.3±1.4(35)	6.6±2.2(39)

Table 2. The CPU time (in seconds) required for training all values of q from 1 to q_{max} by different methods.

Data	train	S2DLDA	2DLDA(1)	2DLDA(4)
FRAV2D	8	4.5	29.7	118.8
PIX	6	1.8	21.7	86.8
ORL	6	2.2	28.1	112.4

Table 2 collects that some results on computation time by different methods for training the bilinear transformation $\mathbf{U}_c$ and $\mathbf{U}_r$ with all values of q from 1 to q_{max}. It can be seen that the computation of 2DLDA is much heavier than S2DLDA. For S2DLDA, we only need to run once for q_{max} and then all $\mathbf{U}_c$'s and $\mathbf{U}_r$'s with q from 1 to q_{max} are automatically obtained due to the separable property. While for 2DLDA, we have to run once for each value of q and thus run a total of q_{max} times. This clearly shows the computation advantage of separable 2DLDA over 2DLDA.

5   Conclusion

In this paper, we propose using separable covariance matrix to model 2D data. Based on this, we propose separable 2DLDA in which a neatly closed form solution of 2DLDA is obtained as that in classical LDA. Compared with the iterative algorithm proposed in Ye et al. (2005), the empirical results show that the performance of separable 2DLDA is satisfactory in terms of classification accuracy, the optimal latent dimensions and computation efficiency.

Acknowledgement

The work of Jianhua Zhao is partially supported by two YNUFE samll project fundings. The research of Philip L.H. Yu is partially supported by a HKU Small Project Funding.

References

ÁNGEL SERRANO, MARTÍN DE DIEGO, I., CONDE, C., CABELLO, E., SHEN, L. and BAI, L. (2007): Influence of wavelet frequency and orientation in an SVM-based parallel gabor PCA face verification system. In *IDEAL 2007*, pages 219–228.

BELHUMEUR, P.N., HESPANHA, J.P. and KRIEGMAN, D.J. (1997) Eigenfaces vs. fisherfaces: Recognition using class specific linear projection. *IEEE Transactions on Pattern Analysis and Machine Intelligence, 19(7):721–720.*

BOUVEYRON, C., GIRARD, S., and SCHMID, C. (2007): High-dimensional discriminant analysis. *Communications in Statistics: Theory and Methods, 14:2607–2623.*

DE MUNCK, J., HUIZENGA, H., WALDORP, L. and HEETHAAR, R. (2002): Estimating stationary dipoles from MEG/EEG data contaminated with spatially and temporally correlated background noise. *IEEE Transactions on Signal Processing, 50(7):1565–1572.*

FUKUNAGA, K. (1990): *Introduction to Statistical Pattern Classification.* Academic Press.

GUPTA, A.K. and NAGAR, D.K. (1999): *Matrix Variate Distributions.* Chapman and Hall-CRC.

HASTIE, T., TIBSHIRANI, R. and FRIEDMAN, J. (2009): *The Elements of Statistical Learning, Second Edition: Data Mining, Inference, and Prediction.* Springer.

INOUE, K. and URAHAMA, K. (2006): Non-iterative two-dimensional linear discriminant analysis. In *Proceedings of the 18th International Conference on Pattern Recognition*, volume 2, pages 540–543.

LI, M. and YUAN, B. (2005): 2D-LDA: A statistical linear discriminant analysis for image matrix. *Pattern Recognition Letters, 26(5):527–532.*

LIU, K., CHENG, Y. and YANG, J. (1993): Algebraic feature extraction for image recognition based on an optimal discriminant criterion. *Pattern Recognition, 26(6):903–911.*

LUO, D., DING, C. and HUANG, H. (2009): Symmetric two dimensional linear discriminant analysis. In *IEEE Conference on Computer Vision and Pattern Recognition*, pages 2820–2827.

MARDIA, K. and GOODALL, C. (1993): Spatial-temporal analysis of multivariate environmental monitoring data. In *Multivariate Environmental Statistics*, pages 347–386. Amsterdam, The Netherlands:Elsevier.

WERNER, K. and JANSSON, M. (2009): Estimating MIMO channel covariances from training data under the kronecker model. *Signal Processing, 89(1):1–13.*

XIONG, H., SWAMY, M. and AHMAD, M. (2005): Two-dimensional FLD for face recognition. *Pattern Recognition, 38(7):1121–1124.*

YANG, J., ZHANG, D., YONG, X. and YANG, J. (2005): Two-dimensional discriminant transform for face recognition. *Pattern Recognition, 38.*

YE, J., JANARDAN, R. and LI, Q. (2005): Two-dimensional linear discriminant analysis. In *Advances in Neural Information Processing Systems 17*, pages 1569–1576.

List of Supplementary Contributed and Invited Papers Only Available on springerlink.com

Supplementary Contributed Papers

Clustering of Waveforms-Data Based on FPCA Direction
Giada Adelfio, Marcello Chiodi, Antonino D'Alessandro, Dario Luzio

Symbolic Data Analysis of Complex Data: Application to nuclear power plant
Filipe Afonso, Edwin Diday, Norbert Badez, Yves Genest

Different P-spline Approaches for Smoothed Functional Principal Component Analysis
Ana M. Aguilera, M. Carmen Aguilera-Morillo, Manuel Escabias, Mariano J. Valderrama

Peak Detection in Mass Spectrometry Data Using Sparse Coding
Theodore Alexandrov, Klaus Steinhorst, Oliver Keszöcze, Stefan Schiffler

A Comparison between Beale Test and Some Heuristic Criteria to Establish Clusters Number
Angela Alibrandi, Massimiliano Giacalone

Estimating Population Proportions in Presence of Missing Data
Encarnaciòn Álvarez-Verdejo, Antonio Arcos, Silvia González, Juan Francisco Muñoz, Maria Rueda

Sub-quadratic Markov tree mixture models for probability density estimation
Sourour Ammar, Philippe Leray, Louis Wehenkel

Data Management in Symbolic Data Analysis
Teh Amouh, Monique Noirhomme-Fraiture, Benoit Macq

Variable Selection for Semi-Functional Partial Linear Regression Models
Germán Aneiros, Frédéric Ferraty, Philippe Vieu

Clustering Functional Data Using Wavelets
Anestis Antoniadis, Xavier Brossat, Jairo Cugliari, Jean-Michel Poggi

Y. Lechevallier, G. Saporta (eds.), *Proceedings of COMPSTAT'2010*,
DOI 10.1007/978-3-7908-2604-3_63, © Springer-Verlag Berlin Heidelberg 2010

Polynomial Methods in Time Series Analysis
Félix Aparicio-Pérez

Cointegrated Lee-Carter Mortality Forecasting Method
Josef Arlt, Markéta Arltová, Milan Bašta, Jitka Langhamrová

Empirical Analysis of the Climatic and Social-Economic Factors influence
on the Suicide Development in the Czech Republic
Markéta Arltová, Jitka Langhamrová, Jana Langhamrová

Yield Curve Predictability, Regimes, and Macroeconomic Information: A
Data-Driven Approach
Francesco Audrino, Kameliya Filipova

Socioeconomic Factors in Circulatory System Mortality in Europe: A Multi-
level Analysis of Twenty Countries
*Sara Balduzzi, Lucio Balzani, Matteo Di Maso, Chiara Lambertini, Elena
Toschi*

Comparing ORF Length in DNA Code Observed in Sixteen Yeast Chromosomes
Anna Bartkowiak, Adam Szustalewicz

Influence of the Calibration Weights on Results Obtained from Czech SILC
Data
Jitka Bartošová, Vladislav Bína

Continuous Wavelet Transform and the Annual Cycle in Temperature and
the Number of Deaths
Milan Bašta, Josef Arlt, Markéta Arltová, Karel Helman

EM-Like Algorithms for Nonparametric Estimation in Multivariate Mixtures
Tatiana Benaglia, Didier Chauveau, David R. Hunter

On the use of Weighted Regression in Conjoint Analysis
Salwa Benammou, Besma Souissi, Gilbert Saporta

Variable Selection and Parameter Tuning in High-Dimensional Prediction
Christoph Bernau, Anne-Laure Boulesteix

A Generative Model for Rank Data Based on Sorting Algorithm
Christophe Biernacki, Julien Jacques

"Made in Italy" Firms Competitiveness: A Multilevel Longitudinal Model

on Export Performance
Matilde Bini, Margherita Velucchi

Statistical Inference on Large Contingency Tables: Convergence, Testability, Stability
Marianna Bolla

A Class of Multivariate Type I Generalized Logistic Distributions
Salvatore Bologna

Adaptive Mixture Discriminant Analysis for Supervised Learning with Unobserved Classes
Charles Bouveyron

Forecasting a Compound Cox Process by means of PCP
Paula R. Bouzas, Nuria Ruiz-Fuentes, Juan Eloy Ruiz-Castro

Cutting the Dendrogram through Permutation Tests
Dario Bruzzese, Domenico Vistocco

Design of Least-Squares Quadratic Estimators Based on Covariances from Interrupted Observations Transmitted by Different Sensors
R. Caballero-Águila, A. Hermoso-Carazo, J. Linares-Pérez

Pseudo-Bayes Factors
Stefano Cabras, Walter Racugno, Laura Ventura

Diagnostic Checking of Multivariate Normality Under Contamination
Andrea Cerioli

On Computationally Complex Instances of the c-optimal Experimental Design Problem: Breaking RSA-based Cryptography via c-optimal Designs
Michal Černý, Milan Hladík, Veronika Skočdopolová

Estimation and Detection of Outliers and Patches in Nonlinear Time Series Models
Ping Chen

Two-way Classification of a Table with non-negative entries: Validation of an Approach based on Correspondence Analysis and Information Criteria
Antonio Ciampi, Alina Dyachenko, Yves Lechevallier

A Mann-Whitney Spatial Scan Statistic for Continuous Data
Lionel Cucala

Quantile Regression for Group Effect Analysis
Cristina Davino, Domenico Vistocco

Regularized Directions of Maximal Outlyingness
Michiel Debruyne

A New Approach to Robust Clustering in R^p
Catherine Dehon, Kaveh Vakili

An Exploratory Segmentation Method for Time Series
Christian Derquenne

Using Auxiliary Information Under a Generic Sampling Design
Giancarlo Diana, Pier Francesco Perri

Improving Overlapping Clusters obtained by a Pyramidal Clustering
Edwin Diday, Francisco de A. T. de Carvalho, Luciano D.S. Pacifico

Visualizing and Forecasting Complex Time Series: Beanplot Time Series
Carlo Drago, Germana Scepi

M-estimation in INARCH Models with a Special Focus on Small Means
Hanan El-Saied, Roland Fried

Score Moment Estimators
Zdeněk Fabián

Testing the Number of Components in Poisson Mixture Regression Models
Susana Faria, Fátima Gonccalves

Support Vector Machines for Large Scale Text Mining in R
Ingo Feinerer, Alexandros Karatzoglou

Computation of the projection of the inhabitants of the Czech Republic by sex, age and the highest education level
Tomáš Fiala, Jitka Langhamrová

Two Kurtosis Measures in a Simulation Study
Anna Maria Fiori

Clustering of Czech Household Incomes Over Very Short Time Period
Marie Forbelská, Jitka Bartošová

Model-Based Nonparametric Variance Estimation for Systematic Sampling.
An Application in a Forest Survey
Mario Francisco-Fernández, Jean Opsomer, Xiaoxi Li

Thresholding-Wavelet-Based Functional Estimation of Spatiotemporal Strong-
Dependence in the Spectral Domain
María Pilar Frías, María Dolores Ruiz-Medina

Boolean Factor Analysis by the Expectation-Maximization Algorithm
Alexander A. Frolov , Pavel. Y., Polyakov , Dusan Husek

Modeling and Forecasting Electricity Prices and their Volatilities by Conditionally Heteroskedastic Seasonal Dynamic Factor Analysis
Carolina García-Martos, Julio Rodríguez, María Jesús Sánchez

Consensus Analysis Through Modal Symbolic Objects
Jose M. Garcia-Santesmases, M. Carmen Bravo

Nonlinear Regression Model of Copper Bromide Laser Generation
Snezhana Georgieva Gocheva-Ilieva, Iliycho Petkov Iliev

Random Forests Based Feature Selection for Decoding fMRI Data
Robin Genuer, Vincent Michel, Evelyn Eger, Bertrand Thirion

Differentiation Tests for the Mean Shape and the Mean Variance of Renal
Tumours appearing in early Childhood
Stefan Markus Giebel, Jens-Peter Schenk , Jang Schiltz

Local or Global Smoothing? A Bandwidth Selector for Dependent Data
Francesco Giordano, Maria Lucia Parrella

Panel Data Models for Productivity Analysis
Luigi Grossi, Giorgio Gozzi

A Stochastic Gamma Diffusion Model with Threshold Parameter. Compu-
tational Statistical Aspects and Application
*Ramón Gutiérrez, Ramón Gutiérrez-Sánchez, Ahmed Nafidi, Eva Maria Ramos-
Ábalos*

On the Correlated Gamma Frailty Model for Bivariate Current Status Data
Niel Hens, Andreas Wienke

Evolutionary Stochastic Portfolio Optimization and Probabilistic Constraints

Ronald Hochreiter

Boosting a Generalised Poisson Hurdle Model
Vera Hofer

Fast and Robust Classifiers Adjusted for Skewness
Mia Hubert, Stephan Van der Veeken

Modelling the Andalusian Population by Means of a non-Homogeneous Stochastic Gompertz Process
Maria Dolores Huete Morales , Francisco Abad Montes

Neural Network Approach for Histopathological Diagnosis of Breast Diseases with Images
Yuichi Ishibashi, Atsuko Hara, Isao Okayasu, Koji Kurihara

Detection of Spatial Cluster for Suicide Data using Echelon Analysis
Fumio Ishioka, Makoto Tomita, Toshiharu Fujita

Time-Varying Coefficient Model with Linear Smoothing Function for Longitudinal Data in Clinical Trial
Masanori Ito, Toshihiro Misumi, Hideki Hirooka

Metropolis-Hastings Algorithm for Mixture Model and its Weak Convergence
Kengo Kamatani

A Method for Time Series Analysis Using Probability Distribution of Local Standard Fractal Dimension
Kenichi Kamijo, Akiko Yamanouchi

Assessment of Scoring Models Using Information Value
Jan Koláček, Martin Řezáč

The Moving Average Control Chart Based on the Sequence of Permutation Tests
Grzegorz Konczak

Depth Based Procedures for Estimation ARMA and GARCH Models
Daniel Kosiorowski

Half-Taxi Metric in Compositional Data Geometry Rcomp
Katarina Košmelj, Vesna Žabkar

LTPD Plans by Variables when the Remainder of Rejected Lots is Inspected

J. Klufa, L. Marek

A Comparison between Two Computing Methods for an Empirical Variogram in Geostatistical Data
Takafumi Kubota, Tomoyuki Tarumi

Improvement of Acceleration of the ALS Algorithm Using the Vector ε Algorithm
Masahiro Kuroda, Yuchi Mori, Masaya Iizuka, Michio Sakakihara

Unsupervised Recall and Precision Measures: a Step towards New Efficient Clustering Quality Indexes
Jean-Charles Lamirel, Maha Ghribi, Pascal Cuxac

Performance Assessment of Optimal Allocation for Large Portfolios
Fabrizio Laurini, Luigi Grossi

Clustering of Multiple Dissimilarity Data Tables for Documents Categorization
Yves Lechevallier, Francisco de A. T. de Carvalho, Thierry Despeyroux, Filipe M. de Melo

Slimming down a high-dimensional binary datatable: relevant eigen-subspace and substantial content
Alain Lelu

Comparing Two Approaches to Testing Linearity against Markov-switching Type Non-linearity
Jana Lenčuchová, Anna Petrič ková, Magdaléna Komorníková

Numerical Error Analysis for Statistical Software on Multi-Core Systems
Wenbin Li, Sven Simon

Sparse Bayesian Hierarchical Model for Clustering Problems
Heng Lian

Data Mining and Multiple Correspondence Analysis via Polynomial Transformations
Rosaria Lombardo

Structural Modelling of Nonlinear Exposure-Response Relationships for Longitudinal Data
Xiaoshu Lu, Esa-Pekka Takala

Empirical Composite Likelihoods
Nicola Lunardon, Francesco Pauli, Laura Ventura

A Fast Parsimonious Maximum Likelihood Approach for Predicting Outcome Variables from a Large Number of Predictors
Jay Magidson

A Bootstrap Method to Improve Brain Subcortical Network Segregation in Resting-State FMRI Data
Caroline Malherbe, Eric Bardinet, Arnaud Messé, Vincent Perlbarg, Guillaume Marrelec, Mélanie Pélégrini-Issac, Jérôme Yelnik, Stéphane Lehéricy, Habib Benali

The Problem of Determining the Calibration Equations to Construct Model-calibration Estimators of the Distribution Function
Sergio Martínez, Maria Rueda, Antonio Arcos, Helena Martínez, Juan Francisco Muñoz

Dealing with Nonresponse in Survey Sampling: an Item Response Modeling Approach
Alina Matei

Estimation of the Bivariate Distribution Function for Censored Gap Times
Luís Meira-Machado, Ana Moreira

Two Measures of Dissimilarity for the Dendrogram Multi-Class SVM Model
Rafael Pino Mejías, María Dolores Cubiles de la Vega

Visualizing the Sampling Variability of Plots
Rajiv S. Menjoge, Roy E. Welsch

Empirical Mode Decomposition for Trend Extraction. Application to Electrical Data
Farouk Mhamdi, Mériem Jaïdane-Saïdane, Jean-Michel Poggi

Dealing with Nonresponse in Survey Sampling: an Item Response Modeling Approach
Alina Matei

The Evaluation of Non-centred Orthant Probabilities for Singular Multivariate Normal Distributions
Tetsuhisa Miwa

Variable Inclusion and Shrinkage Algorithm in High Dimension

Abdallah Mkhadri , Mohamed Ouhourane

Application of a Bayesian Approach for Analysing Disease Mapping Data: Modelling Spatially Correlated Small Area Counts
Mohammadreza Mohebbi, Rory Wolfe

Clusters of Gastrointestinal Tract Cancer in the Caspian Region of Iran: A Spatial Scan Analysis
Mohammadreza Mohebbi, Rory Wolfe

The Financial Crisis of 2008: Modelling the Transmission Mechanism Between the Markets
M. Pilar Muñoz, Maria Dolores Márquez, Helena Chuliá

Data Visualization and Aggregation
Junji Nakano, Yoshikazu Yamamoto

Longitudinal Data Analysis Based on Ranks and its Performance
Takashi Nagakubo, Masashi Goto

Multiple Change Point Detection by Sparse Parameter Estimation
Jiří Neubauer, Vítězslav Veselý

Quasi-Maximum Likelihood Estimators for Threshold ARMA Models: Theoretical Results and Computational Issues
Marcella Niglio, Cosimo Damiano Vitale

A Case Study of Bank Branch Performance Using Linear Mixed Models
Peggy Ng, Claudia Czado, Eike Christian Brechmann, Jon Kerr

Numerical Methods for some Classes of Matrices with Applications to Statistics and Optimization
Juan M. Peña

Maximum Margin Learning of Gaussian Mixture Models with Application to Multipitch Tracking
Franz Pernkopf, Michael Wohlmayr

Low-Pass Filter Design using Locally Weighted Polynomial Regression and Discrete Prolate Spheroidal Sequences
Tommaso Proietti, Alessandra Luati

A Statistical Survival Model Based on Counting Processes
Jose-Manuel Quesada-Rubio, Julia Garcia-Leal, Maria-Jose Del-Moral-Avila,

Esteban Navarrete-Alvarez, Maria-Jesus Rosales-Moreno

Bootstrapping Additive Models in Presence of Missing Data
Rocío Raya-Miranda, M. Dolores Martínez-Miranda, Andrés González-Carmona

On Aspects of Quality Indexes for Scoring Models
Martin Řezáč, Jan Koláček

Data Clustering with Mixed Type Variables and Cluster Number Determination
Hana Řezanková , Dušan Húsek , Tomáš Löster

A General Strategy for Determining First-Passage-Time Densities Based on the First-Passage-Time Location Function
Patricia Román-Román, Juan José Serrano-Pérez, Francisco Torres-Ruiz

Rplugin.Econometrics: R-GUI for Teaching Time Series Analysis
Dedi Rosadi

Computational Statistics, The Symbolic Approach
Colin Rose

EOFs for Gap Filling in Multivariate Air Quality data: a FDA Approach
Mariantonietta Ruggieri, Francesca Di Salvo, Antonella Plaia, Gianna Agró

A Transient Analysis of a Complex Discrete k-out-of-n:G System with Multi-State Components
Juan Eloy Ruiz-Castro, Paula R. Bouzas

Using Logitboost for Stationary Signals Classification
Pedro Saavedra, Angelo Santana, Carmen Nieves Hernández, Juan Artiles, Juan-José González

Test of Mean Difference for Longitudinal Data Using Circular Block Bootstrap
Hirohito Sakurai, Masaaki Taguri

An Empirical Study of the Use of Nonparametric Regression Methods for Imputation
Ismael R. Sánchez-Borrego, Maria Rueda, Encarnación álvarez-Verdejo

A simulation study of the Bayes estimator of parameters in an extension

of the exponential distribution
Samira Sadeghi

A Cluster-Target Similarity Based Principal Component Analysis for Interval-Valued Data
Mika Sato-Ilic

Wavelet-PLS Regression: Application to Oil Production Data
Benammou Saloua, Kacem Zied, Kortas Hedi, Dhifaoui Zouhaier

Bayesian Flexible Modelling of Mixed Logit Models
Luisa Scaccia, Edoardo Marcucci

A Decision Tree for Symbolic Data
Djamal Seck, Lynne Billard, Edwin Diday, Filipe Afonso

The Set of $3 \times 4 \times 4$ Contingency Tables has 3-Neighborhood Property
Toshio Sumi, Toshio Sakata

Visualization Techniques for the Integration of Rank Data
Michael G. Schimek, Eva Budinská

Comprehensive Assessment on Hierarchical Structures of DNA markers Using Echelon Analysis
Makoto Tomita, Koji Kurihara

Non-Hierarchical Clustering for Distribution-Valued Data
Yoshikazu Terada, Hiroshi Yadohisa

On Composite Pareto Models
Sandra Teodorescu, Raluca Vernic

Visualisation of Large Sized Data Sets : Constraints and Improvements for Graph Design
Jean-Paul Valois

Selecting Variables in Two-Group Robust Linear Discriminant Analysis
Stefan Van Aelst, Gert Willems

How to Take into Account the Discrete Parameters in the BIC Criterion?
Vincent Vandewalle

Analysis of Breath Alcohol Measurements Using Compartmental and Generalized Linear Models

Chi Ting Yang, Wing Kam Fung, Thomas Wai Ming Tam

Fisher Scoring for Some Univariate Discrete Distributions
Thomas W. Yee

Constructing Summary Indexes via Principal Curves
Mohammad Zayed, Jochen Einbeck

Censored Survival Data: Simulation and Kernel Estimates
Jiří Zelinka

Supplementary Invited Papers

Heuristic Optimization for Model Selection and Estimation
Dietmar Maringer

Index

A

ABC, 57
actuar, 145
Adams, N.M.., 167
adaptive prediction, 189
affine equivariance, 79
aggregate models, 145
Agostinelli, C., 69
Ahn, S.K., 297
Aitchison geometry, 79
Albrecher, H., 135
Alfò, M., 369
Ambroladze, A., 231
Anagnostopoulos, C., 167
anomalies, 33
approximate Bayesian computation, 47
asymmetry, 315
Aziz, N., 381

B

bandwidth selection, 509
Barth, E., 327
Bayesian analysis, 277, 315
Bayesian hierarchical models, 155
Bayesian inference, 437
Bayesian local regression, 47
Bayesian networks, 549
Bayesian statistics, 469
Benner, A., 19
Berro, A., 89
binary diagnostic test, 533
Blum, M.G.B., 47
bootstrap, 199, 509
Bordes, L., 243
Bottou, L., 177
Bougeard, S., 389
Broccoli, S., 397
Bry, X., 405
Buckley-James estimators, 384
Buckley-James model, 381

C

Cénac, P., 421
Cardot, H., 413, 421

Castellano, R., 429
categorical variables, 389
Cavrini, G., 397
cellular Potts model, 57
censored
– right, 381
censored data, 243, 381
Ceulemans, E., 359
change of support, 285
change point analysis, 501
change-point detection, 557
Chaouch, M., 421
Chauveau, D., 243
Chauvin, C., 389
chi-bar-square distribution, 445
Cho, S., 297
Chung, Y.-K., 437
CLAFIC, 493
classification, 167, 189
clustering, 265, 349
clusterwise regression, 461
co-clustering, 369
coincidences, 33
Colombi, R., 445
colon crypt dynamics, 57
common and distinctive cluster model, 359
compound distribution, 145
computational statistics, 19
computational statistics and data analysis, 19
conditional logit, 369
correlation, 541
Costanzo, G.D., 453
credit default swaps, 429
credit risk modelling, 265
credit scoring, 167

D

data dimensionality reduction, 549
De Bartolo, S., 453
De Carvalho, F.A.T., 461
de Falguerolles, A., 477
Dell'Accio, F., 453

Y. Lechevallier, G. Saporta (eds.), *Proceedings of COMPSTAT'2010*,
DOI 10.1007/978-3-7908-2604-3, © Springer-Verlag Berlin Heidelberg 2010

Demeyer, S., 469
design-based estimation, 413
Dessertaine, A., 413
deterministic algorithm, 589
Devroye, L., 3
diagnostic analysis, 381
dictionary learning, 327
dimension reduction, 305, 349
dimensionality reduction, 337
Dirichlet processes, 277
discrete choice, 369
discrete optimization, 525
discriminant analysis, 189, 389
distance-based model, 517
drift term, 209
Duchesnay, E., 101
DuClos, C., 285
dynamics, 209

E
Edler, L., 19
efficiency, 177
electricity consumption, 413
EM algorithm, 565
empirical Bayes, 47
empirical characteristic function, 501
environmental justice, 277
errors in variables, 285
event-study, 429
evidence approximation, 47

F
face recognition, 597
factor models, 305
Filzmoser, P., 79
financial portfolio optimization., 265
Fischer, N., 469
Fisher Discriminant Analysis, 221
fMRI, 111
forgetting factor, 167
Fortunato, L., 277
Fourier series, 525
Frouin, V., 101
functional data, 189, 453
functional linear regression, 199
functional principal components, 413
functional principal components
    analysis, 199
Fung, W., 437

G
Gaussian copula, 485
Gaussian process, 209
generalization prediction, 231
genetic marker dependency modelling,
    549
genome wide analyses, 101
geometric quantiles, 421
Gibbs sampling, 469
Giordano, S., 445
global optimization, 525
González-Manteiga, W., 199
Gotway, C.A., 285
Goulet, V., 145
Grady, C., 111
Granger causality, 445
graphical models, 445

H
Haas, S., 135
Haasdonk, B., 221
Hadj Mbarek, M., 189
Hand, D.J., 33, 167
Hardy-Weinberg equilibrium, 437
Hayashi, K., 493
health-related quality of life, 397
Heuchenne, C., 509
heuristic algorithms, 89
hidden forces, 33
hierarchical Bayes, 429
hierarchical latent class model, 549
high dimensional data, 349, 421, 573
high-dimensional integration, 135
histogram data, 581
history of statistics, 477
Horvitz-Thompson estimator, 413
Hron, K., 79
Hu, Y.-Q., 437
Hušková, M., 501
Hubert, M., 589
hypothesis test, 199

I
identifiability, 469
imputation, 485
incomplete data, 485
indefinite kernels, 221
information criteria, 297
integral operator, 135

International Association of Statistical
    Computing, 19
interval-valued data, 461
Irpino, A., 581
IRT model, 397
Ishihara, T.., 315

J
Josserand, E., 413

K
Käärik, E., 485
Käärik, M., 485
Kearney, G., 285
kernel methods, 221
Kirch, C., 501

L
Labusch, K., 327
Lalanne, C., 101
Lang, S., 155
Larabi Marie-Sainte, S., 89
LARS, 69
latent variables, 469
Laurent, G., 509
LDA, 597
Lebarbier, E., 557
Lee, J.A., 337
Lee, P.H., 517
Leray, P., 549
leverage effect, 315
Li, S., 597
lifetime data, 253
likelihood ratio, 437
Lim, E.W.C., 525
local influence, 381
logratio transformations, 79
Lopiano, K.K., 285
Luna del Castillo, J.D., 533

M
Müller, H.G., 209
Mahalanobis distance, 221
manifold learning, 337
Markov chain Monte Carlo, 315
Markov switching models, 429
Martínez-Calvo, A., 199
Martinetz, T., 327
matching pursuit, 327

MCMC, 277
Meintanis, S.G., 501
Minami, H., 493
Mittnik, S., 541
mixed stain, 437
mixture models, 243, 277, 359, 517
Mizuta, M., 493
model selection, 69, 231, 297
modified areal unit problem, 285
molecular biomedical research, 19
Molitor, J., 277
Molitor, N.-T., 277
Monte Carlo methods, 3
Montero Alonso, M.A., 533
Mourad, R., 549
multi-move sampler, 315
multi-objective optimization, 265
multiblock PLS, 389
multiblock redundancy analysis, 389
multilevel models, 155
multinomial logit, 369
multiplicative cascade, 453
multivariate outliers detection, 89
multivariate statistical methods, 79
multivariate stochastic volatility, 315
multivariate volatility, 305

N
NAIRU, 123
neural gas, 327
neuroimaging, 101, 565
New, J.R., 525
nonlinear projection, 337
nonparametric, 297
nonparametric regression, 509

O
Oder, A., 111
Omori, J., 315
online estimation algorithm, 421
online learning, 177
operational risk, 541
ordinary least squares, 581
outliers, 589
output gap, 123

P
P-splines, 155
Pękalska, E., 221

PAC Bayes Bound, 231
Pan, J., 305
parameter uncertainty, 123
Parrado-Hernández, E., 231
partial least squares, 101
particle swarm optimization, 89, 525
Paterlini, S., 265, 541
path modeling, 405
penalized discriminant analysis, 111
perturbation, 493
PLS, 405
Poline, J.-B., 101, 565
Polonik, W., 305
population drift, 167
population-based algorithms, 265
posterior distribution of change-points, 557
Preda, C., 189
prediction, 111
prediction intervals, 123
predictive values, 533
principal component analysis, 573
probability distribution function, 581
product-limit estimator, 381
projection pursuit, 89

Q

Qannari, E.M., 389
Queiroz, D.N., 461

R

R, 145
random variate generation, 3
ranking data, 517
Redont, P., 405
reduced k-means, 359
regression, 477
reinsurance, 135
relatedness coefficient, 437
relative, 437
reliability, 243
reproducibility, 111
Richardson, S., 277
Rigaill, G., 557
right censoring, 509
risk capital, 541
risk theory, 145
Robbins-Monro, 421
Robin, S., 557

robust regression, 69
robustness, 69, 79, 421, 573, 589
Rodríguez, A.F., 123
Roldán Nofuentes, J.A., 533
Rousseeuw, P.J., 589
RPCR, 589
RSIMPLS, 589
ruin probability, 135
Ruiz, E., 123
Ruiz-Gazen, A., 89

S

S-estimators, 69
Salibian-Barrera, M., 69
Saporta, G., 189, 461, 469
Scaccia, L., 429
seasonal cointegrating rank, 297
SEER, 405
selection bias, 509
SEM, 405
sensitivity analysis, 493
Seong, B., 297
Shawe-Taylor, J., 231
similarity-based embedding, 337
simulation, 3, 525
simulations, 19
simultaneously comparison, 533
Sinoquet, C., 549
skew normal distribution, 397
Sottoriva, A., 57
sparse coding, 327
spatial heterogeneity, 155
spatial median, 421
spatial models, 565
SPC, 253
Spring, R., 111
state space models, 123
statistical computing, 477
statistical testing, 565
stem cell modeling, 57
stochastic EM algorithm, 243
stochastic gradient averaging, 421
stochastic gradient descent, 177
stochastic orderings, 445
stochastic process, 453
stock returns., 315
Strother, S., 111
structural equation modeling, 469
supervised classification, 389

Support Vector Machines, 231
symbolic data analysis, 461

T

t-SNE, 337
tail dependence, 541
Tasoulis, D.K., 167
Tavaré, S., 57
Tenenhaus, A., 101
THEME, 405
Thirion, B., 101, 565
Timmerman, M.E., 359
Tribes algorithm, 89
trimming. , 573
Trombetta, G., 453
Tucholka, A., 565
two-dimensional data, 597

U

Umlauf, N., 155

V

value–at–risk, 541
Van Aelst, S., 573
Van Deun, K., 349
Van Mechelen, I., 349

Vandervieren, E., 573
Verde, R., 581
Verdonck, T., 589
Verleysen, M., 337
Verron, T., 405
Vicari, D., 369

W

Wang, D.Q., 381
warranty, 253
Wasserstein distance, 581
wearout, 253
Werft, W., 19
Willems, G., 573
Wunder, C., 19

Y

Yao, Q., 305
Yashchin, E., 253
Yener, T., 541
Young, L.J., 285
Yu, P.L.H., 517, 597

Z

Zhao, J., 597
Zhu, D.-G., 437

Printed in the United States
by Baker & Taylor Publisher Services